HANDBOOK OF STRATEGIC ACCOUNT MANAGEMENT

A COMPREHENSIVE RESOURCE

DIANA WOODBURN
AND KEVIN WILSON

Registered office
John Wiley and Sons Ltd, The Atrium, Southern Gate, Chichester, West Sussex, PO19 8SQ, United Kingdom

For details of our global editorial offices, for customer services and for information about how to apply for permission to reuse the copyright material in this book please see our website at www.wiley.com.

Library of Congress Cataloging-in-Publication Data
Woodburn, Diana.
Handbook of strategic account management : a comprehensive resource / Diana Woodburn and Kevin Wilson.
      pages cm
   Includes bibliographical references and index.
   ISBN 978-1-118-50908-1 (hardback)
  1. Selling–Key accounts.   2. Marketing–Key accounts.   3. Customer relations.   4. Sales management.   I. Wilson, Kevin, 1947–   II. Title.
   HF5438.8.K48W66 2014
   658.8–dc23
                                    2014002694

A catalogue record for this book is available from the British Library.

ISBN 978-1-118-50908-1 (hbk)   ISBN 978-1-118-50907-4 (ebk)
ISBN 978-1-118-50905-0 (ebk)

Cover designed by Cylinder

Set in 10/12 pt MeridienLTStd-Roman by Toppan Best-set Premedia Limited
Printed in Great Britain by CPI Group (UK) Ltd, Croydon, CR0 4YY

Contents

CONTENTS

CONTENTS

Acknowledgements

Our heartfelt thanks go to the contributors to this book for their generosity in devoting their time to this project, most especially those contributing new material and extensive syntheses of work for the benefit of interested parties in the hot topic of key strategic account management.

We also acknowledge the patience, guidance and forbearance of all at Wiley, particularly Rosemary Nixon, Ashton Bainbridge and Jonathan Shipley.

Lastly, we thank Cuiling Jiang, research assistant at Kedge Business School, for her amazing dedication, speed and accuracy in combining all the references into one list and rationalizing their almost random presentation in the papers citing them.

The editors

Diana Woodburn, BSc MSc MBA PhD

Diana Woodburn is a key/strategic account management (KSAM) specialist, who has been a major influence on Cranfield University School of Management's initiatives in KSAM since 1997. In 1998 she founded Cranfield's KAM Best Practice Club with Professor Malcom McDonald, which is still running today, and in 2000 she established Marketing Best Practice (MBP), a consultancy that became entirely dedicated to KSAM work, not only teaching and developing people (about 3,000 key account managers and company directors) but also helping companies develop their KSAM programmes and processes.

Working through MBP and Cranfield as a Visiting Fellow, Diana has taught KSAM in numerous diverse sectors all over the world, in major change programmes for global companies and focused support for national companies. At the same time, she has conducted research projects into poorly understood but critical areas of KSAM, resulting in a series of substantial reports and new concepts with theoretical underpinnings and practical applications. Together with Professor Malcolm McDonald, Diana has written one of the most popular books on KAM, *Key Account Management: The Definitive Guide*, as well as a quantity of shorter reports and articles.

Before becoming an academic/consultant, Diana's career spanned most aspects of marketing, several B2B sectors and four continents. She graduated from Manchester University with a 1st Class Honours BSc and MSc in biological chemistry.

Contact: woodburn@marketingbp.com or diana.woodburn@cranfield.ac.uk

Kevin Wilson MBA PhD

Kevin holds the Chair of Selling and Customer Relationships at KEDGE Business School in Bordeaux. He is a researcher, writer and presenter with an international reputation in the field of strategic account management.

He has spent the past 20 years exploring the nature of strategic, national and global account management in more than 1,200 companies and has in excess of 60 refereed and other publications to his credit. He is the author of four books on the subject and has published numerous articles in academic and practitioner journals.

For several years Kevin was a board member of SAMA (The Strategic Account Management Association, based in Chicago), the CEO of the Sales Research Trust, a not-for-profit organization dedicated to the creation and dissemination of knowledge in the field of selling and sales management, and the editor of *The Journal of Selling and Major Account Management*. Kevin has also held full-time academic posts variously at Sheffield, Southampton and the Isle of Man Business Schools.

Contact kevin.wilson@kedge.com

About this book

We, the editors, have long felt that key strategic account management, which we will call KSAM, is sorely overlooked by academia, with the exception of a few experts like those contributing to this book.

As a rule of thumb, products are bought and sold five times over before they reach their final destination with the consumer. There is, therefore, much more commercial activity and many more companies involved in business-to-business (B2B) transactions than in consumer sales. You would not think so, however, if you looked at most universities' business and marketing courses, or even the UK Chartered Institute of Marketing's agenda and publications, in spite of the fact that a majority of its members operate in B2B markets.

Just rebalancing attention between consumer and B2B markets would quickly highlight a key difference: the huge range of customer size and revenues in B2B businesses, which cannot be ignored. All customers are indisputably not equal, and frequently a very few are individually critical to a B2B supplier. The world is littered with companies that have lost one key customer and their whole business with it, whereas consumer marketing does not, and does not need to, consider such a possibility.

Some academics claim that KSAM is just part of relationship marketing, and while it owes a great deal to that stream of thinking, there is much that is different: lumping them together is very misleading. At the same time, sales research literature contributes some valuable ideas to KSAM, but it generally assumes a substantial quantity of unconnected customers and opportunities. That is reversed in KSAM, where opportunities are far fewer, bigger, wide-reaching, linked to the past and the future, critical, and often demanding of significant change in the supplier's business. Also intrinsic to KSAM is its impact on the internal organization and the rest of the company, to which neither relationship marketing nor sales research give much consideration.

Hence this book. Through it, we hope to demonstrate that KSAM is a distinctive and important domain of business that needs to have a place in the minds of academics as substantial as the attention it attracts in companies. This teenager has grown up and deserves a home of its own.

Of course, the philosophy that high-spending customers should receive a different treatment from the norm has been instinctive since the dawn of trading. It began to emerge in academic research in the 1970s and 1980s, so KSAM is not new. However, it is complex in many ways, and while recent years have seen some blossoming of research work, much more is needed. Additionally, students with knowledge of KSAM will be welcomed by all sectors, almost all of which are struggling to implement this poorly understood, difficult and fascinating discipline that severely challenges traditional beliefs and adversarial approaches in business. More universities and business schools should take the opportunity to introduce KSAM to their marketing and management students.

The *Handbook of Strategic Account Management* aims to provide a good look across the KSAM domain so that, in one place, interested parties can see the elements and the issues involved and something of the state of knowledge about them. Authors have been encouraged to include plentiful references to the work of other authors, to make it easier for students and researchers to follow up their streams of enquiry. The reference section at the back of the book therefore provides a definitive list of sources of KSAM research which will be invaluable for students of the subject.

We have solicited contributions from authors as geographically dispersed as possible, although the vast majority have come from across Europe and North America, which seems to be where the bulk of KSAM research originates. Material from Asia seems to be scarce to date, so it would be good, in any future editions, to include Asian perspectives, e.g. how the Chinese concept of *guanxi* relationships relates to KSAM.

The book is comprised of papers by established academics who have made major contributions to our understanding of KSAM. The listing of authors in the section at the back offers a useful guide for those wanting to locate researchers active in KSAM. We have aimed to cover KSAM as broadly as possible, in four sections that group papers addressing similar levels of KSAM:

Section 1: Strategic dimensions of KSAM: looks at the fundamental issues of what and why.
Section 2: Value creation through KSAM: focuses on this core rationale for KSAM success, without which it will fail.
Section 3: Developing KSAM programmes: views KSAM as an organizational change with internal impact across the entire business.
Section 4: Operationalizing KSAM: considers critical elements of execution, wherein lie many of the success/failure points.

Interestingly, while the concept of KSAM is simple, execution generally seems to be much more difficult and complex, and therefore it is doubly important that KSAM principles and practices are clear and agreed, in order that execution might have a chance of success.

The papers vary in their format as authors have necessarily made their own choices over what to communicate and how to present it. Some offer new work and empirical evidence, e.g. Mahlamäki, Uusitalo and Mikkola, and Guenzi, while others offer a thorough review of one aspect of KSAM to identify what we know about it and where to find further information, e.g. Zolkiewski, and Ojasalo. KSAM fails if senior managers are not behind it, so Capon and Mihoc, and Brehmer and Rehme look at making the case for it.

Seminal papers that are as true now as ever are exemplified by Sengupta, Krapfel and Pusateri, and Jensen, Workman and Homburg, with an update on their widely cited findings. The work of the IMP (Industrial Marketing and Purchasing) Group, which has done so much on buyer–seller relationships and value exchange since the 1980s, is well represented by La Rocca and Snehota, Ivens and Pardo, and Henneberg, Pardo, Mouzas and Naudé, while Lacoste contributes a different angle on the vital topic of value creation and competition.

The external context of KSAM can have profound implications, as demonstrated by Piercy and Lane (social and ethical concerns), Croom (customer perspective) and Yip and Bink (global view). Wengler, Storbacka and Woodburn all wrestle with the complexities of internal changes at a programme level, while others consider key issues of execution: Atanasova and Senn (teams), and Wilson and Holt (KAM role) consider people issues, while others look at activity in individual customers, i.e. Gök (account selection and strategies), Wilson (relationships), McDonald and Woodburn (account plans). Lemmens and Vanderbiesen wrap up all those issues in terms of the all-important outcome: customer profitability.

The first part of our editorial addresses KSAM as a whole. We offer a definition of KSAM, which has been sorely missing from the domain: to date we have definitions of key accounts, specification of the KAM job, descriptions and recommendations for ideal KSAM, but no agreed definition of what KSAM is, as a definitive minimum. The lack of a widely agreed definition certainly hampers communication of KSAM from the outset, and it would be a step forward if our proposal were to be generally adopted by the academic community and used by business. The second part of the editorial reviews and summarizes the four sections of the *Handbook* and provides you with a 'fast track' guide to the contents to help you to plan your reading.

Hence the *Handbook of Strategic Account Management* offers a broad and wide-ranging picture of KSAM in terms of researched knowledge. It will be invaluable to students, lecturers and researchers in KSAM, and to rather serious practitioners. Clearly, there is much to be said about KSAM, and much more to be found in the future, and we hope this book will stimulate more academics and practitioners to become engaged in developing our understanding of the domain.

Key strategic account management: where are we now?

BY EDITORS DIANA WOODBURN AND KEVIN WILSON

Key account management has been around a long time. Obviously, business people from time immemorial have recognized the importance of their big buyers, but it took academics a while to acknowledge this simple fact; indeed, it is possible to accuse marketing in academia, which is overwhelmingly focused on consumers, of some responsibility for losing sight of it. Nevertheless, research into key account management kicked off in the 1980s, arguably initially in the USA and soon after, in Europe, fuelled by the Industrial Marketing and Purchasing (IMP) Group's work. At the same time, Citibank's first attempt at global account management (GAM) had been tried, proved successful with customers, been defeated by country managers and reinstated under pressure from strategic customers, all by 1985 (Buzzell). So it is surprising that many companies think key account management/key strategic account management is new, and that there is not a bigger body of research and greater recognition of the economic importance and potential for academic interest in it. We believe that the time has come for both business and academia to give KSAM the position it merits: hence this book.

We suppose that business-to-business (B2B) marketing is overlooked in favour of consumer marketing because anyone may have personal experience of the goods and services explored and the brands are household names, but we have no explanation for why the enormous wallets and life-giving or life-taking demands of key strategic customers have not attracted more attention from B2B marketing and sales research. Losing such a customer because it has not received the treatment it wanted, or keeping it at too great a cost, can both have devastating effects on suppliers, even large companies. For example, the knitwear manufacturer Baird was forced to close 14 factories in the UK and three in Sri Lanka when Marks and Spencer ended their 30-year relationship (Chapman 2004). Uniq (previously Unigate) made an operating loss of £3.6m on a turnover of £736m in 2007 when Marks and Spencer represented nearly 30% of the company's sales and other major retailers contributed most of the rest (Hawkes 2008). Marconi's loss of the BT contract signalled the demise of that business in 2006.

Key strategic customers may be few in number, but the inexorable developments in their increasing power and sophistication, globalization, consolidation and market maturity mean that they are crucial to suppliers in terms of present and future profit. These buyer–seller relationships are arguably the most interesting because of the scale of the rewards and risks and the organizational complexities involved. It really is inappropriate to subsume these relationships into general customer relationship management (CRM) research. KSAM should be seen as a business and research domain in its own right, albeit learning much from other areas of business research, including relationship marketing, selling, management and organizational theory, supply and demand chain management, to list just some of them.

The domain has probably not been helped by the failure to agree a name for it: key account management (KAM), national account management (NAM), global account management (GAM) and strategic account management (SAM) have all been used fairly interchangeably. In the USA, management of the most important accounts is termed SAM or GAM, and key accounts are somewhere down the customer pyramid below national accounts. Elsewhere in the world, KAM is taken to include all the most important accounts, with subdivisions into strategic, global and national accounts. The widely accepted definition of key accounts was formulated by Millman and Wilson (1995a) as 'customers in a business-to-business market defined by selling companies as being of strategic importance', linking the terms 'key' and 'strategic' together. Removing issues of geography, i.e. 'global' and 'national' (these customers are not necessarily key or strategic, although the size and complexity of global customers means they are more likely to be key strategic accounts), we therefore wish to propose a term for universal use for the activity under discussion in this book: key strategic account management, or KSAM.

A definition of KSAM

Clearly, KSAM requires a definition, and the literature is curiously lacking in this respect. While descriptions of good practice and full interpretations abound, they go well beyond a definition of the minimum that qualifies as KSAM. Furthermore, since the treatment of individual key strategic accounts will depend on the nature of each account and vary considerably, we feel that the definition should be positioned at the level of the organization. Companies can then see whether they are, or are not, implementing KSAM, by definition. They may be doing it well or badly, but it should be possible to be clear about whether they are executing what is generally agreed to be KSAM, rather than key account selling or something else. We believe that such a definition does not currently exist, and we therefore offer the definition of KSAM as follows:

> "Key strategic account management (KSAM) is a supplier-led process of inter-organizational collaboration that creates unique value for both supplier and strategically important customers."

This is, we feel, a 'necessary and sufficient' definition of KSAM. Adoption of a definition is important because the lack of it leads to misunderstanding of the requirement, development of inappropriate processes, and problems in operationalization when new processes are not adopted.

KSAM is supplier-led because it is a strategic initiative adopted by senior managers in the supplier organization, who choose which customers are strategically important now and in the future. Customers cannot force their suppliers to offer KSAM, although they may threaten to defect (not always as easy as either side thinks). So the choice of accounts is the supplier's initially, but it needs to be reciprocated: the customer has the choice of collaborating with the supplier, or not. They will need to perceive, or have the potential to perceive, that the supplier could be strategically important to them, too. If they have no wish to collaborate, they should not be a key account, since it is not in the supplier's interests to invest resources where the customer is unresponsive and the return will be poor. For the relationship to work, the benefits must be equitably distributed between both supplier and customer.

KSAM is a process, not a general idea that is open to individual interpretation at any time, parts of which may sometimes be applied and sometimes not. It is a process through which value is created, and sustainable KSAM requires that both customer and supplier should gain value from it. Given the variety and complexity of situations and businesses, it is most unlikely that the value will not be unique, so although there may be parts replicated for other accounts, the total combination of propositions will be different for each key customer.

In order to determine appropriate value for the customer and viable activities that also deliver value for the supplier, the two must work together to determine what exactly that will be. The process involves inter-organizational collaboration because KSAM is not something you do 'to' customers but 'with' them, and therein lies the major difference between KSAM and key account selling or standard account management. Even so, many suppliers are more comfortable with developing ideas internally for, but independent of, the customer and are then disappointed that they do not achieve a better reception when presented.

We would like to qualify this definition with a concept that additionally expresses the purpose and the principal means of operationalization:

> "KSAM offers individual propositions designed to secure long-term profitable business through the coordinated deployment of multi-functional capabilities."

The purpose of KSAM is ultimately profit in a profit-motivated organization (there can be alternative objectives in not-for-profit organizations). KSAM works through a process of investment and return on that investment, which means that its performance must be judged over a sufficiently long term to embrace both. Many elements of KSAM take time to put into place, both in terms of the constituents of the programme on the supplier's side – such as building the competencies of key account managers, modifying and developing new processes, and communicating with and involving the wider organization – and with the customer, building big relationships within their company, gaining a deep understanding of their business, and learning how to work well with them; and in the execution of value-adding projects, to plan, cost and gain approval for them and then to carry them out.

The key account manager is the expert in the customer who gains that deep understanding and from it, working with the customer, determines what value can be created. It is, however, largely the rest of the company that delivers that value, hence the deployment of multi-functional capabilities; indeed, the lack of cross-functional effort has often led to the failure of KSAM since, effectively, nothing has been delivered to the customer. Where functions each provide what they see fit for the customer, without coordination, the impact on the customer is patchy and confusing for them, and unlikely to lead to the required response. Most functions will be involved in some way in the realization of synergistic value in the form of cost benefits, quality enhancement, product development, market exploitation, process enhancement, etc.

Questions for research

In spite of the impressive body of knowledge of KSAM presented herein, there is much that is not yet understood. Ideal KSAM may readily be described, but it would sound like a utopia of altruistic and productive activity which we have never encountered in reality. Underneath the skin, even of programmes that are successful, is a mass of individual insecurities, organizational politics, ignorance of key facts and inertia that will never be examined by relationship marketers and CRM researchers.

Still unanswered are questions such as why, if companies can use their up-to-the-minute systems to determine the profitability of products and regions, they cannot properly account for the profitability of even their most strategic customers? This information is surely critical to the management of accounts that have an alarmingly strong influence on the overall profitability of the supplier's company, and yet our research (Woodburn 2004) questions whether they even want to know, such is the general poor performance in this area. Myths and assumptions abound on this subject which would not be tolerated in other areas of the business.

Although we all know that power has switched from the post-war supply side to the customer side in the 21st century, many companies' customer-centricity is hollow window-dressing. Where claimed, it is often more like sales-centricity, as the customers would attest: constant attendance by sales-targeted individuals is not what customers mean by customer-centric. We have yet to understand how to make the change from competitive, suspicious, defensive cultures towards genuine collaborative approaches throughout an organization. Is it a matter of industrial legacy or human psychology?

The ideal key account manager would have the competencies and personal attributes of a chief executive. Realistically, which of them are essential and which optional? Can missing competencies be adequately covered by members of an account team, or does that undermine the key account manager's credibility? Although key account teams are increasingly an intrinsic part of KSAM, we know little about their functioning and how to optimize this resource.

Very little is clear about how to incentivize KSAM activity, which is made more problematic by its long-term nature. While all are agreed that 'fairness' is paramount (Woodburn 2008b), there seems to be no agreement on how to achieve fairness, except by removing incentives altogether. While companies that had incentives wished to minimize them but were unable to stop them (which some would consider unfair) the companies that had none wanted to introduce them, so no-incentive situations are unlikely. Indeed, in addition to a near-total lack of understanding about how to reward KSAM, little is agreed about what good performance in KSAM is and how it should be measured as well as how it should be rewarded. The whole question of measurement in KSAM is open for research.

A concern for academics, however, is the pressure exerted by journals favouring papers based on quantitative research. While empirical research in KSAM is much needed, the number of key accounts is small, by definition, and when surveys include large numbers of accounts in order to yield statistically significant results, they are almost certainly including non-key accounts. The findings cannot then be confidently extrapolated to key accounts, and since we have identified substantial differences between other customers and the nature and behaviour of key accounts in close relationships with suppliers, there is good reason to believe that they would differ significantly. Consequently, we would expect qualitative research to be much more valid and practical, as well as more informative, than quantitative methods in researching KSAM. Needless to say, however, research projects that can be matched with a sound quantitative design would be very welcome, but we hope that journal editors will appreciate and readily publish qualitative, appropriately researched material on KSAM.

In summary, we are indebted to all 41 of our authors, who have done much in these papers to illuminate this important, challenging and fascinating area, but there is more we desperately need to know about it. The welfare and continued survival of many businesses depend on how they handle KSAM and they are, generally, woefully unprepared to implement it: they really need the knowledge and understanding that academic research could bring to them. This book hopes to stimulate both academic and practitioner interest in progressing our insight into KSAM, which will yield substantial benefits for both 'sides'.

Section 1: Strategic dimensions of KSAM

To many, the case for KSAM is clear and compelling. For those considering the extent of the shift in mindset and culture and the scale of the internal changes required, and for others more detached from the marketplace, the case needs to be made extremely obvious and compelling. Capon and Mihoc make the point that companies, in order to be successful in their fundamental mission to 'make profits today and promise profits tomorrow . . . must attract, retain and grow customers', which they can do only if they create more value for customers than the competition. It then follows that 'if a large percent of revenues derive from a small percent of customers, then those relatively few customers should receive a disproportionately large amount of firm attention and resources'. KSAM is about the optimal application of those resources and management of the outcomes.

***Capon and Mihoc* Making the case for managing strategic accounts**

However, while it is hard to contradict the logic of this argument, many companies and their senior managers find it difficult to swallow the consequences: sometimes because they seem to hold a naive belief that all customers and all account managers should be treated equally; sometimes because they cannot or do not wish to accept the changes to the existing organization that will ensue; sometimes because KSAM requires a degree of trust between trading partners that is simply alien to them. Indeed, in their paper, Piercy and Lane discuss the risks of KSAM, which should be considered alongside the drivers and the opportunities.

Companies are addicted to optimism and tend to assume that they can continue indefinitely as they are, which makes change just one option among others, even a dangerous frivolity to some. Depicting a future of decline is too uncomfortable, even though that would be the logical consequence of failing to adapt to the new reality of market conditions. Across a wide range of sectors, this reality means fewer, larger, globalizing customers seeking more value for their money: especially better integration with their total supply chain, and therefore suppliers with more capabilities operating over a wider geographical area. A supplier denying the impact of such factors is endangering the whole company by delaying the changes needed to protect its business.

Capon and Mihoc set out the pressures in the business environment that demand a KSAM response, together with those from key customers, from smaller, non-key customers, and from the 'new' role of procurement and the application of its techniques. It is critical that everyone in the supplier company embraces the KSAM programme, so they need to understand and fully accept why their company is introducing it – the drivers of KSAM are also the focus of Brehmer and Rehme's paper.

While companies yearn for simplicity, from the outset Brehmer and Rehme recognize its increasingly common presence in bigger businesses and in KSAM. They make an important link between complexity and the form of the KSAM programme designed to respond to it; indeed, they see that KSAM is often introduced to deal with complexity and uncertainty. The nature and source of the complexity – structural and/or operational – will affect KSAM differently, and they identify different types of KSAM programme accordingly:

***Brehmer and Rehme* Drivers for key account management programmes**

- Standard sales situation: low complexity in both dimensions, not requiring KSAM.
- Proactive KSAM programme: high operational complexity, initiated by the supplier internally for coordinating product offers, and driven by sales opportunity.
- Reactive KSAM programme: high structural complexity, driven by external, customer demands for a more coordinated contact and management approach (e.g. international coordination).
- Organization-based KSAM programme: high complexity in both dimensions, driven by belief in customer-centric organizational units.

As they point out, the last of these, i.e. the organization-based KSAM programme, requires the strongest commitment from corporate leadership. Brehmer and Rehme studied ABB over several years, prompting their observation that often 'KAM programmes are established by top management with the notion to increase sales to already established customers in local markets'. As customers become more international, or increase their range of activity or rate of growth, or become more complex in other ways, they demand a more coherent and coordinated approach. The supplier is then drawn towards organization-based KSAM, which is designed to deal with both internal and external issues and complexity, finally requiring its integration into the corporate structure. In her paper Woodburn charts a similar journey, in different terms, of transitioning to KSAM.

Whether KSAM is part of strategy or structure can be debated, and generally suppliers begin by trying to confine it to strategy, often ignoring the impact on structure that, almost inevitably, it will produce, as the company endeavours to work with it. As Brehmer and Rehme say, ultimately 'KAM is both a strategic platform for the sales organization and a part of the overall organizational design'. Perhaps suppliers should recognize the structural implications of what they have started earlier, or accept the limitations of what they can achieve without structural adaptation.

The linkages between strategy and structure occupy a large space in the minds of suppliers and KSAM researchers alike, including Woodburn in her paper on making the transition to KSAM. It would be naive to expect that a stated strategy is automatically embraced by an organization, and KSAM strategy is often diluted or negated by lack of genuine commitment and by general inertia and inability to carry through any kind of organizational change. Development of an effective KSAM programme has to run the gauntlet of a number of cultural factors which frequently frustrate progress, *Woodburn* **KSAM as an organizational change: making the transition** such as a lack of understanding of the difference between sales and KSAM, which can occur both within the sales organization and outside it among the rest of the company.

Resistance is not always owing to misunderstanding: KSAM may be understood but its implications for sales structure are not accepted, when it challenges current allocations of territory or sales results. Sales managers see a loss of status or even of financial incentives if key accounts are removed from their jurisdiction, and they argue against organization-based KSAM even where the customer is seeking this approach. At best, excessive layers of organization slow down appropriate responses to customers and, at worst, prevent KSAM happening. Customers read their importance to the supplier from the distance between their contact and decision-makers on the supplier board.

While suppliers and many academics consider KSAM to be a sales strategy, delivering the value that is intrinsic to KSAM, as discussed by several *Handbook* authors (e.g. La Rocca and Snehota), it has implications for other company strategies, such as product/service strategy, R&D strategy, logistics strategy and financial/ investment strategy. Clearly, the rest of the company needs to accept KSAM and its part in fulfilling the commitments generated, but often other functions stick to their own agenda, which may not be aligned to key customers or to KSAM. A major element in successfully making the change to KSAM is communicating with the rest of the company, understanding and responding to their needs and concerns, and winning their pro-active cooperation.

Woodburn charts the journey towards 'best practice' KSAM taken by companies across a number of sectors (leaving out the cul-de-sacs and errors that they may have entered into along the way) in terms of the actions to be executed to achieve the new way of working. A large, perhaps rather daunting, range of actions needs to be specified and implemented within major streams of activity:

- Strategy and planning: consisting of goals and strategy, planning and objectives, and research.
- Organization and people: addressing key account managers, key account teams and the KSAM community, and the wider organization and senior management.
- Processes: making adaptations in key account manager activities, other KSAM-linked activities and core processes (such as manufacturing, customer services, budgeting, etc.).

Suppliers progress through a series of phases of increasing KSAM sophistication. Many of the early decisions will need to be reformulated and improved as the company learns through its experience of KSAM, and realizes that it and its key customers have outgrown the initial approach, which no longer meets either's needs, as Brehmer and Rehme predicted.

Sengupta, Krapfel and Pusateri tested the common assumption, which clearly some buyers and sellers still harbour, that if the costs of changing a supplier were high, the customer would be obliged to stay with that supplier, to the disadvantage of the customer because the supplier would take advantage of the customer's dependency. This expectation is obviously a significant barrier to developing closer and more cost-consuming relationships; in other words, it undermines the whole concept of KSAM. However, Sengupta et al. were not convinced that this 'rule' applied in KSAM, so they set out to examine the impact of switching costs (the psychological, physical and economic costs

Sengupta, Krapfel and Pusateri
Switching costs in key account relationships

a customer faces in changing a supplier) on both the customer and the supplier, for better or for worse.

Perhaps not surprisingly, switching costs were increased by the customer's relationship-specific investment, but they were also increased by the supplier's adaptations and the incentives it offered to the customer. It might be expected that customers would resist investing in a supplier relationship in order to avoid this vulnerable position, but in longer-term relationships, in which the parties get to know and trust each other, the customer may choose to invest: in products, processes or dedicated people. Higher switching costs increase the importance of the relationship to the customer and its interest in maintaining a high-quality relationship for longer. Sengupta et al. found that higher switching costs resulted in better performance for both supplier and customer, i.e. a win–win situation, rather than the supplier win–customer lose outcome often assumed by customers – and therefore feared and avoided – derived from adversarial relationships. There seems to be a balancing mechanism at work, in which the supplier makes adaptations alongside the customer's investments.

Interestingly, Sengupta et al. also found that 'customers seem to value adaptation in a long-term relationship more than short-term incentives'. They concluded that spending on adaptation was a better use of a supplier's resources than short-term financial incentives such as discounts and sales promotions. So creating high switching costs is a good thing for the supplier, and not a bad thing for the customer. Therefore, logically, key account managers should be considering how they may be increased, even though it is likely that such increases for customers will be matched by the supplier. Although that looks like a job for the key account manager, Sengupta et al. saw it as the responsibility of the whole organization because problem-solving resources will be engaged across the company.

Croom expands on Sengupta et al.'s consideration of the customer's point of view and reminds us that the customer has its own perspective, which suppliers overlook at their peril. Indeed, most of this book takes the perspective of the supplier and looks at the customer through the eyes of the supplier, as the name KSAM implies. In fact, KSAM has always been a customer-driven approach, arising from their exasperation with, as they see it, the short-sighted, short-term, tunnel vision of suppliers. Croom exposes powerful reasons why customers seek KSAM from their key suppliers, many of them emanating from 'new' purchasing practices that buy more intelligently than in the past.

Croom
The strategic buyer: how emerging procurement strategies may support KAM/SAM relationships

Purchasing professionals now employ two kinds of competencies: *operational/technical* skills and *relational/interaction* skills. They have enhanced their capabilities in both areas, e.g. financial literacy, where they are now more interested in total cost and life-cycle cost analysis than price levels, and at the same time they increasingly focus on 'softer skills associated with building long term, collaborative relationships to drive innovation', even though the primary motivation may still be cost reduction. However, we should consider whether KSAM professionals have upgraded their competencies similarly: our experience does not convince us that they have. Most key account managers' financial and analytical skills are still quite poor, and while they would claim superior relationship-building skills, many relate to only a narrow band of contacts in the customer, and especially lack credibility with senior managers.

Importantly, Croom touches on the impact of trust in these relationships: without trust between business partners, very little can be achieved. Trust is often discussed as if it were a binary concept, simply 'on' or 'off', whereas high- and low-trust relationships can be observed, with all gradations in between. High trust has an economic benefit that can be traced through the speed and efficiency of responses, resulting in lower costs and higher revenues, which is reversed in low-trust situations.

Companies need to be internally aligned before they can reasonably expect to align with external partners, but Croom observes that 'even the firm itself may not understand their true capabilities', which is a significant hindrance to achieving internal alignment. 'Alignment between the activities of suppliers and buyers . . . is increasingly considered to be *the* fundamental strategic role for purchasing', but poor communication and low trust are important restrictions in to reaching that goal.

Some key account managers discount the customer's business logic and claim that good relationships are built on their personality and effort, but Croom demonstrates a rational approach to relationships on the customer's side, in which they are clear about the economic benefits they expect. Purchasing professionals, when asked for their reaction to the mantra 'people buy from people', said: 'Amateurs buy from people, and we are professionals.' Another, asked whether liking for the key account manager entered the buying equation, said: 'I like a man who gives me what I like.' Even in cultures that have traditionally placed more emphasis on personal empathy, the key customers are increasingly either global accounts importing well-embedded professional purchasing practices, or the most sophisticated local key accounts. As Croom says: 'The dynamic purchasing executive seeks out suppliers who can articulate a clear relationship development strategy and has developed a strategic account plan *in collaboration* with their customer.' And if that is not the kind of purchasing executive found in the customer, then whether there is any point in nominating them as a key account has to be challenged.

Piercy and Lane
Social and ethical concerns in strategic account management: emerging opportunities and new threats

Finally, Piercy and Lane sound a note – a symphony, in fact – of caution. They suggest that 'the perceived moral intensity of these relationships is commonly low' and therefore 'propose the need for greater transparency and senior management questioning of the ethical and moral issues implicit in strategic account management'. They challenge the ethical position of 'benefiting the few (large, strategic customers) at the expense of the many (smaller customers and other stakeholders)'. The counter-argument would be that B2B markets are increasingly dominated by a few large players; that in order to survive, businesses are obliged to accept, operate in and respond to the market environment that surrounds them; and that if any single supplier does not service a market leader as they require, the whole business could be lost. Nevertheless, they identify the substantial risks in high levels of dependence on strategic customers and raise some very valid issues which suppliers would do well to consider.

Piercy and Lane suggest that no single business is likely to be big enough to cope with the complex and diverse demands of huge, global customers, which are then supported by networks of alliance partners, in which success depends heavily on effectively matching the capabilities of the participating organizations with benefits and trade-offs in the relationship that are favourable for each of the partners. However, they argue that 'this process of matching . . . and realignment of goals and processes is likely to create serious weaknesses . . . and behaviours which would not otherwise be undertaken or . . . regarded as attractive or even acceptable corporate practices'.

Also of concern is the impact of a failed relationship on a company's remaining ability to compete and survive. Certainly, suppliers are acutely aware that the higher the level of dependence on a partner organization, the greater the strategic vulnerability created if the relationship fails. Sengupta et al. suggest that such dependency increases the quality of and commitment to the relationship, but not all relationships endure nevertheless, and the consequences of disruption must be recognized and, ideally, mitigated. With the survival of the company potentially at risk, moral and ethical values may not come to the fore. Indeed, executives may not perceive any ethical dimension in this or 'believe that they or their organizations should consider moral issues as a significant context for collaboration'.

However, mutual trust depends on ethical behaviour between the partners, so in that respect a successful relationship may be self-regulating in that respect to some extent, which is not to say that the collaboration itself might not behave unethically towards other parties. Piercy and Lane identify three aspects of SAM which they consider to 'pose moral and ethical dilemmas: (1) the impact of seller strategy which favours a few customers at the expense of the many; (2) the potentially harmful, though sometimes unintended, consequences of the strategic account relationship; and (3) the dilemmas faced in implementing the strategic account manager role, as it relates to information sharing across organizational boundaries, trust between partnered organizations and the principle of 'keeping promises', and the hidden incentives encouraging unethical behaviour which may be implicit in some strategic account management models'. The editors do not agree with the totality of their analysis, but all concerned should give careful consideration to the issues they raise and determine an appropriate response.

Section 2: Value creation through KSAM

Central themes in KSAM are the concepts of value and value creation. A common view is that KSAM programmes are initiated in the expectation that the potential supplier value embedded in relationships with strategically important customers, represented by turnover or profitability, will be protected and grown by offering buyers enhanced reciprocal value through preferential treatment in respect of prices, terms and individual attention. The contributions to this section suggest that this may be an oversimplified view.

A number of value-related sub-themes can be traced in this section, which suggest that value and value creation are not only central elements of KSAM programmes but also complex issues that are often poorly understood, particularly by senior management.

Some key questions are addressed in this section:

- What is value? (La Rocca and Snehota, Henneberg et al., Ivens and Pardo, Lacoste, McDonald and Woodburn, Lemmens and Vanderbiesen).
- Who creates it and who appropriates it? (La Rocca and Snehota, Henneberg et al., Lacoste, Ivens and Pardo, Lemmens and Vanderbiesen).
- What are the strategic and planning issues in creating value in KSAM? (La Rocca and Snehota, Lacoste, McDonald and Woodburn).
- How is the process managed? (La Rocca and Snehota, Henneberg et al., McDonald and Woodburn).
- Is the value created quantified and sufficient? (La Rocca and Snehota, Lemmens and Vanderbeisen, McDonald and Woodburn).

The idea that value is created by the supplier and appropriated by the buyer is challenged by La Rocca and Snehota, who build upon both the IMP tradition and the more recently emerging concept of service-dominant logic.

La Rocca and Snehota
Value in strategic account management

KSAM from the seller's perspective is about profit, not just about growing revenue, but how to grow profits and how to manage strategic customer relationships are seldom made explicit. Profit is associated with the value created in the relationship between customer and supplier, and traditionally account management has been credited with creating value for customers, by identifying needs and coordinating the activities of the seller organization to meet those needs with bespoke value propositions.

A radical shift has occurred in sales management from transactional to relationship selling and this has been mirrored in KSAM, which has also, until recently, been largely occupied with increasing revenue and share of wallet. The recent change of emphasis towards relationship management is a response to increasingly complex inter-organizational relationships that require higher levels of inter-organizational coordination by account management, and an ability to create new solutions that customers value. The argument put forward by La Rocca and Snehota is that value is created *with* rather than *for* customers. This insight, they claim, is not reflected in the literature.

If value creation is not exclusive to sellers, neither is its evaluation. Value has traditionally been associated with the ownership of goods, and the seller's task has been to discover needs, develop solutions and deliver them to customers in exchange for something else. Value derives from the use of products and services, not solely from their ownership, and value can be determined only from the perspective of the receiver; even then, value assessment will change with the change that occurs in individual and organizational perceptions, understanding, evolution and experience.

Within a B2B context, value does not derive from goods and services but reflects an ongoing process of problem resolution through interdependence, interaction and value creation. Value created through interaction has both costs and benefits to the customer and to the supplier, and solutions to problems may have immediate economic consequences in terms of performance, cost savings and so on, and increasing problem-solving capability.

Value is generated within the relationship, claim La Rocca and Snehota, yet interaction should not be viewed as the means of value creation but 'the very process of value creation itself, which is produced *in between* parties'.

La Rocca and Snehota then go on to discuss how value is generated in business relationships, identifying four *facets* of the process:

1. *Jointness* – the coupling and linking of resources, activities and actors that are jointly used by both supplier and customer.
2. *Solution enactment* – by which players are perceived as participants in the value-creation process: rather than creators or receivers of value, they engage in the solution generation/value-creation process from their own perspective, and interpret that value from their own perspective.
3. *Balanced initiative* – which recognizes that both supplier and customer are active in the search for solutions.
4. *Socio-cognitive construction* – where value is judged from the subjective perspective of individuals. Objective valuation is not possible: it constantly changes in the light of individual responses to experience and context.

This is a complex process involving many individuals from both organizations, requiring connections between customer and supplier organizations and their operations as well as interfacing many different resources and activities. The need is for coordination, both of the internal activities of the supplier and the joint activities with the customer, which suggests a need to go beyond coordination to *relating* (bringing the customer into the value-creation process) through a constant process of adaptation and co-evolution in their ways of working. There is a subtle distinction here that advocates the need to manage *within* the relationship rather than managing the relationship.

What of the skills required to manage this process? La Rocca and Snehota identify what they call the critical capabilities of SAM in light of the changing nature of the process which, they argue, are better perceived as organizational rather than individual abilities. These are presented as 'interaction capabilities, rather than reinforcing analytical skills and practices inspired by a planning logic'. The interactive nature of the process suggests the need for collective (inter-organizational) action rather than individual action. Mutual dependence and the essentially co-creative nature of relationship solution-generating processes leads to a focus upon:

- *Counterpart mobilization:* engaging, mobilizing and integrating the customer in solution generation.
- *Development agility*: developing a tolerance of ambiguity and the ability to innovate and act on partial information while being open to review and reformulate earlier choices.
- *Mindful experimentation*: being willing to experiment/act in times of uncertainty and ambiguity.
- *Persistency and resilience*: the process is ongoing and constantly changing, and the need for adaptation is continuous. Commitment and persistency, if combined with development agility, tend to yield positive economic outcomes over time.

La Rocca and Snehota make a valuable contribution to our understanding of the nature of value in B2B markets, how it is created, how it is interpreted and how it can be managed. They make thought-provoking suggestions as to the nature and form of organizational and managerial competencies necessary to be successful in generating solution-based value within the process of interaction that have important implications for management and approach in KSAM.

Henneberg, Pardo, Mouzas and Naudé Value dimensions and relationship postures in dyadic 'key relationship programmes'

Henneberg, Pardo, Mouzas and Naudé focus upon the management of portfolios of relationships. They also endorse the trend towards relationship-induced value management, the service-dominant logic of Vargo and Lusch, as opposed to the product-dominant logic of traditional marketing. They argue that relationship management processes and capabilities are not embedded in a single party to the relationship but represent dyadic strategic perspectives.

Much extant literature relating to value takes the perspective of the buyer and the value they receive from the seller. This is problematic in that collaboration implies mutual benefits and sacrifices. A dyadically grounded approach is adopted in this offering that takes into account the concept of co-production and mutual benefit, as well as recognizing the concepts of internal and external value.

Value in key relationships can be disaggregated into three levels – internal, exchange and relational:

- Internal proprietary value is created and appropriated by a single actor.
- Exchange value is created by the supplier and exploited by the buyer (or vice versa).
- Relational value is created and appropriated within the relationship.

Both buyer and seller are free to adopt any of these strategies unilaterally but the success of each decision is not independent of the strategic orientation of the dyadic partner. Indeed, some may not be viable or may require ongoing management and coordination.

Thus Henneberg et al. develop a taxonomy of nine relational strategy *postures*. Where strategies concur there is said to be a natural match. Where there are extreme differences between internal value and relational value orientations, then the dyadic relationship may be untenable. Managed relationships are perceived to exist where there is a minor difference between the dyadic partners' value orientation as between internal value and exchange value, and between exchange value and relationship value. Managed relationships occur where both parties in the relationship contribute to making the relationship viable. The four resultant managed relationship states require high levels of dyadic competence and their own specific set of dyadic strategies.

Henneberg et al. make the same point as La Rocca and Snehota, that dyadic competencies are developed not independently but within the context of the relationship, so they reside 'crucially in the resources and activities shared by the dyadic partners'. This paper makes four contributions to our understanding of value creation:

1. A range of value-creation strategies is identified that represents a portfolio of potential strategies that can be adopted by either dyadic partner.
2. Value must be viewed from both buyer and seller perspectives.
3. Value is the product of customer and supplier resources.
4. Actors require specific competencies and insights that are applied in an ongoing process to make the relationship viable.

While the future of KSAM may lie with increasingly collaborative, interdependent and interactive relationship strategies, the reality is that some buyer–seller relationships adopt a competitive stance and are adversarial, competing for transactional benefits. These opposing strategic approaches are argued to have different outcomes. A competitive approach, fuelled by a desire to achieve a greater share of limited transactional benefits, results in one or other party winning a greater share of the 'value pie'. A cooperative strategy, focusing upon deriving benefit from the relationship, results in a larger pie with potentially greater value for both parties. Even where cooperative strategies are pursued, however, buyers often perceive value creation as positive only if they appropriate a larger slice of the value pie.

At either end of the continuum these two approaches are mutually exclusive, but firms often display both, as they operate under the tension of reconciling the need to collaborate to achieve long-term mutual benefit with the need to achieve short-term price transactional benefits. *Lacoste* Lacoste identifies that some key accounts adopt hybrid strate- **'Vertical** gies, combining cooperation and competition, in order to maxi- **coopetition': the** mize their share of the value created. She dubs this relationship **key account** form *vertical coopetition*. It may be necessary for buyers to protect **perspective** their independence of choice within the market rather than select a few dedicated suppliers, while at the same time capturing value from relationship benefits.

15

Adopting relational, cooperative strategies provides buyers with a range of benefits related to product (quality, innovation, etc.), service (supply chain optimization, supplier-specific know-how) and interaction (e.g. problem solving) that is largely non-economic. These benefits are generated through high levels of interaction and mutual knowledge. Competitive strategies, although short term, also deliver benefits to the buyer in the form of achieving best price/quality, at the same time as offering a good overview of the market and allowing them the opportunity to switch suppliers in order to take advantage of innovation or better terms and conditions. This allows the customer to remain relatively independent of individual suppliers.

Two dominant approaches were observed in the adoption of hybrid *coopetitive* strategies: **competitive**/cooperative and competitive/**cooperative**. The first is a primarily competitive approach to the market but with the tactical use of relational approaches, in order to reinforce the competitive strategies. Only after the largest share of pie has been won will non-economic benefits be considered. The second is primarily cooperative, but with the use of competitive tactics to manage a number of aspects of the relationship. For example, transactional approaches are used to deter suppliers from opportunistic activity and ensure competitive prices are maintained. Firms were observed to make use of both approaches. For example, it was found that even where an extreme transactional approach was adopted by the key account, some attempts were made to achieve relational benefits in problem solving by facilitating information exchange.

These observations serve to remind us that although the trend may be towards closer, more collaborative buyer–seller KSAM relationships, not all important customers adopt consistent strategies, whether collaborative or competitive. They can be expected to act in their own best (short- and long-term) interest, adapting their strategic approach to meet the conditions pertaining to individual relationships and market conditions. Suppliers should be aware that from time to time key accounts may adopt strategies aimed at conditioning them to support customers' long- and short-term objectives.

While accepting that these types of customers exist and that many of them are key, the question arises as to whether these relationships are strategic in the sense that we have defined KSAM, or merely key? In some cases (see Lemmens and Vanderbiesen) even global key accounts attempt to extract concessions from their global suppliers for the very reason that they recognize how important they are to them. Evidently many suppliers who have KSAM programmes also have KAM or KAS (key account sales) programmes, highlighting the need for portfolio analysis when striving to create value with and for customers, and for development of different strategies that reflect the reality of relational potential.

Ivens and Pardo
Key account management in business markets: an empirical test of common assumptions

Ivens and Pardo return to the idea that the core objective of KSAM programmes is to create value for both buyer and seller, not to increase prices or share of wallet. They point to a need for a different form of management on the part of suppliers in order to achieve the joint value creation potential that is perceived to be the primary objective of KSAM programmes. Drawing upon the literature, KSAM relationships are identified as delivering benefits in terms of reducing uncertainty for suppliers. A distinction is made between *internal* uncertainty (the supplier's difficulty in predicting the actions of the buyer) and *external* uncertainty (the supplier's difficulty in predicting change in down-steam markets).

The literature also suggests that KSAM relationships are characterized as having:

- Higher levels of relationship-specific investment by the supplier.
- Higher levels of supplier dependence.
- Higher levels of formal contract.
- Higher levels of coordination of the supplier's customer-directed processes.
- Longer duration than ordinary relationships.
- More actors in the relationship.
- Higher levels of financial turnover.
- Customers that pay premium prices.

However, not all of these characteristics of KSAM organization were supported by Ivens and Pardo's research. Specifically, there was no evidence that the supplier's customer-facing processes were better coordinated, that relationships lasted longer, that higher prices were paid or that there were higher levels of formal governance. These apparent anomalies are discussed and the following conclusions are drawn:

1. Key account management programmes should focus on the development of value created for customers and suppliers.
2. To create value there needs to be coordination orchestrated by account managers with power to effect change.
3. Key account status may not be the sole preserve of existing customers but rather may be open to all with the potential for enhanced value creation.

McDonald and Woodburn's paper addresses the need for capturing the value to be created in a form that both organizations can use and execute. They highlight the importance of planning in developing and delivering tangible value to strategically important customers. While their approach stresses the need for suppliers to be proactive, they also point out, citing Henneberg et al., that strategies can be diverse and that they may be aimed at creating different kinds of value, differentiated by who produces and who appropriates the value. The offering from La Rocca and Snehota argues that all value is essentially co-created, but it is perhaps useful to make the distinction that there are occasions when the seller should be proactive, even if only for the purposes of getting the strategizing process started, while acknowledging, as McDonald and Woodburn do, that close customer involvement will ensure greater levels of acceptance of the value offered.

McDonald and Woodburn **Strategic account plans: their crucial role in strategic account management**

Account plans provide benefits at several different levels. They allow customers to express what added value they expect, the supplier to understand how the relationship will contribute to the wider corporate mission, the account team to articulate and understand relational strategies, and opportunities for learning. For the account manager they also provide a clear roadmap for the management of the account.

Value needs to be shared: if either party is appropriating the lion's share of the value then the relationship has no long-term viability. Value, the authors suggest, is finally defined by the contribution it makes to the bottom line for both customer and supplier:

- For customers, the bulk of value creation by suppliers results in lower costs.
- For suppliers, the bulk of value creation by customers results in business growth.

Plans should therefore be aimed at ensuring customer long-term profitability, although McDonald and Woodburn suggest that available tools are often not used to good effect in gauging profit, either of KSAM as a strategy or the value of individual relationships.

They discuss in detail approaches to strategic account planning and propose a number of methodologies for assessing the value that those plans deliver. For KSAM programmes to succeed they need to be supported by quality strategic plans that the company can trust and invest in. McDonald and Woodburn are unsure that many key account managers have sufficient experience and expertise to develop such plans. They are also unsure of the commitment of many supplier companies to the development of these plans, even though they may have rigorous planning processes in other parts of the business.

Adopting a KSAM strategy involves major change in internal culture and alignment of functions, systems and processes to meet the needs and deliver the value promised by KSAM programmes. This cannot be achieved without planning, and effective strategies are unlikely to be developed or implemented without the right quality of people and support from the highest levels within the organization.

Lemmens and Vanderbiesen
Using customer profitability and customer lifetime value to manage strategic accounts

Assessing the economic value of relationships is difficult, but without that knowledge senior management, understandably, has a problem with committing and sustaining investment in programmes that, as we have seen, may cause considerable disruption to the existing organization. This issue is addressed by Lemmens and Vanderbiesen, whose work is designed to quantify the value created in terms of customer profitability. They consider the quantification of value from the supplier's side, admittedly, since it is probably even more difficult to quantify the value the customer receives. They challenge the received wisdom that long-term relationships and customer profitability are necessarily related. They cite the growth in strategic importance, power and professionalism of global procurement in acquiring added value from their suppliers and suggest that account management programmes are a response to the increasing market power of global customers.

Measuring customer and not just product line profitability is important because of the relational costs associated with serving customers through KSAM programmes. Large customers can be unprofitable, not only because of the preferential prices they may have negotiated, but also because of the additional demands they make for account management benefits. These costs may be difficult to identify and quantify, but identifying levels of customer profitability helps to allocate the right costs and revenues at customer account level, leading to a clear view on the profitability of the customers. Lemmens and Vanderbiesen propose that activity-based costing is the only method that can correctly allocate costs accrued through activity around customers and allow the assessment of customer profitability. They provide a number of worked examples that provide clear guidance as to how customer lifetime value (CLV) may be calculated.

Customer profitability can be used as a measure on its own but is also valuable in helping to assess the asset value of customers, the CLV, which is important because it allows customers to be classified into tiers based on their long-term profitability, so that decisions can be taken concerning the allocation of resources to individual customer relationships. CLV can be influenced by the activities of the key account manager in building a closer relationship that facilitates:

- Enhancing cash flows by increasing sales or reducing costs.
- Accelerating cash flows.
- Reducing cash flow vulnerability by increasing customer loyalty, satisfaction and retention.
- Developing servicing propositions and value propositions that provide a platform for future cash flows.

In addition, it is proposed that encouraging customers to participate in co-creation reduces costs and enhances value. The key strategic account manager occupies a central role in facilitating dialogue, ensuring access to information, making everyone aware of the risks and ensuring transparency between all parties involved. The higher the level of his/her engagement in the customer organization and the greater the attention paid to risk reduction, the easier it will be to shorten the decision-making cycle, reducing the time to money.

What is value in the context of KSAM? Ultimately all value in business markets is economic value in terms of profit, but the traditional view of value as being the simple product of economic exchange is too narrow. Increasingly, direct economic and non-economic value is created within the context of relationships and interaction between buyer and seller. 'Non-economic value', in terms of learning, knowledge transfer, process capabilities and innovation etc., translates in the long term into profits and may provide a sounder foundation for long-term growth, so should perhaps rather be seen as indirect economic value.

Value may be created by supplier or customer or jointly and can be appropriated by either party or shared. Traditionally in KSAM, value has been perceived as being created by the account management team for the benefit of the customer, but increasingly customers are drawn towards co-creation with their suppliers and a sharing of mutual benefits. This is not always the case, however; the tendency has been for buyers and sellers to act in ways that support their own, often short-term, best interests and to appropriate a bigger 'share of the pie' where they can. If companies are to benefit from the potential for value creation inherent in interaction and interdependence, this kind of opportunism may not be in their best long-term interests, and a culture of cooperation, trust and mutual interest needs to replace too-blinkered a culture of self-interest.

Section 3: Developing KSAM programmes

KSAM is a strategic relationship marketing initiative that requires its place within the organization and ways in which it can align as one organizational element with others which it relies upon to help deliver value to customers. The issues facing managers designing and implementing KSAM programmes are made more complex because the programme is new: it must ultimately find a way to fit with (or change) existing organizational functions, structures, systems, processes and personnel. A further complexity is encountered because often KSAM is fundamentally different from other elements within the firm, in that it is organized around customers rather than around function, process, technology, product or geography, as traditionally. As such it may challenge existing power bases within the organization and almost certainly challenges existing ways of doing business.

The design of programmes must also address the issue of what it aims to achieve, what it will provide to strategic customers that is not available to ordinary customers, and who will manage the process, both at a strategic level and at the level of the individual relationship. Where will they sit within the organization and how will they interact with other departments in order to coordinate customer-facing activities?

This section offers a number of different perspectives on the problem of how to organize for KSAM. The first two, from Homburg, Workman and Jensen and from Wengler, focus upon those approaches to KSAM that result in superior performance: KSAM effectiveness and overall market performance on the one hand, and economic performance on the other. Yip and Bink identify three GAM organizational configurations and explore one in depth through the medium of a case study. Storbacka offers a framework that emphasizes the interactivity and interdependence of KSAM organizational design elements, stressing the importance of their centrality to the firm. Atanasova and Senn explore the nature of global teams and their role in the GAM process. We see that KSAM is not a solo sales activity, and that teams are becoming increasingly important in its delivery, so their findings are important for KSAM generally. Finally, Guenzi offers a case study of change to KSAM which constitutes a practical look at a company making the transition to KSAM, while so many fail to make the change at all (Wilson and Woodburn 2014), bringing a note of 'the real world' to complete the section.

Homburg, Workman and Jensen have synthesized their seminal papers of 2002 and 2003 to present four decision dimensions relating to KSAM organization, drawing on a wide body of literature:

> **Homburg, Workman and Jensen**
> **A configurational approach to strategic account management effectiveness**

- *Activities* – those things that are done for strategically important customers that are different from what is done for ordinary accounts and which are initiated by the supplier.
- *Actors* – who are responsible for delivering these additional benefits as coordinators (key account managers), contributors (other functional specialists) and supporters/facilitators (senior managers).
- *Resources* – the access that the programme has to sales and marketing and non-sales and marketing resources.
- *Formalization* – the degree to which the programme is formalized.

They posited that decisions made in these areas shape the KAM programme and impact upon performance. These dimensions were further developed into 11 variables, which expand on those dimensions: for example, activities are refined into 'activity intensity – the extent to which the supplier does more for key accounts than for average accounts' and 'activity proactiveness – the extent to which activities are initiated by the supplier'. They present an excellent discussion of these variables and their potential impact upon outcomes.

Homburg et al. drew respondents from companies from a variety of industries with turnovers of $15 million to $1,500 million, and from different levels within the KAM organizational hierarchy. They were asked to rate their KAM programmes on the variables and also to rate their company performance in terms of KAM performance and overall market performance. A taxonomy of KAM organizational clusters was developed, ranging from Top-Management KAM through Middle-Management, Operating Level, Cross-Functional, Unstructured, Isolated, Country Club and No KAM. Each cluster, displaying different levels and combinations of the 11 variables (for example, senior management involvement or formalization), was then associated with KSAM effectiveness.

Two of these clusters amounted to no KAM, i.e. No KAM and Country Club KAM, and two further forms were arguably not really operating KAM either, or at least not KSAM according to our definition, i.e. Unstructured and Isolated KAM. Positive findings included the importance of esprit de corps, proactivity in developing additional offerings for strategic accounts, and the involvement of senior management in the process. In an interesting but controversial finding, Homburg et al. claimed that high levels of formalization may tend to decrease KSAM effectiveness, which was later challenged by Storbacka. This apparent mismatch may reflect different aspects of formalization and the way that it operates: it should be positive for KSAM if it brings clarity to complexity, but it could also have negative connotations if it implies inflexibility and pressure to standardize.

These papers made an important contribution to our thinking about KSAM design and implementation and provided the foundation from which a great deal of

Wengler
The appropriateness of the key account management organization

further research evolved, including a contribution to the next paper in this section. It is surprising that before this article by Wengler, originally published in 2007, no attempt had been made to evaluate the economic effectiveness of KSAM strategies and organizational options by applying transaction cost economics (TCE) theory. TCE is one of the theoretical underpinnings of the IMP interactive, network and relationships approach to industrial marketing and purchasing, and KSAM may be viewed as the operationalization of the IMP approach from the supply side.

KSAM programmes remain popular, despite the difficulties of implementation which commonly result in poor levels of effectiveness and efficiency, because of increasing competition with other suppliers for customers in oligopolistic markets and customer expectations of closer, more collaborative relationships with strategic suppliers. This tension between profitability and competing effectively is accompanied by the tension between a generic KSAM organizational design and one that takes account of the demands of individual relationships. While the literature addresses the issue of different value propositions to meet the needs of different customers, little attention appears to be paid to organizing differently for each relationship. Wengler offers a decision model that he claims will 'help in the process of choosing the most appropriate key account management organization with respect to the characteristics of a specific customer–supplier relationship'.

As a relationship marketing strategy, KSAM organizational decisions need to take account of both internal and external influences, with the consequent need to calculate transaction costs from both inter-organizational and intra-organizational perspectives. KSAM relationships essentially represent the bilateral governance form of economic organization, envisaged by Williamson (1985) as standing (theoretically) between the extremes of firms and hierarchies. TCE has largely ignored the question of internal organization, but Wengler extends the discussion of the traditional transaction costs associated with asset specificity, uncertainty and frequency to questions of intra-organizational design and the impact of organizational design options upon transaction costs. Start-up costs and the cost of organizational resistance to change should also be considered in making cost–benefit comparisons. A decision model emerges that allows companies to assess the appropriateness of existing organizational forms and to choose the most appropriate key account management organizational alternative.

Globalization is one of the most potent factors driving the shift from key account selling to key strategic account management. Global customer organizations are complex and suppliers face a number of inter- and intra-organizational problems in striving to meet global customer design. Global KSAM organizational decisions must address a number of issues: achieving a balance between central coordination and local flexibility; integrating the global programme into the wider organization in an attempt to create internal commitment; resolving global–local authority and power and reporting issues, etc. However, many of these issues also arise with non-global key strategic accounts and should be considered in any KSAM programme.

Yip and Bink outline the main elements of global KSAM organi- **Yip and Bink** zation – i.e. the global account general manager, global steering **Organizational** committee, global account manager, global team and local **structures in** account manager – and discuss the importance of senior man- **global account** agement commitment in terms of executive support and the **management** central role played by information sharing in ensuring pro- gramme effectiveness. Global reporting structures and the use of customer councils at a global level are also addressed.

The global organizational elements may be configured in many different forms, but usually conform to one of three organizational designs:

* Coordination GAM.
* Control GAM.
* Separate GAM.

The nature of these different forms is discussed together with the benefits and problems associated with them. Yip and Bink observe that Control GAM appears to be the approach used most often, with companies tending to move from Coor- dination GAM to Control GAM. A few companies move on to Separate GAM, although this is not the norm. Control GAM appears to be the preferred form adopted by most companies because it provides the ability to balance global power with local knowledge and engage local managers effectively. These advantages and others are demonstrated through the use of a case study exploring GAM at Hewlett-Packard.

The need to integrate KSAM organizational structures within the firm is a central theme in the literature, and equally in this section. The term *integration* implies that something is designed to fit with existing structures, systems and processes, but it should be remembered that KSAM often represents a major shift in the firm's orientation that requires change of existing entities, in order for it to support the fundamental principles and objectives of KSAM. The co-creation of value implicit in organizing for KSAM demands integration and coordination of activities both within the supplier firm and with the strategic customer. KSAM must be viewed not as a sales strategy, therefore, but as a management strategy, geared towards achieving strategic goals as well as the identification of future growth opportunities through a deep understanding of the customer, aligning structures, systems and processes accordingly.

Using an iterative, abductive research process involving sales management experts, as well as participants drawn from a group of nine multi-national firms headquartered in the United **Storbacka** States and several European countries, Storbacka identifies the **Designing** design elements and related management practices of KSAM **strategic account** programmes and differentiates between then according to their **management** impact upon inter- and intra-organizational alignment. His **programmes** framework reflects the necessity for strategy, structure and systems to complement each other and to effect a high degree of internal fit, or configuration. It pinpoints the interconnectedness between different design elements and describes how effectiveness in KSAM programmes is achieved through configuration of the various elements. The research also demonstrates that a number of configurations can be successful, depending on the stage of development of the programme, differing strategic objectives, or industry logic.

Storbacka makes considerable contributions to our thinking about organizational design for KSAM and the conditions under which those designs may be successful. The paper goes beyond the identification of the elements of organizational design for KSAM. From an inter-organizational perspective the model emphasizes the interconnectedness and interdependence of the various elements, the degree to which the initiative is *core*, and demonstrates the centrality of the programme to the firm. An intra-organizational perspective makes evident the value of the bespoke value proposition, an underpinning collaborative customer focus, emphasis on flexibility, and the role of the account team. The value to managers is that the model affords them the opportunity to think through the systematic development of the inter-related elements of the programme in their search for effectiveness.

Atanasova and Senn continue the global theme with the development of an integrative model that sheds light on the performance determinants of global customer teams by combining concepts drawn from both customer management and organizational behaviour research. They see the area as under-researched compared with issues related to programme organization and individual account managers. Indeed, the emphasis in this section on the importance of interdependence, coordination and collaboration makes clear the importance of teams and teamwork in offering value to customers. Global KSAM teams may be structured in a number of ways, but they all involve high levels of vertical and horizontal interaction over multiple geographies, and demand interaction both inside and external to the organization.

Atanasova and Senn
Global customer team design: dimensions, determinants and performance outcomes

The conceptual framework offered by Atanasova and Senn examines the relationship between team design, organizational context and processes and their impact on relational and financial performance. The value of this research is that it moves beyond structural issues to identify key performance indicators, while emphasizing the need for management to take a holistic approach to the composition and management of global customer teams. All of the team characteristics or contextual factors identified were found to have an impact upon performance and, as many of these fall under the control of senior managers, the model provides a practical tool for team design and performance improvement.

So far we have considered the structures and management practices that accompany the effective operation of KSAM programmes around issues of integration, collaboration, internal fit, configuration and so forth. The reality is that the adoption of KSAM nearly always demands radical change within the organization. This is recognized in the last contribution in this section. Guenzi applies the McKinsey 7S framework to an analysis of the change from sales-led to KSAM-focused strategy at Bosch Automotive Aftermarket Italy, which he calls the *key accountization* of the firm. The case study provides a number of general management rules for managing this change process effectively. Core to success is the involvement of senior managers in driving the process, changing culture to reflect customer orientation and stimulating interaction and collaboration between different functional areas. Verbatim comments illustrate many of the issues involved with transitioning to KSAM, but also encouraging responses to progress. The case study brings to life the theoretical contributions to KSAM programme development.

Guenzi
Key accountization at Bosch Automotive Aftermarket Italy: managing and implementing a strategic change

In concluding our review of the contributions to our understanding of the issues facing companies developing KSAM programmes, we note that there are still rich opportunities for further research. Much early research into KSAM has been descriptive and light on theoretical underpinning. Wengler argues that there is an opportunity and a need to carry out more theory-based research, drawing not only on transaction cost economics but also on organizational behaviour, network theory and so on. Storbacka identifies a number of possible avenues for further research and proposes, as do Atanasova and Senn, greater use of quantitative approaches to measure the impact of individual elements of KSAM programmes upon performance. Other areas that remain under-researched include the impact of different types of KSAM structures upon performance, the development of measures for elements that are normally viewed as subjective, what cultural issues might be involved and, perhaps most important of all, more dyadic studies. We have heard in this section that KSAM is of necessity about interdependence, interaction, collaboration, cooperation: so should there not be a focus in our research that takes the dual perspective of buyer as well as seller?

Section 4: Operationalizing KSAM

The principles of KSAM are clear and simple, but its implementation and implications are much more complex and challenging. Indeed, there are many KSAM failures where implementation has never really happened, where only a few cosmetic changes have been made and so, not surprisingly, key accounts have not perceived any material differences and therefore have not responded differently to the supplier either. In Section 1, Woodburn shows some of the common factors inhibiting the operationalization of KSAM, but it is still astonishing that suppliers can do so little to implement their strategy and yet believe that they are pursuing KSAM. Effective KSAM requires concrete change, certainly to attitudes and approaches but also to structures, processes and metrics, much of which is driven by company functions outside the sales and customer management departments. Often their drivers remain unadapted and at odds with KSAM, resulting in a deadlock which is frequently not observed by management; or it may be seen but is left unchallenged and therefore unchanged. This section addresses some of the key elements in KSAM implementation, though it cannot hope to lay bare all the decisions, goals and processes that need to be realigned if KSAM is to succeed.

At its most basic, KSAM could be said to depend on two central decisions: who gets it and what do they get? There is a good argument that key customer selection is a strategic issue, but it is also the key to implementation: suppliers often find that a good starting place is the decision 'who gets it', i.e. key account selection. A concrete listing of named key accounts helps them to move on from the concept of KSAM to actual implementation. On this decision hang many others, about structure, goals, offers, financing, measuring, manning and recruitment and much more. These decisions therefore should be made carefully, objectively and realistically – and often are not, resulting in suppliers with too many key accounts, which they cannot support, and/or the wrong key accounts, from which they will not get the response they require.

Zolkiewski
Recent developments in relationship portfolios: a review of current knowledge

Buyers have long used a matrix approach to the categorization of their suppliers, while numerous KSAM academics have been fascinated by the construction of portfolios of customers, leading to the identification of the most appropriate as key accounts. At the same time, suppliers have generally overlooked all this knowledge and experience, using simplistic approaches that have generally not served them well. They commonly choose the largest customers, regardless of their nature and potential, so greater and very necessary sophistication can be brought to this selection, as Zolkiewski suggests. She looks at customer portfolios as the principal means of selecting key customers and managing relationships with them appropriately.

Customer portfolio analysis is not a trivial matter: it plays a central role in resource allocation decisions, so 'different portfolio models are grounded in different perspectives on how resources should be allocated'. Zolkiewski provides a thorough review of portfolio methods of customer analysis, showing a wide range of factors that may be taken into consideration, and discussing the implications. Indeed, in the following paper, Gök describes in some detail how individual customer strategies, with their resource-demand consequences, are derived from customer portfolios, and Zolkiewski also shows how other authors have demonstrated significant outcomes driven by portfolio analysis.

The question is, then, how should suppliers' construction and use of customer portfolios be improved? Three distinct phases may be identified:

- Determination of an appropriate model to use and the criteria to be assessed; collection of data and construction of the portfolio.
- Use of the portfolio to select key accounts.
- Focus on positions in the portfolio to develop individual customer strategies and assess their resource requirements.

Interestingly, Zolkiewski notes a distinction made by Terho (2009) between portfolio analysis, i.e. the activity of producing the customer portfolio view, and responsiveness, i.e. how the supplier reacts to it. In many cases, there is no specific response to the portfolio analysis, or the response is rather unfocused and dislocated from the portfolio, or no structure exists through which specific decisions and responses at portfolio level can be made, as Woodburn (2004) observed.

In theory, selection is simple: for profit-mission companies, the question to ask would be: 'Over the next X years, which customers will bring us the most profit?' (with X = 3+, depending on the nature of the industry). If that data were available, selection could be automatic; but of course, as all that data lies in the future, it is not available, so the job of the process of portfolio construction and key customer selection is to find indicators that will point to the best profit performers. It is, however, also confused by the influence that the supplier has on the outcomes, which will depend, to some extent, on their own actions, like how much they invest in the relationship and what investments they make, and on their position in terms of relationship, power and trust.

Zolkiewski and other authors highlight the importance of the relationship with the customer and with other members in the network, since these relationships are usually part of a web of interactions between individuals and groups. It may also be considered that the importance of the relationship, for a profit-focused entity, is determined by its capacity, sooner or later, to deliver profits to the supplier. Zolkiewski gives an excellent review of the pros and cons of numerous approaches. She exposes many of the ramifications of customer portfolio analysis: 'Managers need to be aware that portfolios can be used on a number of different levels.' KSAM is emphatically not a 'one-size-fits-all' strategy, and customer portfolios underpin the optimum application of that approach.

In his paper, Gök describes in some detail how individual customer strategies, with their resource-demand consequences, are derived from customer portfolios. He embraces customer heterogeneity and demonstrates how it can be managed, in contrast with suppliers which prefer to avoid complexity by pretending that simplicity and standardization can exist where they do not and cannot. Account portfolio analysis is designed to give prominence to customers to whom the company allocates strategic funds in the hope of developing future business, as well as to emphasize those customers on which the company is dependent. Portfolio analysis helps managers to evaluate customer relationships for development and control purposes, especially in ensuring their long-term profitability, and forces them to adopt a future-oriented perspective. It can also encourage the analysis of the supplier's needs and requirements from the proposed relationship before committing resources toward these objectives, which can easily get lost in the rush to introduce KSAM.

Gök
Account portfolio management: optimizing the customer portfolio of the firm

Through two case studies, Gök shows how the process of portfolio analysis can be applied to the development of strategies for each key customer. A multi-criterion, two-step model is used, whose virtues can be considered in the light of Zolkiewski's review, but Gök demonstrates clearly how such a model drives quite specific customer strategies. Two-step processes have been accused of complexity, but this shows that they are both viable and valuable, when approached systematically. Gök points out that account portfolio analyses are context-dependent, so the criteria used may differ. He also notes that collecting the data can be costly and time-consuming: on one hand, criteria should avoid being so difficult or abstract that the data captured is likely to be highly inaccurate or incomplete; on the other hand, criteria should avoid focusing so much on ease of collection that the analysis becomes primarily backward-looking, or simplistic and unrepresentative of important considerations. Good companies will collect much of the data required anyway as part of their market intelligence and customer insight.

In spite of the many potential criticisms that have been levelled at customer portfolio analysis, careful consideration of the criteria applied can avoid most of them, coupled with regular and active reviews of the portfolio. Companies need to be prepared to change customer positions in the portfolio and refresh their strategies when circumstances change, and to demote accounts when others are promoted, bearing in mind that any company has a limited capacity to offer KSAM treatment. While, in principle, resources should be allocated to high-potential and high-attractiveness customers, in Gök's view such suggestions are rather naïve in terms of addressing the actual direction of allocation and investment decisions, and a thorough account portfolio analysis can be used as a valuable decision support tool in KSAM.

The processes involved in KSAM seem to have received little attention from researchers, and yet many KSAM failures can be attributed to a lack of implementation rather than a lack of intent. We could suggest that if there is no process for doing something, it is not getting done: and this seems to be exactly the situation in many companies – KSAM is just not happening. For example, during a KSAM revival in his company, one key account manager asked 'Are we actually going to 'walk the talk' this time?' Directors tend to make decisions about what they want to see, leaving the 'details' to others, harbouring a surprisingly naive expectation that it will take place. Often very little is executed in reality, partly because of a failure to identify and deal with significant barriers or allocate necessary resources, but also because nobody has worked out the processes of execution. Modifications need to be made in both the supplier's decision-making processes and its delivery processes, since key accounts tend to require variations that involve changing some part of the supplier's normal processes, to offer something different, faster, more transparently, more interactively or whatever it is.

Ojasalo
Strategic account management processes at corporate, relationship and annual level

In KSAM, much of the 'devil is in the detail', but real knowledge in this area is rather scarce. So the extensive review of what has been written about KSAM processes provided by Ojasalo will be invaluable to those endeavouring to understand how KSAM actually works. It offers a great deal of food for thought and should prompt companies transitioning to KSAM to check whether all the processes he highlights have been identified and modified appropriately. It might also trigger the reflection that many of these processes are interlinked and should not be considered in isolation of each other, or of the impact of changing them on the rest of the company's activities. Through mapping KSAM processes at different management levels, Ojasalo emphasizes how critical the commitment and effort of the whole organization is to the success of the KSAM programme, a point that this book reinforces again and again in many different aspects of KSAM.

In order to organize this multitude of implementation activities, Ojasalo offers a three-level framework of processes involved in KSAM: those relating to the corporate level in a supplier company; to the relationships it manages with its key accounts; and to the annual level, which corresponds with the regular and ad hoc activities that deliver KSAM throughout the year. He discusses the hierarchical nature of these levels of processes and their different characteristics, and suggests that this hierarchy also implies an 'order in which these processes have to be tackled if the company is interested in introducing a systematic SAM approach'. Our observations support this notion, since companies are often seen to introduce new processes to implement KSAM at relationship or annual/operational level without having changed corporate-level process, e.g. new account planning not coordinated with existing corporate business unit planning, resulting in misunderstandings and mismatches which cause unhelpful clashes, eventually necessitating a rethink and further changes that are confusing, frustrating, demotivating, exhausting and time-wasting.

Ojasalo notes that, not surprisingly, processes differ according to the task in hand. For example, at the corporate level, the processes involved are different when the company is considering *whether* to adopt a KSAM philosophy; deciding *how* to adopt KSAM; maintaining and improving its KSAM approach; or abandoning its KSAM programme. At the relationship level, processes should take into account the stage of relationship existing with the specific key account. At this level, there must also be processes for developing the value proposition tailored to that account, and selecting and managing the key account manager and team. Rarely considered are the processes that are involved in dissolving or partially unravelling a relationship, but these are also important if negative legacy issues are to be avoided.

According to Ojasalo, annual processes revolve around the annual plan, which is itself subordinate to the long-term relationship plan. The annual account plan details the value to be offered; the outcomes in terms of benefits to the supplier, and customer; relationship development and engagement activities; information exchange; and more. Overall, there should be an appropriate process in place to deliver whatever is specified in the account plans: otherwise, the danger is that they may only represent wishful thinking. KSAM-adapted processes are a fundamental element of implementation into which much more research is needed.

Frequent references to the relationship between buyer and seller in KSAM are made, but not much has been written about what is going on in these relation-

Wilson
Developing
strategic key
account
relationships in
business-to-
business markets

ships and how they work, which, given their core centrality to KSAM, is curious. So Wilson's paper plays a valuable role in exposing what these relationships look like and how they should be managed. Several researchers have identified a series of stages in these connections which, although they may have different points of departure and different labels, are broadly aligned in their charting of the development of such relation-- ships, from more distant and transactional relationships to much closer and more strategic and mutually-supportive relationships. Of these, Millman and Wilson (1994) is probably the most well-known, and Wilson uses that schema to link relationships with the problems addressed by the parties to the relationship through his Product, Process and Facilitation (PPF) model.

We all understand that our behaviour in a relationship is, and should be, strongly influenced by the atmosphere of the relationship: obviously, we behave differently with close family compared with acquaintances, whether we are cooperating together or dealing with conflict. Given that buyers can trade with a supplier without a close relationship, why either side should seek to develop a relationship and what is its purpose for each are valid questions: the reduction of uncertainty is one answer, the need to solve problems another. Wilson goes further and explores how these relationships address the problems identified by Håkansson (1982) of 'limitation', which represents the transaction costs incurred through elements like technology, organizational structure and knowledge; and 'handling', which relates to long-term development and management of the relationship, like power, dependency, cooperation and conflict.

Wilson puts problem resolution at the heart of buyer–seller interaction. There is a hierarchy of problems, some requiring more resources than others for their resolution, which are different according to whether they relate to product, process or facilitation needs. Solutions are more readily determined when the type of problem is understood in these terms. Wilson also links the nature of the problems to be solved with the stage of relationship reached: for example, where sellers concentrate on meeting only product-related customer needs, the relationship 'will be essentially arms'-length, transaction focused and display low levels of customer involvement', and they are unlikely to gain competitive advantage by these means alone. Suppliers that 'can convince their customers of the value of addressing . . . process related issues tend to develop closer relationships with their customers and are less often the victim of competitor activity'.

Facilitation problems are about the way business is done, requiring adaptation on both sides, and their resolution is associated with the closer states of relationship. They involve activities like joint value creation, inter-organizational team-working, and joint development of technology and markets. Through linking relationship stages and problem resolution together, the activities that drive the engine of these relationships can be observed, understood and executed more specifically and usefully and with a higher degree of sophistication than previously. Since a great deal of potential cost and profit depend on them, this understanding is extremely valuable to practitioners as well as to academics.

At the heart of the relationship with the customer is, of course, the key account manager. Once considered a solo, sales-focused role, we now know that successful key account managers lead an account team and contribute widely to the strategies of their own company and the customer's too, which brings the role to a higher, managerial level requiring a substantially different portfolio of competencies. Wilson and Holt show how understanding of the role has changed, partly as KSAM itself has developed, and partly as its implications in terms of the people who deliver it have become clearer. Nevertheless, many companies have yet to recognize that the job demands more senior managers with a much wider range of competencies, for which they will need to pay more.

Wilson and Holt
The role of the key/strategic account manager

Wilson and Holt highlight the differences between strategic key account managers and salespeople, which include the formers' need to work with both external processes, through multiple contacts within the client organization that span functions and hierarchical levels; and internal processes, to manage multi-functional 'virtual' teams, access resources and influence decisions impacting on client relationships. Even so, there is no single configuration of the role that strategic key account managers play: it depends on the relational context; the degree of relational intensity; organizational complexity and cultural diversity; and the customer's demands. Wilson and Millman (2003) summed up the role in the term *political entrepreneur*, which describes people who can recognize and realize the potential for innovation and value creation, and at the same time understand how organizations work, manage people and resources, and influence decisions through networking on both sides. Holt (2003), particularly, focused on the boundary-spanning requirements of strategic key account managers and the importance of their network connections.

Looking at the relational context of the role, it seems clear that various stages of relationship involve different internal and external interactions, different demands, different activities and different decisions, which are, not surprisingly, bound up with the nature of the strategic key account managers' role. Fortunately, since good strategic key account managers are scarce and expensive, that means companies can match their 'inventory' of key account managers with their 'inventory' of customer relationships, reserving their best-qualified and most KSAM-sophisticated key account managers for customers with the KSAM sophistication and business potential to warrant them. Human resources departments should be aware of the implications so that they recruit and develop people to fulfil 'inventory' needs, but many do not have an appropriate understanding of the role and continue to recruit salespeople to the position.

While there is much more to discover about the strategic key account manager's role, enough is already known to see that it changes and often challenges traditional organizational hierarchies and structures and ways of working. In order to carry out the expectations of both supplier and customer, the strategic key account manager needs a higher level of authority, participation in strategy-making, more resources (particularly in terms of an account team), more access to other functions and locations, and a different approach to remuneration, alongside accountability and the competencies to leverage those opportunities appropriately.

Clearly, positioning the strategic key account manager role in the company and making the changes that will allow it to work is a critical part of operationalizing KSAM, but so is identifying the right people for the job. Through demonstrating the scope of the role, Wilson and Holt show the breadth and depth of capabilities now required, while in their paper, Mahlamäki, Uusitalo and Mikkola present empirical evidence of some key personal characteristics that are positive indicators for role performance.

Many companies still recruit key account managers for their track record in sales, and even the more sophisticated suppliers seek a set of task-orientated 'competencies' that, although very important, are not the only factors influencing performance in the job. Personal characteristics affect outcomes too, and whereas competencies can be acquired, it is much more difficult to change personal attributes. A leading exponent of KSAM said her company 'recruited for the attributes and trained for the competencies' it needed in key account managers. However, most companies are wary about discussing personality elements, possibly because of employment legislation, but this reticence is mistaken: most legislation requires a demonstration of the objective relevance to the role, which Mahlamäki et al. have shown.

Using measures of overall job performance and two of its dimensions – relationship performance and sales performance – Mahlamäki et al.'s results suggest that

Mahlamäki, Uusitalo and Mikkola
The influence of personality on the job performance of strategic account managers

life experience or experience working with customers do not necessarily lead to a better-performing strategic key account manager. Correlations between job performance and age, gender, education level, customer work experience and work experience with the company were not statistically significant, although the closest to significance were education level (negative, i.e. not relevant to performance) and work experience with the company (positive, i.e. useful). This suggests that suppliers can look at a wide range of demographic profiles from which to select their key account managers.

Mahlamäki et al. provide evidence that extraversion, agreeableness and conscientiousness contribute to better relationship performance, sales performance and overall performance, particularly extraversion. They also looked at emotional stability and openness to experience, but neither of these seemed to make a difference to job performance. Armed with this information, suppliers can prioritize some characteristics in key account manager candidates over others, which can be very valuable in the often difficult debates that surround selection to these crucial positions.

Clearly, there is much more work to be done to establish the 'ideal' profile for a key account manager, bearing in mind that, as Wilson and Holt showed, the role changes according to the relationship context and therefore also the skills required to fulfil it well, to some extent. Other personality elements, such as curiosity, creativity, gravitas and more, could usefully be exposed to empirical research, so that suppliers could be less dependent on the instinct and intuition of selectors.

While the *Handbook* has included key issues in operationalizing KSAM, there are others we have not covered which are also of interest: for example, rewards and performance measures should be different from those used in sales, but how? Key account managers' leadership of account teams is often poor, but how should it work? Customer profitability is crucial, but which systems provide good information with a manageable amount of effort? Many companies have made their decision to adopt KSAM and now the biggest questions are about how to execute it. Disappointment often seems to be more a failure of execution than of strategy.

SECTION 1

STRATEGIC DIMENSIONS OF KSAM

Making the case for managing strategic accounts

BY NOEL CAPON AND FLORIN MIHOC

Abstract

This paper argues the case for the adoption of account management programmes by first recognizing that all firms in business-to-business markets have a relatively small number of customers (current and potential) that are critical for long-run future health. Because they are so important, the firm should treat them better than it treats its average customer. It further argues that traditional go-to-market strategies are under pressure from a range of environmental and customer-related factors, leading to fragmentation of the traditional system, and that this system will remain but two additional systems are forming – for small customers and for key, strategic and global customers. For the effective implementation of KAM programmes companies must achieve agreement or congruence between the four key organizational elements of strategy, organizational structure, systems and processes, and human resources.

Introduction

The best place to start in making the case for managing strategic accounts in a business-to-business (B2B) environment is with the fundamental business model (Figure 1). This model assumes that the basic operating task for managers and their companies is to make profits today and promise profits tomorrow. If the firm is successful in this task, it will survive and grow, and shareholder value will increase. However, if the firm is unsuccessful in making profits for a sufficiently long time period, it will eventually go bankrupt and likely be forced out of business. Hence, consistent operating success in making profits enables the firm's survival and growth, and leads to enhanced shareholder value.

The managerial imperative to make profits is all well and good, but the causal relationships laid out in the top part of Figure 1 beg an important question: What does the firm have to do to make profits today and promise profits tomorrow? The answer is extremely simple but very powerful: the firm must attract, retain and grow customers. The firm succeeds in this task by delivering value to customers – the vertical dimension of the figure. But merely delivering value to customers is insufficient. The value that the firm delivers must be greater than the one its competitors deliver so that it may secure differential advantage. Securing differential advantage provides the firm with some level of monopoly power (Lerner 1934) and allows it to earn profit margins that exceed the going interest rate.

It is all well and good for the firm to secure differential advantage and to attract, retain and grow customers, but all customers are not equal; some customers are more equal than others (Orwell 1945). The customer revenue distributions of most firms are skewed, following a Pareto distribution (Davis 1941) – more popularly known as the 80:20 rule. In this formulation, 80% of the firm's sales revenues derive from 20% of its customers. Of course, this rule is not exact: for

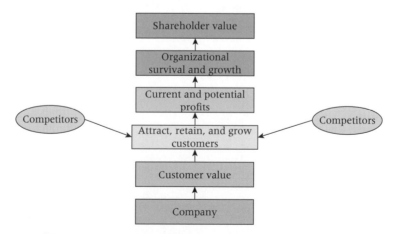

Figure 1   The fundamental business model

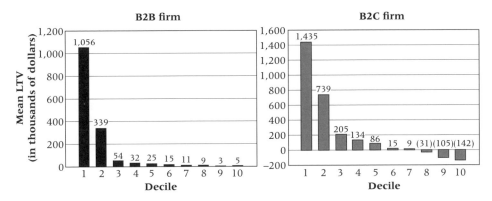

Figure 2 Customer lifetime value distributions

some firms the ratio may be 70:30 and for others 90:10, or even more skewed. (And we should not just confine ourselves to current customers; some customers that provide small revenues today may join the 20% important customers within a few years.)

The implication for the firm is quite straightforward: if a large percentage of revenues derive from a small percentage of customers, then those relatively few customers should receive a disproportionately large amount of firm attention and resources. But where should the firm locate these resources? That is also quite straightforward: if the 80:20 (70:30) rule is true, then the 20:80 (30:70) rule must also be true – 20% of firm revenues derive from 80% of the firm's customers. In general, these 80% of smaller customers are less important to the firm's future than the 20% of larger customers; hence, they should receive less attention and resources. For many managers, this is a harsh truth to stomach, but they cannot escape the reality that resources are scarce. Unless they accept and act on this reality, they will be condemned to the fate of one well-known company. A senior sales manager famously said of this organization: 'The problem we face is that senior management doesn't seem to understand the implications of the 80:20 rule; they want us to be *fair* to all of our customers. The result is quite predictable; we give the same *lousy* service to all our customers.'[1]

We can move beyond revenue distributions and even profit distributions to consider customer lifetime value (CLV) (Capon 2012). CLV is the expected discounted profit stream the firm earns from a customer factored by the retention rate/probability. Figure 2 shows empirical results from two firms: a B2C firm and a B2B firm (Kumar and Shah 2009). The y-axis measures CLV; the x-axis classifies firms by deciles – largest 10%, second 10%, etc. The figure shows that for both firms, the CLV distribution is highly skewed (in excess of 90:10); the top two customer deciles are responsible for CLV for each firm. For the B2B firm, CLV

---

[1] Personal communication to the first author.

just declines as customer deciles become smaller. For the B2C firm, the eighth, ninth and tenth customer deciles incur losses.

To summarize: all firms have a relatively small number of customers (current and potential) that are critical for long-run future health. Because they are so important, the firm should treat them better than it treats its average customer. This admonition may sound unfair, but it is absolutely necessary. However, all firms have traditional organization structures and processes for addressing customers that may have been in place for many years but do not recognize the new reality. In this paper, we present these traditional systems, we discuss the various pressures they face, then we show the ways in which many firms are evolving their go-to-market approaches. These new systems recognize the realities of the fundamental business model and the Pareto distribution that characterizes their revenue sources, and attempt to address their weaknesses in this new and evolving world.

Addressing customers

Most B2B firms' traditional approach to addressing customers typically embraces some form of personal selling effort. The basic choice that firms make is to conduct this activity in-house with an employee sales force or by outsourcing the selling effort to third parties such as agents, brokers, representatives and/or distributors. When the firm decides to conduct the selling effort itself, it must trade off selling effort effectiveness with the cost of sales. Typically, the least costly approach is to organize the sales force by geography – each salesperson sells all of the firm's products to all customers within a well-defined geographic area. However, if customer needs and/or product characteristics vary widely, this approach may not be very effective. For this reason, the firm may specialize its sales effort organizationally by product, market segment, distribution level, current versus potential customers, or some other dimension. Indeed, a large firm may employ multiple types of sales specialization.

The crucial point is that all firms have some traditional sales organization in place. Certainly the organization evolves over time, but historically, firms have not considered customer importance as a key dimension on which to organize. To put it bluntly, the implications of the fundamental business model and the Pareto revenue distribution discussed above have not deeply penetrated many executive suites. But this is changing and in the next section we suggest some critical pressures that are causing firms to think more deeply about their go-to-market strategies and to make significant changes.

Generalized pressures on traditional go-to-market strategies

Regardless of the historic success of the particular go-to-market model the firm currently employs, four general areas – increased competition, environmental forces, globalization and sales force costs – are generating increased pressure on the firm.

Increased competition

There is scarcely any executive today who will tell you that the competitive environment is easing – virtually all will agree that competitive pressures are increasing in depth and scope. The best approach to competitive pressures is to adapt Porter's five forces model (Porter 1980) and consider each of the forces he identified as a competitor (current or potential). In this framework the firm faces five types of competitors:

> *Traditional direct competitors.* These competitors target similar customers to the firm with similar products and services, and similar business models, according to established rules of the game. Typically, neither the firm nor its competitors gain advantage quickly; rather, improved positions result from long-run sustained effort. Regardless, more rapid change may occur when direct competitors merge, or resource availability shifts quickly via acquisitions/divestiture, leveraged buyouts and new capital structures.
>
> *New direct competitors.* These competitors also offer similar products and services but often have some new competitive advantage. Many Western corporations face competition from Asian firms; these new direct entrants often secure price advantage based on low-cost labour. Sources of new direct entrants may be start-ups including former firm employees, firms expanding geographically, organizational networks, new sales and distribution channels, and strategic alliances.
>
> *Indirect competitors.* These competitors offer similar customer values to the firm but with quite different products or technologies. These functional substitutes often appear as different product classes or product forms. Examples are legion: Kodak's chemical film versus electronic imaging; bricks-and-mortar bookstores versus Amazon; and steel versus plastic in automobiles.
>
> *Supply-chain competition.* The firm may face two types of supply-chain competition: suppliers may integrate forward by offering the firm's customers products that the firm currently offers, or the firm's customers may integrate backwards by purchasing from the firm's suppliers and adopting in-house activities the firm currently performs. (Of course, the firm may face severe pressure from suppliers and buyers short of actual competition; we discuss customer pressure in more detail below.)

As a general statement, the overall level of competition faced by most firms is increasing. Different firms face different competitor types and pressures. At any point in time, one competitor or another type may be more significant for the firm. Of course, all firms must consider not only the types and levels of competition they face today but also the potential competitors they may face tomorrow.

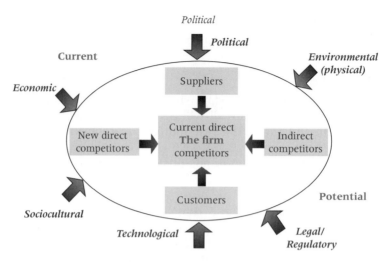

Figure 3 Competitive and PESTLE pressures

PESTLE forces

The firm must address a set of environmental forces that seem ever more complex and subject to change. The PESTLE acronym captures these well: P – political, E – economic, S – sociocultural, T – technological, L – legal/regulatory and E – environmental (physical environment).

Whether it is governmental policy changes, shifting social mores, the impact of the Internet, reregulation and deregulation, or global warming or the fallout from volcanoes in Iceland and Chile, the perturbations caused by PESTLE forces are seriously affecting most firms. Some forces impact the firm directly but, as Figure 3 illustrates, they also have an indirect impact via the firm's competitive environment.

Globalization

A special feature of broad environmental pressures is the seemingly inexorable march towards greater globalization (Friedman 2007). Factors driving increased globalization include a generalized political belief that trade is good; development of organizations such as the World Trade Organization (WTO) to effect increased trade by reducing barriers; the maturing of economic and political unions (like the European Union (EU)) and free trade areas (like NAFTA); greater competitive home-market pressures that encourage firms to venture abroad; opportunities in emerging markets such as BRICI (Brazil, Russia, India, China, Indonesia); improved global communications and the Internet; and improved global transportation – by air for small packages, by sea via containerization, or by widening the Panama Canal.

The combined effect of these factors means that firms conduct increasing amounts of business outside their home-market boundaries. Increased globalization portends major implications for addressing the firm's customers.

Increased selling costs

Most observers believe that corporate expenditures on selling exceed higher-profile advertising and sales promotion, despite the impact of the Internet and customer relationship management (CRM) (Piercy and Lane 2011). For example, rough estimates suggest a 60:40 ratio in Great Britain (Doyle 2002). Until a few years ago, the now defunct *Sales and Marketing Management* annually published survey results on the cost of a sales call. This metric is simply the total cost of the firm's selling effort (including the entire support structure) divided by the number of sales calls. Year after year, this metric increased at a rate greater than inflation – more than doubling during the 1990s (Capon 2001).

Sales and Marketing Management may have perished but leading firms continue to struggle with this issue by making sure they place on-the-road sales effort only on those customers most likely to yield a positive return. Indeed, optimizing resource allocation to various types of selling effort is often a central concern to sales operations departments (Capon and Tubridy 2010).

Summary

All firms face these generalized environmental pressures. Indeed, these pressures have led to major changes in the economies of many countries and the nature of business organizations. The conglomerates of yesteryear have largely disappeared from Western economies as firms have focused their efforts on a restricted set of technologies. Company missions are more narrowly defined and firms increasingly spend resources on those activities where they gain differential advantage. Correspondingly, they prefer to outsource many support processes to specialist organizations. These pressures also impact the way companies address their customers, but we defer that discussion until we have examined a second set of pressures on the firm: those brought by the firm's customers.

Pressures from customers

A major form of economic structure to which many industries evolve is oligopoly. In oligopoly, a small number of firms – maybe just three or four – are responsible for most market share; typically a few smaller firms focus on narrow market segments. A generation ago, in industry after industry, in country after country, many domestic oligopolies flourished (Sheth and Sisodia 2002). To a very large extent, those economic arrangements are a thing of the past, largely as a result of globalization pressures, including cross-border mergers and acquisitions.

In many industries today, it is not a matter of a few firms competing in an industry country by country; rather, it is just a few firms competing globally. Quite simply, we are moving from an economy of multiple domestic oligopolies to a structure of global oligopolies. Consider some examples. The manufacturing industry of passenger jet aircraft that seat over 100 passengers comprises just two firms – Boeing and Airbus. In automobile tyres, three suppliers account for upwards of 60% of global market share – Bridgestone (Japan), Goodyear (USA) and Michelin (France). Add Continental (Germany) and Pirelli (Italy) and market share reaches close to 80%. Perhaps these two industries represent the extreme, but many other industries are moving inexorably in this direction.

Such concentration of economic power has critical implications for suppliers to these industries. The number of potential customers is fast reducing. Suppliers for large passenger jet aircraft have only two potential customers; suppliers to the automotive tyre industry have only a handful. In addition to customer pressure brought on by these external factors, many customer firms are increasing the pressure on suppliers by affirmatively reducing their supplier bases.

Affirmative reduction in number of suppliers

Many firms are deciding that they want fewer suppliers. Table 1 shows a selection of announced supplier reductions by well-known companies, collected over several years. In some cases, supplier base reductions reach 90%.

Several reasons are driving these supplier reductions. First and foremost, customer firms believe a smaller supplier base can help them reduce input costs. Essentially, these firms believe that the traditional purchasing model of many competing suppliers is neither effective nor efficient. Rather, these firms believe that concentrating purchases among fewer suppliers allows these firms to secure economies of scale that will be passed on in the form of lower prices. In addition, fewer suppliers should lead to improved input quality. No matter how effective the firm's quality system, output quality is only as good as input quality. Fewer input sources tighten the quality distribution. Furthermore, the firm can send its

Table 1: Announced supplier reductions

	Previous	*Announcement*	*Percent decrease*
Airbus	3,000	500	83
BAA Airports	11,500	3,000	74
Barclay's Bank	2,000	180	90
Boeing	30,000	10,000	67
Motorola	10,000	3,000	70
Texas Instruments	22,000	14,000	36
Volkswagen	2,000	200	90
Xerox	5,000	500	90

own engineers to help a limited number of suppliers meet its requirements; such resource allocation would be prohibitively expensive for a large supplier base. Relatedly, the firm should receive more consistent service in multiple geographies and generally build closer relationships with suppliers.

Closer relationships between customer and supplier should lead to better communications, strategic pricing, greater transparency into supplier operations, improved operational excellence and enhanced input into supplier activities. Perhaps, even, the supplier–customer relationship could potentially evolve into true partnerships. When partnerships are successful, customer and supplier work together to evolve value further down the value chain.

Rising importance of procurement

A generation ago, purchasing was frequently seen as a managerial backwater. For rising executives, the purchasing department was often a way station where they put in two or three years as part of a learning tour of firm functions, on their way to more attractive and more senior managerial positions. Although firms had functioning purchasing departments, many firms did not build up significant intellectual capital in procurement.[2]

This situation is changing rapidly. Procurement (rebranded purchasing) is becoming a strategic issue for many firms, as we demonstrate using Figure 4. This figure shows simple income statements for two firms, Firm A and Firm B. In each

Company A		
	Original costs	With 10% increase in procurement efficiency
Sales revenue	100	100
Procurement costs	20	18
All other costs	70	70
Total costs	90	88
Profit	10	12
Profit increase (%)		20%

Company B		
	Original costs	With 10% increase in procurement efficiency
Sales revenue	100	100
Procurement costs	70	63
All other costs	20	20
Total costs	90	83
Profit	10	17
Profit increase (%)		70%

Figure 4   The rising importance of procurement

---

[2] See the Merck case in Noel Capon and Christoph Senn, *Case Studies in Managing Key, Strategic, and Global Customers*, Bronxville, NY: Wessex, 2011.

case, revenues are 100, total costs are 90 and profit is 10. The only difference is in the levels of two different types of cost. For Firm A, total costs of 90 are divided between procurement costs – 20 and all other costs – 70. For Firm B, the cost levels are reversed: procurement costs – 70, all other costs – 20. Firm A is perhaps a vertically integrated organization that incurs most costs in-house; by contrast, Firm B is more of an assembly operation of purchased parts.

Setting aside issues of revenue generation, the core question is: where should the CEO of each firm spend their time? The answer is very clear. At Firm A, the CEO should focus on internal operations; these costs are 70, and a modest effectiveness gain would increase profits substantially. By contrast, a 10% effectiveness gain in procurement would reduce costs by only 2 and increase profits by 20%. The situation at Firm B is very different. The vast majority of Firm B's costs – 70 – are in procurement. A 10% cost reduction lowers costs by 7 and profits increase by 70%.

In firm after firm, in industry after industry, firms are shifting their operations from type A to type B. Earlier in this paper we discussed corporate evolution to more focused missions and then identified those activities that lead to securing differential advantage. All other activities are candidates for outsourcing. In many cases, the firm gains return on investment (ROI) benefits, in part by reducing the 'I' – offloading investment to the outsourced supplier. Additionally, the outsourced activity, such as a data centre, may operate more effectively because of the outsourced supplier's greater experience in that particular area.

An important factor driving outsourcing is the rising importance of branding. Not so long ago, customers generally believed that the firm whose name was on the product was also responsible for producing the product. That is no longer the case. The prime contemporary example is consumer electronics where Apple, for example, is highly successful. Apple does not manufacture the iPhone or the iPad; rather, Foxconn (Shenzhen, China) produces these products for Apple. Apple has figured out that manufacturing is not critical to securing differential advantage, so it outsources this process (but has significant competence in logistics and supply chain management). By contrast, Apple focuses on design innovation and its more recently developed competence in retail operations.

The shift from type A firms to type B firms heightens the importance of procurement. Procurement is becoming a strategic function for many firms. Budgets are larger, executive quality is higher, and in general the intellectual capital residing in procurement is increasing dramatically. Such changes imply that the selling job must change also. To address high-quality professional procurement executives, the firm must develop very different approaches than the traditional way of doing business.

Changes in the procurement process

Along with the increased importance of procurement and the increased professionalism of their procurement staffs, many firms have made significant changes in their procurement processes.

- *Strategic sourcing.* A decade or so ago this term did not exist. Strategic sourcing refers to the set of approaches, procedures and tools that organizational customers use to reduce their procurement costs. Consulting firms teach these processes and the movement of skilled procurement executives among companies has led to their widespread, and typically successful, adoption.
- *Centralization.* One of the fundamental managerial challenges today is to decide which functions and activities the firm should centralize and which should be decentralized. In many cases, firms are discovering they can be more effective by centralizing elements of procurement. Several reasons drive purchasers in this direction. First, greater concentration of intellectual capital is likely to spawn more ideas for reducing procurement costs. Second, aggregating purchases of similar products generally leads to larger contracts at better prices. Third, centralized procurement increases the likelihood that the firm can form supplier–customer partnerships to the benefit of both parties.
- *Globalization.* Earlier in this paper we discussed globalization as an important force affecting corporations. As an extension of increasing centralization, many procurement organizations are centralizing globally, entering into global contracts, and procuring certain goods and services on a global basis.
- *B2B exchanges.* Along with the growth of the Internet, many firms are using B2B exchanges to conduct reverse auctions for those goods and services that lend themselves to rigorous definition. When purchasing criteria are very clear, competing suppliers frequently drive down prices to attractive levels for purchasers (if not for suppliers).
- *Insistence on interface simplification.* Many companies now understand that the process of purchasing products and services can be very expensive. Furthermore, dealing with multiple salespeople and other executives from a single supplier can be administratively complex and slow down decision-making. Customers also want a single point of contact so they can secure fast and effective responses when critical issues arise. Hence, many customer firms insist on streamlining the inter-organizational interface, often by requiring that a single supplier executive has overall responsibility for the relationship.
- *Broader scope of responsibilities.* Historically, in many firms, purchasing was confined to quite specific areas, such as supplies or factory inputs. In firms where the procurement organization has successfully reduced spend in these areas, it often secures responsibility for other non-traditional areas of purchasing responsibility such as travel and consulting services.

So, in addition to facing complex competitive and PESTLE pressures, the firm must address pressures from customers. The critical issue for suppliers is deciding how to react to all of these external pressures and customer demands. If the customer requires a single point of contact globally, the firm had better make the appropriate changes or a competitor will emerge to satisfy this specific requirement and the firm may lose a customer.

But there is another perspective: perhaps the supplier can get ahead of the game. Rather than wait to react to customer demands, the firm may put in place the strategy, organization, processes and procedures, and human resources to provide customers with the sort of value that they will require in the future. By offering approaches that address the real problems their customers may face, the supplier may be able to secure significant differential advantage.

Impact of pressures on the firm

The position we take in this paper is that firms have a traditional go-to-market approach. This approach is either indirect through third parties such as agents, brokers, representatives and/or distributors, or direct via an on-the-road sales force. For many firms, this traditional system is under pressure from a series of competitive, PESTLE and customer pressures. As a result, the traditional system is fragmenting. We expect the traditional system to continue and evolve, but the various pressures are leading to two other systems developing. Rather than operate with a single traditional approach to the market, firms will increasingly add two new systems, making three systems in total. We characterize the two new systems as small account management and key, strategic and global account management.

Small account management

The skewed revenue and profit distributions that most firms experience are perhaps the major drivers for seeking alternative ways of dealing with small customers. Low revenues but high costs of traditional on-the-road approaches lead many firms to seek less costly ways of serving these customers. Broadly speaking, the firm has two types of alternatives – selling options and non-selling options:

Selling options. Essentially, the firm decides that some small customers require continued selling effort. Perhaps the revenues are valuable and/or the firm is unable to select which of its small customers may eventually become large revenue sources. Hence, the firm develops a programme to address them but with less commitment than traditionally. The firm may select among several options:
- *Part-time sales force.* In general, part-time, on-the-road salespeople are less expensive than full timers. By careful territory design and astute salesperson selection, the firm may secure good customer coverage yet manage costs effectively. Pharmaceutical firms sometimes use this approach for covering retail pharmacies.
- *Shift to telesales.* Telesales can be very effective and is much less costly than on-the-road salespeople; a telesales operation may even be more effective than traditional salespeople. In Scandinavia, Reebok replaced a sales force calling on small stores with telesales. Customers got to know their sales-

people, who were always available on the telephone. Customer satisfaction increased and costs decreased. Nirvana!

- *Outsource selling effort: assign to agents/distributors.* Frequently, product firms with sales force organizations operate with much higher levels of selling, general and administrative (SG&A) expenses than distribution firms and sales agencies. Furthermore, distribution and agency firms typically earn variable commissions, whereas producing firms typically carry a substantial level of fixed costs. As a result, distribution and agency firms can be profitable with customers and volume levels where producing firms cannot.

Non-selling options. For the options just discussed, the firm decides that none of the selling options is viable. Essentially the firm focuses on less costly approaches to serve these customers, or it decides to stop serving:

- *Traditional direct marketing.* The firm decides to address customers via various forms of direct marketing such as direct mail and other impersonal approaches. Profit margins increase and costs decrease.
- *Electronic contact.* The firm takes advantage of developing digital methods of communicating with customers such as email and websites. The firm may even combine websites with telesales and/or instant messaging. These approaches are far less costly.
- *Raise prices.* Thus far, we have discussed options for addressing the customer profit problem by reducing costs. A viable alternative may be to focus on enhancing revenues. Of course, the firm may lose some customers by raising prices, but customers that remain will be more profitable. Indeed, the firm may discover that its prices have been set too low.
- *Stop serving.* Raising prices is a soft way of losing customers; affirmative decisions to stop serving customers are much tougher. The firm sets performance levels on criteria such as sales units or revenues for a customer to remain a customer and then actively enforces the new rules. Strict implementation of well-chosen criteria will raise profits by ridding the firm of unprofitable customers. Relatedly, some customers may adapt their behaviour to remain customers and hence become profitable for the firm.

Key, strategic and global account management

Figuring out how to address small unprofitable customers is important for firms, but the major implication of the pressures we have discussed concerns what we may label as the firm's strategic (or key) and global account problem.[3] Some executives have a difficult time defining a strategic (or key) account; we take a simple-minded view: a strategic (or key) account is any current or potential customer for which it would be a big deal for the firm to lose or to gain. This is not a terribly precise definition, but in our experience with many companies,

---

[3] Note that key or strategic accounts may be global, but many such accounts are also domestic or regional in scope.

we find that executives have a pretty good general idea of which these customers are.

This definition has an important implication – strategic (or key) is not synonymous with large. Certainly, many of the firm's strategic (or key) accounts are those customers that bring significant revenues today. But equally, some of today's large customers may not be strategic for the firm – perhaps they are declining organizations; perhaps they operate in areas that are no longer strategic for the firm; or perhaps revenues are high but profits are low. Conversely, some of today's small customers may be strategic for the firm because of potential revenues and/or strategic alignment. Remember, if the firm works closely with a small firm, forms a tight relationship, and the small firm is successful and grows substantially, the supplier's revenues will increase along with those of its customer. The supplier simply has to hang on for the ride.

Typically, the firm must take this general definition and work hard to identify the precise set of customers it wants to enter into its strategic (or key) account programme. The core reason is resources. Because they are strategic for the firm, these customers receive additional resources. But the firm can make two potential errors in its nomination and selection process: type A and type B. By making the type A error, the firm enters a customer into its strategic (or key) account programme that it should not have chosen: the firm does not earn an appropriate return on its invested resources – these resources are wasted. The type B error is more subtle but no less important: the firm fails to enter into its strategic (or key) account programme a customer that it should have chosen. Hence, it makes an opportunity loss.

To develop an effective strategic (or key) account programme, the firm should make serious decisions about four building blocks, fundamental elements in the congruence model – see Figure 5.

> *Strategy.* Strategy concerns the allocation of scarce resources to reach an objective or set of objectives. The strategic element in managing strategic accounts has too many dimensions to address in this paper, but certainly nominating and selecting customers for the strategic account programme is central to developing any such programme. Other important issues concern decisions

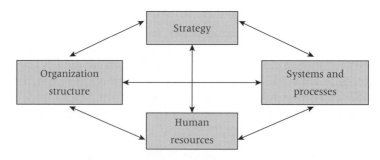

Figure 5 The congruence model

regarding engagement level with customers, developing a vision for the programme, setting objectives, branding the programme to secure external and internal visibility, and organizational commitment. Over and above these programmatic strategic issues, the firm must address a host of strategic issues concerning relationships with individual strategic accounts.

Organization structure. Setting strategy is one thing; designing the organization structure to implement the strategy is quite another. As discussed earlier, typically, the strategic account programme emerges from some former set of internal organizational arrangements. Hence, the strategic account programme may face significant growing pains as the firm struggles with the transition from some former decentralized system to a centralized approach demanded by strategic account management. At one end of a continuum, a strategic account manager has a coordinating role in working with various decentralized players – such as individual sales representatives in geographic territories who retain revenue (and maybe profit contribution) responsibility. At the other end of the continuum, the account manager has total customer responsibility regardless of geographic location; many decentralized employees report to the account manager directly. There are many organizational options between these polar extremes. Related issues concern reporting levels for strategic account managers, the ability to secure high-quality candidates for account manager positions, compensation, the ability to make critical decisions such as pricing, and overall influence within the firm.

Human resources. Many human resource decisions flow from the strategic and organizational factors just discussed. Strategic and organizational demands help frame the knowledge, skills and abilities (KSAs) that candidate strategic account managers should possess. A useful framework classifies KSAs into a four-fold framework embracing strategic acumen, business acumen, relationship acumen and personal acumen. Once the firm has secured agreement on these requirements, it can implement the classic human resource processes of recruiting, selecting, training, retaining and compensating.

Systems and processes. Systems and processes are the grease that allows the organizational wheels to turn smoothly. We can usefully think of three types: soft infrastructure, hard infrastructure and improvement processes:

- *Hard infrastructure.* Items in this category include synchronous information such as real-time communication, and asynchronous information like data storage and retrieval. Other critical areas are financial management systems such as customer profitability measurement, assessing customers' economic value to the firm, and strategic account planning systems.
- *Soft infrastructure.* These items include developing proposals, pricing and contracts, managing opportunities, addressing complaints, and suggestions.
- *Improvement processes.* These items combine hard and soft elements but are focused on improving the firm's approach to managing strategic (or key) accounts. They include monitoring and control systems, customer satisfaction measurement, best-in-class benchmarking, and best-practice

sharing. This category includes meetings such as customer councils and forums, and business opportunity workshops.

Conclusion

In this paper we have attempted to make the case for managing strategic accounts. We have shown that the traditional sales force model is facing several types of pressure – from competitors, PESTLE forces, globalization and increased selling costs, and from customers. This combined set of pressures is leading to fragmentation of the traditional system. This system will remain, but two additional systems are forming – for small customers and for key, strategic and global customers. To develop a successful and comprehensive strategic (or key) account management programme, the firm must implement the congruence model. The firm must make critical decisions about strategy, organization structure, human resources, and systems and processes.

Drivers for key account management programmes

BY PER-OLOF BREHMER AND JAKOB REHME

Abstract

Key account management (KAM) programmes are a way for companies to develop existing relationships and increase sales, thus being proactive and searching for opportunities which are expected of KAM. It is also a way to meet changing customer demands arising from changes in purchasing strategy, buyers' mergers and acquisitions, and the search for synergies in order to reduce costs. This paper analyses the way in which different key account management programmes manage the sales process complexity and customer expectations.

The paper draws on qualitative data collected during a field study of ABB and six of its major customers, based on annual or bi-annual interviews with 50 individuals within ABB from 1996 to 2006, and 3–10 individuals from each of the customers. Interviewees included corporate managers, key account managers and sales personnel/project managers. The customers involved in the study belonged to mining, automotive, process equipment manufacture, building technology, energy production and telecommunication sectors.

In this study three different programmes have been identified and analysed: (1) the proactive programme, which is driven by sales opportunity; (2) the reactive programme, which is driven by customer demands; and (3) the organization-based programme, which is driven by the belief in customer-centric organizational units. With an empirical base the paper provides a basis for understanding the reasons behind the establishment of several KAM programmes in the same corporation. It identifies sales aspects of KAM programmes that are handled in different ways by different types of programmes.

Article reproduced with the kind permission of Emerald Group Publishing: originally 'Brehmer, P. & Rehme, J. (2009) Pro-active and reactive: drivers for key account management programmes, *European Journal of Marketing*. 43(7/8), 961–984.'

Introduction

Research on industrial sales is very much focused on sales personnel and issues such as sales training that use theories, frameworks and constructs from economics and social psychology (e.g. role stress, ambiguity, motivation, rewards), with a focus on individuals (see e.g. Anderson and Oliver 1987; Bush and Grant 1994; Dubinsky 1999; Dubinsky et al. 1986; Walker et al. 1977; Weitz et al. 1986). Practitioners have, however, pinpointed that effective selling requires the participation of many people, and researchers have addressed cross-functional aspects of the selling process (Cespedes 1992; Cravens 1995; Harvey et al. 2003; Narus and Anderson 1995; Natti et al. 2006; Piercy and Lane 2006; Weitz and Bradford 1999). Furthermore, researchers have also addressed that selling and sales organization influence corporate organizations, and corporate organizations heavily influence the way in which sales can be managed and conducted (Galbraith 1995; Rehme 2001).

Many industrial corporations have reduced their supplier base (Abrahamsson and Brege 2005; Sheth and Sharma 1997) and the implementation of programmes such as just in time (JIT), supply-chain management, efficient consumer response (ECR) and joint product development has resulted in the need for tighter linkages with suppliers. In order for suppliers to cater for these customers' needs, specific approaches to the most important customers are needed. For this, KAM approaches are often used, since the selling process is beyond the capabilities of any one individual and may require a coordinated effort across product divisions, sales regions and functional groups.

The literature on KAM can roughly be said to focus on two different factors. One factor concerns small groups of individuals that are formed to service the key account, i.e. selling teams, selling alliances (e.g. Cespedes 1992; Gladstein 1984; Smith and Barclay 1993, 1997). The studies on selling teams have predominantly been concerned with what distinguishes successful from unsuccessful sales teams. The second focus is more concerned with the management concept of KAM programmes, particularly in connection with buyer–seller relationships (e.g. Barrett 1986; Boles et al. 1994; Brady 2004; Natti et al. 2006; Pardo 1997; Pardo et al. 2006; Rehme 2001; Sengupta et al. 1997; Shapiro and Moriarty 1982, 1984a, 1984b). This means a focus on enhancement of the dyadic business relationships and the effectiveness of the KAM programmes from this perspective (e.g. Cespedes 1992; Lambe and Spekman 1997).

Key account management is here defined as the organization that caters for the management and the development of the relationship, in a more or less formal structure. As such it follows that the seller's marketing strategy involves deliberately forming a structure for the largest and most important customers, with the intention to move from interpersonal relationships to group-on-group relationships (cf. Narus and Anderson 1995). Consequently, it can be regarded as the industrial firm's policy to assert that the most important customers really are treated with special care, as an organization with the responsibility to do so is assigned to them. With the exception of the conceptual discussion in Harvey et al. (2003), the literature on KAM seems notably to have missed any discussion on whether KAM is initiated as a proactive, management-driven and opportunity-based solution, or whether it is formed reactively in response to customer needs and wants. KAM is consequently an important ingredient for international and global corporations' sales organizations.

The purpose of this paper is to examine the reasons behind why key account management programmes are formed within corporations, and what factors become important for different types of programmes. Particularly it sets out to understand the development of the key account management organization over time, with a focus on external and internal factors on a company/corporate level. To our knowledge there has been little research covering the development of KAM programmes, particularly following one corporation with both a national and an international scope.

This paper is organized as follows: the next section reviews previous literature on key account management programmes. In the following section the KAM framework developed from previous literature is described with triggers and drivers, as well as a tentative model on the complexity that is present in the industrial sales which KAM programmes tend to handle. A short description of the three programmes follows and the subsequent section contains the analysis. The final section presents conclusions and describes the need for KAM programmes to be able to handle multiple sales situations.

Key account management

The concept of KAM programmes has been developing since the 1960s (Weilbaker and Weeks 1997). It was first designed to handle geographically dispersed customers, with multiple locations, in a systematic manner. Although the approach and content have changed over the years, the international trend of KAM was strong from the 1970s to the 1990s as well as throughout the beginning of the 21st century (cf. Boles et al. 1994; Brady 2004; Natti et al. 2006; Pardo et al. 2006; Weilbaker and Weeks 1997).

Key account management is often defined as a managerial response to sales to large customers. The common denominator in the description of this type of selling is the focus on selling more to established customers, who are significant to the extent that the sales to the specific customer account make up a substantial part of the selling companies' turnover (e.g. Stevenson and Page 1979; Weilbaker and Weeks 1997). Since these 'accounts' purchase a great deal, or have the potential to do so, they represent great sales opportunities, but also, if they already purchase substantially, a great risk (Piercy and Lane 2006; Shapiro and Moriarty 1982). To manage the opportunities and risks it becomes important to try to establish tight and long-lasting relationships with these major or key accounts.

KAM and related terms mean to grant the largest and/or most important customers special treatment since they require special attention (cf. Barrett 1986; Sharma 1997). Shapiro and Moriarty (1982) add that 'a supplier seeks to establish, over an extended period of time, an "institutional" relationship, which cuts across multiple levels, functions, and operating units in both the buying and selling organization'. The term key account management depicts a situation where large customers are handled quite differently from the other customers, inasmuch as there are appointed salespeople, account managers and other dedicated relevant personnel who form the interface to that customer. In other words, this means that there is a selling-side organization that is formed to cater for the special needs of one or more large customers. Particularly, we define a key account management programme as the organization that is formed for large and complex customers where some sales effort coordination is required.

KAM is a way of having one single salesperson, or a sales team, responsible for one major account in a region, one country or globally. One of the benefits for the buyer in having one single salesperson is that the buyer needs to contact only one person, and another is that there may be uniformity in prices for the buyer's divisions even if these divisions are geographically scattered. For the seller, this is a way of ensuring continued orders from the customer. The reason for the continued orders could be the selling company's ability to solve problems, since it now has one dedicated salesperson for each customer who is very knowledgeable about the customer's entire operations (Weilbaker and Weeks 1997). As Natti et al. (2006) debate, KAM can be seen as a knowledge transfer system integrated in the customer management system.

Benefits of key account management programmes

As mentioned initially, the literature on KAM can be said to focus on two aspects, namely sales team articles and KAM programme articles. Studies on sales teams have identified what distinguishes successful from unsuccessful teams. The distinguishing factors include trust, open communication, perceived interdependence between team members (Gladstein 1984; Smith 1997; Smith and Barclay 1997) and issues such as empowerment of sales teams (Perry et al. 1999). Articles on KAM programmes have had a focus on dyadic business relationships (Cespedes 1992; Lambe and Spekman 1997). The questions raised in these articles include the benefits of KAM programmes, the customer's perception of KAM, the people involved, the division of interests and the organization of KAM programmes. Among the benefits of a KAM programme are improved relationships between buyer and seller and thus an increase in sales share, improvements in buyer–seller communication, better quality in sales calls, etc. (Barrett 1986; Boles et al. 1994), but it also incorporates business risks of becoming more reliant on fewer and larger customers (Piercy and Lane 2006).

In an issue of *Thexis* in 1999 there were several insightful studies on how particular companies are managing their key accounts (Millman 1999; Momani and Richter 1999; Wilson 1999). These articles identified drivers that the KAM programme aims to handle, such as shortening distance between seller and buyer (location is shifting to create greater geographical distance), focus on shortening time (coordination, rapidity, timing owing to logistic focus in terms of JIT, ECR) and demand for spreading best practices. Building on Nahapiet (1994), Yip and Madsen (1996) reported that the key driver of account programmes was demand from the rapidly globalizing procurement functions of customers. Using contingency theory, they suggested that a number of industry- and firm-specific factors determine the likelihood of a company forming a key account programme, and of the programme contributing to the successful implementation of global marketing strategies.

Key account management has been credited with a number of benefits. Generally speaking, customers appear to be positive to the KAM approach (Pardo 1997; Pardo et al. 2006). More communication and closer relations (Barrett 1986; Boles et al. 1994), but also more tangible results, such as market and customer share and profits, have been cited as benefits of KAM (Brady 2004; Stevenson 1981). Other identified gains are the development of trust (Doney and Cannon 1997; Smith and Barclay 1997), increased information sharing (Frazier et al. 1988; Mohr and Nevin 1990), reduction of conflicts (Gundlach and Cadotte 1994) and commitment to maintaining the relationship (Achrol 1991; Mohr et al. 1996; Morgan and Hunt 1994).

Internal and external driving forces for KAM programmes

Although the perceived and realized benefits from KAM programmes can be regarded as the rationale as to why companies form these programmes, there are other driving forces that can affect the way in which these programmes are formed, as well as the factors that become important. Naturally enough, the majority of literature has been from the selling firm's viewpoint (e.g. Barrett 1986; Boles et al. 1994; Kirwan 1992; Tutton 1987; Weilbaker and Weeks 1997), but some articles do cover topics from the customer's viewpoint (e.g. Pardo 1997; Pardo et al. 2006; Sharma 1997). The focus of most KAM programmes described is on improving the efficiency and effectiveness of present sales and customer relations. Key factors behind the popularity are promises of dramatic improvements in sales based on a better knowledge of the purchasing demands. The affecting factors are partly internal issues in the selling company and partly related to customer purchasing, i.e. external factors to the KAM programme – see Figure 1 (cf., for example, Cespedes 1992).

The external factors are defined as those that are outside the control of the selling organization and include the purchaser's situation and general environmental conditions and factors. Jones et al. (2005) discuss the external factors affecting sales forces in terms of four categories of influences: customers, competitors, technology and the ethical and regulatory environment. The internal factors are here defined as those factors that are under the domain of control (or appear to be) for the selling organization. This includes the internal organizational issues, as well as the marketing strategies and operations that are handled within the

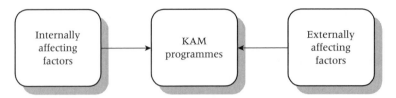

Figure 1   The affecting factors in KAM programmes

seller organization for performance improvements. The aim is to focus on internal factors that target external factors to drive company performance as well as out-perform competitors in creating a better sales offer. Although external factors are outside the direct control of the selling organization they may affect the internal structures and processes (cf. Eisenhardt 2002; Harrigan 2001), having important implications for the focus of the account management. Actions of the seller organization that aim to target internal affecting factors can also affect external factors. KAM programmes are thus regarded as an organizational unit, virtual or formalized, that is directed to handle internal and external factors, and in particu-lar complexities in and between the selling and buying organizations.

Managing industrial sales complexity: A tentative framework

Establishing KAM programmes can, as Jones et al. (2005) discuss, be seen as a way to handle different forms of complexity that derive from internal or external factors. In an article on project complexity, Williams (1999) suggests that, in order to support the management function – in particular planning, forecasting, moni-toring and control – it is vital to model the complexity present. Williams structures the complexity in two dimensions. The first, based on the work of Baccarini (1996), is structural complexity. This applies to different sales dimensions, such as decision-making, management processes, environment, technology, organiza-tion, etc., that are to be handled through the organizational structure or by bun-dling or unbundling the technical complexity of the products and service through the account management. The other dimension involves the complexity originat-ing from the uncertainty present in the sales process.

Uncertainty concerns the instability of circumstances and assumptions upon which decisions are made. Håkansson et al. (1977) describe three types of uncer-tainties for a buyer, and how these are changed during interaction between buyer and seller. Need uncertainty is about uncertainties connected to the levels of demand, and increased interaction might increase or decrease the level of uncer-tainty. Market uncertainty is related to the suppliers themselves, while transaction uncertainty is about the physical transfer of the products from supplier to buyer. In their article they maintain that the buyer strives to keep the uncertainties as low as possible. As a consequence, it becomes important for KAM programmes to be designed so that the uncertainties can be decreased or at least managed, otherwise the complexity might be impossible to manage. Shapiro and Moriarty (1982) and Andersson et al. (2007) also discuss complexity in term of structural and operational dimensions. Based on these authors' discussions, complexity in a KAM setting could be defined along the following dimensions:

1. *Structurally complex*, e.g. a geographical dispersion of customer locations, several units within or across national borders, involvement of multiple functional units.
2. *Operationally complex*, e.g. the need for a variety of product lines, services and/ or technically advanced systems, with demands and needs for advanced fulfilment systems and/or advanced commercial solutions.

The selling organization can be complex along the same dimensions. In order for the KAM to be able to set up a coherent offering, the KAM may need to coordinate geographic dispersion in the seller as well as the buyer organization, manage a variety of goods and services and sometimes entire systems, as well as facilitate logistics solutions for the delivery of these offerings to the customer. In this respect the KAM programme is a tool to decrease the uncertainties in the buyer–seller relationship by coordinating the offering to the customer. Based on different complexities, the focus of the coordination may vary (see Figure 2).

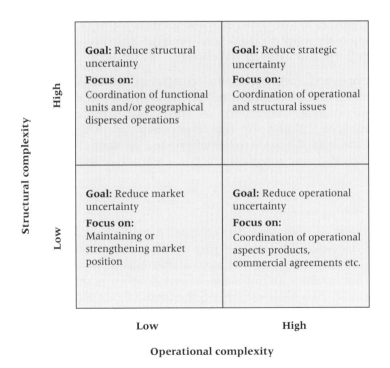

Figure 2 Sales complexity management matrix

In a situation with both low operational and structural complexity the goal should be to reduce the market uncertainty (cf. Håkansson et al. 1977) by clarifying the seller's dedication to be long term and their seriousness as well as commitment to the relationship. The lower left quadrant in Figure 2 concerns the importance of the infrastructure for handling uncertainties during the sales process. It is questionable whether a KAM is needed for this situation since the coordination requirements are low. However, KAM might prove to be a tool to clarify the seller dedication to the customer.

Operational complexity may affect the customer expectations, as in the lower right quadrant in Figure 2, especially in situations where the customer has clear goals and involves the selling organization in design-and-manufacture projects with goals formulated by the customer and accepted by the selling company without discussion. The product structure is a common explanation behind long lead times, high cost of planning, coordination and control, which is also a reason for forming a KAM organization (Homburg and Pflesser 2000). From a KAM perspective, the goal should therefore be to reduce the operational uncertainty by focusing on managing and coordinating aspects related to operational complexity that is a result of many product varieties, complexity in logistics solutions, etc.

High structural and low operational complexity mean that the seller needs to focus on the coordination of organizational units. The industry context affects the structural complexity that causes uncertainties for the customers, that needs to be managed, as in the upper left quadrant in Figure 2. Sales management must subsequently adapt to contextual prerequisites such as national cultures, corporate cultures and external stakeholders' demands.

High structural and high operational complexity means that the focus is to coordinate both operational and structural issues. The goal is to reduce what we have termed 'strategic uncertainty' and involves comprehensive coordination. Harvey and Speier (2000) use the term 'relational richness' to capture the net uncertainties in the KAM relationship, and as Natti et al. (2006) observe, knowledge sharing and integration are of great importance from a long-term perspective.

Research method

The paper draws on qualitative data collected during a field study of ABB and six of its large customers. The study is part of a longitudinal study of the management of industrial sales, its development and its effects on strategy, relations and customers. Since ABB is an international and global corporation with a presence in all regions of the world, we limited the focus in this paper to the European continent and focus here on examples from the Nordic countries, Ireland, Germany and the UK. The customers in the study belong to mining, automotive, process equipment manufacture, building technology, energy production and telecommunication sectors.

With 50 interviewees we conducted 2–3 interviews within ABB from 1996 to 2006 and with each of the 6 customers 3–10 interviewees were interviewed 2–3 times. Interviewees included corporate managers, key account managers and sales personnel/project managers. The three-layered interview design was explicitly planned to gather data on the same topics from different hierarchical levels. We did not develop performance measures to assess the effectiveness of the three different key account management programmes. Interviews were semi-structured and lasted between 90 minutes and 3 hours. In addition we participated in annual European sales managers' conferences arranged in order to share experience and customer knowledge and inform on strategic changes.

Data from these interviews were elaborated to produce mini case studies of the three KAM programmes as well as the customers involved in the study, enabling identification, evaluation and matching of patterns as they emerged from within individual cases (Eisenhardt 1989). We then cross-compared the mini cases to identify common patterns in the account management programmes. Following Gummesson (2005), we worked with comparisons, condensing the data in order to identify patterns and independent variables to preclude the presence of other independent variables of the three KAM programmes. The use of the pattern-matching tactic strengthens the internal validity of the research. Here the multiple case research design is of importance as the multiple empirical setting contributes to high external validity (Gummesson 2005).

Three key account management programmes at ABB

KAM programme – ABB Swedish Market

In order to deal with the coordination problems for the Swedish market, senior management in ABB Sweden initiated a project entitled ABB Swedish Market (Svensk Marknad). ABB Swedish Market was formed officially in 1996 (although it was initiated earlier). It consisted of the Swedish ABB companies and their sales organizations. For the strategic development of ways to work within specific customer segments and towards specific customers, the market for ABB in Sweden was divided into nine industry segments:

1. Power generation (hydro power, nuclear, large steam turbines, power heating and industrial turbines).
2. Power distribution.
3. Government/environment/water.
4. Total installations.
5. Metal.
6. Pulp and paper.
7. Chemicals, pharmaceuticals and food.
8. Integrated manufacturing.
9. Original equipment manufacturer (OEM) products.

Instead of operating through the internal ABB segment structure, this was an attempt to divide the market from a customer perspective. For each industry 'segment' there was one principal company, i.e. one ABB company, assigned. The principal company employed the industry segment manager and together they held responsibility for the strategic development of the business within the designated industry.

In the different industry segments, a number of KAM teams were formed, consisting of sales people from relevant ABB companies covering that particular customer. The team members each represented one ABB sales organization. The KAM teams were given the task of focusing on the processes and applications of key customers in order to be able to supply as correct a solution as possible regarding that specific customer.

The key customers were all large, or potentially large, customers. It was especially important to focus on customers with which at least one of the ABB companies had good relations, and where there were opportunities for other ABB companies to move in. Not uncommonly this could be the case in many of ABB's customer relations, and subsequently this was seen as an opportunity for the ABB group to expand sales in the Swedish market.

The forming of a geographical divide, industry segmentation and KAM teams was not intentionally designed to change the organization. The ABB companies were meant to function as separate entities, then and in the future. The project could be seen as something of a 'virtual organization', with the intention to develop the way ABB approaches the Swedish market. This is a 'best of both worlds' vision, to coordinate sales efforts but retain the benefits of the decentralized organization – see Figure 3.

One of the main assumptions of this work was the need to have good and visible contacts at all levels in the customer's organization. Since one of the major aims was to address large customers, it meant that normally the customer's organizations were fairly complex, so enjoying good relations with a customer could mean only for one specific part or department of the customer's organization.

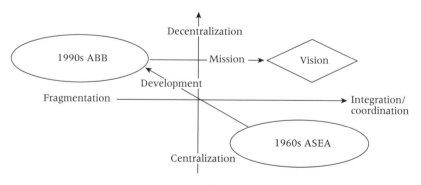

Figure 3   The development of ABB sales (ABB internal material 1996)

In October 1996 the ABB Sweden management presented a leaflet in which the ABB Swedish Market's strategic goal and vision were presented. It outlined the importance of Sweden as an ABB home market and that this market was changing:

"The customers are concentrating on their core business and therefore demand simplicity and more comprehensive solutions." *(ABB leaflet on strategy and action)*

In strategic terms, the ABB Swedish Market's development and the current task were expressed as the:

"[Development] from a centrally controlled ASEA to a decentralized organization with ABB companies. Our task is to move towards a more coordinated ABB, a network, whose primary task is to simplify things for the customers and help the customers with total solutions, without changing the good things with our decentralized organization." *(ABB internal material translated)*

In the same leaflet an action plan in three steps presented the ABB management view of the content of this work:

Step 1. Simplicity for the customer – geographical division, regional management, KAM teams, ABB coordination increases, more market knowledge.
Step 2. Cost effectiveness – avoid duplicate work, coordinate and plan, learn from each other, develop IT support.
Step 3. Increased revenue – segment orientation, new total view of the market, offer comprehensive solutions in a correct manner, listen to the customer, meet all levels in the customer company.

ABB Swedish Market was clearly a top management initiative. The focus of the approach was to create simple contact for the individual customers. The managing director for ABB in Sweden described it thus:

"An important principle is to always try to make the relation as simple as possible. That is the basic idea for ABB Swedish Market. The intention is that for you as a customer, provided you do not need contacts with specialists, it should be sufficient with one contact person at ABB."

Moreover, the preconceptions on which ABB Swedish Market rested were:

1. The fragmentation of ABB sales experienced by customers.
2. The demand to buy more complete systems as opposed to mere product increases.
3. Too many sales calls by sales engineers from different ABB companies.
4. Fragmented sales are not cost effective.
5. Coordinated sales efforts will aid in the efforts to increase market share and subsequently sales.

The ABB Sweden customer base had some interesting characteristics. One estimate from ABB concluded that the division of customers was disproportionate with regard to large and small customers. Of an estimated 11,000 ABB customers in total, only 50 were said to account for approximately 60% of the ABB Swedish sales. When the company looked into this in greater detail it discovered the total customer base to be in the region of 40,000, where 100 customers accounted for 60% of sales. After the divestment of the distributor business in the Nordic countries, i.e. ASEA Skandia, the top 100 customers were accounting for almost 80% of the total sales. With such an asymmetric customer base, there was obviously a tendency to prioritize the large customers over the small.

KAM programme in the ABB business area for industrial products and systems

The ABB business area for industrial products and systems had several coordination groups especially aimed at coordinating efforts for international customers. International customer coordination was seen as one way to try to win these large accounts, by starting initiatives towards these customers.

In 1992 the business area started a distributor coordination project for its largest wholesale customers in order to be able to follow the international expansion of those customers. In 1995 the business area 'low-voltage apparatus' started another project called Original Equipment Manufacturer (OEM) Customer Coordination, which followed international OEMs' business. In 1998 ABB combined the two key account projects into a common key account organization for both distributors and OEM.

Whereas market segmentation was a way to understand the needs of different customer groups, in particular with regard to the technical requirements and their application needs, key account management was a way of paying special attention to large customers and their specific needs. From a selling company perspective there might be more issues that are common to different large customers than there are to companies belonging to the same application segment. The major determinant for ABB to coordinate sales activities, however, was from the beginning to achieve door-openers to customers with operations in different geographical markets and to benefit from benchmarking within different application segments.

The work for the coordination of international accounts was divided into two different tracks, one for OEM customers and one for the electrical wholesale business. For OEM the international accounts were subdivided in accordance with their application needs into a number of segments. The idea was to have one coordinator for each of these segments to be responsible for the coordination of all international accounts within the same segment. All in all 20 international accounts for the OEM segment were active at the same time, whereas the wholesaler international KAM programme was for 10 customers.

For the coordination of international OEM customers there was a group for the facilitation of international key account management. This group consisted of

12–15 international and national key account managers from Europe and the USA, who met on a regular basis 3–4 times a year, with a special focus on a few selected OEM segments (windpower, HVAC, generator sets and drives). They had around 20 KAMs under their wings. One of the major drivers for the group was to take advantage of the application segmentation and use this knowledge to reach other customers within the same OEM segment.

Each account had one international account manager responsible for the ABB contacts with the whole customer organization. In each country where the customer had local presence, the organization assigned one national key account manager. The national key account managers were responsible for the day-to-day needs of the customer business, as well as for keeping track of movements and activities that might have changed the way in which the customer wanted to do business. Furthermore, whereas the international KAM was responsible for the strategic partnership, and thus agreements, the national key account managers were responsible for the local partnership agreements – see Table 1.

The international key account managers came from both producer companies and pure sales companies, where one key element determining who should be assigned as KAM was the location of the businesses' headquarters, although a few of the KAMs also came from production companies outside the headquarters' country, particularly when there were special needs that could be resolved only with producer intervention of some sort. The overriding determinant for international KAM was still, however, the main location of the customer's business. Furthermore, the majority of key account managers had more than one assigned key account, both nationally and internationally. Some of the account managers had the KAM work merely as a part-time assignment whereas others were kept fully occupied by it.

Key account management for organizational reorientation

In November 2000 ABB announced a change of chief executive officer. The new CEO was appointed in January 2001 and this signalled a major reorganization scheme for the whole group. This new organization was based on four application-oriented industrial segments and two product segments – see Figure 4.

In this layout the product segment, i.e. Power Technology Products and Automation Technology Products, contained all the producing companies, which were transformed into divisions within either Power Products or Automation Products. This organization was implemented throughout the ABB world. The product segments were to be responsible for product development, production and production-associated operations.

The application-oriented organization was based on the customer segments manufacturing and consumer industry, process industry, oil, gas and petrochemicals and utilities. This organization became responsible for all selling, relationship-building and application-oriented systems and product development in their respective industry segments. It contained the KAM organizations, which became

Table 1: The schematics of ABB international customer coordination, the segments and the KAM programme

Market segment	Market sub-segment	Key account	International KAM	National KAM						
				AT	DE	DK	FR	SE	UK	US
OEM	Gen set	KA No.1	KAM No.1	X		X		X		
		KA No.2	KAM No.2		X	X		X		
	Air cond.	KA No.3	KAM No.3			X	X			X
	Wind power	KA No.4	KAM No.4	X		X				X
	Pumps	KA No.5	KAM No.5		X			X	X	
		. . . . . .	. . . . . .							
Wholesaler		KA No.6	KAM No.6	X		X		X		
		KA No.7	KAM No.7		X		X		X	X
		. . . . . .	. . . . . .							

AT = Austria, DE = Germany, DK = Denmark, FR = France, SE = Sweden, UK = United Kingdom, US = United States

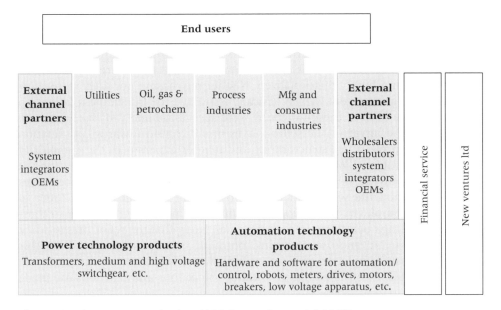

Figure 4 The 2001 organization (ABB internal material 2001)

even more important. The basic idea was that the producers were to sell their products or systems via the customer segment sales organizations. An exception to this was the supply to wholesalers and OEMs, etc., which would be taken care of by the product segments themselves. A remnant from the former organization was the business area structure. The producers were measured by their performance in the individual customer segment and by business area, but not as separate entities.

This was the biggest organizational shake-up since the merger between ASEA and BBC into Asea Brown Boveri Ltd (ABB) in 1987. It was based on certain assumptions. First, it was more important to be customer- and customer-application oriented than previously. Particularly in order to supply an industry segment with systems or entire plants, this organization was meant to be equipped to deal with the coordination of ABB activities and products. Second, globalization of the business was increasing and the organization re-emphasized this fact by strengthening the international KAM programme. Third, it addressed the issue of differentiation and fragmentation experienced both internally and externally. The predominant factor underlying this was the formation of larger units for the producing divisions and the coordination aspect in the sales divisions.

The reorganization also entailed problems and challenges, particularly related to the centralization component in the new organization. Ultimately, the global KAM programme defined 30 global customers as key accounts with top executive sponsors, thus clarifying the strategic importance of these customers for the ABB group.

KAM programme drivers

Low purchasing coordination and low sales coordination in some respects constitute the starting point of this study. Both seller and buyer are organizations that are large and highly divisionalized. Neither purchasing nor sales were coordinated to any great extent, which basically also fitted the individual relationship fairly well since both of these functions were specialized and thus fairly narrow. When either the buyer or the seller moves in a direction towards coordination the relationship has a less structural fit and neither experiences the complexity present as a problem. When the buyer takes action it is fairly natural for the seller to react to the new customer demands and thus coordinate their sales operations. When the seller initiates actions for sales coordination in order to reduce some complexity dimensions it is difficult to persuade the buyer to coordinate purchasing operations. Instead it is more likely that the seller tries to adapt to the buyer's organization, maintaining coordination in the sales operations. This makes sales task completion more complicated and increases the complexity in the sales process. In cases with joint actions, the actions and reactions are made reciprocally.

In the ABB Swedish Market case it was ABB that had been pursuing the issue of coordination prior to any clear customer requirement to do so. This is a clear indication that this ABB sales organization in some respects was leading the way for these approaches, and in some instances has actually created the prerequisites for altering its customers' way of buying products.

ABB identified that a number of its customers experienced technical problems as a result of the current purchasing strategy, problems that were impossible to overcome without coordination of sales activities. The programme was thus formed to support system selling or selling of technical solutions that includes a number of new products or services from other companies in the ABB group. In ABB the focus of the KAM programme and its managers was mainly on establishing and managing an internal cross-divisional sales organization in order to increase the sales for the group and creating an awareness of the competences that ABB had, so that each sales engineer had the ability to channel business opportunities to the right ABB division. Consequently, the characteristics of each KAM differ since they aim to reflect the characteristics of each customer, focusing on a combination of goals formulated in terms of technical problem solving, a reduction in the customer supply base or business opportunities for ABB. The focus of the KAM programme has been to anticipate these customers' buying organizations' efforts in coordinating their purchases between different units – see Figure 5.

The focus for this programme was the coordination of products and systems to create a more complete ABB offer to key customers. The idea was to make the product and structure simpler by forming KAM teams, and from a customer perspective make both the technical and commercial offer less complex. However, by starting this programme the complexity in coordinating technical and com-

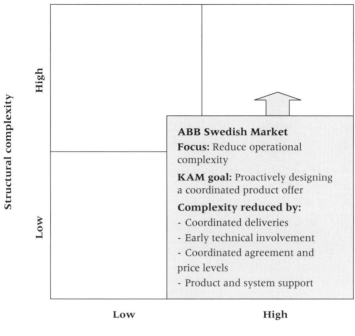

Figure 5 The sales process focus of the Swedish Market programme

mercial issues increased for the internal ABB team (depicted by the arrow in Figure 5), thus increasing the structural complexity since the programme puts pressure to coordinate an uncoordinated organization.

In the international KAM programme the situation was somewhat different. The buyer drive for this programme was relatively strong. Furthermore, some of the relationships that constituted the reason for the programme contained elements whereby the buyer laid coordination requirements on the seller organization. This meant that the buying organization produced a more integrated way of organizing the purchasing organization. It was therefore the buyer organization's dedication to purchasing coordination that resulted in more ABB sales coordination within the realm of the KAM programme. For example, ABB had an established relationship with a customer but the customer demanded not only the supply of parts but also that ABB should pre-assemble the parts into sub-systems. This required competences of several companies in the ABB group and the KAM programme was set up around the specific project/solution – a temporal solution-based KAM programme.

Furthermore, in instances of a joint action in the formation of KAMs, there appears to be a joint effort also in trying to achieve benefits from the programme. The rationale for moving towards more sales coordination when the buyer organization is coordinated is much stronger than when sales coordination influences

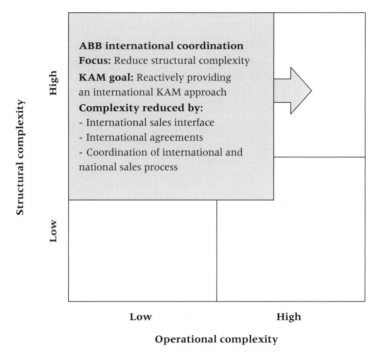

Figure 6 The business area KAM programme

purchasing. A result of this is that customers who have experienced the benefits of the temporal solution-based KAM programme compare how they have been approached in different geographical or product areas. Hereby the buyer often spots commercial gains if the selling group coordinated their offer, products and services worldwide. For the ABB group this means that a KAM programme must be established, initiated by the customers' demand for decreasing the costs, to identify in which way the customer is to be approached and to establish a common way initiated by the customer – redundant activities and sales work have to be changed. The programme also aims at commercial coordination on a group level and consequently there will be few possibilities for geographical and product companies to be unique, increasing the operational complexity – see Figure 6.

This programme had a focus on coordinating geographical units, thus making the commercial deal more consistent and, from a customer perspective, less complex. This means that the sales processes become more complex, since the sales have to be handled on different levels and at different locations in the customer's organization (depicted by the arrow in Figure 6). Much of this complexity stems from the geographical dispersion and the resulting geographical coordination that is emphasized in this programme. From the customer perspective, commercial and market complexities are expected to decrease with the introduction of this programme.

The Global KAM programme was initiated as a response to changes among customers in different industries, characterized by tighter economic conditions, in order to increase their competitiveness, common legislation in several countries regarding standards (i.e. electricity safety standards), deregulation of industries and markets as well as the introduction of more advanced technology. The focus was to coordinate a large variety of products, commercial agreements and fulfilment systems across different units as well as national borders.

The requirement laid on ABB, as a supplier of parts and sub-systems, was to take responsibility for the customers' final products, manufactured at different locations, functioning together independent of the intended market. Mergers among ABB customers led to a more polarized and divided market, with on one hand large global companies and on the other small local companies. For ABB, its products and solutions were still the basis of the offering, but to be a competitive supplier to the large customer the company also had to understand the requirements that its customer faced in its markets. To do that, the KAM organization had to be present in all parts of the world and be relatively more customer- than product-centric. Consequently, an organizational structure based on the key customer's demands was formed to gain internal coordination through dialogue and communication of customer requirements, identifying areas to increase sales. This also appears to be a development from the preceding KAM programmes, which developed to become designed to manage both structural and operational complexity – see Figure 7. The Global

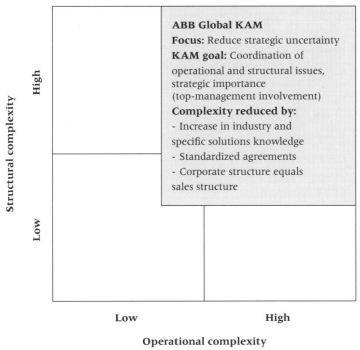

Figure 7   The Global KAM programme

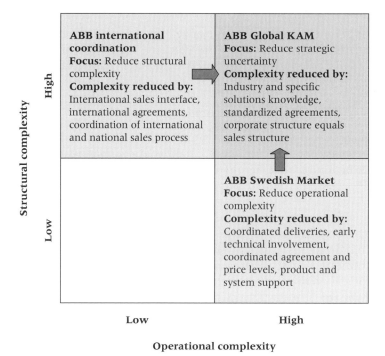

Figure 8 Complexity and KAM programme development

KAM also entailed increased importance for 30 global customers that all required top management attention, making the KAM a strategic important sales action.

By implementing KAM programmes in buyer–seller relationships the complexities change over time. Furthermore, it becomes important to manage these uncertainties in order to achieve the benefits that are associated with KAM programmes – see Figure 8. For different types of programmes, the complexities are different, and the way in which they are managed differs. There are two factors that stand out (cf. Shapiro and Moriarty 1982):

1. *Structural complexity* (location dispersion, units in different regions and nations).
2. *Operational complexity* (need for multiple products, technically advanced systems involving engineering know-how).

These two factors have had a substantial impact on the design of the programmes. The reasons behind the different programmes have also differed where the structural complexity has been caused by a response to customer requirements, whereas product complexity was based on a proactive implementation of a KAM programme. For the Global KAM the coordination becomes a highly strategic issue for the ABB group, thus involving top management to reduce the strategic uncertainty.

Situations that entail both low operational and structural complexity (low–low) have not been reported in this study since this is a sales situation that will not benefit from KAM programmes. This is not surprising since the coordination requirements are low both in structural and operational dimensions.

Conclusions

Although there is much talk about having customer focus and pursuing customer-centric marketing, there are still large discrepancies between the marketing strategy and the way buying companies perceive their own role. Whereas the focus on the buying counterpart is aimed at cost reductions, sales organizations' primary focus is on selling more. In marketing strategy, reducing total costs in the relationship is not the first priority. This reasoning is very much associated with the marketing and purchasing strategies encountered in the buyer and seller firms. The marketing strategies contain the focus on systems and international selling as well as the focus on customer share. Similarly, the purchasing strategy contains the coordination of corporate purchasing nationally and internationally as well as the degree of functional buying. This also means that marketing and purchasing strategies are important reasons for KAM programmes being established.

Coordinated purchasing and selling may be perceived both as a structural issue, i.e. how we structure the organization, and a strategic one, i.e. how we want to direct our efforts in purchasing and selling. This also boils down to the long-debated issue of strategy and structure and their effects on firms (cf. Chandler 1962, 1998; Harris and Ruefli 2000). The ability to coordinate is strongly affected by the structure in the firm, whereas the strategy directs coordination efforts.

Particularly interesting with regard to this is the strategic/structural fit between buyer and seller in the different KAM programmes. This was seen especially in respect of action and reaction towards coordination. Buyer action to coordinate purchasing results in considerable importance for sales coordination and thus KAM programmes, whereas solely seller-initiated KAM programmes entail more organizational adaptations from the seller party, since it appears to be more difficult to persuade buyers to coordinate their operations on the basis of the seller wanting it. Moreover, in a seller-reactive programme the KAMs are more compelled to do the coordination and are thus more focused in their efforts. In a proactive programme the efforts to be coordinated are less defined and therefore need to span a larger scope, at least initially.

Furthermore, whereas seller strategy in KAM programmes is directed towards selling more by being the preferred or sole supplier (cf. Barrett 1986; Shapiro and Moriarty 1982), buyer strategy is more often than not aimed at cost reductions by development of closer supplier relationships (cf. Dwyer et al. 1987; Kalwani and Narayandas 1995). This means that in a reactive KAM programme the coordination is directed more by the customer requirements, whereas a proactive KAM programme is more reliant on a teamwork coordination containing a larger scope, but also more opportunity based. From this proactive/reactive perspective, three different types of KAM programme focus can be discerned.

In the division between proactive and reactive KAM situations there are strong indications of differences with regard to competitive force. In a reactive situation the seller organization needs to be able to respond to a demanding customer, be it for an international commercial deal or for individual projects, since the customer has the initiative. In a proactive situation the seller organization, although subjected to competitive forces, has more leverage in trying to present an attractive offer to the customer, thus avoiding directly comparable competition. In the proactive situation the knowledge base is important to handle matters in a coordinated manner that combines the system-wide resources and capabilities in unique ways to provide more value through the offerings to its key customers (Teece et al. 1997). The dynamic capabilities of the supplier are based on internal resources of knowledge (in some situations scattered in different organizational units) and market awareness, which the competitor will find very difficult to replicate, imitate or trace the origin of. This is KAM providing a competitive advantage compared with its potential rivals based on the specific features of each market/customer.

Whether or not coordinated selling, or for that matter purchasing, is more related to structure than strategy is not that easy to discern. We acknowledge that there can be strategic considerations from top management that distribute power and mandate in the organizational structure of the company. This means that the structure enables the coordination of KAM sales and therefore also the implemented marketing strategies. The strategy behind the establishment of the KAM programme has to be incorporated in the strategy and business scope of the entire enterprise, otherwise it can harm the effectiveness of the supplier (Weilbaker and Weeks 1997).

We show that KAM programmes are established for a number of reasons and that different dimensions direct the workings of the programme towards addressing different terms of complexity. One is that KAM is supposed to handle sales complexity in terms of structural aspects and uncertainty. KAM should also be a response to external aspects, deriving from customer expectations, as well as a way to handle internal aspects in the sales process (see Figure 1). In this study four different strategic dimensions have been identified, resulting in conditions requiring different types of KAM programmes (see Figure 9):

1. The standard sales situation – a situation with low complexity in both dimensions, which is a situation that does not require a KAM programme.
2. The proactive KAM programme – which is driven by sales opportunity.
3. The reactive KAM programme – which is driven by customer demands.

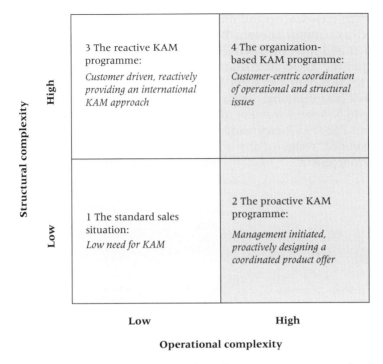

Figure 9 The four strategic dimensions and resulting KAM programme development

4. The organization-based KAM programme – which is driven by the belief in customer-centric organizational units.

The fourth dimension and resulting KAM programme requires the strongest commitment from the corporate leadership, where KAM becomes one of their top priorities.

Performance implications of new ways of organizing marketing and sales activities have been examined in a number of contexts (Anderson et al. 1994; Morgan and Hunt 1994; Workman et al. 2003). The development in KAM practice has gone from being an over-layered dimension in the organization to a situation where KAM is one of the main dimensions in the corporate structure (e.g. Galbraith 1995; Rehme 2001). Subsequently, KAM has also developed from being mainly an operational sales coordination topic to a strategic coordination for the entire organization. The main motivation behind this is that it is becoming a prerequisite to coordinate the corporate structure from a customer perspective to be able to handle large global customers.

Studying an organization over time makes this development fairly clear. More often than not KAM programmes are established by top management with the notion to increase sales to already established customers in local markets. When customers demand more coherent and coordinated international contracts, this drives the establishment of international KAM programmes and thus coordination across national borders. With the potential to handle both the internal shortcomings and the external needs emanating from customer development, it is logical that the KAM programme is integrated in the corporate structure. In this sense KAM is both a strategic platform for the sales organization and a part of the overall organizational design. From being a sales opportunity, KAM is thus developing to become a reaction to larger customers' centralization or coordination of purchasing. As Piercy and Lane (2006) observe, this development, if not carefully handled, could involve a number of hidden risks that can restrain the strategic development.

KSAM as an organizational change: making the transition

BY DIANA WOODBURN

Abstract

Once convinced of the efficacy of KSAM, companies need to consider how to achieve the vision that academics have painted for them, but the literature has very little to say about how to make the change. Success is not guaranteed. This paper looks at the journey to best practice KSAM and identifies early and later phases of activity that mark the development of the organization as a KSAM operator. The different elements and actions that comprise these phases are determined in terms of strategy and planning, organization and culture, and processes.

Introduction

Academic literature is largely focused on the very important need to paint the picture of how key strategic account management (KSAM) should look or does look. However, as increasing numbers of companies have ceased to challenge the KSAM vision and accepted the concept, their attention has shifted to issues of implementation and particularly how the transition can be achieved. Research has concentrated on inter-organizational relationships (e.g. Ford 1980; Gosman and Kelly 2000; Ivens and Pardo 2007; Millman and Wilson 1995) rather more than intra-organizational structures and adaptations for managing them (Kempeners and van der Hart 1999; Zupancic 2008).

Indeed, KSAM failure is not uncommon (Napolitano 1997; Wilson and Woodburn 2014) and companies are understandably anxious to avoid it, although academics may be more interested in examining the issue of why failure is so common (Wilson and Woodburn 2014). While this paper is concerned with exploring how transitioning towards best practice is achieved, there is more than a suspicion that many failures may be because the company never actually made the transition to KSAM. Homburg et al. (2002) identified several forms of KSAM, some of which are not KSAM at all ('Country club KSAM') or are so inefficient that they barely qualify, i.e. 'Middle management' KSAM, 'Operating level' KSAM, 'Unstructured' KSAM, 'Isolated' KSAM.

In 2005/2006 a group of global and national companies at different stages in their KSAM development together charted the various actions they had completed to establish KSAM in their organizations (Woodburn 2006). Much of the material in this paper was discovered and developed through that project, particularly the KSAM transitioning journey, which mapped out the actions and changes that each phase of development had demanded. The findings and model of KSAM development in Woodburn (2006) were later corroborated by quantitative research in Davies and Ryals (2009).

This project soon made it clear that establishing KSAM is a journey which is not completed quickly (Capon and Senn 2010; Wengler et al. 2006; Woodburn 2006): indeed, it may be seen as an extended and possibly never-ending journey, as suppliers are obliged to continually develop the ways they work with their key customers. Progress post-introduction is rarely linear, and can go backwards as well as forwards (Capon and Senn 2010), so continuous improvement cannot be assumed: constant pressure is needed to maintain forward momentum. Indeed, whatever has already been done to develop KSAM, there is more yet to do because, as it develops, it touches more people and processes in the supplier company and in the customer too.

Companies normally find change difficult, and suppliers often underestimate the time, effort and investment needed to achieve KSAM success. It is a major organizational change, not just the latest sales initiative (Capon and Senn 2010). Underestimating the scale of the change is likely to mean that the development process is set unrealistic deadlines, is under-resourced, is unsupported by senior management across the board and ultimately fails against impracticable short-term expectations.

KSAM strategy

Strategy should, of course, lead any organizational change, although observation suggests that it is often not the case, and existing structures, culture and objectives often override the optimum expression of the strategy. KSAM is an organizational change, though suppliers frequently do not recognize it as such and make the mistake of underestimating what is required to achieve what they seek.

Introducing KSAM is itself a strategy, but like any strategy, it requires further expression before it becomes a direction that people can understand, align with and implement. While KSAM is itself focused on the interface with key customers, it needs to be related to other company strategies in order to be effective and to deliver the promised value to key customers (see 'KSAM structure' on page 83). Strategies from supply chain, product development, customer service through to marketing, finance and human resources should all take account of KSAM demands, and need to be aligned accordingly.

KSAM strategy is implemented at both a programme level – developments in organization, recruitment, resources, processes, etc. – and the level of individual key accounts. The strategies formulated for customers will specify what value is appropriate for each of them, and will therefore collectively define what operational strategies the supplier needs to adopt to fulfil those promises. Companies may realize the modifications they need in KSAM-linked strategies top-down, by developing the programme at a high level, or bottom-up, through collating their strategic account plans (see Woodburn 2006), which gives them a more concrete view of the changes required, or probably a combination of both. Whatever the process applied, the reformulation of all functional strategies to align them around KSAM at the time of its introduction should not be overlooked or delayed.

A strong, even painful stimulus often launches a company's desire to introduce KSAM. Identifying the stimulus is useful in demonstrating the need for change: it helps enormously if the whole organization knows what the driver(s) is and can appreciate why the company has to change. Not only does everyone then understand the importance or even necessity of the initiative, but they are more likely to identify appropriate responses to the company's specific drivers.

Drivers of KSAM

Organizations rarely make the effort to adopt KSAM unless there is a powerful driver behind it, often triggered by a particular issue or event. An event may be a symptom of an underlying trend or need that has not gained credibility or urgency until the event drew attention to it, such as the loss of a major customer because of the inflexibility of the supplier's approach, or a punitive drop in profit owing to mistakes made through poor coordination. The 'tipping point' for action

	Internal	External
Positive	• Desire for growth • Capitalizing on broad offering • Multiple channels to same customers • Fashionable/useful bandwagon? • Better MIS systems	• Customer demand – one company, less time, spent better • Customer demand for strategic partnership • Globalizing/cross-boundary customers
Negative	• Pressure on margins • Pressure on resource • Organizational change/low internal cohesion • Need for cover for failing offer	• Mature market • Embarrassment in the marketplace • Customer loss/potential loss/pre-loss feedback

Figure 1 Drivers of KSAM

is often provided by negative stimuli such as the loss of a major contract, a public brawl between companies or other adverse publicity, or unexpectedly or persistently bad results.

However, drivers for KSAM can be positive as well as negative, and may originate from inside or outside the organization. Negative external drivers are powerful, but there are also positive drivers that may be leveraged to promote the initiative or to make it possible – see Figure 1. Organizations often contain a potential champion for KSAM (McDonald et al. 2000) who has observed an opportunity or an alarming trend and is convinced that KSAM is the route to dealing with it. Champions who have not yet gained the attention and support of the company to take action may use untoward events and wield them as 'sharp sticks' to goad their companies into action.

External drivers

Customers have wanted KSAM treatment from their suppliers for a long time (Yip and Madsen 1996; Woodburn and McDonald 2001); indeed, KSAM is basically a customer-driven approach so, unsurprisingly, a large part of the external drivers originate with customers. Responding to them may be seen as positive, while the fear of actually losing a key account is certainly negative, as is embarrassment in the marketplace arising from, for example, poor coordination or opportunism made visible. In a mature market, products become commoditized and price pressures more severe, leaving KSAM as one of the few differentiators still available.

Internal drivers

Where key accounts are a substantial amount of a company's profits, the supplier may see that the best growth opportunity lies with those customers, especially as they tend to be market leaders growing at a greater rate than their competitors. KSAM then potentially becomes the main contributor to the supplier's ambition. Furthermore, where the supplier has a wide offering across a range of routes to market, it can gain synergy and cut waste and confusion through coordinating its offer, and that coordination needs KSAM for its delivery. Better management information systems (MIS) provide the mechanics for coordination and information supply, which makes effective KSAM more possible now than in the past.

Negative internal drivers, such as pressure on margins and resources, may drive companies to deal with them through KSAM, but they pose problems for the initiative too: KSAM is not a cost-saving solution, although longer term it should provide a good return, albeit not guaranteed (Kalwani and Narayandas 1995; Reinartz and Kumar 2002). Some companies have tried to compensate for a failing offer or service through KSAM ('putting lipstick on the pig') but it is unlikely to succeed in such circumstances and is not recommended until the underlying issues have been fixed.

Often at the outset KSAM champions emerge who will identify the most powerful drivers and decide how they can best be employed. However, even if there are clear reasons for change, there will also be strong resistance from internal forces: from people who simply do not like change, or who consider any new approach to be a criticism of what they have done to date, or who see the new way of working as eroding their territory or power base. The company needs to be constantly reminded of the compelling reason why it opted for KSAM, as the champion inevitably meets resistance.

Customer demand for KSAM treatment is a strong driver (Buzzell 1985), but some suppliers still fail to recognize it (or prefer not to). Indications that customers are either consciously seeking KSAM or are unconsciously ready for it include customers who are:

- Communicating opportunities and initiatives and involving the supplier in their strategies.
- Expecting an understanding of their business: inviting the supplier to meet a wider range of people in their organization and giving a broad range of information about their business and marketplace.
- Wanting to explore joint projects involving more commitment.
- Wanting to talk longer term and develop strategies together.
- Asking for a more senior account manager with more authority and/or competency.
- Wanting a transparent or integrated approach and a single point of contact, dealing with them as a single entity.

This list can be turned into a simple 'litmus' test, which can quickly show whether the supplier has customers who are ready for KSAM. Not all of the indicators in the list need to be positive to make the case for KSAM: any one of them could be sufficient. Furthermore, it is clearly not necessary for all of a supplier's customers to want KSAM in order to instigate a programme – many do not qualify anyway, nor is there any point in forcing it on those who do not want it. The crucial question is whether a significant amount of the business is tied in with customers who do want KSAM treatment and will respond to it.

KSAM strategy implementation

A wide range of KSAM success factors has been studied (e.g. Stevenson 1981; Workman et al. 2003; Wotruba and Castleberry 1993; Zupancic, 2008), mostly focusing on specific elements of programmes that have proved successful, assuming that, once identified, companies can adopt these elements. And yet KSAM failure is all too common. Studying the failure factors can help to illuminate the success factors. Natti and Ojasalo (2008) found four barriers to the utilization of customer knowledge originating in the supplier organization, while Wilson and Woodburn (2014) also found that less tangible elements relating to culture and norms were more often cited as causes of failure than were the formal elements of KSAM, which can be written down and documented. In fact, Workman et al. (2003) found that KAM formalization was negatively correlated with KAM effectiveness.

Problems were less about whether the KSAM strategy was clear or appropriate (though a lack of clarity was also mentioned) and more about whether the company as a whole was really committed to it and could apply that commitment consistently. Challenges to companies' capability of changing at all were also common. These were called moderating factors, which undermine and compromise the KSAM initiative from the outset. Also collected were a number of intervening cultural factors, which indirectly but effectively obstruct the implementation of KSAM. Figure 2 depicts a model of KSAM-relevant organizational elements, showing both of these types of factor.

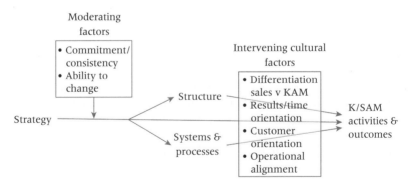

Figure 2 A model of the linkages between organizational elements in KSAM (Wilson and Woodburn 2014)

This model suggests that companies should change their behaviour very visibly, communicate the strategy and the change in their expectations clearly and with conviction and consistency (across the organization and across time), and instigate a process of change that will prevent recidivism. If, in reality, there is very little change activity, coupled with ambivalence about moving to KSAM, the people concerned will reflect that inertia and ambivalence and either be slow to respond, while they wait to be convinced that the company is serious about KSAM, or not change at all.

However, the model suggests a further set of failure factors which can also frustrate KSAM strategy, even if the strategy has clear and consistent commitment: those emanating from the culture. For example, Workman et al. (2003) found that 'it is not so much the extent of team use that matters but rather the development of an organizational culture that is committed to supporting KAM'. In Wilson and Woodburn (2014) negative cultural aspects included a lack of differentiation between sales and KSAM, over-strong focus on results in the short term, a lack of genuine customer orientation and a lack of alignment with KSAM in the operational functions. These issues also require conscious action to change them both initially and on a continuing basis. Without continued focus and effort, companies easily slide back to their pre-existing orientation and ways of working, some of which are destructive to the KSAM strategy.

KSAM structure

All structures in companies of any size carry with them intrinsically anti-KSAM features, so companies have to choose the structure that seems the least unhelpful, rather than an ideal. Indeed, organizational structure in KSAM poses a conundrum: key customers expect to be influential and therefore close to the supplier's senior management (which implies that the key account manager should be in such a position). At the same time, they expect prompt and consistent delivery of value, which suppliers feel requires the key account manager's proximity to operations – they are concerned that key account managers may become divorced from reality at ground level (Woodburn 2006). Many-layered structures in which the position of the customer representation (i.e. key account manager) is structurally distant from senior managers are not welcome to key customers and may be read, not unreasonably, as indicative of their true importance to the supplier.

Positioning KSAM in the organizational structure

Difficulty in devising an ideal structure does not mean that all structures are equally good for KSAM: there are forms of organization that make KSAM particularly difficult. The (very common) multi-level hierarchy shown in Figure 3 is not popular with key customers, who see the key account manager in this kind of structure as having very low levels of seniority, influence and decision-making power, which is probably true. Normally, each key account manager is not

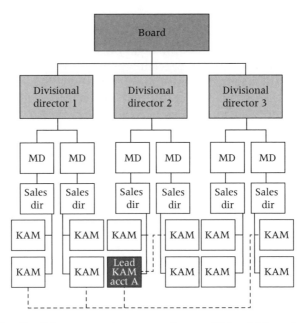

Figure 3   Adding 'lead' key account managers in a multi-level hierarchy

empowered to speak for other divisions in the company from which the customer might also purchase, and has to refer discussions to other key account managers, but to achieve better coordination and satisfy the customer's desire for 'single point of contact' while avoiding structural change, some companies nominate a 'lead key account manager', as shown in Figure 3.

Table 1:   Advantages and disadvantages of lead key account managers

Advantages	Disadvantages
Improves communication and coordination	Does not deliver genuine integration, sub-optimal for customers
Keeps key account managers close to delivery, keeps them 'real'	Key account manager promotes home business more strongly: works in comfort zone, responds to 'home' senior management
Does not disturb current structure in the rest of the company	Not good for growing new business from other divisions, maintains status quo
Aligned with current role and competencies of key account managers	Limited empowerment, hard to operate, involves constant, difficult internal negotiations
Flexible	Complicated, difficult for others to understand and work with

The 'lead' is normally positioned in the division that already does most business with the customer because the existing relationship is seen as a deciding factor. The figure shows an example of one lead key account manager but in reality there would be at least several more working with other key accounts, and then the picture becomes complex and difficult to manage. Key account managers in such situations generally have limited empowerment and are trying to operate a difficult model from a relatively weak position.

While this least-disturbance approach is popular with supplier management, the majority of companies struggle to make this model work well enough to meet the expectations of key customers – see Table 1.

The critical issue is the key account managers' degree of empowerment, especially outside their 'home' organization. Elevating the key account managers in the hierarchy or flattening the structure helps, as in Figure 4, but internal divisional or geographical boundaries, normally strengthened by financial targets, will give rise to most of the same problems. These matter when the most important customers interact with more than one supplier-defined strategic business unit (SBU).

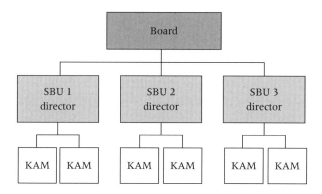

Figure 4   Regional structure with more senior key account managers

To overcome the shortcomings of the preceding structures, some suppliers have introduced high-level KSAM units where key account managers operate at only one level removed from the board and their line manager sits on the board – see Figure 5. This structure is designed to minimize internal competition and reduce the distance between the board and the key account manager representing the customer, but strong, clear links need to be made with the operational delivery functions in the company to enable it to work as it should, without introducing new internal boundaries. Companies with a single product division operating in one country with national key accounts can organize themselves in this way more easily than multi-nationals and multi-product companies.

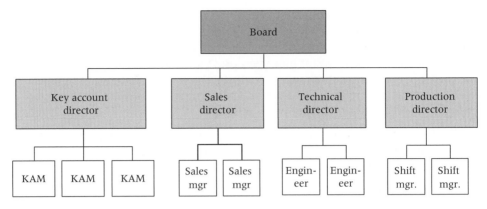

Figure 5 High-level KSAM structure

Ultimately, strict hierarchies are not conducive to the flexibility required for KSAM, leading suppliers towards a matrix structure, preferably with two dimensions reflecting both product/service and customer requirements. Most companies need to operate with a strong structure around their products/services, in order to achieve and maintain excellence in what they offer. For a similar reason, to maintain excellence in how they offer it, they also need a strong structure around their customers, particularly their key customers. When suppliers operate a third axis as well (normally geography), one or two axes generally emerge as stronger and it often appears to be the customer dimension that is weakest (Woodburn et al. 2004).

Because the key account manager needs to pull activities together across the company, any structure will have its shortcomings. Companies accustomed to working in a matrix structure are likely to find the change easier than traditionally hierarchical companies in which attitudes and habits will need substantial recasting. Ideally, the organization should be flexible enough to mirror the customer's organization, but companies struggle with managing the complexity and general untidiness of such a variable approach.

Change in organizational structure is not sufficient on its own: it is supported or defeated by formal and informal networks, systems and processes, objectives and targets and also by attitudes and cultural norms. All need to be addressed at an early stage to achieve a successful transition (for a case study in change, see Guenzi et al. 2009).

Positioning KSAM and sales

A lack of understanding of the nature and purpose of KSAM, and therefore a lack of differentiation between sales and KSAM, leads to inappropriate decisions on its positioning in the organization (Wilson and Woodburn 2014). Key account managers cited the conflict between the 'opposing philosophies of traditional sales and account management' as a cause of KSAM failure, especially when the management of both sales and account management programmes falls under sales management, who are 'uneasy with the process'.

Sales directors/managers find it difficult to treat their two types of reports differently and tend to apply familiar, traditional sales management practices, such as short-term sales targets, call number targets and standard resource allocation, which are inappropriate in KSAM. Key accounts require more varied, customer-specific approaches and lower-quantity, higher-value activity. In addition, sales managers often promote traditional territory sales people to the role of key account manager, who are largely moulded by their previous experience in traditional selling. In Wilson and Woodburn (2014), key account managers reported a poor understanding of the role as a common cause of failure. It was 'perceived as being primarily a sales role rather than a management role', with key account managers judged on their ability to grow sales rather than nurture customers. Their companies reflected a mentality of 'it all comes down to sales in the end'.

To achieve the required change, sales directors' attitudes should be addressed, as well as those of key account managers with sales backgrounds. New person and job specifications, together with new recruitment and personal development policies and new terms and conditions, are required: a sales department that has simply been renamed is likely to revert to selling behaviour, as Woodburn (2006) found. Factors originating in both the organization's sales culture and the key account managers themselves work against the change to KSAM:

- Strong, even relentless, focus in the business on current sales results.
- Reward systems designed for sales (Ryals and Rogers 2006; Woodburn 2008).
- Salespeople like it (they feel successful when they close a deal).
- Security and familiarity ('we know how this works').
- Confidence in outcomes (clearer cause and effect linkages).

The way in which key account managers spend their time is a key indicator of KSAM development progress. Woodburn (2006) found that companies operating KSAM believed that only 5–10% of a key account manager's time should be spent on selling (when defined as converting specific opportunities to wins, i.e. managing the sales cycle, gaining bid sign-offs, pitching and closing the deal). While selling is clearly an important element of the key account manager's role, it is one among others. Table 2 shows how supplier KSAM programme managers thought key account managers' time should be allocated, alongside how they feared their people were currently deploying their time.

Key account teams

Key account teams have become common in the management of key accounts in companies that have realized the range of activities involved in KSAM. Members are drawn from a variety of functions, depending on the needs of the business with the customer – customer service and technical specialists are frequently members, but marketing, product management and finance are also often included. Members are almost always only partially dedicated to the key account,

Table 2: Key account manager's use of time

Key account manager activity	Actual	Should be
Developing relationships	25%	20%
Implementing and motivating the deal operationally	25–30%	15%
Developing industry knowledge/understanding strategy/planning	0%	5–15%
Selling/achieving sales result, bid. sign-off	30–50%	5–10%
Internal alignment for deal commercially	0–15%	5–10%
Internal day-to-day problem solving	15%	5%
Internal understanding of capability	0%	5%
Promoting brand/business	0%	5%
Reporting/providing information	0–10%	5%
Training and education	0–5%	5%
Team management	0%	5%
Other	?	10%
Total (of mid-points of ranges)	**113%**	**100%**

so in most cases they have 'dotted line' reporting to the key account manager and 'solid line' reporting to their functional head. Commonly, team members have other key customers with which they work and/or they also have objectives set by their 'home' function. As a result, the biggest single issue in the effective operation of key account teams is the cooperation of team members and allocation of their time, given the conflicting demands of their functional head and key account manager(s), as Figure 6 suggests.

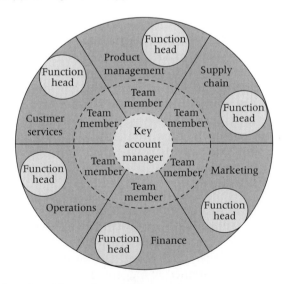

Figure 6 Cross-functional key account teams

These teams are tasked with the long-term management of the customer. Team members are a fundamental part of the relationship and are highly valued by the customer, so there should be a consistent core of team members at least. However, functional heads who are the 'resource owners' do not always see continuity as an issue and may reallocate members quite casually, overlooking the importance of the relationship with customer staff and the fit with the customer's business.

The dimensions of the following characteristics of key account teams seem to define their 'atmosphere', ways of working and success (Atanasova and Senn 2011; Woodburn 2009):

1. The nature of the leadership (usually by the key account manager).
2. The scope of the team's authority and decision-making power.
3. The team's objectives, their nature and alignment with the company's objectives.
4. Recognition of the importance of the team by the company and the team members themselves.
5. Persistence, i.e. the team's length of life and continuity of team membership.

Support for key account teams is critical to their success and that of KSAM as a whole. Because of their relatively informal nature they can be invisible in the organization and membership may be seen as extra work with very little recognition for it. Atanasova and Senn (2011) found that their performance was directly influenced by three team processes: communication and collaboration, conflict management and proactiveness. Where key account teams work well, the supplier organization makes a particular effort to communicate and celebrate their role and efforts in the view of the rest of the company.

Making the change

KSAM is probably difficult to implement because it is a cultural as well as a business initiative. Effective cultural change starts with an exploration of the gap between the current situation and the desired situation and a stage of 'unfreezing' (Lewin 1946) to allow people to move on. Successful change programmes demand sensitivity, political awareness, clarity, consistency, translation into practicalities, energy and stamina from the people determined to make the change happen. In some companies a KSAM champion emerges or is appointed, with or without the support of a core team.

A KSAM champion with a high level of seniority in the organization can make a huge difference to success: they can maintain a focus on pushing KSAM through and keeping development on track, not just to kick-start the programme but also to keep up the forward momentum over the next few years. The KSAM champion must convince senior management of the imperative for change and sustain that view over a long period of time and through some tough battles, particularly with the sales force.

Commonly, a large proportion of the sales force, regardless of seniority and sales experience, will lack much of the skill set required to fulfil key account manager positions. Nevertheless, the current sales force and its management generally need to be won over, which may be difficult: KSAM is often seen as challenging the status quo and territorial interests, and indeed it does. Their development should be recognized and training and learning opportunities offered at an early stage, rather than later, still making the requirement to adapt very clear.

There will be others around the organization who are threatened by the change, both in reality and in their imagination, and their issues must be recognized too. Overlaying the corporate culture are national cultures in international companies and all the sub-cultures of functions such as sales, supply chain, service, marketing, etc. Furthermore, underlying the corporate culture in all companies are informal networks and links: the 'under-culture'. People who currently feel comfortable and in control will have to move to situations that they cannot yet visualize and where, honestly, their control and comfort are likely to be diminished. Others will find their power and influence increased, and some may be uncomfortable with that too. A significant change like KSAM has strong political overtones, both during set-up and in later implementation (Wilson and Millman 2003).

A common vision of what KSAM means for the organization should be created and communicated widely, whereas companies frequently embark on KSAM with vague and various ideas of what is involved, including the widespread belief that it is a sales function initiative whose implications will be limited to sales. Broad senior management support and engagement must be gained for sustainable KSAM (Brady 2004; Wilson and Woodburn 2014) in order to achieve cross-functional support for major change and for serious investment. 'A firm commitment from senior-level management won't ensure a program's success, but the lack of commitment can seal a program's failure' (Stevens 2009).

Interestingly, KSAM champions are not always entirely frank with senior management in explaining the extent of change required for successful KSAM (Woodburn 2006). Quite frequently, they describe an intermediate, transition stage of KSAM to senior managers, in order not to alarm them and risk an adverse reaction, unless the CEO or MD is also the KSAM champion.

The KSAM champion or core team will need to:

- Articulate what KSAM is and how it differs from existing approaches.
- Agree KSAM's priority versus other initiatives.
- Specify the effort and supporting action required from senior managers.

Companies can take one of three approaches to the speed and scale of the change: revolution, 'step-change' or incremental evolution. Some companies would like to run a pilot programme, but it is debatable whether a valid pilot is possible. Given the inevitable limitations in duration, completion and commitment, the trial will be deficient as a microcosm of eventual reality and may not expose or illuminate important issues, leaving companies not much the wiser about the chances of success or the issues they will meet in a full implementation.

Although incremental evolution is seen as safer, it may not even be noticeable and therefore gets little attention and response, so it stands a greater risk of fizzling out, which is itself a risk. However, few companies seem able to cope with revolution and 'step-change' is probably the most common approach. 'Step-change' is also advisable where a powerful or urgent driver exists because it creates urgency, gets noticed and highlights the need for action, reaches critical mass and delivers a result, but it will also create 'problems'. However, if a significant corporate initiative is not creating problems, change is probably stalled.

As Wilson and Woodburn (2014) suggest (see above), in order to be successful through KSAM, and particularly in order not to start and fail, companies should see it as an important corporate change programme and give it the commitment, attention and resources to work.

The KSAM transitioning curve

The transitioning curve describing how KSAM development proceeds in most organizations (Woodburn 2006) is shown in Figure 7. The curve is assembled from the actions taken by companies from different sectors in their KSAM

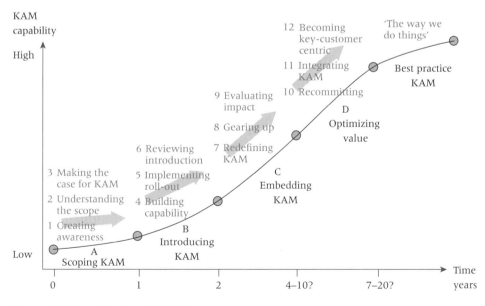

Figure 7 Transitioning to KSAM

development journeys. It represents a fairly realistic picture, neither idealized nor peppered with mistakes, but it does include sub-optimal stages through which most companies pass. Most companies take a wrong turn at some point and head into a cul-de-sac from which they have to extricate themselves, but these individual excursions have been omitted.

Normally, KSAM development seems to be organized into five principal phases:

A. Scoping KSAM.
B. Introducing KSAM.
C. Embedding KSAM.
D. Optimizing value.
E. Best practice.

The first four phases are discussed here, but not the last, i.e. arrival at 'Best practice KSAM', since that occupies much of the literature. The phases can overlap, as some companies emphasize certain elements more than others and advance faster in those areas. In particular, the early phases, A 'Scoping KSAM' and B 'Introducing KSAM', may not be cleanly divided into the sequence of action charted (Davies and Ryals 2009), as suppliers sometimes commit themselves to KSAM and start to introduce elements of it before having completed their evaluations. Time to introduction, the end of Phase B, consistently takes about two years, but can take longer. Shorter periods seem rare, so suppliers contemplating introduction need to adjust their expectations accordingly.

The time required for Phases C and D seems less consistent, but 5–10 years is likely even for suppliers steadfast in their determination to make progress. However, Phase C, 'Embedding KSAM', often takes that amount of time on its own and many companies get stuck there, never reaching Phase D, 'Optimizing value', because deep down they are not ready to take on some of the organizational changes and power shifts involved. Some companies have been implementing KSAM in various forms for 20 years but still could not say they had reached best practice. Capon and Senn (2010) describe slightly different stages, taking potentially even longer, and still best practice is not guaranteed.

Each phase can be divided into three periods or sub-phases, following on from each other approximately chronologically, in which different actions are executed or initiated. There will undoubtedly be considerable overlap between the sub-phases, so any sequence of actions should not be taken as set in stone – in some focus areas action might be quite advanced, while others have been left unattended.

A wide range of action is involved in implementing a KSAM programme. The necessary actions can be grouped into three coherent streams of activity observable across all KSAM phases. Suppliers will, at most times, have some development activities running that address:

• Strategy and planning.
• Organization and culture.
• Processes.

The balance of activity changes across different phases. A heavy focus on strategy and planning would be expected at the outset, with little, if anything, developing in processes at that point. Action addressing process adaptation increases later on, as the focus is rebalanced from strategy towards implementation. Development can be further described as contributory streams of activity within each broad area of the initiative, as shown in Table 3. In addition, at some points there will be critical milestones to pass, such as the point when a company decides whether or not to adopt KSAM, or to recommit to KSAM at a later stage.

The early stages

Phase A: Scoping KSAM

This first phase is a crucial one in which the decision to embark on KSAM – or not – is taken. Champions of KSAM look outside at the marketplace for their

Table 3: Activity streams in KSAM development

Stream of activity	Contributory streams	Description
Strategy and planning	Goals and strategy	Vision and overall aims
	Planning and objectives	Specific planning activities and quantified forecasting
	Research	Finding out information needed from internal and, importantly, external sources
Organization and people	Key account managers	Changes in the role, rewards and development of and for the individual
	KSAM teams and the KSAM community	People consistently working on a key account or the KSAM programme
	The wider organization and senior management	Addressing the rest of the company
Processes	Key account manager activities	Processes engaging individual key account managers and generally their responsibility
	Other KSAM activities	Processes involving the KSAM community, typically customer service, monitoring and review
	Core processes	Operational processes run by the rest of the organization, not specifically for KSAM

justification, at what their most important customers are saying and doing, and at what approaches their competitors and other leading companies are taking. Ideally, the KSAM champion defines what success in KSAM would look like for the company and describes the journey towards that success, taking into account outcomes for the company, the individuals involved and the customers. 'Scoping KSAM' can be divided into three sub-phases, as Table 4 shows. Phase A may easily take up to a year and involve a good deal more effort, discovery and political activity than anticipated.

Phase A should end with a formal approval decision, but often the process leading up to it is quite chaotic and political. Putting together the business case for a major change like KSAM is very difficult because of the range of implications and the uncertainty associated with assessing a complex position in the future. Most organizations will look for strong justification before taking on KSAM, but the extent of the initiative and the difficulty of quantifying the outcomes still means that they have to take their decision with less than cast-iron proof. Consequently,

Table 4: Phase A sub-phases in scoping KSAM

Sub-phase	Key actions
1. Creating awareness	Identify a powerful driver, which could be positive but is generally negative.
	The KSAM champion (often self-appointed), who recognizes the possibility of KSAM as a solution, works to generate awareness of KSAM.
2. Understanding the scope	Appoint a KSAM programme team to work with the champion.
	Get to grips with how KSAM addresses the issues through research, putting it in context and communicating with stakeholders.
	Begin to look at which customers would be involved.
3. Making the case for KSAM	Clarify specifics of strategy, objectives, costs and customers.
	Assemble the business case with what KSAM will look like in the organization and expected outcomes.
	Position and define the job of key account manager.
Milestone: senior management approval	Critical decision point: stakeholders should have been identified and hearts and minds won over.

the convictions of key players and internal politics play a large part in the decision, and the supplier may become committed to KSAM, even though cross-company understanding, assessment and acceptance have not been achieved.

Companies that miss out elements of Phase A may embark on KSAM on a false premise, considering it to be a short-term initiative from which they can readily disengage. When they fail to get a quick and unequivocal pay-back, they may waver in their commitment to the KSAM programme, described as 'corporate wobble' by one company (Woodburn 2006), which may have disastrous effects on key account managers and customers who have committed to KSAM. Companies should see KSAM as a longer-term programme and be adequately prepared for the journey.

The KSAM programme is likely to be challenged internally at all stages of its existence, so companies need a good understanding of the financial implications from the beginning. There may be cost savings emanating from KSAM ways of working, but investment is also required, and generally KSAM does not save cost, for two reasons:

- KSAM generally increases the cost of running the customer interface for key customers. Companies often find those resources by withdrawing them from other smaller or less important customers, but the resource requirement is rarely better than cost-neutral.
- KSAM is more likely to increase volumes or maintain business that might be lost, rather than save cost or raise prices (Kalwani and Narayandas 1995; Ivens and Pardo 2008): key customers are adept at bargaining away cost savings but they do award more business to key suppliers.

The business case can look misleadingly unattractive if an unrealistic baseline is used, i.e. if it were assumed that current levels of business would be maintained in the absence of KSAM, whereas in a KSAM-ready marketplace a failure to change the approach to key customers is likely to lead to a decline in business. Such a decline should be applied as the most probable baseline underlying the case for KSAM.

Phase B: Introducing KSAM
The launch phase is often a chaotic period in which the organization finds that it is still 'making it up as it goes along', depending on the amount and depth of scoping carried out in the first phase, but it is understandably difficult to coordinate such wide-ranging changes. However, once certain elements are put into place, others need to be implemented within a fairly short space of time – see Table 5. Action should be planned in advance and then implemented simultaneously around the launch. Key account managers are generally appointed at varying times before the launch, but other launch actions should then follow as soon as possible, since delay in completing them has a wide range of implications. For example, key account managers will start developments with customers from the time that they are appointed, sometimes before important support elements

Table 5: Phase B sub-phases in introducing KSAM

Sub-phase	Key actions
4. Building capability	Finalize goals and the plans to meet in greater detail, highlighting specific, actionable requirements.
	Appoint competent key account managers with high priority.
Milestone: launch	Coordinated launch: though capability building and roll-out are likely to merge in practice.
5. Implementing roll-out	Build specific internal support rapidly so that key account managers can function effectively.
	Inform the rest of the organization about the new approach.
	Adopt feedback- and progress-monitoring processes.
6. Reviewing KSAM introduction	Review the introduction and make adjustments to structure and ways of working at an early stage (too soon to review revenue or profit).
	Publicize good/new practice and actively discourage bad/old practice to make the commitment to change clear: identify issues.

are in place inside the supplier, with the resultant danger of making and having to break promises to key customers.

The appointment of appropriate key account managers is a crucial action: the job should be carefully described together with the competences and attributes required to fulfil it. Key account managers can be recruited internally, from sales and other functions within the company, and even externally from candidates who match the profile. The quick and easy way is to appoint current relationship owners and/or senior salespeople as key account managers, but many of them cannot meet the requirements of the job and removing them, once appointed, causes a great deal of trouble and bad feeling.

Key account teams have an important role in execution as a large part of the 'specific internal support' required to ensure delivery of customer commitments, and are best appointed as early as possible. Some suppliers decide that they will set up account teams 'next year, when we understand better what we're doing', but by that time the customer is likely to have concluded that the whole thing was just sales talk and empty promises, and withdrawn their commitment, which will be much more difficult to regain.

At the end of the introductory phase, some of the organizational issues that might cause friction and disruption begin to emerge. Cross-boundary issues (whether national, divisional, cultural or just departmental) will undoubtedly arise. If left unattended, they sow the seeds of poor performance against high expectations that will eventually undermine and potentially destroy the whole KSAM approach.

Even at this point there will be people who are already asking for evidence of the value of KSAM in terms of increased revenue, margin or profit. However, KSAM is a medium- to long-term strategy and should be judged accordingly. Meanwhile, companies have specific anecdotes about how KSAM has helped the business with customers which they can use for the purpose of encouragement rather than evaluation.

The later stages

Phase C: Embedding KSAM

Even by the end of Phase B (Introduction), suppliers can see that KSAM is not quite as simple as first envisaged, and there are elements that need to be reconsidered and re-specified. The organization recognizes that it has only reached the end of the beginning and should expect to make further, substantial developments. Organizations that get KSAM all 'right first time' do not appear to exist. At this stage there is a period of redefining various elements of the programme that were put in place in Phase B at a basic level, such as the customer categorization criteria, roles and rewards, followed by a period of intense activity to 'gear up' to the new perception of the requirement, as in Table 6.

So, for example, in Phase B the selection criteria for key customers usually emphasize current volumes of business, but the limitation of this approach becomes clearer with experience of working with those customers who take large volumes but remain uninterested in closer collaboration. In addition, as suppliers recognize the amount of resource absorbed by key customers, they understand the importance of ensuring that only those who will respond at a satisfactory level should receive such expensive treatment. The criteria for selecting those customers need to be more sophisticated, along with the process for applying them.

Again, key account plans should have been produced in Phase B, but commonly they will be incomplete, lack explicit strategies and have a short-term focus. Suppliers begin to see the need for genuine strategic account plans in whose development the customer has been heavily involved. The plan format is upgraded, more training on producing strategies and plans is delivered to key account managers (and teams, ideally) and the requirement for quality is clarified and followed through.

Process development becomes a major focus. Processes should be adapted to facilitate the implementation of strategies with key customers, whatever their nature, with the emphasis on maintaining flexibility. Since key customers will always 'push the boundaries', suppliers developing processes to support them

Table 6:   Phase C sub-phases in embedding KSAM

Sub-phase	Key actions
7. Redefining KSAM	Tighten up some elements, such as customer criteria and account plans, in terms of both specification and quality of execution. Relax other elements to allow more flexibility in response to customers and circumstances.
8. Gearing up	Invest seriously in KSAM; in the key account managers, support, feedback and more. Develop processes to operationalize KSAM, to manage it more professionally and to ensure alignment of KSAM strategy with application.
9. Evaluating impact	Clarify expected outcomes of KSAM. Evaluate results versus expectations and impact internally and externally, reviewed by senior management.
Milestone: review commitment	Decision on whether and how to continue with KSAM now the organization understands what it is and what its outcomes can be: agree to commit to decision.

should avoid rigidity and excessive standardization. Effective processes designed to deliver to KSAM needs should replace 'rules' and 'compliance', unless legally required.

By the end of this phase, the supplier has a functioning KSAM approach that is valued by customers, is properly embedded in the organization and is producing results, but the supplier can still improve its approach to KSAM and get more out of it. The company should take the opportunity to:

- Complete a thorough review.
- Check that the decision to operate KSAM is still valid.
- Gain the unequivocal commitment of all senior and middle managers to KSAM and their role in it, at least.
- Prepare to revise, upgrade, reconfigure and take all elements to another level.

However, evidence that companies complete this very useful stage is patchy, to say the least. If the company carries out a review, and assuming that it confirms the decision to operate KSAM, it should now have sufficient confidence in the approach and the individuals it has made responsible for it to allow KSAM to be delivered with the flexibility and variety that it requires.

Table 7: Phase D sub-phases in optimizing value

Sub-phase	Key actions
10. Recommitting	Senior managers recommit to KSAM very publicly and re-energize the programme. KSAM is accepted as a permanent part of the culture and operations of the organization.
11. Integrating KSAM	KSAM and key customers are represented in all major forums and plans. The needs and operation of KSAM are integrated into all relevant business processes.
12. Becoming key-customer centric	Information is seen as central to proper management and is not subservient to traditional metrics. KSAM's strategic position and contribution are recognized and accepted.

Phase D: Optimizing value

By the end of Phase C, KSAM should be really embedded in the company and the supplier should be ready to move on to Phase D, in which it now has the experience and understanding of KSAM to increase the benefits from KSAM and to improve its performance and outcomes. By this stage, the supplier has successfully negotiated difficult issues and identified positive outcomes. With a more confident mindset, companies can embark on making some of the changes that they were unwilling to implement earlier. Internally, operations and management might become more complex (Brehmer and Rehme 2009), but if that complexity allows the supplier to offer more powerful customized solutions for key accounts, then managing that complexity is a valuable capability – see Table 7.

In Phase B, the mediocre quality of the account plans meant that they were probably not good enough to make a contribution to the business planning cycle for the whole organization, but if the quality of the plan has been lifted in Phase C, they should now take up this role. Strategic account plans show the supplier how a very significant part of its business will develop over the subsequent three plus years – where its key customers are heading, which strategies it needs to support and invest in, what resources it will require, what outcomes it can expect and whether the overall direction is aligned with its own strategies. These plans represent an invaluable source of information that should be feeding the development of the corporate business plan, but which will require a defined process to make that input.

Any processes that are intransigent, inflexible and unhelpful to key customers should be investigated with a view to making them more KSAM-friendly. All senior managers and function heads, rather than seeking how KSAM fits into their function's priorities and ways of working, can be proactively exploring what their function can do for KSAM. The needs of key customers are explicitly acknowledged in their plans. Senior managers of all functions are vocally and visibly supportive of KSAM, which is part of the consistent and continuous communication about what KSAM and key accounts mean to the supplier's business that enables the whole company to achieve best-practice KSAM.

KSAM should be fully integrated into the working of the organization at all levels (see Table 8). It now holds a permanent and appropriate place in the structure, the planning cycle, budgeting and resourcing, career development for key account managers, etc. The focus shifts from how to install, communicate and operationalize KSAM to how to manage, implement and extract maximum benefit from the exciting raft of key customer programmes and projects that are enabled through KSAM. KSAM is accepted as the normal way of working: 'why' and 'how' are no longer challenged and are replaced by a focus on 'what' in terms of the business with customers. Key indicators that the company is genuinely

Table 8:   Signs of embedded KSAM

Organization	*Key account managers*
• All senior managers talk openly and frequently about key customers and their key account managers.	• They have identified all the account team members and defined their roles in the relationship with the customer.
• The company is prepared to invest in key customers (against a business case with returns expected beyond one year).	• Their strategic account plans cover at least three years and are complete, in live use and up to date.
• Strategic account plans play a major part in the corporate planning process.	• They have a business-focused relationship with at least one of the customer's board directors.
• Profitability (not just gross margin) of individual key customers is measured.	• Key customers rate key account managers' understanding of their business and their marketplace at or over 8/10.
• Key account managers are paid at a similar level and on a similar basis to strategic business unit directors (rewarded on company rather than personal performance).	• They can define the added value the company brought to the customer in the last year.

operating an embedded KSAM programme include both the wider organization/ senior management and key account managers.

With confidence in their own experience of KSAM, suppliers should be able to improve performance further through wholeheartedly embracing the concept of the importance of key customers. That also means that, having developed the people to manage them, key account managers should be fully competent and trusted to take over as the 'managing director of the customer' in terms of the supplier's business with them, backed by a suite of management information that readily and accurately represents the position with each customer individually. The company is now ready for best-practice KSAM.

Conclusion

Making the transition to KSAM is not easy or quick. Eventually, it will touch almost every part of the company and people at all levels in the organization, and make changes in the way they work and with whom they work. The early stages, in which suppliers research and explore what KSAM will mean for them, are very important in making the smoothest possible transformation. That is not to say that there will be no resistance to the change because, in our experience, resistance from some quarters is inevitable. Success requires political skills, robustness, persistence and the backing of senior management.

Transitioning occurs through taking action across strategy and planning, the organization and culture, and processes. Early approaches are likely to be revisited as the company learns more about KSAM, and the original idea reworked with increasing sophistication and subtlety. KSAM is not simple: it is predicated on treating key customers individually and differently according to their needs (and those of the supplier), and uniform and standardized approaches and processes will, by definition, not meet the expectations of most key customers. Suppliers start by making fairly superficial adaptations for key customers, but go deeper as they learn from their customer partners and reap the business benefits.

Key account managers that start out as salespeople also have to transform themselves to play their role as a leader. Sensible companies help them in every way to achieve the required level, both through training and development and through removing barriers and supporting them as much as possible. Companies that have strong functional and divisional structures with weak customer orientation are often asking key account managers to execute a high-pressure job in a generally hostile environment, inevitably with limited levels of success and retention.

KSAM teams have become a very important part of the offer to key customers – their broad and mixed skill set and specialized knowledge provide a great deal of the value a customer receives from the supplier. Team members are mostly only partly dedicated to any one customer, so both the organization and the key account manager that leads the team need to make substantial and continued efforts to give and gain recognition for the team, communicate objectives and ways of working, and attract buy-in from team members and their functional heads.

Suppliers with mature KSAM programmes tend to come to the conclusion that the only way they can achieve the business synergies they seek is through a centralized unit of key account managers working with key customers across all geographies and products, not attached to a local or specialist structure. They recognize, however, that this approach still requires major efforts to keep operational delivery links close and realistic. Whatever the structure, successful KSAM requires a willingness to share and to work across boundaries in teams, for corporate rather than territorial objectives.

Competitors catch up, customers want more innovation, and newly appointed directors arrive with different ideas about customer management to challenge the KSAM programme. Alternatively, complacency and slippage can surface if companies become so used to KSAM as 'the way we do things round here' that they forget what made it successful. The KSAM approach should constantly be reviewed, revised and kept fresh and up to date. Ultimately, companies need to recognize that transitioning to KSAM is a long haul, but very worthwhile, and maybe even obligatory, in current markets.

Switching costs in key account relationships

*BY SANJIT SENGUPTA, ROBERT E. KRAPFEL
AND MICHAEL A. PUSATERI*

Abstract

Companies are increasingly implementing key account management for their most important business customers. Relationships between key account managers and their customers are intended to be long-term strategic partnerships resulting in competitive advantage for both. Switching costs include the psychological, physical and economic costs a customer faces in changing a supplier. The main question we seek to investigate in this paper is whether customer switching costs are good or bad for both the customer account and the selling firm. Further, we examine the factors leading to switching costs so that key account managers may influence the outcomes in these relationships.

From Journal of Personal Selling & Sales Management, *vol. 17, no. 4 (Fall 1997): 9–16. Copyright © 1997 by PSE National Educational Foundation. Reprinted with permission of M.E. Sharpe, Inc. All Rights Reserved. Not for Reproduction.*

The authors gratefully acknowledge the assistance of the National Account Management Association (NAMA) in collecting the data for this study. This article was invited and did not go through *JPSSM's* regular review process.

Companies are increasingly implementing key or major account management for their most important business customers (Sengupta et al. 1997a). In some companies, these are also called national or global accounts. Key account managers (KAMs) should develop and build long-term relationships with each of their customer accounts. The account manager helps the customer solve operational and strategic problems by providing research and analysis. As part of the deal, the customer commits to large volume purchases of products and services over a long period of time. This is a challenging boundary role suited only for the best sales professionals.

Selected sales management literature has examined the role of the key or national account manager (for an overview, see Weilbaker and Weeks 1997). Numerous conceptual articles and case studies have described the benefits of implementing such programmes, the traits, skills and knowledge required of key account managers, and the environmental conditions under which such programmes would flourish. However, there has not been an integration of the sales management literature with the literature on relationship marketing (Biong and Selnes 1996; Lambe and Spekman 1997a). We agree that such a move is necessary and desirable because relationships between key account managers and their customer accounts are intended to be long-term strategic partnerships resulting in competitive advantage for both.

The relationship marketing literature (Dwyer Schurr and Oh 1987; Morgan and Hunt 1994; Webster 1992 are just a few examples) has a number of constructs, frameworks and empirical generalizations that can be useful to improving the efficiency and effectiveness of KAM relationships. While the relationship marketing literature discusses both vertical buyer–seller and horizontal relationships (Bucklin and Sengupta 1993), KAM relationships fall into the vertical category. An important concept in vertical buyer–seller relationships that can be applied to KAM relationships is switching costs, the focus of this paper.

Conceptual framework and hypotheses

Switching costs were popularized by Jackson (1985) in her study of industrial marketing relationships. She defined switching costs as the psychological, physical and economic costs a customer faces in changing a supplier (Jackson 1985, p. 13). When contemplating a switch in suppliers, a customer faces setup costs and takedown costs (Weiss and Anderson 1992). Setup costs include the cost of finding a replacement supplier who can provide the same or better level of performance than the current supplier or the opportunity cost of foregoing exchange with the incumbent (Dwyer et al. 1987). Takedown costs include relationship-specific or idiosyncratic investments made by the customer that have no value outside the relationship with the current supplier and have to be written off (Anderson and Weitz 1992). The net result of switching costs is

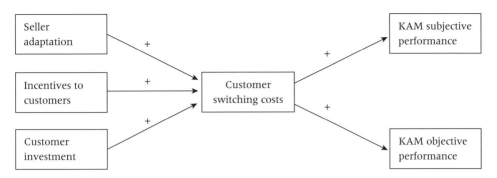

Figure 1   Conceptual framework

that they produce inertia for the customer to remain in the relationship with the current supplier.

The main question we seek to investigate in this paper is whether customer switching costs are good or bad for the customer account and the selling firm in key account relationships. Further, what factors lead to the creation of switching costs so that key account managers may exert some influence over the outcomes in these relationships? To this end we develop a conceptual framework (Figure 1) incorporating relevant antecedents and consequences of switching costs based on the existing literature.

Antecedents of switching costs

In the relationship marketing literature, much has been written about the concept of interfirm adaptation (Dwyer et al. 1987; Johanson et al. 1991). Adaptation promotes efficiency and brings about balance between an organization and its environment (Johanson et al. 1991). In key account relationships, the selling firm often faces changes in its own or customer environment that call for adaptation in products, policy, systems or organization. Seller firm adaptation has symbiotic benefits for both seller and customer. For instance, like many other corporations (Spiro 1996), Marriott faces the technological challenge of fixing the 'Year 2000' problem in its online reservation system which will affect all its major customers and travel agents. To the extent that this technological adaptation is successful, Marriott increases its value to its key customer accounts. Most key customer accounts appreciate flexibility on the part of their suppliers. The enhanced value from seller adaptation increases customer switching costs in relation to other potential suppliers. Thus, we put forth our first hypothesis:

> H1: The greater the adaptation undertaken by a selling firm, the greater the switching costs faced by a customer account.

The underlying rationale for key account management is that when selling firms focus their resources on serving a few important customers, it pays off in terms of sales and profits (Sengupta, Krapfel and Pusateri 1997). A major item of promotional expenditure in key account sales is 'push' money. When dealing with retail customers, for example, manufacturers may offer slotting allowances for carrying new products or special allowances for in-store promotions (Greenwald 1996). Another form of incentive offered to key customers is aimed at creating 'pull' or loyalty with their end-users through co-branding or joint advertising efforts. For example, Black and Decker made use of both 'push' and 'pull' incentives in launching its DeWalt line of power tools through key retailers like Home Depot (Dolan 1995). When such incentives are offered by the selling firm, they also create customer switching costs in relation to other potential suppliers. This leads to our next hypothesis:

H2: The greater the incentives offered by a selling firm, the greater the switching costs faced by a customer account.

Relationship-specific investments are investments in assets which are specialized to the exchange relationship (Heide and John 1988). If the relationship were to be terminated, the value of these assets would be largely lost because their salvage value outside the relationship is very low. For instance, a customer of ocean shipping services may have to invest in containers and material handling equipment tailored to the ships and dock facilities of a particular carrier. If the customer wanted to switch to a new supplier, it would have to forego this investment and reinvest in containers and equipment for a new carrier. In a similar vein, selling firms sometimes ask key customers to invest in customized hardware and software so that they can do electronic data interchange (O'Callaghan et al. 1992). Such non-redeployable assets give rise to switching costs (Heide and John 1988):

H3: The greater the customer's relationship-specific investment, the greater the switching costs it faces.

Jackson (1985) suggests that switching costs are likely to be higher when the product is technologically complex and requires a high level of service to be provided to the customer. While we do not put forward a formal hypothesis for product complexity, we do include it as a control variable antecedent of switching costs.

Consequences of switching costs

Switching costs create dependence of the customer on the supplier (Morgan and Hunt 1994; Biong and Selnes 1996). The questions is, is this dependence good or bad for the relationship? The earlier literature on sales management and channel theory (summarized in Gaski 1984) suggests that in conventional arm's length relationships, this situation of asymmetric dependence is good for the selling firm which can exploit the dependence of the customer. However, key account managers cannot be so short-sighted. For a different approach, we turn to insights from relationship marketing.

Dwyer et al. (1987) propose that when a relationship develops over time, the two parties gain experience and learn to trust each other. Consequently, they may gradually increase their commitment through investments in products, processes or people dedicated to that particular relationship. The customer may incrementally invest resources in the relationship and voluntarily increase its switching costs and dependence on the supplier (Anderson and Narus 1991). Dwyer et al. (1987) suggest that the customer's anticipation of high switching costs gives rise to the customer's interest in maintaining a quality relationship. These anticipated high switching costs lead to an ongoing relationship being viewed as important, thus generating commitment to the relationship.

Morgan and Hunt (1994) found a direct, positive empirical relationship between termination costs and commitment, a negative relationship between commitment and propensity to leave, and a positive relationship between commitment and cooperation. Biong and Selnes (1996) found a positive relationship between dependence and continuity of the relationship. Therefore, switching costs should result in favourable relationship outcomes for both parties.

KAM performance depends on favourable relationship outcomes for both seller and customer. The selling firm is more interested in achieving financial objectives such as account market share, sales volume and profitability. However, the key customer is more interested in meeting their own objectives and being satisfied with the products and services provided. Thus, we conceptualize two dimensions of KAM performance, subjective and objective. KAM subjective performance is what the KAM accomplishes for the customer in terms of meeting the latter's objectives, continuity, cooperation and satisfaction. KAM objective performance is what the KAM achieves for the selling firm. We put forth these final two hypotheses on the relationship between switching costs and KAM performance:

H4: The greater the switching costs faced by a customer account, the higher the subjective performance of a key account manager.
H5: The greater the switching costs faced by a customer account, the higher the objective performance of a key account manager.

In testing the last two hypotheses, we include seller firm size, a proxy for resource availability, as a control variable that can affect KAM performance.

Data collection

This study is part of a larger study that the National Account Management Association[1] (NAMA) commissioned us to do in spring 1996 on best practices in key account management among its member companies. We began our study with in-depth exploratory interviews of five key account managers (KAMs) and their supervisors with the aim of obtaining face validity for our framework and generating items to operationalize our constructs.

Following the exploratory interviews, a structured survey questionnaire was designed to tap into all the relevant constructs in our framework using multiple item Likert scales wherever feasible. We borrowed items from existing literature where available and formulated our own questions for new constructs. The survey questionnaire, reply-paid envelope, and requests for participation were mailed to 528 NAMA members in February 1996. One hundred and seventy-six completed, usable surveys were returned, giving a respectable 33% response rate. Our respondents were front-line KAMs from a broad cross-section of US firms across many different industries (55% manufacturing, 43% service). Firms represented were large, with median sales of $3 billion and 14,000 employees. Our KAM respondents had a median age of 41 and were well-educated (61% had a bachelors degree, 28% had a graduate degree). They had a long tenure within their firm, median 12 years, 10 in sales and of those, 3 as a KAM.

Each respondent provided data for a specific customer account they were responsible for. If they handled three or more accounts, they were asked to provide data on the account they spent the third largest amount of time with. If they handled two accounts, they were asked to provide data on the account they spent the largest amount of time with. If they handled just one account, they provided data on that account. This procedure was followed to minimize self-selection bias in the reported account.

A reliability analysis was done for each multiple-item variable. Some individual items were dropped to increase reliability using Cronbach's alpha. The final operationalization of variables along with respective Cronbach's alphas is reported in Table 1.

We also did an exploratory factor analysis on all 18 items in Table 1 and found that they load cleanly on the underlying 8 factors. This provides some evidence for the convergent and discriminant validity of our measures. Means, standard deviations and correlations for all our eight variables are presented in Table 2.

---

[1] Now Strategic Account Management Association (SAMA).

Table 1: Variable operationalizations and reliabilities

No.	Construct	Item	Cronvach's alpha
1.	Seller adaptation	During this relationship with the customer account: a. our firm has often made adjustments in its role in response to changing circumstances. b. our personnel have not adapted to changing expectations of their duties and obligations.[R] c. our firm has reallocated resources and effort when unexpected situations have arisen.	0.63
2.	Incentives to customers	Our firm: a. provides financial incentives to the customer account that help their bottom line. b. provides incentives to the customer account's end-users to keep them as loyal users.	0.58
3.	Customer investment	The customer account has invested in systems and procedures tailored to our firm.	N/A
4.	Product complexity	Our firm's product/service offerings to this customer account are technically complex.	N/A
5.	Customer switching costs	The customer account: a. will find it very difficult to replace us as a supplier. b. faces low switching costs in terminating their business relationship with us.[R]	0.63
6.	KAM subjective performance	As KAM representative, I have: a. helped the customer account meet their objectives. b. not created a satisfied customer.[R] c. promoted future cooperation with the customer account. d. built a productive, worthwhile customer relationship. e. built a customer relationship that will outlive my tenure with the customer account.	0.80
7.	KAM objective performance	For your firm's last operating year: a. What percentage of this customer's purchases in your product/service category did you get? b. What percentage of your annual profit objectives have you achieved with this customer account? c. What percentage of your annual sales volume objectives have you achieved with this customer account?	0.71
8.	Seller firm size	How many employees in your firm?	N/A

[R]reverse-coded
Response scales for most items were 5-point Likert scales going from Strongly Disagree (1) to Strongly Agree (5) except items under 6, 7 which had open-ended response scales

Table 2: Means, standard deviations, correlations

	Seller adaptation	Incentives to customers	Customer investment	Product complexity	Customer switching costs	KAM subjective performance	KAM objective performance	Seller firm size
Seller adaptation	3.61 (0.74)	0.17[a]	0.17[a]	0.15[a]	0.25[a]	0.35[a]	0.14	0.07
Incentives to customers		3.13 (1.04)	0.10	0.12	0.18[a]	0.07	0.04	0.10
Customer investment			2.63 (1.20)	0.25[a]	0.34[a]	0.24[a]	0.12	0.17[a]
Product complexity				3.33 (1.23)	0.19[a]	0.04	0.09	−0.04
Customer switching costs					3.17 (1.03)	0.23[a]	0.21[a]	0.07
KAM subjective performance						4.16 (0.58)	0.23[a]	0.17[a]
KAM objective performance							57.50 (29.55)	0.22[a]
Seller firm size								41,471 (139,976)

In diagonal cells, numbers outside parentheses are means and numbers inside parentheses are standard deviations
[a]significant correlations at $p = 0.05$

110

Results

In order to test our conceptual framework and hypotheses (Figure 1), we used path analysis with ordinary least squares regression. The results are presented in Table 3.

In column 2 of Table 3, we regress customer switching costs against the three antecedent variables – seller adaptation, incentives to customers, customer investment – and the control variable, product complexity. We find that seller adaptation and customer investment are strongly and positively associated with customer switching costs (H1, H3), while incentives to customers are weakly and positively associated with switching costs (H2). Contrary to expectation, product complexity was not related to customer switching costs in our sample.

In column 3 of Table 3, we regress KAM subjective performance against customer switching costs and seller firm size. As expected, switching costs were strongly and positively associated with subjective performance (H4). In a similar vein, switching costs were strongly and positively associated with KAM objective performance (H5) in column 4 of Table 3. Seller firm size had a positive

Table 3: Ordinary least squares regressions

Independent variables	Dependent variable: customer switching costs	Dependent variable: KAM subjective performance	Dependent variable: KAM objective performance
Seller adaptation	0.15 (1.99)[a]		
Incentives to customers	0.12 (1.68)[b]		
Customer investment	0.28 (3.81)[a]		
Product complexity	0.09 (1.15)		
Customer switching costs		0.22 (2.84)[a]	0.18 (2.24)[a]
Seller firm size		0.15 (2.01)[a]	0.21 (2.68)[a]
Adjusted R^2	0.15	0.06	0.07
F-test	$F(4, 166) = 8.43$[a]	$F(2, 157) = 6.45$[a]	$F(2, 150) = 6.49$[a]

Parameter estimates outside parentheses are standardized betas, numbers inside parentheses are t-statistics
[a]significant at $p = 0.05$
[b]significant at $p = 0.10$

significant relationship with both KAM subjective and objective performance in Table 3.

The explained variance in the dependent variables in Table 3 is modest, indicating that our study omitted some variables that also affect switching costs and KAM performance.

Discussion

In this paper, we have demonstrated the importance of customer switching costs in key account relationships. Customer switching costs have a significant positive impact on both aspects of performance – the achievement of seller firm objectives based on objective criteria such as account market share, sales volume and profitability, and the achievement of customer objectives and satisfaction by more subjective criteria. They help to achieve a win–win for both parties in the relationship. This is a marked departure from conventional thinking in adversarial relationships where customer switching costs were considered good for the seller but not for the dependent buyer.

What is the mechanism by which this win–win is achieved? As our results indicate, the biggest factor that gives rise to customer switching costs is customer investment in relationship-specific assets. If this was the only factor at work, it would make the customer dependent on the supplier and the relationship unbalanced, with unfavourable relationship outcomes.

However, our results show that relationship-specific investment by the customer is not the only factor affecting customer switching costs. There is a dependence balancing mechanism at work by way of seller adaptation. Notwithstanding customer relationship-specific investment, the adaptability or flexibility of the seller firm demonstrates to the customer that the seller is not going to be opportunistic or exploitative. This is reassuring to the customer, helps balance the relationship, and further increases the commitment and switching costs of the customer. This reciprocity or balance is the essence of the win–win in key account relationships. The value of balance or mutual dependence, sometimes called interdependence, has been studied in a channels context with results consistent with our own (Gundlach and Cadotte 1994; Kumar et al. 1995).

Interestingly, we found that 'push' and 'pull' incentives offered to customers do not do much to increase customer switching costs. Customers seem to value adaptation in a long-term relationship more than short-term financial incentives. While adaptation does require investment on the part of the seller firm, this may be a more cost-efficient use of resources than directly offering incentives. The soft-sell of adaptation may yield better results than the hard-sell of push–pull money in key account relationships.

Finally, when we look at the empirically validated antecedents of customer switching costs, we realize that creating these is the responsibility of the entire selling firm, not just the responsibility of the individual KAM. In order to adapt, the selling firm will need to allocate resources from all over the organization in order to solve specific problems that come up. The KAM can bring the requirements to the attention of the selling firm and can do his or her share of internal marketing. Ultimately, a higher level of management within the selling firm must take responsibility for allocating the necessary resources for adaptation or financial incentives.

The strategic buyer: how emerging procurement strategies may support KAM/SAM relationships

BY SIMON CROOM

Abstract

This paper reviews key strategic account management from a purchasing and supply perspective. The purchasing function has experienced a major strategic shift in the last 20 years. More professionals are highly qualified, well remunerated and great strategists.[1] The article looks at the increasing adoption of an interaction approach by purchasing – we are interested in how purchasing contributes to business performance by placing collaboration with key suppliers at the centre of its strategies, why trust-based relationships are important and how innovation can be gained from partnerships with key suppliers.

---

[1] See both the Institute for Supply Management, USA and the Chartered Institute of Purchasing and Supply, UK.

Introduction

A strategic account is a source of significant benefit to an organization's prosperity and future development. Customers are also increasingly stating that suppliers are among their most important assets. Scan the annual accounts of most leading corporations and suppliers not only warrant a mention, they are cited as a vital resource. Apple and Nike, to name but two, list their suppliers in their annual statements and on their websites, emphasizing the importance to their own brand reputation of their suppliers' capabilities and reputations. Mutual dependence is becoming a way of life for world-class supply organizations. Furthermore, the financial and technological advantage to be gained through world-class supply management has positioned the function into a core role in corporate governance.

In this paper, the focus is on a customer's view of their upstream supply. Critical issues on the agenda for supply professionals are discussed, opening with the strategic and financial importance of their role and the advantage that can be applied to corporate performance through strategic purchasing decisions. Achieving such influence requires attention to building collaborative relationships with suppliers, central to which is the phenomenon of trust. While trust is often talked about as though it is a 'soft' or intangible characteristic arising from human interaction, we will examine the notion of the economics of trust, aiming to articulate some of the tangible or quantifiable ways in which a number of thought leaders and practitioners build their case for more attention to the dynamics of interaction between the actors in a buyer–seller relationship.

Managing interaction between supply chain partners has become an imperative, one that reflects the view that 'competition no longer takes place between companies but between supply chains'. Since this phrase became popularized by Professor Martin Christopher of Cranfield University in the early 1990s, it now reverberates around the halls of corporate HQs and academia alike, a homily that has become a modern-day trope for business. Aligning supply chain partners to a common purpose, however, is not such a simple process. Clarity of purpose and clear consistency of decisions to that purpose are, at the very simplest level, the key requirements for alignment between supply chain partners. If an organization cannot get its suppliers to align with its own strategic aims, this causes significant problems for the execution of strategies in support of those aims. In essence, this is at the heart of our concern for buyer–seller interactions in this paper.

We examine some of the challenges that arise when one side to a transaction fails to account for the other's position and power in the transaction. As much as we would all like to exert power over our partners in business, this is clearly not the case, and the use of purchasing portfolio and customer portfolio analyses provide an insight into how misalignment can emerge from one-sided strategic analysis.

The point of building collaborative relationships with suppliers is very much in response to the demands presented by rapid technological innovation, shortening life cycles and step-change transformation. We see the move towards collaborative innovation as gaining significant momentum under such dynamic conditions. Apple, Procter & Gamble, Nike (and many others) are using the power of their suppliers' technical capabilities to work collaboratively on their product and service innovations. Such collaborative innovation is characterized by interdependence tempered with a clear view of where the locus of change can most readily emerge.

The article concludes by examining how the role and contribution of purchasing function and purchasing professionals continue to transform given the pressures and opportunities we discuss here.

The strategic importance of purchasing

Strategic account management is increasingly being considered as one of the components of supply chain performance. Interest in global supply chains reflects their increasing importance to our economic life. In 2009 world exports of intermediate goods exceeded the combined export values of final and capital goods, representing 51% of non-fuel merchandise exports,[2] indicating the importance of business-to-business transactions on a global scale. Thus as global economic systems have become highly interconnected, with many consumer products tracing their supply chains across multiple continents involving a range of industries, organizations cannot operate as if they are in a vacuum.

In addition to the shifts in global economic activity, localized events are having a more pronounced impact on global business prospects. Major natural disasters such as the 2011 Tohoku earthquake and tsunami, the Thai floods that same year, and human-caused disasters such as the Rana Plaza building collapse in Dhaka, Bangladesh in April 2013 have been seen to reverberate around the world. These tragedies had a significant human toll, but also exacted a profound effect on business activities across the globe. Supply shortages arising from the events in 2011 closed many auto manufacturing sites around the world, disrupted computer production, led to increased prices for memory chips and impacted market deliveries. The media coverage of the Rana Plaza collapse claimed that it occurred partly as a result of low-cost country (LCC) sourcing strategies employed by Western fashion brands, which led to a major reassessment of their collective responsibilities for ensuring safer supplier working practices, conditions and facilities. Looking to suppliers for a proactive approach to supply chain safety and disaster response is one of the building blocks of supply chain risk strategy. Relying on 'good partners' who share in the analysis and response phases of risk management can help avoid recent event biases and provide direct input to contingency plans.

---

[2] World Trade Organization and Institute of Developing Economies (2011) Trade patterns and global value chains in East Asia: From trade in goods to trade in tasks. Geneva and Tokyo.

Corporations are increasingly sensitive to the political impact of their strategic decisions relating to global sourcing; the debate whether to offshore, near-shore or re-shore has implications far beyond the walls of the boardroom. In 2010 Steve Jobs, former Apple CEO, responded to President Obama's query about why Apple did not manufacture in the USA with the now infamous statement that 'those jobs aren't coming back'. As an indication of how political sensibilities can shift corporate strategy, by 2012 Apple's new CEO Tim Cook had taken a more positive position on the company's global production system, which led to re-shoring of Mac Pro production to Texas. This required manufacturing suppliers to refocus on the strategic advantages of local sourcing for Apple, such as speedier delivery, shorter supply lines and lower total costs. Getting 'inside the head' of the customer in this instance was a critical driver for the sourcing decision and their supplier's account management teams had a major role to play in both the evaluation and execution of a viable near-sourcing plan.

Case Example 1: Taylor Guitars, El Cajon, California

Securing vital resources for production can be a major challenge if it so happens that your major input is an endangered species. Taylor Guitars of California faces immense challenges in securing the woods needed to provide the high sound quality and durability from a number of endangered timber species such as mahogany. One strategy the company has adopted is to collaborate with a Spanish furniture manufacturer to acquire a mahogany plantation in Cameroon, thereby securing a sustainable source of supply while simultaneously ensuring that there are more socially responsible practices being employed in the company's supply chains.

Thomas Friedman's thesis in his highly popular (and populist) book *The World is Flat* is that key changes in technology and global sourcing, plus the emergence of both large and developing economies in China, India, Brazil and, to a lesser extent, Russia, were driving more interdependent, collaborative and open global supply chains. Taking the discussion further in terms of our interest in account management and purchasing, Håkansson and Snehota (2006) state in their influential article 'No business is an island' that this interdependence between actors in networks requires that business strategy decisions need to be reoriented to embrace the context of the networks in which businesses find themselves.

In the purchasing field, the importance of managing across boundaries with suppliers has long been viewed as critical to the strategic success of the firm, with Monczka and Morgan (2000) highlighting in particular the impact of an increasing trend for outsourcing, LCC sourcing and collaborative design. Thus modern business practices have embraced the notion that to produce goods and provide service experiences they will have to increasingly rely upon an extended network of suppliers, collaborators, service providers, distributors and customers, all of whom have a significant impact on their performance and development.

When we begin to think about the 'extended enterprise' (Dyer 2000) as the mechanism through which competitive activity takes place, decisions about the nature of strategic relationships between customer and supplier, the potential for capitalizing on the creative power of multiple actors and the importance of collaborative operations begin to take the front seat in how such decisions are shaped. The purchasing function, by virtue of its role as a boundary-spanning function, naturally has a major part to play in such decision-making, but it cannot operate alone.

Case Example 2: Medical supply chains

The healthcare sector in the USA has considerable cost and profit pressures due to governance structures, which have increasingly expanded the strategic role of purchasing and supply functions across the sector. The costs associated with medical products and service provision, technology-driven price inflation, demographic pressures, diverse stakeholder pressures from clinicians and administrators, challenges of managing complex inventory systems and the criticality of providing responsive service levels are the key challenges in this sector. For many supply professionals, it is the management of inter- and intra-organizational challenges that causes the greatest headaches:

"Our consultant surgeons are amongst the best in the world, are at the top of their game. They work closely with the local university, again, one of the best medical research schools in the world. So, we are frequently at the leading edge of medicine. Which presents me with big problems trying to get a good deal on some of the new equipment that is still at an early stage of development.

My job is to provide them with the best value for money products, tools and equipment, which may clash with what they want – typically they only want 'the Rolls-Royce' instruments. And to be honest a lot of people around here think that makes them some real SOBs! Sure, they are opinionated, egotistical and at times self-righteous, but I would be too in their shoes. So, I find it really helps to listen to them, figure out what is important about their needs and ask their advice. I always put it this way: 'I'm here to make it easy for you. I'm not a physician, but I am a market expert – I can search the market, evaluate the options, provide you with a thorough breakdown and then together we can figure out our best choice.' That seems to work well most of the time.

My job is really about financial stewardship, but since we are not a manufacturing business, but a caring business, I find it better to couch this in terms that resonate with whoever I'm talking to – but the bottom line is, it's about the bottom line!"

Ryan Harrison, Buyer

(Continued)

"A lot of our consumables are really pricey – we spend millions on infection-prevention supplies. A few years back we were buying from around 300 different suppliers in this category alone and it was impossible to manage relationships, gain economies of scale or be sure our costs were contained. So many users within the hospital group were ordering directly off of suppliers, we had some major work to do to bring that all in line.

Then we reached out to one of the major distributors in the sector and were pretty candid with them. 'We need to consolidate our supply base and reduce our total spend by 25% in the next year. How can you help us?' They embraced this with open arms and not only helped meet our targets, but their intranet is aligned to ours so users can order with ease and we have 100% transparency as well as really great pricing and discount deals.

I know how competitive our purchasing was – this is the third hospital district I have been at in seven years and I still have good 'intel' on my previous hospitals. I know they came in and really pulled out all the stops for us. As a result, we have just 30 suppliers in the category now and (X) is our number one strategic alliance partner. They even have a team permanently located on one of our central sites to help monitor, manage and evaluate our supply. This has been a great partnership so far and our financial impact has been pretty impressive, saving the group over $1.5 million in the last year alone."

Jose Ottega, Vice-President

Supply base reduction can be a major opportunity to turn a customer into a strategic account. Naturally, this depends on scale (can you provide all of the products and services in an enlarged category?), but it can also mean that a more collaborative position with current competitors and suppliers is necessary to deliver the full service expected from sole sources. It is also critical to realize that this move to a smaller supply base is not just about trying to secure economies of scale. The notion here is that buyers are seeking 'full service supply' as a means to gain value-added benefits from their suppliers, such as vendor-managed inventory (VMI), synchronous delivery, or service innovation. Fortuitously, this also resonates with many in strategic account management – adding value through service (Grönroos and Ravald 2011) offers significant potential for business growth.

Given the focus that many organizations place on the evaluation of purchasing policies, practices and projects, financial literacy is an important attribute. The ability to articulate the benefits of purchasing actions and strategies across the business in a convincing manner is a fundamental skill purchasing executives need to acquire. One framework that has been used to promote the impact of the function has been DuPont ratio analysis (illustrated below), which was originally developed by the DuPont Corporation in the 1920s.

Using basic financial ratio analysis, DuPont analysis indicates the hierarchical relationships that exist between purchased material costs and return on net assets

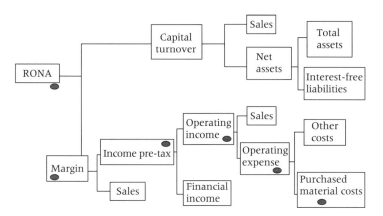

Figure 1 DuPont ratio analysis model

(RONA), as illustrated by the highlights in Figure 1. The use of ratio analysis as a means of presenting the impact of purchasing decisions helps convey a consistent message across the business, where responsibility for specific elements of financial performance is shared – for example, the connection between operating income and purchased costs is a significant shared concern between purchasing and operations. So while it has been acknowledged that communication skills are critical for purchasing professionals (Guinipero and Pearcy 2000), the calibre rather than the content of such communications has been the dominant focus of research (Claycomb and Frankwick 2004).

The Institute for Supply Management[3] has stressed financial literacy as a core component of purchasing's internal and external communications with stakeholders. Expect buyers to focus increasingly on the RONA/ROI of any purchase contract and relationship. At the very least, it helps to be able to measure the financial benefits available over the life cycle of your products or services. This makes great sense for most marketers – identifying the economic value to customers is a core marketing concept – but it is also becoming an aspect of financial literacy for buyers.

In addition to DuPont ratio analysis, life cycle cost analysis (LCCA) is becoming a critical analytical approach used by purchasing professionals, emphasizing the importance of a focus on total cost rather than price in the evaluation and management of supplied goods and services. Figure 2 indicates the main building blocks of a simple LCCA.

Building an LCCA requires data and participation from across the business and from suppliers, as Case Example 3 illustrates.

---

[3] http://www.ism.ws

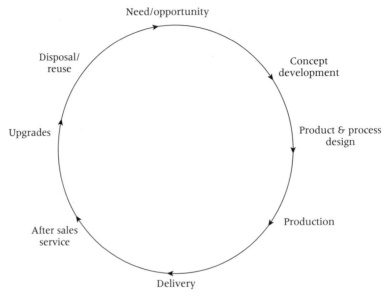

Figure 2 Life cycle analysis

Case Example 3: Defence sector

"We have to buy at the lowest price for sure, but unlike back in the days when that was the prime issue, now our burning platform is to lower total life cycle costs. I can't do that on my own. I need the estimators, operations, maintenance and finance guys from across the (Y) sector of our business. But I also need DoD (Department of Defense) and the Navy since they're our customers. Suppliers have a massive role to play too – after all, we outsource so much manufacturing and assembly now that they are the ones with the first-hand experience and knowledge.

It doesn't help that our prime suppliers are also our biggest competitors though. Trying to get them to share what they think is proprietary data is a real pain. So the best we can do sometimes is give it our best guess. Well, we do more than guess as we have pretty good knowledge around the place that helps us build our LCCA models, but in the end, it is a guess. We do have one supplier account manager (Z) who is amazing and will really go the extra mile with us on LCCA and most efforts we have to build closer working together. But they're unusual. This industry is an insular, exclusive and very protective one. Everyone thinks they own the secret to the Holy Grail and are not willing to share it!"

James R. Smithers, Vice-President

The role and skills required by purchasing professionals have been shown to have changed as the purchasing has shifted from tactical to strategic (Burt et al. 2003; Guinipero and Pearcy 2000), shifting the emphasis to negotiation, interpersonal and teamwork skills in addition to enhanced technical skills (such as financial literacy). Croom (2001) and Bowersox et al. (2005) discuss the strategic role of the purchaser as embracing two distinct sets of skills: operational/technical skills and relational/interaction skills. Competence in the operational 'stagecraft' of supply – sourcing, contracting and negotiating – has long been at the heart of a purchasing professional's success. Nevertheless, an increased focus on the softer skills associated with building long-term, collaborative relationships to drive innovation is recognized as central in any function aiming to influence its network of stakeholders. That the IMP (Industrial Marketing and Purchasing) Group expounded on this issue in the early 1980s merely underlines the significance of adopting a relational network perspective when thinking about business practice. It also aligns with the increasing importance given to the need for SAM/KAM (Wilson and Millman 2003) to operate within a dynamic organizational context to resolve customer problems and challenges.

Case Example 4: Global electronics

"We don't actually manufacture anything! All of it is outsourced, but that does not mean we don't manage our manufacturing chain. I spend at least two hours every day video conferencing with our factories in China, Taiwan and Vietnam. I used to be on planes all the time, but now I travel probably once every five or six weeks at most. Not only do I video conference (with HD-quality video) but we all share exactly the same databases and ERP [enterprise resource planning] systems, use wikis and blogs to help build our knowledge management as well.

I have great relationships with the teams at all our supplier manufacturing plants since I have met all of them multiple times over the years. Video conferencing also means we can archive the calls, and I can make sure we have translators involved in the calls to help clarify technical points or emphasize any issues. If there's a problem, I can be woken at night and deal with it within minutes. I do send engineers and experts into the plants as and when needed and I know we have developed some unique cross-cultural working relationships with our plants."

Supply Chain Manager, Cisco Systems

Building close working relationships with suppliers has been one of the key transformations in the roles and responsibilities of purchasing and has been heavily explored from an academic perspective (Spekman and Carraway 2006). Gadde and Snehota (2000), for example, state that 'developing partnerships with suppliers is resource-intensive and can be justified only when the costs of extended involvement are exceeded by relationship benefits'. Building on this, both Möllering (2003) and Johnston et al. (2004) found in their research that close, trust-based relationships do not mean that these relationships will become collaborative or strategic – an issue we will return to in 'Power-based relationships', below. Emphasizing this point, Cousins and Spekman (2003) found that purchasers' motivation for partnership relationships was primarily cost-based rather than to drive collaborative innovation or reduce time to market. There is still a dependence on price-based negotiations, relative inertia in buyer–supplier relationships and a more arm's-length form of interaction. In these cases (Beth et al. 2003) we will still encounter tactical-based relationships with purchasing, and it is also likely in these cases that efforts to build a strategic account relationship will emphasize critical internal stakeholders who exert far more influence over sourcing and supplier relationships than the purchasing department. In this paper we are addressing strategic shifts in purchasing, which means there are laggards as well as leaders.

The economics of trust

One topic that has been significant in the supplier relationship literature is trust, recognized as a major issue in determining the nature of supplier–customer relations. It is viewed as a foundation for cooperation and as the basis for stability (see, for example, Dyer et al. 1998; Helper and Sako 1995; Lamming 1993; Sako and Helper 1998), and it has been argued that it can be a significant source of competitive advantage for suppliers and buyers (Cousins and Stanwix 2001; Zaheer et al. 1998).

Kim et al. (2010) conducted a dyadic study of cooperative buyer–seller relationships, finding that switching costs and technical uncertainty – in essence, inertia for changing suppliers – were far more significant determinants of supplier relationships for buyers. This contrasted with suppliers in the same relationships who had a much higher concern for reciprocity in the relationship than their customers. However, relatively few empirical studies have been conducted into trust-based supplier relationships, as noted by Emberson and Storey in 2006. There has been a more concerted effort to examine trust-based relationships and relational strategies in the SAM/KAM literature. Guenzi et al. (2009) found that employing a strong customer (or customized) orientation has a significant impact on building trust with customers, along with employing cross-functional teams for the account interactions (see also Gounaris and Tzempelikos 2012; Guesalaga and Johnston 2010; Zhizhong et al. 2011). De Ruyter et al. (2001) and Gosselin and Bauwen (2006) have also emphasized the importance of a customized approach to managing relationships with customers in order to enhance the integration between the two parties. De Ruyter et al. in particular found a strong connection between commitment to a customer and trust between customer and supplier as having a positive impact on the development of the strategic account relationship, findings validated by Alejandro et al. (2011).

The drivers and consequences of trust have been addressed in a fascinating article by Paul Lawrence and Robert Porter Lynch and published as a leader article in *European Business Review* (Lawrence and Lynch 2011). They set out a compelling catalogue of success stories and principles for collaborative innovation, and provided a clear support for the principles of trust-based relationships. Porter Lynch in particular has been an active exponent of the value of trust-based relationships and much of his work reflects the works on the economics of trust by Stephen M. Covey Jr (Covey and Merrill 2008) and others.

Research into the impact of behaviour of individuals and groups on economic decision-making has been growing in the last two decades. Pollitt (2002) discusses the increasing interest for economists of social capital and highlights the impact that trust between management and employees can have on innovation, citing HP, 3M and UPS as three exemplars of how encouraging social interactions and trust building can stimulate corporate levels of innovation. The new field of behavioural economics essentially questions the validity of long-held assumptions of rational behaviour by market actors (for example, the work of Dan Ariely). In examining the impact of positive and negative emotional responses upon economic decision-making, Andrew Oswald has written extensively on the 'economics of happiness', his thesis being that it is possible (and valuable) to model the behavioural, social and psychological effects of economic activity. The corollary for supply relationships is that one could expect to find a significant variation in economic performance because of different behaviours within and across the dyadic links between supplier and customer.

In *The Speed of Trust* (2008), Covey claims that 'trust makes the world go around', exploring the strategic and economic value of building trust within and between organizations. Very much in line with the behavioural economists' theses, he highlights the importance of trust between customer and supplier not just as a 'social virtue' but as having clear economic benefits in speeding up interactions and lowering costs. Covey argues that as trust in a relationship reduces, it takes longer to get things done. Process inefficiencies emerge, costs increase and revenues decline, thereby constraining profitability. Beth et al. (2003) discussed this in their *Harvard Business Review* panel discussion on relationships, noting the premium earned from high-trust versus low-trust relationships. Porter Lynch has illustrated this graphically in Figure 3.

The methodology used, which we have employed at the University of San Diego Supply Chain Management Institute for many years, is to solicit executives to analyse two supplier relationships – one that they consider 'high trust' and another they consider 'low trust'. Discussion then takes place around the performance and operational characteristics of interactions and processes with each supplier. If possible, actual performance metrics are used to discuss the advantage of high trust over low trust in dimensions such as speed of response, degree of supplier-led productivity (cost) and effectiveness – see Figure 3 for an illustration of the framework. We typically find a performance advantage of 60–110% for high-trust supplier relationships over low-trust.

This is a critical tool for both buyers and SAM/KAMs in presenting the case within one's own organization for adapting relationships with strategic partners. Trust is also a major asset in building strategic relationships, as Case Example 5 illustrates.

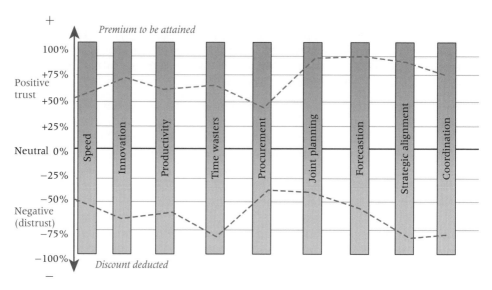

Figure 3 The Economics of Trust Framework
Note: With thanks to Robert Porter Lynch

Case Example 5: Corporate banking services

John McCallum is the Vice-President of Banking Operations at GlobalBank Corporate Services in Phoenix, Arizona. Mail operations spend for the bank is around $28 million per annum, all of it outsourced to three suppliers. Supplier A is John's 'high-trust' supplier and Supplier B his 'low-trust' supplier:

> "A and B are both fairly competent suppliers, they are regarded as the top two in the industry and use much the same technology and processes as each other. When we visit their operations, to be honest you would at first be hard pushed to tell much difference – but boy, do we have polar opposites there.
>
> I love working with A – their account team and service guys are available 24/7, know my people by name and are always checking how things are going. Their account management approach means they review their weekly performance with us by comparing data and have adapted their metrics to suit our experience (and to be honest, told us where we are measuring things the wrong way, like on-time delivery). We had one issue where a major mailing campaign had been incorrectly packed – one of the inserts was missing. They caught it before it went out and started reworking the whole batch of 450,000 overnight, resulting in the mailing hitting the mailboxes only one day later than planned but with no errors. And they remitted us the cost of the mailing.
>
> Supplier B, however, is very confrontational almost as their default state. We have to call them, constantly monitor their performance and if ever there is a problem we spend too much time haggling over blame rather than resolving the

(Continued)

problem. If I could I would put all my business with A, but they just don't have the capacity available when we need it – our mailings run in cycles which sometimes overlap with their other customers' cycles.

When I went through the economics of trust exercise I didn't at first buy into it 100%, but when I did the analysis (I called back to the office three times over lunch to get the data right) it was clear that we get a 30–40% total cost advantage from A through significant efficiencies and performance benefits even though the prices we pay look much the same. Less hassle, more improvement ideas and just a much easier way of managing our campaigns. It's now an important question I ask of our suppliers – 'What is your key account strategy' – as I want to know they are focused on serving their customers."

John McCallum, Vice-President

Over the course of 15 years of running executive events across the world, our informal data gathering typically indicates a 'value advantage' for high-trust over low-trust relationships. Trust is often considered in the literature to be 'built over time', the consequence of multiple interactions between the parties to a long-term relationship (Sahay 2003). It is not something that 'just happens' but is a result of a conscious effort to build the relationship by both parties, customer and supplier.

There remains general disagreement over whether trust can be intentionally created and managed in an economic environment (Blois 1999). It is contended (Sydow 2001) that the processes, routines and settings in a relationship that can influence the development of trust can be managed and that even if trust cannot be managed, the agents 'can certainly act in a trust-sensitive way when building and sustaining inter-organizational relations or networks'.

In building high-trust relationships one of the primary aims is to achieve improvement in the alignment between the activities of suppliers and buyers. Increasingly this is considered to be *the* fundamental strategic role for purchasing – much as it is for strategic account managers.

Strategic alignment

At its simplest, individuals at various organizational levels should agree on criteria such as cost, quality and flexibility, whichever are believed to be crucial to the success of that organization (Boyer and McDermott 1999). This internal consensus is considered to be an important requirement for developing the alignment between an organization and its external environment in order to achieve competitive success (Miles and Snow 1978).

One of the more recent schools of thought in the field of strategic management, the resource-based view (RBV), emerged more than 20 years ago and provides a valuable insight into competitive advantage. According to one of the pioneers of the RBV, Jay Barney (2001), organizations improve their performance by employing competitive strategies based upon their capabilities. But the dynamic nature of strategic capability (Teece et al. 1997), the idiosyncratic nature of such capabilities and at times the fact that capabilities can even be thought of as somewhat ethereal ('you know it when you see it') may mean that even the firm itself may not understand its true capabilities.

Capabilities are essentially contingent – their very existence depends upon the environment or relationship networks within which they are deployed – and thus the core concern in the RBV for our consideration is how such capabilities arise from the alignment of resources to customer requirements and experiences. Croom (2001) has examined strategic alignment between a customer and its suppliers, noting that misalignment frequently arises from poor communications and low trust. He further examined the role of customer–supplier (dyadic) alignment in driving shared innovation between the parties. Slack and Lewis (2011) discuss strategic alignment between one organization's operations and its market requirements as a process of 'reconciliation' between the two parties' often diverse objectives and requirements.

Case Example 6: The automotive industry

CovPressWorks, founded in 1890 in Coventry, UK, is a long-time supplier to Jaguar Cars of pressed steel components such as petrol (gas) tanks. For much of the company's history it was a typical 'metal bashing' operation, content to build products to customer specifications as well as offer a range of its own proprietary products.

In the early 1990s the company found that its main automotive customers were increasingly demanding it developed its operations processes to provide more synchronized deliveries, employed lean processes and engaged with the workforce in *kaizen* practices to drive continuous improvements. Perhaps the most significant strategic shift was the expectation that suppliers should increasingly shoulder responsibility for new product development, collaborating with their customer's engineering design team and at the same time taking on what is known as *system supply*, requiring delivery of complete gas tank assemblies. This meant not only taking responsibility for the pressed steel operations but incorporating the assembly of all valves, pumps, gauges, electronic components and pipework required for the completed assembly. CovPress invested in a dedicated clean room, which was a significant change from its traditional presswork operations.

> "We could see significant business opportunities even though they were some way in the future as we had a very steep learning curve when we moved into assembly rather than our usual press and weld operation. What convinced us was, I guess, Jaguar's commitment to the move to system supply and the higher

(Continued)

level of assembly we needed to employ, whilst we also saw a radical shift in their supplier strategies. It is fair to say that for years we had been too focused on the regular pricing battles we had with their purchasing department (and they with us). What changed was they really reached out to us to take ownership for the whole assembly, and have a major design input.

Contractually I think we felt fairly comfortable, but it was the really positive attitudes from the top down all the way to the expeditors that made us feel so good about this move. And here we are, 20 years later, with a radically different business, a broader product portfolio and, I have to say, really great relationships with the buyers. They wanted us to focus on building a cross-functional team to serve them, and we decided that we needed to adopt a strategic account management approach. That's how I ended up moving from the shop floor to management, though I do seem to still spend half my life with the operations and pressing guys."

Gary Mason, Strategic Account Manager and former foreman

In building a coherent strategic alignment at an operational level between supplier and customer, Slack and Lewis's Strategy Matrix (2011) model has provided a very useful framework for the strategic design of alignment between supplier processes and customer requirements, as illustrated in Figure 4.

This framework connects customer requirements (which are classified in terms of five generic objectives of cost, flexibility, dependability, speed and quality) to the core supply decision areas of capacity, supply network design, technology and

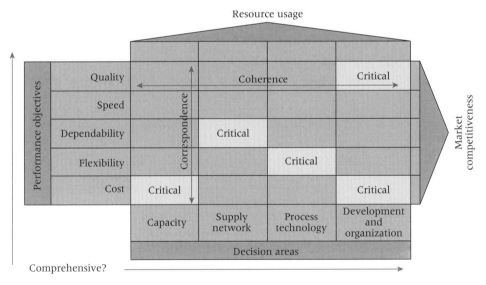

Figure 4 Slack and Lewis's Strategy Matrix
Source: Slack and Lewis (2002, 2008)
Note: Reproduced with the kind permission of Pearson Education, from *Operations Strategy 3rd edition* by Slack and Lewis, ISBN 978-0-273-69519-6. Copyright Nigel Slack and Michael Lewis 2002, 2008.

development. The core premise here is that decisions relating to improvements and investments in an area such as capacity (i.e. the size, scope and location of process resources) must align to the requirements of the customer. For example, if customers are demanding low-cost supply then decisions about location and economies of scale must support low-cost supply.

Slack and Lewis also highlight the importance of logical consistency when taking supply strategy decisions. There needs to be alignment of decisions to each specific objective (coherence), decisions in any aspect of the operation (such as technology) must reflect or correspond to the ranking of performance priorities, and such strategies must be complete (comprehensive). While this sounds trivial, often there are significant misalignments and confusions in dyadic relations. Buyers and suppliers have different priorities for the same supply process, have confusion between measures and a lack of consistency with their respective organizations. It is vital to overcome these disconnects and gaps, since they are extremely common, as Case Example 7 illustrates.

Case Example 7: Researching alignment

"We decided to survey our suppliers to find out precisely what they thought our priorities were for them. It was a sobering experience. Fair enough to say hardly any of our suppliers understood our requirements as clearly as we thought they could. It was obvious we were doing a lousy job of communicating both internally but especially with our suppliers. So, we brought them all together for a couple of days' workshop with our buyers, engineers and product managers. Only then did the penny really drop that we had a major task on our hands to really clarify for ourselves what were the 'right' objectives and how to achieve them in collaboration with our suppliers.

Quite a few of our suppliers seemed wary of asking us too many probing questions in case we thought any less of them, yet we also had suppliers who clearly believed it was 'their way or the highway', so we couldn't just take one approach when trying to align ourselves and our key suppliers. After all, not all suppliers are equal, and not all customers are, so it now seems.

We also found that our view of the suppliers' performance was at odds with how they thought they performed. Sometimes it was as simple as using different reference points – schedule and delivery dates, for example. We would measure response in terms of how long from our signal the supplier took to deliver; they would measure against scheduled date. Neither is wrong, just different. We also found that our own production team had a worse view of delivery performance simply because they did not focus on when goods arrived, just when they got to the production line. Our own internal logistics performance was conflated with supplier delivery, confusing the data point."

Garry McMann, Purchasing Director

One of the most insightful ways to investigate alignment/misalignment between buyers and their suppliers has been to conduct a series of interviews and surveys across the two parties' operations, sales, marketing and service departments. Using a structured approach to obtain responses about the supplier's view of customer needs and the customer's views of supplier performance helps to provide a valuable insight into the potential for 'gaps' in understanding and communication between the parties. Croom et al. (2014) studied 3,600 respondents, analysing the degree of consensus between supply chain partners about customer needs and improvement priorities. A statistically significant gap was found between the respondents in terms of the alignment of key performance criteria and the known demands of customers – in essence a cognitive dissonance where the customer's priorities are known but often ignored.

Illustrating this while also providing a useful framework for analysing misalignment, Slack et al. (2001) developed the notion of a gap model in the 1990s to illustrate the possible sources of misalignment and to highlight precisely where such gaps arise – see Figure 5.

From an operational perspective, buyers increasingly focus on the value of data for measuring supplier performance, yet find that there are significant relationship issues associated with gaining a clear, accurate and relevant view of their performance. In fact, Cousins et al. (2008) found that 'monitoring supplier performance is not of itself sufficient, rather, it is the process of socializing the buyer

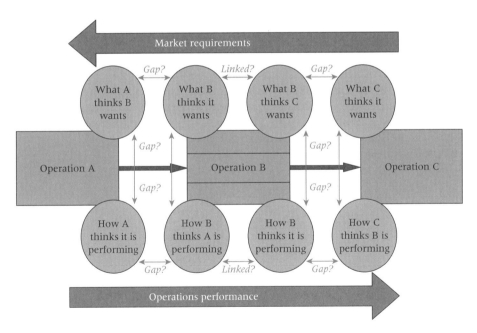

Figure 5 Perception gaps in supply chains
Source: Slack and Lewis (2002, 2008)
Note: Reproduced with the kind permission of Pearson Education, from *Operations Strategy 3rd edition* by Slack and Lewis, ISBN 978-0-273-69519-6. Copyright Nigel Slack and Michael Lewis 2002, 2008.

and supplier that is critical to success'. Previously, Yorke (1984) had commented that 'if objectives are to be met in both the short and the longer terms, dimensions for a strategic portfolio should be market- or customer-oriented and not based solely on the perceptions of the supplier's own management thinking, even though it claims to be outward looking to the marketplace'.

How buyers and their supplier relate is thus not a 'trivial' issue. The context within which relationships operate has a profound impact on performance, the development of their commercial relationship and the strategic value added through the (buyer–supplier) dyad. The perceptions of the actors involved in the relationship thus have a primacy in shaping decisions and consequently directing sourcing decisions and innovation. How trust is built within the relationship also has a significant impact on the contribution to be gained from the relationship. It is self-evident that engagement with key accounts will involve clearly defining current and expected performance. It is also clear that just asking a buyer is not necessarily sufficient. Buyer–supplier interactions involve multiple touchpoints (Gadde and Snehota 2000) and bringing together the key actors in the relationship, soliciting their involvement and clarifying and agreeing on critical metrics and measures offers a valuable way to reduce the expectation and perception 'gaps' in the relationship. This helps to identify how your customer views you, and shapes how you view your customer.

Power-based relationships

For purchasing professionals, Peter Kraljic's 1983 purchasing portfolio is still regarded as the seminal framework for supplier positioning and segmentation (see Figure 6). It is used to help define the measures for managing each form of relationship based upon two criteria: the levels of supply market risk being faced in each category and the potential financial impact of that category of purchases to overall business performance.

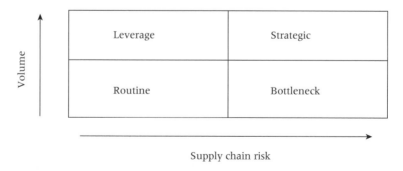

Figure 6   Kraljic's purchasing portfolio matrix

How does your supplier allocate risk?

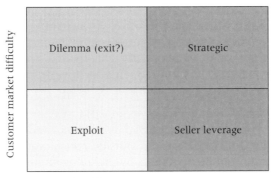

Figure 7 Typical supplier's risk matrix

Kraljic's thesis is that one should adopt different strategies depending on the impact and risk faced with a supplier. For items that have a major impact financially (i.e. they are a large-expenditure item) and where there is medium risk in the supply market, he recommends an exploitative strategy; where buyers' strength is low relative to that of suppliers, he recommends efforts to diversify or seek alternative sources. It is common to find that sourcing and supplier management strategies utilize the Kraljic matrix to define the position of individual suppliers and/or categories. However, there are some significant concerns with this one-sided approach.

Zolkiewski and Turnbull (2002) reviewed the literature on customer relationship and supplier relationship portfolio analyses, concluding that many existing approaches are too simplistic, do not take into account the interactions between the different members of the relationship and often focus on attributes that are difficult to evaluate (including profitability potential of a relationship).

Considering a typical customer portfolio approach which takes the common dimensions of financial return and risk (Zolkiewski and Turnbull 2002), Figure 7 illustrates how suppliers view their customer portfolio utilizing high market risk and high return to categorize their accounts and identify their potential. Almost by definition, suppliers and customers view their relationships as having different opportunities for 'leverage' or exploitation.

The GenCo case (Case Example 8) illustrates a common dilemma in buyer–seller relationships. If a supplier is very important to the customer, is that view reciprocated? If a buyer wants to exploit a particular supplier, as Kraljic claims, what if the supplier really does not view the buyer as important? In other words, buyer–seller relationship behaviours are determined by *both* sides of the relationship. In the majority of the literature (as Zolkiewski and Turnbull (2002) noted), researchers have failed to consider the relationship from the viewpoint of all those within that relationship.

Case Example 8: GenCo Supplies

GenCo Supplies is an MRO (maintenance, repair and operating, or indirect) supplier serving major manufacturing and assembly operations for its customers in southern California. The company sells tooling, steel bar, sheet metal, welding supplies and ancillary components for a wide range of medium- to high-volume customers.

One of the company's major initiatives in 2011 was to reassess its strategic accounts. It had five customers it classed as strategic, and ten more that were 'important'. Under guidance from an outside consultant, GenCo decided to enrich its classification of its customers by including strategic dimensions such as 'ease of interaction', delivery performance/service levels, per annum growth, technological advantage and reputational benefits in addition to the typical measures of volume, turnover and contribution. This led to it reclassifying its customer base into six strategic accounts (of which two were newly classified as strategic, replacing one customer 'relegated' out of the classification) and seven 'important customers'.

> "We realized that whilst we thought that our biggest customers should be our strategic accounts, they didn't all offer strategic opportunities for us. One in particular just happened to be a large global corporation with a big spend, but really didn't offer us many avenues to develop competencies we thought would be strategically valuable to us. Plus, they could be really difficult at times."
>
> Andrew Cozimel, Strategic Account Director

The consultant then spent time talking with each of the strategic and important accounts, focusing first on their buying department and then on their operations department.

> "I found that GenCo had failed to realize that they were an important source for one of their customers. The more I talked to everyone involved in that dyad, the clearer it became that there was 'something there between them'. What really impressed GenCo with our approach was that we had taken into account the views and opinions of both sides of the relationship. Just having the conversation seems to have been a real catalyst for some interesting account relationship developments."
>
> Jimmy Callahan, Supply Chain Consultant

Figure 8 highlights one of the common dilemmas within dyads where there is high volatility yet high potential return. If both parties view the other as 'strategic', does that mean they will build a collaborative relationship? Almost by definition, where both parties are attracted to each other there is a strong possibility that there will be mutual desire for partnership. However, the remaining three

It may not be where you think!

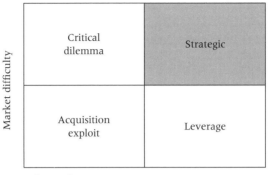

Figure 8   The dyadic relationship dilemma

quadrants present some real dilemmas for one or other party. What if I feel I can 'exploit' you, yet you do not view me as significant? Efforts on my part to 'tighten the screw' may simply result in you exiting from the relationship (Helper 1993). It can thus be extremely difficult to build a strategic relationship when you have far less power than the other party.

For this reason, purchasers are increasingly recognizing that they not only want to have strategic suppliers in order to build long-term value but they also want to be *preferred customers*, opening up the willingness of suppliers to work closely over the long term in a tight, collaborative and innovative manner.

Collaborative innovation

Joseph Schumpeter coined the term *creative destruction* to describe the economic impact of replacing existing products and processes with new ones. His work was based in part on the notion of Kondratieff cycles – the long-wave economic cycles characterized by technological shifts such as the advent of digital communications and media. The seminal work on sources of innovation has been that of Von Hippel (1978, 1985, 1986), in which he concluded that the process of product development is an interactive process between manufacturers and users. He hypothesizes that two different paradigms describe the generation of new ideas: the manufacturer active paradigm (MAP) and the customer active paradigm (CAP). Simply put, the first paradigm sees new products emerging from the innovative endeavour of the manufacturer, while in the second paradigm the customer identifies ideas and chooses the means of development. In his later works of 1985 and 1986, Von Hippel discusses the notion of *lead users* as custom-ers who are the main drivers of particular innovative efforts. In other words, not every customer is going to be a dominant innovator in the marketplace, and thus

Table 1: Foxall and Johnston's locus of responsibility for product development (1987)

Manufacturer-initiated innovation (MII)	Manufacturer performs all stages in the new product development process (Von Hippel's MAP)
User-initiated innovation 1 (UII1)	User develops new product for internal use
User-initiated innovation 2 (UII2)	The user-initiator approaches manufacturer with innovation for manufacturer to supply (Von Hippel's CAP)
User-initiated innovation 3 (UII3)	In addition to UII2, user commercially exploits the innovation
User-initiated innovation 4 (UII4)	User is responsible for all stages in the development process, including consumption

innovation by manufacturers may in fact be strongly determined by the activities of one or two customers.

Foxall (1986, pp. 23–24) contended that in fact there is not a simple dichotomy between CAP and MAP and he later (with Johnston 1987) further extended this perspective by identifying five sources of innovation between the extremes of manufacturer-led to user-led, shown in Table 1.

Recognizing that responsibility for the exploration and exploitation of innovation may occur in a number of ways, involving varying degrees of interaction between customer and supplier, raises a fundamental question: how do the various collaborative forms of innovation occur? Von Hippel (1978) claimed that the clarity of customer need and the accessibility of the supplier to the new product activity constituted the determining factors.

Addressing this point, Asanuma (1989) offers a useful categorization of suppliers in which he posits that the extent to which suppliers contribute to the development of new products can be considered in terms of their 'degree of technological initiative' (which is much the same as Von Hippel's view that a manufacturer's accessibility is important). Asanuma contends that the approach employed is determined by the characteristics of the origin of product or component being supplied. He observed that Japanese auto manufacturers had three broad types of product: those for which the customer provided the full specification, those parts which the supplier specified and the customer approved, and components which were proprietary, which he called 'marketed goods'.

Bititci et al. (2004) examined a range of innovative networks and contrasted the structures they found – essentially highlighting the different forms of collaboration between partners in the supply chain and the role of suppliers and buyers in supply chain innovation. Lewis (1990) also examined collaborative alliances and explicitly highlighted the value of trust-based relationships in driving innovation. Many of the examples he drew upon were large, Fortune 500 corporations such as Procter & Gamble, GE, IBM (Owen et al. 2008), Apple, Sony and Kraft, all of which embrace their suppliers and network partners into their innovation practices.

Greer and Lei (2011) highlight the impact of customer involvement and customer engagement in the process of joint development for innovation – a strong encouragement for buyers and their colleagues to take a lead in such collaboration. Payne et al. (2008) employ service-dominant logic to highlight the impact of strong relationship management of customers, by suppliers, in value creation. Whichever way you look at it, collaborative innovation is seen to be a world-class practice.

Case Example 9: Supplier involvement in new product development

During the 1990s, we conducted a longitudinal study into the introduction of supplier involvement in new product development at Jaguar Cars in the UK. Over the course of the two years of the Jaguar XJ8 development programme and a similar timescale for subsequent X-type development, we observed the development programme's evolution. We participated in an extensive series of interviews with suppliers, engineers, buyers, product managers, programme managers and production managers with the primary purpose of examining the collaborative nature of the vehicles' development.

Prior to Ford's purchase of Jaguar in 1991, new vehicle development was the province of Jaguar's engineering functions. Suppliers were invited to respond to designs, with no guarantee of any contractual involvement upon launch and subsequent production runs. Indeed, the company had a practice of using prototype suppliers for the development process and using production suppliers only after competitive tendering for the pre-launch and production supply. One consequence of this was that the development of Jaguar's XJS model had taken more than 12 years and had continued to encounter quality and design problems throughout its life. The XJ8 was very different for Jaguar – suppliers became involved at the concept stage, participated actively in the development programme and had a powerful voice in design issues. Consequently, the programme was extremely successful and was considered a 'proof of concept'.

"Ford instilled in us the Ford Product Development System where suppliers had a major role to play from day one. We selected suppliers based on capability, rather than price, and had to work very closely with them to make sure we all pulled together. I was sceptical at first because we had always taken a more adversarial approach to our suppliers. But I was delighted that we came in on time, on budget and had one of the highest quality products in the history of the company. And we won the annual Ford Best Program award for our efforts. It was a joy to work this way."

Paul Stokes, Supply Director, Jaguar Cars Ltd 1997

The transformation of purchasing and supply

Buyers are typically represented as confrontational, hard dealing and tactical individuals focused on getting the cheapest price they can. While this is still a valid stereotype in many companies, there is another side of the profession. These are the buyers and supply managers who understand that no business is an island. They see their role as one that focuses on managing total life cycle costs in order to increase the financial health of their business. They appreciate the critical role that trust-based relationships can play in supporting their strategic goals because they know their suppliers are vital sources of competitive advantage. They can articulate the economic benefits of their supplier relationships. They know that they need a comprehensive strategic approach in order to benefit their supply chains. They can work in a range of relationship situations no matter who appears to hold the power. They want suppliers to share information, knowledge and creativity, and drive innovation in both of their operations. Above all, they want to be preferred customers. In fact, they want to see account strategies that are thorough, value adding and well articulated. They want to deal with account managers who are strategic thinkers, can make things happen in their own business and are focused on joint problem resolution.

In conclusion, the following three quotations appear to capture the changes now making purchasing and supply professionals engage proactively with their suppliers, seek out professional strategic account managers and take major steps towards closer integration of their supply chain partners:

> "In order for organizations to maintain a competitive advantage, more focus will be placed on trust building, communication, and joint planning and developments. Dedicated groups of individuals will be charged with handling the strategies of relationships with suppliers and customers." (*Institute for Supply Management, USA*)

> "Our vision is to obtain best value for AstraZeneca from all its external expenditure by leveraging and linking our resources to fully meet business needs and exploit our suppliers' capabilities." (*Astra Zeneca Purchasing Vision*)

> "Supplier relationship management is a cornerstone of delivering results from cost-down and cost-out focused initiatives over a sustained period. It is often tempting to pressure for price-down in markets where margins are thin, but this behaviour often has the cost of losing the faith of the supplier when it comes to more radical process-based cost savings. . . . Those suppliers chosen as business partners will be expected to engage in a series of initiatives to attack cost and process innovate. These activities will be at different degrees of magnitude, but their outcomes will be clustered around improving quality, assuring supply, cost down or cost elimination." (*Mark Day and Scott Lichtenstein, Exploiting the Strategic Power of Supply Management, 2008*)

The dynamic purchasing executive seeks out suppliers who can articulate a clear relationship development strategy and have developed a strategic account plan in collaboration with their customers. Buyers know that to deliver great results, they need to have a few strategic suppliers helping drive value across the supply chain. In many ways, purchasers are becoming strategic account managers who just happen to be looking in a different direction up the supply chain.

This article has examined how purchasing executives look at collaboration with key suppliers as a core element of their strategic actions. Understanding the expectations, perceptions and needs of customers is at the heart of strategic account philosophy as a means of obtaining value from the account, but it should also add value for the customer to embrace such strategies. Alignment between buyer and supplier is a concept that seems self-evident, yet it is not a natural state in inter-organizational relationships for such alignment to occur. Efforts by SAM/KAMs to drive strategic alignment will need to look at the precise nature of the customer's needs, wants, processes, strategies and desire for close relationships. Increasingly we are seeing that the literature in both the SAM and purchasing fields views a win–win approach as one of the most effective options for driving innovation, value creation and strategic growth. Like any relationship, business or otherwise, understanding the needs of the other party and recognizing where alignment is beneficial requires a conscious and explicit effort.

Implications for future SAM/KAM research

Three areas for future research from this paper offer complementary streams for SAM/KAM researchers.

One of the dimensions of research in the supply chain management and procurement field is the operational alignment and product/process elements of relational interactions. In our discussion of the economics of trust, it is apparent that a total life cycle approach to collaboration with key accounts is an area worthy of further examination. Financial pressures are never far away in our discussion of strategic account relationships, but for purchasing and supply professionals such issues are typically at the forefront of their concerns. Building strategic supplier relationships naturally focuses on the value-added benefits from such relationships; whether this involves value analysis/value engineering approaches to product and process challenges, TCO (total cost of ownership) analyses or category pricing programmes, such financially driven issues are deserving of further study.

The second theme is that of risk management, contingency planning and risk mitigation, which are particularly intriguing areas for corporations with extensive global supply chains. The incidence of natural and man-made disasters has increased significantly over the last 40 years (Bournay 2007) and supplier involvement in contingency planning offers considerable benefits for SAM/KAM research into risk-assessment methodologies, disaster-response strategies and strategic resource positioning.

The third stream of research would address the increasing reliance on collaborative networks for product, process and market innovation, emphasizing a critical contribution for strategic account management in the innovation field. Both in terms of exploration and exploitation of novel ideas, the role of SAM practices addresses issues of intellectual property (IP) ownership, processes of new product/process/service development and factors driving or inhibiting collaborative partnerships.

Conclusion

The role of purchasing and the tools it employs have changed almost beyond recognition over the last 20 years. Purchasing has undoubtedly ascended to a far more central and strategic role in major corporations, a transformation that will continue to impact on SAM/KAM. In some ways, it might be viewed as a balancing of the power equation, but it is much richer than this. Purchasers have long been regarded as the tough negotiators, squeezing every last cent out of suppliers. That undoubtedly is going to continue, but a significant shift towards value-rather than cost-focused supplier negotiations and supplier management offers immense opportunities.

We are seeing the agenda move towards the benefits of collaborative innovation, supplier-led improvements and joint strategies for adding value to the end customer while enhancing return on investment. Procter & Gamble is probably one of the world's leaders at capitalizing on supplier innovation. It exemplifies the strategic value of looking outside its four walls for new products, new processes and new markets. This mirrors the aspirations of strategic account managers. Building business on price is never seen as a sustainable or desirable strategy, yet frustratingly has been the scene too often faced when interacting with purchase agents. As purchasing moves to a more central and strategic role, a common ground is emerging for both parties to focus on common goals, a clear plan for engagement and a mutual respect between transacting parties as they move towards longer-term and fruitful partnerships.

Social and ethical concerns in strategic account management: emerging opportunities and new threats

BY NIGEL PIERCY AND NIKALA LANE

Abstract

While ethical and moral issues have been widely considered in the general areas of marketing and sales, similar attention has not been given to the impact of strategic account management approaches to handling the relationships between suppliers and very large customers. These relationships are generally characterized by high levels of buyer–seller interdependence and forms of collaborative partnership. Observation suggests that the perceived moral intensity of these relationships is commonly low, notwithstanding the underlying principles of benefiting the few (large, strategic customers) at the expense of the many (smaller customers and other stakeholders), and the magnitude of the consequences of concessions made to large customers, even though some such consequences may be unintended.

Dilemmas exist also for executives implementing strategic account relationships regarding such issues as information sharing, trust and hidden incentives for unethical behaviour. We propose the need for greater transparency and senior management questioning of the ethical and moral issues implicit in strategic account management. Relatedly, we also give attention to the linkages between corporate social responsibility (CSR) initiatives in business organizations and the imperatives of strategic marketing to compete effectively through creating superior customer value for strategic customers. The expanding scope and domain of CSR leads us to identify an array of factors placing CSR at the heart of insightful market and segment choices by managers and the building of strong and sustainable competitive position with a company's most important accounts.

Introduction

Strategic relationships between organizations

Strategic account management (SAM) strategies are a prime example of the new type of collaborative, strategic, value-chain relationship which is coming to characterize the route to market for many major supplier organizations (Piercy 2009). Although a distinct strategy in its own right, SAM shares many of the characteristics of other strategic inter-organizational relationships, which underlines the benefits of a broadening perspective concerning the management issues faced in sustainable and effective SAM.

In fact, the formation of strategic relationships among suppliers, producers, distribution channel organizations and customers (intermediate customers and end-users) occurs for several reasons. The goal may be gaining better access to markets, enhancing value offerings, reducing the risks caused by rapid technological change, sharing complementary skills, learning and acquiring new knowledge, building sustained close relationships with major customers, or obtaining resources beyond those available to a single company. Strategic relationships of these kinds are escalating in importance because of the complexity and risks in a global economy, the skill and resource limitations of a single organization, and the power of major customers to insist on collaborative relationships with their strategic suppliers. Strategic alliances, joint ventures and strategic account collaborations are examples of cooperative relationships between independent firms (Cravens and Piercy 2013). We will argue that SAM should be understood as one example of the increasingly complex networks of connections between organizations.

Our reasoning is that along with other strategic inter-organizational relationships, SAM represents an important transformation taking place in industry after industry, driven by two factors. First, the age of mass production is largely over and customers demand unique value, so value is shifting from products to solutions and experiences, and consequently relationships are taking over as the central element of exchange. Second, no single business is likely to be big enough to cope with complex and diverse customer demands. This underlines the importance of alliances and networks to deliver customer value – constellations of suppliers that can be configured in different ways to meet different customer needs. Success will involve managing through new collaborative networks (Prahalad and Krishnan 2008).

Consider, for example, the transformation at IBM. A key element of IBM's business services strategy has been to multiply collaborative projects across all the major parts of the business. Collaborating with customers and even competitors to invent new technologies is part of IBM's strategy of openness. Sharing intellectual property in the form of software, patents and ideas is intended to stimulate industry growth and create opportunities for IBM to sell high-value products and services that meet new demands. IBM's 'collaboratories' are joint ventures for research with countries, companies and independent research establishments throughout the world. Through its collaborative strategy IBM has been transformed into a borderless organization working globally with partners to enhance the value of offerings to customers on a worldwide basis (Hempel 2011; Kirkpatrick 2005). Our logic is that SAM represents one form of inter-organizational collaboration, and that it shares the characteristics of other forms of this phenomenon.

Strategic account management relationships

It is clear that in managing relationships with large corporate customers, many selling organizations have moved to the adoption of SAM and global account management (GAM) approaches as ways of building teams dedicated to managing the relationship with the most valuable customers (Capon 2001, 2012). Procter & Gamble's 200-person team to manage its relationship with Wal-Mart, its biggest retailer customer, is illustrative. Importantly, strategic, key and global accounts (customers) are increasingly considered strategic partners.

Indeed, it appears increasingly the case that some customers may dominate a supplier's customer portfolio. These customers may pose substantial challenges because of their ability to exert considerable influence and control over suppliers. For example, like P&G, more than 450 other suppliers have established offices in Wal-Mart's home town of Bentonville, Arkansas, in order to be close to their largest customer, and Tesco exerts a similar effect in the UK (Wiggins and Rigby 2006). Nonetheless, it may be mistaken to regard dominant customers as strategic relationships or partners – they may simply be very large accounts with a conventional, though possibly imbalanced, buyer–seller relationship with suppliers.

However, the strategic significance of customer dominance should not be underestimated. For example, the merger of Gillette with Procter & Gamble in 2006 created the world's largest consumer brands group, with a combined portfolio of brands that gives the company a much stronger bargaining position with major retailers like Wal-Mart, Carrefour and Tesco. However, the merger also represents a significant change to P&G's business model, with a new focus on lower-income consumers in markets such as India and China. In positioning in these emerging markets, P&G is deliberately not partnering with powerful global retailers. In China, Gillette offers P&G access to a huge distribution system staffed by individual Chinese entrepreneurs – what P&G calls a 'down the trade' system ending up with a one-person kiosk in a small village selling shampoo and toothpaste. Importantly, the intent of P&G's strategy should be to achieve growth in Asian markets and reduce dependence on mature markets dominated by powerful dominant retailers (Grant 2005).

The general view seems to be that real strategic customers are those with which the relationship is based on collaboration and processes of joint decision-making, where both buyer and seller invest time and resources in the strategic relationship. For a growing number of companies SAM provides an innovative model for managing relationships with their most important customers.

Of course, the importance of these developments is underlined when customers actively promote concentration in their supply base and attempt to restrict supplier numbers. For example, in September 2005, Ford Motor announced its intention to cut its supply base of 2,000 by around half to reduce its $90 billion purchasing budget and to improve quality. By 2009, Ford had more than halved its global supply base from 3,300 in 2004 to 1,600, with a goal of quickly getting down to 750 suppliers. Ford targets seven 'key suppliers' covering about half its parts purchasing, with enhanced access to Ford's engineering and product planning. Ford will work more closely with selected suppliers, consulting them earlier in the design process and giving them access to key business plans on future vehicles, and committing to giving them business to allow them to plan their own investments (Mackintosh and Simon 2005; Simon and Mackintosh 2009). Interestingly, Ford cut the development cost of seats for the Focus sedan by awarding the entire global contract to a single supplier – Johnson Controls (Simon 2010).

The underlying rationale for SAM is that a supplier's most important customers require dedicated resources and special value-adding activities (such as joint product development, business planning, consulting services) in the value offering. Importantly, SAM is increasingly understood as a new business model that goes beyond conventional buyer–seller relationships to establish partnership and joint decision-making between the customer and the supplier. Nonetheless, there are substantial risks in high levels of dependence on strategic customers. Investments should be weighed against the risks of customer disloyalty and strategic change, as well as the perception of strategic customer privileges by the rest of the customer base. The attraction of SAM may rest on a degree of market and relationship stability which may not exist.

For example, in 2005 Apple Computer announced an end to its long-term strategic relationship with IBM as the supplier of microprocessors for Apple desktop computers, and named Intel as the replacement. Apple believes that Intel can provide components for the products of the future, with higher performance and lower prices. Supplier switch is increasingly viewed as a strategic move by companies like Apple to leverage their competitive position, which takes higher priority than loyalty to existing strategic suppliers. Indeed, supplier switch of this kind may be an inevitable consequence of strategic change (Morrison and Waters 2005).

Importantly, if we see SAM as an alliance-based relationship rather than a simpler buyer–seller linkage, then it is likely that the success of the relationship will depend heavily on effectively matching the capabilities of the participating organizations and on achieving the full commitment of each partner to the relationship. The benefits and the trade-offs in the relationship must be favourable for each of the partners. The contribution of one partner should fill a gap in the other partner's capabilities. However, we will argue below that the unintended consequences of this process of matching and the realignment of goals and processes that is likely to ensue may create serious weaknesses. Alliance-based relationships may create behaviours which would not otherwise be undertaken and which would not otherwise be regarded as attractive or even acceptable corporate practices.

For example, one important concern in the alliance-based SAM relationship is that the partner (buyer or seller) may gain access to confidential technology and other proprietary information, which may be detrimental to the interests of third parties. While this issue is important, the essential consideration is assessing the relationship's risks and rewards and the integrity of the SAM partner. A strong bond of trust between the partners exists in most successful relationships. The purpose of the relationship is for each partner to contribute something distinctive rather than to transfer core skills to the other partner. It is important for the managers in each organization to evaluate the advisability and risks concerning the transfer of skills and technologies to the partner. Poor judgements in this area may lead to breaches of ethical standards and even unlawful degrees of collaboration.

Relatedly, it is important to recognize that strategic account relationships may be fragile and difficult to sustain effectively, particularly if there is a lack of trust or mutuality of interest between partners. Moreover, careful analysis is required of the impact of a failed relationship on a company's remaining ability to compete and survive. The higher the level of dependence on a partner organization, the greater the strategic vulnerability created if the relationship fails.

Broadening the management perspective on SAM

Our goal here, drawing on the comments above, is to suggest a number of ways in which the management approach to SAM may usefully adopt a broader perspective than has been the case in most instances to date. In part this reflects the maturing of the SAM concept itself, as well as important changes in the business environment. The questions we address are concerned with opportunities to build stronger and more sustainable relationships with strategic customers, but also with highlighting the risks and pitfalls that may be encountered and that should be avoided before they become damaging.

Specifically, we wish to draw attention to the following issues.

Ethical dilemmas to be resolved in making SAM effective and sustainable

It is in the nature of SAM that in many situations one side of the relationship will be dominant, e.g. by constituting a disproportionately large proportion of the other partner's business, or controlling access to a critical resource. The concern is that the resulting dependence will create an unconsidered and unattractive level of business risk for the weaker partner and that dependence may lead to behaviours which would not otherwise be undertaken. The implications of dependence require careful management attention from both these viewpoints.

However, our immediate focus is based on the observation that the perceived moral intensity of SAM relationships is commonly low, notwithstanding the underlying principles of benefiting the few (large, strategic customers) at the expense of the many (smaller customers and other stakeholders), and the magnitude of the consequences of concessions made to large customers, even though some such consequences may be unintended.

Dilemmas also exist for executives implementing strategic account relationships regarding such issues as information sharing, trust and hidden incentives for unethical behaviour. We propose the need for greater transparency and senior management questioning of the ethical and moral issues implicit in strategic account management. The unprecedented level of scrutiny of corporate ethical issues underlines the urgency for these issues to be examined and where possible dilemmas to be resolved before they become damaging to the business relationship (Piercy and Lane 2007, 2009).

Corporate social responsibility as a dimension of strategic customer relationship

Related to ethical mandates, the pressure on business to undertake corporate social responsibility (CSR) initiatives from a defensive or more strategic perspective is also unprecedented. Advocates urge companies to incorporate societal benefits within their business models to deliver value against both commercial and societal goals, whether in environmental protection, sustainability, supply chain and employment behaviours or ethical standards (Piercy and Lane 2011).

In the context of SAM, three issues are emerging and deserve management attention. First, the match between social initiatives may become an important part of the process of identifying potential strategic account relationships. Second, shared CSR goals and programmes can be an important part of a strategic account relationship that helps sustain the relationship. Third, an unintended consequence of enthusiasm for CSR initiatives between seller and buyer may be to transgress competition law. Carefully handled, CSR provides an additional dimension to building sustainable strategic account relationships.

Ethical dilemmas in SAM and how to avoid them

The domain we examine in this section of the paper is defined by the relationship between the strategic account manager in a selling organization and the purchasing organization of the large and very large customer. More generally, the advance of the study of marketing ethics has been supported by studies carried out at what may be called critical stress points, such as the ethics of marketing research or salesforce management behaviour. Such critical junctures are points at which marketing ethics considerations are both important and highly problematic. In this tradition, our study is concerned with a critical juncture in the value chain relating to the relationships between sellers and large buyers, most particularly where these are formalized into strategic account management arrangements.

However, it is likely that, as with many marketing and selling situations, many executives will not perceive strategic buyer–seller relationships situations as manifesting ethical issues (Singhapakdi 1999). This differentiation is reflected in the concept of moral intensity – 'the extent of issue-related moral imperative in a situation' (Jones 1991). Moral intensity consists of six components: magnitude of consequences, social consensus, probability of effect, temporal immediacy, proximity and concentration of effect. The suggestion is that issues of high moral intensity will be recognized more readily and ethical intentions established more frequently than is the case with issues of low moral intensity (Singhapakdi and Vitell 1990). Nonetheless, manager perceptions of low moral intensity do not necessarily align with realities, particularly as those realities are perceived by others, such as regulators.

Our concern is that major selling and buying organizations have, in effect, created a new type of boundary-spanning role or interface, the successful performance and operation of which potentially requires an individual executive to covertly undertake behaviours which are potentially unethical, possibly dubious morally, and in extreme cases even unlawful. We will provide examples to illustrate the basis for this concern. Our case suggests the need to assess more carefully the definition of the role of the strategic account manager to accommodate stricter limits on what is, and what is not, acceptable behaviour, regardless of short-term performance imperatives.

In spite of the growth of SAM approaches in many sectors, recent studies suggest that while SAM is one of the most fundamental changes in marketing organization, it is one where a sound research foundation to guide management decisions remains largely lacking (Homburg et al. 2002; Workman et al. 2003). In particular, we can find no sign in the relevant literature that any critical study has been undertaken of the potential for ethical problems or moral conflicts in the SAM relationship itself or in its consequences. Certainly, it has been suggested that policies of active collaboration between companies and their suppliers are attractive in avoiding the 'dog eat dog' philosophy of buyer–seller confrontation, and that the implementation of these buyer–seller collaborations should be based upon 'deep-rooted ethical values' (Valenzuele and Villacorta 1999). However, what has not been considered are the outcomes if collaborative buyer–seller relationships are not, in fact, based on deep-seated ethical values, or if the collaboration is not perceived by executives as having an ethical dimension, or indeed if executives do not believe that they or their organizations should consider moral issues as a significant context for collaboration.

The urgency and topicality of the issue we address is underlined by contemporary suggestions that increasingly corporate incentive structures and business strategies push in directions that are at odds with ethical behaviour, producing a situation where executives may feel penalized, not supported, for raising ethical questions. This personal conflict may be exacerbated by the short-term bias of investors providing yet more pressure to support unethical behaviour in critical business relationships (e.g. Plender and Persaud 2005, 2006).

In this part of the article, we examine and illustrate three aspects of strategic account management relationships which pose moral and ethical dilemmas: (1) the impact of seller strategy which favours a few customers at the expense of the many; (2) the potentially harmful, though sometimes unintended, consequences of the strategic account relationship; and (3) the dilemmas faced in implementing the strategic account manager role, as it relates to information sharing across organizational boundaries, trust between partnered organizations and the principle of 'keeping promises', and the hidden incentives encouraging unethical behaviour which may be implicit in some strategic account management models. Finally, we consider the ways in which organizations may address the dilemmas we have identified.

Our argument is framed around what we suggest to be some of the important ethical and moral dilemmas faced by senior corporate managers, strategic account managers and strategic purchasing executives in the way they reach decisions relating to the strategic account/strategic supplier relationship, i.e. the moral judgements, standards and rules of conduct they generate and apply (Gundlach and Murphy 1993). In fact, it could be argued with some merit that in fact what we are considering is not an attribute of SAM per se but rather of the relationships that suppliers have with their large and very large customers. This is to some extent true, since the dilemmas on which we focus largely exist because of the imbalance of power and the exercise of that power by one party over the other, albeit in the guise of collaboration and partnership. However, it is also the case that by creating a new organizational role to contain and isolate these problematic relationships, organizations have not removed but have at best obscured the dilemmas we identify. Worse, the SAM role, typically held by a relatively junior executive, is in danger of becoming a way for more senior management to disclaim responsibility for moral issues in relationships with large customers.

While accepting that the situations we describe characterize the supplier–large customer relationship, we are particularly concerned about the effect of strategic account management roles on the reality of that relationship and the risk that this new management approach introduces additional moral and ethical hazards.

Interestingly, analysts of strategic alliances have drawn attention to several aspects of relational risk, including when a partner undertakes self-interested opportunistic behaviour at the expense of the other party (Das and Teng 2001). Several theoretical frameworks indicate that the opportunity to take advantage of the other party in an alliance negates the advantage of strategic alliance, and that opportunism should be replaced by cooperation. However, the mutual trust necessary can be achieved only through ethical conduct between the parties (Daboub 2002; Daboub and Carlton 2002). A study by Daboub and Calton (2002) adds further insight to the nature of the emerging ethical and moral dilemmas faced in strategic account relationships. They argue that the complexity and change in the business environment have mandated the development of new inter-organizational relationships, which importantly 'has resulted in the disaggrega-tion of the value chain and the disaggregation of ethical and legal responsibility' (p. 96). If strategic account relationships are a relatively new manifestation of the network forms evaluated by Dabaub and Calton, then a similar conclusion about the loss of ethical foundations may hold true. However, while these issues have achieved some recognition in the strategic alliances literature, they have been largely ignored in the study of strategic account management. We propose that dilemmas exist with respect to several characteristics of strategic account management/strategic supplier management relationships.

The good of the few versus the good of the many

The attractions of a relationship marketing strategy that focuses attention and resources onto strategic accounts have been widely rehearsed in the literature. The underlying logic is that favoured treatment of key partner organizations, as strategic accounts, can reduce customer costs, increase product quality and increase customer satisfaction, while at the same time reducing seller expenses, achieving economies of scale, gaining access to markets and technology, and creating barriers to entry for competitors (e.g. see Fontenot and Hyman 2004; Gundlach and Murphy 1993; Kalwani and Narayandas 1995). SAM offers the promise of sustainable competitive advantage by developing intense, long-term marketing relationships with key partners that are difficult for competitors to duplicate, and by vertical integration, possibly to the extent of exclusive dealing or single-source relationships (e.g. see Buchanan 1992; Weitz and Jap 1995).

However, by implication, strategic account management is a policy that favours the few (the strategic accounts) at the expense of the many (smaller accounts and other organizational stakeholders). The fact cannot be avoided that such focus on strategic accounts can be achieved only at the expense of others who are not party to the collaboration between buyer and seller and its details. Indeed, if there were no such advantage for the buyer, then there would be no basis for a strategic account/strategic supplier relationship. For example, most obviously, concessions and special treatment for strategic accounts may be at the expense of the supplier's smaller customers, who pay higher prices and receive less advan-tageous terms of trade. This may have a two-fold effect: first, smaller accounts receive poorer value than strategic accounts, thus negatively influencing their profitability; but second, if they compete with the same strategic accounts in a shared end-user market, their competitiveness is undermined and their long-term survival may be threatened. In a very real sense, smaller accounts may pay more not because they are more expensive to serve but because they lack the power to demand and obtain lower prices. A business model which institutionalizes and legitimates this form of cross-subsidy raises a moral question of whether it is right or fair to treat smaller customers in this way. (Relatedly, policies of cross-subsidy are actually illegal in some countries and can attract substantial legal penalties if they are uncovered.)

Alternatively, it can be argued that advantageous terms offered to strategic accounts are at the expense of shareholder interests. Interestingly, while formal strategic alliances are normally matters of public contract and open to scrutiny, and financial mergers are subject to shareholder permission by ballot, strategic account relationships are not normally subject to the same scrutiny or right to reject by the owners of the business. Indeed, conceding excessive advantages to strategic accounts may also be to sacrifice the long-term value of the company to its owners, by sacrificing long-term profitability for short-term gains in sales and market position.

Advocates of SAM would doubtless argue that the natural process of market concentration means that some customers will be more important than others, and that it is therefore both reasonable and perhaps inevitable that they will receive more advantageous terms of trade from suppliers than other, less important customers. There is a degree of truth in this viewpoint. However, it is also the case that for suppliers who conform to this pattern of behaviour, one consequence is that they further enhance the bargaining power of their major customers and have to live with the consequences, which may be undesirable both for themselves and for others. Customers with market power are likely to use that power in their own interests, and to use additional power yet more. Of course, there remains the unresolved question of whether any supplier is likely to jeopardize future relationships by making such a formal complaint about a dominant customer.

Importantly, there seem to be some doubts that customers treated as the 'favoured few' will actually reciprocate this favour with their suppliers. Strategic account relationships may in this sense be based on an implied promise of loyalty and collaboration which is not kept. Consider, for example, the troubled automotive parts supply marketplace. For some years, suppliers have experienced pressure from their major carmaker customers to hold down or reduce prices, while raw material costs have been escalating. Faced with stagnant demand for cars, and increasingly fragmented markets, car manufacturers have moved back towards treating suppliers as adversaries rather than 'trusted partners'. Suppliers with long-term strategic relationships with major customers are now faced with the reality that the concessions they have made to sustain a relationship may have been in vain because the customer may not keep the implied promise of partnership. In this sense, inter-organizational relationships that are not grounded in ethical exchange may also be highly unattractive in commercial or economic terms.

Lastly, there are risks that the relatively covert operation of buyer–seller collaboration formalized in the SAM strategy may also lead towards actions that are prohibited under competition law and that are hidden until late in the day. Since the object of relationship marketing and SAM is to create mutually beneficial alliances with strategic accounts, they are likely to restrict trade among competitors by creating barriers to entry (Williamson 1979). If the relationship is coercive, restricts competition, discriminates among different classes of customer or inhibits innovation, then it may violate competition law in several parts of the world, but importantly in such situations 'stakeholders such as employees, customers, communities, channel members, competitors, and governments may be harmed' (Fontenot and Hyman 2004). If, for example, a supplier sells products and services to a strategic customer at prices that are less than variable cost, while charging other customers prices higher than variable cost, there is a prima facie case for anti-competitive behaviour.

While global generalizations are difficult, due to differences in legal systems and enforcement policies in different countries, it is certainly valid to underline the pragmatic need to balance ethical, legal and economic responsibilities (Carroll 1991). However, constructs like Carroll's 'pyramid of social responsibilities' underline the case that to rely only on legal frameworks to judge the acceptability of buyer–seller relationships is a relatively weak way of confronting issues which may simply be judged as 'wrong' against many prevailing sets of norms. The legal boundaries separating abuse from normal business practice are somewhat blurred and are apparently becoming more so (Buck 2005). The puzzle of equating that which is unpunished with that which is morally justified suggests that the rightness or wrongness of actions in managing strategic account relationships may require other forms of evaluation than the purely legalistic.

More generally, it is suggested that the law alone is insufficient to ensure that corporate behaviour does not act against the interests of owners, third parties or the wider interests of society. Legal regulation may simply codify the lowest common denominator, while lagging behind the way in which markets and corporate strategies have evolved. In addition, business strategies have side effects – externalities – that are typically not considered in regulation. Hence, 'there is a need for ethical behaviour that goes beyond complying with the law, especially in the gray areas where managers face conflicting priorities' (Plender and Persaud 2006).

Our study of the available literature on strategic account management has failed to locate any consideration of ethical or moral dimensions of this business model. We suggest that perceived moral intensity is low. Nonetheless, a prima facie case can be made for the view that, at least in some cases, strategic account relationships are morally undesirable if they are unfair to smaller customers, introduce or reinforce competitive distortions in end-user markets, provide a vehicle for covert anti-competitive behaviours and lack shareholder mandate. Guidelines for ethical exchange propose principles of equality, commitment, equity and loyalty, while anecdote and observation suggest broken promises, one-sided commitment and illusory reciprocity between partners. It would be exaggerated to suggest that all strategic account relationships are flawed in this way, but we do suggest that the potential for abuse underlines the need for more searching scrutiny of the moral and ethical foundations of strategic account relationships than appears to be the case currently.

The unintended consequences of concessions to strategic accounts

A second area of concern relates to the consequences of concessions and advantages developed by suppliers for their strategic accounts, which may be unintended but which nonetheless are damaging to themselves and to others. The dilemma is that while there is increasing recognition that companies should manage their businesses in such a way that they are not detrimental to society (Carroll 1993), there appear to be an increasing number of situations where successful marketing activities by firms impact negatively on consumers, society or other stakeholders in ways that have not been planned or anticipated (Fry and Polonsky 2004). For example, recent estimates suggest that Britain's farmers are forced to throw away as much as one third of their home-grown fruit and vegetables because of the 'rules' imposed by supermarkets relating to the cosmetic appearance of produce (Leake 2005).

While intended exchange effects with key customers are clearly expected to be positive, they may in fact have certain negative consequences as well as or instead of the positive outcomes planned. One of several possibilities may explain this: the buyer and seller may miscalculate the effect of their exchange on others; they may adopt an egoist perspective and ignore the effect of their exchange on others; or they may not have the power to control the effect in question (Mundt 1993).

From an ethical perspective, it has been suggested that the prescriptive priority is for executives to accept the moral obligation to carefully consider not only the intended exchange-related activities with the customer, but also the unintended consequences of marketing activities on the primary stakeholders in the network of exchanges that comprises the marketplace (Fry and Polonsky 2004). This obligation is perhaps more related to exhibiting a reasonable level of due care to others than to suggest all possible outcomes can be predicted or, indeed, avoided. Nonetheless, while evaluation may take place only within reasonable boundaries, the priority of that moral obligation is supplemented by the knowledge that unintended consequences may be severely harmful to the originators as well as to bystanders, and enlightened self-interest may also be relevant, since economic damage may ensue for the originator. For example, companies that divorce themselves from the employment concerns of their key suppliers are taking a large risk and may even be considered morally and economically irresponsible.

In short, an ethics perspective suggests that buyer–seller relationships of the type described here can produce several types of socially undesirable consequences and harm to third parties, and these consequences appear to have been largely ignored in the literature. There are many supporting examples. Principles of ethical exchange are breached in situations where exchange partners not only harm other stakeholders but ultimately damage their own organizations as well. We suggest there is a compelling case for greater scrutiny of strategic account relationships by senior management to evaluate the possible consequences in moral terms as well as economic ones. It is perhaps apposite to note the argument that ethical behaviour in business is more rational, more intrinsically valuable and more profitable than unethical behaviour (Velasquez 1996).

Moral dilemmas in implementing the SAM executive role

In addition to the unintended consequences of decisions made to very large customers, and the degree to which favouring one small customer group at the expense of others meets reasonable standards of fairness and equity, attention should be given to the effects of strategic account management approaches on the individual executives concerned. In particular, these concerns revolve around the possibility that in order to effectively implement the organizational role which has been allocated, executives may be in a position where they are de facto required to take actions and make decisions which offend their own codes of conduct, their own organizations' ethical and governance standards, and more general concepts of fair dealing between buyers and sellers. Indeed, as noted earlier, executives in some circumstances may be placed in a situation where the SAM role presses them to undertake behaviours which may be or may become unlawful. This argument is illustrated by considering the questions of information exchange between buyer and seller within the strategic account relationship, and the degree to which actual or implied promises between the parties can be kept, as well as the incentives for unethical behaviour implicit in the strategic account model.

Information sharing

One characteristic of the operation of strategic account management is a high degree of information sharing between seller and buyer. This may include sensitive information regarding costs and prices, new product plans and other strategic developments. For example, in a workshop presentation at our university between a strategic account manager and his purchaser in the strategic account, both executives placed much emphasis on the trust between the two parties, and particularly the sharing of proprietary information. When pressed, the executives reluctantly admitted that their own organizations and their chief executives did not know how much information had actually been shared and were unlikely to have formally approved. Nonetheless, they maintained that the strategic account relationship could not operate effectively, other than through intense information sharing. A critical question therefore is whether information sharing by the executives concerned is limited to that sanctioned by the organization, or whether it goes further.

The risk is that the SAM model imposes a requirement for information sharing on individual executives in buying and selling organizations that goes beyond that sanctioned and approved by the organization. To perform well in the SAM role, the individual must choose whether or not to breach organizational policies and management practices by disclosing confidential information selectively to their counterpart in the partner organization. To choose not to undertake this behaviour is probably to choose to perform the SAM role poorly (against the goals set by management). To ignore organizational policies and share confidential information raises the issue of the contravention not only of formal governance but possibly also of personal codes of conduct.

While offering senior management the advantage of 'deniability' if accused of anti-competitive behaviour, the SAM role transfers the onus for this decision to relatively junior executives. This appears unattractive in terms of governance but also in the way an organization treats its managerial employees. A business model that imposes an unfair burden on individual executives to make strategic account management work through behaviours not approved by the organization is morally questionable. Further, the same pressure may also result in information sharing that reaches the level of anti-competitive behaviour, so individual executives may actually have to choose whether to follow the law (and do their jobs less well, with whatever corporate penalties may ensue) or to ignore the law (and perform the job better).

Partnership, trust and the principle of 'keeping promises'

Some suggest that the reality of modern buyer–seller relationships underlines the death of reciprocity and the illusion of expecting customer loyalty. It is certainly the case that there have been fundamental changes in the relationships between buyers and sellers in business-to-business situations. However, there seems some tendency for analysts to have adopted a somewhat biased view of those changes and for managers to build strategies that rely on assumptions about reciprocity in buyer–seller relationships and customer loyalty.

Consider the potential for broken promises of several kinds that exists in strategic account relationships. For example, mid-2005 saw the giant UK hardware retailer Focus writing to suppliers demanding that they pay more towards distribution costs and increases in cash discounts for invoice settlement. This action effectively changed payment terms with suppliers mid-contract. Around one third of Focus's suppliers were dropped because they rejected the new terms (Tooher 2005). The Focus example is only one of many. However, perhaps more pervasive than the breaking of contractual promises between suppliers and buyers is the breach of the promises implied by the apparently cooperative and collaborative partnership relationship.

For instance, telecommunications equipment supplier Marconi in the UK had a strategic relationship with British Telecommunications Group that went back several decades. As one of BT's largest suppliers of network equipment, BT was Marconi's largest customer, accounting for 25% of sales. In April 2005, BT announced the supplier network for its £10 billion spend on the massive '21st Century Network' project. Marconi was not included as a supplier. Notwithstanding the long-term relationship with Marconi and the company's research and development strengths, BT made its decision based on price, and Marconi was unable to reduce costs to the levels of overseas competitors, even though it had been prepared to run at a loss. Marconi's market value almost halved when BT's decision was made known. By late 2005, the main part of Marconi's business had been purchased by Swedish telecoms company Ericsson, leaving Marconi with just its UK-based services operations (Odell 2005). Commentators conclude that Marconi's biggest mistake was believing that BT would remain a loyal customer (Durman and Box 2005). Marconi did not simply lose a customer, it lost the whole business.

However, what remains elusive is the degree to which Marconi had the right to believe that BT would remain a loyal customer because of the decades-long strategic relationship between the companies. For a collaborative or partnership-based relationship to have endured for such a period of time suggests the existence of trust and cooperation between the buyer and seller. But that would then suggest an implied 'promise' to continue or sustain the relationship, or at least to make clear when it was likely to come to an end. The unilateral abandonment of a partner through a single phone call, as was the case with Marconi and BT, raises serious questions about the reality of buyer–seller partnerships, which remains unresolved. It is unclear in this case whether the outcome represents misjudgements by individual actors or the breaking of implied promises between the two organizations. Certainly, the degree to which promises were implied underlines the pressures placed on the account management and purchasing executives concerned and the dilemmas they face.

The point we would emphasize relates not to corporate relationships as such but rather to the impact of such situations on the individual executives responsible. The managers in BT who chose to drop Marconi as a key supplier and those who exert market power to refuse to accept price increases from suppliers are unlikely to be the same individuals who operate the buyer–seller relationship. Those who partner across organizational boundaries develop relationships, offer commitment, cooperate, make or imply promises as to future behaviour, and assume duties towards each other, and do so to make strategic account management work effectively. When their own organizations subsequently adopt policies that lead to broken promises, breaches of commitments and other harmful effects to others, the question arises whether organizations have a moral and ethical basis for treating their executives in this way.

Interestingly, the notion of 'trust equity' captures the idea that trusting relationships between organizations are attractive because they reduce the costs of doing business – less time is devoted to monitoring compliance, negotiations, contractual details, for example (Landry 2000). However, it seems that one signal of the dysfunctional supply chain is where trust exists between individuals but the organizations that employ those individuals do not behave as though encumbered by the obligations of a trusting relationship. In this sense, the promises made or implied by individual executives in a strategic account relationship can be no more than conditional, even if this is not recognized by the individuals concerned. The individual executive's dilemma hinges on making relational promises which may be broken by the company, in spite of the assumed existence of 'trust equity' and the advantages of 'trusting relationships' between seller and buyer organizations.

The hidden incentive for unethical behaviours

There is also some precedent for believing that dilemmas are heightened in impact on the individual executive by perceptions that those who perform 'best' in the customer-facing role are less likely to be challenged on their ethical standards than those executives who perform less 'well' against organizational objectives. There is empirical evidence in the sales area, for example, that there is a general tendency for sales managers to discipline top sales performers more leniently than poor sales performers for engaging in identical forms of unethical behaviour (Bellizzi and Hasty 2003; Bellizzi and Bristol 2005).

While the proposition has not been tested in the strategic account management area, these findings provide a relevant insight into how executives responsible for managing buyer–seller relationships may themselves be managed. In this sense, the account executive who achieves considerably higher sales, or the purchasing executive who achieves outstanding cost savings, may face less scrutiny of the behaviours undertaken to achieve these results. The personal risk is that if performance against organizational objectives suffers, then all aspects of individual behaviours may well come under additional scrutiny by management. The incentive is thus placed on continuing and extending behaviours that achieve 'results', regardless of their nature, to avoid being 'brought to account' for current and past behaviours. This suggests the existence of a 'slippery slope' for executives regarding standards of behaviour, from which it may be difficult to exit once momentum takes over.

Corporate self-harm

Finally, there is some concern that SAM strategies may be harmful in a variety of ways to the long-term interests of suppliers themselves. This would suggest that SAM executives are placed in a position where to meet the responsibilities and goals of their role, they are obliged to undertake actions that are fundamentally harmful to their own companies and the various stakeholders involved, and they are responsible for 'corporate self-harm'. This poses a difficult choice for executives – to go ahead with enacting the role they have been given, taking no heed of the possible long-term consequences for their companies, or to incur the organizational unpopularity, and possibly worse personal consequences, by making the case that some SAM activities should be constrained by the long-term interests of the company.

For these reasons, an ethics perspective raises questions about the 'rightness' of a business model that rests on the willingness of individual executives to take personal risks in breaching organizational policies to perform the job effectively, and to make undertakings to partners in other organizations, knowing that promises may be broken if top management decides to abandon the strategic account relationship in search of other priorities. It appears in some cases that executives are expected to manage relational exchange on the covert understanding that ethical foundations may be abandoned by their seniors, when opportunistic behaviour appears to be advantageous. In addition, a reputation for bad behaviour in managing inter-organizational relationships may undermine the reputation of the organization and its executives, thus undermining ability to partner in the future. The ways in which these substantial dilemmas are to be handled provides a major test for the moral and ethical foundations of strategic account management.

Addressing the moral and ethical dilemmas in strategic account management

Nonetheless, we have seen that the business attractions of SAM as buyer–seller are substantial. So the question becomes, how should executives protect a valuable business approach from the moral and ethical dilemmas we have identified? At its most extreme, our concern is that the increasingly widely adopted strategic account management approach to managing buyer–seller relationships is a seriously flawed means to achieve an end that may itself be morally dubious. It arises from the relationship between selling organizations and their most important customers – often very large, powerful customers. The existence of the dilemmas we have identified has been largely ignored or denied in the extant literature. For this reason, a significant enhancement of current practice would involve actions simply designed to leverage perceptions of moral intensity in the management of strategic account relationships. At present, this major area of business concerned with critical buyer–seller relationships appears to exist and operate in a moral vacuum, where policies, actions and their consequences are framed only by relatively short-term economic criteria. We suggest that there are a number of ethical and legal considerations, which should be evaluated concerning the operation of SAM/strategic supplier relationships.

The responsibility for stimulating an enhanced moral intensity rests with senior management, not with the relatively junior executives tasked with executing strategic account relationships. In particular, there is no reason why stakeholders should not expect the same standards of due diligence and fiduciary duties from top management in managing these new collaborative forms of buyer–seller relationship, as are commonly expected in other governance situations. This would suggest that senior executives should be asked to indicate the ways in which they have examined all aspects of strategic account relationships and to prove that they have not damaged the company and do not pose excessive risks to its survival and value, by virtue of the way in which these relationships have been enacted and managed. Such scrutiny could encompass wide-ranging issues – from the moral and ethical to the economic – allowing stakeholders to make informed judgements regarding the adequacy of management diligence in managing strategic account relationships. While managers may be misled or simply make errors of judgement, for them not to make a reasonable effort to recognize the plausible effects of strategic account relationships and their consequences for relevant stakeholders would appear to be morally unacceptable.

One starting point would be embracing a degree of openness and transparency in the conduct of strategic account relationships comparable to that required in situations where inter-organizational relationships involve formal mergers or acquisitions or contractual relationships. Generally it appears that strategic account relationships are shrouded in secrecy, conducted with a degree of covertness, and their operations often not fully revealed even inside the companies in question (for example, in terms of information sharing and price concessions). The defence of this lack of transparency is that proprietary and share-sensitive information is at stake, and norms of commercial confidentiality should prevail in considering sensitive relationships with major customers. However, by comparison, mergers and acquisitions involve substantial disclosure and a major duty of due diligence, and formal contractual alliances between companies possibly demand something similar.

We should be wary, of course, of substituting a legal or economic dilemma for an ethical one. For example, under US price-fixing laws, it is illegal under some circumstances to communicate pricing information to competitors (which could occur if a supplier publicized price structures to all buyers) (Fontenot and Hyman 2004). Equally, disclosures that reduce a company's competitiveness by better informing competitors about its strategies may be unreasonable. However, notwithstanding such constraints, there appears little real reason why the existence of 'strategic partnerships' between buyers and sellers should escape all disclosure requirements, by virtue of appropriate corporate governance rather than external mandate. Indeed, such disclosure should provide a level of detail allowing relevant stakeholders to evaluate the impact of strategic account strategy on their own interests, although clearly there is no guarantee they would do so.

For example, in a strategic account relationship the almost inevitable reality is that the purchaser will know the prices paid by other (usually smaller) customers, though possibly not always those paid by other strategic accounts. However, it is rare for smaller customers to be informed of the prices paid by larger, strategic accounts. A governance mandate of transparency for strategic account relationships would suggest that buyers and sellers should declare openly prices being paid, so that they are known to all relevant stakeholders. Indeed, this would potentially also expose whether the lower prices paid by strategic accounts do actually reflect economy of scale (which is probably unobjectionable) or whether they are the product of the use of market power by the large customer (a matter of considerable concern to smaller customers who consequently pay higher prices, as well as to shareholders who might question the attractiveness of allowing the majority of customers to effectively subsidize the largest customers). There appears a compelling case that enhanced transparency surrounding strategic account relationships would help to reinforce an ethos of ethical behaviour by executives.

There might also be appeal, given the strategic significance of large customers to suppliers, in providing a simple ethical framework for managers to consider. Here we draw on the recent work of Plender and Persaud (2006), who propose that developing an ethical culture surrounding a corporate issue may be approached more effectively by senior managers routinely asking probing questions about the nature and consequences of decisions being made, than by adopting formalized and complex ethical guidelines that reduce business ethics to a 'box ticking' exercise. In the area of strategic account management and strategy, such interrogation might take the form of such questions as:

- Who are all the people affected by the strategic account relationship with this customer – employees, managers, shareholders, competitors, other third parties, and the wider community and environment?
- Does this customer relationship actually or potentially cause harm to any of those affected, beyond the acceptable effects of fair competition? Are there reasonable things we can and should do to avoid or compensate for this harm?
- Has our behaviour been deceptive? Would you regard it that way if you were in any of the other stakeholders' positions?
- Are there disguised conflicts of interest between parties to the strategic account relationship, shareholders and those affected by the customer relationship?
- If everyone behaved in the way we are behaving, what would happen? If harm would result from everyone treating customers, third parties and shareholders as we are doing, should we refrain from continuing this customer relationship in its current form?

In addition, such questions should be incorporated in the training and development of executives for strategic account management positions, and addressed in personal appraisals. It has been suggested that in addition to the role of codes of ethics and ethical policies to promote ethical practice, one major impact on achieving ethical standards in marketing can be achieved by encouraging executives to consider the importance of ethics as a determinant of business success (Singhapakadi 1999). Asking questions becomes more significant if the questions are perceived to address issues that are truly important to executives.

However, while advances may be made through greater transparency and designing training and development activities that help executives to identify ethical issues in the situations they face, and to develop appropriate ethical responses, as well as designing evaluation and compensation plans that motivate and reward ethical behaviour (Roman and Ruiz 2005), this does not address the proposal that organizational conduct relies on top management leadership. Indeed, one long-standing argument in marketing is that because of its importance, ethics should be made an explicit and integral part of the strategic planning process (Robin and Reidenbach 1987; Wotruba 1990).

In the broader terms of developing appropriate governance mechanisms for new types of buyer–seller relationships, Daboub and Calton (2002) underline the importance of emerging frameworks, such as: (1) global corporate citizenship, emphasizing the links between financial performance, social performance, sustainability and environmental performance, to address the claims and rights of all stakeholders (Waddock 2002; Wood and Logsdon 2002); (2) the integrated social contracting theory of economic ethics, concerned with generating ethical norms appropriate to particular economic groupings, for example in the form of specific corporate- to industry-wide codes of ethics (Donaldson and Dunfee 1999); and (3) stakeholder learning dialogues, as a way of handling complex, interdependent and awkward problems, involving the social construction by shareholders of a trust-based form of governance (Daboub and Calton 2002). Approaches of these kinds provide mechanisms for addressing ethical concerns across partnered organizations, but also involving business leaders as well as more junior executives.

Certainly, Daboub and Calton (2002) provide an optimistic point to conclude. They underline the potential for developing relationships and culture for new organizational forms, such as buyer–seller collaboration, that are not only functional in delivering business success but are also consistent with legal and ethical norms. They stress the goal of governance that includes the voices of all stakeholders, particularly those with legitimate moral claims, but without the power to establish those claims. The challenge here is for managers to respond to these challenges in strategic account management.

SAM and corporate social responsibility

We now turn our attention to another dimension to the integrity and social standing of business that is also relevant to broadening the SAM concept, in the form of corporate social responsibility. Certainly, there is plenty of evidence that interest and concerns about ethics and social responsibility are escalating rapidly in importance for business organizations throughout the world, impacting on SAM and other new business models. In part these issues are driven by the belief that businesses should behave in an ethical way because it is the right thing to do, but also that they should deliver social benefits as well as meeting business goals. Importantly, perceptions of a seller's ethical standing and social contribution can have a direct impact on its attractiveness to customers and their willingness to buy (Piercy and Lane 2009, 2011). For this reason ethics and social responsibility questions are increasingly significant to the creation of effective customer relationships, the central issue in effective SAM.

The expanding scope and domain of CSR

As conventionally understood, corporate social responsibility spans economic, legal, ethical and philanthropic concerns by an organization and its stakeholders (Carroll 1991). The objective is a favourable impact on society and eliminating or reducing the negative effects which a business may have. Importantly, while at one time mainly an issue of 'corporate philanthropy', or entirely a question of moral obligation or pure altruism, CSR has been increasingly recognized as a source of competitive advantage, as well as an important part of how competitive relationships operate (Porter and Kramer 2002).

From this perspective, CSR encompasses company activities that integrate social and environmental concerns into business operations, and into the company's interaction with other stakeholders, on a voluntary basis (Piercy and Lane 2009). Importantly, the 21st century has seen issues of social responsibility and the morality and ethics of company practices become key elements in managing customer relationships and particularly how companies are perceived and understood by their customers. Nonetheless, research suggests that an integrated approach to CSR in marketing is largely missing in both theory and practice (Maignan et al. 2005).

Factors underpinning the growing attention by executives to issues of corporate social responsibility are the new concerns and expectations of consumers, public authorities and investors in the context of globalization and industrial change; social criteria increasingly influencing the investment decisions of individuals and institutions; increased concern about the damage caused by economic and business activity to the physical environment; and the transparency of business activities brought about by media and new information and communication technologies (Commission of the European Communities 2001).

Business norms across the world have moved CSR into the mainstream of business practice. Non-governmental organizations such as the World Resources Institute (WRI), AccountAbility, Global Reporting Initiative (GRI), International Standards Organization (ISO 14000) and the United Nations all have major initiatives aimed at improving the social involvement and performance of the world's business community (Godfrey and Natch 2007). Indeed, there is an increasingly widespread view that sustainability is now the key driver of innovation for companies (Nidumolo et al. 2009).

Central interests in CSR in business strategy include the impact of ethical and social performance on corporate reputation, the growing role of ethical consumerism in shaping new market segments and the demands for higher ethical standards and social initiatives placed on suppliers by business-to-business customers (Piercy and Lane 2011).

Already, some companies have made high-profile efforts to position themselves as socially responsible as an explicit part of their strategy. Some go even further in advocating the combination of business and social goals. Rosabeth Moss Kanter (2009) uses the term 'vanguard companies' to describe those that are ahead of the rest and provide a model for the future, because they aspire to be both big and human, efficient but innovative, global but concerned about local communities, using their power and influence to develop solutions to problems the public cares about. She concludes from her studies of companies such as IBM, Procter & Gamble, Publicis, Cemex and Diageo that humanistic values and attention to societal needs provide the starting point for effective strategy in the global information age. Nonetheless, social purpose creates strategic advantages because those social commitments have an economic logic that attracts resources to the firm (Moss Kanter 2009).

Another view is that the key issue is the search for business models that create shared value. Porter and Kramer (2011) propose an extension to earlier views of CSR and argue that societal needs, not just economic needs, define markets, and that viewing markets through the lens of shared value opens up innovation and growth opportunities. Their logic also rests on closely linking social goals with business goals. They define shared value as policies and operating practices that enhance a company's competitiveness while simultaneously improving the economic and social conditions in the communities in which the company operates. They argue that creating shared value supersedes CSR. Shared value initiatives are under way at companies such as Google, IBM, Intel, Johnson & Johnson, Unilever and Wal-Mart.

Addressing societal concerns can provide major productivity improvements for the firm. For example, by reducing its packaging and cutting 100 million miles from its trucks' delivery routes, Wal-Mart both lowered carbon emissions and saved $200 million in costs. Shared value opportunities are created from re-conceiving products and markets and redefining productivity in the value chain.

In short, the scope of CSR has gone way beyond just meeting society's new standards, to become an essential part of how we compete and of the relationships between sellers and strategic customers (Hooley et al. 2012). For example, it is no small matter when companies like Wal-Mart and Unilever look to the Rainforest Alliance to certify the coffee and tea they sell (Skapinker 2008).

CSR and SAM relationships

In the new business environment, CSR may be linked to effective SAM in several ways that illustrate both the potential threat to strategic customer relationships and emerging opportunities to make those relationships more sustainable and effective.

Becoming toxic

In many sectors, strident demands from business-to-business customers for their suppliers to implement CSR policies and initiatives that are acceptable to the customer organization are escalating rapidly. In fact, at one extreme, a poor corporate reputation – regarding handling of suppliers and customers, honesty and fairness in deals, behaviour towards the environment, the working standards for employees in the value chain, and so on – can actually make a company toxic. Customers may reject a supplier because they do not want to be contaminated by association and to face the criticisms of their own customers and shareholders. This risk is avoided by buying and partnering with others.

The 'vendor compliance' programme at Target Corporation is illustrative. Purchasing officers are required to uphold Target Corporation social responsibility standards wherever they buy in the world, even when these exceed the requirements of local laws. Target engineers inspect suppliers' factories not just for product quality but also for labour rights and employment conditions. Similarly,

Home Depot, the American DIY chain, insists that all its wood products are sourced from suppliers who can provide verifiable evidence of their sound forest management practices. Home Depot is one of the largest buyers of wood products in the country, and the company wants to be seen as taking a strong position on sustainability (Senge et al. 2008).

Companies like Target and Home Depot are no longer unusual in giving attention to the ethical and social responsibility standards demanded of their suppliers throughout the world. Recently, Gap withdrew a line of children's clothes from its shelves, following allegations of forced child labour at Indian subcontractors. In common with other clothes retailers, Gap monitors the behaviour of suppliers in its value chain, and in 2007 it stopped working with 23 factories (Johnson and van Duyn 2007).

At its simplest, one test of the robustness of a SAM relationship is becoming the acceptability of the supplier to the buyer on an array of ethical and social issues. Relationships are not likely to survive failure of that test.

Competitive disadvantage

The very real business risk tied up in this is that judgements of supplier ethical standards and commitment to social responsibility are increasingly linked to the attractiveness as a supplier and as a candidate for a strategic relationship. This is a particular disadvantage when competing suppliers are more attractive in these terms. Quite simply, a supplier's value offering may be undermined because of its company CSR position. Buyers will either genuinely not want to do business because of what you stand for, or they will not want to buy or partner for fear of sin by association – they do not want to be castigated by their own sharehold-ers or by the media and lobby groups for doing so. When other suppliers can evidence superiority in ethical and social contributions, this may be a decisive competitive advantage.

For example, in the USA, many large companies, including Microsoft, already insist on good diversity practices from suppliers, and are reducing or terminating the business they do with suppliers who fail to heed requests to diversify their workforces. Indeed, while many US-based multi-nationals have adopted volun-tary corporate responsibility initiatives to self-regulate their overseas social and environmental practices, pressures mount for more active involvement of the US government in mandating such regulation (Aaronson 2005). British-based com-panies that operate 'supplier diversity policies' include Morgan Stanley, BAA, and car rental group Avis Budget (Taylor 2007). Suppliers unable or unwilling to meet the social responsibilities defined by major customers stand the considerable risk of losing those customers, notwithstanding the existence of a strategic relationship.

Similarly, in the UK, the late 2000s and early 2010s saw an 'environmental arms race' between retailers, each claiming to be greener than the other. Marks & Spencer's announcement that it intended to be carbon neutral led to claims from Tesco that it would carbon label all its products, and similar eco-promises from

Sainsbury's. While responding to competitors' CSR moves may not always be the best approach, the strategic significance of CSR to competitive positioning and buyer–seller relationships is growing.

Building attractiveness for strategic customers

A strong corporate reputation driven by CSR initiatives may make a supplier more attractive than competitors to some customers, because they benefit by being associated with these initiatives in the eyes of their stakeholders. In that sense, CSR adds to the value of the relationship. It provides the customer with an assurance of the supplier's good standing and that it is safe to deal with them without risking their own reputation.

Leading computer supplier Dell Inc faces challenges in rebuilding its value proposition after losing market leadership to the competition. Dell is leveraging its distinctive competitive competences in initiatives with both business and social benefits – using the strengths of its direct business model to generate collective efforts to reduce energy consumption and protect the environment. The initiative centres on improving the efficiency of IT products, reducing the harmful materials used in them and cooperating with customers to dispose of old products. Dell's environmental strategy focuses on three areas: creating easy, low-cost ways for businesses to do better in protecting the environment – providing, for example, global recycling and product recovery programmes for customers, with participation requiring little effort on their part; taking creative approaches to lessen the environmental impact of products from design to disposal – helping customers to take full advantage of new, energy-saving technology and processes, and advising on upgrades of legacy systems to reduce electricity usage; and looking to partnership with governments to promote environmental stewardship. The link between this CSR initiative and the company's business model, value proposition and relationships with major corporate customers is clear.

Partnering with strategic customers in social initiatives

It is likely that many CSR initiatives will be based on partnerships between organizations rather than a single organization acting on its own (Senge et al. 2008). For example, Microsoft partners with governments in less developed countries to offer Microsoft Windows and Office software packages for $3 to governments that subsidize the cost of computers for schoolchildren. The potential business benefit for Microsoft is to double the number of PC users worldwide and to reinforce the company's market growth. The social benefit is the greater investment in technology in some of the poorest countries in the world, with the goal of improving living standards and reducing global inequality. Similarly, many of Unilever's CSR initiatives involve collaboration with governmental and non-governmental organizations throughout the world.

The collaborative nature of CSR initiatives in many sectors underlines the potential for incorporating CSR into the SAM business model as a way of matching buyer and seller aspirations and reinforcing the strength of the relationships between them.

Nonetheless, while CSR-based relationships between buyers and sellers are an attractive way of building sustainable, long-term relationships, and at the same time responding to demands for integrity and social benefit in business models, a note of caution should be sounded. Even the pursuit of corporate social responsibility initiatives on a collaborative basis potentially raises several antitrust issues.

The pursuit of corporate social responsibility initiatives has led to several industry-based alliances to tackle environmental and social risks – for example, Hewlett-Packard, Dell, IBM and others have launched an industry code of conduct for suppliers; big brands like Mattel and Hasbro have said their suppliers must meet the jointly agreed standards of the International Council of Toy Industries. The idea is to pool experience and to reduce the inefficiencies when all companies in a sector attempt to individually audit suppliers' environmental and employment practices. Nonetheless, the collaborative nature of these arrangements means participants must pay attention to competition legislation. If companies are regarded as too deeply entwined, regulators may find that competition between them has weakened and take action.

Industry alliances for any purpose must avoid certain key behaviours: market manipulation – corporate alliances must demonstrate that their joint activities do not lead to price fixing or other forms of market limitation; boycotts – codes of conduct must be voluntary and individual companies must address issues of breach of the code by suppliers; and benefits – an alliance should demonstrate the low risk of anti-competitive harm and pro-competitive benefits and efficiencies to be gained. Indeed, in North America, alliances can seek an official 'comfort letter' from bodies like the US Justice Department stating the authority does not intend to challenge the activities of the alliance.

While CSR initiatives offer a way of demonstrating both social responsibility and general contributions to meeting societal needs, they must not be implemented in ways that can be regarded as anti-competitive' (Murray 2006; Wright 2006).

Conclusions

Our focus here has been on the relationships between suppliers and large, often situationally powerful customers, which are at the centre of SAM models. Our goal was to broaden the SAM model to incorporate dimensions related to ethical and moral concerns and the related impact of corporate social responsibility on buyer–seller relationships. The first part of the paper started with the observation that the ethical and moral issues implicit in SAM relationships have been largely ignored by the literature, perhaps because of the relative newness of the SAM approach, and perhaps because of the somewhat different scope of the model.

First, we raised questions about the moral attractiveness of a business model that favours the few (large customers) at the expense of the many (smaller customers, shareholders, third parties). Indeed, the relationships formed may even move into the forms of anti-competitive behaviours, which are unlawful. The morality of business decisions being made on the basis of the unbridled use of bargaining power by buyers, and the consequent concessions from suppliers, with scant regard to the harm caused to others, appears questionable. The evidence suggests also that those entering into such relationships should be aware that implied promises of loyalty and partnership may be an illusion, suggesting that economic consequences may also be unattractive in some cases.

Second, we considered the consequences of strategic account management relationships between suppliers and their large customers, albeit that some of those consequences may have been unintended. We suggest that the more harmful consequences of strategic account relationships appear to be neglected or perhaps unimagined by those establishing this type of business model. Whether those (unintentionally) harmed are employees, managers, competitors or society at large, there appear to be major ethical concerns about a business model that produces such consequences.

Third, we examined the potentially unfair and harmful impact of strategic account management on executives responsible for the implementation of this strategy, concerning primarily the potential for hidden incentives for unethical behaviour.

We suggest that the ethical and moral dilemmas in strategic account management approaches, and more generally in the relationships between suppliers and large customers, should be made more explicit, i.e. that management should make efforts to heighten the moral intensity surrounding these relationships. The ethical climate of strategic account relationships could also be enhanced by far greater transparency and openness and the pursuit by management of basic questions of fair and ethical conduct with those executives responsible for strategic account relationships. Progress could be made by recognizing moral and ethical issues in the training and development of executives for these management roles, as well as reflecting ethical standards of behaviour in evaluation and reward approaches. However, the underlying issue is more broadly about developing governance systems that address the impact of increasingly common inter-organizational business models on all stakeholders in the value chain, and that address issues of ethical and moral behaviour as well as economic interests.

In the second part of the paper, we turned to the related issue of the societal dimension of SAM, as it related to corporate social responsibility initiatives. At one level, it is clear that the minimum acceptable standards for ethical behaviour and social impact in business organizations have increased and continue to do so. Some of the behaviours of the past and denial of social responsibility are no longer sustainable by companies pursuing market success. Yet some of the case examples we have examined of 'vanguard companies' and a push for 'creating shared value' in new business models point the way to something more exciting than compliance and defensiveness. They underline the real and pragmatic potential for business models that deliver against both social and ethical mandates and against commercial business goals. However, we retain the argument that a starting point in linking CSR initiatives more closely to strategic marketing imperatives lies in the concept of customer value and particularly the development of value propositions built around CSR which resonate with customer priorities and needs. We argue that CSR will be important to strategic relationships with customers from several perspectives: the danger of becoming toxic and unattractive to the buyer because of poor CSR performance; the risk of competitive disadvantage if competitors can offer a better match with a customer's CSR aspirations and goals; but the opportunity to build real competitive edge based on matching CSR with customer strategy and partnering to deliver both commercial and social benefits.

While not welcomed wholeheartedly by all executives, we believe there is growing evidence that CSR will be a significant way of how business is done in the future, with particular implications for successful SAM.

SECTION 2

VALUE CREATION THROUGH KSAM

Value in strategic account management

BY ANTONELLA LA ROCCA AND IVAN SNEHOTA

Abstract

Strategic account management (SAM) is responsible for adding value to customers and capturing value for the supplier in customer relationships. It is generally accepted that effective account management is vital for generating value in relationships with strategic accounts. The authors integrate this idea by examining value creation in business relationships, arguing that value is generated in interaction between the supplier and the customer, rather than within the supplier organization. This aspect of the value-generating process in business relationships affects the task of SAM and calls for specific skills. Since the task of managing strategic accounts involves allocating resources and efforts in the relationships, and enabling the customer to create value together with the supplier, understanding the relational interaction and the interaction skills involved is crucial to SAM.

Introduction

While few will contest the premise that strategic account management is about profit and not just about revenues, opinions on how to grow profits from strategic accounts and how to manage them are seldom made explicit, and when they are spelled out, they tend to vary a great deal. This paper starts by assuming that the profitability of an account for the supplier company is related to the value created in the relationship between the customer and the supplier, and examines how that is achieved in companies operating in business markets. The authors first explore the value-creating process in relationships with truly strategic customers that, given the limits on management attention, can number only a few, and then discuss the capabilities and skills required to create value in relationships with such strategic accounts.

Effective business strategy, particularly in business markets, hinges on creating economic value for and with strategic customers. Analysing, conceiving and delivering value in relationships with strategic accounts requires systematic account management. This has been traditionally credited with the responsibility of adding value to customers by coordinating activities within the own organization and, more recently, the activities in the relationship between the parties. This paper will develop this idea further and integrate it by examining the value-creation process and then outlining how competent strategic account management can enhance value-creation performance in customer–supplier relationships.

The authors build on the idea that value is co-created in a relationship between the supplier and customer, rather than produced by the supplier and then delivered to the customer (Vargo and Lusch 2008). Consequently, the article specifically examines how relational factors that go beyond the product service content of the relationship actually concur in generating value and how they are linked to value performance in a relationship. Starting from the idea that value generating is a multi-dimensional construct (Grönroos 2011), the authors examine three factors of value performance – cost efficiency, relational quality and innovativeness (Jaworski and Kohli 1993) – from the supplier's and the customer's perspective. This part is wound up by identifying the critical managerially-relevant value-generating processes and then explores effective managerial practices in generating value in customer relationships. This emphasizes that effective value-generating practices go beyond the coordination of ongoing activities, and in particular implies integrating the customer's operations with own activities at various levels and on various objects in order to develop novel solutions. Against the background of effective value-creation practices in business relationships, the authors conclude by discussing the competencies and capabilities required for strategic account management.

The changing role of strategic account management

The changing role of SAM is best discussed against the background of a major shift taking place in the sales management landscape. Sales management is increasingly taking a relational rather than a transactional focus, particularly in business-to-business (B2B) markets where there has been a shift in sales management from an emphasis on closing the deal to a relationship selling approach (Moncrief and Marshall 2005). Relationship selling means that salespeople have a key role in the formation of buyer–seller relationships (e.g. Piercy 2006). Indeed, selling companies increasingly seek a greater level of partnership with their most important accounts, and that has spawned interest in strategic account management (Leigh and Marshall 2001). The importance of account management in business and industrial markets derives from the fact that in such markets not all customers are equal and that a few customers (often no more than a handful) represent a dominant part (often more than two thirds) of the sales revenues of companies operating in such markets (Håkansson and Snehota 1995; Sheth and Parvatiyar 2002).

This shift has implications for marketing practice in the B2B field as suppliers pay more attention to the maintenance and enhancement of specific relationships with selected customers (Napolitano 1997). Managers are becoming increasingly eager to understand and manage the quality of individual business relationships as well as the whole portfolio of relationships (Cater and Cater 2010). Furthermore, suppliers find it very difficult to differentiate themselves from competitors solely on the basis of product quality (Ulaga 2003) and the focus of differentiation is shifting to building unique relationships with business partners.

Experience of handling key accounts has taught that approaching strategic accounts strategically is anything but simple since these are, as the Strategic Account Management Association (SAMA) suggests, 'complex accounts with special requirements, characterized by a centralized, coordinated purchasing organization with multi-location purchasing influences, a complex buying process, large purchases, and a need for special services' (in Storbacka 2012, p. 259). Furthermore, the complexity of the purchasing organization is often mirrored by the complexity of the supplier organization that often supplies multiple products or product lines from several production sites with various complementary services and administrative and logistical arrangements. This complexity, on both the customer and the supplier side, makes the relationship content multi-faceted and complex.

Difficulty in managing strategic accounts is related to this complexity of relationships in terms of products/services transacted and to the number of interacting individuals. As the complexity of customer–supplier relationships increases, considerable management effort is needed (and is actually spent) on coordinating various activities both internally within the supplier organization and externally between the customer and supplier organizations, and in relationships with other suppliers and customers. Experience from the practice of key account management shows that the most important ingredients of effective account management are the coordination of key personnel intra-firm (Lambe and Spekman 1997), minimizing conflict and improving communication between buyer and seller (Barrett 1986) and generally coordinating activities effectively (Workman et al. 2003). But managing the business relationship with a strategic account entails more than coordinating existing activities; it involves, in particular, conceiving, developing and providing new solutions that customers value. At the same time, managing strategic accounts is not only a matter of suppliers' programmes or strategies because in business markets customer value is not produced by the supplier and subsequently delivered to the customer; rather, it is co-created interactively between the supplier and the customer (Vargo and Lusch 2008).

In marketing practice, a boundary-spanning function such as strategic account management has an important role in relationships with customers and in creating value in these relationships. The complexity of relationships with 'strategic accounts' makes the strategic management of these critical for a company's overall market performance, and the supplier's competence and ability to manage strategic customers appears to be positively correlated with market performance (Berghman et al. 2006; Bowman and Narayandas 2004; Sullivan et al. 2012). As B2B firms are increasingly moving from transactional to relational logic, scholars acknowledge that the role of sales has to reflect the relational nature of sales processes (Sheth and Sharma 2008). However, the view of sales prevailing in the extant literature, that sales contribute to conceiving, producing and delivering customer value by understanding customers' and/or sellers' needs and fulfilling them with the bundle of goods and services fitting these needs (e.g. Weitz and Bradford 1999), remains transactional.

The situation is similar for SAM. SAM is moving towards a relational perspective, similar to the way sales has done. However, although the management of strategic accounts revolves around value creation, recent research that addresses the issue of value has been limited to a few studies (Pardo et al. 2006; Storbacka 2012). The role of SAM in the creation of value in business relationships appears underresearched and remains somewhat ambiguous. It deserves to be examined more systematically. In the next section, the paper starts from the way in which the value concept is currently presented in the marketing literature in general, and in industrial marketing in particular, in order to provide a framework for value generation in strategic customer relationships.

Value in business relationships

Understanding the factors that influence the value of an account (a customer) can help to allocate the account management efforts across various activities more effectively. While most decisions in management practice are taken with reference to the economic value of the various alternatives considered, the concept of value is not always easy to translate in business practice even if it is intuitively appealing. This section therefore starts by taking a closer look at the idea and meaning of value.

The concept of value

In marketing literature, value is traditionally defined as a bi-partite construct consisting of benefits and sacrifices. Traditionally, the concept of value has been defined as the trade-off between the benefits and costs of ownership (Monroe 1990; Zeithaml 1988). In business markets, value to the customer is commonly defined as 'the perceived worth in monetary units of the set of economic, technical, service and social benefits received by a customer firm in exchange for the price paid for a product offering' (Anderson and Narus 1999, p. 5). The traditional notion of value in exchange assumes that value is embodied in the products and services that are conceived, designed, produced and delivered to customers. This notion is linked to a rational sequence of uncovering the needs, devising solutions, producing the solutions and transferring them to customers in exchange for something else.

When value is defined as the consequences of ownership (and use) one tends to overlook that value depends on the subject of value for whom one considers the consequences, and cannot be simply unequivocally derived from the object (Holbrook 1994; Monroe 1990; Woodruff 1997). Even when value refers strictly to economic value, the value is not given from the object of exchange as such, but always related to the subject and its context, which has interesting implications. As value is related to the consequences for 'a subject' it means that it is also dependent on the knowledge, understanding and perception the subject has of the consequences. Furthermore, it is the expected rather than the actual value that is a reference for behaviours and decisions in business and in markets. Value is linked to knowledge, perceptions and expectations, and assessing value involves 'a judgment comparing what was received (e.g. performance) to the acquisition costs (e.g. financial, psychological, effort)' (Oliver 1997, p. 28).

Value is thus subjective and dependent on subjects' knowledge and perceptions with regard to consequences, and therefore value and value judgements are intrinsically emergent and changing. Value assessment in hindsight is different from the value expected because value subjects – people as well as organizations – evolve and change; their perceptions of the context and value of objects change, and so does their understanding of what consequences may arise. Besides, the context itself keeps changing, with consequences for the benefits and costs for the owner and user that can be derived from a product or service. Value is thus not static; it is an inherently transient entity.

The intricacy of the value concept is certainly a reason why it is common in business not to assess value analytically but to use norms and heuristics to assess and measure value. Indeed, in business practice many improvements are about putting to the fore aspects and consequences previously ignored or neglected and linking these to economic outcomes.

Value of a business relationship

The relational turn in marketing and sales literature has spawned interest among B2B marketing scholars for modelling and measuring the value of

Table 1: Economic consequences of supplier relationships

Relationship costs	Relationship benefits
Direct procurement costs	Cost benefits
Direct transaction costs	Revenue benefits
Relationship-handling costs	
Supply-handling costs	

Source: Gadde and Snehota, 2000

customer–supplier relationships (Anderson and Narus 1998; Lindgren and Wynstra 2005; Palmatier 2008; Ulaga and Eggert 2006). Adopting the relational perspective has set in motion considerable efforts to rethink the value-generating process, acknowledging that value originates in relationships rather than being embodied in products or services transacted between buyers and sellers (Gadde and Snehota 2000; Palmatier 2008; Payne and Holt 1999; Ulaga and Eggert 2006). The idea that inspired the bulk of the recent research on the value of business relationships is that the value of a relationship can be explained by its content and the consequences for the two companies involved.

Table 1 shows one of the models proposed in the research to frame the cost and benefit consequences for the business customer (Gadde and Snehota 2000). It classifies the customer's cost of a relationship with a supplier in direct procurement costs (mainly the price paid for the goods or services purchased), direct transaction costs (costs of carrying out the transaction, e.g. various logistics costs such as packaging and transport and stocking, order processing and other administrative costs), relationship-handling costs (broadly, the cost of personal and impersonal communication) and supply-handling costs (cost of the infrastructure for handling the purchasing). It also suggests that there are two types of benefits that a business customer derives from a supplier relationship: revenue benefits and cost benefits. The former includes consequences for the customer's own product and market performance, which translates into increased revenues. The latter consists of cost savings that the supplier relationship in question permits; these can involve the direct product costs and/or various indirect cost items.

Similar models have been proposed for the value of a relationship to a supplier but these are used much less commonly (e.g. Turnbull and Zolkiewski 1997). The value of the relationship to a supplier includes various factors that go beyond current profitability and should include the potential of the existing relationship and the estimated pay-offs from alternative levels of involvement in the relationship and in other relationships of the supplier company. The economic value of the customer is not easy to assess; it is linked to customer attractiveness and reflects benefits other than the direct monetary revenue stream from the customer and its profitability (La Rocca et al. 2012). In assessing the economic value of a customer, development effects and consequences of the relationship for other customer relationships of the supplier must also be considered.

The value of a customer relationship to a supplier and that of a supplier relationship to the customer in business markets derives from how the supplier's and the customer's operations are connected (Cespedes 1995). Tuli et al. (2007) have shown that benefits and costs to customers stem from solutions applied in the relationship, and these originate in a set of customer–supplier relational processes such as understanding and defining mutual requirements, integrating goods and services, and deploying various support activities. Value consequences of a relationship for both the supplier and customer depend on the solutions and arrangements for how operations of the two companies are linked. In this sense, the value originates in linkages and interactions between the parties in the relationship (Edvardsson et al. 2011; Grönroos 2011) and relationships have a distinct and different value for each of the parties. Value of the relationship depends on how the content of the relationship has been configured in various aspects including, but going beyond, the product and service offered.

Arguing that value consequences, both costs and benefits, originate from numerous elements beyond the goods exchanged and stem from what is going on in the relationship and in connected relationships, Walter et al. (2001) opine that 'despite the growing trend toward considering and using business relationships as means of value creation, the marketing literature is deficient in some important ways' (p. 366). First of all, the actual economic value of a solution is always relative to the context of reference and never absolute. A crucial aspect of value formation in business relationships is that solutions in business relationships are not conceived and implemented a priori by one of the parties; rather they are outcomes emerging from joint action (Dhanaraj and Parkhe 2006; Perks and Moxey 2011; Ritter and Gemünden 2003). Solutions in business relationships arise concurrently with problem identification that occurs during interactions between producers and users (Harrison and Finch 2009; Johnson and Ford 2007), which makes value dynamic rather than static.

When we consider value from the relationship perspective, what comes to the centre of attention is the interdependence of the parties to the relationship, the interactive nature of customer–supplier relationships, and the resulting dynamics of such relationships that affect the process of value generation (e.g. Ballantyne et al. 2011; Lindgren and Wynstra 2005; Ulaga and Eggert 2005; Vargo and Lusch 2004). The relational perspective on value implies other priorities and critical issues than those resulting from the traditional linear logic of conceiving, producing and delivering value. In particular, it highlights the fact that in business relationships value is actually produced in interactions that take place among the individual actors involved in the relationship (Corsaro and Snehota 2010; Edvardsson et al. 2011; Grönroos 2011). Consequently, interaction should not be interpreted as simply a means of value creation but rather as the very process of value itself, which is produced 'in between' parties (Håkansson et al. 2009; Storbacka and Nenonen 2009). Hence, conceptualizing the generation of value in business relationships has to reflect the nature and characteristics of the interaction processes going on.

Generating value in business relationships

Economic consequences of a business relationship for the supplier and the customer, and thus its value, originate in the solutions and arrangements put in place in the relationship, as these give rise to costs and benefits for both the supplier and the customer. Solutions in customer–supplier relationships in B2B markets involve myriad elements of the relationship content, such as product features' performance and quality, production volumes and methods, logistical arrangements, communication and administrative routines, and quality control procedures and financing, among others. Even in relationships of medium complexity, the solutions and arrangements are so multi-faceted that a priori blueprinting is impossible: it can even be difficult to map these in hindsight.

Since the value derives from solutions applied in the relationship, one needs to address the question as to how the various solutions emerge and are put in practice. Value generation in relationships between customer and supplier is a process of finding solutions. The content of customer–supplier relationships tends to be composite in terms of the product and the service content, activities carried out, and number of individuals involved, with their different roles and agendas. The solutions that emerge in relationships result from the complex interaction between individuals, who are often numerous, representing the two business organizations (Ford et al. 2011). They also involve connections between the customer and supplier organizations and their operations (Cespedes 1995). Numerous heterogeneous resource elements and activity flows that characterize the two businesses and their operations must be configured and interfaced.

There are always some adjustments going on in every business relationship. In most cases, the relationship content morphs relatively fast and the solutions as to how the two organized systems are related are never really stable. The continuous adjustments in customer relationships are always worked out jointly between the parties who, in turn, need to carry out various adaptations (Hallen et al. 1991). The connections between the two businesses are made in interaction between actors on both sides. Because both the cost and benefits are consequent to the interaction about solutions, interaction is the key process in generating value in business relationships.

From the supplier's point of view, interacting with customers always entails costs, but integrating the customer in their own operations can result in cost efficiencies and can be beneficial in generating ideas for new solutions and implementing them (Johnson and Ford 2007; von Hippel 1988). It has been shown that interaction intensity in business relationships is positively related to the innovativeness of the supplier business (Coviello and Joseph 2012; Hult et al. 2004). Benefits from interaction in business relationships occur because in customer–supplier relationships the 'produce perspective' is confronted with a 'use perspective' (Harrison and Waluszewski 2008; Ingemansson and Waluszewski 2009; Wilkinson and Young 2002) and the solutions emerge as various issues of concern arise and are jointly addressed. Since 'learning evolves through a combination of discoveries, positive and negative feedback and the creation of additional creative propositions' about innovation (Hoholm and Olsen 2012, p. 344), the confrontation of supplier and customer knowledge and logics favours the production of new knowledge about possible solutions (Tuli et al. 2007; Young and Freeman 2008).

Various studies of business relationships confirm that interaction is a determinant of the development of the relationship and crucial for innovation in solutions which, in turn, determine the potential value of the relationship (Håkansson et al. 2009). This aspect of generating value, although not easy to assess and measure, becomes highly relevant, particularly in relationships involving strategic accounts.

While both parties to the relationship jointly concur in generating the value of the relationship, the relationship does not have any value independent of the benefits and costs of the two parties. While the solutions and arrangement are arrived at jointly, who bears the costs and who is entitled to the benefits that can accrue is always negotiated and determined between the parties. The customer and supplier generate value jointly but the claim to the value from a relationship is always individual and distinct. For either of the two parties to a business relationship, there are always differences in terms of the appropriation of the value generated in the relationship, and thus in the economic value of a relationship (Pardo et al. 2006).

The traditional transactional perspective on value in market relationships, which tends to assume value is produced by the supplier, embodied in products and services and then transferred on to the customer, does not properly capture the more dynamic aspect of value generation in circumstances where relationships matter, as in industrial markets. Instead, taking the relational perspective leads to highlighting the interactive nature of the value-generating process and underscores that value is actually generated jointly between the supplier and customer. It also stresses the notion that the value of business relationships is dynamic rather than static, and points to the critical role of innovation in value formation. That has consequences for the role account management can play in generating value between supplier and customer businesses.

Before the implication for strategic account management is discussed, we will examine a few features of the value-generating process as they have emerged in recent research. This research has identified four facets of the process that generates solutions in business relationships and ultimately accounts for the economic consequences for the businesses involved: jointness, solution enactment, balanced initiative and socio-cognitive construction (Haas et al. 2012). The paper will first look at these and then proceed to examine the consequences these features of the value process in customer–supplier relationships are likely to have for the task of SAM and the capabilities and skills required to handle the task. The four features are interrelated but we will first treat them separately.

'Jointness'

The idea of 'jointness' as an important aspect of the value-generating process in business relationships refers to the fact that workable solutions always involve coupling and linking of resources, activities and actors of supplier and customer organizations. The notion of jointness with respect to solutions means that these cannot be operated separately by two disjointed entities; rather, they are always operated jointly by the supplier and customer.

The minimal form of jointness required in order to determine and apply any solution within relationships is the consent of the counterpart to the solution adopted and/or to eventual adaptations. However, the mutual involvement is generally deeper than that. No solution can be developed and applied, and no value can be generated in the absence of the other party, which means that value is co-created only when the parties join. For the supplier, this means no value is produced until the customer joins in the process and uses the solutions, as the value is always 'value-in-use' (Grönroos 2011). The solutions and arrangement have different value consequences for each of the parties to the relationship, but in principle, the value of relationships originates mainly in sharing and integrating resources, especially non-material resources such as skills and knowledge, between the supplier and the customer organizations (Lusch and Vargo 2006; Vargo and Lusch 2008).

Value generated for the customer and the supplier in relationships reflects not only connections and adaptations within the single specific relationship but also how the two businesses are connected to the wider network of resources, activities and actors in their own context. This is not only the customer but also the organization's partners throughout the value network who collaborate with other entities and integrate resources to provide a solution from a combination of specialized competences and complex services (Cova and Salle 2008).

Solution enactment

Jointness does not mean that the supplier and the customer necessarily fully agree and share perspectives, develop identical understanding and pursue the same goals. In practice, the way parties understand the context and their intent is likely to differ significantly. Furthermore, both the supplier and the customer act under considerable uncertainty when they identify and apply various solutions. Their uncertainties can stem from the complexity of the offering, from the continuous changes within the two related businesses, and from changes in the context of the supplier and customer business. Under such circumstances, planned action, based on thorough analysis of the situation, identification of the goals and choice of action, becomes problematic. When the individuals who act on behalf of the supplier or customer organization look for solutions to problems that arise, the encounters and interaction between those involved may provide the missing information and may help to uncover parties' tacit knowledge that is relevant for devising effective solutions. The actual solutions are 'interacted' in the sense that rather than being conceived, designed and implemented, these solutions can stem from quite divergent understanding and motivations and are actually enacted as the parties interact. Given the rate of change in customer–supplier relationships, solutions are more or less continuously re-invented.

Different streams of research have explicitly defined value creation as interactional (Haas et al. 2012; Vargo and Lusch 2008), claiming that value in business relationships is interacted. This means interaction should not be interpreted simply as a means to facilitate the value creation but rather as the very process by which value is produced 'between parties'.

The mechanism of enactment makes value relationships specific and therefore impossible to determine from the features of the relationship or of the individual actors. This idea adds to the concept of perceived value of an interactional element, as value images are enacted by the parties while they interact. Therefore, they continuously evolve as interactions unfold. Scholars who developed the Service-Dominant Logic (SDL) framework (Vargo and Lusch 2004, 2008) tend to highlight that with multi-sided or reciprocal propositions (Ballantyne et al. 2011) there are no longer any message makers and message transmitters. Instead, we see participants in interactive communication processes in which (latent) customer requirements and (unanticipated) solutions emerge through a mutually creative constructed dialogue. The perspectives of at least two parties are linked in a business relationship in reciprocal promises, while each party looks for an equitable exchange (Ballantyne and Varey 2006).

Balanced initiative

The initiatives of the supplier and customer in defining solutions are more balanced than is usually thought. In marketing literature in general it is common to assume that the seller/supplier takes the initiative and responsibility for the development of various solutions to be offered to the customer and strives to control the marketing process for the organization's own advantage. The role of customers is assumed to be that of a passive 'price-and-offering taker', albeit a competent one who knows what their needs and desired solutions are and who is looking for the most efficient supplier of such solutions. This view of the initiative between the buyer and seller is related to the idea that solutions (as bundles of products and services) are first conceived, then produced and finally sold and transferred to the customer. This is not a realistic picture of what is going on in customer–supplier relationships in business markets, where it has long been recognized that customers tend to play an active part in the process by which effective solutions are brought about and often come to play a major role in identifying and producing such solutions (Levitt 1960; Webster 1984).

Recent research clearly shows evidence that the solutions' effectiveness is not related to supplier-controlled variables only, but several customer-related variables concur in defining the solutions (Tuli et al. 2007). Customers in business markets, certainly those in strategically relevant relationships, are not simply passive price-and-offering takers; rather, they often lead the development of the relationship and its content (Johnson and Ford 2007). It is not a rare occurrence for customers to take the initiative and define most of the solutions regarding the way in which the product features are defined, the production process is organized, the control procedures are executed, and how administrative routines are configured, and so on. The development of a solution entails a set of relational processes from the requirement definition to after-sales support in which customers' involvement is critical. Customers' involvement limits the supplier's autonomy because the effectiveness of the solution depends on several customer variables and is not related to supplier variables only (Tuli et al. 2007).

Socio-cognitive construction

The role played by knowledge-related factors in generating value leads to the consideration that value generation in business relationships involves 'socio-cognitive construction'. It has been shown that the assessment of a solution's value is not a linear function of the qualities or attributes of a certain offering or of a certain relationship; value judgements depend on individual perceptions and interpretations that parties hold of situations and of the consequences of adopting certain solutions (Corsaro and Snehota 2010; Vargo and Lusch 2008) to such an extent that one can talk about value images. The link of value to cognitive factors and perceptions means that a strictly objective determination of value in relationships is ruled out; in customer–supplier relationships value is a product of individual perceptions rather than a function of the qualities or attributes of a certain offering (Lamont 1955) or of a certain relationship.

This resonates well with the argument in service marketing that 'value is always uniquely and phenomenologically determined by the beneficiary' (Vargo and Lusch 2008, p. 7). In mundane terms this means that the value of a relationship is in the eye of the beholder and that what parties see is never a given because the perceptions and interpretations are formed in the various interactions in which a party is involved. This also means that since parties tend to have different and unique positions in other relationships, their understanding of the implications of a certain solution's effects will be different and likely to lead to different reactions.

Value images are formed as parties interact and each develops their own idea about which are the key value elements. As parties interact they both learn and teach each other about solution consequences and thus form value judgements. This mutual learning and teaching actually amounts to creating value. Consequently, narratives become particularly important sense-making tools through which actors construct their reality and express their idea of value (Weick 1995). In a wider context it has been argued that 'markets are ideas and activities that exist because actors in the context seek to get access to new resources that they can integrate with their other socio-cultural resources in order to create value' (Storbacka and Nenonen 2010, p. 2). Parties to a relationship negotiate and define mutual obligations and responsibilities, which has consequences for how the value generated becomes appropriated between the partners. The dependence of value on the socio-cognitive elements means that interactive communication impacting the understanding, interpretations and perceptions that those involved have of the consequences of given solutions assumes an important role in creating value.

The four features of the value-creation process in business relationships with strategically relevant customers discussed above have consequences for account management. They affect the task of strategic account management and have implications for the skills and capabilities required to cope with the value-generating process in customer relationships. Considering SAM as a function that is in principle accountable for generating value in relationships with strategic customers, one can turn to the question of how these features of the value-generating process affect the task and practices of SAM.

Managing value generation in strategic account relationships

The very idea of account management stems from concerns about coordinating various activities of the supplier at the interface of the own organization with an important customer in order to create incremental value in customer relationships (Georges and Eggert 2003; Pardo et al. 2006; Workman et al. 2003). Since several different organizational units such as production, research and development, procurement, marketing, sales, technical support, logistics and administration are more or less directly involved with the corresponding functions of the customer, such interface activities can be numerous and entail substantial costs. Tighter coordination of such activities can prevent conflicting and dysfunctional behaviours, enhancing the relationship quality and making the involvement of various functions more cost efficient. Coordinating the various activities is certainly an important contribution of account management to generating value in and from customer relationships.

While the coordination function within the own organization that makes relationships more cost efficient is important in account management, there are two other aspects that are important for the formation of value in relationships: interdependences and interaction in customer–supplier relationships. The first is related to the need to coordinate not only activities within the own organization but also the joint activities with the customer (Napolitano 1997). Extending the task of coordination from the internal activities of the supplier to joint activities is highly relevant for the economic outcomes of the relationship for both the supplier and the customer as it affects both parties' relationship costs and the relationship quality.

The second aspect is related to the need to continuously adjust existing solutions and thus develop the relationship. Such adaptations require developing novel solutions and involve a certain degree of innovation that can become highly significant for the economic outcomes of the relationship for the supplier and the customer. Innovation in relationships with customers tends to be positive and significant for the development of the supplier business (Hult et al. 2004; von Hippel 1988). Because the economic consequences of coordinating joint activities and innovative relationship solutions can be more significant than the cost-efficiency effects of internal coordination, the extension of the coordination from internal to joint activities and from managing existing solutions to developing new ones is highly relevant for strategic account management.

The task of account management in a company's main business relationships can best be described and defined as *relating* the own and customer's organizations, rather than simply coordinating existing activities. Relating involves connecting different resources and activities of two organizations and adjusting and developing existing connections. The issues that need to be addressed in this process of relating are likely to be so numerous that it is impossible to establish a priori a blueprint for the configuration of the relationship, and the problems that arise cannot be addressed and solved unilaterally. Relating the own and customer organization is demanding because the solutions are conceived and implemented between customer and supplier in an interactive process that usually starts from the 'unknown' and proceeds to a tangible configuration of the relationship on which its economic outcomes depend. Developing an economically viable relationship implies not simply listening to customer requests and adapting to these; it requires 'bringing the customer into' the value-generating process and integrating the customer's operations with own operations – making the customer create value. Relating involves a process of reciprocal enactment (Danneels 2003) between the customer and the supplier. Relating implies building the supplier's offering, but the customer's involvement means trade-offs between the own and the counterpart's short- and long-term costs, and benefits need to be addressed and settled.

Regardless of how economically and strategically convenient and advantageous the configuration of a relationship is, it is never accomplished, and the need to adapt the solutions in the relationship is, in principle, never-ending. Connecting the two related systems of the supplier and the customer is not a single event but a process of *adapting* over time since the network context and consequently the relationship are in perpetual motion. This process of adapting follows the evolving issues and problems each company faces in its operations. There are always reasons to modify the existing offering, either internal to the relationship, to improve its performance or economics, or external, to relate it to the other relationships of the counterparts or the evolving network. Because of the mutual adaptations, the development of the two companies' resources follows a particular path, their activities become more or less specialized and the two actors co-evolve their ways of working (Ford et al. 2011; Håkansson et al. 2009; Sanchez et al. 2010). What makes relationships with the main customers strategically relevant and important is that these involve unique interaction processes that result in unique relationships that will significantly affect the supplier's current economic performance and are critical for the supplier's future performance potential.

The broadening of the scope of account management towards relating rather than activity coordinating, especially with respect to strategically relevant customers, makes the task of SAM more demanding. Managing relating is challenging because developing a viable relationship and offering involves combining elements of the activities, resources of the supplier and the customer, as well as the actions of different individual actors in the two companies into a configuration that will be functionally feasible and economically sustainable. Relational solutions are likely to be complex not only because they are built on a composite set of resources, and interdependent activities, but also because they require the joint action of actors who have different ideas, perceptions and agendas. Relating is demanding also because every relationship connects and confronts two business systems, two business models and two 'thought worlds' which are never stable or in equilibrium but always in motion and always exposed to pressure for change and in need of adaptation.

The task of account management with respect to generating value in business relationships to strategically relevant customers is challenging for at least three reasons. One is that the task of account management becomes broader because coping with value generation in relationships adds to, and does not substitute, the task of coordinating the own organization's interface activities. Another reason is that the active engagement with customers limits autonomy in choices; being dependent on counterparts' actions and reactions requires an interaction orientation in order not to lose the benefits of added value emerging from interaction which, in turn, implies following the actions and reactions of the counterpart. On the whole, the task of account management becomes more of managing within a relationship rather than managing the relationship. Since interaction continuously changes the course of action and choices, a key account is required to scrupulously manage interactions with customers as these are critical events in the generation of value. Finally, effectively contributing to the generation of value in customer relationships entails the need to balance own vs. joint interests, and the somewhat contrasting requirements for coordinating the existing configuration of the relationship vs. developing it in innovative ways. Organizationally, this involves continuously seeking a balance between opening for developmental reasons and closing for producing workable solutions.

Furthermore, the balancing act among contrasting criteria in SAM is to be carried out in a context in which those in charge of the account management are exposed to contrasting pressures from the own and customer organization. Taking charge of value generation in relationships with critical customers is thus a tall task that requires extraordinary capabilities.

Conclusions

In light of the features of the value-generating process in business relationships and the task of value creating in relationships with strategically relevant customers, one can now discuss the skills and capabilities required to cope with such a task. Rather than reinforcing analytical skills inspired by a planning logic, what is needed is to develop and strengthen 'interaction capabilities'. However, to acquire and grow interaction capability for a supplier company is not simply about developing individual abilities; rather, it is about developing organizational practices and routines. Such routines and practices should build on shared identification and understanding of interdependencies in the own and customer organizations.

Mutual interdependence and jointness in the value-generating process implies the necessity to think in terms of collective rather than individual action and to involve a set of actors in collaborative relationships in order to make use of a 'distributed knowledge system' (Tsoukas 1996). Engagement of others needs to be elicited in order to make use of various elements of the distributed knowledge system, or in other words, of the existing networks. Engaging others who can contribute to developing effective solutions in relationships implies managing interdependent rather than unilateral autonomous action. That, in turn, requires accepting co-leadership and the necessity to orchestrate the distributed competences for better performance (Dhanaraj and Parkhe 2006). Since generating effective solutions in a relationship depends on knowledge and perception-related factors, interactive communication plays an important role, and there is a need to consider mutual learning and teaching in customer–supplier relationships. Because the actual solutions are enacted rather than the result of a linear analytical process, interaction orientation (Ramani and Kumar 2008) is required to cope effectively with the solution-generating process.

While the need for developing interaction capability is evident, both management practice and research currently offer only partial indications and conjectures as to what the interaction capabilities consist of and how they can be fostered. Extant research on interaction capabilities appears to converge on four broad aspects of interaction capability (Coviello and Joseph 2012; Håkansson et al. 2009; Ramani and Kumar 2008) as being important for outcomes of business relationships.

Counterpart mobilization

There is a need to engage the customer (and others) in the process of identification and implementation of solutions that generate value in a relationship. Engaging others requires identification of the key connection between the own and customer organizations, understanding of the economic consequences of these connections and elaboration of an actionable map of the value-formation process in the relationship. It also necessitates understanding the effects of the customer involvement for the own organization's autonomy (Ford et al. 2011). Understanding value formation in relationships involves analysing costs and value for both companies in the short and long term, and involves the capacity to view value at the level of the relationship over time rather than for single transactions, for both counterparts rather than one, and the ability to identify often contrasting value consequences of the offering (Ulaga and Eggert 2006). Development of new solutions requires engaging an entire set of actors, who can offer different contributions, and facilitating the flow of information among the relevant actors. Engaging others is not simply about being adaptive; rather, it means pursuing the logic of 'effectuation' (Read et al. 2009) or 'enactment' (Weick et al. 2005), which implies accepting the principle of co-creation. Engaging the counterparts also involves fostering the mutual creation and sharing of information among various actors implicated in the relationships.

Development agility

Commitment to exploratory learning (Miner et al. 2001) favours the development of solutions that effectively lead to generating value for the parties in a relationship through innovation. Development agility means a willingness to act on partial information but at the same time being open to review and reformulate past choices. Rather than seeking more complete information and solving the ambiguity of choices through scenario planning or extensive analysis, coping effectively with the interaction process in a business relationship requires tolerance for ambiguity. Ultimately, development agility is about the ability to question and probe one's own and the other's experience and decisions, and the openness to accept the effectuation logic of the enactment of solutions as various issues in the relationship emerge. This means following the logic of jointly creating developments in relational solutions, rather than simply unilaterally adapting to each other's actions and reactions (Ford et al. 2011). Development agility entails commitment to the development of the relationship, rather than an opportunistic pursuit of perceived market opportunities and a crowd-following mentality. Effective joint development requires acceptance on both sides of the relationship that outcomes of the interaction processes in relationships are contingent on the reciprocal process of enactment (Danneels 2003).

Mindful experimentation

Given the ambiguities management faces in business relationships, finding novel solutions in relationships requires experimentation. When the set of options open to management is unclear, even unplanned action can inform managers. Experimenting can help to generate new options as long as it is mindful and not erratic. Mindfulness requires afterthought and elaborating the experience. It has been shown that a blend of planned and unplanned actions can inform future decisions on solutions in relationships (Weick et al. 2005) and it has been suggested that, under the circumstances, adaptive experimentation can favour learning among the parties (Day 2011). Enacting workable solutions and couplings in the relationship through a trial-and-error process in which both parties engage is an important component in innovating the content of relationships and thus producing value for the parties. Also, studies on innovation have shown that developing novel offerings and relationship solutions requires extensive experimentation, engagement in a joint trial-and-error process, and reviewing one's own understanding of key relationships (Chesbrough 2010, p. 356). Innovation requires the ability to simultaneously open existing designs and procedures and to operate closure to put solutions in place (Håkansson and Olsen 2012). Therefore, finding new solutions through experimenting can put the own organization under considerable stress to manage such seemingly contrasting requirements at the same time.

Persistency and resilience

No point of equilibrium in a relationship can remain stable for long, and the need to adapt existing solutions is continuous. Relationships develop because participants become committed to some future states, which involves accepting an investment logic, in the sense that efforts and cost to solve emergent contingencies precede potential beneficial returns. The latter are always deferred. Accounting for the costs and benefits of various choices always has a time dimension that needs to be considered. Opportunity identification and exploitation is not a single event; rather, both are a continuous ongoing activity (O'Connor and Rice 2001). In exercising relational choices there is no given time horizon but commitment and persistency, if combined with development agility, tend to yield positive economic outcomes over time (Ghemwatt 1993). Competencies for change (Peterat and Helfatl 2003) and resilience (Hamel and Välikangas 2003) are involved in the supplier and customer organizations, because mutual adaptations in strategically relevant business relationships require that both the supplier and the customer have a modicum of capacity to meet the unexpected. Building competences to cope with change involves fostering non-routine experiment orientation in the organization and accepting the temporary nature of success.

Developing such capabilities in companies that operate in business markets requires establishing appropriate organizational routines and practices, not only in the marketing and sales functions but in all organizational functions that operate at the company boundaries interfacing with customers. Since managing value in strategic relationships is not about combining ready-made elements and applying known solutions but is about innovating, it is necessary to make use of a distributed competence in the own organization and elsewhere in the business network. That entails greater organizational complexity. Since the competences needed to actively relate to specific individual customers are distributed throughout the supplier organization, various organizational units need to be engaged in the external relationships and such engagement cannot be delegated to traditional boundary units as, for instance, sales or marketing (Gummesson 1991; La Rocca and Snehota 2012). SAM cannot be a substitute for the involvement of these units; it can provide support and some guidance for their engagement.

That leads to a final consideration of the management style and approach to strategic account management when it becomes a distinct and formal unit in the supplier organization. The active involvement of others, within the own organization, in the customer organization and eventually among third parties in the value-generating process, necessitates non-hierarchical decision and management processes because the resulting interaction in business relationships can never be fully controlled and directed by one of the parties. For better performance of the networked actors, the distributed competences need to be collectively orchestrated (Dhanaraj and Parkhe 2006) and the roles of those involved need to be continuously negotiated and renegotiated among the parties.

SAM can perform an active role in orchestrating the activities, but without the possibility of relying on centralized control. Furthermore, management in the supplier organization must experiment with organizational solutions differentiated in relation to value-creation processes for different customers (La Rocca and Snehota 2014). Since diversity has been identified as a driver of success in innovative projects, the provision of a diverse team for each strategic account, a team that understands the ongoing process and capacity to leverage and integrate diverse ways of thinking, is an important ingredient of successful SAM.

Value dimensions and relationship postures in dyadic 'key relationship programmes'

BY STEPHAN HENNEBERG, CATHERINE PARDO,
STEFANOS MOUZAS AND PETER NAUDÉ

Abstract

Business-to-business marketing is often concerned with the way in which companies manage strategically important relationships with their counterparts: their key relationship programmes (KRPs). These relationships can be managed through the implementation of specific managerial and organizational structures, commonly implemented via key account programmes (on the supplier side) or key supplier programmes (on the customer side). Underlying this managerial process is an implicit assumption that these important relationships bring some form of additional value to one or both parties involved. However, a dyadic view of how this value is created and shared between the parties remains an under-researched area.

In this conceptual paper, we use the multi-faceted value construct introduced in Pardo et al. (2006) and posit that the buyer's or seller's value strategies can be best understood as being *internally*, *exchange* or *relationship* based. This in turn allows us to analyse the value gained as being the outcome of one of nine generic key relationship postures within any dyadic KRP. We focus on an analysis of so-called 'managed' relationship postures and identify a number of dyadic activities and competences that we hypothesize are important in managing such KRPs, and which can form the basis for further empirical research.

Introduction

Strategically important business-to-business exchanges often foster the development of specific managerial and organizational structures that enhance these interactions. They are commonly implemented via key account programmes (on the supplier side) or key supplier programmes (on the customer side). These programmes are hypothesized to provide benefits for both exchange partners and foster long-term, cooperative and collaborative business relationships (Pardo 1999; Shapiro and Moriarty 1982; Sheth and Sharma 1997; Stevenson 1980; Stevenson and Page 1979). Such relationship-induced value management is increasingly being seen as a dominant logic for marketing (Vargo and Lusch 2004).

In order to achieve the managerial and organizational structures that facilitate such key relationship interactions, certain organizational and strategic competences, i.e. specific combinations of resources, are hypothesized to exist (Homburg et al. 2002). However, we argue that these competences cannot be seen as 'entity-centric' and simply embedded in the actors, activities and resource composition of one organization, and that key relationship programmes and the mutual value that is created and delivered by them are characterized by 'dyadic' strategies that go beyond the frame of single organizational entities, as proposed by Möller (2006). Therefore, we focus on strategically important dyadic relationships as part of companies' management of their specific focal net (Alajoutsijärvi et al. 1999).

Based upon a review of previous work and further conceptual development, we posit that a competence-based perspective of relationship building in strategically important inter-organizational exchanges needs to be analysed, first, from a value perspective in order to understand the different facets of relationship outcomes (Lindgreen and Wynstra 2005; Möller and Törrönen 2003), and second, from the perspective of a dyadic interaction in which the inter-organizational relationship itself becomes the focus of attention (Ford and Håkansson 2006). Research on key account management (KAM) as well as on key supplier management (KSM) and supply chain management has hitherto neglected researching organizational interactions in terms of the value concept or with regard to competence-based management, i.e. a competence-based view of the firm (Day 1994; Reid and Plank 2000; Srivastava et al. 2001).

Before introducing our strategic and competence-based considerations, we will establish in the next section the importance of value in dyadic exchanges as the core concept for an analysis of KRPs.

Value and key relationship programmes

The importance of value for theorizing in marketing is widely recognized (Anderson 1995; Eggert et al. 2006; Georges and Eggert 2003; Holbrook 1994; Ulaga and Eggert 2006; Walter et al. 2001), and it can be posited that value constitutes a pivotal underlying concept in explaining exchange constellations. Collaborative relationships have always been clearly associated with the concept of value, with Anderson (1995) arguing that value is the *'raison d'être'* of that kind of relationship. However, except for the work by Georges and Eggert (2003), Ulaga and Eggert (2005 and 2006) and Pardo et al. (2006), the very specific context of key account management and key supplier management (collaborative relationships by definition) has not been investigated from the value point of view. In the case of Georges and Eggert (2003), value is observed only from the buyer's perspective. This is problematic in the sense that collaboration implies mutual benefits and sacrifices, i.e. a dyadically grounded perspective (Bonoma and Johnston 1978; Wilson 1978). Ulaga and Eggert (2005 and 2006) and Eggert et al. (2006) report empirical findings on perceived relationship value. However, the focus is not dyadic but organization-centric (in this case focusing on purchasing managers), dealing exclusively with value that is created by suppliers *for* customers. Developing this further, Pardo et al. (2006) posit a multi-faceted concept of value for KAM and derive key account value strategies (KAVS), focusing on static and dynamic aspects of value strategy. However, the dyadic perspective is not consequently employed, neglecting the interactions between suppliers and customers within a key relationship programme. The only existing dyadic perspective on value creation is provided by Möller (2006) in the context of the strategic competences necessary to sustain general business interactions. Möller's (2006) model, which shares some similarities with Henneberg et al.'s (2005) work, will be discussed below and the distinguishing features of our model will be outlined.

In this way, this paper addresses existing shortcomings in the literature by building on the multi-faceted value construct previously introduced in Pardo et al. (2006) and linking this to different value strategies that are available to supplying and buying organizations utilizing key relationship programmes. This is done based within an axiomatic framework that focuses on the exchange dyad between supplier (key account management) and customer (key supplier management), operationalized as the specific relationship context of a key relationship programme (McDonald 2000; Missirilian and Calvi 2004). In contrast to Möller (2006), we thus posit for our analysis an 'incremental' value concept, analysing specifically the 'extra' or additional elements that characterize KRP exchanges over and above mere business transactions (Homburg et al. 2002).

Compared with Möller (2006), our proposed model is more specific in two ways and is therefore 'nested' within the 'value-producing system' approach (Möller et al. 2005). First, we focus on relationships which are embedded within specific organizational structures geared towards expressing the 'logic' of this relationship (i.e. KRPs). Second, we analyse concretely the value aspects which can be linked to the decision of committing organizational resources to 'structure' this relationship. In this way, the value-production logic as analysed by Möller and Törrönen (2003) represents the general exchange morphology, while our model emphasizes the specific KRP relationship. By including a value logic which can be internally focused, as well as by separating value creation from value appropriation, our model enriches the proposed business-to-business value strategies in Möller (2006). In fact, by allowing for 'internal' value focus, we enlarge the 'value production' perspective used by Möller and Törrönen (2003) and Möller (2006) by a further element.

In our argument, we thus link the specific elements of value strategies in KRPs, operationalized as a taxonomy of nine different strategic exchange postures, to an understanding of necessary competences to manage these exchange situations and introduce 'dyadic' competences as underlying managerial and organizational structures that facilitate optimal value interactions in strategic business-to-business relationships. Our specific focus will be on the so-called 'managed' relationship postures. Finally, their viability and economic suitability as well as the underlying facilitating dyadic competences are discussed.

Key relationship value strategies

We posit that a dyadic perspective of value in KRP interactions needs to start with a conceptual understanding of the multi-faceted nature of value (Biggart and Delbridge 2004; Ulaga and Eggert 2005; Wengler et al. 2006), and that value in KRPs can be usefully disaggregated into three levels: internal, exchange and relational value (Pardo et al. 2006). While *internal* (or *proprietary*) *value* is created and appropriated by a single actor in the dyad (Wilson et al. 2002), *exchange value* is based on the efforts of the supplier and appropriated by the buyer (and vice versa) (Abratt and Kelly 2002; Ulaga 2003; Ulaga and Eggert 2006; Weilbaker and Weeks 1997). *Relational* value comes into existence because of a collaborative relationship between key account management and key supplier management programmes, i.e. it is created and appropriated within a relationship (Anderson et al. 1994; Pardo et al. 2006).

Such a multi-level value perspective allows us to consider the different value strategies open to players within a KRP, thereby specifying the value production types as introduced by Möller and Törrönen (2003). Both buyer and seller in a KRP need to be aware of all the different value aspects that may characterize their interactions. However, they need to be unambiguous about their specific value focus within the dyadic relationship in order to optimize the activities, processes and resource allocation related to this focus. Furthermore, as part of their value strategies, they also need to take into account the specific focus of the dyadic exchange partner and align their value strategy with that of their counterpart (Möller 2006).

Based upon this approach, we are able to identify three different value strategies available to players within a KRP, these being the strategic postures that we can then use to map the companies' strategy matching activities. It has to be noted that these actor-centric strategies are specific to the rationale of engaging in a

KRP, i.e. the strategic relationship with key exchange partners and the associated investments in processes, organization and offering (Homburg et al. 2002):

1. An *internal value strategy* is a strategy where the supplier or/and the customer create key relationship structures primarily for reasons of internal efficiency and effectiveness. In this case, internal organization around KRPs provides cost reductions in managing the exchange, or facilitates new opportunities. For this key relationship value strategy no 'relationship' is necessary as value is intrinsic (i.e. proprietary) to each individual exchange entity. It can be argued that many food retailers such as Tesco and Sainsbury's in the UK operationalize their category management via key supplier programmes using such a strategy which, although guaranteeing the supplier a certain long-term demand, provide internal value to the retailers through process and interface optimization. This strategy is characterized by direct and immediate value appropriation; with the dyad being used merely to substantiate an intra-organizational strategic focus (Gosselin and Bauwen 2006; Wengler et al. 2006).

2. An *exchange value strategy* is based on delivering value to the exchange partner (e.g. a customer) in order to achieve certain exchange characteristics that are profitable for the selling company, such as customer loyalty, cross- or up-selling, or strategic information gathering (Weilbaker and Weeks 1997). It has been shown that providing exchange value is directly linked to rela-tionship quality (Walter et al. 2003). Although this strategy is based on an appreciation of the dyadic characteristics of the exchange, the value can still be delivered in a long-term 'transactional' mode, i.e. a real relationship, based on trust, commitment and interdependency, may not exist (Lambe et al. 2000). Such a value strategy is at the core of the KAM logic as applied by most FMCG manufacturers in their relationship with retailers. Through the bundling of regional, national and international sales, as well as category-enveloping agreements, companies such as Unilever and P&G are able to deliver superior value to strategic account clients. The deployment of ECR systems is a manifestation of such exchange value strategies (Mouzas and Araujo 2000).

3. A *relational value strategy* presupposes a 'deep' relationship between the dyadic exchange partners. Value in this strategy cannot be managed or created by individual organizational entities alone, and the 'relational rent' is deter-mined by cooperation (Dyer and Singh 1998). It is intrinsically linked to the cooperative and collaborative activities and the commitment of both parties. An example of a knowledge-sharing network based on relational value is Toyota's net of strategic relationships with suppliers as analysed by Dyer and Nobeoka (2000). A clear decision is made to invest in key relationships with important suppliers in order to collaboratively develop knowledge which is useable by all network members. By fostering a 'strong tie network', based on a shared identity, multi-directional value flows come into existence which manifest themselves in production process knowledge being 'owned' by the

network partners and not individual players (Dyer and Hatch 2006; Håkansson and Pedersen 1999).

It needs to be noted that while exchange and relational value strategies are similar to the dimensions introduced in Möller and Törrönen (2003) and used in Möller (2006), our internal value strategy has no equivalent in their categorization. This is mainly due to the fact that our focus is on a specific inter-organizational relationship context, namely KRPs, which are influenced by manifold motivations by actors which can be internally focused or externally oriented (Pardo et al. 2006).

Strategic matching of relationship postures

While companies can choose to focus on one of these value strategies as a rationale for their investment in KAM or KSM, or possibly on a portfolio of these strategies (Campbell and Cunningham 1983), the success of such a decision is not independent of the strategic orientation of the dyadic partner. The value strategy chosen by the dyadic exchange partner may be conditional or influential for its own strategic positioning regarding its value focus (Parolini 1999). That means that certain value relationships are not necessarily complementary. In fact, they may be non-viable or need active management and coordination. Based on the three identified value strategies, Figure 1 shows nine generic dyadic key

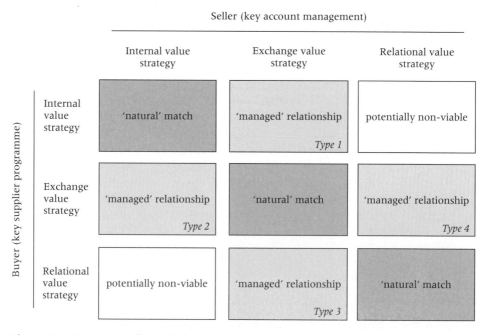

Figure 1   Nine generic key relationship postures in a KRP

relationship *postures*, indicating some possible mismatches. This approach is iso-morphic with the dyadic interaction approach as suggested by Campbell (1985) and also used by Möller (2006) for an analysis of general value strategies within business-to-business marketing. Therefore, part of the strategic decision-making in KRPs must be a 'matching' exercise which can be determined through negotia-tion (Möller 2006; Mouzas et al. 2007; Pardo 1999).

The grid of key relationship postures shows that both parties are able to focus on each of the three key relationship value strategies independently, i.e. they are autonomously able to decide on different internal and external ways of value creation and on the appropriation aims of their value orientation. However, we posit that not all combinations of strategies, i.e. dyadic postures, are viable. A natural match exists when both parties individually focus mainly on the same facet of KRP value. For example, if both seller and buyer organize and manage their respective KRP structures so as to optimize proprietary value (i.e. in our terminology, both sides use internal value strategies), a workable equilibrium between both companies exists: expectations regarding the essence of the KRP are aligned, incremental value is not contested between both sides, and organi-zational structures and processes do not overlap, i.e. the KRP as such does not need to be 'managed'. Consider, for example, the relationship between Sinalco-Cola and the retailer Rewe in Germany. Both manufacturer and retailer organize and manage their respective KRP structures in order to optimize proprietary value as both parties use internal value strategies. Rewe needs SinalcoCola, a relatively small player in the caffeinated beverage market, to leverage its power during the annual negotiations with Coca-Cola and PepsiCo. Meanwhile, Sinal-coCola treats Rewe, one of a whole range of possible distribution channels, as a strategically important account in order to achieve the internal operational efficiency which allows the management of such a diversified distribution network. Manufacturer's and retailer's expectations are aligned, incremental value is not contested, and organizational structures and processes do not overlap.

The situation, however, is different when both parties do not use the same value strategy focus. If we envisage the selling company focusing its key account man-agement on an internal value strategy, while the buying company aligns with an exchange value strategy, a dyadic 'mismatch' exists: the buyer has expectations regarding value appropriation that are not necessarily reciprocated by the seller. In this example, the seller appropriates value that exists because of its own key account programme. On top of that, it receives value from the customer through its key supplier management programme. Obviously, the buyer expects long-term gains from this exchange (Blois 1999), e.g. in the form of incremental value delivered by the seller and appropriated by the buyer. If both parties implement their part of the dyadic exchange in isolation, this long-term reciprocity (or value equilibrium) would not be achieved. This could mean that such a 'relation-ship' would not be formed in the first place. However, the situation is not neces-sarily non-viable (i.e. would result ultimately in a breakdown of the strategically important relationship). We characterize it as a 'managed relationship'.[1] This means that besides the dyadic interactions that constitute the underlying exchange, this situation is workable if dyadic negotiations and alignment on the level of value strategies exist (Ritter et al. 2004). This would potentially allow for a system to be developed between both parties, based on a mutual understanding of the specific rationale as to why both are engaging in the dyadic KRP. Therefore, both parties could continue their 'non-matching' value strategies within a framework that establishes an equilibrium of mutual value. However, such a 'managed relationship' is less stable than a 'natural match' and needs to be negotiated and monitored constantly (Mouzas et al. 2007). This means a much higher level of interactivity and information-sharing is necessary between both parties within the KRP, i.e. the 'networking overheads' are higher. In order for this to happen, certain 'dyadic competences' are necessary, as discussed below.

In our grid, we indicate that two postures are potentially non-viable, so that even strategic matching exercises would not allow a 'managed relationship' to be developed. Consequently, it is posited that such postures would be unstable in the medium to longer term and would ultimately cause the disintegration of the dyadic KRP. Such a situation is envisaged when any matching between an internal value strategy and a relational value strategy is attempted. By definition, these strategies are antagonistic towards each other: relational value depends on the co-creation of value while an internal value strategy is based on an intra-organizational orientation towards incremental value. In this constellation, one party is not willing to engage in value creation by the relationship. In its extreme form, where there is an incommensurable dyadic position regarding the mutual expectations of the two parties, no amount of negotiation between the parties short of a value strategy change would make this posture viable.

A competence view of key relationship postures

Implied in the discussion of relationship postures is the argument that the optimal design of a KRP is not primarily an intra-organizational task focusing on the recombination of resources (as, for example, implied in the analysis by Homburg et al. 2002). Such a focus would work only in the cases of the three 'natural match' postures shown in Figure 1. In such cases there is a workable equilibrium in the dyadic relationship, even if the relationship value itself is not fully exploited. In addition, we can assume a migration over time of a particular relationship from top-left to bottom-right in Figure 1, as the two parties continue to work

---

[1] Note that a 'managed relationship' does not imply 'managing a relationship'. A managed relationship points towards the fact that dyadically, i.e. by mutual understanding, both parties in the relationship can contribute to making a relationship viable in a concerted way. This can be contrasted with managing a relationship which is about one party attempting to frame the modalities of a relational interaction (Ford et al. 2003).

ever closer together, thereby reducing uncertainties and increasing cooperation (Anderson and Narus 1991; Ford et al. 2003).

However, many KRPs are likely to lie in the four 'managed relationship' postures. In such cases, typified by slightly differing strategic value orientation between the two parties, a successful working relationship depends crucially on strategic matching (Möller 2006), and consequently on the ongoing process of negotiating and re-negotiating the KRP relationship. This cannot be done by one organization alone, and it is therefore a 'dyadic competence' that is important, if not necessary, for any matched KRP. This dyadic competence depends on the interaction patterns of both partners: their ability to understand the value strategy focus of their exchange partner; their ability to communicate their own value strategy focus and the shifts in it; their empathy about what is possible within a specific posture defined by the respective value strategies of both partners; their willingness to find a 'value match' and to manage this agreed posture constantly via interactions; their ability to measure value not just for themselves but also for their exchange partner; and their (often lack of) willingness to use power to enforce a solution (Mouzas et al. 2007). Such matching strategies have been discussed not just in terms of marketing strategy but also regarding supply chain alignment (Prévot and Spencer 2006). This is in line with a dyadic interpretation of the concept of 'network competences' as introduced by Ritter and Gemünden (2003). Such competences in an inter-organizational exchange system have been described as contributing to organizations' 'network insight' (Mouzas et al. 2007).

To achieve this competence, it is not enough to build efficient and effective key account management and key supplier management structures independently. This competence, in line with its characteristic of being dyadic, resides crucially in activities and resources that are shared between the two exchange partners (Golfetto and Gibbert 2006; Möller 2006). We can hypothesize that each of the four 'managed relationships' shown in Figure 1 would require its own particular set of dyadic value strategies. These are shown in Table 1 and discussed briefly in turn, always with the perspective of moving the relationship from 'top-left' to 'bottom-right' as noted above, in order to achieve maximal value from the relationship over time.

Type 1: Seller's exchange orientation, buyer's internal orientation. In these situations, it is the seller who is seeking to focus on the longer-term exchange and to provide exchange value to the buyer, whereas the buyer seeks predominantly internal, transactional value. Examples of such a dyadic KRP can be found in the automotive industry, e.g. in the case of Recaro and DaimlerChrysler, where manufacturers built key buying relationships with first-tier suppliers mainly to streamline their internal production logistics processes (e.g. via build-to-order programmes or the co-location of suppliers with plants). The supplier, meanwhile, treats the automotive manufacturer as a key account by providing additional offering benefits (e.g. by managing the whole logistics and 'safety inventory'

Table 1: The four different 'managed relationships'

Type 1: Seller's exchange orientation, buyer's internal orientation

Seller drives managed relationship
- Reduce perceived risk of a deeper relationship
- Reduce cost of buyer doing sourcing business
- Offer complementary products/services and long-term structural solutions

Type 2: Buyer's exchange orientation, seller's internal orientation

Buyer drives managed relationship
- Reduce perceived risk of a deeper relationship
- Reduce cost of supplier doing selling business
- Offer complementary and bundled demand

Type 3: Seller's exchange orientation, buyer's relational orientation

Buyer drives managed relationship
- Deepen relationship
- Joint process innovation
- Buyer key network integration of supplier

Type 4: Buyer's exchange orientation, seller's relational orientation

Seller drives managed relationship
- Deepen relationship
- Joint process innovation
- Reduce perceived risk for buyer

---

process of an integrated JIT system for the manufacturing plant) (Dyer and Hatch 2006; Howard et al. 2006).

In such cases, it is the task of the seller to move the buyer from an internal to an exchange value orientation. One possible way for the seller is a re-interpretation of the exchange value as focusing on cost reduction of the exchange via better supplier know-how and quicker time-to-market cycles (Cannon and Homburg 2001), in line with the efficiency aim of the buyer. Furthermore, the seller can build risk-reducing benefits into their offering, e.g. upgrading their product/ service offering to 'solutions', which provide long-term, structural benefits for buyers and seller. Newman's concept of 'cross-sourcing' (1989) can also be actively employed by the seller, e.g. by providing a sourcing consortium, in line with Möller and Törrönen's (2003) emphasis on the 'supplier-network function'.

Type 2: Buyer's exchange orientation, seller's internal orientation. This represents the flip-side of the type 1 posture: the seller establishes KAM programmes for internal efficiency purposes, while the buyer focuses on providing exchange benefits to the seller through a KSM. Examples for such a dyadic posture can be found in situations where the consumer demand-oriented product life cycle management is heavily linked to supply chain management competences (Jüttner et al. 2006). In such a case a buying company would want to provide added value to its suppliers (e.g. customer knowledge transfer) in order for them to assist in competence development and optimized product life cycles. However, this is not always directly reciprocated by these suppliers with an aligned KAM value strategy, often causing them to unilaterally focus on internal efficiency gains.

The focus in type 2 cases is on reducing the seller's perceived risk of deepening the relationship (e.g. risk of dependency on key customers), by relating the exchange value for the seller to the network context (Ehret 2004). This can, for example, be done by providing supplying companies with long-term contracts, supply bundling and supply complimentarity offers, or through joint interaction process development to induce the development of their KAM strategy from an internal to an exchange focus.

Type 3: Seller's exchange orientation, buyer's relational orientation. While the customer in this scenario is interested in generating collaborative relationships, the KAM focuses on exchange value to the buyer. For example, providers of smart phone operating systems such as Microsoft and Symbian (and to a lesser extent, Apple) are currently trying to provide added benefits in terms of implementation/pre-configuration value to some of their core customers in mobile phone production (e.g. Sony Ericsson) and mobile phone distribution (e.g. Carphone Warehouse) in order to become a standard operating system for a newly developing market. The mobile phone manufacturers, meanwhile, are interested in a more collaborative value strategy as part of their new product development (NPD) efforts, e.g. by developing new applications together with their key suppliers to increase the penetration of smart phones in the end-consumer market. This mismatch can potentially be explained by what has been called the distinction of 'know-how' compared with 'capacity' projects: while the supplying software companies think of their key customers as part of a 'capacity exchange' aimed at providing incremental value improvements, the phone manufacturers look for 'know-how exchanges' via utilizing supplier knowledge through an integrative partnership (Wagner and Hoegl 2006).

While type 3 postures structurally favour the buyer, they may nevertheless frustrate the customer's key supplier programme as the exchange does not create the added benefits of relational value as expected because of sellers not realizing potential collaborative interactions. Therefore, one would expect the buyer to mobilize the inherent potential of its key supplier programme via an emphasis on relationship value, especially personal interactions (Ulaga 2003). Furthermore, it can be hypothesized that buyers will encourage (and potentially give incentives to) joint process or NPD innovations, maybe based on co-location agreements or joint ventures. Certain ICT-based relationships (JIT, KANBAN systems) could also encourage the supplier company to engage in a deeper and collaborative exchange (Myhr and Spekman 2005). It is also possible to achieve this by incorporating the supplier company into the wider key network of the buying organization (Ojasalo 2004).

Type 4: Buyer's exchange orientation, seller's relational orientation. In this situation, the supplier is interested in collaborative relationships, while the customer is focusing on exchange value, e.g. to retain a key supplier. Consider the example of the discount retailer ALDI and a small manufacturer of breakfast cereals. ALDI is focusing on the exchange value that comes about through the production of standard cereals as retailer brands, while the manufacturer sees retailer brands as a means to create collaborative relationships with ALDI and thus to promote other manufacturer brands. It is likely that the supplier of cereal products will seek to adapt its key account programme as a means to developing deep and collaborative exchanges necessary for a real relational value strategy, i.e. a natural fit. In this case, key account managers will have a kind of pedagogical role towards the customer, aiming at interpreting and displaying interest for the customer to develop different kinds of collaboration. This necessitates a deep knowledge of the customer's value chain and strategy (Jüttner et al. 2006). The key account manager will certainly have to reassure the customer about the costs of such a relational value strategy (e.g. through risk-reducing measures). The move from the customer's exchange orientation to a relational orientation must be supported by a clear exposé of the benefits for the customer: enhanced value created for the customer, respect of confidentiality, low cost of implementation, etc.

Conclusion

This paper develops an initial conceptual grounding regarding value dimensions and strategies in dyadic business-to-business exchanges that are perceived to be of strategic importance to both exchange partners. As such, it specifies some of the more general findings in Henneberg et al. (2005), Möller (2006), and Möller and Törrönen (2003). For this purpose, we have introduced the core *explanandum* of the key relationship programme as a special case of close and collaborative dyadic exchanges. Based on the dimensions of value creation and appropriation within an exchange environment, we use a multi-faceted perspective of value available to each exchange partner: proprietary value, exchange value and relational value. The explicit incorporation of internal KAM and KSM value elements provides further elaborations of existing literature in this area. These dimensions allow for the derivation of three corresponding key relationship value strategies open to buyers and sellers: an internal value strategy, an exchange value strategy and a relational value strategy.

However, within a dyadic KRP choices regarding these value strategies cannot be made autonomously without taking into account the value orientation of the exchange partner. Using the three key relationship value strategies for buying and selling companies, we conclude that nine generic postures exist within a KRP. While three constitute a natural 'dyadic match', two are deemed potentially non-viable. The majority (four postures) depend on the value dyad to be managed in order to achieve a long-term and viable value exchange. This finding leads us to the introduction of 'dyadic competences' which are necessary to build these managed relationships. We posit that this will be the case if 'strategic matching' is achieved as part of the management of focal net relationships, underpinned by competences which reside in the interactions/activities and shared resources between both companies (Alajoutsijärvi et al. 1999; Möller 2006). As such, we specifically clarify the value appropriation and creation strategies in dyadic key relationship programmes and so contribute to a better understanding of value within deep business relationships, which was singled out by Lindgreen and Wynstra (2005) as one of two important research avenues regarding the value concept in business markets.

The contribution of this paper stems from four different sources. First, our value point of view allows us to clarify the idea that a key relationship programme must be seen as a set of different value-creation strategies, including internally focused ones. KRPs cannot be considered as a homogeneous set, but much more as a portfolio of different value strategies. Second, and contrary to much of the earlier work on value, our departure point is the one of 'value in and by the relationships' (Pardo et al. 2006). This means that we are considering value both from supplier and customer perspectives in an integrated (dyadic) manner. Third, our work supports the idea that relational value (the most efficient value strategy) cannot be disconnected from a dyadic perspective in the sense that it results from a combination of both customer's and supplier's resources. Finally, our work points to the fact that specific competences and strategic insights of actors engaging in key relationships are necessary. These competences are not the ones that are mobilized to build the KRP, but more specifically relate to match the customer's and the supplier's value strategies in order to make the relationship viable, sustainable and develop further. These competences, ranging from the knowledge of the exchange partner's position in the value strategy matrix to the ability to incentivize an exchange partner's evolution towards a relational strategy, are complementary and ongoing competences that people in charge of KRPs must display (whether as key account managers, key supplier managers, or the heads of key relationships divisions). As such, our work on how dyadic relationships between companies are affected by value strategies and their matching contributes to a better understanding of networked marketing entities (Achrol 1997; Achrol and Kotler 1999) that are characterized by collaborative interactions as a foundation of marketing management (Vargo and Lusch 2004).

Nevertheless, we recognize that as a conceptual proposal, our work displays several obvious limitations. At present it lacks empirical evidence, and has not been verified in managerial actions. Further research is necessary to develop our multi-faceted value concept in key relationships. Initially, the underlying value strategy constructs need to be operationalized. The overall model must be tested empirically, and work carried out to identify more clearly those additional 'dyadic' competences thought to support specific value strategy postures. For example, it remains to be seen whether or not non-viable dyadic postures actually exist and for what reasons they may be perpetuated. In addition, the performance relations of the different postures must be clearly established, particularly the effect on profitability obtained, and the impact of 'managing' certain KRPs. While a development from more internal to fully relational dyadic value strategies is implied, it may be that such a development is not in the interest of all exchange partners (barriers and limits to development), is suboptimal (inefficient development), or does not contribute to the overall profitability of the key relationship (short- as well as long-term bottom-line impact).

The impact of a portfolio of value postures and strategies within several key relationships also remains to be analysed in more detail, as does its relationship with different organizational forms of KAM and KSM programmes. This would contribute towards redressing the current imbalance in research where the focus tends to be on explaining organizational performance through entity-specific constructs, and rather neglecting relationship characteristics and network participation as crucial explanatory variables (Gulati et al. 2000). Furthermore, a true network perspective needs to be adopted by putting the dyadic relationships into a systemic environment (Håkansson et al. 1999) which makes it possible to ascertain the necessary networking competences to manage the proposed value strategies within complex inter-organizational structures of exchange relationships (Ritter 1999). The degree to which certain aspects of the key relationship postures and associated value strategies are relationship-specific or can be used cross-relationally remains open to further research (Ritter and Gemünden 2003; Ritter et al. 2004).

'Vertical coopetition': the key account perspective

BY SYLVIE LACOSTE

Abstract

Why do key accounts combine opposing types of relationship with their suppliers? The author has chosen to term this new hybrid form of supplier relationship management, which combines cooperation and price-competitive transactions and reflects the tension between value creation and value appropriation, 'vertical coopetition'. She investigates the use of this concept in the context of an in-depth qualitative study, involving, first, an exploratory field study and, second, four case studies involving leading industrial MNCs (multi-national companies). The results indicate that 'vertical coopetition' occurs in two forms: when the price-competitive approach is predominant but some cooperation features are still to be found; and when cooperation is predominant, but appeals to competition are still made. Mutually opposed aspects of each form are linked and explained by three pivotal mechanisms, which the author calls 'strengthening', 'correction' and 'commuting'. Finally, the study reveals that, increasingly, the key account's brands or business unit value are explanatory forces of 'vertical coopetition'.

Reproduced with the kind permission of Elsevier, from Lacoste, S. (2012) Vertical coopetition: the key account perspective. *Industrial Marketing Management*, 44(S), 202–218.

Introduction

'Coopetition' is a term which arose in the 1980s to refer to inter-firm relationships that involve simultaneously both 'cooperation' and 'competition'. The concept links two mutually exclusive types of relationship and merges them into a hybrid form. The concept has attracted an increasing amount of interest on the part of academia since the 1990s, marked especially by the seminal work of Brandenburger and Nalebuff (1995, p. 59) who used game theory to 'encourage thinking about both cooperative and competitive ways to change the (strategic) game'. From a managerial perspective, companies that are competitors are increasingly cooperating to improve their competitive advantage over their other global competitors (we have numerous examples in the automotive industry, such as the recent discussions between BMW and Peugeot:[1] 'BMW is examining whether to share platforms with French rival PSA Peugeot Citroën for its Mini small car'). However, the 'coopetition' approach is often restricted to 'horizontal' relationships, e.g. among competitors (Bengtsson and Kock 1999, 2000) and there is little academic research applying the concept to 'vertical' relationships, e.g. between customers and suppliers.

Exploring the concept of 'vertical' coopetition

Heide and Wathne (2006, p. 98) 'posit that exchange relationships may simultaneously involve different types of orientations . . . Although we endorse this view as it applies to individual transactions, our framework is based on the assumption that actual shifts among fundamentally different relationship orientations are both possible and likely.' Most researchers find it conceptually easier to work on the polar aspects of the relationship continuum, rather than on the 'hybrid' forms combining these two aspects.

Consequently, many researchers have shown that a relational and cooperative orientation is key, in customer–seller relationships, to improving value creation and the customer's competitive advantage (Anderson and Narus 1991; Cardozo et al. 1992; Day 2000; Dunn and Thomas 1994; Dyer and Singh 1998; Ford 2001; Grönroos 1997; Jap 1999; Morgan and Hunt 1994) and is increasingly the norm in buyer–seller relationships (Walter et al. 2003). For these academics, value creation is optimized via cooperative relationships (Ulaga and Eggert 2006), even if they recognize that 'customer firms perceive value creation as positive only if they appropriate a larger slice of the bigger value pie' (Wagner et al. 2010, p. 1).

If we leave the subject of value creation to one side and turn our attention to the appropriation of value between customers and sellers, we find that some

---

[1] Some industrial firms have strong product brands (i.e. within the FMCG industry) whilst others, in industrial products, do not have branded products but differentiate their products within the organization of their Business Units.
See *Financial Times*, http://www.FT.com, Daniel Schäfer (05/08/2009), 'BMW eyes Peugeot tie-up for Mini.'

researchers have demonstrated that both parties could also 'compete' in terms of value sharing in a game theory setting (Zerbini and Castaldo 2007). Value sharing between customer and supplier can lead to competition between both parties as value appropriation is a zero sum game: the more one party appropriates value, the less will be left to the other. As we discussed above, customers will want the largest possible share: they will move value competition between them and their suppliers to competition among their suppliers. By forcing suppliers to compete among themselves, customers lead such suppliers to offer the largest possible value share to customers to win or keep the business from other suppliers. This is a way for customers to make sure they optimize value sharing in their best self-interest. This is how competition, and more specifically price competition, among suppliers reflects 'value sharing' competition between suppliers and customers. These two different ways of managing value are referred to as 'pie expansion' (Jap 1999) – the creation of value within a cooperative relationship – in contrast to 'pie sharing' (Jap 2001) – sharing value, competing to get the biggest slice. These two approaches complement each other while using opposite relational tools: cooperation and competition.

Within the relationship-marketing paradigm, we also find a conceptual approach that opposes two types of marketing: transactional and relational marketing are mutually exclusive at both ends of a continuum (Day 2000). On the one hand, we have the search for cooperation to gain mutual benefits (Dunn and Thomas 1994); on the other, an emphasis on short-term transactions with price-related benefits designed to attract new customers (price competitive transactions). There has as yet been little academic interest in the 'grey area' in which transactional and relational features are supposed to become intertwined in the middle of the continuum, or how 'pie expansion' and 'pie sharing' can overlap and merge. The paradox inherent in combining these two mutually exclusive forms of relationship has been recognized. Indeed, some researchers from the IMP Group,[2] who study both the marketing and procurement perspectives, agree that buyer–supplier relationships encompass both cooperation and conflict (Håkansson and Snehota 1998), but the area in which transactional and relationship marketing co-exist remains unexplored.

Furthermore, the polarization of transactional and relational features is reflected in marketing literature, in which the supplier's viewpoint is emphasized; but how appropriate is it to prioritize the point of view of the supplier over that of the customer (Blois 1996)? What happens if it is in the interests of the customer to safeguard his or her independence of choice within the market rather than select a few dedicated suppliers, or if the customer prefers to combine both approaches? Is it not the customer who creates a paradoxical tension between capturing value from relational benefits provided by key suppliers (Ulaga 2003; Ulaga and Eggert 2006) and takes advantage, at the same time, of price-competitive market transactions (Gummesson 1997), and organizing tenders?

---

[2] *Industrial Marketing and Purchasing Group* – http://www.impgroup.org.

Exploring 'vertical' coopetition from the key account perspective

If we take a specific customer perspective – the key account perspective – we focus our analysis on those customers who 'purchase a significant volume, buy centrally for a number of geographically dispersed organizational units and desire a long-term, cooperative working relationship as a means to innovation and financial success' (Colletti and Tubridy 1987; Stevenson 1980). Their key account status is defined by their expectation that they will represent for their suppliers 'a natural development of customer focus and relationship marketing in business-to-business markets' (McDonald et al. 1997). Such customers therefore symbolize the 'New frontier in relationship marketing' (Yip and Madsen 1996). At the same time, they may set up their own e-market places (as Danone, Henkel and Nestlé did with the CPG Market), including electronic auction tools, and use transactional tools to manage their supplier relationships though price competition.

Electronic bidding tools, such as reverse auctions, have decreased the transactional cost of selecting from an enlarged supplier base. Jap (2003) shows that electronic auctions can reduce a negotiation process lasting six weeks to only a few hours, while Smart and Harrison (2003) use a case study to demonstrate that e-tender can generate a 30% price decrease. Electronic tools have sparked a renewed interest in the transactional approach that marketing researchers believed had been swept away by the relationship marketing paradigm (Day 2000; Grönroos 1994). Thus, key accounts do combine cooperation and competition in the form of price-competitive transactions, paving the way for 'vertical coopetition' as a new and hybrid form of supplier relationship management.

Research objective

From a conceptual viewpoint, we need to understand why key accounts create this 'hybrid' form of relationship with suppliers. As yet, no one has examined the reasons why customers 'coopete' with suppliers.

In this paper 'vertical coopetition' is thus analysed from the sole perspective of key accounts acting in their own self-interest and disregarding the optimization of mutual welfare. Our analysis is grounded in managerial practice, we study 'vertical coopetition' as a tool designed to optimize value creation and appropriation for key customers, whose status is characterized by an asymmetrical position imbuing them with a certain amount of power.[3] We explore a specific relationship background and do not study the conditions of a Walresian buyer–seller network

---

[3] As key accounts are strategic customers from their suppliers' perspective, it may be expected they are in power dominant position versus their suppliers, although a study by Caniëls and Gelderman (2007) produces evidence of supplier dominance in which the item being supplied is considered to be of strategic importance. However they admit that this is an unexpected and 'provocative result' (Caniels and Gelderman 2007, p. 227).

equilibrium (Corominas-Bosch 2004; Kranton and Minehart 2001). Although the literature on networks in buyer–seller relationships includes a study of two polar features encompassing non-cooperative behaviours and some link (relationship) patterns, the quest for economic balance depends on prices. Our study, meanwhile, analyses value as a 'coopetitive' relational driver.

Our research challenges the prevalent view of normative, collaborative buyer–supplier relationships and it attempts to provide a more nuanced theory. From the literature on relationship marketing, we analyse the benefits of relational and transactional exchanges with a view to gaining an insight into why key accounts prefer to combine aspects of both approaches. We then examine the concepts, most of them originating in the field of strategy, that explain 'horizontal coopetition' (Bengtsson and Kock 1999, 2000; Garrette and Dussauge 1995) and check whether and how they can be applied to 'vertical coopetition'.

From a managerial perspective, a greater understanding of the drivers used by key accounts in setting up hybrid forms of relationship is required to help organizations analyse emerging purchaser roles more effectively. Our goal is to study how the concept of 'vertical coopetition' can be applied to key accounts and to dissect the whole mechanism of combining polar forms of relationships.

The paper is structured as follows. First, positioning the research within the academic literature on hybrid forms of relationships, combining opposing concepts. Second, describing the research methodology. To reach our goal, we conducted a qualitative research programme including an exploratory survey involving ten in-depth interviews of senior purchasing managers from ten different manufacturing or service MNCs, refined by four case studies, taking a more balanced view of purchasers and 'internal' customers (users or influencers) within the key customer organization. We also checked data with respondents collected from their supplier companies (key account directors). Our analysis and interpretation of the results led us to define two major types of 'vertical coopetition': a cooperation predominant form of coopetition and a price-competition predominant form of coopetition, each of them including three different types of 'pivots' linking cooperation and price-competition approaches: 'strengthening', 'correction' and 'commuting'. Finally, we discuss the factors explaining the use of vertical coopetition. We conclude with the managerial implications of our findings and provide directions for further research.

Relational versus transactional benefits

To understand why key accounts should consider combining cooperative and price-competitive relationships, we will first examine what benefits they can derive from each type of relationship. We will define those benefits based on an analysis of definitions derived from previous scholarly work on polar relationships (Dwyer et al. 1987; Grönroos 1994; Macneil 1978, 1980; Payne et al. 1995).

Mostly non-economic in nature, relational benefits are derived from cooperation and based on value creation and sharing (Anderson and Narus 2004, 1999). Value creation based on long-term cooperation can be broken down into product-linked benefits (quality, innovation, etc.), service-linked benefits (supply chain optimization, supplier's specific know-how, etc.) and interaction benefits, such as problem-solving (Ulaga 2003). Some direct economic benefits may also be added, such as cost-reduction programmes and bonuses, but they are generally the outcome of the relational benefits alluded to above. These benefits can be generated only if both key account and supplier achieve a high level of interaction and mutual knowledge which enable them to work continuously on the principle aspects of the value chain (Porter 1980, 2008).

As well as cooperation and relational benefits, competitive market price exchanges generate transactional benefits. Competitive market price exchange enables key accounts to achieve the best price/quality ratio in their offer. Being a short-term transaction approach, it provides customers with a good overview of the market and, therefore, furnishes them with the opportunity to change suppliers whenever they want, a useful capability in terms of exploiting market innovations. This type of exchange enables key accounts to remain relatively independent from their suppliers and to act according to their best self-interest.

Understandably, key accounts want to combine both types of benefit simultaneously exploiting relational benefits and achieving the best price (for a specific offer). However, the problem here is that the two types of relationship are paradoxical. This implies a choice between either a long-term relationship with pre-selected suppliers and joint efforts to create value from non-economic benefits, or a transaction-by-transaction approach designed to benefit from the best specific offers. We will now investigate how key accounts can overcome this paradox by means of 'vertical coopetition'.

From horizontal to vertical coopetition

Aliouat (1996), whose research is based on the seminal work of Axelrod (1980; Axelrod and Hamilton 1981), suggests one major explanation for the paradoxical use of the two approaches within a 'horizontal' context that can be applied to 'vertical' relationships. There may be a paradox associated with a situation characterized by interdependence: key accounts may combine cooperative and aggressive behaviours to maximize their earnings. This can be illustrated by means of game theory.

If we refer to Aliouat's cooperation benefit matrix (1996, p. 74), cooperation can generate mutual earnings of 100 to both the key account and the supplier. But if aggressive behaviour is added by the key account to the cooperation, for example, the launching of a competitive bid, those earnings can reach 200 and be doubled for the key account. Such an approach will bear fruit until such a time as the supplier becomes wary and starts to mistrust the key account, at which point it will inevitably begin to incur losses. Thus, it is in the key account's interest to find a trade-off between cooperation and calling for competitive bids to optimize earnings.

As early as 1989, Braddach and Eccles had rejected the transaction cost economic continuum with two mutually exclusive poles going from market to hierarchy. They 'emphasize how transactions controlled by one mechanism are profoundly affected by the simultaneous use of an alternative control mechanism'. Here, they hint at an unbalanced interaction between two mechanisms, in which a less powerful one influences its more powerful counterpart. Developing this line of reasoning, we can surmise that one type of relationship is used to soften the impact and 'correct' the other one. An example would be the use of market price competitive exchange to 'correct' inherent problems in the cooperative approach, i.e. the risk of opportunism on the supplier side.

The notion of correction suggests that coopetition does not necessarily imply a perfect equilibrium between cooperation and price competition: one form of relationship may be predominant, with the other appearing as secondary, mitigating the effects of the first one.

In the field of strategy, Bengtsson and Kock (1999, 2000) have produced in-depth studies of coopetition within horizontal alliances in B2B networks, analysing how firms combine the advantages of competition and cooperation. The authors define three forms of coopetition: when cooperation dominates, when competition dominates and when cooperation and competition play equal roles.

The choice of each form is defined by the specific resources available to individual competitors. This approach can be applied to 'vertical coopetition' to produce a description of the same three forms of coopetition. The more the suppliers have strategic resources required by the key account, the more cooperation is predominant. The scarcer those resources are and the more fragmented they are among a large number of suppliers, the higher the level of price competition.

To complement the insights from the literature review, which reveals three forms of coopetition, we will now turn to an initial empirical study both to justify and to refine our theoretical framework.

Development of theoretical framework

The empirical stage of our research involves firstly a field study; the objective of which is to define whether the findings of our review of the literature on horizontal relationships can be applied to vertical relationships.

Field study

We decided to select ten MNCs that are the leaders in their respective industries and would have key account status with their suppliers. We purposely selected MNCs from both the industrial and service sectors with a view to maximizing the sample's diversity and uncover a wide variety of supply relationships within the business-to-business sector.

We conducted ten in-depth interviews with purchasing managers and directors with substantial experience in the field of purchasing. The interviewees were contacted through the alumni network of a business school. On average, the interviews lasted between an hour and 90 minutes. We applied a semi-guided interview technique developed by a French researcher (Romelaer 2005, p. 114). All the interviews were audio-recorded and transcribed by the author within 72 hours. We used thematic coding and mapped relationships conceptually (Miles and Huberman 1994, 2003).

Refined theoretical framework

This initial field study confirmed that out of the ten companies interviewed, nine had hybrid forms of relationship with their suppliers. The exception to this rule was provided by a company dealing with purely relational features in an industry in which prices are fixed by law.

The field study revealed that two hybrid forms of vertical relationship are predominant:

1. Relationships based on competitive pricing (mostly via tenders) but including a certain degree of cooperation.
2. Predominantly cooperative relationships, including some calls for competition (competitive bids).

This is consistent with Bengtsson and Kock (1999, 2000), except that in vertical relationships, at least among the companies studied, no balanced form of relationship between competitive pricing and cooperation was to be found: there was always one predominant form mixed with a secondary, weaker one.

We also found some interesting mechanisms linking the two forms of relationship. As hinted at by Braddach and Eccles (1989), one form of relationship would 'correct' the weaknesses of the other, but could also 'strengthen' the qualities of the other form. In certain circumstances, one form would also 'substitute' another.

Case studies

To complement the insights from the field study, we carried out four comprehensive case studies (Yin 2003) as we needed to understand in detail how the mechanisms and the dimensions described here work.

We chose to study four global MNCs, leaders in their industry in three different sectors: industrial equipment (Case 1), packaging (Case 2) and FMCG (Cases 3 and 4). To keep things even, we decided to focus on four manufacturing MNCs. When there was a need to focus on a specific supplier or product, this choice was determined by the Anderson and Narus study (1991), which points out that corrugated cases were on the transactional (price-competition) side of the relational continuum whereas industrial equipment was on the cooperative side. By selecting 'polar' products, we were able to gain an insight into the influence of specific products on the choice of relationship. Since it was of critical importance to question influential decision-makers involved in selecting and monitoring supplier relationships, we conducted in-depth interviews with senior executives.

We selected global and European purchase managers/directors (six informants) and 'users' (four informants, including a project director, a corporate technical manager and a sensory panel manager). In the interests of external validity (Yin 2003) and to avoid a strictly dyadic approach, we also interviewed suppliers (key account managers and directors – five informants) working with a number of the MNCs in the sample. We also selected 'expert' CEOs who were heading up different organizations, one of them stressing marketing and KAM roles, the other a procurement role. To ensure that the data derived from the interviews were valid, we organized a number of presentations with key informants during which we asked them to assess our conclusions. During these presentations we had the opportunity to clarify some minor findings. Our final sample consisted of around 25 informants (including informants from the field study). For the case studies, we applied the same interview and analysis technique as for the field study. We also used thematic coding (Miles and Huberman 2003, 1994). The original coding schemes from the field study were modified and refined as analysis progressed in the case studies and new concepts were uncovered.

Key findings

Key Finding No. 1: The pivotal points associating a relationship primarily based on competitive pricing with a number of relational features and the impact on value management.

Some key account buyers prefer to remain in an 'adversarial' type of relationship and put a lot of pressure on their suppliers with recurrent (sometimes unexpected) tenders to ensure the best price/offer from the market.

> **Expert**: "What we have found is that when you purchase, in a sense, you often get the best terms when there is a degree of uncertainty and you get less good terms when you become obvious in the way you operate."

> **Case 1: European Purchase Director**: "I purposely do not develop long-term, committed and stable relationships."

Although the type of relationship alluded to above is primarily based on the short-term transactions with price as a mediator, rather than the relationship itself (Dwyer et al. 1987; Grönroos 1994), it does include some relational features which 'correct' the strictly price-competitive approach. This is not merely due to the fact that transactions may be sustained (Dyer et al. 1998; Palmer 2007), but also due to the fact that key accounts want to compensate for the disadvantages of a lack of cooperation, especially in cases in which there is a commercial dispute to settle. Even if there is no commitment on the part of the key account, an element of trust will 'correct' the pure price focus and introduce some relational benefits, mostly in terms of information-sharing (Ulaga 2003).

Although self-interest is dominant, key accounts will not let supplier trust decrease below a certain threshold and thus will not focus exclusively on a transaction-based relationship in order to optimize their profits:

> **Case 1: European Purchase Director**: "In all cases, key account status is going to help you, specifically if you have a commercial dispute . . . If the problem is enormous, you need somebody (the supplier) who can solve the dispute in a global way."

If one relational benefit has to be sustained, within a predominantly transactional relationship, it is information-sharing focused on problem solving, especially if the problem arises from the key account's end customer.

In such situations, value is primarily derived from competitive prices (pie sharing) but one relational element may ease the pressure on the supplier during negotiations: a proven ability to settle problems rapidly, especially when such problems impact the end-user. This is in line with Abratt and Kelly's study (2002, p. 473) showing that the ability of 'managers to identify problems and provide solutions within their key accounts is ranked as the number one success factor in key customers' perception of customer–supplier partnerships.

Some relational features may also 're-enforce' the price-competitive exchange: Sheth and Parvatiyar (1995, p. 399) recall the major axiom of this price-competitive approach ('transactional marketing'): 'One axiom of transactional marketing is the belief that competition and self-interest are the drivers of value creation. Through competition, buyers can be offered a choice.'

To get the best choice in a 'bounded rationality' situation (Simon 1959) a key account will maintain a certain rapport with a panel of suppliers in order to 'optimize' its market information gathering capabilities and obtain the elements enabling it to launch competitive bids at the appropriate time (fixing prices for a certain period of time when the market starts to rise, for example) and to work with the most appropriate players.

> **Case 1: European Purchase Director**: "The important thing is to understand your supplier's sales strategy. So it's better to keep in touch with suppliers because it increases your negotiating capabilities. This is the reason why I never kick out a supplier: I just lower the volumes I grant them. Otherwise, you lose market knowledge and there is a loss of effectiveness."

Here, and as paradoxical as it may seem, the relational benefit derived from information-sharing is used to reinforce the transactional approach and the appropriation of value on the part of key accounts: the focus is on 'pie sharing' and on obtaining not only the lowest prices but also the lowest sustainable prices.

The primary tactic used to achieve this is tendering before market prices pick up and negotiating the length of contracts to prevent suppliers from recovering the full extent of price increases. Fine-tuning transactional strategies requires a great deal of market information and a degree of cooperation on the part of suppliers in terms of providing such information (certain suppliers may deem it in their interest to conduct some of their business at low profit levels in view of economies of scale).

Last but not least, once key accounts believe that the limits of the transactional approach have been reached, they often introduce a number of relational elements. Key accounts 'commute' from a predominantly transactional relationship to a more collaborative approach. Pillai and Sharma (2003) have studied how a mature buyer–seller relationship can follow a reversed U curve, migrating from a relational orientation towards a transactional one. This process can follow the opposite course with a relational orientation replacing a transactional one (Webster 1992). When buyers believe they have exhausted the possibilities of a transactional approach (achieving and maintaining the lowest prices on the market), they may choose to focus on relational benefits, such as improved quality, innovation, etc. (Ulaga 2003).

> **Study 7: Purchase Support Manager**: "We can't pressurize suppliers on a long-term basis: if we do, we run the risk that a supplier may end the contract or cut corners on quality or on supply chain efficiency. In the end, we may suffer as a result or our end-customers may suffer.
>
> We have more than met our cost-saving targets. So, we proved that we achieve cost-savings. We have worked with our suppliers on a variety of products, but we can't go below the lowest price. We can lower the price once, or twice, but we reach a limit when this is no longer possible . . . What we then try to do is to keep on working on price fairness, but we do this alongside product improvement, processes improvement, product differentiation and services. Today, we are in an innovation workshop."

In such instances, value management is definitely sequential. The first task is to obtain the biggest share of the pie, after which the aim is to add non-economic benefits to that share.

Whatever the type of pivot used to introduce a relational orientation to a price-competitive relationship, it is always deployed as a kind of 'incentive' to obtain the most competitive market price while simultaneously keeping the supplier relatively happy. Key accounts will 'soften' the relationship, introducing relational benefits as incentives for the supplier. Those 'incentives' can take the form of information transfer (in the case of joint problem solving), which can help suppliers gain customer share, integration into the key account's long-term strategy, which can help suppliers to increase profits by reducing costs (Kalwani and Narayandas 1995), and increased value sharing (quality or innovation improvements), which can help suppliers to sustain wallet share.

Key Finding No. 2: The pivotal point associating a relationship primarily based on cooperation with a number of price-competitive features and the impact on value management.

Although this type of relationship is primarily collaborative and based on a quest for mutual relational benefits within a long-term relationship, rather than on short-term transactions designed to achieve the best market price (Dwyer et al. 1987; Grönroos 1994), some transactional features (Ivens and Pardo 2005) 'correct' the relational approach. The major reason is key accounts' fight against suppliers' opportunistic behaviour (Wathne and Heide 2000). Buyers want to be sure that, even when they have a long-term contractual commitment with a supplier, they will still get the most competitive price throughout the length of the contract.

> **Case 3: Global Purchase Director – Packaging**: "If I have a price-competitiveness guarantee, I can commit to a supplier for a very long time. The price, as well as the margin, must be competitive in the appropriate market. I buy the largest volumes possible; I wouldn't be properly representing the interests of my company if prices were blocked at an initial level. If a gap between the supplier and market prices gradually develops, the supplier must return to the market level, even if this involves reducing his margins. If the supplier is unable to do this, then we have a major concern. I check the market price level all the time. Everybody wants to work with us."

> **Case 4: European Purchasing Group Manager**: "We have 'framework agreements' and we have an indexation clause on raw materials. (Nevertheless) we never accept a supplier's price without checking it with another supplier. In our contracts, it is stated that we can give any new project to any supplier. We have an obligation to discuss the matter with the ('preferred') supplier and he has a priority in terms of new business, but if his price is not good enough, we can give the new project to another supplier. Otherwise, it would be too easy! We systematically put out calls for tender for all new products."

Although value is derived from creativity and a will to 'increase the pie', rather than just optimize their slice, key accounts do not want to suffer at the hands of suppliers increasing their own slice, and will make sure that, in relative terms, the slice they get is the largest proportionately to the increase in the value of the pie achieved in conjunction with the supplier.

Another reason why transactional features have the effect of 'correcting' the relational approach (a reason which has not been discussed in the academic literature, and a driving force in our sample), is that the competitive price approach is a way for key accounts' buyers to assert their role and credibility within their own companies. While they find it difficult to turn certain relational benefits into economic data, they can more easily use tenders to help them demonstrate any cost reductions they have made.

> **Expert**: "So, it sounds peculiar, but in many large companies, purchasing departments are happy enough to see prices from their incumbent suppliers kind of moving

up because they may have an opportunity to bring them down when it comes to the point when everybody is really watching their performance; this opportunity is the tender process."

Calls for competition are also the symbol of the buyers' power, whereas some relational benefits (product development, quality improvement) fall within the remit of other key account departments (R and D or production).

It is at this point that 'vertical' coopetition is closest to 'horizontal' coopetition. As Bengtsson and Kock (2000, p. 419) observed, 'Individuals in the material development departments at both companies cooperated with each other, while individuals in the marketing and product development departments competed with each other. Goals were jointly stipulated in their cooperation, but not, of course, in their competition.' We find the same type of synchronic approach (Perret and Josserand 2003) when the coopetitive process is 'compartmentalized': the buyer takes care of the transactional orientation, whereas other actors or departments, which use the purchased product, will take care of the relational approach.

> **Study 3: Director, Global procurement EMEA**: "(With users) you have this relationship (with the supplier) that may be very strong and erase all rational and unbiased decision-making. The role of the purchasing director is to bring some in-depth thinking to the relationship and provide opportunities; finding out whether we can find something better or cheaper on the market."

Value creation is often difficult to turn into numbers, in the sense of well-defined economic benefits (how much is information-sharing worth?). Such cooperative strategies may appear to be subjective, and buyers often prefer the 'objectivity' associated with calls for tender (based on objective figures which can be used to calculate margins).

> **Case 3: Global Purchase Director – Packaging**: "In the end, the power of the buyer resides in the fact that he can launch calls for tender . . . Savings exist because purchasers can demonstrate them; otherwise they are invisible."

Coopetitive approaches of this kind reveal a desire to clarify value calculations: when the limits of the value pie are blurred, key customers go back to basics, calculating the size of their slice if they are not sure they can optimize it. Although it may seem paradoxical, some 'price competitive' features help to 're-enforce' the predominant relational approach. Key accounts want to be reassured that suppliers are not behaving opportunistically. Calls for tender may be launched, but only for a few products or as a 'benchmark', leaving the supplier with most of its existing business with the key account. The supplier or a consulting company may be requested to benchmark a strategic product against a similar product in the market. Whatever the outcome, the supplier will not be at risk of losing the business but may be asked by the key account to re-align prices to reflect the market. The aim of the key account is to strengthen the relationship while ensuring that the supplier does not view it as a 'captive' customer. The price control mechanism is primarily used to reinforce suppliers' level of trust.

> **Case 3: Global Purchase Director – Packaging**: "When we reach that point (with the supplier), we start to abandon the purely transactional approach. We talk more about projects and less about prices. We check whether the price is competitive, but we trust those people, since we know the gap between them and the other suppliers. We do not fool around challenging them every two months. When we (at the CEO level) talk about new technology, they answer: 'Where you want to go, we will go.' There is a strong trust relationship and they are able to react appropriately, whatever the situation. I see a future with them."

In such a coopetitive strategy, value is almost exclusively derived from creation based on relational benefits (rather than directly economic ones). Interestingly, however, since the level of trust is very high, suppliers must 'prove' (by providing evidence) that they offer the largest value slice to the customer. This reinforces the willingness to work together to expand the size of the pie. The relationship thus becomes self-reinforcing.

Key accounts may also 'commute' from a predominantly relational approach to a formalized transactional one. Some key accounts will deploy a relational approach through the duration of a particular contract and then systematically renew it by means of a call for tender. They may also launch a competitive bid when the supplier's turnover with a specific product has reached a fixed limit. In such circumstances, the supplier's turnover may be at risk, but if it wins the tender, the relational approach will move forward.

> **Case 4: European Purchasing Group Manager**: "We launch tenders, for instance, when we renew contracts. We do this with standard suppliers every year, with 'key' suppliers every two or three years, and with 'strategic' partners every five years."

This last coopetitive approach demonstrates that an optimum level of trust can never be attained and that key accounts are keen to check on a regular basis that the non-relational benefits they derive are not detrimental to their goal of obtaining the largest possible slice of the pie. They also want to ensure that they will be able to modify the relational orientation if they fail to obtain the kind of slice they feel they are entitled to.

Again, whatever the mechanism used to add transactional content to a collaborative relationship, it will always be a form of 'control': calls for tender are used by the key account to 'control' their relationship with the supplier. Mirroring this inter-firm control mechanism is an intra-firm control mechanism in which key buyers apply a transactional approach to suppliers to control their own internal environment.

Key accounts have developed new 'hybrid' forms of vertical exchange with their suppliers, combining calls for tender with cooperation, applying either 'incentive' mechanisms to upgrade their supplier's level of commitment or inter-firm 'control

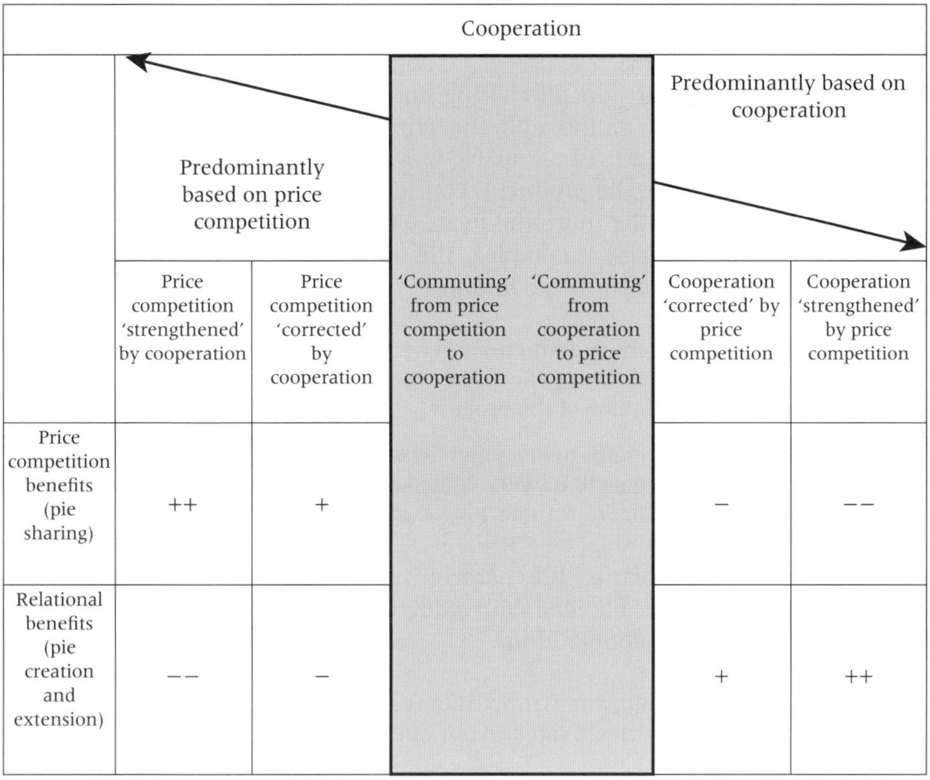

		Cooperation						
						Predominantly based on cooperation		
	Predominantly based on price competition							
	Price competition 'strengthened' by cooperation	Price competition 'corrected' by cooperation	'Commuting' from price competition to cooperation	'Commuting' from cooperation to price competition		Cooperation 'corrected' by price competition	Cooperation 'strengthened' by price competition
Price competition benefits (pie sharing)	++	+				−	−−
Relational benefits (pie creation and extension)	−−	−				+	++

Figure 1 The 'coopetition' continuum

mechanisms' to counter their opportunistic behaviour or, paradoxically, to maintain a high level of trust.

'Correcting' and 'strengthening' pivotal points alter the respective influence of predominant and secondary approaches. The 'strengthening' pivot emphasizes the predominant form, while the 'correcting' pivot emphasizes the secondary form. This leads me to define a vertical 'coopetition' continuum starting from price competition to a strong form of cooperation, as described in Figure 1.

Figure 1 represents a continuum along which the strengthening mechanism is located towards the polar end of the continuum. The 'correcting' mechanism, on the other hand, includes a number of advantages deriving from the second form and this mitigation places it half way between the middle and the end of the continuum. The 'commuting' pivotal point switches from one form of coopetition to the other and is located right in the middle of the continuum. These three mechanisms bring a degree of dynamism along the relationship continuum.

We have to understand why key accounts choose either a cooperation-predominant form of coopetition or a price-competitive one, and gain an insight into each of the two sub-dimensions of each predominant form.

Key Finding No. 3: The purchased product as an explanatory factor of the form taken by coopetition.

In the academic literature on purchasing and marketing, there is a direct link between product segmentation and the choice of relationship to be applied (Anderson and Narus 1991; Bensaou 1999; Kaufman et al. 2000; Kraljic 1983). In other words, the more the product is considered a commodity and the simpler the purchase process is, the more the focus will be on price; while the more the product or purchase process is complex, the more the focus will be on the relationship. My studies confirm these findings:

> **Case 1: European Purchase Director**: "I checked that those processes (competition based on price) would work effectively when raw material makes a significant contribution to the final price of the product.
>
> We don't have much room for manoeuvre: Coca-Cola varnish is Coca-Cola varnish. The day you want to change it, it's very difficult, extremely difficult. So you end up signing long-term agreements with people (suppliers)."

Nevertheless, the approach is still characterized by 'coopetition'-based relationships: price competition is blended with a degree of cooperation, and cooperation is blended with calls for competition.

> **Case 4: European Purchasing Group Manager**: "We don't go in for single sourcing. We never develop a single supplier (for one product range)."

In reference to Kraljic's (1983) seminal work, non-critical and leverage products can be associated with price competition as the predominant form of coopetition, while bottleneck and strategic products can be associated with cooperation as the dominant form. Furthermore, it transpired from this study that it is not only in terms of product segmentation that the choice between predominantly cooperative and predominantly price-competitive coopetition can be analysed. A new moderating variable appeared in the value of the key account brand or BU (business unit) in which the purchased product is incorporated. Key accounts choose their different relational orientation with their suppliers in reference to the value these specific brands or BUs bring to their global business.

Key Finding No. 4: The key account's brand or BU value as a major explanation of the coopetition form.

The case studies mentioned above (specifically Cases 3 and 4) reveal a trend towards a greater sophistication in purchaser analysis. Buyers have moved from purchased product analysis towards a value analysis of their own brands and product ranges. As for products in Kraljic's matrix, brands or BUs are positioned on a continuum defined by the relative competitive advantage they provide in comparison with the other key account brands or BUs.

If the comparative competitive advantage is high and the brand or BU generates a high level of value for the key account, supplier relationships will be predominantly cooperative. According to Porter's classification, the purchase strategy will be based to a larger degree on differentiation mode and relational benefits will be sought. If the comparative competitive advantage is low and the brand or BU generates a low level of value for the key account, the supplier relationship will be predominantly based on price competition. According to Porter's classification, the purchase strategy will be based to a larger degree on a cost domination mode and the lowest purchase prices will be sought.

Within the same key account, a supplier of the same (purchased) product may be confronted with different relational orientations according to the brand or BU it is selling to. Buyers are, nowadays, increasingly involved in the process of creating value by means of brands or BUs and will therefore define their relationships with suppliers, not only in relation with the purchased product segmentation, but also according to their own brand or BU value segmentation.

> **Case 4: European Purchasing Group Manager**: "In my team, people are organized in business units, which means that a European buyer will be responsible for a specific 'spend category', like solid board, but he or she will be responsible for one or two businesses (lines of final products). A pan-European supplier may work with different businesses, but he will not deal with the same buyer.

> Obviously, the specific marketing strategy of each business will directly influence the type of relationships we want to have with the suppliers. In highly competitive markets, we may only apply a cost approach, on other high-range products [In this context, products are to be understood as products to be sold to the end user by the key account.], we will go for partnerships. The purchase strategy doesn't just involve looking for the best suppliers, it also implies matching the needs of our marketing people. Some businesses don't have the same needs as the others. From there, we will develop relationships (with suppliers) that we will differ according to our product lines."

> **Case 3: VP Procurement**: "(Buyers) are interested in brand profit, thus they are as interested in increasing brand profit and decreasing the cost of the product as they are in boosting the top line, the sales value of the brand."

> **Case 3: Global Purchase Director – Packaging**: "The future of our company is that buyers will be less and less connected to markets, but more and more connected to our brands. Some buyers will join marketing teams. These are senior buyers, who have experience in several markets. Their mission will be to improve the brand and work to develop it."

In conclusion, we have two moderating variables that influence the choice of the dominant form (either cooperative or price-competitive) of coopetitive relationships; on the one hand, purchased product segmentation, and on the other, the value classification applied to sold product (brand or BU).

These two variables are not of equal weight: the sold product (brand or BU) classification takes precedence over product segmentation in determining the relational orientation to be applied. For instance, in terms of a purely purchased

Value of brands or BUs

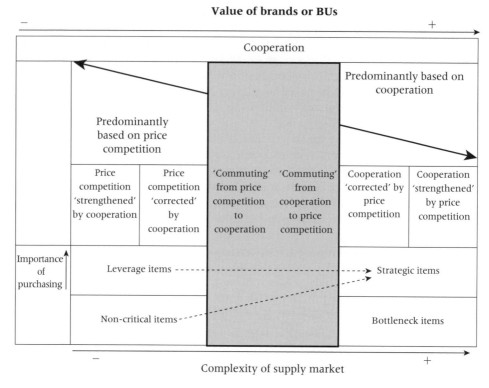

Figure 2 The 'vertical coopetition' synthesis

product segmentation, corrugated cases will be considered as non-critical or leverage products for which a coopetitive relationship, predominantly based on price competition, will be applied. But if the corrugated cases are used by the key account as RRP (retail ready packaging) for a high-value brand, then a coopetitive relationship, predominantly based on cooperation, will be developed with suppliers.

The Kraljic (1983) purchasing portfolio model is based on two aspects (Dubois and Pedersen 2002): the importance of purchasing and the complexity of the supply market. Our model adds a third aspect: the value of the sold brand or BU line of products. This means that a non-critical or leverage product may become a strategic product and that, in consequence, the 'coopetitive' orientation may transform from a predominantly competitive one to a predominantly cooperative one, as described in Figure 2.

'Vertical coopetition' has become a key concept in understanding the sophisticated and dynamic approach taken by key accounts to their relationships with suppliers. As we have demonstrated, the relationship is characterized by a combination of cooperation and price competition, but the respective roles of the two approaches within that combination may be influenced by two major variables: the purchased product itself and, more importantly, the value of the brand or BU in which the purchased product is incorporated.

Discussion and managerial implications

According to our research, this is the first time that an attempt has been made to conceptualize, using an approach grounded in managerial practice, the notion of 'vertical coopetition'. Thus, my research contributes to a better understanding of the relational strategies applied by key accounts, outlining as it does a number of new trends in purchasing strategies.

Contribution from the key account's viewpoint

The first major change is a more pronounced internal trend away from purchasing and towards marketing. This means that major companies now place a greater emphasis on mitigating potential conflicts between purchasing and marketing and setting up working procedures that involve purchasers in the marketing decision process. Purchase managers may come to play an integral role in defining marketing strategy. They are increasingly expected to contribute at an early stage to key accounts' value creation processes. As such, they play an important role in selecting suppliers who 'fit' key account marketing needs as effectively as possible, while at the same time playing a more traditional role by ensuring that their companies achieve the best value share possible (the biggest slice of the pie). This may create a certain degree of conflict, in that purchasers are expected to find suppliers with whom they can optimize relational benefits while still maintaining a degree of price competition, which implies a relationship characterized by proximity tempered by a certain degree of distance (to safeguard independence of choice). In order to resolve conflicts over roles, purchasing organizations are using different tools. A new type of structure is emerging in which cooperation and calls for tender are managed by different people. Senior buyers take care of cooperation, which is often considered the 'strategic' part of the relationship, while junior buyers follow a defined process to organize tenders and supplier benchmarking mechanisms.

When this 'split' between different people within an organization is not possible, framework contracts (Mouzas and Ford 2006) are sometimes used to avoid role conflict. By defining, in an umbrella contract, both the relationship and long-term expectations, on one hand, and detailed rules for price competition (Request for Quotation) on the other, buyers become less schizophrenic since they are aware in detail of how coopetition strategies will be applied. Thus, buyers can maintain a certain distance simply by applying defined rules (even if they are the ones who have defined those rules).

These emerging trends may be food for thought for other customers, not necessarily key accounts, who wish to optimize their relationships with their suppliers.

Contribution from the supplier's viewpoint

The implications of our research are also extremely important for suppliers. Suppliers can use this input to construct their own marketing strategy and, more especially, their key account programmes. Our research emphasizes the fact that suppliers must primarily focus on the brands or lines of products which their key customers believe deliver high value to them. This may provide a new vision of key account management in which key customers are no longer considered as a whole but in which specific segments of key customers are targeted – the fact that purchasers' responsibilities are defined along individual business terms may help to define this segment-based strategy within key accounts' range of brands. Furthermore, suppliers may also adopt a number of very different strategies with the same key customer: they may decide to go for price competition and standard products if they have a predominantly price-competitive relationship with their key accounts, or they may choose to position themselves at the other end of the relational continuum and work on relational benefits. The new perspective that our research offers can help suppliers to define a relational strategy based not on individual customers, but on their customers' brands and product lines. Following that line of reasoning, it is possible to imagine that key account management could become key (customer) brand management. Insofar as purchasing managers 'merging' into the marketing team is concerned, suppliers will have to focus on the competitive advantages they can bring to their key accounts, considered not in terms of their identity as single companies but in terms of specific brands and product lines.

Because of the key account 'coopetitive' approach, suppliers who want to work on a cooperative basis will always have to face pressure from key customers to lower their prices. Views on the nature of 'cooperation' have increasingly veered away from Jap's (1999) definition of '(creating) mutually beneficial outcomes for all participants'. Today there is greater pressure from key accounts to obtain a larger share of the 'pie' and 'mutual' is far from meaning 'equal'. Suppliers have to think of relational benefits for their key customers not only in terms of delivering competitive advantages, but also in terms of doing so at a lower cost than other suppliers. This should encourage them to attempt to find synergies (to share development costs) and create relational benefits that can be offered to different, non-competitive key accounts. In order to do so, they will have to 'decompartmentalize' their key account management structure.

Thus the major conclusion of our research (within the limit of its exploratory nature) is that the concept of key account management may, in years to come, undergo major changes, as suppliers will need to develop transversal management approaches to their portfolio of key accounts in order to take advantage of the latter's most valued brands and share the development costs of relational benefits among different accounts if they want to guarantee success.

Conclusion and directions for future research

In this paper we attempt to bridge the gap between transactional and relational purchasing (derived from the relationship marketing paradigm) by defining the concept of 'vertical coopetition', which helps to understand the dynamic approach taken by key accounts in managing their relationships with their suppliers.

As we have demonstrated, this vertical relationship is characterized by a combination of cooperation and price competition, but the weight of each antagonistic approach within that combination may be influenced by two major variables: the purchased product itself (reference Kraljic's (1983) seminal article) and, more importantly, the value of the brand or business unit in which the purchased product is incorporated.

Our paper may provide practitioners with a new tool (Figure 2) that will help them to fine-tune their relational strategy:

- Suppliers may assess the coopetitive mix in their relationships with key customers and use it to segment such customers or to define the level of resources they wish to allocate to them. They may no longer have a monolithic customer approach but decide to adjust their key customer relational strategy according to the value of the customer's different final product lines or brands and focus their efforts where they can add and appropriate more value.
- Key customers may also define the coopetitive mix in their relationships with suppliers according to the latters' contribution to the added value of their final products. As defined in our article, the coopetitive mix may be used to segment suppliers as a dynamic approach and an incentive for suppliers to dedicate more efforts to collaboration and innovation.

In short, our research is a pragmatic attempt to fill in the 'middle' of the relationship continuum, which has been left blank by academic scholars, and qualify the relationship marketing paradigm with the practitioner's perspective.

Our findings establish the relevance of defining key account–supplier relationships as 'coopetitive' and provide a framework for describing such relationships, but as is true of all research projects, this study could be a stepping-stone for further research opportunities.

First, this research programme focused on a limited number of case studies. The key accounts selected are global companies wielding a good deal of power in their respective industries, implying that their suppliers found themselves in an asymmetrical power relationship. It would be interesting to broaden this research approach to other standard customers.

Second, we deliberately chose to emphasize the key accounts' point of view. The perspective of suppliers was taken into account, but only in order to gain a critical insight into the viewpoint of the key accounts. We did not study any specific dyadic relationship or any network perspective. The results of the study would have to be consolidated by taking such perspectives into account.

Third, although we include some 'users' from departments other than procurement in our key account informants, the study focuses on buyers, which may have created some potential bias. Further research could deal with this input at a later date.

While the need for further research has to be borne in mind when considering the results of the study, we have nevertheless introduced new insights into customer–supplier relationships that may be of use to both academics and practitioners and offer an alternative to the bipolarization of such relationships in current present scholarship. Further research should attempt to corroborate the results of the study against a broader background (quantitative research) and apply other perspectives (standard suppliers).

Key account management in business markets: an empirical test of common assumptions

BY BJÖRN SVEN IVENS AND CATHERINE PARDO

Abstract

Purpose – The concept of key account management (KAM) has received considerable attention from practitioners and scholars for well over 20 years now. However, numerous articles build on a set of tacit assumptions for which we lack empirical evidence. This paper seeks to propose an empirical test of several of these assumptions.

Design/methodology/approach – The contribution draws on a study conducted among 297 purchasing managers in two industries (packaging goods, market research data).

Findings – The findings indicate that parts of the foundations of KAM are not as solid as they may appear at first sight.

Practical implications – This paper invites managers of KAM programmes to carefully consider the objectives they assign to such programmes by integrating the idea of value created both for key customers and for suppliers implementing such programmes.

Originality/value – The article extends knowledge of key account management in the business field by providing new – and, in the light of the extant literature, sometimes rather counter-intuitive – insights into this important management phenomenon. It does this by systematically comparing key account relationships and non-key account relationships.

Reproduced with the kind permission of Emerald Group, originally Ivens, B. and Pardo, C. (2008) 'Key-account-management in business markets: an empirical test of common assumptions', *Journal of Business & Industrial Marketing*, Vol. 23/5 pp. 301–310.

Introduction

As a reaction to changes in environmental factors, in their customers' purchasing behaviours and demands, and in their own strategies, many suppliers in the business-to-business field have introduced key account management (KAM) programmes. The aim of these programmes is to serve strategically important customers in a more individual manner than minor accounts (Pardo 1997, 1999; Workman et al. 2003).

Reflecting the increasing practical importance of key account management, marketing has developed an important body of literature that deals with various aspects of key account programmes (Homburg et al. 2002; Weilbaker and Weeks 1997). However, even when authors draw upon theoretical frameworks (such as power-dependence theory or transaction cost analysis for instance), empirical tests are more often called upon in the 'further research' section than conducted in the field. More specifically, an issue remaining particularly opaque is the question to what extent key account relationships can be clearly distinguished from 'normal' buyer–seller relationships. Many authors posit differences without providing empirical evidence. In fact, studies opposing key account dyads to non-key account dyads are extremely rare.

Therefore, our main purpose in this paper is to compare both types of relationships on a selected number of specific aspects that we derived from the KAM literature.

In the following section, we briefly present a description of the nature of key account management. Following this review, we develop a set of hypotheses. We then show the results of an empirical test conducted in two industries opposing 91 key account relationships to 206 traditional relationships. The final section contains a discussion of implications for key account theory and practice.

Key account management

Suppliers increasingly pay attention to the maintenance and enhancement of important customer relationships. This particular attention is often manifested by the establishment of key account programmes (Kempeners and van der Hart 1999), with the overall objective of occupying a marketplace position of competitive advantage (Hunt 2000).

In the extant literature a panoply of different terms is being used to designate the specific organizational solutions this paper deals with, e.g. national account management, large account management or strategic account management (Boles et al. 1999). Based upon a discussion of these terms, Pardo (1999) pleads for the use of key account management (KAM), a position shared in this article. The central characteristics of KAM are summarized by Pardo (2006, p. 115):

"In a firm's customer portfolio, there is a central core (of customers). The supplier believes that if the exchanges with these customers are managed in a specific way, they can offer greater commercial efficiency. These are the customers the supplier designates as his firm's key accounts. To manage them in a specific way means a different form of management than that usually used for his customers. More specifically, this means the creation of a new mission (thus the creation of a new job, new practices, etc.) and its integration into the existing structure. This mission involves coordinating supplier information and action in time and space in relation to a customer in its entirety."

Recently, Homburg et al. (2002) and Workman et al. (2003) have underlined the importance of the KAM topic but have also mentioned that 'the survey research has primarily presented descriptive data concerning various aspects of KAM programmes, with little theoretical development and few hypotheses tested' (Workman et al. 2003, p. 4).

Our objective is to contribute to a stronger empirical foundation of assumptions made about key account relationships. For this purpose we draw upon propositions about key account management relationships that have been made in the extant literature. We raise them as hypotheses by narrowing them down to different theoretical frameworks and test them empirically.

Central constructs and hypotheses

Constructs drawn from the 'resource dependence' and the 'transaction costs' approaches

Discussing inter-organizational governance, Heide (1994) identifies three frameworks that are particularly relevant for the study of key relationships: resource dependence theory, transaction cost analysis (TCA) and relational contracting theory. Ivens and Pardo (2003) provide an analysis of differences between key and non-key relationships regarding the norms discussed in the latter framework. Hence we focus, in this paper, on the resource dependence approach and TCA. The aspects of key account management we study are derived from the extant literature.

KAM and uncertainty

According to Boles et al. (1996, p. 7), 'through their interaction with a buyer or buying team [key account managers] can increase the confidence in the supplier. This helps reduce uncertainty and increase trust'. Uncertainty is an important element of the atmosphere surrounding exchange relationships. Higher degrees of uncertainty either induce transaction costs to safeguard against risk or oblige managers to bear mental pressure.

What impact could key account management have on uncertainty? To answer this question, we suggest that a differentiated perspective is required. It has been argued that a too broad definition of uncertainty leads to conflicting results (Balakrishnan and Wernerfelt 1986). Thus, for the purpose of our study, we rely upon the TCA approach of uncertainty and isolate two forms of uncertainty: internal and external uncertainty.

1. We define internal uncertainty as the difficulties a supplier meets in predicting a customer's future behaviour in an ongoing relationship. Internal uncertainty is also called 'behavioural uncertainty' by Rindfleisch and Heide (1997) and defined as 'the difficulties in verifying whether compliance with established agreements has occurred' (p. 31).
2. We interpret external uncertainty as a supplier's inability to forecast accurately the evolution of its own and its customers' downstream markets as well as of the environmental factors influencing these markets. This definition is not far from the one given by Heide (1994) for whom 'external uncertainty is a property of the decision environment within which the exchange takes place' and is linked to the fact that 'relevant contingencies are too numerous or unpredictable to be specified ex ante' (p. 73). It is also called 'environmental uncertainty' (Rindfleisch and Heide 1997) and explained by the fact that the 'circumstances surrounding an exchange cannot be specified ex ante' (p. 31).

We can now discuss what impact key account management may have on both external and internal uncertainties. By implementing a key account management programme, a supplier creates a new organizational solution which should serve his customers' needs better than the preceding one. This implies higher satisfaction of customers' needs and leads to higher levels of commitment (Wilson and Mummalaneni 1986). Summarizing, the installation of key account management increases the customer's perceptions of the supplier's attractiveness and underpins the strength of mutual bonds. Hence, the supplier perceives less internal risk than in a non-key account (non-KA) relationship. We formulate the following hypothesis:

> *H1a.* In KA relationships, there is less internal uncertainty than in non-KA relationships.

A different causal relationship may be expected for external uncertainty. Williamson (1985) argues that firms seek to minimize transaction costs and, under conditions of environmental uncertainty, move from market forms of governance toward hybrid forms or vertical integration. We nevertheless argue that key account management can be interpreted as a type of hybrid form of governance, and, as such, the implementation of a key account management programme is a reaction to external uncertainty. Hence:

> *H1b.* In KA relationships, there is a higher external uncertainty than in non-KA relationships.

KAM and supplier's relationship specific investments

The specificity of what is done for a customer by a supplier implementing a key account management programme seems to have always been at the core of the definition of key account management. For instance, in one of the fundamental academic contributions to key account management, Stevenson and Page (1979, p. 94) explained that key account management implies that 'special marketing procedures are followed'. For Workman et al. (2003) key account management can be defined as 'additional activities, actors or resources' directed to specific customers. Lambe and Spekman (1997, p. 64), comparing key account relationships and alliances, describe the former as relationships where 'buyer and seller share a relatively high level of dependence based on relationship-specific investments that elevate switching costs for both parties'. As a matter of fact, a supplier implementing a key account management programme wishes a long-term relationship with his customer. In this sense, he is encouraged to make relationship-specific investments. Specific investments – or asset specificity – is a dimension of exchange largely discussed in the transaction cost framework. It refers to the degree to which a supplier's investments represent sunk costs in case a customer terminates their relationship. We then propose the following hypothesis:

> *H2.* In KA relationships, the supplier's relationship-specific investments are higher than in non-KA relationships.

KAM and supplier dependence

By implementing a key account management programme a supplier signals that a customer (the key account) is important to him. This importance can stem from various sources. Resource dependence theory (e.g. Pfeffer and Salancik 1978) posits that few organizations are internally self-sufficient with respect to their critical resources. Rather, they need to cooperate with partners disposing of resources critical for their success (Ulrich and Barney 1984). Key account management can be interpreted as a link a supplier attempts to create with a customer because he believes the customer to be a critical resource (or to dispose of critical resources). Not only does the key customer represent a source of business a supplier wants to secure, the key customer is a critical resource for number of other reasons. The customer's reputation, his capacity and willingness to cooperate in R&D projects with the supplier, his ability to serve as a benchmarking partner are some aspects that could make the customer a valuable resource. And the list is much longer (Walter et al. 2001). Accordingly, from the vantage point of resource dependence theory, the introduction of a key account management programme is a possible response to a supplier's dependence on his customer. Therefore we can raise the following hypothesis:

> *H3.* In KA relationships, the supplier's dependence is higher than in non-KA relationships.

KAM and formal contracts

On the basis of their empirical study, Workman et al. (2003) conclude:

> "Our results indicate that formalization of key account management programs actually reduces key account management effectiveness. Having a formalized program can impede flexibility and the ability to customize offerings to specific customers" (pp. 14–15).

These results appear to the authors to be relatively counter-intuitive because, as they note, 'in marketing, effective effects of formalization have been empirically shown' (Workman et al. 2003, p. 11). Sharma (1997), several years before, also hypothesized that 'higher levels of formalization [of the decision process] are associated with lower levels of preference for key account programmes' (p. 31), and this hypothesis proved to be supported (p. 32).

However, if we consider a supplier's dependence to be higher in a KA relationship (see hypothesis *H3*) then a reverse hypothesis can be formulated for non-KA relationships. In the case where there is unilateral dependence, Heide (1994) empirically demonstrates that bilateral governance has less chance to be used to regulate exchanges. Hence, governance will take either a unilateral or hierarchical form. Moreover, let us assume that contracts explicitly state, in the present, how situations will be handled in the future. We are then authorized to consider that for customers, the presence of a contract provides rules on how the supplier may behave in the future, and at the same time stipulates the consequences (both legal and economic) of a supplier's potential violation of these rules. This framework can reassure the customer by reducing the uncertainty he is facing when working with a given supplier, and thus allow him to commit more strongly to the relationship. That kind of regulation then appears to be adapted to key account exchanges. Building on this interpretation of the possible role of formal contracts we then chose to raise the hypothesis the following way:

> *H4.* In KA relationships, contractual governance is higher than in non-KA relationships.

KAM process coordination

Numerous are the authors underlining the aspect of supplier's process coordination in key account management: coordination seems to be regularly quoted as a characteristic attribute of key account management programmes within companies. For instance, Lambe and Spekman (1997) underline key account managers' 'ability to coordinate key personnel intra-firm' (p. 71). Shapiro and Moriarty (1984) also note that 'much of the [key account management] concept revolves around the coordination of all elements involved in dealing with the customer' (p. 2). Barrett (1986) stresses the role of key account programmes in minimizing conflicts and improving communication between buyer and seller. He also puts into evidence the role of the key account team in ameliorating the process of coordination within the supplier organization: 'the [key account] team, working in a well-coordinated fashion, is able to "pull" the buying decision through the organization' (p. 69). Shapiro and Moriarty (1984) point out that 'much of the [key account management] concept . . . revolves around the coordination of all elements involved in dealing with the customer' (p. 2). And very recently, Workman et al. (2003) argue that 'successful key account management requires the coordination of activities' (p. 10). The authors explain that this supplier coordination is demanded by the key account as far as 'many buying firms have centralized their procurement and expect a similarly coordinated selling approach from their suppliers' (p. 38).

Stevenson (1981) seems to be the only author in the KAM literature who – based on his empirical survey – cannot conclude that 'an advantage of [key account management] is improved internal seller coordination' (p. 121), even if, as he recalls, 'normatively speaking, a reason for adopting a national account system is to improve internal coordination' (p. 122). He explains this result by arguing the time needed to attain such coordination: it needs time before key account management effectively improves internal coordination.

On the basis of these different works, we choose to test the following hypothesis:

> *H5.* In KA relationships supplier's customer-directed processes are better coordinated than in non-KA relationships.

KAM and relationship duration

In their work, Boles et al. (1996) show that key customers 'often face long time horizons associated with major purchases' (p. 14) and state that 'for this reason, the issues of keeping a long-term perspective [is] of relatively greater importance [than for] small accounts' (p. 14). For Millman and Wilson (1995), the development of a key account relationship can be modelled through a six-stage process. They explain that before implementing a key account management programme, the supplier must develop a network of contacts with the customer and gain knowledge about it. These early stages of the key account management (or pre-key account management) process take time. Pardo et al. (1995) use the term 'key accountization' to describe 'the process of adaptation of the organization with a view to managing exchanges with high stakes customers' (p. 127). Thus, the implementation of a key account programme – as any organizational adaptation process – takes time. Moreover, a key account management programme contributes to stabilize the relationship between a supplier and a customer. As Homburg et al. (2002) point out, the additional activities performed by the supplier for key account customers (what the authors call 'activity intensity') 'can lead to customers wanting to maintain and deepen the relationships' (p. 8). The picture drawn by all these authors of the key account relationship is similar to the one of 'relational exchange' described by Dwyer et al. (1987).

To summarize, time and more specifically relationship duration can be associated in two ways to key account management. First, because companies often wait before attributing a KA status to a customer to be sure he requires a specific treatment, we can anticipate that, in KA relationships, the duration of the relationships is higher than in non-KA relationships. Second, we must also consider the fact that key account management programmes are associated – in essence – with a long-term perspective: they are implemented to stabilize and secure a relationship between a supplier and a customer where specific assets are developed and the problem of sunk costs is always present. Using Dwyer et al.'s words, they create 'barriers to switching [and] provide a competitive advantage' (Dwyer et al. 1987, p. 14). Hence, we raise the following hypothesis:

> *H6.* In KA relationships, the duration of the relationships is higher than in non-KA relationships.

KAM and the number of actors

In his work describing customers preferring key account management programmes, Sharma (1997) indicates that 'firms that use a multi-functional and multi-level form of decision making prefer key account programmes' (p. 35). The author also hypothesizes in his work that 'higher numbers of people involved in decision making are associated with higher levels of preference for key account programmes' (p. 31), and this hypothesis is supported (p. 32). One of the reasons why key account management programmes are created is the complexity of customers' structures and the number of actors involved. Decision-making processes within customer firms often include people from different hierarchical levels and different functions. We then follow Sharma's argumentation that the number of actors involved – on the customer side – in the relationships is higher than in non-KA relationships. Therefore we choose to test the following hypothesis:

> *H7.* In KA relationships, the number of actors involved – on the customer side – in the relationship is higher than in non-KA relationships.

Customer turnover

The importance of the customer (in terms of turnover) seems to have always been at the core of the definition of what a key customer is. Turnover is the most quoted criterion for attributing to a customer a KA status (Napolitano 1997). For instance Boles et al. (1994) explain that 'volume' is 'necessary to provide national account[1] type service to a customer' (p. 268). Their survey proves that 'the first criterion for a firm being labeled a national account' is volume of potential business and the second 'volume of past sales' (p. 270). Lambe and Spekman (1997), recalling Shapiro and Moriarty's works, state that key account management pro-

---

[1] As explained earlier in this paper, we consider the denomination 'national account management' to be equivalent to 'key account management'.

grammes are 'most likely to be formed when a customer is relatively large' (Shapiro and Moriarty 1984, p. 62). Sharma's (1997) work shows that 'larger organizations preferred key account programmes' (p. 35). For Barrett (1986), key account management 'simply means targeting the largest and most important customers . . .' (p. 64), and going further, 'most companies established [key account programmes] based on existing or potential dollar volume. This is the primary criteria established by companies' (p. 65). More than 20 years ago Stevenson (1980), basing himself on a set of previous works and communications, raised the following hypothesis – '[key account] customers tend to exceed a threshold level of dollar volume of purchases' – and confirmed it. Tosdal (1950), quoted by Stevenson (1980, p. 134) noted that the key account status 'was given to a firm which used a large quantity [of products]'. Lang (1973), also quoted by Stevenson (1980, p. 134), noted that a key account customer should have 'large volume potential'. Corbin and Corben (1973), quoted by Stevenson (1980, p. 134) noted that key account management is needed due to 'bigger customers'. Previously Stevenson and Page (1979, p. 97) had already put into evidence such a factor: 'findings tend to verify that large buyer size is a critical factor related to the use of national account marketing'. Building on this abundant literature, we choose to test the following hypothesis:

H8. In KA relationships, the average turnover of customers is higher than in non-KA relationships.

Price level

For Boles et al. (1994), by implementing a key account management programme a supplier can expect to 'increase margins based on the premise that major accounts will pay more for the value added by the holistic approach of [the key account program]' (p. 26). Such increases can stem from different effects. An important driver of revenue and contribution margin is price. In the same perspective, Sharma (2006) recalls that 'the assumption underlying these practices is that long-term customers are more profitable because they pay higher prices' (p. 145).

On the opposite, Stevenson and Page (1979) expect that 'once a customer is designated a [key] account, it may . . . receive price . . . concessions' (p. 94). However, they have no empirical support for their hypothesis. But there is, nevertheless, a growing debate on the real profitability of long-term relationships, e.g. Reinartz and Kumar (2000, 2002) as well as Dowling and Uncles (1997) for consumer goods markets; Naidu et al. (1999) for the health care sector. As Pillai and Sharma (2003) point out, 'recent findings have cast doubt on some of the fundamental assumptions of relationship marketing theory. In fact, some research has suggested that transaction-oriented strategy may be more profitable for firms' (p. 643).

More generally, the relationship marketing literature suggests that companies can improve their profitability through the establishment of loyalty bonds with customers. Profitability can be impacted through cost reduction and revenue increase. Rosenberg and Czepiel (1984) argue that retaining customers is less expensive than competing for new ones, and Jacobs et al. (2001) show that increasing customer loyalty has a positive effect on revenue. One could also argue that suppliers who manage to satisfy their professional customers through key account management create a quasi lock-in effect. Moreover, in key account management programmes the purchaser's objective is not so much to obtain low costs per unit but rather to reduce total cost of ownership (Cannon and Narayandas 2000). This shifts the focus from reducing unit price to obtaining a broad range of tangible and intangible benefits.

On this basis, keeping in mind that there is no common and consensual position on this question, we choose to raise the following hypothesis:

> H9. In KA-relationships customers' perceived price level is higher than in non-KA relationships.

Note that by raising this hypothesis, we focus on customers' perceived price level because for the participants in the study it is easier to provide a general evaluation of a supplier's price level relative to the market than information based upon a precise calculus; and because overall price perceptions rather than single price information on a specific product or transaction have an impact on the long-term evolution of business relationships.

Empirical study

Study design: sample and questionnaire

The study is based on a written survey among managers involved in professional purchasing processes. Two industries were selected. The packaging industry represents a classical industrial goods market whereas the market research sector was chosen as an industrial service market. In both industries, long-term relationships play an important role.

Questionnaires were distributed to purchasing managers for packaging goods at the leading German trade show 'FachPack'. Potential participants were identified at the entrance, asked to complete the questionnaire at their office and to return it within four weeks. Only German participants were included in the final sample in order to control cultural bias in this study. On the market research side questionnaires were sent out to those members of the leading German market research association (BVM) which is concerned with the purchasing process of market information.

The questionnaire contained only closed questions. The respondents were asked to answer by concentrating on one selected supplier with whom they had been working for at least two years. The selection of the supplier was left to them. A total of 1,142 customer companies in two industries (packaging goods and market research) were contacted. A total of 340 questionnaires were returned, 43 of which were insufficiently completed or which referred to foreign suppliers. In order to control cultural bias, only questionnaires referring to German suppliers were taken into account. Hence, the available database consists of $n = 297$ cases.

In all cases, the respondents had been involved in the relationship for at least two years, so that we assume that they are knowledgeable. The participating customer companies cover all three major industry sectors (industry, retail and services). On the customer side, the sample consists of SMEs as well as large companies. The size structure of the supplier companies is closely correlated to the relative importance of these types of companies in their markets. Hence, sample representativity appears to be established.

In order to identify whether the replying customer is a key account the question-naire contained the following question:

What is your company's position in the relationship with this supplier?

- The supplier defines us as key account.
- The supplier does not define us as key account.

A total of 91 participants answered that their supplier defined them as a key account (KA) while the remaining 206 customers referred to themselves as cus-tomers without key account status. In order to check for classification error, we asked participants to name the customer they evaluated. About 40% of the respondents provided a company name. We reached half of them by telephone and asked what status they attributed to the customer. No differences between the customer and the supplier answers appeared. Hence, the sample consists of 70% non-key account customers (non-KAs) and of 30% KAs, which indicates a slight bias as compared with average KA/non-KA ratios. However, this deviation from the expected distribution appears to be of an extent that remains tolerable for the aim of this study.

Measures

The variables developed in the hypotheses section are partially hypothetical con-structs, partially observable facts. Whereas relationship duration (in years), cus-tomer turnover and number of actors involved (on the customer side) can be measured directly, multi-item scales were developed for the measurement of the remaining concepts:

- *Uncertainty.* The construct has often been operationalized for the purpose of empirical tests of the transaction cost framework. The uncertainty scales used in this study describe the external and internal uncertainty surrounding the supplier's decisions in the relationship with his customer. Because their studies focus on vertical long-term business relationships our scales are based on the measurement instruments developed by Noordewier et al. (1990) and Heide and John (1990).

- *Relationship-specific investments.* This scale describes the investments made by the service provider in physical assets, procedures, and people that are tailored to the relationship. It is based on the scale used by Werner (1997).
- *Supplier dependence.* This scale is drawn from resource-dependence theory. It describes the extent to which the supplier is dependent on the customer and his resources. The measure is based upon an instrument developed by Jap and Ganesan (2000).
- *Contractual governance.* In order to measure the extent to which the relationship is being governed through formal contracts we based ourselves on the work of Macauley (1963).
- *Supplier internal coordination.* This construct describes the extent to which the supplier is able to control the internal flow of goods and information without inefficiencies at interfaces (single item measure).
- *Price level.* Through this measure we establish whether the prices the supplier charges for his products are (clearly) above, equal to, or (clearly) below the average market price for comparable goods or services (single item measure).

All multi-item scales meet the criterion of $\alpha \geq 0.7$ (Nunnally 1978). The confirmatory analyses of the factors are also indicative of a good fit. The values all lie above the critical thresholds of 0.6 for factor reliability and 0.5 for the average variance extracted (Homburg and Baumgartner 1998). The intercorrelations among the constructs are moderate (all under or equal to 0.5), confirming the measures are distinct. Each item loads significantly ($p < 0.05$) on its corresponding factor, providing further evidence for convergent validity.

Tests of hypotheses

Figure 1 (means) and Table 1 (*t*-tests) present the core results of the inter-group differences in means. The nine hypotheses are only partially confirmed. Key account management programmes prove to imply: higher supplier investments, higher supplier dependence, a large number of actors involved on the customer side and an increased customer turnover, higher levels of external uncertainty, and lower levels of internal uncertainty. But, at the same time, key account management programmes do not lead to better process coordination, are not reserved for long-term customers, they do not allow suppliers to realize price premiums, and they do not rely upon higher levels of formal governance through contracts than relationships in which customers are treated as ordinary accounts. Note that we also conducted the analyses for each one of the two sub-samples (packaging goods and market research data) and that no significant differences were observed.

Discussion

Four hypotheses among the ten we raised are not confirmed by our empirical survey. As such, they constitute rather counter-intuitive results. Let us have a precise look at these results.

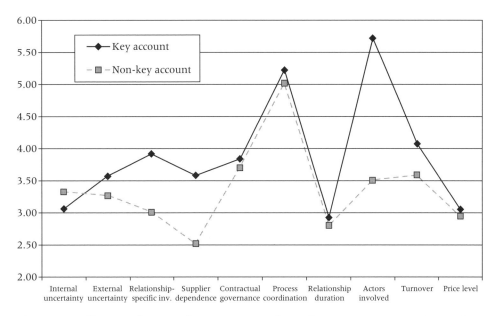

Figure 1 Differences between key accounts and non-key accounts concerning various dimensions of business relationships

The first result indicates that key account management programmes are not associated with better process coordination. Our initial hypothesis was formulated on the basis of a literature review where a majority of authors linked the key account management process to an improved coordination process on the supplier side. Common wisdom also tells us that the essence of a key account management programme is coordination. Nevertheless, as mentioned initially, through his empirical survey Stevenson (1981) could not establish a link between key account management and improved internal seller coordination. What does this result teach us about key account management? Stevenson explained that time was needed to attain such a coordination. As most of the key account management programmes within firms have been implemented only recently, we can imagine that this coordination is still in process on the supplier side. We can also consider that the coordination task is more difficult in KA relationships than in non-KA because the relationship to be managed is more complex. Our result may also point to the problematic situation many account managers face. They have to translate key customer problems into supplier solutions. In order to do so, they need to obtain the cooperation of other functional departments. Homburg et al. (2002) show that account managers' access to marketing as well as non-marketing resources inside their company varies tremendously among different types of KAM programmes. In their study, the best-performing KAM programmes are the ones where cooperation between internal suppliers and the account manager is particularly good. Low-performing KAM types lack this support for

Table 1: Hypotheses and results of *t*-tests

Hypotheses	Variable	Mean		Predicted relationship	OK?	Significance (t-test)
		KA	NKA			
H1a	Internal uncertainty	3.06	3.33	KA < NKA	✔	*
H1b	External uncertainty	3.57	3.27	KA > NKA	✔	**
H2	Relationship-specific inv.	3.92	3.01	KA > NKA	✔	***
H3	Supplier dependence	3.58	2.52	KA > NKA	✔	***
H4	Contractual governance	3.84	3.71	KA > NKA	✔	n.s.
H5	Process coordination	5.22	5.02	KA > NKA	✔	n.s.
H6	Relationship duration	2.92	2.80	KA > NKA	✔	n.s.
H7	Actors involved	5.71	3.50	KA > NKA	✔	**
H8	Turnover	4.08	3.59	KA > NKA	✔	***
H9	Price level	3.05	2.94	KA > NKA	✔	n.s.

Notes: Significant at the level of *90%, **95%, ***99%, n.s. not significant

the account manager. Against this background, it may well be that in many of the programmes comprised in our sample, key account managers do not have the means to achieve their goal of process coordination because other functional units do not support them enough, such that key customers suffer from this lack of coordination.

The second result indicates that key account management programmes are not reserved for long-term customers. When we raised our hypothesis we indicated that relationship duration could be associated to key account management in two ways. Because companies often wait before attributing a KA status to a customer to be sure it requires a specific treatment, we can anticipate that in KA relationships, the duration of the relationships is higher than in non-KA relationships. We must also consider the fact that key account management programmes are associated – in essence – with a long-term perspective: they are implemented to stabilize and secure a relationship between a supplier and a customer.

But none of these explanations seems to be valid with regard to our results. Does this mean that 'relationship duration' and KAM are not associated in any way? In a sense, yes. If key account management means creating value through a specific organizational design dedicated to a customer, the choice to implement a key account management programme can be made without reference to 'relationship duration'. A prospect can be treated as a KA. A key account manager can dedicate his time to penetrate an account with which, to date, no major business has been conducted. Simply, the organizational design called 'key account management programme' is the most adapted for penetrating this customer. After all, this result is in line with the customer value literature (e.g. Walter et al. 2001) that posits that the importance of a customer to a supplier firm does not merely stem from accumulated turnover. Instead, a large number of value drivers, such as know-how, innovativeness, or network integration, determine the customer's importance to the supplier.

Third, the results indicate that key account management programmes do not allow suppliers to realize price premiums. On this last result, we must admit that when raising our hypothesis we were quite interested to establish a link between the presence of a key account management programme and a possible price premium. The positions of different authors were not so clear. We must certainly wonder about the significance of 'price premium'. The objective is not to raise prices but to create value that can mean the same prices (or even lower prices) but higher volume. This is exactly what is done in cross-selling – the same prices but more products and services sold. It may also mean the same prices but fewer costs for the supplier. The result is of utmost importance for the KA research as it allows us to position once again key account management in a value-creation perspective, which is a far richer concept than achieving price increases.

Let us finally note that *H4*, which was raised on divided opinions about the link between contractual governance and key account management, is not confirmed. It appears that the question whether the parties involved in exchange believe that a formal agreement is required to specify the conditions of exchange is not correlated to the customer's importance to the supplier. Other factors serve as predictors of the level of contractual governance. Potential antecedents are the level of trust established in the dyad or the supplier's dependence on the customer. And other governance mechanisms, such as norms or pledges, complete the overall governance structure regulating a business relationship. Hence, it may be more relevant to analyse the complete governance system rather than one individual mechanism.

Managerial implications

Managers in charge of key account management, whether directly (as key account managers) or indirectly (as managers of key accounts divisions or sales managers), should consider the outputs of our research. We can summarize our findings as follows:

- Managers should recall exactly what the objective of a key account management programme is. It is not to obtain higher prices but to work on a perspective of value creation. As Wilson (2000) points out, we are in an 'integrative relationship' perspective where value is created both for the customer (Ulaga and Chacour 2001) and the supplier (Walter et al. 2001; Walter and Ritter 2003).

- If coordination (of the supplier action towards the customer) is at the core of a key account management programme, the complexity to be managed in a KA relationship is so important that the efforts to be granted are very important to obtain a good level of process coordination. Managers must not underestimate this investment and be prepared to allocate sufficient resources to this coordination task. Their superiors need to understand this problem, too. It may well be that for an account manager to be effective, a certain amount of power is required. Otherwise, his dependence on his colleagues' goodwill may simply be too high and, over time, discouraging. This power does not need to be exclusively of the hierarchical type. For instance, recent results from SAMA[2] indicate that less than one third of the key account teams are formal ones (e.g. with a hierarchical link between the key account manager and other team members). Power can be conferred by individual behaviours, charisma, career path in the firm, etc.
- New customers or even prospects can be granted key account management treatment. If you can demonstrate that with such treatment you are going to create more value than without, then do not hesitate: launch a key account management programme!

Limitations

Although we believe that our work represents a valuable contribution to the development of a solid empirical foundation to the field of key account management, we acknowledge a series of limitations to this study. First, it was conducted in one country only (Germany). Given that culture may have an impact on some of the variables we studied (e.g. perceptions of external and internal uncertainty), a replication in a different country market would be useful. Furthermore, we relied upon respondents from only two industries. While this focus on two fairly different industries allowed us to control certain environmental influences, a replication with a truly cross-sectional sample would provide more robust results. Finally, our study is based on a single-sided and single-respondent design. All three limitations provide potential directions for future research.

Executive summary and implications for managers and executives

This summary has been provided to allow managers and executives a rapid appreciation of the content of the paper. Those with a particular interest in the topic covered may then

---

[2] 2002 Survey of Strategic Account Management Practices – www.strategicaccounts.org.

read the paper in toto to take advantage of the more comprehensive description of the research undertaken and its results to get the full benefit of the material present.

Key account management programmes, as we know, aim to give a rather more personal and individualistic treatment to those customers we regard as more strategically 'key' to the company, than we do to minor accounts. What we do not always know is whether the assumptions we are making in allocating this status are based on solid ground.

To be certain that such customers deserve the extra attention they get by way of a KAM programme, many companies often adopt a 'wait and see' approach before promoting them from the ranks of the more 'ordinary' customer. Key account management programmes are associated, in essence, with a long-term perspective – implemented to stabilize and secure a relationship between a supplier and a customer where specific assets are developed and the problem of sunk costs is always present.

But if we are to assume from this that new customers, or even prospects, should not be granted KAM status, we might be wrong and consequently missing out on good business.

Concerned that some of the tacit assumptions on which we base KAM activity are not backed up by empirical evidence, Björn Sven Ivens and Catherine Pardo demonstrate that some of its foundations are not as solid as they might first appear. On the question of new customers and prospects having KAM treatment, for instance, they say: 'If you can demonstrate that with such treatment you are going to create more value than without, then do not hesitate: launch a key account management programme!'

A key account manager can dedicate his time to penetrate an account with which, to date, no major business has been conducted. The key account management programme is the most adapted for penetrating this customer. The importance of a customer to a supplier firm does not merely stem from accumulated turnover. Instead, a large number of value drivers, such as know-how, innovativeness, or network integration, determine that importance.

Managers, whether in charge of KAM directly (as key account managers) or indirectly (as managers of key accounts divisions or sales managers), should have in mind exactly what the objective of a key account management programme is. It is not to obtain higher prices but to work on a perspective of value creation – what's been described as an 'integrative relationship' perspective where value is created for both the customer and the supplier.

If coordination (of the supplier action towards the customer) is at the core of a key account management programme, the complexity to be managed in a KA relationship is so important that the efforts to be granted are very important to obtain a good level of process coordination.

Managers must not underestimate this investment and be prepared to allocate sufficient resources. Their superiors need to understand this problem, too. It may well be that for an account manager to be effective, a certain amount of power is required. Otherwise, his dependence on his colleagues' goodwill may simply be too high and, over time, discouraging.

This power does not need to be exclusively of the hierarchical type. For instance, recent results from a Strategic Account Management Association survey indicate that less than one third of the key account teams are formal ones. Power can be conferred by individual behaviours, charisma, career path in the firm, etc.

The Ivens and Pardo study indicates that key account management programmes are not associated with better process coordination, contrary to the view of a majority of authors, and the common wisdom which tells us that coordination is the essence of a KAM. As most of the key account management programmes within firms in their study had been implemented only recently, perhaps this coordination is still in process on the supplier side. What also must be considered is that the coordination task is more difficult in KA relationships than in non-KA because the relationship to be managed is more complex.

If key account managers do not have the cooperation of other functional departments to achieve their goal of process coordination, key customers suffer from this lack of coordination.

The study also indicates that key account management programmes do not allow suppliers to realize price premiums. The objective is not to raise prices but to create value which can mean the same prices (or even lower prices) but higher volume. It may also mean the same prices but fewer costs for the supplier. The result is of importance as it allows key account management to be positioned in a value-creation perspective, which is a far richer concept than achieving price increases.

Strategic account plans: their crucial role in strategic account management

BY MALCOLM MCDONALD AND DIANA WOODBURN

Abstract

Strategic account plans sit at the core of KSAM: they specify the value to be offered to the customer and received by the supplier. They should be what gets done, and yet very little has been written about them. This paper discusses the essential elements of strategic account planning: the purpose of strategic account plans; their role in value creation; the importance of understanding and quantifying customer profitability; the key account manager's role in their development; and the plan production process, linked to corporate planning. Since these plans are highly confidential and rarely available for study, almost nothing has been documented on what they look like and what they contain, so their structure, format and content are described. With so much business at stake, plan quality needs to be excellent, but unfortunately quality is an issue, as is implementation. Finally, the information captured in these plans can quantify the value created by KSAM at the level of individual customers and the more aggregated levels of all customers and the whole company, although the equation is far from straightforward. Overall, strategic account plans play a critical but overlooked role in successful KSAM.

Introduction

A great many excellent and important ideas about key strategic account management (KSAM) programmes have been researched and discussed by many authors, particularly in terms of structure, selection of key customers, profitability, actors, and the core requirement of value creation for customers (Pardo 2006). Many good suppliers already give key customers plenty of attention, but they are often not clear about what tangible difference implementing KSAM makes to their approach to a key customer. We believe the problem lies in their failure to articulate, specify and plan for the value they need to create for these customers.

In the absence of tailored value created for the customer, KSAM will fail. As Piercy and Lane (2014) say, 'A supplier's most important customers require dedicated resources and special value-adding activities. . . . If there were no such advantage for the buyer, then there would be no basis for a strategic account/ strategic supplier relationship.' We contend that, unless the value is defined and described in a plan dedicated to each key customer (and implemented, of course), there may not be any real value creation and that, even if a valuable concept has been developed, it is unlikely to be realized and delivered without a reasonably formal mechanism to inform and gain the commitment of the customer and the rest of the business. This puts key account plans at the very heart of successful KSAM, and yet very little has been written about them: this article seeks to begin to redress that balance.

Essential elements of KSAM planning

The key account plan should pull together all the knowledge and thinking around each customer to identify powerful and affordable value recipes for them. Without such a plan, it is impossible to begin to assess whether the customer will respond, and to what extent, and whether the response justifies the costs. The plan needs to address how the value 'recipe' will be converted into action, and that must be made sufficiently clear to all deliverers for them to understand what they need to do, and to gain their commitment to doing it. We contend the following:

- KSAM strategy will not be enacted unless aligned strategies are developed at the level of individual key accounts and made explicit in key account plans.
- Sustainable KSAM requires the creation of customized value for both parties, made explicit in key account plans.
- Customer profitability is best assessed, optimized, forecast and managed through the key account plan.
- The key account manager (and team) knows more about the account than any other supplier function and has responsibility for developing account strategies and plans.
- Account plans should have a consistent format to ease assessment, information sharing and business planning.

- Effective implementation of account plans requires approval by the organization, acceptance and support from the customer, adequate resource provision, aligned action and monitoring for plan progress, as well as results.

These principles are all concerned with the production, viability and implementation of each plan, and hence KSAM as a whole. While they are clearly interlinked, we will look at them separately in order to consider the scope and importance of each.

The purpose of strategies and plans for individual strategic and key accounts

KSAM is itself a corporate strategy at the highest level (*ibid.* Piercy and Lane 2014), but in order for KSAM to be realized, its precise meaning in each supplier requires further clarification. Many companies mistake their objective as their strategy in KSAM. They describe their aspiration in terms of growth in sales and/or profits from key customers, apparently failing to notice that simply stating a number does not achieve it. Until *how* they will achieve the desired outcome is specified, i.e. the strategy/ies, there is no defined route to success that people can enact.

KSAM strategies, even at a high level, can be very varied: they may focus on the introduction of new products; greater supply chain flexibility; extra capacity; new technology or services that will add value to key customers; and they may include initiatives that offer more efficiency or effectiveness for the supplier, such as production savings, joint marketing, or other strategies that may be both powerful and worthwhile when implemented for large customers, but not necessarily for the whole customer base. Certainly, vague assumptions about future activity are no substitute for explicit, customer-specific strategies. As Pardo et al. (2006) say, 'Suppliers need to be clear about their specific value focus in the relationship in order to optimize activities, processes, and resource allocation.' These authors identified several kinds of value, depending on which party creates and which consumes or appropriates the value (Biggart and Delbridge 2004):

- Exchange value, created through the supplier's KSAM activities and consumed or appropriated by the customer, e.g. tailored product offering.
- Proprietary (supplier) value, created and appropriated by the supplier (alternatively, proprietary customer value would be found where it is created and appropriated by the customer), e.g. supply chain efficiencies.
- Relational value, co-created value appropriated/consumed by both parties (Payne et al. 2008), e.g. joint new product development.

At a high level, a supplier's KSAM strategies may favour one or more of these values overall, although a strong focus on proprietary supplier value with limited attention to the other types of value is unlikely to appeal to customers, and therefore leads to unsuccessful KSAM. The emphasis and expression of the high-level strategy should be different in each customer.

Strategic account managers are often disappointed when their company rejects some of their ideas for customer strategies, and yet they have not articulated those ideas in a structured plan that allows the company to assess those ideas strategically, operationally and financially in a rational manner. The plan can be as important to the customer as it is to the key account manager and the supplier: as Pardo et al. (2006) say, 'Customers that are key accounts should have an understanding of the value strategy that is pursued by the supplier in order to optimize their own position'. Through the account plan, both parties can see how their strategies can be aligned to optimize the benefits they gain from the relationship.

Godfrey (2006) placed the key account plan at the heart of KSAM when he identified four functions for the plan which address key actors in KSAM:

- For the customer, to make visible and explicit the added value they could expect.
- For the supplier, to show how the plan contributes to the corporate vision expressed in the corporate business plan.
- For the key account team, to specify and clarify strategies and objectives so they could understand what success was and know when they achieved it.
- For other key account managers, to share their plans and experiences for others to learn from them.

Additionally:

- for the key account manager, to provide a clear roadmap for management of the account and to gain the organization's approval and support for it.

Many companies pride themselves on being 'action-orientated' and do not genuinely value strategy. Indeed, according to Collis et al. (2008), 85% of American directors do not know what the components of a strategy are, with the result that organizations drift aimlessly until financial disaster strikes. That failing is manifested by a lack of KSAM strategy at the higher level, which translates into a lack of strategy at the customer level too. If good-quality strategic customer plans are not required by top management, key account managers see their production as a waste of time. In the absence of an explicit strategy captured in a plan, the key account manager falls back on day-to-day activity, which is perceived by the customer as traditional selling and normal customer service. Consequently, the customer just responds to the supplier's approaches in the same way as before, and not to the supplier's inflated expectations – while there may not be a plan, there is always an objective.

Planned value creation

Value is seen as the driver of the exchange process, and the fundamental basis for all marketing activities by Holbrook (1994), while Anderson (1995) considered value to be the reason for the collaborative relationships that Lambe and Spekman (1997) put at the heart of KSAM relationships. Sustainable KSAM should offer value for both supplier and customer (Pardo et al. 2006). We all acknowledge that in the last quarter of the 20th century commercial power moved from producers to customers, but many suppliers still operate a product- and production-orientated culture and keep customers at arm's-length. Vander-merwe (1999) goes as far as suggesting that traditional capitalism has become irrelevant and needs to be replaced by new business models based on 'customer capitalism'.

Successful KSAM should balance the value appropriated by the supplier and customer, but it is often not so. Some suppliers making healthy profits from a big business with the customer give nothing special in exchange; and some customers have captured the lion's share of the value available in the current business model, leaving the supplier with a poor return on their investment in the cus-tomer. Neither of these situations is sustainable in the long term but, even so, the winning partner is often deaf to suggestions that the balance should be adjusted voluntarily before the loser takes drastic action, like switching to another supplier, demanding major price increases or even withdrawing supply. As Ander-son and Narus (1999) point out, however, value does not exist in isolation, but is relative to competitive offers.

While value can be created through a variety of different strategies, in most cases it will finally be defined as a benefit feeding through to the bottom line, although suppliers are becoming increasingly involved in supporting their customers' 'green' reputation or social responsibility agenda. Cynics might suggest that these strategies are really aimed at profit sustainability anyway, and most value initia-tives are directly linked to profit improvements. These will, broadly, stem from reducing costs or from business growth. Woodburn et al. (2004) concluded that:

- For customers, the bulk of value creation by suppliers results in lower costs.
- For suppliers, the bulk of value creation by customers results in business growth.

That is not to say that customers would not welcome suppliers who helped them raise their prices or grow volumes with their customers; or that suppliers would not be delighted if their customers enabled them to save costs and, indeed, such initiatives do occur. However, Kalwani and Narayandas (1995) also showed that customers were adept at bargaining away supplier cost savings. Generally, cus-tomers expect suppliers to cut costs for them (directly or indirectly) and are receptive to that approach, and suppliers expect to increase the volume of busi-ness they have with customers: therefore most effort seems to be directed towards these kinds of value creation.

Planning for customer profitability

Managing powerful customers profitably is perhaps the biggest issue facing sup-pliers today, as markets mature, particularly in Western Europe and America, and as inexpensive versions of goods which were hitherto only supplied by the West flood into their markets from lower-cost countries such as China. Most organiza-tions respond by putting pressure on their suppliers because the easiest and quickest way to increase margins which are being challenged is to cut the price paid for external goods and services. The problem with this approach, however, is that price cutting is finite, whereas value creation is infinite and is limited only by creativity and imagination.

It seems self-evident that KSAM programmes should aim to acquire and retain customers that have the greatest potential for profit (Ryals 2005; Thomas et al. 2004) which assumes that the costs of acquiring and supporting these customers do not outweigh the benefits (Blattberg et al. 2001; Gupta et al. 2004). However, Woodburn and McDonald (2001) showed that even suppliers claiming to have a good idea of customer profitability (i.e. the profit the supplier makes from its business with the customer) only captured data in terms of product-based gross margins, while some of their customers were clearly 'voracious consumers of resources' (p. 86), which were not quantified and recorded.

Differences in buying power, strategy, structure, buying mix, sector and activities result in profitability varying widely between customers (Ryals 2005; Storbacka et al. 2000; Wilson 1999), so this lack of understanding of how much the supplier is actually making from each key customer is clearly dangerous. This degree of variation between customers implies that the issue should be addressed at the level of the individual account, not customers overall or even key customers as a group. Cooper and Kaplan (1991), Kalwani and Narayandas (1995), Wilson (1999) and others have shown that some of a supplier's largest customers had eroded supplier margins to such an extent that the business with them made a loss for the supplier. Furthermore, Van der Sande et al. (2001) found that Henkel's expectations of which customers were most profitable were wrong in many cases. Similarly, the key account manager of a leading financial services company's biggest customer found, having completed a special project to establish the actual profitability of this, his only customer, that his (and his company's) expectation was '100% wrong'. Such discoveries should constitute a 'wake-up call' for all suppliers.

The account plan is the most appropriate place to analyse, develop and manage a key customer financially. Bradford et al. (2001), Ryals (2005), Van Raaij et al. (2003) and many others have demonstrated how customer profitability affects strategies for and management of key customers, so logically they should be discussed and integrated within the same instrument. Just as strategies are meaningless without numbers, numbers are meaningless without strategies and explanations of what will be spent and why and what returns can be anticipated. A strategic key account plan should show the earnings from the customer in the past and in the future, assuming that the strategies described in the plan are implemented. In addition to the income, it needs to make visible the costs, both direct product/service/logistic costs, and indirect costs like marketing, project and relationship costs, including those of the key account manager and team. Furthermore, any investments which will deliver beyond the current financial year need to be included in an appropriate manner, e.g. expressed in discounted cash flow terms like any other investment. Indeed, rather than being presented with a single number, finance departments would prefer forecasts given as a range around the mean with a probability of achievement attached to it (Woodburn 2008).

Role of the key account manager in plan development

It seems self-evident that the key account manager is the prime mover and person responsible for developing and delivering the account plan, together with the account team. We have observed a distinctly higher quality in plans (wider-ranging, better informed and more strategic) developed in conjunction with a multi-functional account team, compared with those produced by key account managers working solo. Achieving a good-quality outcome requires considerable skills on the part of the key account manager (Woodburn 2006a): of leadership, inter-personal and political awareness, diplomacy and coaching; of competences like analysis, financial understanding, technical and product knowledge, and knowledge of their own company's capabilities; and of vision, strategy development, forecasting and the ability to communicate with clarity and impact in writing and in person. Not surprisingly, not all key account managers possess such a range of skills at a sufficiently high level.

To an extent, shortfalls in the key account manager's portfolio of competences and personal attributes can be compensated by team members, provided that the key account manager has the ability to gain their participation and commitment to the planning process, and capture the outputs in the plan. However, there is a minimum level of competency below which the key account manager's ability to understand the team's contributions, render them into a well-organized plan and represent it to others internally and externally would be compromised.

The literature on the competences of key account managers, e.g. Sengupta et al. (2000), Wotruba and Castleberry (1993), initially focused on selling as the principal requirement, although Wilson and Millman (2003) shifted the focus with their paper on the key account manager as 'political entrepreneur'. The view of the key account manager's role changed, for some at least, towards a more managerial position. Holt (2003) noted that good global account managers spent 10% of their time on account planning and Woodburn (2006b) found suppliers from diverse sectors who agreed that 5–15% of time should be spent in this way, but believed that, in reality, it was next to zero in their companies. Otherwise, very little attention has been given specifically to the key account manager's role in successful account planning and the competences it demands. In this respect academia mirrors suppliers themselves, which generally do not emphasize planning competences in their recruitment and requirements of key account managers. However, if the key account plan is at the heart of KSAM (Godfrey 2006), the key account manager is at the heart of the planning process, and needs to apply the time and competences it deserves.

The strategic account manager will need project management competency to manage the planning process and coaching skills to support team members playing their part in it. In addition to developing the plan, the strategic account manager and team play a crucial role in presenting it, both internally to senior management and externally to the customer. While key account managers are commonly trained in presentation skills, strategic account team members often are not. We have seen many examples where the supplier's senior managers and the customer have found team presentations more productive than a solo performance by the key account manager (still the norm), but team members probably require extra training in communication and inter-personal skills to fulfil this valuable role.

The planning process

Little enough has been written about account plans as a whole, and virtually nothing about the planning process. The process generally takes weeks, even months, so it is necessary to map it out to ensure that steps are planned in advance and that those involved have set aside the time and resources to complete it to schedule. Shortcuts tend to be at the expense of involving the customer and the account team, which is a false economy if the process fails to engage the commitment of either. Plans written by key account managers on their own are usually limited in scope; often based on incomplete information; and tend to struggle to get buy-in from the rest of the company.

Customers may or may not wish to be part of the process. Refusing the supplier's invitation to participate is probably an indicator of a fairly distant relationship, not the kind of collaborative relationship sought in KSAM. These more distant relationships are limited in their short-/medium-term potential, so if the customer does not choose to contribute to the planning process, the supplier should recognize the business-limiting nature of their current position with that customer and plan accordingly.

Consideration of the five stages of strategic account planning shown in Figure 1 demonstrates why the key account manager needs to dedicate a significant amount of time to it. They must expose the planning process and solicit the time of customers, team members and senior managers in order to secure their contribution. The plan should be ready in time to make an input to the supplier's overall business planning process (see pages 253–5).

The plans for strategic accounts together represent a substantial amount of business, and probably represent an increasing proportion of the business in the future. This increasing dependency is a risk to the supplier (Piercy and Lane 2014) that needs to be recognized, but the alternative, to limit or give up some of this business, may be even more risky. At least, the supplier should acknowledge the expectations of strategic customers, the strategies planned for them, and the business that is anticipated; and build those expectations and its response to them into its overall business plan.

In order to achieve that coordination, there needs to be a process whereby the individual account plans inform and feed into corporate planning. It should be backed by a process of iteration, in which the account plans bid for resource and

Preparation	• Identify team involved • Train team in analysis, objectives and strategy setting, writing plans • Brief on form and timeframe of plans, and timing of process

Analysis and strategy setting	• Conduct workshops on customer analysis/understanding • Collect missing information • Conduct workshops on objectives and strategies • Check feasibility of strategies and integration with other strategies and plans

Plan production	• Identify responsibilities in producing plan document • Write plan in company format: executive summary, main plan, appendices for detail • Present plan to senior management • Get informed approval, commitment and resources from all functions

Implementation	• Identify teams to develop and enact implementation plan • Develop communication programme for plan • Agree responsibilities for action and ways of working together • Implement responsive communication across the company • Implement!

Monitoring & measurement	• Set up measures against plan objectives and actions • Set up review and renew process with team and customer • Give feedback on strategies and results to senior management at suitable and intervals

Figure 1   The account planning process

demonstrate the return that can be expected for it; the company decides what it will and will not support; and the account plans are adjusted accordingly and resubmitted to the corporate planning process. In our experience, corporate planning and account planning operate independently, with the latter process 'freewheeling' within the sales function. The consequences are that the corporate plan sets customer performance targets which, unrelated to the account plans, may be quite nonsensical; and the company may miss out through not providing resources to fulfil productive strategies, and possibly failing to recognize critical market changes.

KSAM plans in the context of corporate planning

According to McDonald (2012), KSAM planning should take place before draft plans are prepared for a strategic business unit, or at least at the same time. As a general principle, planning should start in the market where the customers operate. Indeed, in anything other than small organizations, it is clearly absurd to think that any kind of meaningful planning can take place without the committed inputs from those who work with the customers, particularly key accounts. Yet many companies develop their business plans by a separate process run by Finance, without the inputs of customer managers, who are then on the receiving end of the outputs of the process, i.e. sales targets.

At the same time, individual customer strategies must be developed in the light of the supplier's corporate strategy, or they run the risk of depending on propositions that the supplier will never implement. This suggests another reason why customer strategies must be explicit and documented, i.e. to ensure that they are sufficiently aligned with corporate strategy. However, they need not passively comply with current corporate strategy, but should seek to influence future strategy to ensure the inclusion of key customer expectations and opportunities. So those aspirations need to be both visible and specific enough for the supplier to be able to evaluate them properly.

Kicking off the annual business planning round, key account strategic plans should represent messages from and responses to the marketplace, especially the most influential customers, i.e. key accounts, but also reflect the overall, longer-term corporate strategy. Figure 2 illustrates the relationship between plans in the organization. It does not include the plans of other functions, like supply chain, research and development, customer service, etc., but since the fulfilment of key account strategies will often fall to them, those plans also need to be informed by the key account plans.

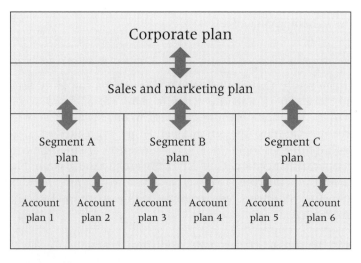

Figure 2 Hierarchy of strategic plans

Research into the efficacy of strategic plans for marketing and strategic accounts (McDonald 2012) has shown that such plans, when well conceived and executed, make a significant contribution to commercial success, the main effects being:

- The systematic identification of emerging opportunities and threats.
- Preparedness to meet change.
- The specification of sustainable competitive advantage.
- Improved communications between different functions and their managers.
- Reduction of conflicts between individuals and departments.
- The commitment of key departments and individuals to delivering the value promised to customers.
- More appropriate allocation of scarce resources.
- A more market and customer-focused orientation across the organization.
- Better, sustainable financial performance.

KSAM plan format and content

Again, very little has been written about the actual content of key account plans. As the content is specific to each account, and companies consider the material to be highly confidential, general discussion is difficult. However, some elements should be common to most or all plans, which we identify here, but clearly there will be variations depending on, for example, the market sector, the company's business model and the position of KSAM and the key account manager in the organization.

Drivers of format and content

We suggest that the content and the form in which it is presented should be driven by a number of practical principles, relating to the plan's:

- Scope.
- Authority.
- Audience.
- Usage.
- Duration.

Scope

KSAM is much more than a selling activity, so other functions are involved in delivery of its strategies. Furthermore, the account plan is generally the only plan in a supplier's business that is dedicated to an individual customer. The account plan should therefore represent the whole of the supplier's interaction with the key account, not just the endeavours of the key account manager. Unless totally independent of each other on the customer side, it should also represent all product groups and locations.

Authority

Since the plan is prepared by the people who know most about the customer, having consulted any others with knowledge or influence, it should be the most authoritative document the supplier produces relating to the account. It should be neither unrealistically optimistic nor conservative/pessimistic, but should present viable strategies and the most realistic expectations of the future. It may raise questions, but it should also answer them. It is no use to the supplier (or customer) unless it means what it says and will do what it says.

Audience

The plan will be read by a range of readers, from senior managers to operational people, and needs to be intelligible to all of them; therefore it should not assume that they are already well acquainted with the account. The plan needs to understand the readers' context; ensure that they will find what they want to know; and anticipate their queries and deal with them. For example, the executive summary is designed for senior readers who may be reading 20 or more of these plans, so it needs to be a succinct collection of the information they seek, including profit forecasts.

Usage

Initially, the plan is employed to gain the supplier's and customer's commitment. There should be a formal approval process in the supplier, including all functions involved in delivery: without it, the key account manager cannot rely on getting the resources needed to implement the plan. Formal approval from the customer may be a legal step too far, but most of the plan should be shared (or even prepared) with them, to gain their agreement to fulfilling their part of it. Subsequently, the plan should act as a blueprint that is used as a live working document, not an 'academic exercise', that guides the activities of the key account manager and team, informs the rest of the company and gains their cooperation with implementation, and is the basis for assessing progress.

Duration

Three years is a minimum span for the plan regardless of sector, and it will be longer in some, e.g. large capital projects. Even in fast-moving sectors, the direction of change is generally known and can be planned for. Failure to do so leaves suppliers 'on the back foot', just reacting to external forces and far from control of their own destiny. Normally, plans show strategies and projections for three years, with one year of action. In order to make the case for some strategies which take a while to implement, the plan period should be even longer so that the return on investment can be shown in a realistic timeframe, which will extend beyond implementation and its costs.

Structure and format

Clearly, account plan structures and formats vary, but the ones we have seen show a great deal of commonality. It is no help to a company to use a free-style

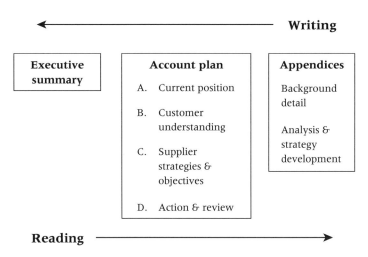

Figure 3 Account plan structure

approach: readers waste time trying to find information that is located and pre-sented differently in each. Similarly, the key account manager's time is better spent on populating the plan than working out how to structure it. For everyone's convenience and comprehension, suppliers should work out an appropriate format and insist that key account managers use it. It should not, however, con-strain what they have to say. The length of the plan and level of detail are critical choices. We have read short plans containing meaningless generalities, and long plans specifying an over-detailed breakdown of action that will, and should, be recast by those carrying out the action. While short plans are popular in theory, when the customer represents significant amounts of money, the plan should be of sufficient length to cover the business properly.

Figure 3 shows how an account plan may be composed. Cherished detail and workings can be housed in appendices where they do not obscure important points: those who wish to go to this depth can find them there, while others need only read the body of the plan to find what they have to do and why. The figure makes the point that plan development starts with analysis and ends with the writing of the executive summary, but the writer should remember that it will be read in reverse order.

There is a substantial body of scholarly evidence concerning the appropriate components of world-class strategic marketing plans (McDonald 1986; Smith 2003), i.e:

- A mission or purpose statement.
- A financial summary.
- A market summary/overview.

Table 1:   Account plan content

Action plan sections	*Section content*
Account plan	
A. Current position	Supplier account team
	Principal customer relationships
	Customer history with supplier
	Current issues
B. Customer understanding	Customer's market position
	Role/participation in marketplaces
	Market/business environment
	Key external issues for customer
	Competitive position
	Customer objectives
	Customer strategies
C. Supplier objectives and strategies	Customer critical success factors
	Supplier's environment in this customer
	Key external issues for supplier
	Competitive position
	Supplier objectives
	Supplier business strategies and costs
	Supplier relationship strategies
	Plan risks (external) and dependencies (internal)
D. Action and review	Key action plan
	Review

- SWOT analyses on key segments/decision-makers.
- Λ portfolio summary.
- Assumptions.
- Objectives and strategies.
- Financial implications/budgets.

These elements can be conveniently housed in the structure in Table 1.

Plan quality

Clearly, plans need to be of sufficient quality to hold their position at the heart of KSAM and bring the benefits described here. Table 2 shows guidelines for assessing plan quality gained from experience of reviewing some hundreds of plans.

Table 2: SAM plan evaluation guidelines

Plan element	Reference sections	Level 1	Level 2	Level 3	Level 4	Level 5
Overall presentation of business issues	Executive summary Section A: Current position Section B: Customer understanding	Excellent understanding of SA Complete, coherent Addresses key issues Appropriate emphasis Focused and clear Creative	Good understanding of SA Mostly complete, some visible coherence Addresses key issues Clear	Acceptable understanding of SA Essential components No significant contradictions or omissions	Weak understanding of SA Significantly incomplete or incoherent	Little or no understanding of SA Incomplete and/or includes major contradictions
Analyses, esp market map	Appendices	Comprehensive & effective use of tools Valid conclusions drawn Deep understanding of customer	Significant & effective use of tools Illustrates main points of customer situation	Some use of tools Elucidates key issues facing customer	Little use of tools Does not draw valid conclusions	Little or no use of tools No conclusions, poor customer understanding
Objectives	Section C: Supplier strategies and objectives	Realistic Joined up with customer situation, customer and supplier strategies	Realistic Connects current situation and supplier strategies	Statement building from current situation	Unclear or not well connected to situation	Not stated, or just sales targets
Strategy	Section C: Supplier strategies and objectives	Clearly stated Targeted Added value for customer Feasible, clear resource requirement Consistent with objectives	Clearly stated Targeted Added value for customer Feasible, clear resource requirement Consistent with objectives	Clearly stated Targeted Added value for customer	Strategy simply stated	Strategy not stated, and/or stated strategies are outcomes or actions
Action	Section D: Action and review	12-month development 3-year major action Matched with strategy Thorough measurement framework	12 month development 3 year major action Matched with strategy Focused measurement framework	12-month development Limited measurement framework	Short-term action Measurement is just sales targets	Short-term action No control mechanism

Plan implementation

The account plan exists to ensure that the right things are planned, agreed and done. Implementation is critical: a plan is only a plan, and although it has a crucial role to play in getting everyone prepared to play their part from top to bottom of both organizations, it clearly should not be mistaken for action. Implementation is not an easy subject, as each company and each plan will have different actions to implement, leading to a huge variety of activities. Since companies are normally unwilling to share their plans outside their organization, making any generalizations about the activities and quality of execution, barriers and successes is almost impossible. However, some characteristics of effective implementation can be identified from comments of key account managers describing what does *not* work (Wilson and Woodburn 2014).

Requirements for effective implementation

In addition to a good quality plan, implementation requires:

- Cross-functional and cross-location alignment.
- Customer commitment.
- Sufficient resource.
- Identified responsibilities.
- Realistic timeframes.
- Good project management.
- Clear goals and measurements.
- Pragmatic adherence to the plan.

Cross-functional and cross-location alignment: where the team of people required to take action do not understand the purpose, importance and benefit of the SAM programme, they are likely to be reluctant to prioritize its actions against their other activities, and may not make the right decisions about interpretation of the tasks assigned to them. They should be kept fully informed.

Customer commitment: the commitment of the customer is vital: key account managers are wont to complain that they did everything they were supposed to do, but the customer did not. That begs the question of whether the customer sees sufficient value for them in the plan: presumably not, if they did not carry out their actions. Unimplemented plans are often still really supplier sales plans.

Sufficient resource: in our experience, the majority of account plans do not specify the quantity of resources required, and certainly not the cost. Clearly, resource availability and cost are fundamental elements in the assessment of the profitability, desirability and feasibility of a plan. Resource information should be part of the plan: yet few key account managers appear to have access to resource planning and costs.

Identified responsibilities: resources are more often people and time than cash, and a core element of implementation is finding the people to do the work and ensuring that they and their managers accept these responsibilities. Since the perfect marriage of tasks with people and competencies is not always available, assigning responsibilities early and clearly helps to indicate where resource prioritization and building may be required.

Realistic timeframes: key account managers, under pressure from the organization, frequently underestimate the time required to execute action and receive the return, which will only begin to appear when the action has been fully completed. Unrealistic timing expectations can turn real success into apparent failure.

Good project management: strategic account plans will contain numerous projects, some led by the key account manager, others by another function, e.g. product development or supply chain changes. Customers get frustrated if they cannot see good progress on initiatives important to them (and why would they be involved in ones that are not important to them?) and costs tend to mount with delays, so any project management, regardless of who is the project manager, needs to be excellent.

Clear goals and measurements: quantification of expectations is arguably the most straightforward way to ensure that everyone understands what is intended. A mix of ultimate and interim goals helps to keep implementation on track, backed by measurement systems to ensure that the course of progress is accepted by all, and is not a matter for debate. Measurements and collection systems shared with the customer are ideal for all-round clarity.

Pragmatic adherence to the plan: account planning is a not a perfect science, and plans should be applied in a pragmatic and practical way. Accommodations to events and unanticipated details are likely, but in consultation with those involved and within the spirit of the plan. It should be reviewed regularly and changes identified either as minor 'noise' or major unforeseen events: the latter should be very few in a well-analysed and constructed plan.

Companies often fail to implement their plans. A plan that is not applied is pointless. It should be a blueprint for implementation across the company, and if it is put away and forgotten, the supplier cannot be surprised if it fails to reach its goals. Unused plans presumably represent poor plans or reactive panic action: neither should be acceptable to companies pursuing KSAM. Bradford et al. (2012) propose that implementation should not be seen as a giant leap of faith at the end of a process but something that is built in throughout the planning process.

Measuring KSAM value

KSAM requires a major commitment from suppliers, not least the time and effort put into the account plans that are the engine central to the initiative and the resource commitments they incur. So it is reasonable to ask, 'Is it worthwhile?' or 'Does it add value?' However, the question might be asked at the level of an individual key account; or at the level of all key accounts; or of all customers or, in fact, the company overall, so the answer is not simple. Although establishing systems to capture revenues and costs for key customers enables the supplier to monitor value at the first two levels, i.e. for individual key accounts and for all key accounts, measuring the value of KSAM to the company as a whole is clearly more difficult. Indeed, some companies have found that, at the same time as focusing very successfully on key accounts and growing business with them, sales to other customer groups have fallen, so assessing added value from KSAM is complex.

The term 'value added' has its origin in a number of different management ideas, and is used in very specific ways by different sets of authors. Most of the ideas come from the USA, and originated in business school and consultancy research in the mid-1980s.

Value-chain analysis

Porter's well-known concept of value-chain analysis (Porter 1980) is an incremental one that focuses on how successive activities change the value of goods and services as they pass through various stages of a value chain. 'The analysis disaggregates a firm into its major activities in order to understand the behaviour of costs and the existing and potential sources of differentiation. It determines how the firm's own value chain interacts with the value chains of suppliers, customers and competitors. Companies gain competitive advantage by performing some or all of these activities at lower cost or with greater differentiation than competitors.'

Shareholder value added

Rappaport's (1986) research on shareholder value added (SVA) is equally well known: his idea of value added focuses less on processes than Porter's, and acts more as a final gateway in decision making, although it can be used at multiple levels within a firm. The analysis measures a company's ability to earn more than its total cost of capital. Within business units, SVA measures the value the unit has created by analysing cash flows over time.

There are a number of different ways of measuring SVA, one of which, market value added (MVA), needs further explanation. MVA is a measure first proposed by consultants Sterne Stewart in 1991, which compares the total shareholder capital of a company (including retained earnings) with the current market value of the company (capitalization and debt). When one is deducted from the other, a positive result means value has been added, and a negative result means investors have lost out. Within the literature, there is much discussion of the merits of this measure versus another approach proposed by Sterne Stewart, i.e. economic value added (EVA). MVA is one of a number of tools that analysts and the capital markets use to assess the value of a company. As a research topic, it focuses more directly on the processes of creating that value through effective marketing investments.

Customer's perception of value

Value added can also be seen as the customer's perception of value. Unfortunately, despite exhaustive research by academics and practitioners around the world, this elusive concept has proved almost impossible to pin down: 'What constitutes [customer] value – even in a single product category – appears to be highly personal and idiosyncratic', concludes Zeithaml (1988), for instance. Research has not found a neat, causal link between offering additional customer value and achieving value added on a balance sheet. That is, good ratings from customers about perceived value do not necessarily lead to financial success (and financially successful companies do not always offer products and services which customers perceive as offering better value than competitors). Nevertheless, the individual customer's perception of the extra value represented by different products and services cannot be easily dismissed: in the guise of measures such as customer satisfaction and customer loyalty, it is known to be the essence of brand success, and the whole basis of relationship marketing.

Accountancy value add

The accountant's definition of value added is 'value added = sales revenue – cost of purchased goods and services'. Effectively, this is a snapshot from the annual accounts of how the revenue from a sales period has been distributed, and how much is left over for reinvestment after meeting all costs, including shareholder dividends. Although this figure will say something about the past viability of a business, in itself it does not provide a guide to future prospects.

All these concepts of value, although different, are not mutually exclusive. Porter's value-chain analysis is one of several extremely useful techniques for identifying potential new competitive market and key account strategies. Rappaport's SVA approach can be seen as a powerful tool which enables managers to cost out the long-term financial implications of pursuing one or other of the competitive strategies which have been identified, including KSAM strategies. Customer perceptions, especially those of key customers, are clearly a major driver (or destroyer) of annual audited accounting value in all companies, whatever strategy is being used. Walters and Halliday (1997) usefully sum up the value added discussion thus: 'As aggregate measures and as relative performance indicators they have much to offer . . . [but] how can the manager responsible for developing and/or implementing growth objectives identify and select from alternative [strategic] options?'

Even if the concepts of customer loyalty and customer satisfaction are insufficient to explain results a link may exist between more complex and wide-ranging customer-orientated strategies and financial results, which requires a far more rigorous approach to forecasting costs and revenues than is common in KSAM planning, coupled with a longer-term perspective on the payback period than a single year. This longer-term cash-driven perspective is the basis of the SVA approach, and can be used as a basis for establishing the value of and in strategic account plans.

Nevertheless, several surveys (e.g. KPMG in 1999, CSF Consulting in 2000) have found that less than 30% of companies were pushing SVA-based management techniques down to an operational level, seemingly because of difficulties in translating cash targets into practical, day-to-day management objectives. Expenditure on key accounts is rarely treated as an investment which will deliver results over an extended period, whereas other expenditure in a company is requested in a business case made via a capital expenditure proposal process and assessed on its ROI over a number of years. The account plan, showing the specific strategies, action, resource requirement and results, is effectively a capital expenditure proposal and should be treated as such, both in its preparation and in its approval. Well-developed account plans are the way forward for these accounts to receive the resource required to deliver the powerful strategies that will make substantial differences to the business.

Conclusion

In order for KSAM to be taken seriously and managed properly in a supplier, it should be underpinned by strategic account plans for individual key customers covering at least a three-year period. These plans need to be of sufficient quality to allow the company to trust them and invest as necessary. Sadly, they often are not of such quality. Without doubt, one of the biggest barriers is the people who are asked to write strategic account plans. Key account managers who have spent most of their career in sales have not previously been required to develop long-term, strategic and financially comprehensive plans with careful, analysis-based forecasts. They need to have the competences of experienced senior executives, fully trained in analytical techniques, financial analysis, strategic planning, political and interpersonal skills: indeed, the very skills required by a successful general manager or chief executive officer.

The determination of the supplier company to achieve such plans is also often in doubt, even though their approach to other forms of planning may be much more rigorous. Unless the company insists on the development of strategic account plans to a satisfactory level, key account managers will interpret its reticence as an escape clause, since many key account managers pride themselves on their action rather than their thinking and planning and, as Woodburn (2008) shows, are rewarded for the former rather than the latter.

Needless to say, however good the plans, they are of very little value unless they are implemented. KSAM is without doubt one of the major challenges facing business today. It is fraught with difficulties in conceiving, planning and implementing it, because it requires major organizational change and substantial shifts in the supplier's view of customers, and in its internal culture, in order to align its R&D, purchasing, manufacturing, logistics, IT, finance, service and other functions with the equivalent functions in its customers' businesses. Clearly, all this cannot be achieved without a good plan. This alignment will only occur in relatively few special cases but, when they happen, such relationships represent a well-spring of profitability for both parties.

Using customer profitability and customer lifetime value to manage strategic accounts

BY RÉGIS LEMMENS AND TOMAS VANDERBIESEN

Abstract

Today's economy is characterized by an increasingly globalized business-to-business environment, whereby a very large proportion of a supplier's overall revenue stream is generated by a very small number of customers. Because of the strategic importance of these customers, they should be considered assets of the company and treated accordingly. The performance of these customers should no longer be based on their revenues but on their profitability and lifetime value. This paper explains the concepts of customer profitability and customer lifetime value at an individual key account level. It also proposes a framework that guides strategic account managers during the account planning process, to improve the relationship with their strategic customers in a profitable way.

Introduction

Sales, and more particularly strategic account management, is undergoing a paradigmatic shift that involves a change in focus from managing customer accounts based on revenues to managing the accounts based on profitability for planning and follow-up; and to managing based on valuation for long-term strategic resources and investment-allocation purposes. This is triggered by an ever rising globalized business-to-business (B2B) environment, whereby a very large proportion of a supplier's overall revenue stream is generated by a very small number of customers. These customers, referred to as strategic customers, are often the product of close relationships that have been built over a period of many years and can therefore not easily be replaced. Losing such a customer can, for many organizations, never be compensated by the number of new customers acquired during that year. This means that losing a strategic customer may be decisive in failing to reach the organization's sales targets.

Many supplier organizations have responded to this situation by implementing special account management procedures and teams within their organizations, whereby each individual strategic customer is considered an asset of the company and no longer a commodity that comes and goes (Gupta and Lehman 2007). These intangible assets are critical and often dominant determinants of an organization's value (Srivastava et al. 1998). The people managing these strategic customers are no longer seen as salespeople but as managers or custodians of these high-value assets. Their task is to closely follow up and monitor the relationships based on account plans, and at the same time they have to nourish long-term relationships by managing the investments that the organization is willing to make for these customers.

Customer loyalty does not mean customer profitability per se

Relationship marketing emphasizes the need for maintaining long-term customer relationships. Customer profitability is supposed to be positively related to customer loyalty and customer satisfaction. This link between customer satisfaction and profitability is one of the cornerstones of customer relationship management (CRM) (e.g. Anderson and Mittal 2000; Reichheld and Sasser 1990). In recent years this link has been questioned by several researchers (Helgesen 2006; Reinartz and Kumar 2002; Soderlund and Vilgon 1995; Zhang et al. 2010), and while several studies found a link, others, such as Reinartz and Kumar (2002), found that the relationship between loyalty and profitability is much weaker – and more subtle – than the proponents of loyalty programmes claim. They found little or no evidence to suggest that customers who purchase steadily from a supplier over time are necessarily cheaper to serve, less price sensitive, or particularly effective at bringing in new business.

Very large customers are powerful and demand highly customized solutions, have high demands in terms of sales and account management, and are challenging in terms of profit (Brady et al. 2004; Piercy 2006; Sawhney 2004). They know their value to their suppliers and use it to get premium services or price discounts (Reinartz and Kumar 2002). They are also more knowledgeable about product offerings and are better able to assess the quality. In general, purchasing has become a strategic function with responsibilities for profitability, cost control and shareholder value (Janda and Seshadri 2001; Piercy 2006). Furthermore, many organizations have recognized the strategic value-adding potential of global procurement (Ellram and Carr 1994) and have therefore adopted integrated centralized purchasing practices (Olsen and Ellram 1997; Sheth and Sharma 1997). These organizations have reduced their number of suppliers by 40–90% (Emshwiller 1991; Ulaga and Eggert 2006). This enables them to increase their buying power and achieve further price reductions or transaction cost reductions with a smaller subset of suppliers (Ulaga and Eggert 2006). When professional purchasing managers use complex sourcing metrics to select the 'right' suppliers, and dictate terms on how they will be supplied, more than ever before supplier profitability is determined at the point of sale (De Boer et al. 2001; Piercy 2006; Talluri and Narasimhan 2004).

As a response, supplier organizations have been implementing special account management procedures and sales teams. Strategic account managers nurture long-term customer relationships (Arnold et al. 2001) by becoming trusted advisors for their accounts and by demonstrating a solution-driven focus (Sheth 2000). They are in charge of sales, customer satisfaction and ultimately profitability and customer value (Harvey et al. 2003).

Traditionally, the benefits of customer profitability and customer lifetime value (CLV) are discussed at an aggregated level for a customer segment or even the complete customer base. Such aggregated levels allow the calculation of customer equity linked with shareholder value, but we believe that there is a gap in the literature showing how these concepts can be used at an individual account level. This paper aims to contribute to the existing literature on customer profitability and CLV by focusing on an individual key account.

To implement CLV and reap the rewards we need a framework to guide strategic account managers during their account planning process. The measurement of customer profitability and CLV, and the definition of the optimal account development strategy, are the core of our proposed CLV management framework for strategic accounts. Kumar et al. (2008) developed a CLV management framework and field tested it at IBM, in order to better allocate visit frequencies to customers. Inspired by their work, we propose the CLV framework in Table 1 for a strategic account management setting.

We first discuss the importance and the methods available to measure customer profitability. Several cost-allocation methods are discussed, whereby arguments are presented in favour of activity-based costing. Second, we discuss the importance and relevance of measuring CLV. The limitations of using an individual measure rather than the traditional aggregated one are discussed briefly. Third, we will analyse in detail the financial and non-financial drivers of CLV. Finally,

Table 1: CLV framework for a strategic account management setting

Process	Purpose
Measure customer profitability	Determine the methods for calculating the profitability of each customer
Measure CLV	Determine the lifetime value of strategic accounts
Define the drivers of CLV	Determine which factors influence the CLV of each account
Define the optimal account development strategy	Determine the optimal mix of activities that is likely to increase the overall lifetime value of the account

we will present an integrated account development framework which strategic account managers can use during their account planning process.

Measuring customer profitability

What is customer profitability?

Customer profitability is the arithmetic difference between earned revenues and associated costs of an individual customer relationship, measured over a discrete time period such as a year (Jacobs et al. 2001).

$$CP_t = Revenue_t - Cost_t$$

where: $t =$ the discrete time period over which the customer profitability is calculated.

The calculation of customer profitability is based on information of actual purchases the customer has made in the considered past time period and on the associated costs (Ryals 2008, p. 22). These data should be available within the company.

Why is customer profitability relevant?

The costs of marketing, selling and servicing customers can vary significantly (Benson et al. 1987). As a result, it is possible for a company to have profitable products and at the same time incur customer-related costs that make certain customer relationships unprofitable (Hilton 2008). Research shows that not only small customers but also large customers can be unprofitable (Reinartz and Kumar 2000; Sharma 2003, 2006). Customer profitability management helps to allocate the right costs and revenues at customer account level, leading to a clear view on the profitability of the customers. Since the ultimate objective of companies remains to make a profit from selling products and services, measuring and managing customer profitability has become an essential part of customer relationship management.

How can customer profitability be measured?

Costs

In their zeal to delight customers, some companies actually lose money with their customers because they become customer-obsessed rather than customer-focused. They want to satisfy their customers at all costs and in this light they offer additional product features and services but fail to receive prices that cover the costs. To avoid this, suppliers need an in-depth understanding of the total cost of the delivered products and services (Kaplan 2005).

Costs can be split into two main categories: the first contains all costs linked to the production of goods, i.e. the 'cost of sales', while the second covers the costs generated by servicing the customers, i.e. 'cost to serve'. In standardized production and service environments the 'cost of sales' will not be impacted by customer behaviour, allowing suppliers to focus on determining and controlling the 'cost to serve' (Shapiro et al. 1997). Costs of serving customers can vary significantly, triggered by the fact that some buyers can negotiate more aggressively, or take advantage of differential discounts because of their size, or because they can perform functions themselves, such as in-house maintenance or technical support (Benson et al. 1987). When working with strategic accounts, strategies, processes and systems become interwoven, leading to a situation where the split between the two cost categories becomes less obvious. It is therefore important that in the first step, costs of all natures are considered and listed and in the next step, only the costs caused by the customer and funded by the supplier are assigned (see Table 2).

Revenues

Depending on the industry and products that are sold, different revenue types can be more or less important. Each organization has to decide which revenue types they want to include. Some types, such as gross sales income, fees, commissions, margins, discounts, rebates and refunds, are generic and quite simple

Table 2: Cost nature categories

Cost nature	Short description
Pre-sale costs	All costs related to activities in the sales process, prior to the moment that the contract is closed
Production costs	Contains both the one-off costs such as design, set-up, testing, regulatory and the recurrent production costs
Distribution costs	All costs made to transfer the goods to the supplier
Post-sale service costs	This category is often neglected. Sometimes customer training, installation, technical support, and repair and maintenance are profit-making operations, but businesses bundle such services into the product price and the buyer pays 'nothing extra' for them

to allocate, while others, such as financial interests, exchange of assets, exceptional revenues and any other increase in owner's equity, can be more complicated. As soon as the activities or behaviour of a customer generates revenues, the effort to link the revenues to the customer should be made. The majority of revenues that can be influenced by the account manager are generated by the gross sales income, which is calculated by multiplying the price at which goods or services are sold by the number of units or amount sold. Customized pricing policies are at the heart of any strategy to manage customer profitability.

Multiple pricing strategies exist: there is not 'one pricing strategy' that is the best in all situations, so the adoption of a pricing strategy is a learning curve driven by studying the needs and behaviours of customers.

The most commonly applied pricing strategies are:

- *Cost-based pricing*: the price is determined by adding a profit element on top of the cost of the product. The main advantage of this approach is that prices are relatively easy to calculate. If the profit element is applied consistently, the business can also predict more reliably what the overall profit margin will be. The main weakness of cost-based pricing is that aspects related to demand (willingness to pay, price elasticity) and competition (competitive price levels) are ignored. In the context of strategic account management, cost-based pricing is rare because customers often have a good view on the actual costs since they are more involved in the total production process. Some customers even demand total transparency of the costs of the products that they buy and often they are not prepared to pay a price higher than the intrinsic value of the offer.
- *Value-based pricing*: the approach uses data on the perceived customer value of the product or service as the main factor for determining the final selling price. This approach is driven by a deep understanding of customer needs, customer perceptions of value, price elasticity and customers' willingness to pay. The big disadvantage is that this information is usually hard to find and interpret. Furthermore, a customer value-based pricing approach may lead to relatively high prices, especially for unique products. Though that will have a positive impact on the customer profitability in the short run, this pricing approach may spur market entry by new entrants offering comparable products at slightly lower prices. Finally, it is important to note that it is an error to assume that customers will immediately recognize and pay for a truly innovative and superior product. Marketers must educate customers and communicate superior value to customers before linking price to value. Customers must first recognize value in order to be willing to pay for value, rather than basing their purchase decision solely on price (Hinterhuber and Liozu 2012). In the context of strategic account management it is often the uniqueness of the combined offer of products and services that creates an added value for which the customer is willing to pay a supplement (Woodburn et al. 2004).
- *Risk-based pricing*: this pricing strategy has already been used for years in the financial sector. Engagement with customers or assets with a higher risk

profile has to be compensated by higher returns. In the context of strategic account management, the risk element is represented by the stability of the relationship, both commercially (e.g. has this company already been a customer for many years?) and financially (e.g. does this customer always respect payment agreements?). The more 'stable' a customer is, the better the pricing conditions that can be awarded. However, risk-based pricing also brings a perverse effect, which occurs because higher-risk customers are charged a higher margin on products and services, so revenue from them is higher than from a lower-risk customer. If not properly managed, account managers could become motivated to promote deals with customers that offer higher risks.

- *Competitor-based pricing*: this approach uses price information from actual or potential competitors as a primary source to determine appropriate price levels. The strategy should be used only if price is one of the most important purchase criteria for customers. The main advantage of this approach is that the competitive situation is taken into account, while the main disadvantage is that aspects related to the customer's demand function are ignored. Competitor-based pricing should be used with caution, to avoid a price war (which has happened in both the car and the airline industries).

Allocation methodology

The biggest challenge in calculating customer profitability is reliably measuring and assigning the costs to the customers. Unlike revenues and direct costs, indirect costs require a method to allocate them to individual customers. Management accounting systems often treat these indirect costs coming from marketing, finance, IT, facility management, HR, and customer service as a layer of overheads to be spread evenly over all customers. It is simply not true that customers buying the same amount of goods or services need the same amount of time and attention (Ryals 2002). Costs of different types will be influenced by a number of customer-specific elements (see Table 3).

A uniform spread of indirect costs over all customers can be triggered by the faulty impression that prices and costs are correlated, but research (Berger et al. 2006) suggests that usually they are not, which produces a broad dispersion of account profitability. Instead of valuing customers based on an arbitrary cost distribution, installing a cost-allocation method that assigns the indirect costs based on a rationally supported methodology allows much better assessment of the value of a customer (Gupta and Lehman 2007). Cost-management systems have to be used to determine the activities, costs and profit associated with serving particular customers (Hilton 2008). Different cost-allocation methods are possible, but each of them will lead to a different result and thus different estimates of customer profitability. Establishing reliable profitability figures for customer accounts is not straightforward, but the following methods are in use:

- *Cost/Income ratio*: all indirect costs are spread proportionally over all customers according to their gross revenue.
- *Standard unit costing*: this method allocates the company's fixed costs over a given period of time to the items produced during that period. The standard

Table 3: Cost type influencers

Cost type	Influencers
Pre-sale costs	Different entities of the customer that need to be visited can be spread over multiple locations which are geographically dispersed and located far from the salesperson's home base. Some customers require seemingly endless sales calls, while others place their orders without delay. Some must be courted with top-level executives backed up by sophisticated account management techniques, while others need little special effort.
Production costs	Order size influences cost, as do set-up time, scrap rate, custom designs, special features and functions, unusual packaging, and even order timing. Off-peak orders cost less than those made when demand is heavy. Some orders call on more resources than others. A company that stores products in anticipation of orders, however, will have difficulty tracing production costs to particular orders and customers.
Distribution costs	Fast delivery costs more. Costs vary with the customer's location. Shipping via preferred transportation mode. Lack of back-haul opportunities. Special logistics support such as a field inventory entails cost.
Post-sale service costs	Post-sales is completely customer specific and these costs must certainly be individually monitored.

unit costing method can provide added value in a production environment, but it will not be very effective in those organizations where non-standardized products are manufactured and services are rendered.

- *Volume-based costing* (also called traditional costing): this product-costing system allocates overhead costs to a single cost pool (e.g. factory overhead) and then volume-based cost drivers are used to allocate the overhead costs to individual products or services. The cost drivers mostly depend on the number of units manufactured. Cost drivers, which can be plant-wide or departmental, often include labour hours, machine hours and labour costs. This method is best applied where large, unique, high-cost items are built to order rather than mass produced, and when many costs can be directly traced to each job.
- *Activity-based costing*: ABC, described by Cooper and Kaplan (1991), is a costing model that identifies all activities performed in an organization and assigns the costs linked to each of these activities to all products and services, to the extent of their actual consumption of these activities. As such, ABC translates indirect costs into direct costs. In this way an organization can establish the true full cost of its individual products and services. The ABC methodology assigns all of an organization's resource costs, through activities, to the products and services provided to its customers. ABC is generally used as a tool

for understanding product and customer service costs, and has predominantly been used to support strategic decisions such as pricing, and identification and measurement of process improvement initiatives. It enables companies to have a better understanding of their cost structures and the profitability of their customers. Armed with this information, companies are better able to drive down the cost of sales and focus on those customers that are profitable (Sheth and Sharma 2008).

Choosing a method

To calculate trustworthy customer profitability, revenues and cost must be correctly allocated to the right accounts. The main difficulty lies in the assignment of indirect costs to individual customers on a reliable basis, which is essential for changes in customer behaviour to be translated into costs assigned to them. The first three cost-allocation methods (cost/income ratio, standard unit costing and volume-based costing) allocate costs without sufficiently taking into account customer behaviour and individual customer characteristics. The correct costs of a customer can be calculated only by determining all activities and costs associated with serving particular customers (Hilton 2008). The ABC method is the only method where different consumption of services directly influences the costs allocated to the customers. Moreover, a change in behaviour of the account will only be reflected in the costs allocated to the account via ABC and not via any of the other allocation methods (Benson et al. 1987; Nachnani 1998; Woodburn et al. 2004). Even though implementing ABC is time consuming and thus expensive, it is the only methodology that returns a meaningful cost at customer level which can be used in a strategic account management approach. Alternatively, time-driven ABC also provides a meaningful cost at customer level but at a lower level of complexity and thus at a lower cost.

What are the shortcomings of using customer profitability?

The idea that customers are to be considered as assets is gaining acceptance, which leads to the development of literature on how to measure customer value (Berger and Nasr 1998; Gupta et al. 2004; Jain and Singh 2002; Mulhern 1999; Reinartz and Kumar 2002; Rust et al. 2001). The most important responsibility of key account managers is to retain and develop their accounts in order to maximize the value of the customers to the supplier organization. But what is the value of a customer? How can we use customer profitability as a measure of current and future value?

Calculating the value of a customer is not possible with financial metrics based on past performance, such as accounting-based profitability (Gupta et al. 2006; Stahl et al. 2003). Estimation of the total value of all customer assets, also called customer equity (CE), is made by taking the sum of the current and projected future cash flows of all customers (Blattberg and Deighton 1996). Future-oriented customer profitability calculates the net present value (NPV) of future expected costs and revenues associated with serving a customer over their entire future life. This is also known as customer lifetime value analysis (e.g. Berger and Nasr 1998; Dwyer 1989; Hoekstra and Huizingh 1999; Jain and Singh 2002).

Measuring customer lifetime value

What is customer lifetime value?

CLV is a central metric for assessing the profitability of customers: it equates to the present value of all future profits generated by a customer. The idea of CLV is derived from NPV analysis, where the NPV of a financial asset is the sum of the discounted future cash flows that will be generated from the asset. Effectively, CLV is the NPV of a customer's future profits. One common approach is to assume that we know the duration of a customer's lifetime, and then calculate a discounted cash flow for that time period (Berger and Nasr 1998; Blattberg and Deighton 1996; Gupta and Lehman 2007; Jain and Singh 2002).

The CLV measure incorporates the probability of a customer being active in the future, the future contribution margin and the future costs required to retain the customer. All these factors, used to calculate CLV, are essential for designing account management strategies. It is important to understand that CLV is a method to predict or forecast future customer behaviour.

Other methods such as recency, frequency and monetary value (RFM), share of wallet and past customer value also allow the prediction of customer behaviour. RFM is a technique widely used in marketing to predict future customer buying behaviour based on the customer's past purchasing patterns, and therefore requires a past purchasing history database in order to forecast future customer behaviour. The share of wallet of a customer consists of comparing the level of spend of an existing customer on a particular product or service category with the supplier versus the complete spend of a customer, which requires an estimate of the customer's complete spend in a particular product or service category. Past customer value is based on past cumulative customer profitability adjusted for the time value of money.

These techniques rely on past data and performance to predict future performance and are based on the assumption that the customer will be active in the future. They lack the probability of the customer being active in the future, as well as an estimate of the costs required to retain the customer. They also rely on the availability of a lot of historical data from which they compute averages. Key accounts are not average accounts and therefore none of these techniques is appropriate for valuing key accounts.

Why is customer lifetime value relevant?

By using CLV an organization can rank its customers or classify them into tiers based on their expected profitability, so firms can appropriately allocate resources across high- versus low-value customers (Reinartz and Kumar 2003; Rust et al. 2004; Venkatesan and Kumar 2004). An analysis of customer profitability may well show that some of the large customers are in fact unprofitable customers (Cooper and Kaplan 1991; Niraj et al. 2001). CLV may also help in revising existing discounting structures to improve profitability (Kalafatis and Denton 2000), and it may be used for making customer acquisition decisions so that a firm does not spend more on acquiring a customer than the CLV of that customer (Gupta and Lehmann 2003; Gupta and Zeithaml 2006). It allows firms to balance their resources between customer acquisition and customer retention (Reinartz et al. 2005). Recent studies also show that CLV can provide a link between customer value and firm value (Gupta et al. 2004). The CLVs of all the current and potential customers form a firm's customer equity (e.g. Rust et al. 2004; Villanueva et al. 2008), which has been found to be a good proxy measure of the firm's equity-market valuation (Gupta et al. 2004). Thus, the CLV framework helps bridge marketing and finance metrics.

How can the CLV of an individual customer be measured?

Traditionally, CLV is calculated by discounting future cash flows over the lifetime of the customer.

$$CLV = \sum_{t=1}^{T} \frac{(Cash\ flow\ In_t - Cash\ Flow\ Out_t)}{(1+r)^t}$$

Cash flow in = revenues in time period t
Cash flow out = costs in time period t
r = discount return
t = time period
T = the number of time periods for which the CLV is estimated.

The discount rate is based on the cost of capital of an organization. The minimum discount rate of an organization is its weighted average cost of capital (WACC). WACC is defined as the weighted average cost of debt and the cost of levered equity (Gallagher 2000) and is calculated as follows:

$$WACC = \frac{Equity}{Equity + Debt} \times Cost_{eq} + \frac{Debt}{Equity + Debt} \times Cost_{deb} * (1-t)$$

$Cost_{eq}$ = cost of equity
$Cost_{deb}$ = cost of debt
t = marginal tax rate.

The WACC is the cost of equity ($Cost_{eq}$) multiplied by the proportion of equity funding and the cost of debt ($Cost_{deb}$) multiplied by the proportion of debt funding reduced with corporate tax benefits (t) (see Tables 4 and 5).

The feasibility of making accurate estimates for revenue and cost is most significant in setting a realistic time horizon. According to Gupta et al. (2004), a time period from three to five years is appropriate for the following reasons:

Table 4: Example of calculation of WACC (assuming corporate tax rate of 20%)

	Amount	Cost
Equity	75,000	10%
Debt	50,000	5%
Tax	20%	
WACC	0.076	

Table 5: Example of calculation of CLV using WACC (assuming WACC of 7.6%)

	This year	Year +1	Year +2	Year +3
Revenue	100	104	108	112
Cost	60	62	65	68
Profit	40	42	43	44
Discount rate		7.60%	7.60%	7.60%
NPV risk corrected profit	40	39	37	35
CLV	151			

- Estimates further in the future will be less reliable and therefore undermine the confidence that is put in the resulting measure.
- Information of later years will have significantly less impact on the customer value due to the applied discount factor.

Further, in most cases the majority of a customer's lifetime value is captured within the first three years (Gupta and Lehmann 2005).

Traditionally, CLV calculations assumed a contractual setting between the customer and the supplier whereby future cash flows are known. While it is reasonable to assume that relationships between an organization and its key customers are based on contractual agreements, it is not reasonable to assume that therefore all future cash flows are known. Key account relationships often comprise a multitude of products and services that are sold in the form of projects and contract agreements. Although existing projects and agreements come to an end, new ones are constantly being formed based on new business opportunities at the account. Even existing contracts are often renegotiated through the contracts life cycle. For these reasons a supplier needs to know the probability of its future cash flows:

$$CLV = \sum_{t=1}^{T} p(Purchase_t) * \frac{(Cash\ flow\ In_t - Cash\ Flow\ Out_t)}{(1+r)^t}$$

where: $p(Purchase_t)$ = probability the customer will purchase or continue purchasing in period t.

The formula assumes that there is only one project or contract agreement with the customer, which is often not the case with key accounts. Therefore, we first need to calculate NPV of each individual project or contract, taking into account the purchasing probability. CLV is then the sum of the probability-adjusted individual NPVs for the account:

$$NPV = \sum_{t=1}^{T} p(Purchase_t) \times \frac{(Cash\ flow\ In_t - Cash\ Flow\ Out_t)}{(1+r)^t}$$

where: NPV = net present value of an individual project or contract at the customer
$p(Purchase_t)$ = probability the customer will purchase or continue purchasing in period t.

The current formula includes the sales/account management costs as part of the outgoing cash flows. However, a large amount of these costs will be generated regardless of whether the customer purchases or not. Costs related to the acquisition, development and retention of key accounts need to be included in the overall CLV, which raises the question of whether to include these key account management costs at the level of the individual project or contract, or at the overall customer level. The answer depends on how the key account management programme is organized.

As explained in Gupta and Zeithaml (2006), depending on the use of model, acquisition costs have to be included implicitly where the lifetime value of an as-yet-to-be-acquired customer is considered. If, however, expected residual lifetime value is calculated, the acquisition cost should not be included. For example, large matrix organizations, such as IBM, have dedicated key account managers and technical architects for specific customers, whose costs are attributed at individual customer level. However, when they are selling a particular solution they include product experts who are salespeople working in specific IBM business units. If there is no opportunity, these specialist salespeople will not be called upon, so their costs are specific to each individual business opportunity.

Following Reinartz and Kumar (2003), we can adjust the formula as follows:

$$NPV = \sum_{t=1}^{T} p(Purchase_t) \times \frac{(GC_t)}{(1+r)^t} - \frac{(S\&MCost_t)}{(1+r)^t}$$

where: GC = Gross Contribution Margin

$S\&MCost$ = Sales and Marketing Costs.

CLV is the sum of the NPVs of all existing and potential projects and contracts minus the costs associated with developing and retaining the key account.

$$CLV = \sum_{n=1}^{N} NPV_n - \sum_{t=1}^{T} \frac{(KAMCost_t)}{(1+r)^t}$$

where: N = number of existing and potential projects and contracts

n = current project or contract

$KAMCost$ = costs of managing the key account as whole.

Several methods exist to calculate the probability that a customer will purchase or continue to purchase. Choosing a method depends on the characteristics of the customer exchange process. In the context of managing strategic accounts, the knowledge available from the account managers takes precedence over statistical calculation based on averages.

Scoring is a qualitative way of measuring specific types of probabilities based on understanding of the accounts. The scorecards usually consist of a set of opportunity qualification criteria which, when weighted, provides a probability of success. The advantage of this method is that it makes it very clear what are the drivers for winning the opportunity.

Example
A highly simple form of scoring opportunities is to assign probabilities to each stage of the sales process. The total value of the opportunity is multiplied with the probability factor, resulting in a forecast value:

Process stages	Lead	Prospect	Presentation	Negotiating	Sales
% Probability factor	5%	10%	25%	50%	100%

For existing contractual business it is common to take a probability of 100% for the duration of the contract. The renewal of the contract can be considered as a new opportunity for which probability can be scored based on the 'strength of the relationship'. Strength can be measured based on a number of weighted relational elements, where the most important are longevity of relationship, number of different products/services that are bought, quality of relationship and number of contacts between supplier and customer (in both directions). This approach to measuring the 'strength of the relationship' refers to the customer portfolio strategy matrix developed by McDonald et al. (1997), which can then be used as a basis for determining the probability of retention.

Defining the drivers of CLV

According to Srivastava (2001) there are four key financial drivers through which a strategic account manager could create shareholder value:

- Enhancing cash flows by selling more or reducing costs. Strategies to increase the share of wallet, increase pricing and increase cross-selling to existing customers lead to higher sales. Costs can be reduced by improving the efficiency of internal processes or by leveraging external resources, such as involving the customers in completing certain parts of the value-creation process.
- Accelerating cash flows, as earlier cash flows are preferred because of the risk and time adjustments of later cash flows.
- Reducing vulnerability and volatility of cash flows. Vulnerability of cash flows can be reduced by increasing customer satisfaction, loyalty and retention. Cash

flow vulnerability can also be reduced by cross-selling products and services less vulnerable to competitive actions.

- Augmenting the long-term value of the account by carefully investing in servicing processes and value propositions that will provide a platform for future cash flows.

A strategic account manager can influence these drivers by developing better relationships, adding more value and reducing the time to money of future business opportunities.

Developing better relationships

Beside calculating and knowing the lifetime value of a customer, key account managers need to know how they can actually influence it. So far we have looked at the probability of purchase at an opportunity or contract level. However, a key account is more than the sum of the underlying opportunities and contracts. The relationship is often cited as the additional element that keeps all the individual business opportunities together.

A number of researchers have identified a series of relationship stages associated with different levels of intimacy (Dunn and Thomas 1994; McDonald et al. 1997; Palmer and Bejou 1994). Specific drivers of customer relationships are interdependence, trust, joint planning, dedicated teams and multi-level contacts. These relationship levels are defined by the frequency of interaction, the depth of the interactions and their scope. The more people from both the seller and the customer organization in communication with each other over a wide range of issues, the higher the level of intimacy that will develop. According to Oliver and Winer (1987), customers who buy more, more frequently and across different categories will have a better relationship with their suppliers. While selling across different categories will help to build relationships, so will selling across different departments or business units within a single customer. According to Srivastava and Shocker (1997), a customer's switching costs increase with multiple relationships with the same supplier. When these relationships are satisfactory and frequent they lead to a greater level of trust, which again leads to longer and more intimate customer–supplier relationships (Morgan and Hunt 1994).

Reinartz and Kumar (2003) researched the drivers of CLV. While their research focused on a business-to-consumer setting, their findings are, to some extent, transferable to a business-to-business setting. They categorized the drivers as exchange characteristics and customer heterogeneity. Exchange characteristics describe the process and nature of the exchange between the supplier and the customer, including elements such as cross-selling, spending levels and customer royalty levels. Customer heterogeneity describes the type of the customer, such as industry sector, size or other demographic variables (see Table 6).

Adding more value

In a business-to-business setting, relationships are built only if they add value to both parties. According to Grönroos (2008), value for customers means that they

Table 6: The drivers of CLV

Drivers	Impact	Impact on customer profitability
Spending level	Average monthly spending level over a given period	(+)
Cross-buying	Number of different products/categories purchased	(+)
Focused buying	Purchase within one category	(−)
Inter-purchase time	Average number of days between purchases	(∩)
Loyalty instrument	Customer's ownership of company's loyalty instrument (B2C) or availability of line of credit (B2B)	(+)
Mailing effort by the company	Number of mailing efforts of the company (B2C) or the number of contacts (B2B)	(+)
Income	Income of the customer (B2C) or income of the firm (B2B)	(+)
Population density	Number of people in a two-digit zip code (only B2C)	(−)

Source: Reinartz and Kumar (2003)

are or feel better off than before after having been assisted by the provision of resources or by a process or a set of processes. So what can strategic account managers do in order for their customers to feel better during and after purchasing their products and services? According to Prahalad and Ramaswamy (2000), customers want to exercise their influence and interact with their suppliers and thereby co-create value. They argue that by implementing co-creation the customer is being involved in marketing and product development activities to strengthen a sustainable relationship. Increasing customer loyalty or reducing market research costs are other examples of drivers for companies to engage in the process of co-creation (Nambisan 2002; Payne, Storbacka, and Frow 2008).

Suppliers in co-creation also benefit from productivity gains, whereby customer labour substitutes for supplier labour (Fitzsimmons 1985; Lovelock and Young 1979; Mills and Morris 1986). In all cases, transforming the customer into an active participant is the central concept, in order to be able to deliver them maximum value. The process relies on a meaningful dialogue between the customer and the supplier whereby both gain access to knowledge and transparency of information. In return, customers will also bear more responsibility for dealing with the risks associated with the co-creation process. Prahalad and Ramaswamy (2005) conceptualized the co-creation process in a model called the DART (dialogue, access, risk–benefits, transparency), which allows strategic account managers to add value to their customers by:

- Enhancing the dialogue, which means more than listening to the customer, and involves sharing information and learnings across the whole co-creation process, not only with the customer but also with other parties involved.
- Ensuring that all parties involved in the process have complete access to all the necessary information and tools.
- Ensuring that all parties are fully aware of the risks associated with the co-creation process.
- Ensuring transparency between all parties involved.

Reduce time to money

The time horizon is an important element in CLV, whereby earnings today are more valued than earnings tomorrow. What can a strategic account manager do to shorten the length of time before earning any revenues?

The more people involved in making a purchase decision, the more complex the decision-making process and the longer it will take. Often in a B2B context the person or department who experiences the problem is not the same as those who can make the purchase decisions: a decision-making unit analyses the problem and the proposed solutions in order to make a purchase decision. The 'time to close' for business opportunities can be shortened by selling high into the customer organizational hierarchy. Often the higher people are in the hierarchy, the more authority they have to make purchase decisions. By focusing the sales effort on demonstrating how the supplier's products and services can solve their problems, strategic account managers can shorten the sales cycle.

The amount of risk the customer perceives with the purchase also causes long purchasing cycles. According to Shapiro (2001), perceived risk levels can be reduced by offering:

- A trial or pilot project to demonstrate the benefits of the value proposition.
- A 'Trojan Horse', which is a limited module of the whole value proposition, so the customer gets better acquainted with the system and what it can mean for them. This can be a module with one of the most popular features which make the initial first module purchase attractive.
- Usage- or performance-based pricing.
- Special introductory discounts.

Define the optimal account development strategy

Most studies focused on the value of calculating CLVs in order to segment customers and allocate resources accordingly. This raises the question: 'What is the value of calculating the CLV for an account manager who manages only a few key accounts?'

Calculating customer profitability and CLV for key accounts is really useful only if account managers use them to manage their accounts. In our view, the value lies in the insight provided by the analysis of the CLV and how it can be improved.

We compared our approach with an existing key account planning approach used in a large international systems integrator. While their approach encompassed most of the components of CLV, they did not calculate it into a single value. In their view the benefit of calculating the CLV of their strategic accounts would not be the value itself but to provide a framework of how all these components relate to each other. To that extent we further developed an account development framework linking all the financial and non-financial drivers of CLV (see Table 7). We proposed this framework as a tool to help strategic account managers to analyse their accounts and develop optimal account development strategies.

Table 7: Framework linking financial and non-financial drivers of CLV

Drivers	Impact	Impact on customer profitability
Increase share of wallet	Increase in the customer share of wallet enables a supplier to sell more and to reduce their costs through economies of scale.	Increase cash flows
Increase cross-selling	Cross-selling products enables a supplier to sell more, to establish more revenue streams from one account, thereby reducing their vulnerability and volatility of their revenues. Number of different product/categories purchased (Reinartz and Kumar 2003).	Increase cash flows Reduce vulnerability Reduce volatility
Increase co-creation with customer	Involving the customer in the design, production and delivery of the value proposition offers the possibility of reducing costs for the supplier and increasing value for the customer.	Reduce vulnerability Reduce volatility
Changes in pricing model (volume based, usage or performance based pricing)	Introducing new pricing models such as volume, usage or performance based pricing reduces the customer perceived risk in the purchase. Some business buying has converted to a subscription model already in order to reduce the perceived risks of their customers.	Accelerate cash flows Reduce vulnerability
Offer special discounts	Cash flows can be accelerated by offering special discounts (Shapiro 2001).	Accelerate cash flows
Offer pilot projects or paid proof of concepts	The financial exposure of a customer can be reduced by scaling down the size of the purchase. A pilot project or even proof of concept can help the customer to reduce their perceived risk in the purchase (Shapiro 2001).	Accelerate cash flows

Table 7:   (Continued)

Drivers	Impact	Impact on customer profitability
Gain access higher up the customer's organizational hierarchy	Selling directly to people higher up in the organization's hierarchy can lead to shorter and less complex (costly) sales cycles.	Increase cash flows Accelerate cash flows
Provide more customized solutions	Providing customized solutions allows suppliers to become more embedded in their customers' operations, which increases customer loyalty and decreases the probability that customers can replace the firm with a competing supplier (Sawhney 2004).	Reduce vulnerability Increase long-term value of the account
Increase multi-level contacts	Increasing contact frequency across multiple levels of both organizations leads to higher customer profitability (Reinartz and Kumar 2003). Dialogue between different levels in the organization is essential to promote co-creation and to develop a climate of trust (Prahalad and Ramaswamy 2000).	Reduce vulnerability Increase long-term value of the account
Introduce a joint planning process	Joint strategic planning process, where the customer is actively involved, increases the commitment levels of the customer and is linked to customer satisfaction and loyalty (Woodburn et al. 2004).	Reduce vulnerability Increase long-term value of the account
Increase customer satisfaction levels	Customer satisfaction influences repeat purchase behaviour (Bolton 1998), 'word of mouth', (Anderson 1998), cross-selling rates (Verhoef et al. 2001), purchase of premium options (Ngobo 2005) and price premiums (Homburg et al. 2005). Highly satisfied customers are likely to recommend the firm's products to other consumers (Anderson 1998), generate additional business at a lower cost for the firm (Villanueva et al. 2008) and reduce suppliers' operating costs associated with defects and complaints (Fornell and Wernerfelt 1988).	Reduce vulnerability Increase long-term value of the account

Conclusions

There is mounting evidence that organizational structures are evolving towards closer alignment with their markets (Day 2006). This development has been applauded by organizational theorists who endorse smaller, customer-responsive units, in which focus is shifted from products to service and from products to solution. In this customer-focused selling or consultative selling model (Arnett and Badrinarayanan 2005), the sales organization owns the relationship with the customer and is responsible for its own balance sheet.

In strategic account management, firms increasingly need to assign sales/profit responsibilities to the sales organization (Millman 1996). Sales directors realize that long-term profitable relationships with customers ask for long-term investments. The multi-year customer lifetime value approach is the only method to determine whether these long-term investments in customers are paying off. CLV analysis needs to be included in account management processes and, more specifically, in the account planning process. In this paper we have presented a framework through which strategic account managers can use customer profitability and CLV as a framework to define their account strategy.

Besides the financial value, captured in the CLV calculation, customers have a relational value. According to Ryals (2008), there are four sources of relational value. The first is the reference value, which is generated by associating with customers (hence high-profile customers shown in business brochures, for example). The second is the referral value, which is created when existing customers recommend the supplier to a potential new customer. Third, the learning value comes from the process and quality expertise customers pass back to their supplier. The last is the innovation value which is triggered by customers who push their suppliers to participate in their joint product or process innovation. The first two types will simplify the attraction of new customers and therefore reduce the costs for acquiring new customers, while the last two result in a cost decrease and even a revenue increase. This explains why customers with negative CLV can be retained, because of the relational value generated. Future research will show how to calculate the relational value of a customer and include it in the calculation of their lifetime value.

SECTION 3

DEVELOPING KSAM PROGRAMMES

A configurational approach to strategic account management effectiveness

BY CHRISTIAN HOMBURG, JOHN WORKMAN, JR. AND OVE JENSEN

Abstract

At the turn of the millennium, most firms struggled with the challenge of managing their strategic accounts. Adopting a configurational perspective on organizational research, this paper reports the empirical state of SAM implementations at the time. Eight prototypical SAM approaches are described based on a cross-industry, cross-national study. The results show significant performance differences between the approaches. The prototypes are based on an integrative conceptualization of SAM that defines key constructs in four areas: (1) activities, (2) actors, (3) resources, (4) approach formalization. Finally, the paper reports findings on the effectiveness of SAM approaches. Internal culture matters a great deal while the formalization of the SAM approach does not. Overall, the study shows that companies should proactively manage their strategic accounts.

Introduction

This paper summarizes the findings of empirical research that was conducted in 1999 and published in two articles. One article, Homburg et al. (2002), focused on configurations of strategic account management. The other, Workman et al. (2003), focused on determinants of strategic account management effectiveness. At the time, the research project was the largest – and still is among the largest – empirical study on strategic account management ever done. In this paper, the summary of the two articles offers a description of the state of strategic account management at the turn of the millennium. Beyond the historical documentation, the research findings on SAM effectiveness are as provocative and challenging to managers and academics as they were at the time of their original publication.

The challenges in SAM have changed through the years as SAM matured as an instrument. We observe that much of the SAM-related debate today revolves around processes. At the time when we conceived our study, none of the expert interviews strongly emphasized this view. The professionalization of selling processes and the widespread adoption of selling process methodologies like Miller-Heiman, Solution Selling, and Target Account Selling, took place in the decade after we conducted our research. At the time of our research, the challenges resided more in the area of organizational structures (Whom should we appoint as account managers? To whom should they report?) and authority (How do we get local sales entities to cooperate with the account managers?). While the organizational structures seem to have moved out of focus, the authority challenge appears to us as an evergreen of SAM. This is where our research results are as current as ever.

In the business arena, at the turn of the millennium, many companies were faced with powerful and more demanding customers. These powerful buyers had in many industries been shaped through corporate mergers, typically in industry sectors such as retailing, automotive, computers and pharmaceuticals. These large customers often rationalized their supply base to cooperate more closely with a limited number of preferred suppliers (e.g. Dorsch et al. 1998; Stump 1995). They demanded special value-adding activities from their suppliers, such as joint product development, financing services or consulting services (Cardozo et al. 1992). Also, many buying firms centralized their procurement and expected a similarly coordinated selling approach from their suppliers. For example, global industrial customers demanded uniform pricing terms, logistics and service standards on a worldwide basis from their suppliers (Montgomery and Yip 2000). Internal organizational structures often hampered a coordinated account management, such as when the same customer was served by decentralized product divisions or by highly independent local sales operations. In addition, the complex set of activities for complex customers could not be handled by the sales function alone, but required participation from other functional groups. These developments had induced many suppliers to rethink how they manage their most important customers and how they design their internal organization in order to be responsive to these key customers. Firms increasingly organized around customers and shifted resources from product divisions or regional divisions to customer-focused business units (Homburg et al. 2000). This was when many firms established specialized key account managers and formed customer teams that were composed of people from sales, marketing, finance, logistics, quality and other functional groups (Millman 1996; Wotruba and Castleberry 1993).

In the academic literature just before the turn of the millennium, Millman (1996, p. 631) commented that 'Key account management is under researched and its efficacy, therefore, is only partially understood.' Kempeners and van der Hart (1999, p. 312) argued that 'organizational structure is perhaps the most interesting and controversial part of account management'. In a qualitative study of marketing organization (Homburg et al. 2000), we had found the increasing emphasis on key account management (KAM) to be one of the most fundamental changes in organizations.

At the time of our research, while some research had focused on global accounts (Montgomery and Yip 2000; Yip and Madsen 1996), the term *key account management* (KAM hereafter) – rather than strategic account management – appeared to be the most accepted term in publications (Jolson 1997; McDonald et al. 1997; Pardo 1997; Sharma 1997) and the most widely used term in Europe. In our original research we used the words key account management and defined it as 'the designation of special personnel and/or performance of special activities directed at an organization's most important customers' (Homburg et al. 2000, p. 463). This paper sticks to our original terminology. We subsume under key account management all approaches to managing the most important customers that have been discussed under such diverse terms as key account management, key account selling, national account management, national account selling, strategic account management, major account management or global account management. 'National account management' clearly has become a misnomer as business with important customers increasingly spanned country borders (Colletti and Tubridy 1987).

The paper is organized as follows. We begin with the results of the Homburg et al. (2002) article on configurations.

1. We derive the core design dimensions of KAM approaches from the KAM literature and from related research areas to develop an integrative conceptualization of key account management.
2. We identify the key constructs within these design dimensions.
3. We identify prototypical approaches to key account management in practice based on a cross-national, cross-industry taxonomy.

This is followed by an exploration of how the different approaches perform. We explore the outcomes of different KAM approaches and report the findings of the Workman et al. (2003) article on KAM effectiveness. We conclude by discussing implications of our research for theory and for managerial practice.

Given that taxonomies are less frequently developed than conceptual models, a few comments on their value are in order. As Hunt (1991, p. 176) has noted, classification schemata, such as typologies or taxonomies, 'play fundamental roles in the development of a discipline since they are the primary means for organizing phenomena into classes or groups that are amenable to systematic investigation and theory development'. Given that the conceptual knowledge about the design of KAM is at an early stage and that our research endeavour is to expand its scope, a taxonomy is particularly useful in providing the field with new organization. By means of the taxonomy, we are studying the complex KAM phenomenon through holistic patterns of multiple variables rather than isolated variables and their bivariate relations. This research approach is consistent with the configurational perspective to organizational analysis that has been gaining increasing attention (Meyer et al. 1993). The basic premise of the configurational perspective is that 'Organizational structures and management systems are best understood in terms of overall patterns rather than in terms of analyses of narrowly drawn sets of organizational properties' (Meyer et al. 1993, p. 1181). Thus, the configurational perspective complements the traditional contingency approach (Mahajan and Churchill 1990). Two alternatives of identifying configurations have been distinguished: *typologies* represent classifications based on a priori conceptual distinctions, while *taxonomies* are empirically derived groupings (Hunt 1991; Rich 1992; Sanchez 1993). Hunt (1991) notes that grouping phenomena through taxonomies as opposed to typologies requires substantially less a priori knowledge about which specific properties are likely to be powerful for classification, because taxonomical procedures are better equipped to handle large numbers of properties.

State of KAM literature at the turn of the millennium

Four main themes emerged from our review of literature on key account programmes. First, key account programmes encompass special (inter-organizational) activities for key accounts that are not offered to average accounts. These special activities pertain to such areas as pricing, products, services, distribution and information sharing (Cardozo et al. 1992; Montgomery and Yip 2000; Shapiro and Moriarty 1984b). Second, key account programmes frequently involve special (intra-organizational) actors who are dedicated to key accounts. These key account managers are typically responsible for a number of key accounts and report high in the organization (Colletti and Tubridy 1987; Dishman and Nitse 1998; Wotruba and Castleberry 1993). They may be placed in the supplier's headquarters, in the local sales organization of the key account's country, or even on the key account's facilities (Millman 1996; Yip and Madsen 1996). It is frequently stressed that key account managers need special compensation arrangements and skills, which has implications for their selection, training and career paths (Colletti and Tubridy 1987; Tice 1997). Third, key account management is a multifunctional effort involving, beside marketing and sales, functional groups such as manufacturing, R&D and finance (Shapiro and Moriarty 1984b). Fourth, the formation of key account programmes is influenced by characteristics of buyers and of the market environment, such as purchasing centralization, purchasing complexity, demand concentration and competitive intensity (Boles et al. 1999; Stevenson 1980).

We observed a number of shortcomings in prior research. First, the design issues above have mostly been studied in isolation and have not been consolidated into a coherent framework. Shapiro's and Moriarty's (1984a, p. 34) assessment that 'the term national account management program is fraught with ambiguity' was still valid. Second, there was a general lack of quantitative empirical studies on the design issues above, particularly on the cross-functional linkages of KAM. Where quantitative research had been undertaken, it had essentially been descriptive and has not systematically developed and validated measures. Third, much of the empirical work that had been done (and has driven conceptual ideas) was based on observations in large, Fortune 500 companies with sophisticated, formalized key account programmes. This excluded small and medium-sized companies that actively manage relationships with key accounts, but do not formalize the key account management approach. Quantitative empirical research had not taken up a comment by Shapiro and Moriarty (1984a, p. 5) in their early conceptual work that 'the simplest structural option is no program at all'. Fourth, given that conceptual work had mentioned a variety of structural options (Shapiro and Moriarty 1984a), there was no broad-based empirical work that allows generalizations about how KAM is done in practice.

An integrative conceptualization of KAM

Approach to the conceptualization

In this section, we will blend the insights from prior literature into an integrative conceptualization of KAM. Our conceptualization is composed of fundamental dimensions of KAM, each of which comprises several key constructs. We will distinguish between two types of variables in developing our taxonomy. First, we will identify a parsimonious set of theory-based key constructs that serve as 'active' input variables for the cluster algorithm. Second, we will complement these with a number of 'passive', non-theoretical, descriptive variables which will be used to further characterize the clusters.

Fundamental dimensions of KAM

We begin our conceptualization of KAM by identifying the fundamental dimensions of the KAM phenomenon. Prior research on dimensions of KAM can be summarized in terms of three basic questions: (1) What is done? (2) Who does it? (3) With whom is it done? However, as we have elaborated in the literature review, the scope of prior research has been limited to formalized key account programmes with designated key account managers in place. We claim that to formalize or not to formalize the key account approach represents a decision

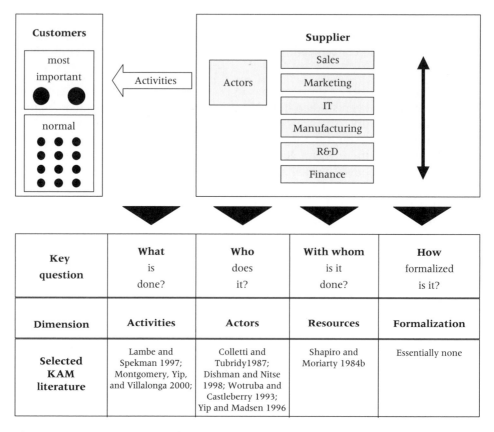

Figure 1 Conceptualization of key account management

dimension of its own. Therefore, we add a fourth question to KAM research: (4) How formalized is it? This leads us to conceptualize four dimensions of KAM. Drawing on research on the management of collaborative relationships that has distinguished between activities, actors and resources (Anderson et al. 1994; Narus and Anderson 1995), we refer to the four dimensions as (1) Activities (2) Actors (3) Resources and (4) Formalization. The first dimension refers to inter-organizational issues while the other three refer to intra-organizational issues in KAM. Figure 1 visualizes our conceptualization of KAM.

Previous definitions of KAM have tended to focus on specific dimensions of KAM. Some authors focus on special activities for key accounts. As an example, Barrett (1986, p. 64) states that 'National account management simply means targeting the largest and most important customers by providing them with special treatment in the areas of marketing, administration, and service.' Others emphasize the dedication of special actors to key accounts. Yip and Madsen (1996, p. 24), for example, note that 'National account management approaches include having one executive or team take overall responsibility for all aspects of a customer's business.' Our conceptualization is more integrative because it encompasses both activities and actors, and additionally resources and formalization.

We will now go through each of the four fundamental dimensions of KAM to identify a parsimonious set of theoretically based key constructs. Those will be used as (active) input variables for the cluster algorithm leading up to the taxonomy. We will then identify additional descriptive (passive) variables that will help to enrich our descriptions of the clusters.

Activities

Both the KAM literature (e.g. Lambe and Spekman 1997; Montgomery and Yip 2000; Napolitano 1997; Shapiro and Moriarty 1984b) and the relationship marketing literature suggest inventories of activities that suppliers can do for their key accounts. Among these are special pricing, customization of products, provision of special services, customization of services, joint coordination of the workflow, information sharing as well as taking over business processes that the customers outsource. The first question that arises with respect to organizational activities is how intensely they should be pursued. Shapiro and Moriarty (1980, p. 5) argue: 'A key issue here is: How will or does the servicing of national accounts differ from that of other accounts?' Therefore, we define *activity intensity as the extent to which the supplier does more for key accounts than for average accounts.*

Beside the level of intensity on an activity, another important conceptual issue is the origin of that intensity. Given that powerful customers are often forcing their suppliers into special activities, the question arises whether the supplier or the key account proposes a special activity. Millman (1999, p. 2) observes that 'some . . . programs are seller-initiated, some are buyer-initiated'. Empirical results by Sharma (1997) and by Montgomery and Yip (2000) indicate that supplier firms indeed use KAM in response to customer demand for it. According to Arnold et al. (1999, p. 15) 'the proactive-reactive dimension matters a great deal'. Hence, we define *activity proactiveness as the extent to which activities are initiated by the supplier.*

Actors

Probably the most frequently discussed topic in key account programme research is which special actors participate in key account activities. These specialized actors can be viewed as a personal coordination mode in KAM. The participation of special actors has a horizontal and a vertical component. The KAM literature suggests that there are many possibilities for horizontally placing KAM actors, ranging from a line manager who devotes part of his time to managing key accounts to teams who are fully dedicated to key accounts (Shapiro and Moriarty 1984a). Similarly, Olson et al. (1995) present a range of coordination mechanisms with a permanent team at one end of their continuum. Marshall et al. (1999, p. 96) note 'that team work is a fairly new concept in managing accounts and that salespeople are working in a team format much more today than in the past'.

Cespedes et al. (1989) even argue that 'selling is no longer an individual activity but rather a coordinated team effort'. It has been suggested the use of teams is a reaction to the use of purchasing teams on the buyer side (Hutt et al. 1985). We define *the use of teams as the extent to which teams are formed to coordinate activities for key accounts*.

While teams refer to the horizontal participation in KAM, another fundamental issue pertains to vertical participation. KAM actors may be placed at the headquarters, at the division level or at the regional level (Shapiro and Moriarty 1984a). The importance of senior executive involvement in KAM has frequently been underscored in the KAM literature. As Millman and Wilson (1999, p. 330) note: 'Key account management is a strategic issue and the process should therefore be initiated and overseen by senior management.' Napolitano (1997) points out that 'top management must also play the lead role in securing business unit management support for the program.' This is supported by writers on strategy implementation who argue that the organization is a reflection of its top managers (Hambrick and Mason 1984). Empirical support for the importance of top management has been provided by Jaworski and Kohli (1993) who have found market orientation to be positively related to top management emphasis on it. Therefore, we define *top management involvement as the extent to which senior management participates in KAM*. Hence, the top management involvement construct adopted from the literature on strategy implementation and on market orientation is conceptually close to the centralization construct used in organization theory, which refers to the extent of decision authority being concentrated on higher hierarchical levels.

Resources

As Shapiro and Moriarty (1984a, p. 2) have noted: 'Much of the NAM concept as both a sales and a management technique revolves around the coordination of all elements involved in dealing with the customer.' The KAM literature and the team selling literature have pointed out that support is needed for key account activities from such diverse functional groups as marketing and sales, logistics, manufacturing, IT, and finance and accounting (Moon and Armstrong 1994; Shapiro and Moriarty 1984b). 'The key question, then, is: . . . how can a salesperson obtain needed resources?' (Moon and Gupta 1997, p. 32). Obtaining resources has a pull and a push component.

In some cases, key account managers have special organizational power to ensure full cooperation from other organizational members. In other instances, key account managers have to rely on their informal powers and interpersonal skills (Spekman and Johnston 1986, p. 522). As the key account manager is typically part of the sales function (Shapiro and Moriarty 1984a), this lack of authority is most obvious for functional resources outside marketing and sales. We define *access to non-marketing and sales resources as the extent to which a key account manager can obtain needed contributions to KAM from non-marketing and sales groups*.

However, even within the marketing and sales function a key account manager may face difficulty in receiving support for his tasks (Homburg et al. 1999; Platzer 1984). One common problem is the lack of authority over regional sales executives who handle the local business with global key accounts (Arnold et al. 1999). For example, regional sales entities often resist company-wide agreements on prices or service standards. Therefore, we define *access to marketing and sales resources as the extent to which a key account manager can obtain needed contributions to KAM from marketing and sales groups*.

While access to resources refers to pulling on resources, research on team selling has frequently emphasized that the achievement of cross-functional integration in the selling centre is facilitated if the participating functions themselves push cooperation (Smith and Barclay 1993). Day (2000, p. 24) notes that in order to develop strong relationships with customers, 'a relationship orientation must pervade the mind-sets, values, and norms of the organization'. Jaworski and Kohli (1993) refer to this concept of inter-departmental culture as esprit de corps. Culture is often viewed as a resource: 'Organizational resources are the assets the firm possesses that arise from the organization itself, chief among these are the corporate culture and climate' (Morgan and Hunt 1999, p. 284). Fisher et al. (1997) note that esprit de corps fosters the exchange of customer and market information. Therefore, we define *the esprit de corps of the selling centre as the extent to which selling centre participants feel committed to common goals and to each other*.

Formalization

As Shapiro and Moriarty (1984a) note, one of the 'major organizational decisions that must be made as a company approaches a NAM program' is: 'Should there be a NAM program or no program?' We believe that the distinction between more or less programmed approaches is highly relevant. As we have shown in our literature review, KAM approaches that do not have a key account programme in place are under-researched.

Characteristics of KAM programmes are the definition of reporting lines and formal linkages between departments, the establishment of formal expense budgets, the documentation of processes, and the development of formal guidelines on how to handle the accounts (Boles et al. 1994). Thus, in essence, the design decision of installing a key account programme revolves around the question to what extent KAM should be formalized. Consistent with writers on marketing organization (Olson et al. 1995; Workman et al. 1998), we define *the formalization of a KAM approach as the extent to which the treatment of the most important customers is governed by formal rules and standard procedures*. Hence, formalization can be viewed as an impersonal coordination mode, as opposed to top-management involvement and use of teams, which represent personal coordination modes in KAM.

Additional descriptive variables

In addition to the theoretical constructs developed above, the KAM literature also suggests a number of descriptive variables to characterize KAM approaches. These variables refer to very concrete, mostly demographic features of KAM approaches, such as the positions of key account managers. Because these variables are not theory based, we will not use them as input to the cluster procedure. However, given that these variables have frequently been discussed in KAM publications, we will use them to enrich our interpretation of different KAM approaches.

In many companies, KAM teams are led by a key account manager. We define the key account coordinator as the person who is mainly responsible for coordinating activities related to key accounts. The first descriptive variable refers to the position of the key account coordinators. One possibility is to establish dedicated full-time positions for the coordination of key accounts (Pegram 1972). A fundamental question in this context is whether key account coordinators are placed in the supplier's headquarters or locally in the country or geographic region of the key account's headquarters. An alternative to the full-time option is a part-time responsibility. As Shapiro and Moriarty (1984a, p. 5) note, 'the task is often taken on by top-level managers . . . In other companies top marketing and sales managers and/or field sales managers take the responsibility.'

The second descriptive variable connects directly to this question of part-time vs. full-time responsibility. We define *the key account coordinator's dedication to key accounts as the percentage of their time they spend with managing key accounts vs. average accounts*. Another question concerning the allocation of time is how much time is spent with customers compared to the time devoted to internal coordination. Colletti and Tubridy (1987) report that 40% of a major account sales rep's time is administration work. We define *the internal orientation of key account coordinators as the percentage of their time they spend with internal coordination vs. externally with customers*. A final descriptive question that has frequently been raised in KAM studies is how many accounts key account coordinators are typically looking after (Dishman and Nitse 1998; Sengupta et al. 1997a; Wotruba and Castleberry 1993). We define *the span of accounts as the number of accounts for which key account coordinators are responsible*.

Outcomes

One of our objectives is to go beyond the conceptualization of KAM approaches and the taxonomy to explore the performance effects of design decisions. We distinguish between outcomes with respect to key accounts and outcomes on the level of the overall organization. Given that KAM involves investing in special activities and actors for key accounts which are not available for average accounts, we define *KAM effectiveness as the extent to which an organization achieves better relationship outcomes for its key accounts than for its average accounts*. While the benefits of KAM have often been claimed in the KAM literature, empirical evidence on the outcomes of KAM is rare and methodologically limited to *t*-tests or correlations of single item ratings of performance (Platzer 1984; Sengupta et al. 1997a; Stevenson 1981). A much better understanding of the outcomes of collaborative relationships has been developed by relationship marketing research (e.g. Kumar et al. 1995). This literature suggests that firms, through building relationships, pursue such outcomes as long-term orientation and continuity (e.g. Anderson and Weitz 1989; Ganesan 1994), commitment (e.g. Anderson and Weitz 1992; Geyskens et al. 1996; Gundlach et al. 1995), trust (e.g. Geyskens et al. 1998; Moorman et al. 1993; Rindfleisch 2000), and conflict reduction (e.g. Frazier et al. 1989).

Some authors indicate that KAM not only has outcomes with respect to key accounts, but also organization-level outcomes. As Cespedes (1993, p. 47) notes: 'Another benefit is the impact on business planning. Salespeople at major accounts are often first in the organization to recognize emerging market problems and opportunities.' Of course, organization-level outcomes are also affected by average accounts. Following the terminology of Rueckert et al. (1985), we distinguish between adaptiveness, effectiveness and efficiency. We define:

- *Adaptiveness as the ability of the organization to change marketing activities to fit different market situations better than its competitors.*
- *Performance in the market as the extent to which the organization achieves better market outcomes than competitors.*
- *Profitability as the organization's average return on sales before taxes over the last three years.*

Sample

Given our research objective of identifying prototypical approaches to KAM, we collected data using a mail survey in five business-to-business sectors in the USA and Germany. Based on the field interviews, we determined that the most appropriate respondent is the head of the sales organization. As Table 1 shows, our respondents are high-level managers. We received responses from 264 German firms and 121 US firms for effective response rates of 31.8% and 14.6% and an overall response rate of 23.3%. Our measures are reported in the Appendix. The details of the measurement and clustering procedures are documented in the original articles.

Key account management configurations

We will now interpret the clusters identified and will assign labels to the approaches (see Table 3). Although there are risks of oversimplification in using such labels, they serve the didactical purpose of highlighting empirically distinct aspects of different approaches and facilitate the discussion of the results.

Table 1: Sample composition

a) Position of respondents	Total (n = 385)
Managing Director, CEO, VP of Region, Head of Bus. Unit	19%
VP Marketing, VP Sales, VP Sales & Marketing	49%
Head of KAM, KA Manager	9%
Sales Manager, Product Manager	19%
Other	3%

b) Demographics of the firms		Germany (n = 264)	USA (n = 121)	Total (n = 385)
Industry*	Chemical & Pharmaceutical	24%	18%	22%
	Machinery	22%	30%	25%
	Computer & Electronics	17%	14%	16%
	Banks & Insurances	17%	11%	15%
	Food & Packaged Goods	20%	27%	22%
Annual Revenues*	<$15 Million	5%	10%	6%
	$15–30 Million	14%	11%	13%
	$30–60 Million	20%	15%	18%
	$60–150 Million	17%	24%	19%
	$150–300 Million	13%	11%	13%
	$300–600 Million	11%	13%	12%
	$600–1500 Million	5%	10%	6%
	>$1500 Million	14%	11%	13%

* Equal structure of subsamples based on $p(l^2) > .05$

Top-management KAM

This approach truly deserves the name 'programme'. These companies highly formalize the management of their key accounts. Over 60% of companies in this cluster have dedicated sales managers to coordinate activities for key accounts, which is consistent with the finding of 73% of key account coordinator time being devoted to key accounts. Top management manifests the highest degree of top management involvement in KAM. Hence, it is not surprising that this approach is managed out of the company headquarters (86.1% of key account coordinators are based in the suppliers' headquarters). In addition to heavy top-management involvement, these companies make intensive use of teams. Activities for key accounts are intense and are proactively initiated. An interesting finding is that selling centre esprit de corps is high, whereas access to both marketing and sales and over non-marketing and sales resources is low. This may suggest that access to resources is barely needed. Top management might negotiate umbrella contracts, which are carried out by operative teams based on highly standardized procedures.

Table 2: Cluster description

Dimension	Variable	Cluster								
		Top-management KAM	Middle-management KAM	Operating-level KAM	Cross-functional, dominant KAM	Unstructured KAM	Isolated KAM	Country club KAM	No KAM	Total
		n = 37	n = 76	n = 57	n = 44	n = 38	n = 40	n = 37	n = 46	n = 375
Activities	Activity intensity	**medium–high**	medium	**medium–high**	**high**	medium	medium	low	low	
	Activity proactiveness	medium	medium	low–medium	**high**	low–medium	medium	low	low–medium	
Formalization	Approach formalization	**very high**	high	rather high	**very high**	low	Rather low	very low	low	
Actors	Top-management involvement	**very high**	medium	low	high	very low	medium–high	high	low	
	Use of teams	much	little	**much–very much**	**very much**	little	medium	very little	very little	
Resources	Selling centre esprit de corps	rather strong	rather weak	rather strong	**strong**	**strong**	weak	rather weak	weak	
	Access to marketing and sales resources	rather low	high	low	**very high**	rather high	medium	**very high**	very low	
	Access to non-marketing and sales resources	low	medium	low	**high**	medium	low	medium	low	

(Continued)

Table 2: (Continued)

Dimension	Variable		Cluster								
		Top-management KAM	Middle-management KAM	Operating-level KAM	Cross-functional, dominant KAM	Unstructured KAM	Isolated KAM	Country club KAM	No KAM	Total
		$n = 37$	$n = 76$	$n = 57$	$n = 44$	$n = 38$	$n = 40$	$n = 37$	$n = 46$	$n = 375$
Additional, descriptive variables	Dedication to key accounts	**73%**[c]	66%[abc]	**70%**[bc]	**73%**[c]	*57%*[a]	**66%**[abc]	62%[abc]	57%[ab]	66%
	Internal orientation	50%[ab]	49%[ab]	49%[ab]	46%[a]	**62%**[c]	51%[ab]	49%[ab]	**58%**[bc]	51%
	Span of accounts (median)	5	5	5	5	5	5	8	10	5
KAM performance	KAM effectiveness	**5.39**[b]	**5.39**[b]	**5.53**[b]	**5.63**[b]	**5.46**[b]	*5.01*[a]	**5.41**[b]	*5.04*[a]	5.37
Overall organizational performance	Performance in the market	5.03[bc]	**5.23**[cd]	5.04[bc]	**5.51**[d]	5.19[cd]	4.72[ab]	5.16[cd]	*4.54*[a]	5.07
	Adaptiveness	4.75[bc]	**4.87**[b]	4.46[ab]	**5.43**[d]	4.85[bc]	*4.25*[a]	4.50[abc]	*4.23*[a]	4.68
	Profitability	**6.38**[b]	*4.98*[a]	*4.98*[a]	5.64[ab]	5.84[ab]	5.23[ab]	*4.82*[a]	*4.80*[a]	5.27

Reported values are mean values if not otherwise noted. In each row, cluster means that have the same superscript are not significantly different ($p < .05$) on the basis of Duncan's multiple-range test. Means in the lowest band are assigned [a], means in the next highest band [b] etc. Means in the highest band are printed in bold, means in the lowest band in italics.

Middle-management KAM

This approach manifests a high level of formalization, but, in contrast to the first approach, top-management involvement is medium. Intensity and proactiveness with respect to activities are also on a medium level. These results may suggest that these companies have installed a formal key account programme, but on a middle-management level. Our interpretation is supported by the finding that 28.8% of key account coordinators are locally based in this approach, compared to 13.8% in Top-management KAM. The fact that key account managers are often locally based may also explain the high access to marketing and sales resources. On the contrary, selling centre esprit de corps and access to non-marketing and sales resources are low, which leads to the overall impression that KAM in these companies is mainly driven by (local) middle management in the marketing and sales function.

Operating-level KAM

These companies are doing a lot for their key accounts and have considerably standardized procedures. In these aspects, this approach is comparable to Top-management KAM and Middle-management KAM. However, top-management involvement is lower than in these other approaches. Not surprisingly, access to functional resources is low. While the VP of sales or marketing is the key account coordinator in 27.4% of Top-management KAM companies and 23.1% of Middle-management KAM companies, this is only the case for 9.8% of companies in this cluster. The low degree of top-management involvement together with fairly developed activities and teams may suggest that this KAM approach is mainly borne by the operating level. None of the other approaches has such a high percentage of companies with dedicated sales managers for key accounts (70.8%), 17.1% of which are locally based.

Cross-functional, dominant KAM

This cluster has the highest values for nearly all variables. First, activities are very intense and are proactively created. Second, formal procedures and team structures are fully developed. Top management is strongly involved. Third, selling centre esprit de corps and access to functional resources are high. 65.6% of Cross-functional KAM companies have dedicated sales managers as key account coordinators. Their share of time spent externally with the customer is the highest of all approaches, as reflected by the 46% on internal orientation. The overall picture suggests that these companies are completely focused on their key accounts. It seems that, in these companies, customer management is virtually identical with key account management.

Unstructured KAM

As shown by the low values on formalization, top-management involvement, and use of teams, these companies have not created special organizational structures for key accounts and do not have a programme in place. This is consistent

Table 3: Position of key account coordinators

Position of key account coordinator	Total (n = 375)		Top-management KAM (n = 37)		Middle-management KAM (n = 76)		Operating-level KAM (n = 57)		Cross-functional, dominant KAM (n = 44)		Unstructured KAM (n = 38)		Isolated KAM (n = 40)		Country club KAM (n = 37)		No KAM (n = 46)	
	Head-quarter	Local quarter	Head-quarter	Local quarter	Head-quarter	Local quarter	Head-quarter	Local quarter	Head-quarter	Local quarter	Head-quarter	Local quarter	Head-quarter	Local quarter	Head-quarter	Local quarter	Head-quarter	Local quarter
Normal sales manager	7.8%	5.9%	3.4%		5.8%	3.8%	2.4%	7.3%	6.3%		14.8%	3.7%	7.4%	11.1%	19.0%	14.3%	8.3%	8.3%
Dedicated sales manager	35.8%	15.9%	48.3%	13.8%	44.2%	17.3%	53.7%	17.1%	40.6%	25.0%	44.4%	7.4%	18.5%	33.3%		4.8%	22.2%	5.6%
VP of sales	18.5%	3.2%	24.1%		17.3%	5.8%	9.8%		15.6%		11.1%	3.7%	14.8%		28.6%	9.5%	30.6%	5.6%
VP of marketing	3.4%		3.4%						3.1%		3.7%		3.7%		9.5%		8.3%	
General manager	4.6%	0.4%			1.9%	1.9%	4.9%				11.1%		3.7%		9.5%		8.3%	
Other	4.5%		6.9%		1.9%		4.9%		9.4%				7.4%		4.8%		2.8%	
Total	74.6%	25.4%	86.1%	13.8%	71.1%	28.8%	75.7%	24.4%	75.0%	25.0%	85.1%	14.8%	55.5%	44.4%	71.4%	28.6%	80.5%	19.5%

with the observation that activities are more a reaction than a proactive initiative, as indicated by the 3.83 mean on proactiveness. KAM comes mainly out of the headquarters and key account coordinators are often normal sales managers (18.5% compared with 6.3% in Cross-functional KAM). An interesting observation is that 62% of key account coordinator time is spent on internal coordination, the highest percentage of all clusters. This may account for the fact that selling centre members have an extremely high esprit de corps for KAM and that it is no problem obtaining contributions from either marketing and sales or other functional resources. The overall impression is that these companies are pursuing KAM on an ad-hoc basis, mobilizing internal resources only when the key accounts ask for it. Interestingly, 11.1% of these companies name the general manager as the key account coordinator, although top-management involvement is the lowest of all approaches. This suggests that the general management's responsibility exists on paper only.

Isolated KAM

Intensity and proactiveness of activities as well as formalization and use of teams manifest mid-range values in this cluster. This seems to imply that these companies are trying to do something for key accounts, which is supported by the finding that top management is fairly involved. The most striking feature about this cluster is that in 44.4% of companies in this cluster, key account coordinators are locally based. This may explain why this cluster has very low values on selling centre esprit de corps and on access to non-marketing and sales resources. Hence, the overall picture is that KAM is a rather isolated, local sales effort in these companies which, despite some effort from the side of the top management, struggles for cooperation from the central business units.

Country club KAM

The striking characteristic of this cluster is a high degree of top-management involvement that goes along with low values on most other variables. The management of key accounts in these companies is not guided by formal procedures and teams are hardly ever formed. Special activities are performed less intensely and less proactively than under the other approaches. Most importantly, there are basically no dedicated key account coordinators. KAM coordinators are often the VP of sales, a general manager, even the VP of marketing. The comparatively low level of activities combined with high top-management involvement and high access to sales may suggest that, in these companies, KAM is little more than representation by senior managers. In 33.3% of these firms, key accounts are simply handled by normal sales managers. With the exception of the top-management involvement, this approach is fairly close to the 'No KAM' cluster.

No KAM

This cluster has the lowest values on nearly all variables: comparatively little activity is performed, but not proactively. Formalization is low, just as cross-functional cooperation and esprit de corps. It is interesting that mainly VPs of marketing and sales or general managers are named as key account coordinators, though top-management involvement in this cluster is low. This suggests that the VPs have responsibility on paper, but do not actually perform that role. The interpretation of this approach is straightforward: these companies do not manage their key accounts. Or some companies may only have started to manage their key accounts, given that they profess to have dedicated key account coordinators.

Key account management effectiveness

We now turn to the success of the various KAM approaches. In interpreting the results in Table 2, one has to pay attention to whether the outcome variable is on the level of the key accounts or on the level of the organization as a whole. KAM effectiveness can be assumed to be strongly influenced by how key accounts are managed and is thus our main outcome variable of interest. On the contrary, variance in organization-level outcomes, such as performance in the market, adaptiveness and profitability, can be explained by many factors other than KAM. In fact, a firm may be driving its performance, for better or worse, through the average as opposed to the key accounts.[1]

On both the KAM level and the organization level, the 'No KAM' and the 'Isolated KAM' approaches perform the worst. On the organization level outcomes, 'Cross-functional KAM' companies stand out with respect to both performance in the market and adaptiveness. As far as profitability is concerned, 'Top-management KAM' companies perform best. The fact that the most effective approaches are not the most profitable ones may be explained by the fact that some approaches, besides generating higher revenues, also involve higher costs.

A second observation in Table 2 is that several KAM approaches are equally successful. This finding is consistent with the concept of 'equifinality' emphasized by the configurational approach (Meyer et al. 1993). However, given our key informant design, it raises the issue of whether a common method bias is present in the data. Two facts from our data speak against the presence of a bias. First, a possible key informant bias should affect the subjective performance measures (e.g. KAM effectiveness), but not the objective performance measure (i.e. profitability). The fact that several configurations also manifest the same level of objective performance supports the validity of our findings on the subjective measures. Second, even in very active approaches (e.g. Top-management KAM), there is a lot of variance across the respondents concerning the performance variables. Indeed, the lack of significant differences between some approaches is due to the high variance rather than a tendency of all key informants to rate their own approach high.

---

[1] We owe this idea to an anonymous reviewer.

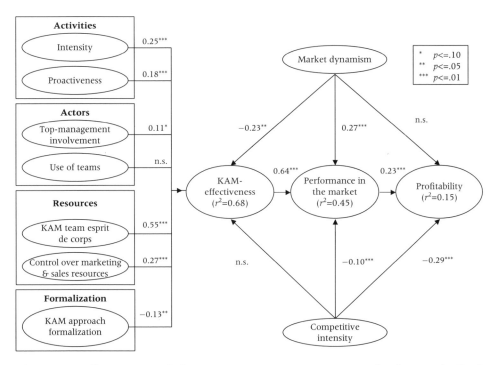

Figure 2 Effectiveness of key account management (completely standardized coefficients)

Figure 2 shows the results of a structural equation model on the performance relationships that is part of the Workman et al. (2003) article. We find that the dimensions of the KAM approach which positively affect KAM effectiveness (in decreasing order of effect) are KAM team esprit de corps, access to marketing and sales resources, activity intensity, activity proactiveness and top-management involvement in KAM. On the other hand, formalization of the KAM approach, a design parameter emphasized in the KAM literature, is negatively related to performance. The most surprising aspect of our findings is that the softer factors (e.g. top-management involvement, KAM team esprit de corps) matter more than formalization of the approach. One downside of formalizing the approach to key accounts is that this may lead to bureaucracy and impede flexibility in responding to the demands of different key accounts. To the extent that there is heterogeneity among key accounts, formalized approaches may get in the way of providing special treatment to customers.

One might argue that KAM effectiveness is especially important in the case when a large percentage of revenues come from key accounts. We analysed the potential moderating effect by a multiple group LISREL model. The sample was split by the median of the percentage of sales derived from key accounts. In the group with a high percentage of sales to key accounts, the effect of KAM effectiveness on performance in the market is stronger than in the group with low percentage of sales to key accounts. However, in both sub-groups, we observe strong and highly significant effects of KAM effectiveness on performance in the market (standardized effect of .40 in the case of low percentage of sales to key accounts and .55 in the case of high percentage). The significance of this moderating effect can be tested. In the first multiple group LISREL model, we freely estimated the parameters in both groups. In a second model, we introduce an identity restriction: we set the effect of KAM effectiveness to market performance equal in both models. If this restriction significantly deteriorates model fit (measured by chi-square), there is a significant moderating effect. As chi-square deteriorates by 4.3 (which is larger than the threshold value of 3.84), the moderating effect is significant at the 5% level. These findings are consistent with those of Birkinshaw et al. (2001) who find a significant difference in the effectiveness of global account structures for conditions of high vs. low dependence on global customers.

Discussion

Comparison of KAM configurations with existing research

While prior research has never classified KAM approaches empirically, there is some discussion of options companies have in implementing KAM. McDonald et al. (1997) suggest ideal types of KAM, assuming KAM approaches to line up along a continuum from pre-KAM to synergistic KAM (Millman and Wilson 1995a). Along the continuum, the activity intensity, use of teams and top-management involvement are implied to rise, which actually implies a correlation among these design variables. Our results do not support this ideal continuum nor the correlation. As we have shown, high degrees of top-management involvement occur in combination with both high and low degrees of activity intensity and in combination with both high and low degrees of use of teams.

A second typology of KAM programmes has been proposed by Shapiro and Moriarty (1984a) based on qualitative interviews in 19 large manufacturing and service companies (see also the supplementary comments by Kempeners and van der Hart 1999). These researchers distinguish between six types of KAM programmes which resemble the KAM approaches we identified. More specifically, their national account division resembles 'Cross-functional KAM', their corporate level programme is similar to 'Top-management KAM', their operating unit programme at group level is similar to 'Middle-management KAM', their operating unit programme at division level parallels 'Operating-level KAM', their part-time programme resembles the 'Country club KAM', and their no programme option is close to the 'No KAM' approach. However, our work goes beyond the prior work by identifying the design variables behind the approaches, by providing richer descriptions of the approaches, and by supplementing the descriptions with quantitative data. We also detected two additional KAM approaches, the 'Unstructured KAM' and the 'Isolated KAM'. These two carry out a considerable amount of activity for key accounts while not formalizing the approach. In conclusion, our findings seem to indicate that we have not overlooked KAM approaches that occur in practice. This speaks for the validity of our taxonomy and for the absence of a non-response bias.

Research contribution to KAM configurations

Despite the immense importance of KAM in managerial practice, prior research in this area has been very fragmented and sound empirical studies have been scarce. Our contributions come from both the conceptualization and the taxonomy.

The first contribution is to provide conceptual clarity to KAM design decisions and to lay the basis for future research. Besides synthesizing the existing literature, this research extends the conceptual scope of KAM research by drawing attention to the fact that previous research has not gone beyond the boundaries of formalized KAM programmes to study non-formalized KAM approaches. We derive an integrative conceptualization of KAM identifying four key dimensions: (1) Activities (2) Actors (3) Resources and (4) Formalization (see Figure 1). We also develop scales for key constructs related to KAM.

A second contribution of our work consists in being the first study to empirically classify designs of organizational approaches to selling. While taxonomies exist for the buyer side (Bunn 1993) and for the relationship between buyer and seller (Cannon and Perreault 1999), there has been no taxonomy for the organization of the seller side. Moncrief (1986) has created a taxonomy of *individual* sales position designs, but the level of analysis in selling research has shifted to the selling *team* in the decade that followed (Weitz and Bradford 1999). As Marshall et al. (1999, p. 88) state: 'Clearly, the operative set of sales activities representing a sales job in the mid-1980s is deficient to accurately understand and portray sales jobs of today.' Hence, our taxonomy closes a gap in empirical knowledge about organizational approaches to selling.

A third contribution is the refinement of existing KAM typologies. We confirmed the types of KAM postulated by Shapiro and Moriarty (1984a), supplemented them with empirical detail and detected two additional approaches. These two carry out a considerable amount of activity for key accounts while not formalizing the approach.

An additional contribution of our taxonomical research is to provide deeper insights into the performance aspects of KAM approaches. On a general level, it is important to note that the same level of performance can be accomplished through different approaches. This is consistent with the concept of equifinality emphasized by the configurational approach (Meyer et al. 1993). Yet some approaches perform significantly worse than others. The finding that 'No KAM' companies are behind on all performance dimensions represents the most comprehensive empirical demonstration so far that suppliers benefit from managing their key accounts. The similarly mediocre performance of 'Isolated KAM' indicates that half-breed approaches to KAM are likely to fail. These results suggest that failure to achieve access to, and commitment of, cross-functional resources seems to play a critical role for the success of KAM programmes. This reinforces recent research on marketing organization that recognizes the cross-functional dispersion of marketing activities (Workman et al. 1998).

Research contributions to KAM effectiveness

One contribution is the identification of specific aspects of a KAM approach that lead to effectiveness. Prior KAM research has not been able to demonstrate which aspects of a KAM approach are most important. Our results indicate formalization of KAM programmes actually reduces KAM effectiveness. Having a formalized programme can impede flexibility and the ability to customize offerings to specific customers. Additionally, it may be more costly, due to administrative costs, or dedication of the best salespeople to these accounts when they might be more productively used elsewhere. Rather than a formalized programme, our results indicate the important factors are whether firms do different things for their key accounts, do them proactively, and then provide an overall culture and organization environment that provides the resources needed to support the KAM effort. Top-management involvement is important, not only for its direct effect on KAM success, but also for sending signals to the organization that support of the KAM effort is important. In terms of the categories of our model, activities and resources are more important than actors and formalization. Given the prior emphasis on KAM programmes and KAM managers (formalization and actors), our results indicate a shift in research direction towards better understanding the activities and resource dimensions that may be needed.

A second contribution is our finding concerning teams. It is not the extent of team use that affects KAM effectiveness, but rather the development of esprit de corps among those involved in the management of key accounts. The coordination of activities across the organization requires a common commitment to serving the needs of key accounts. Similar to the research on market orientation, our results indicate that development of an organizational culture that supports customers is a key driver of performance. Research on marketing's role within the organization has started to examine conditions which lead to marketing having relatively higher or lower levels of influence (Homburg et al. 1999) and the knowledge and skills necessary to connect customers with the firm's product and service capabilities (Moorman and Rust 1999).

While there is a long tradition of studying power and influence within the sales organization (e.g. Busch 1980) and within channels of distribution (e.g. Frazier 1983; Gaski 1984), there is a lack of research on cross-functional influence of the sales organization and competition for resources within the organization. Since KAM is primarily about managing and coordinating the activities of people over whom the key account manager does not have formal authority, additional research is needed to understand how key account managers can best accomplish their goals and obtain the needed resources. Research on product managers and new product development team leaders may be a good source of theoretical frameworks for addressing this issue of access to resources and 'responsibility without authority'.

A third contribution is our finding that KAM effectiveness leads to profitability in the market. KAM effectiveness has a direct effect on performance in the market that then leads to profitability. Since performance in the market encompasses all accounts (not just key accounts), this result implies that there is a relationship between how well firms do with key accounts and their general performance in the market. This link between KAM performance and firm performance highlights the importance of the topic of KAM and the need for additional research on organizing to manage key accounts.

On a more general level, a fourth contribution of our research is that it highlights the importance of studying how firms manage their intra-organizational relationships. While there have been calls for field research that helps refine conceptualizations of buyer–seller relationships and the process by which these form and evolve (Narus and Anderson 1995), there has been relatively little examination of the intra-organizational processes involved. These relationships are complex due to the multiple people, products, functional groups, hierarchical levels and geographies represented on both buyer and seller sides. By identifying issues involved in the intra-organizational management of relationships, our study serves as a bridge between the relationship marketing literature and the marketing organization literature (e.g. Moorman and Rust 1999; Workman et al. 1998).

Managerial implications

One of the most fundamental managerial tasks is designing the internal organization. These design decisions are typically taken on the level of the organization rather than the level of individual accounts. Thus, the organizational perspective adopted in this research has particular appeal to top executives.

The key message to managers is not to take a 'laissez-faire approach' to KAM. Given that the 'No KAM' option is markedly less successful than other approaches, our results clearly call managers to actively manage key accounts. The fact that there are significant performance differences between the more actively managed approaches demonstrates that it is important to think consciously about how to design the approach in detail. Our work also shows that KAM requires support from the whole organization. Therefore, top managers should not leave the design of the KAM approach to the sales organization.

The conceptualization of KAM developed in our research provides managers with a systematic way to think through designing the KAM approach. As Day and Montgomery (1999, p. 12) note, 'conceptual frameworks, typologies, and metaphors that are the precursors to actual theory building' provide valuable guidelines for managers. Managers should work through four questions: (1) What should be done for key accounts? (2) Who should do it? (3) With whom is cooperation in the organization needed? (4) How formalized should the KAM approach be? We particularly emphasize that managing key accounts does not necessarily require setting up a formal key account programme.

The taxonomy developed further supports managers in designing their KAM. Managers can categorize their own company's approach based on the prototypical implementation forms identified. Based on the taxonomy, they can discover neglected design areas and develop alternative designs.

Specifically, managers involved with key accounts need to consider and debate the following questions:

- To what extent does your firm actually do different activities for your key accounts?
- Does your firm proactively initiate these activities?
- Is top management involved with KAM?
- Has your firm developed a culture that develops an esprit de corps among those involved in KAM?
- Do key account coordinators have sufficient access to marketing and sales resources?

Finally, our empirical results on effectiveness provide managers with guidance concerning factors having the greatest effect on KAM effectiveness.

- KAM team esprit de corps and access to marketing and sales resources by key account managers are particularly important. Because KAM is fundamentally about relating better to the firm's most important customers, changes are required throughout the organization and not simply in sales and marketing.
- Proactiveness has a significant effect on outcomes. Sales managers should not wait for customers to request special treatment, but rather should be proactive. In so doing, they can differentiate themselves from competitors and design KAM activities in a way that leverages their core competencies.
- Managers should involve the top managers in their firm in KAM. While prior research has claimed that top-management support is important (Napolitano 1997; Platzer 1984; Weitz and Bradford 1999), there has been lack of empirical support. Our data indicate a significant positive association between top-management involvement in KAM and success.
- Finally, managers should exercise caution in regard to formalization of KAM. Our results indicate a negative association between KAM formalization and KAM effectiveness. As emphasized above, the activities, actors and resources seem to matter more than formalization.

Conclusion

KAM continues to be a highly relevant issue for marketing and sales managers. In addition, it is still a highly interesting area for academic research. The research reported in this paper has provided the basis for future research through contributing an integrative conceptualization of KAM. It also filled a gap in knowledge about how firms actually design their approach to key accounts. Finally, it showed that actively managing key accounts leads to significantly better performance than neglecting them.

Appendix

Scale items for theoretical measures

Construct	Items
Activity intensity (reflective scale, scored on 7-point scale with anchors 1 = not more than for average accounts and 7 = far more than for average)	Compared with average accounts, to what extent do you do MORE in these areas for key accounts? • Product-related activities (e.g. product adaptation, new product development, technology exchange) • Service-related activities (e.g. training, advice, troubleshooting, guarantees) • Price-related activities (e.g. special pricing terms, corporate-wide price terms, offering of financing solutions, revelation of own cost structure) • Distribution and logistics activities (e.g. logistics and production processes, quality programmes, placement of own employees in account's facilities, taking over business processes from customer) • Information sharing (e.g. sharing of strategy and market research, joint production plans, adaptation of information systems, access to top management) • Promotion activities to final customers (e.g. joint advertising and promotion programmes to help the account sell your products)
Activity proactiveness (formative scale, scored on 7-point scale with anchors 1 = not more than for average changes and 7 = far more than for average)	Do the activities in these areas derive more from customer initiative or more from your own initiative? *(items equivalent to activity intensity)*
Top-management involvement (reflective scale, scored on 7-point scale with anchors 1 = strongly disagree and 7 = strongly agree)	Within our organization . . . • even small matters related to key accounts have to be referred to someone higher up for a final decision • very few decisions related to key accounts are made without the involvement of senior managers • top management often deals with key account management
Use of teams (reflective scale, scored on 7-point scale with anchors 1 = strongly disagree and 7 = strongly agree)	Within our organization . . . • when there is a problem related to our key account relationships, a group is brought in to solve it • key account related decisions are made by teams • we have teams that plan and coordinate activities for key accounts

(Continued)

Construct	Items
Selling centre esprit de corps (adapted from Jaworski and Kohli 1993; reflective scale, scored on 7-point scale with anchors 1 = strongly disagree and 7 = strongly agree: R = reverse scoring)	People involved in the management of a key account . . . • are genuinely concerned about the needs and problems of each other • have a team spirit which pervades all ranks involved • feel like they are part of a big family • feel they are 'in it together' • (lack an esprit de corps R) • (view themselves as independent individuals who have to tolerate others around them R)
Access to marketing and sales resources (reflective scale, scored on 7-point scale with anchors 1 = very difficult and 7 = very easy)	How easy is it for the key account coordinator to obtain needed contributions for key accounts from these groups? • Field sales • Customer service • Product management
Access to non-marketing and sales resources (reflective scale, scored on 7-point scale with anchors 1 = very difficult and 7 = very easy)	How easy is it for the key account coordinator to obtain needed contributions for key accounts from these groups? • Research & development • Manufacturing • Logistics • Finance/accounting • Information technology • General management
Approach formalization (reflective scale, scored on 7-point scale with anchors 1 = strongly disagree and 7 = strongly agree)	Please indicate the extent to which you agree with the following statements. • We have established criteria for selecting key accounts. • Within our organization, formal internal communication channels are followed when working on key accounts. • To coordinate the parts of our organization working with key accounts, standard operating procedures have been established. • We have put a lot of thought into developing guidelines for working with our key accounts.

Construct	Items
KAM effectiveness (reflective scale, scored on 7-point scale with anchors 1 = very poor, 4 = about the same, and 7 = excellent)	Compared with your average accounts, how does your organization perform with key accounts with respect to . . . • achieving mutual trust • achieving information sharing • achieving a reputation of fairness • achieving investments into the relationship • maintaining long-term relationships • reducing conflicts • meeting sales targets and objectives • (making sales of those products with the highest margins) • (making sales from multiple product divisions)
Performance in the market (reflective scale, scored on 7-point scale with anchors 1 = very poor, 4 = about the same, and 7 = excellent)	Relative to your competitors, how has your organization, over the last three years, performed with respect to . . . • achieving customer satisfaction • providing value for customers • attaining desired growth • securing desired market share • successfully introducing new products • keeping current customers • attracting new customers
Adaptiveness (reflective scale, scored on 7-point scale with anchors 1 = not more than for average accounts and 7 = far more than for average)	Relative to your competitors, how has your organization, over the last three years, performed with respect to . . . • adapting to changes in the business environment of your company • adapting to changes in competitors' marketing strategies • adapting your products quickly to the changing needs of customers • reacting quickly to new market threats • exploiting quickly new market opportunities
Profitability (interval item with 10 levels of variable provided)	What was your company's average pre-tax profit margin over the last three years? 1 = negative; 2 = 0–2%, 3 = 2–4%, 4 = 4–6%, 5 = 6–8%, 6 = 8–10%, 7 = 10–12%, 8 = 12–16%, 9 = 16–20%, 10 = more than 20%

(Continued)

Construct	Items
Competitive intensity (adapted from Jaworski and Kohli 1993; reflective scale, scored on 7-point scale with anchors 1 = strongly disagree and 7 = strongly agree)	Please indicate the extent to which you agree with the following statements. • Competition in our industry is cut-throat. • There are many 'promotion wars' in our industry. • Anything that one competitor can offer, others can match readily. • Price competition is a hallmark of our industry. • One hears of a new competitive move almost every day. • (Our competitors are relatively weak. R)
Market dynamism (adapted from Jaworski and Kohli 1993; reflective scale, scored on 7-point scale with anchors 1 = strongly disagree and 7 = strongly agree)	Please indicate the extent to which you agree with the following statements. • In our kind of business, customers' product preferences change quite a bit over time. • Our customers tend to look for new products all the time. • We are witnessing demand for our products and services from customers who never bought them before. • New customers tend to have product-related needs that are different from those of our existing customers. • (We cater to many of the same customers that we used to in the past. R)

The appropriateness
of the key account
management organization

BY STEFAN WENGLER

Abstract

Key account management programmes often lack efficiency and effectiveness, as most key account management organizations are inadequately designed for specific customer–supplier relationships. In this paper, a decision model based on transaction cost economics is developed that allows for individualized decision-making on the most appropriate key account management organization: by defining the transaction cost economics determinants *uncertainty* and *frequency* in more detail companies will become able to refine their decision on the key account management organization alternatives with respect to the characteristics of their individual customer–supplier relationship.

Reproduced with the kind permission of the *Journal of Business Marketing*, originally Wengler, S. (2007) 'The appropriateness of KAM organization', *Journal of Business Marketing*, 1(4), 253–272.

Inefficiencies and ineffectiveness of key account management programmes

Since the late 1960s and early 1970s, key account management (KAM) has belonged to the most popular concepts in marketing management, which suggests serving important customers specifically (Weitz and Bradford 1999), i.e. differently from 'ordinary' customers. Over the years, research in KAM has predominantly focused on the objectives and structure of KAM (Kempeners and van der Hart 1999; Pardo 1997; Shapiro and Moriarty 1982, 1984a/b), the selection of key accounts (Gosselin and Bauwen 2006; Napolitano 1997), and only recently on performance issues in KAM (Boles et al. 1999; Homburg et al. 2002; Ivens and Pardo 2007; Pardo et al. 2006). The economics of KAM, i.e. the mechanisms determining why and when to implement as well as how to organize KAM in specific business relationships, has merely been of implicit interest in previous research and neglected so far.

This lack of research in the economics of KAM is accompanied by a rather remarkable anachronism: though various empirical studies report poor efficiency and effectiveness of most KAM programmes (e.g. Napolitano 1997; Sengupta et al. 1997), Wengler et al. (2006) find in an exploratory study that more than 20% of the 91 interviewed companies from diverse industries (e.g. telecommunication, mechanical and electrical engineering, chemical, and the automotive industry) still plan to implement KAM, while more than 50% have already implemented KAM. These findings therefore suggest that the popularity of KAM is still rather strong – despite the empirical findings that added value will be difficult to extract from most KAM programmes. Only as soon as the intensity of competition and/ or the intensity of coordination between supplier and customer increases does KAM seem to be the most appropriate marketing management organization alternative (Wengler et al. 2006).

A model will be proposed in this paper that will help in the process of choosing the most appropriate KAM organization with respect to the characteristics of a specific customer–supplier relationship. Based on transaction cost economics reasoning, the model allows for a qualitative assessment of various KAM organization alternatives and will thereby support the decision on the most appropriate one. Before laying out the decision model, the questions regarding what is understood by KAM and how the concept fits in recent marketing management research need to be defined.

The concept of key account management

Key account management is considered as a focused, supplier relationship marketing programme (Weitz and Bradford 1999) which aims at establishing, developing and maintaining a successful and mutually beneficial business relationship with the company's most important customers. KAM embraces strategic, functional and organizational dimensions – see Figure 1.

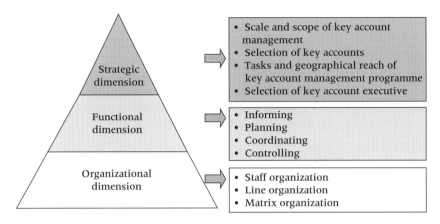

Figure 1 The dimension of KAM

The strategic dimension of key account management

As KAM takes on an important part within the company's marketing management, it needs to know which strategy it has to follow: depending on the corporate or business strategy as well as the key account itself, KAM has to develop an individual marketing concept for each key account (Sheth et al. 2000), a concept that encompasses the scale and scope of KAM, the selection of key accounts, tasks and geographical reach, as well as the selection of a KAM executive and a KAM team.

The functional dimension of key account management

The formulation of the tasks within the functional dimension of KAM is the result of its strategic objectives. This includes all customer-oriented tasks that are necessary to reach the strategic goals, i.e. informing (Weilbaker and Weeks 1997), planning (Pegram 1972), coordinating and controlling.

The organizational dimension of key account management

After the KAM programme strategy is set and its tasks are formulated, the company needs to consider its institutionalization (Shapiro and Moriarty 1984a). The complete KAM programme has to be reflected by its formal organization (Grönroos 1999).

Within organizational science, researchers differentiate between three general organizational principles: the staff organization, the line organization and the matrix organization (Schreyögg 2003), which can all be applied to KAM. KAM as a staff organization takes on a more supportive role by specializing in analysing, planning and controlling; in contrast, KAM as a line organization will be more appropriate if a self-responsible KAM unit is desired, which manages its customers by itself and influences the internal coordination processes considerably.

KAM as a matrix organization is established – at the least – alongside two dimensions, e.g. the customer and product management, and is thus very powerful, but often characterized by internal conflicts.

As companies are also characterized by hierarchies, these organizational design alternatives might be implemented on different organizational levels (Shapiro and Moriarty 1984a), i.e. the level of the sales representative, the regional level, the functional level, the divisional level or the corporate level – see Figure 2.

At which of these organizational levels KAM is implemented depends on the marketing management of the supplying company as well as the individual characteristics of each supplier–customer relationship. It is therefore necessary to appreciate

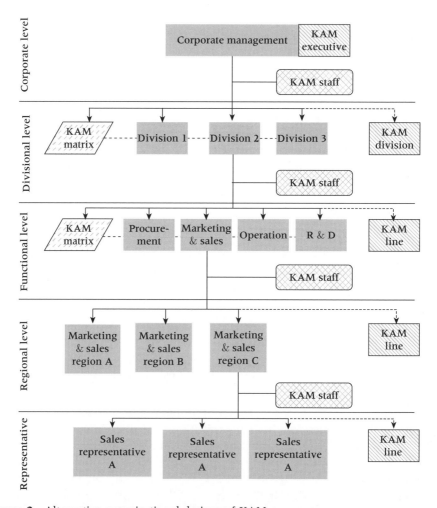

Figure 2   Alternative organizational designs of KAM

KAM as a relationship marketing programme – and not solely as a personal selling approach, as it had been considered until the 1980s (Wotruba 1991).

Key account management in the context of relationship marketing

The insistence on shifting the focus of KAM from personal selling to relationship marketing (Weitz and Bradford 1999) considerably alters KAM's character: it overcomes the limiting aspects of personal selling and allows for analysing and managing KAM with an awareness of its wider context – a business-to-business relationship. Therefore aspects completely neglected so far in KAM research, such as its implementation or its adequate design with respect to the business relationship, have become more relevant in KAM research.

In business-to-business markets, the marketing function often seeks to fulfil the needs and desires of each individual customer; companies are increasingly focusing their resources on their most profitable customers and are starting to implement the adequate organizational structures to fully integrate all customer-facing activities (Sheth et al. 2000). KAM is one structure, but the most expensive alternative for designing the supplier–customer interface, and its implementation may be less attractive than has been generally thought (Piercy and Lane 2003). It is therefore a strategic investment decision that needs to be evaluated carefully in advance (Blois 1997).

As the organizational design of the marketing management organization and, in our case, the KAM programme are predominantly determined by internal as well as external factors (Webster 2000), we need to turn to an economic theory that enables us to derive relevant decision determinants and to evaluate organizational alternatives based on their economic value. Although both economic theories, the resource dependence approach (Pfeffer and Salancik 1978) and the network approach (Hakansson 1982; Sydow 1992), allow for an analysis of supplier–customer business relationships, neither encompasses both perspectives simultaneously in their economic analysis, the intra-organizational as well as the inter-organizational perspectives (Schreyögg 2003). In addition, both theoretical conceptions lack a comparative, economic approach on choosing between organizational alternatives.

In the following, we will turn to transaction cost economics, because it focuses on the economic exchange process and the internal organization, and offers a powerful economic theory approach based on transaction costs as well as a comparative cost calculation based on a qualitative assessment that is needed for choosing the most appropriate KAM organization.

Transaction cost economics and marketing management

Transaction cost economics (Williamson 1975, 1985, 1996) is traditionally concerned with the analysis and the evaluation of the most efficient organizational mode of completing and executing a transaction or a related set of transactions – on the basis of transaction costs (Williamson 1975).[1]

Transaction cost economics differentiates mainly three organizational arrangements by which exchanges can be carried out: firms (hierarchies), markets and bilateral governance (hybrids). Based on the transaction costs resulting from the transaction's *asset specificity, uncertainty* and *frequency*, the agent will choose the most efficient organizational arrangement. The efficacy of the alternative organizational mode (firm, market or bilateral governance) must be assessed thereby in a comparative analysis. 'Which transactions go where depends on the attributes of transactions on the one hand, and the costs and competence of alternative modes of governance on the other' (Williamson 1996).

Although Williamson was convinced that bilateral governance would be of negligible relevance, as he assumed the hybrid economic organization to be inherently unstable and difficult to organize in the presence of uncertainty and transaction-specific assets (Williamson 1975), his reservations vanished over time (Williamson 1985, 1996), and he acknowledged that these hybrid economic organizations might even pose interesting organizational problems.

Within bilateral governance, such an organizational problem particularly arises as soon as two autonomous agents strive for the establishment of a long-term relationship with their transaction partner. Depending on the scale and scope of the business relationship as well as their activities, the supplying company needs to decide on the organization and design of its marketing management. Even though these intra-organizational aspects are increasingly determining the efficacy and success of business relationships, transaction cost economics has disregarded the relevance of the internal organization in intermediate market exchanges so far (Theuvsen 1997). With its three determinants (i.e. asset specificity, uncertainty and frequency) transaction cost economics is merely able to decide on the transactional arrangement, but not on the intra-organizational design of each of these arrangements – depending on the transaction's situational factors.

The decision on the most appropriate marketing management organization is therefore different from traditional transaction cost economics considerations as it does not represent any of the governance modes, i.e. market, bilateral governance or hierarchy. Applying transaction cost economics analysis to such internal organizational matters as the decision between alternative marketing and sales organizations therefore requires an extension of traditional transaction cost reasoning. For such a comparative institutional approach, wherein the most efficient marketing organization can be chosen, further determinants are necessary to enable informed choices among these complex alternatives. Particularly, the

---

[1] Transaction costs are defined as the 'costs of running the economic system' (Arrow 1969), i.e. they include the costs of planning, adapting and monitoring transactions (Williamson 1985).

transaction characteristics *uncertainty* and *frequency* seem to play a key role in this context and may help to determine the most efficient marketing organization design – with respect to a specific business relationship.

The determinants of the decision model

Extending the focus of transaction cost economics research to intra-organizational design matters, such as the decision on the appropriate marketing management organization, will require a detailed analysis of the relevant transaction characteristics (1) *asset specificity*, (2) *uncertainty* and (3) *frequency*. In the following sections, we will demonstrate that, besides asset specificity, uncertainty and frequency are also of particular relevance in the decision on the appropriate organizational design (Joshi and Stump 1999a; Menard 2004) as the embeddedness of the company, i.e. its institutional environment, increasingly matters (Cannon and Perreault 1999; Li and Nicholls 2000; Williamson 1996).

Asset specificity

Asset specificity has traditionally played a major role in transaction cost economics. Williamson is particularly concerned with transactions which involve a high degree of asset specificity, as companies need to economize on the latent hazards of opportunistic behaviour (Heide and John 1990; Klein 1996). Depending on the degree of asset specificity, Williamson proposes different organizational arrangements for the execution of transactions, i.e. the market, bilateral governance or firm.

Recent research in transaction cost economics, however, finds that asset specificity does not necessarily need to result in an asymmetrical commitment of a transacting party within a business relationship (Ganesan 1994; Heide and John 1990; Joshi and Stump 1999a). Due to such relational institutions as private ordering, credible commitment and relational norms, opportunistic behaviour might be attenuated in relational exchange situations. An effect similar to those relational institutions might also have the implementation of a specific marketing management organization (e.g. key account management): though it increases the supplying company's asset specificity on the key account, since it needs to be seen as an investment in the business relationship (Blois 1997), KAM facilitates the control of the customer's behaviour and reduces – due to its closeness – the hazards of opportunistic behaviour.

In the presence of asset specificity, the implementation of a specific marketing management organization might thus be helpful. Within the transaction mode of bilateral governance there will be various design alternatives of such a marketing management organization that will primarily depend upon the scale and scope of the business relationship's asset specificity. For reasons of simplicity, we will suppose in the following a middle to high degree of asset specificity that requires the implementation of KAM; this assumption will enable us to show how the design of the KAM organization will vary, depending on the company's perceived uncertainty and frequency.

Uncertainty

In his approach on transaction cost economics Williamson (1996) simply assumes a certain, but constant, degree of uncertainty and acknowledges three main forms of uncertainty, namely primary uncertainty, secondary uncertainty and behavioural uncertainty. The distinction between primary and secondary uncertainty can be traced back to Koopmans (1957). From Koopmans' perspective, uncertainty consists of aspects that are unpredictable and take the agent by surprise, i.e. primary uncertainty, as well as aspects that can be influenced by the economic agent, i.e. secondary uncertainty. Even though both forms of uncertainty can be considered equally important (Koopmans 1957; Williamson 1996), only secondary uncertainty issues appear to be relevant in the decision on the appropriate marketing management organization, as these issues can be influenced and are more predictable: they will include internal organizational issues as well as external factors, like the institutional environment or current market characteristics surrounding the transaction/relationship (Joshi and Stump 1999b; Windsperger 1998).

Drawing from recent research in marketing and organizational science, our assessment of sources of uncertainty reveals four uncertainty clusters:[2] (1) intra-organizational complexity, (2) environmental complexity, (3) environmental dynamics and (4) interdependencies.

(1) *Intra-organizational complexity:* as research in organizational and marketing science has confirmed, one of the main sources of uncertainty and thus fostering organizational change within marketing management is intra-organizational complexity (Shapiro and Moriarty 1982). Rather than satisfying the customers' needs, centralized marketing management units are often implemented to improve internal coordination matters. Increasing internal complexity results primarily from the firm's size (Gupta et al. 1986; Olson et al. 1995; Shapiro 1977; Shapiro and Moriarty 1982; Sharma 1997), the sales task complexity (Berry 1983; Moon and Gupta 1997; Rueckert and Walker 1987), and the product complexity (Kohli and Jaworski 1990; Moon and Gupta 1997; Shapiro and Moriarty 1982; Sharma 1997).

(2) *Environmental complexity:* this includes every factor which is external to the supplying company, but influences the supplying firm's action considerably. This complexity represents the second cluster of secondary uncertainty and includes factors such as the customer (Pardo 1997; Shapiro and Moriarty

---

[2] In this paper, complexity will be understood in the following as an antecedent of uncertainty – drawing upon organization theory and its research on complexity for the categorization of complexity.

1982; Sharma 1997; Szymanski 1988; Wengler et al. 2006), the competitor (Moon and Gupta 1997; Shapiro and Moriarty 1982; Wengler et al. 2006), the partners (Day and Klein 1987; Spekman and Strauss 1986), and the wider relevant environment (e.g. technology (Workman et al. 1998), governmental regulation (Sheth et al. 2000)).

(3) *Environmental dynamics:* intra-organizational and environmental uncertainty already pose severe problems to a company's marketing management – even from a static point of view. As both forms of complexity are sometimes subject to change, environmental dynamics arise from a higher frequency of disturbances at the same number of disturbance effects, from the intensity of the disturbances, or from their predictability (Achrol and Stern 1988; Schreyögg 2003; Williamson 1996). In the presence of environmental dynamics, additional complexity and thus uncertainty occurs (Palmer and Bejou 1994).

(4) *Interdependencies:* interdependency as the fourth cluster of secondary uncertainty needs to be particularly emphasized in a world of increasing cooperation and collaboration (Day and Klein 1987; Heide and John 1990; Spekman and Strauss 1986). Complex and individualized product-service offerings as well as the reduction of the value-adding activities to the company's core competencies increasingly require cooperation and collaboration across functional as well as organizational boundaries. In order to realize their tasks, the different functions and organizations become more and more interdependent (Gundlach and Cadotte 1994), i.e. if disturbance effects occur in one function/organization, these will also affect another function/ organization (Rueckert and Walker 1987). The higher the interdependency between these functions/organizations, the higher is the resulting uncertainty the economic agents have to cope with.

By a more in-depth differentiation of secondary uncertainty, it is possible to make this term more explicit, instead of leaving it as abstract as it has been within transaction cost economics so far. Clustering these sources of secondary uncertainty into intra-organizational complexity, environmental complexity, environmental dynamics and interdependencies also improves the analysis from the perspective of marketing management.

Besides primary and secondary uncertainty, behavioural uncertainty is rather important within transaction cost economics. In the context of opportunistic/ strategic behaviour, behavioural uncertainty mainly determines adequate governance structures to safeguard the economic agent with the transaction-specific assets against the expropriation hazards (Williamson 1996). The design of a specific marketing management organization may constrain the customer's strategic behaviour as intensified coordination and collaboration efforts make strategic behaviour – and thus behavioural uncertainty – more unlikely.

Uncertainty in all its facets therefore influences the design of the internal marketing management organization. Besides uncertainty, frequency also impacts the internal organizational design of KAM and is thus of higher relevance than transaction cost economics has suggested so far.

Frequency

The third determinant of Williamson's transaction cost economics approach, besides asset specificity and uncertainty, is *frequency*. From the traditional perspective on transaction cost economics, Williamson assumes frequency as a relevant, but not necessarily decisive, determinant. The transaction costs decrease if the transactions are of a recurrent kind. Williamson does not emphasize the relevance of frequency, but instead supposes a middle degree of frequency in bilateral governance (Williamson 1996).

Frequency, however, plays a more dominant role than transaction cost economics has suggested so far: transactional exchange applies only to pure or almost market transactions. Particularly in recent decades the character of most economic exchanges has changed from a transactional to a more relational one, which means that transaction cost economics needs to consider the business relationship (Kleinaltenkamp and Ehret 2006). The transaction cost economics determinant *frequency* will then include (1) the number of transactions of a recurrent kind, which are part of a single market transaction, (2) the number of market transactions, which are characterized by their interconnectedness, and (3) the key account's relational intent.

(1) *Number of transactions*: in traditional transaction cost economics, it is assumed that transaction costs decrease the more often transactions of the same kind are realized. These transactions of a recurrent kind are regularly part of a single market transaction: in the beginning of the exchange process both economic agents agree upon the exchange conditions ex ante (e.g. in the form of a sourcing agreement). As the amount to be exchanged and the prices are fixed, the following transactions thus take place within this exchange agreement. The market transaction is therefore realized by several transactions of a recurrent kind (Kleinaltenkamp and Ehret 2006). The number of transactions determines the transaction costs within the single exchange, i.e. it is highly transaction cost relevant.

(2) *Number of market transactions*: in contrast to traditional transaction cost economics reasoning, which considers only the number of transactions, its extension in the context of business relationships requires the differentiation between transaction and market transaction as well as the inclusion of the number of market transactions as determinants in the decision model: as transactions are part of a single market transaction, market transactions themselves are independent of, as well as interconnected with, each other (Kleinaltenkamp and Ehret 2006). Business relationships are characterized by the existence of at least two market transactions, which are often realized in a successive form: as soon as one market transaction is terminated, the existing exchange agreement is prolonged or a new one is negotiated. Executing various parallel market transactions implies a considerably greater challenge to the marketing management organization; more complexity may increase the resulting transaction costs significantly.

(3)   *Key account's relational intent*: besides the number of transactions and the resulting market transaction, the business relationship is also characterized by the relationship-building activities, the duration, and the customers' time horizons on the business relationship (Rokkan et al. 2003). The supplying company therefore needs to enable its marketing management organization to handle as well as respond to the key account's relationship building activities – besides the realization of market transactions. 'Customer relationships start as soon as one party starts to act on expectations beyond a single market transaction' (Kleinaltenkamp and Ehret 2006), i.e. business relationships result primarily out of the desire for, as well as the expectation of, continuity (Anderson 1996).

The economic agent's relational attitude, also called relational intent, has gained considerable attention in recent articles on relationship marketing (e.g. Ganesan 1994; Kumar et al. 2003; Pillai and Sharma 2003). The relational intent is thereby defined as the 'willingness of a customer to develop a relationship with a firm while buying a product or a service attributed to a firm, a brand, and channel' (Kumar et al. 2003). The relational intent is often accompanied by various relationship-building activities (e.g. informal information exchange, meeting of corporate members, etc.) which are realized in addition to and outside of the ordinary market transactions. Responding to these activities implies additional transaction costs for the supplying company: depending on the relationship-building activities as well as the marketing organization design, the transaction cost economizing effects will vary. From a transaction cost economics perspective, *relational intent* therefore indicates how efficiently the organization may be able to handle, or rather respond, to the relationship-building activities of the buying company. As the resulting transaction costs are mainly determined by the frequency of interaction, relational intent therefore needs to be recognized as a separate but relevant decision determinant within the traditional transaction cost determinant *frequency*.

In contrast to its traditional understanding, in the context of business relationships, *frequency* comprises more than the number of transactions. In addition, the determinant includes the number of market transactions as well as the customer's relational intent.

In the previous section, the main determinants in transaction cost economics (i.e. asset specificity, uncertainty and frequency) were extended and defined in more depth. As the analysis of these variables in the context of the design of the marketing management organization has demonstrated, asset specificity, which primarily determines the transaction cost economizing governance mode, remains an important factor, as it mainly influences the mode of the marketing management organization; but transaction cost determinants, uncertainty and frequency, become more important in the context of the intra-organizational design, like the decision on the adequate marketing management organization, and mainly determine the design of these internal organizations.

The decision on the most appropriate KAM organization

The decision on the most appropriate KAM organization consists of a two-step procedure. In the first step, the economizing effects, i.e. the efficiency of the KAM organization alternatives, needs to be determined; the second step, the cost–benefit assessment, in which the transaction cost economizing effects are weighed against the set-up costs of implementing the organizational alternative, enables the supplier's management to decide on the most appropriate KAM organization. The most appropriate KAM organization alternative therefore is not the most efficient alternative, but the one with the best cost–benefit trade-off.

In the following, (1) the principles and structure of the decision model will be explained, (2) the economizing effects of the KAM organization alternatives will be determined and (3) the cost–benefit assessment will be carried out. However, it is important to notice that the following statements need to be understood as initial conceptual reflections, which are still subject to empirical testing. In addition, the analysis of the economizing effects as well as the cost–benefit assessment will remain rather abstract, as the decision can be best made with respect to a specific supplier–customer business relationship.

The principles and structure of the decision model

In transaction cost economics, traditional decision-making is largely based on comparative analyses. Although researchers in transaction cost economics are increasingly trying to quantify transaction costs as well as to develop complex mathematical models (Anderson 1996), Williamson stays in the tradition of transaction cost economics and in his analysis of the institutions of governance – referring to Simon (1978) – compares the transaction cost economizing effects of his alternative governance modes. This way, all governance modes are compared simultaneously and in relation to each other (Williamson 1985, 1996); therefore the quantity of transaction costs is not decisive, but rather the transaction cost economizing effects of each of these governance modes. We will follow Simon and Williamson in their approach and favour a comparative decision model – based upon the extended transaction cost economics decision determinants.

For the decision model, we will focus completely on the economizing effects of different KAM organizations and describe all the other alternatives as 'no KAM'. With regard to the above mentioned KAM alternatives, we suggest ten decision alternatives that are rather common in the context of KAM. There are four basic decision alternatives: no KAM organization, a staff KAM organization, a line KAM organization, and a matrix KAM organization; depending on the organizational level (regional, functional, divisional, corporate), variations of these basic decision alternatives are conceivable.

The decision model is structured rather simply – see Table 1. It consists of two dimensions, the alternative KAM organizations as well as the relevant transaction cost economics determinants. These consist of the determinants asset specificity,

Table 1: The structure of the decision model

		KAM organization alternatives									
	No KAM	Staff organization			Line organization				Matrix organization	
Determinants		functional	divisonal	corporate	regional	functional	divisonal	corporate	functional	divisional
Asset specificity										
Uncertainty Primary uncertainty										
Secondary uncertainty Internal complexity Environmental complexity Environmental dynamics Interdependency										
Behavioural uncertainty										
Frequency Number of transactions Number of market transactions Relational attitude										

uncertainty and frequency – as Williamson's approach suggests. Asset specificity will not be of high relevance in our model as we assume a middle to high degree of asset specificity, which requires the implementation of KAM. More important to the decision process is the determinant uncertainty: it will be distinguished between primary, secondary and behavioural uncertainty. The dominant role of secondary uncertainty within the decision model becomes evident as it is categorized in its four sources of uncertainty, i.e. internal complexity, environmental complexity, environmental dynamics and interdependency. The third determinant of transaction cost economics, frequency, will include the number of transactions, the number of market transactions and the customer's relational intent.

Whereas the relevant transaction cost economics determinants represent the vertical part of the decision model, the KAM organization alternatives correspond with the horizontal part.

The economizing effects of the KAM organization alternatives

The following transaction cost economics analysis of the ten marketing management organization alternatives reveals the transaction cost economizing effects of each alternative. Whereas 'no key account management' means that there will be no economizing effects at all and should be proposed only if there is no asset specificity, uncertainty and frequency, KAM as a staff organization allows for various economizing effects; at the functional as well as the corporate level, staff KAM represents a centralized planning and coordination unit. At the functional level, i.e. as a part of the marketing and sales function, strategic management processes and procedures are centrally coordinated across the regional marketing and sales units, whereas operational customer service is as decentralized as possible. The same is true for 'staff key account management' at the corporate level, though the coordination takes part across divisions, requires massive support from the corporate management, and is better equipped for dealing with – besides internal complexity – environmental complexity and environmental dynamics. As soon as a company prefers to centralize the strategic aspects of KAM and to leave operational tasks such as serving the key account within the marketing and sales function, the company should decide for staff KAM at the divisional level, which economizes partly on internal and environmental complexity.

In contrast to staff KAM, which represents a separate unit external but still partly attached to the line organization, 'line KAM' is fully integrated within the company's organization. 'Key account management as a line organization at the regional level' is the lowest-level KAM programme within the line organization, and economizes best in situations with medium internal coordination needs and partial external integration within an existing business relationship, while the product portfolio does not require any major adjustments. Concerning 'key account management as a line organization at the functional level', the decision alternative seems to be a particularly appropriate choice in business relationships if the key account requires – to a certain extent – a customization of the supplier's product-service offerings.

Table 2 The economizing effects of KAM organization alternatives

		Key account management organization alternatives								
	No KAM	Staff organization			Line organization				Matrix organization	
Determinants		functional	divisional	corporate	regional	functional	divisional	corporate	functional	divisional
Asset specificity	0	0	0	0	0	+	++	+	+	+
Uncertainty										
Primary uncertainty	0	0	0	0	0	+	++	+	+	++
Secondary uncertainty										
Internal complexity	0	+	+	+	+	++	++	+	++	++
Environmental complexity	0	0	+	+	+	+	++	+	++	++
Environmental dynamics	0	0	0	+	0	+	++	+	++	++
Interdependency	0	0	0	0	0	0	+	+	+	+
Behavioural uncertainty	0	0	0	0	0	+	+	+	+	+
Frequency										
Number of transactions	0	0	0	+	+	+	++	+	+	++
Number of market transactions	0	+	+	+	+	++	++	+	++	++
Relational attitude	0	0	0	0	+	+	++	++	++	++

From a hierarchical point of view, KAM is equally as powerful as the other organizational functions and may thus be able to influence these functions in favour of the customer's requests. However, the transaction situation should be characterized by only a medium degree of environmental complexity, environmental dynamics, behavioural uncertainty and relational attitude. 'Key account management as a line organization at the divisional level' is exceptional within the decision alternatives as it represents a separate and independent business unit in the corporation. This organizational alternative should be pursued only in those transaction situations characterized by a completely distinct product-service offering for one or a small group of important customers. 'Key account management as a line organization at the corporate level' is represented by a member of the management board. The key account alternative's economizing effects on asset specificity as well as on uncertainty are characterized by a medium degree, due to its limited involvement in KAM's day-to-day-business (see Table 2). Instead, 'key account management as a line organization at the corporate level' is best suited for transaction situations in which the key account requires specific treatment at the board level, but not at the operational level of the business relationship.

A more adequate KAM alternative for high-frequency and high-involvement business relationships in dynamic and interdependent market environments is represented by the matrix organizations of KAM. 'Matrix KAM' at the functional level seems to be the best alternative if the intense business relationship is characterized by a highly competitive environment where product and process adjustments are often required, and the key accounts are both demanding but also rather valuable for the corporation. The economizing effects of 'key account management as a matrix organization at the divisional level', however, are the most powerful, as this KAM alternative moves the supplying corporation close to a quasi-integration without setting up a completely distinct business unit. Its internal processes are fully capable of enacting transaction cost economizing in situations characterized by high environmental complexity, high environmental dynamics and high interdependency.

The assessment of alternative KAM programmes from a transaction cost economics perspective reveals their comparative advantages and disadvantages in different transaction situations (see Table 3). Although we are now able to decide on the most efficient transaction cost economizing organization – with respect to specific transaction situations – our assessment of the economizing effects of the various KAM alternatives has so far neglected the (somewhat vast) costs of implementing these alternatives. For a comprehensive discussion, management needs to assess not only the benefits (transaction cost economizing effects) but also the costs (set-up costs) of implementing one of these decision alternatives (Blois 1996). Only if the trade-off between the benefits (transaction cost savings due to efficient information processing, etc.) and the costs (e.g. costs of implementation, costs of organizational resistance, etc.) is positive may altering or adjusting the marketing management organization's design or setting up a new organizational design be sensible (Windsperger 1996).

Table 3 The transaction cost economizing effects and the relevance of KAM alternatives

Key account management organization alternatives

Determinants	No KAM	Staff organization				Line organization			Matrix organization	
		functional	divisional	corporate	regional	functional	divisional	corporate	functional	divisional
Asset specificity	0	0	0	0	0	+	++	+	+	+
Uncertainty										
Primary uncertainty	0	0	0	0	0	+	++	+	+	++
Secondary uncertainty										
Internal complexity	0	+	+	+	+	++	++	+	++	++
Environmental complexity	0	0	+	+	+	+	+++	++	+++	+++
Environmental dynamics	0	0	0	+	0	+	+++	++	+++	++
Interdependency	0	0	0	0	0	0	+	++	+	++
Behavioural uncertainty	0	0	0	0	0	+	+	+	+	+
Frequency										
Number of transactions	0	0	0	+	+	+	++	+	+	++
Number of market transactions	0	+	+	+	+	++	++	+	++	++
Relational attitude	0	0	0	0	+	+	++	++	++	++

Cost–benefit assessment of the KAM organization alternatives

The assessment of the costs and benefits will permit decisions on the relevance and irrelevance of each KAM alternative, as some of the KAM alternatives would require massive investments/costs for realigning processes and/or might induce organizational resistance. We are therefore able to exclude several alternatives on the basis of a theoretical assessment: 'staff key account management at the divisional level' lacks influence across functions and has conflicting interests, particularly with the marketing and sales function; 'line KAM at the regional level' does not have sufficient authority concerning cross-functional coordination as long as it remains organized within the existing sales force; 'key account management as a line organization at the corporate level' guarantees top-management involvement in the KAM process, but is completely detached from operational activities; and finally, 'key account management as a matrix organization at the divisional level' requires enormous implementation effort and costs necessary for setting up a functioning, cross-divisional KAM programme.

A positive benefit–cost trade-off, however, might be achievable in the context of the other KAM alternatives: 'no key account management' requires no implementation costs at all; the functional as well as the corporate 'staff key account management' enable the company to achieve considerable coordination synergies across the marketing and sales function or the divisions' KAM programmes, respectively; 'line key account management programme at the functional level' represents a sole, but powerful, organizational unit detached and independent of the marketing and sales function; 'matrix key account management at the functional level', though rather expansive, represents the most adequate and efficient alternative in dynamic market environments; 'line key account management at the divisional level' represents rather an exception, since these organizations might be cost efficient as well as effective, but only in rare situations.

As the preceding cost–benefit assessment has revealed, some KAM organization alternatives are more relevant than others. One needs to keep in mind that the 'relevance' of these organizational alternatives has been determined on a very abstract level.

Conclusion

This paper proposes a decision model on the adequacy of the design of KAM organizations. Based on transaction cost economics, an easy-to-handle decision model has been developed that supports companies in their decision on the most appropriate KAM organization – with respect to their specific customer–supplier business relationships.

The application of transaction cost economics to the analysis of the marketing management organization required two extensions: its application within business relationships and the development of a multi-dimensional concept of uncertainty as well as frequency. Based upon these decision determinants, the proposed organizational KAM alternatives were qualitatively assessed concerning their cost–benefit trade-off, i.e. transaction cost savings minus set-up costs (e.g. costs of implementation/organizational resistance). By evaluating these alternatives, companies will be able to choose their most appropriate KAM organization alternative. In effect, the decision model will also be applicable for reviewing the appropriateness of existing KAM organizations.

Our analysis of the most appropriate KAM organization is the first theory-based approach to making informed choices on various KAM organization alternatives. For too long, KAM research has neglected economic theory, though increasingly researchers have been recognizing the relevance of the economic perspective in KAM (e.g. Homburg et al. 2002; Pardo et al. 2006). Although the economic perspective encompasses both efficiency and effectiveness, the prime focus in this paper is on transaction cost economics, which seems to be rather suitable. First, the decision on the marketing management organization is primarily concerned with the supplier's internal organizational design, i.e. the supplier's efficiency; second, due to the extension of the determinant uncertainty, the customers'/ markets' requirements are considered, although indirectly; and finally, recent research by Ivens and Pardo (2007) suggests that KAM does not necessarily increase customer satisfaction or trust.

The application of the decision model is based on initial conceptual reflections. Further refinement of the decision determinants as well as empirical research and testing will be indispensable. A start for more theory-based research in key account management has, however, been made.

Organizational structures in global account management

BY GEORGE YIP AND AUDREY BINK

Abstract

The key elements of global account management organizational structure include the global general manager, global steering committee, global account manager, global account team, information management, executive sponsorship, local account managers, global reporting structure and customer councils. Although the organizational structures of GAM programmes can take a multitude of forms, all of them are variations of three basic approaches, each of which strikes different balances between global integration and local (or national) autonomy. We call the three Coordination GAM, Control GAM and Separate GAM.

Reproduced with the kind permission of Oxford University Press, originally Chapter 4, 'Structuring the global customer management programme' in Yip, G.S. and Bink, A.J.M. (2007) *Managing Global Customers: An Integrated Approach.*

Introduction

The organization structure of the global account management (GAM) programme forms the bedrock of the total GAM effort. But there is, of course, no one best way of organizing GAM, as the right structure depends on the company and its situation. This article will describe the various elements that make up a GAM organization. We will also discuss the three major forms of GAM organization, along with their benefits and possible pitfalls.

While there is a large literature on strategic account management (SAM), there is a much smaller one about GAM and even less on GAM organizational structures. GAM research probably started with Yip and Madsen's (1996) article with five case studies. Most recently, Shi et al. (2010) have provided both a full conceptual framework and empirical test. In between, key publications include Arnold et al. (2001a, 2001b), Capon and Senn (2010), Hennessey and Jeannet (2003), Homburg et al. (2002), Montgomery and Yip (2000), Shi et al. (2004, 2005), Verra (2003), Wilson et al. (2002), Yip and Bink (2007a, 2007b) and Yip et al. (2007). Some of these publications address the role of organization structure, but only Yip and Bink (2007a, 2007b) address this issue directly.

Case Example 1: Citibank's evolving GAM programme

Citibank has been pioneering global account management for its corporate customers since the 1970s and has since rebranded and reorganized the programme to better answer customers' needs.

The worldwide customer group (WCG) started in the late 1970s, was rebranded in the mid-1980s and continued to exist more or less in the same form until the mid-1990s. The group worked with about 250 corporate clients. Those companies were all global players, mainly in the chemical, pharmaceutical, automobile and retail industries, but no financial institutions. In some ways, WCG was never disbanded, but the name was dropped in 1984 and brought back in the late 1980s. The WCG was replaced in 1995 with the Global Relationship Bank (GRB) programme. The new GRB organization seeks to create and add more value by focusing on industries. The GRB covers about 1,400 multi-national customers, made up from Fortune Global 500 and other companies with global presence and/or global activity (e.g. some UK financial institutions, such as fund managers, do not have overseas branches but do trade extensively overseas).

Elements of a GAM organization

There seem to be as many organization forms for GAM as there are companies, given the need to tailor for the situation of each company. In particular, each company implements each element of GAM in a somewhat different way, producing unique configurations. These elements of GAM structure include the global general manager, global steering committee, global account manager, global account team, information management, executive sponsorship, local account managers, global reporting structure and customer councils.

Global general manager

A GAM programme needs a global general manager who is responsible for the programme and its strategy and operation. This needs to be a senior manager at the corporate or business unit level. Many companies, however, do not have such a position in place, or in some cases the responsibility is given to a manager who also has other duties. For some smaller global companies, having a general manager who is solely responsible for the development of the global programme is a luxury they cannot justify. DMV International, a European supplier of ingredients for the food and pharmaceutical industries, has its global key account managers reporting into the (European) regional sales manager, who is also responsible for all other sales in that particular region. Even though the regional sales manager strongly supports the global account management, there is still the possibility of conflict of interest between local and global issues.

When there is no opportunity to have a global general manager who is dedicated to the programme, companies should at least use a reporting structure that minimizes conflict. This can be achieved by giving overall responsibility for GAM to a high-level manager who has no direct links with any particular geography. Whether there is a dedicated general manager or a shared one, this person needs to have the authority and the desire to help develop the programme in the best way possible. Many company examples show that as soon as there is a person at the head of the programme who really believes that global relationships are the way forward, things change for the better. For example, when Unilever appointed a new senior vice-president for global customer development, the existing situation, in which there were no systems, processes or real support for the global account managers, started to evolve into a more empowered organization with more dedicated teams, and that is more embedded in the total Unilever organization.

Global steering committee

Many companies with successful GAM attribute part of this success to having a global steering committee. Such a committee typically comprises a group of senior executives committed to the global programme, but with other general responsibilities. The global steering committee will meet on a regular basis to decide on the overall strategy and objectives for the programme and monitor the development. The collective power of the executives should outweigh any country or regional managers to make sure that any conflicts on allocating resources or global–local friction can be easily resolved.

Having a global steering committee means that it is easier for the company to handle the tension that comes with the global–local disparity, and it creates much visibility for the company's dedication to global relationships. Some companies even have separate global steering committees for specific relationships, in which case there is often a direct relationship between the members of the committee and senior managers at the customer or supplier. Admittedly, a structure like this is very costly in terms of executive resources, and will realistically be created for only very special relationships.

Having global steering committees can be just as valuable for a global customer as for a global supplier. In the case of British energy company, BG Group, there are currently two relationships with suppliers that are deemed important enough to invest in a steering committee. For each global relationship, BG Group has established a committee consisting of senior managers from both BG Group and the supplier. These committees meet on a regular basis and aim to focus on strategic issues that arise within the relationships. Both global steering committees are being chaired by a BG Group executive vice-president, which embodies the high level of commitment BG Group has to the global relationships.

Global account manager

A good GAM is key to a successful global account relationship. The GAM is responsible for the relationship with the account and the resulting performance. Ideally, the GAM is dedicated to one global account, although in some smaller companies it is necessary to spread GAMs over multiple accounts. In many less advanced GAM programmes, the GAM is a mid-level manager with a career background in sales. As managing global customers is about more than just the GAM programme, so it is also about more than just sales. More and more companies are starting to realize that the relationship with important global accounts should not just revolve around the transactional aspects but be more integrated with other parts of the company in order to achieve a more rounded relationship that is a good foundation for creating more opportunities between the companies in the long run. Therefore, it is important to realize that the skill set of a GAM is not, as the head of one GAM programme put it, 'the same set of skills as a local account manager, plus having a passport'.

It is also not unheard of any more to have GAMs who do not have a background in sales. Xerox realizes the importance of knowing the customer's industry and takes this into account when choosing the right GAM for an account. The GAM for global bank HSBC spent a large part of his prior career in finance, and the GAM for the Volkswagen account used to be a Volkswagen employee.

Besides knowledge about the customer's industry, other necessary GAM skills include cultural awareness, team management and sensitivity. In general, a GAM takes responsibility for the strategic planning of the account, deciding on goals, and determining and obtaining the right amount of resources. Furthermore, often the GAM will lead the team of people that supports the global account: the global account team (GAT). The GAM needs to guide the GAT members in their particular roles and help them develop their individual relationships with the account. Sourcing of information is also an essential task for the GAM. They need to be the ultimate expert on the account, and combine all the information that is available with the separate GAT members or local account managers. The GAM should, however, also have thorough knowledge about the capabilities of their own company, and how these can help the customer. At Xerox, many of the GAMs have a background in either Xerox itself or the specific account they are managing. The GAM for Volkswagen has more than 25 years of experience in positions either with or relating to this customer. A complete outsider would have a much harder job getting to know all the ins and outs at both companies, and therefore find it harder to identify combined, or other, opportunities for the two companies.

In terms of organizational position, many companies have a structure in which the GAM reports within the geographic area in which they are based. This occurs when no separate reporting structure exists for the GAM programme. But to avoid conflicts of interest between the global and local parts of the company, it is better to have the GAM reporting to a senior manager at the corporate level.

Global account team

The composition and organization of the GAT provides a good indicator of the level of integration of global customer management (GCM). When a GAT is very informal, and consists only of the different local account managers, then the GAM programme probably focuses only on sales, and the GAM does not have enough authority to be able to take full responsibility for the relationship with the account. A company with an integrated approach to managing global customers will have formal global account teams that are both cross-function and cross-country. For example, DMV International works with global account teams that consist of both sales managers for the account from different geographies and representatives from different functional areas that have contact with the customer (e.g. R&D).

The GAT plays a crucial role in getting the relationship with the customer beyond the transactional phase into a partnership. The GAT needs to implement the global strategy for the account while taking into consideration the existing organization of the company. Having a cross-functional team helps to get all relevant views on board, keeps the links with the different departments, and ensures that the global account organization will not lead a life of its own separate from the existing organization. The GAT is also key in building the network of customer relationships that pulls in many participants from both the supplier and the customer. Building on existing relationships, the GAT can engage the customer in new plans and opportunities.

The team members will also be an invaluable source for getting information from different parts of the customer's company, supported by a good information system that can handle this. In the relationship between ABB and its supplier, Xerox, the latter achieves a broad range of contact points by mirroring the ABB organization. ABB has a group supply chain management function that is divided into direct and indirect activities and a national procurement organization in each of the top 22 countries. Xerox maintains a customer contact person in all of these countries, so ensuring a broad basis for relationship management and information gathering. Furthermore, the team members act as 'ambassadors' for GCM in their respective departments, ensuring support throughout the company.

Some companies have full-time team members, but it is not always optimal to have employees dedicated to one account. Best-practice sharing and integration of the global programme with the rest of the company come as important benefits of having GAT members with multiple roles. Which way to go will differ between companies and needs to be determined based on the company's situation.

Case Example 2: Young & Rubicam's global account team

To develop a global account strategy, Young & Rubicam established a global management structure that oversees both the development and the execution of every global campaign. Global managing directors and their teams represent the core of the company's global management structure. Each global managing director provides a corporate global perspective for each campaign and is responsible for all communications with the client. Team members must be devoted to the client, have a global perspective and a broad understanding of not only their client's markets but also the key success factors of each region. Furthermore, because execution is always carried out locally, the firm must have access to and be able to coordinate a wide network of resources. Few clients begin with the premise of establishing a globally integrated campaign. Typically, campaigns are developed for one country and diffused to other countries once proven successful.

Information management

As managing global customers comes with a complex structure of relationships, measurements and information streams, a sound information-management system is essential for the success of the programme. The GAM needs to be very knowledgeable about the customer and its industry, but they will not be able to gather this information without the help of the GAT and a well-functioning information system. Two types of information management systems are important here: first, the results measurement system and second, the customer relationship management (CRM) system.

Many companies still have trouble getting both types of systems geared up for global relationships. Measurement systems need to track the sales of the global accounts and therefore the results of the GAM programme. A common problem is that most of the current systems identify every delivery address as a separate customer, and when a manager wants to see the results for a complete account, this has to be combined manually, which is complicated by differences across regions. Another common problem is that many GAMs do not have easy access to a good overview of the complete results of their account. Besides missing a good management tool, this can make things very complex when it comes to remuneration of the GAM. Many companies traditionally link remuneration for national account managers to the account's revenues. This link should be less strong for global account management, as it should be based more on long-term relationship development than short-term sales. But not having information on global revenues for an account really undermines the ability to judge a GAM's performance. This shows, once more, how important it is to have the GAM programme integrated within the whole company.

When choosing and implementing a new information system, managers need to think about the necessary capabilities of the system, including tracking global sales and profits. While the situation for sales measurement can be bad, it is often even worse for the internal information systems that support CRM. Almost all big companies have some form of internal information system, such as Siebel, Lotus Notes or Livelink. But when we asked if these systems were used to their full potential, the majority of global managers had to admit that they were not.

Many companies implement these costly systems without thinking about their actual use. Training people how to use them is necessary, but incorporating the actual use in their everyday tasks is at least as important. People will go looking for information at the moment they need it, but what is the incentive for loading information they already have into the system, and how will they find out that there is vital information for them on the system if they do not know they should be looking for it? Often this situation ends up as a negative cycle of thinking: there is no useful information on the system, therefore never going on the system and never uploading information.

HSBC encourages its relevant employees to visit its Lotus Notes system at least once a day to deposit or access information. Other firms, such as engineering company Schlumberger, have integrated the internal information system with measurement and logistics systems, to make using the information system a natural thing to do in everyday tasks.

Executive sponsorship

GAM will be successful only with a high level of executive sponsorship. The complex nature of managing global customers needs a high-level executive to whom to escalate conflicts between global and local business units. Even though the executive sponsor should not be involved in operational problems, having the position in place will give a visible signal to the organization that GAM is something for top-level management, thus helping to gain support and commitment at lower levels. Having executive support also helps in getting essential people and other resources for the global account. So, in addition to a 'programme champion' in the form of, ideally, a board-level director who has overall responsibility for the GAM programme, many companies choose to have a system of executive sponsorship for the different accounts that involves more top-level executives.

In an executive sponsorship system for GAM, every global account is assigned a senior manager, such as chief financial officer or chief technical officer, who keeps in contact with a senior manager on the customer side. This shows the customer that it is important to the supplier, and helps to develop the relationship. The executive sponsor will often be able to help the GAM to overcome barriers and to open doors that would be closed to the GAM alone. The executive sponsors should not be assigned at random. Ideally, the executive sponsor is someone with specialist knowledge about the industry of the account, or possibly with a previous relationship with the account. They need to be a good conversation partner for the customer.

Furthermore it is very important that the sponsor be fully committed to the success of GAM. In some companies the executive sponsor also acts as a mentor for the GAM, helping them to set goals and strategy for the account. This system also works for customers with a global supplier management programme. A global purchasing officer for Royal Dutch Shell said: 'There is endorsement and support for global supplier management from the highest level on. The boss saying "I want it to happen" is not enough, but it does help.'

Local account managers

In general, any company with big international customers will have different national account managers (NAMs) dealing with the separate parts of the account. When the big international customer becomes a global account, these local account managers will need more coordination. Also, the NAM becomes more than a local sales manager. They have to realize that they are part of a global team and that sometimes a global objective will ask for local sacrifices. In regard to global accounts, the main GAM-related task of NAMs becomes the local implementation of global agreements, in addition to the usual selling and maintenance responsibilities for the local unit of the global customer. Therefore, it is important for the NAM to keep informed about activities on the global level. On the flipside, the GAM is dependent on the NAM for information at the national level, in order to get a good overview of the total situation with the account. In a way, the NAMs are the eyes and ears of the global account team. They have the most direct links with different parts of the customer and will gather information not available at the global level. For example, the Unilever GAM for Wal-Mart works with about 50 people worldwide to set foundation objectives and operational guidelines.

Some companies have the luxury of having NAMs who are dedicated to a specific global account, but in many cases they will have to be spread across different accounts, global and otherwise, as the local business volume with the global account is not big enough to justify a dedicated person. But even though these local managers work for the global account for only a small percentage of their time, it is important that the GAM knows exactly who is working on the account. The GAM should be able to communicate with these NAMs on a regular basis.

Sometimes one or more NAMs may even be part of the global account team. As the global account organization, by its nature, is very complex, companies should keep to a minimum changes to the local responsibility for the global account. At Unilever, GAMs complain about the high turnover of personnel on the local level, due to the personal career development strategy that Unilever follows. One GAM said: 'I have an annual worldwide meeting with all the local managers who are responsible for my account. Every year, half of the people there are new, and I will be outlining my strategy for the account all over again.'

Global reporting structure

The global reporting structure is the backbone of the GAM programme. The reporting structure gives the overall image of what position the GAMs have in the total organization. The position they are reporting to can say much about the GAM programme and the commitment a company has to make it successful. In general, there are three streams of reporting structures: reporting in the geographical organization, reporting in a matrix organization and reporting in a GAM-specific organization. In the first type of reporting structure, the balance of power lies with the country sales managers. The GAM will report into the country manager of the country in which they are based, often the HQ country of the account.

DMV International works with a regional system in which the global key account managers report into their own regional manager. Many of the global accounts have their HQ in north-west Europe, and therefore a lot of the global key account managers report into the same regional manager, which helps with any local versus global barriers, as this manager is particularly supportive of the GAM project. Having a direct line into the country or region is often the first reporting structure with which a company starts off its GAM programme, as it is easier to implement than the other two structures. A negative aspect of this structure is the potential friction between benefits for the country and the global account. A country manager might prefer the GAM to work on the part of the account that is based in their country, as any business with the rest of the account will have no influence on the country P&L.

In the second type of reporting structure the GAM will be positioned in a geographical area and will report to a geographical manager, but will also report to either a corporate executive responsible for global accounts, or a corporate manager of the particular business line in which the account is active. This way it is easier to get a power balance between local and global interests. In the third structure, the power balance lies with the global account manager. They have authority over local account managers, and might even have them reporting to them. The GAM will report to an executive manager responsible for global account management, and the global accounts seem to have priority over other accounts. Citibank global relationship bank (GRB) employees report to both industry groups and country management.

Customer councils

Customer councils are not reserved for GAM only, but they can be particularly interesting in this situation. As having global relationships is a relatively new situation for most companies, customer councils can help determine what services can be developed to really help the customer create added value. In a customer council, relevant executives, ideally as senior as possible, are brought together with the GAM and possibly the global steering committee. These events provide an opportunity to understand the customers' needs in doing global business. The setting is particularly inviting for the customers to open up about their needs, wants and possibly complaints.

Vodafone runs a testimonial programme in the form of a customer council with six global accounts. A two-day advisory board with two senior representatives from every global account was used to form working groups on different subjects that are relevant to global relationships, such as 'global contracts' and 'service management.' Each work group has a representative of all the six accounts, chaired not by a Vodafone representative but by one of the account representatives. Although Vodafone has 50 global accounts in total, it uses this select group of accounts to test new products, services and ideas, and to roll out these products to the other global accounts when they turn out to be successful.

Case Example 3: How Royal Dutch Shell customizes its GAM programme for Unilever

Establishing a global customer management (GCM) programme is only the start of the process. Suppliers must ensure that their programmes' design and implementation meet the needs of their customers and must refrain from establishing a GCM programme for its own sake. Real competitive advantage comes from a GCM programme that complements customers' business processes, as does Shell's programme for Unilever. This programme is customized to Unilever's needs and focuses on helping Unilever to implement its Total Productive Maintenance (TPM) programme at its plants.

Both Shell and Unilever see this as a partnership in which they can find synergy that gives them an edge over competitors. While Unilever sees Shell as the ideal partner to contribute to TPM, it is beneficial for Shell to customize its GCM programme for Unilever this way, as the TPM knowledge gained helps Shell to become Unilever's preferred supplier for lubricants. As Shell develops a good relationship in more Unilever plants, it can start gaining more leverage through global coordination of the entire relationship.

Different forms of GAM organization

There are many different forms of GAM organization, but they normally seem to be variations on three different approaches: Coordination GAM, Separate GAM and Control GAM. When implementing a GAM organization, a company needs to find a balance between central coordination and local flexibility. Furthermore, the programme needs to be integrated into the total organization of the company in order to create the informal organization that gets the whole company involved in managing global customers. Whatever organization form is chosen, the GAM programme will have a particular effect on the other account organization in the company as it will often change the responsibilities and communication lines for the national account managers. In companies that have various independent national account structures, it may even lead to standardization among these national programmes. These changes will be less intense with Coordination GAM, but the effectiveness of this form can be disputed. The typical sequence is for companies to start with Coordination GAM, then move to Control GAM, then lastly to Separate GAM, although few have gone that far.

Coordination GAM

The Coordination GAM organization structure takes the existing company organization and adds a coordination layer of GAMs (see Figure 1). The main task of these GAMs is to coordinate among the relevant geographical areas when the customer asks for a global deal. Furthermore, the GAM will try to develop the account into other areas where the company previously had no business. In general, the GAM in a Coordination GAM organization will not have any authority over the local operations but needs to get their consent for any activity on a global level. Many banks use a Coordination GAM structure because of the importance of local relationships and a relatively low need to globally standardize the services provided to global customers.

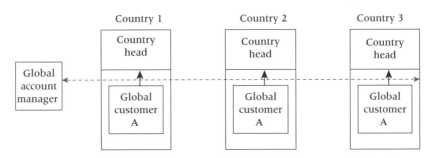

Figure 1   Coordination GAM

Case Example 4: Vodafone's Coordination GAM

Vodafone, the world's largest mobile telecommunications company, based in the UK, provides an example of a Coordination GAM approach. The company is relatively young and has seen strong growth in the last few years, mainly through takeovers. As there is still a high level of autonomy in the different countries, Vodafone finds it difficult to work with customers on global deals. Previously, the company took an ad hoc approach to demands for global business, often meaning that the national account manager of the country with the biggest part of the global deal would lead the communications with the other involved countries. As Vodafone grew and global business became increasingly more common, the company employed an extra coordination level in the form of the international account manager (IAM).

The tasks of this IAM differ from those of the national account managers. The IAM negotiates central deals, but further local implementation is negotiated on a local level by NAMs. The IAM does not have any control over the P&L of the countries involved. Because of the high level of external growth, the different countries have different structures for national account management, which does not help in making the coordination role easier.

A benefit of Coordination GAM is the ease of implementation, as it does not disturb any existing organization structures. The drawback arises from the GAM programme not being as effective as it could be. The lack of authority means there is room for disagreements between local subsidiaries, and it will often be very difficult to come to a global agreement when all local subsidiaries are working for themselves. For many companies, the Coordination GAM programme is the first step, and the programme often evolves over time into a more structured and powerful organization. Managers should take these future developments into account before embarking on global account management, as sometimes it can be hard to change from the early perceptions about the position of the GAM programme and the position of the GAM. It might be better to incur more disruption in the start-up phase of GAM in order to send the right message: that this company is fully dedicated to making global relationships work.

Separate GAM

Separate GAM is in some ways the opposite of Coordination GAM. In the Separate GAM organization, the company creates a completely new, separate business unit for the global accounts (see Figure 2). This can be a complete separation where the employees are dedicated to Separate GAM and the GAM business unit operates its own support activities, such as technical support and sales services. Separate GAM may run some functions as a separate entity, but also share other functions with the organization of the geographic structure.

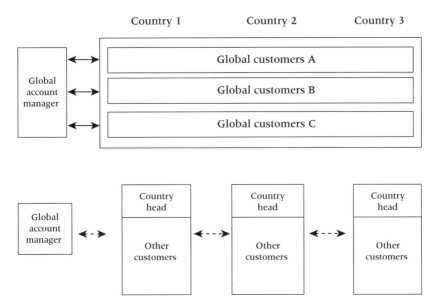

Figure 2 Separate GAM

In Separate GAM, global accounts that were previously served by several different geographies are completely lifted from the geographic structure to the new business unit. The complete responsibility for the global accounts now rests in the new business unit, which operates alongside the existing geographic units that still take care of the non-global accounts. In addition, the global account manager may have some coordinating responsibility for other customers that have not been pulled into the separate, global organization (as shown in the lower part of Figure 2).

Case Example 5: IBM's and Hewlett-Packard's Separate GAM

Using a Separate GAM structure for its top 100 or so customers, IBM has three different models in place to deal with account management: territory coverage for smaller customers, an aligned model in which account management is organized around customer industry sectors, and an integrated model. In the integrated model, account management forms a business unit in its own right, and is used for only very large global accounts. The P&L for these accounts is measured on a global basis, and a global team is in place to manage the accounts.

Hewlett-Packard also tried this approach in the late 1990s, breaking out its top 100 accounts. This approach lasted only a short time before it was overtaken by a decision to reorganize HP into a front-end (customer-facing) and back-end (operations) structure.

The main benefit of Separate GAM is the total control the global unit has over the relationship with the global accounts. There is no reason for friction between global and local subsidiaries and it is easier to manage information about this account. The customer gets the attention it needs from a unit that is experienced in handling global accounts and has employees who are dedicated to global accounts. This structure also makes the interface with the account clearer, so that the customer always knows where to go with questions. However, this approach, which can have 'silo' aspects, also has its disadvantages. First, it is a very expensive solution that can be implemented only by companies that have a substantial amount of global business. Furthermore, the separating out of the GAM programme means there is less overlap with other account organizations, which means less sharing of best practices.

Control GAM

Control GAM is the most common organizational form of GAM. It means that the responsibility for the account essentially lies with the GAM programme and there is some level of authority to enforce that in the local subsidiaries (see Figure 3). Often Control GAM is set up in a matrix organization in which all employees who work with a global account on the local level report not only to their geographical line manager but also to the GAM. The GAM reports to a senior executive at the corporate level, who is responsible for the whole GAM programme, and sometimes also to a regional manager if this is necessary within the company's organization structure. The reporting lines from the local account managers to the GAM and their geographic managers will differ.

Typically, in the early days of a GAM programme, the reporting line to the geographic manager will be a lot stronger than the, often dotted, reporting line to the GAM. When the programme earns more credibility over time, the balance between those two reporting lines typically moves more in the direction of the GAM. In some companies, the regional managers report into the same person as the GAMs or the GAM general manager, typically a vice-president or director for sales. This helps in resolving conflicts, as problems can escalate to the VP's level.

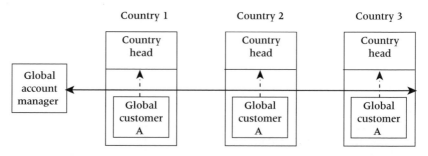

Figure 3   Control GAM

In Control GAM, conflict can arise about authority over the local subsidiaries where global accounts operate. The GAM needs some level of authority to make sure that global agreements can be enforced on the local level, but most companies try to steer away from taking all autonomy from the local subsidiaries. Enforcing plans on local subsidiaries without any discussion leads to resistance towards the global programme, which damages the programme in the long run. Therefore, GAMs should involve local subsidiaries in global decisions that affect their local customers. This not only motivates local managers more to execute these decisions, but involves them as a good source of information about the local implications of global decisions.

Case Example 6: JWT's and Royal Dutch Shell's Control GAM

The world's oldest advertising agency, JWT (formerly J. Walter Thompson), now part of WPP, runs a Control GAM programme. The agency has approximately two decades of experience with its GAM organization, in which each global client is assigned its own global business director (GBD). This GBD takes responsibility for the qualitative and quantitative results of the business with the client and has executive authority over all business with the client, including the interaction in the different regions. As it will frustrate employees when this authority is used often, the GBD aims to resolve problems by mutual consent, but if there is real friction they have the power to do something about it.

Royal Dutch Shell also operates a Control GAM programme. In 2004, Shell had a standard regional approach (EU/USA/Latin America/Asia), with regional (zonal) account teams and global account teams for the customers selected to be global accounts. Each global account has a responsible GAM who reports to the respective business manager for their sector (e.g. automotive). The global key account management programmes are similar across the different business groups, with minor differences. In most cases the local account managers are dedicated to one account, but in some sectors (e.g. food producers) this is not feasible and the local account managers have to serve several customers. The local account manager reports directly to the GAM, but has a dotted line to the local commercial manager and the local Shell organization, as they depend on local functions such as marketing and supply chain.

Benefits of Control GAM include the balance between global power and local knowledge, and engagement of local managers. For most companies this seems to be the best way to work with global accounts, and the many benefits outweigh the disadvantages of possible friction and the need to make changes in the company's organization structure.

Global account management at Hewlett-Packard

Hewlett-Packard is one of the pioneers and leaders in the use of GAM. We describe the HP programme in some detail here in order to illustrate how the different elements of a GAM programme can work together and evolve.

In the past two decades HP has developed a globally oriented organization to serve strategic global accounts. The original driver for this development was globalization of the computer systems industry and accompanying changes in customer behaviour. Originally, HP's GAM programme covered only certain segments of its business, but as customer needs became more sophisticated, the programme was gradually expanded to the whole company. Key for HP's programme is the balance between a single customer interface in the form of the account manager and account team on a global level, and specialist support for products, service and solutions on a local level.

Globalization drivers affecting the computer systems industry

Since the late 1980s there has been increasing pressure for globalization in the computer systems industry. A growing number of multi-national customers have centralized or coordinated purchasing and vendor selection. These multi-nationals require vendors to have the ability to serve them as a single entity around the globe. Furthermore, the customer focus has shifted from the product itself to its functionality, which has increased customer demands for global standardization and consistent services. Fast-changing technology accelerated the evolution from centralized mainframes to decentralized computer networks that are linked worldwide. Additionally, the importance of continuous innovation and time to market increased because of the opportunities that fast-changing technology provided. All these changes led to a revision of the traditional relationship between vendor and customer. Customers expect vendors to be strategic partners who understand their business needs and are able to provide appropriate products, services and solutions to their activities across the world.

HP strategy towards global account management

HP wants to be the trusted information technology (IT) advisor for its global accounts by increasing customer intimacy and satisfaction. This strategy is supported by building a strong competency in higher value-added services and driving HP further up the IT value chain. With the aim of providing direct customer support for key global accounts, HP has been expanding its global account management programme since 1991.

Currently the top 200 corporate accounts are classified as global accounts and handled in the HP GAM programme. Important components of this programme include having unified, empowered corporate account teams combined with strong specialist support, assigning executive sponsors for major accounts, having a worldwide company look and feel, and selecting the right accounts to be a corporate global account.

HP's account organization model

Creating a single interface to the account, HP designates a global client business manager (GCBM) for every global account. This GCBM is assisted by a global account team that comprises different HP disciplines. For major accounts, a high-level executive is also assigned to support the account interface. This encourages HP executives to be actively involved with accounts that are considered crucial to the company's long-term success. Furthermore, customers highly appreciate this direct connection to upper management. In addition to the global account interface, the customer can rely on local support. A number of regional account managers are responsible for the local management of the account. Product, service and solution specialists also work on this local level. These specialists can give the customer dedicated support and create a local closeness of experts to the different customer divisions.

To achieve a worldwide company look and feel, HP works with globally uniform commercial terms, infrastructure and company policies. Synchronization of company processes over the different regions ensures the delivery of similar services worldwide.

Role of the global client business manager

The GCBMs play a critical part in HP's GAM programme as they are responsible for the worldwide relationship with the customer. Key responsibilities of the GCBM include:

- Identifying and creating 'valued' opportunities that are beneficial to both the customer and HP.
- Marshalling and coaching HP and partner teams to pursue opportunities and execute commitments made to the customer.
- Measuring and improving customer satisfaction and loyalty.
- Meeting HP financial targets.
- Providing the primary focal point for managing executive communications and relationships between HP and the customer's management.

To live up to these responsibilities the GCBMs need to understand and communicate HP's capabilities in products, services and solutions. They also need a thorough understanding of the customer's business and business environment.

Selecting global accounts

Obviously, not all of HP's accounts are suitable for global account management. A typical global account would be a large multi-division, multi-national company that is one of the leaders in its markets. The customer does significant business with HP or shows potential for such. A good fit with HP's market focus and culture is also necessary to ensure the optimal results from global account management.

Value of the GAM programme to customers

Customers generally respond positively to the HP GAM programme. Most global accounts have a complex multi-national decision-making process. Therefore, HP's single focal point for account communications provides the clarity that customers value in a supplier. As the account team has a thorough understanding of the customer's business, they are able to bring proactive solutions and deliver best practices. The empowered GCBM and account team ensure fast decision making, which customers also appreciate. HP sees the programme as an important differentiator from its main competitors such as IBM and Xerox.

In line with its strategy, HP aims for long-term, mutually beneficial relationships with its strategic customers and makes major commitments to achieve these. Since its inception, HP considers its GAM programme to be a very successful way to realize these relationships and to develop a truly global organization.

Conclusion

This article shows that there is no single best way of organizing GAM. Managers need to find a suitable implementation of GAM elements for their own company situation. However, some best practices are valid for most companies:

- The right balance of global control and local flexibility.
- High-level executive support for the GAM organization.
- A clear, formal GAM programme that is neither too ill defined nor too rigid, and that is visible to the whole company.
- Integration of the GAM programme with the rest of the company organization; it needs to become part of the company culture.
- A cross-functional global account team.
- A workable and effective balance of power within the GAM programme.

There is plenty of scope for further research. Key issues to be explored include:

- When and how to make the transition from one structure of GAM to another.
- The performance consequences of different types of structure.
- Which types of processes best support the different structures.
- What variants there are for the three structures.
- How the different elements of organization structure can be best configured together under the different modes.

Designing strategic account management programmes

BY KAJ STORBACKA

Abstract

This paper aims to generate a better understanding of the design elements and related management practices of strategic account management programmes, in order to assists firms wishing to design such programmes. The research process is based on systematic combining of literature, empirical data from interviews with nine multi-national firms, interaction with the firms during the research, and the knowledge resource base of the Strategic Account Management Association.

A strategic account management programme (SAMP) is defined as a relational capability, involving task-dedicated actors, who allocate resources of the firm and its strategically most important customers, through management practices that aim at inter- and intra-organizational alignment, in order to improve account performance (and ultimately shareholder value creation). The research identified four inter-organizational alignment design elements – account portfolio definition, account business planning, account-specific value proposition and account management process – and four intra-organizational design elements – organizational integration, support capabilities, account performance management, and account team profile and skills. The management practices pertinent to each element are discussed.

Firms need to ensure that a SAMP is configured so that there is fit between the design elements discussed. Focus should be put on identifying framing elements that set the foundation for configuring effective programmes, as they determine the prerequisites for other elements.

The paper contributes to the literature on strategic account management by summarizing extant research and developing an organizing framework, informed by an empirical study.

Reproduced with the kind permission of Emerald Group Publishing: originally Storbacka, K. (2012) Strategic account management programmes: alignment of design elements and management practices. *Journal of Business & Industrial Marketing*, 27(4), 259–274.

Introduction

This paper is built on the premises that an under-investigated source of firm performance heterogeneity is the firm's ability to identify and manage customer relationships that contribute, or could contribute significantly (or critically), to the achievement of corporate objectives, present or future (Burnett 1992), or which are pivotal to a compound success in a market (Abratt and Kelly 2002). The unit of analysis in the paper is the management practices related to the management of strategically important customer relationships, or strategic accounts, defined by the Strategic Account Management Association (SAMA) as 'complex accounts with special requirements, characterized by a centralized, coordinated purchasing organization with multi-location purchasing influences, a complex buying process, large purchases, and a need for special services'.

Strategic account management focuses on co-creation of value (Vargo and Lusch 2008) and is both 'inside-out', that is, implements strategy in order to achieve agreed corporate goals, and 'outside-in', that is, identifies business and renewal opportunities by deeply understanding the customer's value-creating process, and influences the firm's strategic process (Gosselin and Heene 2003). According to Homburg et al. (2002), strategic account management programmes include 'special activities . . . such as pricing, products, services, distribution, and information sharing' that they involve 'in addition to marketing and sales, functional groups such as manufacturing, research and development, and finance' (pp. 40–42). Strategic account management is, hence, a set of boundary-spanning (McDonald et al. 1997; Piercy 2009; Singh and Rhoads 1991) management practices between the firm and the selected customers, between different functional groups and hierarchical levels within the firm and the customer's organization, and often between geographical areas (and, thus, cultures).

Piercy and Lane (2006) conclude that there are substantial risks related to the whole notion of strategic account management and specifically to the implementation of strategic account management programmes. Guesalaga and Johnston (2010) identified internal alignment as a key area of research and proposed that 'there is a need for a conceptual model for alignment' in strategic account management (p. 1067). This research answers to this call by focusing on both intra-organizational alignment of goals, principles and practices across functions, and inter-organizational alignment between the firm and its strategic accounts. Inter-organizational fit can be described as a 'high level of agreement or consistency between two interacting organizations' (Toulan et al. 2002, p. 3). Strategic account management can strive to influence intra- and inter-organizational fit by changing elements of the firm's business model and/or improving the interconnectedness of firm and customer business models. The alignment aims at improved performance of the account, both in terms of value creation for the strategic account and value capture for the firm.

Homburg et al. (2002) have suggested a configurational approach to key account management. A particularly important aspect of a configuration is to create harmony, consonance or fit between the elements of the configuration (Meyer et al. 1993; Miller 1996; Normann 2001). According to Meyer et al. (1993), configurations are constellations of design elements that commonly occur together because their interdependence makes them fall into patterns. Miller (1996, p. 509) suggests that configuration 'can be defined as the degree to which an organization's elements are orchestrated and connected by a single theme'. Miller suggests that typical themes could be innovation or efficiency. We argue that strategic account management can be a theme around which a pattern or programme can be orchestrated (Hui Shi et al. 2004).

This opens up questions regarding the opportunities for firms to design aligned and effective strategic account management programmes (or configurations). Baldwin and Clark (2000) suggest that a design can be viewed as an abstract description that encompasses both structure and function. Designs can be broken down into smaller units, called design parameters or elements. The elements of a strategic account management programme are management practices.

This article addresses the above research gaps and aims to generate a better understanding of the determinants of an aligned strategic account management programme in order to assist firms wishing to design such a programme. More precisely, the purpose of the article is to develop an inclusive and comprehensive framework that identifies the design elements and related management practices of strategic account management programmes. The paper contributes to the literature on strategic account management by summarizing extant research and developing an organizing framework, informed by an empirical study (MacInnis 2011).

The paper is structured as follows. First, we describe the research process and the methods used. Second, we give a broad description of the developed framework and the design elements of strategic account management programmes. Third, we describe the identified sets of management practices within each design element. Finally, we conclude by discussing implications, future research opportunities and managerial implications.

Research process

The research discussed in this paper was carried out in the Netherlands between September 2007 and April 2008, and involved a group of five sales management experts, as well as a group of nine multi-national firms headquartered in Belgium, Finland, Germany, the Netherlands and the United States, operating in different industries: management consulting, textiles, consumer electronics, elevators and escalators, office furniture, insurance, document handling, engineering and training. The case firms participated in the process as they have a keen interest in investigating the effectiveness of strategic account management programmes. The interaction with the participating firms involved senior-level executive vice-presidents and their direct reports.

The research process consisted of three phases: (1) the design elements phase, aimed at identifying possible design elements and creating a first version of a framework of strategic account management programmes; (2) the management practices phase, aimed at investigating various management practices, or sets of practices, for each design element; and (3) the interpretation phase, with the aim to finalize the framework and describe the management practices for each design element.

Between the phases we conducted two full-day research workshops with 2–3 representatives from each participating case firm. In the workshops the results of each phase were discussed with the firm representatives and initial results were refined according to comments received in the workshops. This process of member checks increased trustworthiness of our results (Lincoln and Cuba 1985; Wallendorf and Belk 1989). During the workshop, the researchers documented the discussions and collected written feedback and firm-specific examples of account management practices.

Eisenhardt (1989) has pointed out that conceptual frameworks are typically based on combining previous literature, common sense and experience. Our abductive research process was based on the systematic combination (Dubois and Gadde 2002) of literature, empirical data from interviews, interaction with the firms during the research seminars, and the knowledge resource base of SAMA. Abductive research strives to match theory and reality by a non-linear, path-dependent process of systematically combining empirical observations and insights from a continuous exposure to literature. According to Dubois and Gadde (2002, p. 555), matching is 'about going back and forth between framework, data sources, and analysis'. The research process followed this approach as we combined literature reviews with experience and learning from field-based research with reflective practitioners (Schön 1983). The author was working closely with some of the case firms, also conducting other forms of action research together with the companies (Gummesson 2000). The author is, additionally, closely linked to SAMA, and a regular contributor in its research seminars and conferences. As a consequence, informal and consulting-based interactions created common sense and experience that, together with the literature and the formal data collections, established a basis for the emerging framework explained below.

As the research proceeded, continuous iterations were made partly with extant literature (as listed in the references) and with the rich knowledge resource base of SAMA. The knowledge base, which is available online for members of SAMA, consists of research reports commissioned by SAMA, articles published in *Velocity* magazine (and its predecessors), white papers, and handouts from presentations by business executives (strategic account managers, SAMP managers and their superiors), consultants who focus on strategic account issues and academics. The material covers a period starting from 1997 and can be sorted by subject, keyword, author, title and other criteria. In addition to the *Velocity* articles, there are 68 research reports, 12 white papers and 651 presentation handouts covering every conceivable aspect of strategic account management.

In order to deepen the understanding of existing management practices, nine personal interviews with executives from the participating case firms were carried out, lasting between 73 and 187 minutes. The respondents were all senior managers (all with 15-plus years of industry experience) with titles such as Senior Vice-President Sales, Senior Partner, Business Unit Head, Vice-President Sales, Account Executive and Partner. This data generation aimed to provide a rich description of the strategic account management practices and followed a purposive sampling approach (e.g. Eisenhardt 1989; Patton 2002; Wallendorf and Belk 1989), where the content of each discussion was built on the basis of previous responses. As the interviews progressed, a framework was gradually built. After each set of interviews the data were categorized according to the data-analysis process of Spiggle (1994) and Strauss and Corbin (1990), building on emerging previous categories.

The narrative used in presenting the qualitative research is a combination of findings from the interactions with the representatives of the participating case firms, the expert interviews and the literature review. Due to the extent of the data, we have chosen to focus on presenting the final results of the research instead of the intermediary results or direct quotes or comments by the case firm representatives. In the text we indicate clearly when the comments by the participating firms have influenced the outcome.

In assessing the trustworthiness of the qualitative research we draw on Flint et al. (2002), who used assessment criteria from interpretive research and grounded theory. Building on Lincoln and Guba (1985), Miles and Huberman (1994), Spiggle (1994), Strauss and Corbin (1990), Wallendorf and Belk (1989), we focus on credibility, transferability, dependability, conformability, integrity and utilization. Based on the assessment elaborated in Table 1, we consider that our research met these criteria.

The design elements of a strategic account management programme

In this paper, a strategic account management programme is defined as a relational capability, involving task-dedicated actors, who allocate resources of the firm and its strategically most important customers, through management practices that aim at inter- and intra-organizational alignment, in order to improve account performance (and ultimately shareholder value creation). Account performance is to be viewed as both value capture and value creation (Storbacka and Nenonen 2009).

Table 1: Trustworthiness of the qualitative research process

Criteria	Method of address
Credibility (internal validity, authenticity) Extent to which the results appear to be acceptable representation of the data.	• Eight months of continuous interaction with industry representatives resulting in sufficient member checks. • Continuous process of combining literature findings with interview findings and inputs from workshops. • Two full-day workshops with 18–22 industry representatives from nine firms in different industries. *Result:* emergent framework was altered together with firm representatives as well as a result of dialogue among research team members, i.e. initial assumptions were refuted.
Transferability (external validity, fittingness) Extent to which the findings can be applied to other contexts.	• Nine multi-national firms representing nine different industries and four different European nationalities were interviewed and participated in the workshops. • Use of purposeful sampling. *Result:* findings can be transferred/generalized across several industries and European and possibly global business practices.
Dependability (reliability, auditability) Extent to which there is consistency of explanations.	• Workshop participants reflected on their current and previous experiences as individuals and as representatives of their firms. • Written feedback was collected during the workshops. *Result:* consistency across participants' stories and feedback.
Conformability (objectivity) Extent to which interpretations are the result of the participants and the phenomenon as opposed to researcher biases.	• A total of 22 representatives of the case firms gave feedback on the emergent results during two workshops. • Both the researcher and the informants were active participants and knowledge was constructed collaboratively. • Findings were presented to the participating firms and found useful. *Result:* interpretations were altered, expanded and refined.
Integrity Extent to which interpretations are influenced by misinformation from participants.	• Interviews were professional, friendly and anonymous. • Case firms participating in workshops were selected on a non-competitive basis in order to ensure openness. • Workshops were participative and dialogue centered: securing that all participants were able to express their view. • Participants were asked to voice their views in various ways and no forced conclusions were made. *Result:* participants were not trying to evade the issues being discussed.
Utilization (applicability, action orientation) Extent to which the findings are relevant for and can be used to benefit the participants.	• Two workshops were held where the research findings were discussed together with practical recommendations. • Case firms have adapted new practices based on the research. • The results have been presented in several executive education context and countries and managers have found the results useful. *Result:* participants benefited from the framework and conclusions of the research.

Based on the research process we developed a framework of a SAMP consisting of four inter-organizational alignment design elements – account portfolio definition, account business planning, account-specific value proposition and account management process – and of four intra-organizational design elements – organizational integration, support capabilities, account performance management, and account team profile and skills.

The elements in Figure 1 are divided into two groups – intra- and inter-organizational alignment – and organized on a circle around the raison d'être of the SAMP (roles and goals), in order to illustrate that all elements have to echo this meaning, and to highlight the interconnectedness and configurational fit between all elements: change of one element may require change of several others.

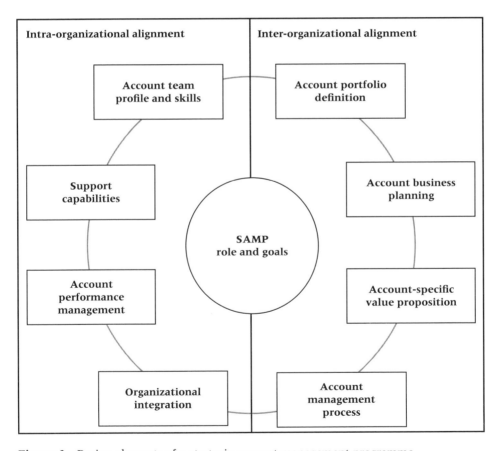

Figure 1 Design elements of a strategic account management programme

Piercy and Lane (2006), Wengler et al. (2006) and Sherman et al. (2003) suggest that many organizations have not yet recognized that there is a difference between strategic account management and key/major account selling. Sherman et al. (2003) suggest that a SAMP should be viewed as a business rather than a sales initiative. A SAMP should implement strategy in order to achieve agreed corporate goals, but it should also be a vehicle for top management to identify business and renewal opportunities, and influence the firm's strategy process by providing deep understanding of the customer's value-creating process, and align functional and business unit processes accordingly.

Typical goals that can be achieved with a SAMP are growth, improved profitability, reduced risk due to asset and information sharing, reduced risk due to volume commitments, reduced risk due to joint planning for future, trust and interdependence, reduced risk due to increased dependency by the customer, cost savings due to reduced production costs, reduced transaction costs due to better information, reduced uncertainty and routinized transactions, consistency leading to better fit which ultimately leads to increased efficiency and effectiveness, and facilitation of introduction of new products and services due to increased trust (Ellram 1991; Harvey et al. 2003; McDonald 2000; Senn 2006).

Inter-organizational alignment – practices related to aligning with customers

Napolitano (1997) suggested that the primary focus of strategic account management is to orchestrate the inter-organizational relationship in order to ensure the attainment of mutually beneficial goals. Inter-organizational alignment is defined as a process of increasing the organization's understanding of the selected customer's business concerns and opportunities, and jointly developing a value proposition and an encounter process for the delivery of the value proposition. It may require adaptation of both firm and customer business models and relational norms (Tuusjärvi and Möller 2009). Next, the four inter-organizational design elements of SAMPs (i.e. account portfolio definition, account business planning, account-specific value proposition and account management process) and the identified management practices will be presented in more detail.

Account portfolio definition

According to the case firms and the literature it is clear that selecting the right accounts for a SAMP portfolio is one of the keys to effectiveness (Woodburn and McDonald 2011). The opportunity costs of selecting the wrong accounts are considerable. Not only will the firm waste resources on the wrong account, but it may also lose the potential upside of deepening cooperation with a truly valuable account.

The case firms report that problems may arise if accounts are selected based only on a retrospective analysis, leading to increased resource allocations to accounts with a 'brilliant past'. In account selection, firms should focus on indicators that depict the future performance potential of the account (Spencer 1999).

What makes a customer relationship strategic varies among the case firms, based on their strategy, competitive situation, structure of customer base, industry logic and geographical spread (Gosselin and Bauwen 2006; Homburg et al. 2002; McDonald et al. 1997; Piercy and Lane 2006; Workman et al. 2003). Strategic accounts are to be viewed as relationships that are of strategic importance both to firm and customer (Gosselin and Heene 2003), indicating that the collaborative element requires commitment also from the customer. This notion is echoed by research findings indicating that the configurational fit between firm and customer business models is a key variable to explain account management performance (Gosselin and Heene 2003; Homburg et al. 2002; Workman et al. 2003).

The final portfolio of accounts can, based on the interaction with the case firms, be analysed in terms of homogeneity, i.e. does the firm select customers that portray similar strategic characteristics, or does it acknowledge that customers can be valuable and strategic for many reasons? Yorke and Droussiotis (1994) suggest that a combination of customer share and customer perceived strength could be used to differentiate between accounts. Storbacka (2004, 2006) suggests that customers can be divided into capacity optimization, cash flow maintenance, and renewal and growth portfolios, based on their role in supporting the firm in improving its performance.

Based on the interaction it seems that managing the selection process can be more important than setting the selection criteria. The SAMP needs to establish a management process, on a programme level, that defines a goal for the number of strategic accounts it plans to manage, defines how to establish and apply the selection criteria, and defines a decision-making procedure.

The decision-making process relates both to selecting and de-selecting strategic accounts. As the account environment is dynamic and dependent on competitive action, accounts that have been viewed as strategic at one stage may later develop in ways that do not warrant the strategic account investment level. This raises two important questions: how often is the choice made, and who makes the decision? McDonald et al. (1997) suggest that it takes time to align and develop an account in such a way that its performance improves. A particularly important view advocated by several case firms is that the development work needs to be done according to a certain procedure that is driven by the annual planning process of the firm. In many cases, firms' decisions on selection and de-selection are taken once a year. A typical decision-making process is based on the executive committee making yearly decisions based on suggestions by the SAMP organization's analysis and consequent proposals.

Account business planning

The case firms view strategic account management as a long-term activity, building on resource allocations that should not be changed lightly or too frequently.

SAMP could be viewed as an investment process, whereby the firm (and the customer) invests in their relationship in order to balance risks and return. There could, according to McDonald et al. (1997, p. 742), be a ten-year span from 'identifying the attractiveness of an account to achieving the full potential of the relationship with that organization'. Decisions about such investments require an investment plan, called in this context an account business plan.

Based on the research we conclude that the plan and the planning process fulfil three roles. The account planning process is, first and foremost, a mechanism for enhancing organizational (Senge 1990) or network (Peters et al. 2010) learning by involving information acquisition, information dissemination and shared interpretation activities, often executed using a database that could be viewed as an organizational memory (Slater and Narver 1995). According to Abratt and Kelly (2002), the firms and the account teams need to acquire information that helps them to understand the customer and their main concerns, problems and strategic issues. The information and the conclusions drawn from it should be recorded in a database. The case firms report that the information acquisition is a team effort that crosses functional borders and involves top management.

Second, as all case firms establish, the account business plan is a tool to get commitment from firm management to assign the resources needed to develop the account in such a way that the identified potentials can be realized. Gosselin and Heene (2003) argue that in order to secure the performance of the account, a strategic account manager must be able to address all the existing competences of the company.

The third role relates to inter- and intra-organizational alignment. The case firms use the account business plan as a tool for communicating about the account's business internally in the firm, in order to create awareness and promote an account-oriented culture, and within the customer organization in order to stimulate demand (cf. Millman and Wilson 1999).

The plans discussed with the case firms typically cover issues such as description of the strategic account (business environment, technical environment), extant offering and relationship process, analysis of the relationship (customer's value-creating process, value capture, future business potential), resource allocation and responsibilities between account manager and team, opportunity articulation, monetary and operational goals, action plan (generic, common actions, account-specific actions) and a contact matrix (describing the contact patterns between firm team members and customer representatives).

The resource allocations, defined in the case firms' account business plans, can be divided into 'P&L investments' (i.e. cost allocations from increased activity levels) and 'balance sheet investments' (i.e. actions that are visible in the balance sheet and influence the level of capital invested in the account). Examples of account investments are sales projects, joint R&D projects, product, service or customer service process adaptations and customizations, financing of inventory, distribution channel financing, investments into business process alignment initiatives, marketing support to channel companies, discounting schemes, and opportunity costs for the resource allocations made.

A strategic account business plan should be firmly rooted in corporate strategy as it taps into the firm's strategic resources. The case firms report that hence the planning process needs to be connected to the yearly planning cycle of the corporation, given that such a cycle exists. Corporate planning needs to give its input to strategic account planning, specifically focusing on the goal setting for the strategic accounts, and conversely, strategic account planning should feed corporate planning with investment needs and ideas for new offerings.

Account-specific value proposition

Homburg et al. (2002), McDonald et al. (1997), Millman and Wilson (1999), Sengupta et al. (1997b), Sherman et al. (2003) and Wengler et al. (2006) show that the key difference between account selling and strategic account management is that the value proposition for the selected strategic customers is 'special', specific to the account and different from what other customers are being offered. Literature discusses issues such as 'outsourcing of non-core processes', 'moving downstream in the value chain', 'transitioning from products to services' and moving 'from selling products to selling solutions' (Auguste et al. 2006; Oliva and Kallenberg 2003; Wise and Baumgartner 1999).

According to Vargo and Lusch (2008), firms can only make value propositions: since value is always determined by the customer (value-in-use), it cannot be embedded through manufacturing (value-in-exchange). A value proposition is defined as the firm's suggestion to the customer on how its resources and capabilities, expressed as artifacts (goods, service, information and processual components, such as experiences), can enable the customer to create value (Flint and Mentzer 2006). Anderson et al. (2006) suggest that a firm should identify all benefits customers receive from the offering, identify the favourable points of difference, and pinpoint the one or two aspects of difference whose improvement will deliver the greatest value to the customer.

The idea of a value proposition relates to the discussion about solutions referring to the practice of integration or adaptation of firm processes to create a better fit with the customer's processes (Brady et al. 2004; Davies et al. 2006; Miller et al. 2002) and 'systems selling' (Millman 1996). Millman (p. 632) sees systems selling as 'delivering a comprehensive "package" or "bundle" of product/service attributes and benefits to selected customers. The package may comprise both standardized and customized components; including hardware, software, installation, product/process know-how, maintenance, consultancy, training, etc., normally promoted to customers as a "total solution" from a single source.'

The case firms pinpoint that from an operations management point of view, a firm has to do trade-offs in relation to its strategy. Siggelkow (2002) argues that flexible manufacturing systems and wide product variety reinforce each other: the wider the product variety, the more valuable are investments in increasing the flexibility of the manufacturing system, and conversely, the more flexible the manufacturing system, the greater the benefit (i.e. the lower the cost) of increasing product variety. However, a firm has to choose between various dimensions of operational performance as no plant or operations system can provide superior performance in all dimensions simultaneously (Heikkilä and Holmström 2006). A typical trade-off that needs to be discussed is the trade-off between standardization and customization: an increase in product variation increases the average unit cost if operating policies remain unchanged.

In many case firms the outcome of standardization/differentiation optimization would be to find a balance between standardized modules and a capability to efficiently assemble different module combinations in order to customize account-specific offerings (cf. Böttcher and Klingner 2011; Raddats 2011). In order to make sales and marketing of solutions more effective, some firms make predefined combinations or solutions. These give the customer the possibility to select a suitable module combination which is close to the ready-made solution. Predefined solution configurations make sales easier because there is less need for tailoring.

Account management process

Abratt and Kelly (2002) argue that strategic accounts have complex needs and require individual attention through a carefully established relationship process. Millman and Wilson (1999) argue that strategic account management processes are 'those activities, mechanisms and procedures which facilitate the effective management of [strategic] accounts' (p. 328).

Based on the research, the account management process has four roles, which can be interpreted as process steps. First, the process aims at generating knowledge and disseminating a shared interpretation of this knowledge as a foundation for value creation. This is called 'customer knowledge competence' by Campbell (2003). Knowledge flows can, based on Gebert et al. (2003), be classified into three categories: (1) knowledge for customers, i.e. knowledge of products, markets and suppliers; (2) knowledge about customers, i.e. customer histories, connections, requirements, expectations and purchasing activity; and (3) knowledge from customers, i.e. knowledge gathered to sustain continuous improvement or new product development (Nicolajsen and Scupola 2011).

Several of the case firms had invested in processes aimed at supporting all these knowledge flows simultaneously and reciprocally. These processes are related to lead customer involvement and customer value research. Involving lead customers was viewed as essential for the success of account management, especially if the value proposition is complex and developing. By conducting customer value research the firms aimed at mapping the customers' processes, identifying business concerns and opportunities, and understanding what is valuable for them. A particularly important aspect was to focus on untapped needs or proactively sense customer expectation and specifications that are not expressed explicitly.

Another key issue was to analyse the customer's situation as a part of the complete value chain or network.

Second, the process involves the sales process, whereby value propositions are turned into orders. According to Tuli et al. (2007, p. 14), 'selling solutions is a complex exercise that involves the consideration of conflicting requirements of multiple stakeholders in a customer organization and sales cycles lasting up to two years'. For the case firms, sales and sales management were, therefore, mostly seen as a sub-activity (although an essential one) of strategic account management. The total account management process aims at ensuring continuous business and generating business opportunities. The role of the sales process is to cultivate the opportunities for orders.

Third, the role of the process is to secure the delivery of the agreed value proposition. Tuli et al. (2007) report that customers view a solution as a set of customer–supplier relational processes comprising customer requirement definition, customization and integration of goods and/or services, their deployment, and post-deployment customer support. This highlights the role of the strategic account manager as the champion of value creation and not only as the salesperson. It also pinpoints the need for 'after-sales' support in the form of various services (Kowalkowski et al. 2011).

For the case firms, the account management process begins by establishing a view on the encounters necessary in order to deliver the value proposition. These encounters will be handled by different functions and on different organizational levels. In addition, encounters may be carried out in different channels.

Fourth, the process builds relationship strength and longevity, by attaining goal congruence and systematically constructing bonds, consisting of mutual resource dependencies with relationship-specific resource allocations or investments (Sengupta et al. 1997a). Hui Shi et al. (2004) discuss this in terms of achieving configurational fit in a global account management context. There are two specific types of fit to be achieved: standardization fit refers to the supplier standardizing its products to match the standardization demand of the strategic account, while coordination fit refers to the extent to which value-adding activities are planned and executed interdependently in a coordinated manner.

The case firms see the symmetry of relationships in terms of power and resources as a central tenet in managing relationships with strategic customers. Reciprocity has been shown to be important in symmetric relationships. Demonstrating flexibility to the customer shows that the firm is not exploiting the customer's commitment and creates the infrastructure of long-term orientation in buyer–seller relationships: i.e. trust (Ganesan 1994).

The role of personal relationships as social bonds was debated during the research process. The trend seems to be towards matched systems and processes (Sharma 2006) instead of purely personal relationships. One particular viewpoint that the case firms highlighted was top-management involvement, which grows in importance as the accounts become more strategic. Senn (2006) reports that Siemens is experiencing success using a top executive relationship process that aims at 'orchestrating contact among customers and Siemens executives; obtaining executive support for the contact planning; establishing a consistent process for executive meetings and actions; and systematically managing information gained from the executive engagement' (p. 29).

Intra-organizational alignment – practices related to creating a collaborative culture of commitment

The intra-organizational alignment relates to creating a collaborative culture of customer focus, flexibility and commitment. According to the case firms, this requires that all employees and functions of the firm understand the strategic account's status and needs, the value proposition given to the account, and that they are committed to provide the resources necessary to support the account's performance (Abratt and Kelly 2002; Day 2011; Millman and Wilson 1999). This alignment is often referred to as one of the central determinants of SAMP effectiveness. Homburg et al. (2002) report that cross-functional KAM companies stand out with respect to both performance in the market and adaptiveness.

Next, the four intra-organizational design elements of SAMPs (i.e. account team profile and skills, support capabilities, account performance management and organizational integration) and the related management practices will be discussed in more detail.

Account team profile and skills

McDonald et al. (1997) conclude that in order to coordinate day-to-day interaction under the umbrella of a long-term relationship, selling companies typically form dedicated teams headed up by a strategic account manager. The strategic account manager can be defined as the custodian of the strategic customer relationship, orchestrating the deployment of firm-wide resources to provide the delivery of the value proposition.

A strategic account manager is a role that can be characterized as boundary spanning (Singh 1993; Singh and Rhoads 1991) and as such characterized by issues related to autonomy, authority and consideration (i.e. levels of support from superiors, co-workers and customer representatives). Millman and Wilson (1999) refer to an account manager as a 'political entrepreneur', highlighting the strategic, business management and relational requirements.

The experience backgrounds, competences and skills needed to perform the task of a strategic account manager are far beyond those of a salesperson (Gosselin and Heene 2003). As McDonald et al. (1997, p. 748) state: 'A key account manager needs far more skills than a sales person. In fact, it is misleading to consider it as merely an extension of a sales career.' In order to manage across firm–customer, functional and cultural boundaries they have to have knowledge and/or experience from sales, marketing, business development, strategy, control and operations, as well as command high levels of authority and status in both their own company and the customer's organization (Cespedes et al. 1989).

According to Gosselin and Heene (2003), the strategic account manager 'must be positioned and viewed in the company as a senior executive, responsible for participating in shaping the business strategy through his competence and knowledge of key customers' (p. 25). The case firm interaction indicates that the strategic account manager needs the credibility of seniority to be able to convincingly discuss strategic and financial issues with the customer (and firm) top management. The strategic account manager has to have the willingness to develop the account on a long-term basis. They are not necessarily the best salesperson, or the one with the longest experience of the customer, but the one who is best positioned to improve the performance of the account.

The skill sets are, hence, very close to those of a general manager. McDonald et al. (1997) report that typical account manager skills would be integrity, product/ service knowledge, communication skills, understanding the customer's business and business environment, and selling/negotiating skills. Sherman et al. (2003) refer to a specific skill set for the strategic account manager: the ability and willingness to take initiative, commit time and effort to ensure success, provide proactive assistance/support, develop technical competencies and train others. Capon (2001) defines and differentiates between business management skills, boundary-spanning and relational skills, leadership and team-building skills.

The skill sets required to successfully manage strategic accounts are varied and usually require a team of individuals – sometimes on both the firm and the customer side (Narus and Anderson (1995) refer to this as 'group-on-group sales'). Weitz and Bradford (1999) argue that cross-functional teams are necessary because the individual salesperson does not cover all the facets of firm resources and competences, nor will they by themselves possess enough intra-firm influence to propose and implement value propositions that create competitive advantage. Increasingly, managing the strategic account is a team effort involving sales, marketing, operations, finance/control and logistics (Jones et al. 2005; Kempeners and van der Hart 1999).

The number of team members and the formalization of the team effort in the case firms vary, based on SAMP goals and characteristics, between formal and informal teams; they may even involve representatives from the customer organization. There is surprisingly little research on factors influencing the effectiveness of team selling, although most researchers argue for a shift of focus in the unit of analysis from the individual sales person to the selling team (Workman et al. 2003).

A central theme related to the role of a strategic account manager, identified in the interaction with the case firms, is their ability to deal with conflicts (Atanasova and Senn 2011) and influence people both within and outside the firm. If the team-building is informal, strategic account managers exert influence without any formal authority. Helsing et al. (2003) provide the following model for creating impact without authority: establish personal credibility, build internal network, create customer advocates, determine organization feasibility, apply influence skills and involve senior management. Cohen and Bradford (2005) have identified five different types of organizational currencies that can be exchanged as a basis for exerting influence: inspiration (providing inspirational visionary goals), task (providing support, resources, assistance and knowledge), position (providing possibilities to enhance career and become recognized by higher-ups), relationship (providing closeness, emotional backing) and personal (providing learning and creation of self-esteem).

Formal account teams may perform more effectively in more complex relationships where the value proposition requires both input from many functions in the firm and ability to change elements of the customer's business model and value-creating process. In formal team arrangements, team members need to allocate time that they devote to their account. Team members spend less time in front of the customer than the strategic account manager, but they ensure that everything happens smoothly in each encounter. As McDonald et al. (1997) conclude, the strategic 'account manager conducts the orchestra' (p. 753).

The findings from the case firms emphasize the difficulty in finding individuals with the necessary skill sets required for strategic account management. Many of them are increasingly recruiting strategic account managers who do not have a sales background. Experience of managing teams or business units is perceived as more important than sales experience. The team set-up varies greatly. Most of the case firms report more interest in defining formal rather than informal account teams. The reasons seem to concur with the suggestions of Jones et al. (2005): increased complexity of the firm's offering, the need for a richer set of information exchange between firm and customer, and the relative size and inherent risks of the account.

Support capabilities

There are several 'sub-capabilities' needed in strategic account management programmes. Already in the research project on national account management, launched by the Marketing Science Institute in the early 1980s, it became evident that account management is an organizational process and that the account managers need support systems. Shapiro and Moriarty (1984) suggest that certain parts of the organization, beyond account managers, need to be integrated: information systems, administration, field and technical service, logistics, manufacturing/operations management, application engineering, development and product engineering, finance, legal, control and marketing. Based on the interaction with the case firms it can be concluded that all of these are true also today. The level and content of support are dependent on the firm's strategy, the SAMP content and roles, and the dynamic of the industry.

Effective organizations are configurations of management practices which facilitate the development of knowledge that becomes the basis of competitive advantage (Day 2011; Slater and Narver 1995). Gosselin and Heene (2003) claim that a SAMP is involved in the process of building competences. Hence, the role of information processing and sharing is key for effectiveness (Birkinshaw et al. 2001), and technology can be a central tool (Sharma 2006) in terms of sales force automation or CRM systems that facilitate a common database and support tools for encounters.

Based on Day (1994, 2003) and Sharma (2006), it can be suggested that the creation of environmental (market sensing, technology monitoring) and competitive scanning processes is important as inputs to the account business planning process (focusing on 'customer scanning'). The case firms argue that customers are often conservative. Hence, investing only in 'customer listening processes' may become a barrier against renewal and innovation. Customer insight, therefore, has to be matched with business intelligence. Day (1994) argues that there needs to be a matching of outside-in processes and inside-out processes of technology, manufacturing and logistics.

The interaction with the case firms identified two specific capabilities, which usually reside outside the account management teams, that the teams need to be able to access. First, support in value quantification and account performance monitoring from business controllers is needed in order to show to firm and customer that the account performs according to the role and goal definitions. Second, account teams may need extensive support in contract management from legal departments – especially in cross-national contexts, involving cross-legal structures and/or changing earnings logics (for instance, long-term service contracts) – to manage the long-term legal risks.

Account performance management

Building on Workman et al. (2003), strategic account management effectiveness is defined as the extent to which account performance improves. The underlying assumption is that relationship goals – such as development of trust, increased information sharing, reduction of conflicts and commitment to maintain the relationship – lead to positions of advantage (Day 1994) and this in turn leads to improved performance in the market, such as revenue growth, market share, customer satisfaction and retention of customers.

The argument by Ulaga (2003) that measurement of value creation in buyer–seller relationships is still in its infancy seems to fit with the empirical reality. Flint and Mentzer (2006) argue that customer business value can be viewed in several ways. Pardo et al. (2006) have identified three categories of value in an account management context: exchange value, which is the value originating in activities by the firm and being consumed by the customer; proprietary value, being created and consumed only by the firm (or the customer) as it creates and operates its account activities for its efficiency or effectiveness exclusively; and relational value, the co-produced value (for firm and customer) that emanates from being party to a relational constellation embedded in collaborative and cooperative activities.

Account performance is defined as the total value formed during the interaction between firm and customer over time. According to Storbacka and Nenonen (2009), an essential managerial aspect of account performance is to define how the value is shared between the firm (value capture) and the customer (value creation). Blois and Ramirez (2006) argue that although firms exist to help customers and organizations to create value, they do so only in order to capture part of that value for themselves. However, it is important to note that long-term value capture is not possible if the customer does not perceive that the relationship creates value to the customer. Value creation is hence a prerequisite for value capture (e.g. Gosselin and Bauwen 2006).

Storbacka and Nenonen (2009) suggest that value capture can be measured by the discounted present value of all future economic profit that the customer relationship generates, and this can be used as a proxy for the shareholder value creation. Economic profit defines the net operating profit after tax (NOPAT) and subtracts the cost of capital for the economic book value of firms' assets used in the customer relationship under analysis. Thus, the key components of economic profit on a dyad level are revenue from the relationship, total cost incurred by the relationship and the capital invested in the relationship.

The case firms report that as strategic account management is a long-term investment, it is of particular importance not to rely on retrospective (lagging) indicators of value but also take a longitudinal view (developments over periods of analysis) and identify prospective (leading) indicators. Examples of leading indicators used are customer acquisition cost, customer retention or turnover of customer base, number of long-term contracts, order backlog, communication efficiency, advance payments, receivables turnover, inventory turnover, invested capital, automation rate of repetitive core tasks, make/buy ratio of non-core tasks, sales funnel size and new product development.

A value proposition should also involve the process of quantifying the effect of applying the proposition to the customer's value-creating process. Sherman et al. (2003) report that firms that quantify the value they deliver to customers tend to be more successful in their strategic account management programmes. Anderson et al. (2006) suggest that, based on case evidence, value propositions must be distinctive, measurable (quantifiable in monetary terms) and sustainable for a significant period of time. The quantification of value can be done for each account-specific value proposition using 'value word equations' (i.e. demonstrating the logic by which a feature turns into a benefit and how this can be measured), or based on long-term evidence from similar accounts, using 'value case histories' (i.e. to demonstrate the value generated in previous situations and use these as references).

Organizational integration

For the case firms, a SAMP was above all an organizational challenge. Most organizations tend to have a structure focusing on product and geography. Adding the 'third dimension', i.e. the customer or account viewpoint, raises questions relating to efficiency, complexity and flexibility. Within a product-focused organizational structure, salespeople are essentially product specialists (Homburg et al. 2000). The idea of a SAMP is to enable account managers to build value by understanding and responding to concerns and opportunities that customers encounter. This may require the ability to assess the whole value chain, including customers' customers and possible end-users. According to the case firms, the difficulty of an account management organization stems from the fact that the strategic account manager (and his team) does not only act as a liaison, or coordinator, but rather as the 'single point of contact' for the customer, interpreting the customer's situation, making value propositions and ensuring that the promised value is delivered.

The research shows that a firm wanting to succeed with a SAMP needs to design its structure and management process in order to be responsive to the strategic customers. Strategic account management cannot be confined to the sales functions, but rather it crosses the boundaries between several functions, product areas, geographical areas and hierarchical levels (Storbacka et al. 2009). Hannan et al. (1996, p. 506) suggest that an organizational element is part of the 'organizational core if changing it requires adjustments in most other features of the enterprise . . . coreness means connectedness, elements in the core are linked in complicated webs of relations with each other and with peripheral elements'. Based on the research, we suggest that a SAMP is a core element of the organization for the firm that chooses to implement it (Piercy 2010).

Strategic account management usually entails quite a lot of conflicts (Atanasova and Senn 2011) as there may be poor goal congruence both across functions in the firm and across organizational boundaries. Some of these cannot be solved structurally; instead management may need to focus less on solving conflicts and more on reconciliation of dilemmas (Trompenaars and Hampden-Turner 1998). What is required is contextual ambidexterity, defined by Gibson and Birkinshaw (2004, p. 209) as 'the behavioural capacity to simultaneously demonstrate alignment and adaptability across an entire business unit'. Furthermore, Workman et al. (2003, p. 10) show that esprit de corps – defined as the 'extent to which people involved in the management of [strategic] accounts feel obligated to common goals and to each other' – is a key determinant of effectiveness.

The above analysis puts emphasis on the firm's top management (Workman et al. 2003). Based on the interaction with the case firms it is evident that strategic integration needs to happen in the executive committee. Senior management need to steer a balance between driving innovation together with customers and improving firm efficiency by standardizing, being centralized and decentralized, and focusing on short-term and long-term simultaneously (Gibson and Birkinshaw 2004).

With a few exceptions (generally very large global accounts that are organized as separate business units), the case firms' SAMPs are structurally organized in some matrix with regard to the prevailing product and/or geographical structure. This creates a need for transparency – solving issues related to measurement, remuneration and management of strategic account managers is essential to succeed. The matrix leads to a situation where strategic account managers have a solid line to a specific business unit and a dotted line to the account (sometimes semi-formal) team. In addition, there usually is a dotted line to a SAMP office or a senior manager in charge of the SAMP. McDonald et al. (1997) claim there is need for a steering committee at top management level, where the strategic account team and functional teams can troubleshoot implementation. Gosselin and Heene (2003) claim that the strategic account manager must be a part of the firm's executive decision process. The case firms pinpoint that being part of the process may mean there are rules for escalation, i.e. when there is need to secure access to resources (such as production capacity) in order to deliver the value proposition promised to the strategic account, the account management team needs to have access to functional or business unit decision-making.

Discussion

This research responds to recent calls to improve firms' capability to connect business processes that cut across traditional organizational silos (Bolton 2006) and to a more general call for conceptual articles in marketing (Yadav 2010). More specifically, the research deals with concerns, expressed by Guesalaga and Johnston (2010), about the lack of academic research on strategic account management topics viewed as important by practitioners. They particularly identified four areas where there is lack of or no academic research available: organizing for key/strategic account management, adaptation of key/strategic account management approaches, the role of senior management in key/strategic account management, and internal alignment as a critical determinant of performance with key/strategic accounts.

The SAMP framework developed contributes to the above mentioned research gaps. Informed by an abductive empirical process, a framework was developed that summarizes and organizes extant research into a managerially actionable form (MacInnis 2011). In addition to the internal alignment issues it acknowledges the need to find a balance between internal and external alignment. Hence, alignment was chosen as the key dimension in the framework.

Alignment, configurational fit, equifinality and formalization

As the research aimed at developing an inclusive and comprehensive framework, the paper covers and summarizes a wide variety of literature pertinent to the adaptation of an effective SAMP. The discussion of the design elements illustrates the complexity of the task: alignment requires the simultaneous and cross-functional development of a multitude of capabilities and management practices.

A central contribution to the strategic account management literature, and specifically to the alignment issue, is the argument for a configurational approach.

Miller (1996, p. 511) argues that 'the fit among the elements of an organization may be evidenced by the degree to which strategy, structure and systems complement one another'. Elements are said to interact if the value of one element depends on the presence of the other element; to reinforce each other if the value of each element is increased by the presence of the other element; and to be independent if the value of an element is independent of the presence of another element. A firm with many elements that reinforce each other is said to have a high degree of internal fit (Siggelkow 2002). Creating a successful configuration implies that the core elements are reinforcing, such that the overall system is in a state of coherence or consistency (Siggelkow 2002), or as Miller and Friesen (1984, p. 21) argue, 'configuration, in essence, means harmony'.

This is depicted in the framework (Figure 1) by the circle that illustrates that alignment starts with a clearly articulated raison d'être for the SAMP, and pinpoints the interconnectedness between all design elements: change of one element may require change of several others. Hence, the contribution of this research is not so much in the identification of any specific new aspect of strategic account management; the contribution centres on describing how effectiveness in a SAMP is achieved by securing configurational fit between the various design elements and management practices. The research suggests that the vulnerabilities and risks of strategic account management (Piercy and Lane 2006) can be decreased and controlled by creating a SAMP with high levels of configurational fit.

Homburg et al. (2002) report that several approaches to strategic account management are equally successful. This supports the argument often discussed in the configurational approach (Meyer et al. 1993; Miller 1996): the idea of equifinality. Equifinality implies that different configurations can be effective as long as they are configured in such a way that there is internal fit or congruence between the elements. The SAMP elements discussed in the paper are likely to be present in all configurations of programmes; elements will interact, be reinforcing and independent, but they will be configured differently in different contexts. As a result of the research method used in this paper, it was not possible to systematically compare the SAMP configurations of the participating case firms. Based on the interactions during the process it is clear, however, that the configurational set-ups were quite different, due not only to the development stage of the SAMP but also to differences in strategies and industry logics. This constitutes a very interesting area for further research, as discussed in the next section.

The research results can be viewed to contradict some of the earlier findings by Workman et al. (2003) on whether strategic account management needs to be formalized in order for it to be effective. Workman et al. (2003) define formalization as the 'extent to which an organization has established policies and procedures for handling its most important set of customers' (p. 11). Surprisingly, they do not find a positive correlation between formalization and effectiveness and conclude that 'activities and resources are more important than actors and formalization' (p. 16).

Rather than a formalized programme they claim that firms need to do differential things for their strategic accounts, they need to do them proactively, and align their organization in order to provide the support needed to deliver on the promises made to strategic accounts. This prescription, however, easily sounds like a prescription of formalization – creating an interesting conflict in the interpretation of their research. They also conclude – in a footnote – that powerful, and maybe therefore not so profitable, customers demand highly formalized programmes and that this has had an impact on their empirical results.

Building on Wengler et al. (2006), this research suggests another explanation. Wengler et al. suggest that there is a difference between 'strategic account management' and 'key/major account selling' (cf. Piercy and Lane 2006; Sherman et al. 2003). If the organizations are focusing only on the latter, they often feel that there is no need for formalization outside the marketing/sales organization. As a SAMP requires cross-functional alignment, our research suggests that it benefits from a formalized configuration.

Further research avenues

There are several possible avenues for further research. First, the management practices identified can be developed into measures for a quantitative study, aimed at comparing capabilities and management practices between firms. This assessment should be combined with firm performance measures, in order to create more understanding of how effective SAMPs can support firm performance.

Second, more understanding should be created of different types of SAMP configurations; are there possibly generic configurations? This can be viewed as a limitation of the present research as it does not investigate how the differences in firm strategies, industry characteristics or business logics influence the configurational set-up of a SAMP. Several attempts have been made to classify strategic account management configurations. Millman and Wilson (1995) developed a typology for the different (life cycle) stages of development of strategic account relationships. This typology was developed by McDonald et al. (1997) and finally by McDonald and Woodburn (1999) into a continuum from exploratory to integrated. Piercy and Lane (2006) distinguish between major accounts and strategic accounts. Homburg et al. (2002) arrive at a taxonomy of eight approaches or configurations of [key] account management, ranging from 'No KAM' and 'Country club KAM', to 'Cross-functional, dominant KAM' and 'Top-management KAM'. Gosselin and Bauwen (2006) have created a typology of accounts (transactional, captive, key and strategic accounts) and claim that there are only two types of relationships that will be possible in the long run: the partnership-based strategic accounts and transactional sales-based accounts. Arnold et al. (2001), Birkinshaw et al. (2001), Gosselin and Bauwen (2006), Harvey et al. (2003), Millman (1996), Montgomery and Yip (2000), Senn (1999), Wilson and Weilbaker (2004) and Yip and Madsen (1996) pinpoint the fact that the geographical dimension drives both intra- and inter-organization complexity, which warrants for the distinction between key account and global account management. Finally, Al-Hasan and

Brennan (2009) argue that there are cultural issues to consider when applying key account management practices in developing countries.

In addition to the above proposed categorizations, efficient configurations of the SAMP elements can be dependent on a number of internal issues, for example whether the programme focuses on innovation and exploration or on efficiency and exploitation. Configurations can also be determined based on relationship characteristics such as customer buying behaviour (Bensaou 1999; Kaario et al. 2004; Kraljic 1983), customer asset management portfolios (Storbacka 2004, 2006) and relationship patterns (Anderson and Narus 1991; Ford et al. 2003).

Finally, configurations can also be determined based on industry characteristics and business logics. Eisenhardt and Martin (2000) explore differences between moderately dynamic and high-velocity environments. The research process suggest that firms operating with an installed base of captive equipment (Oliva and Kallenberg 2003) adapt different configurations compared with process industry firms supplying offerings that function as inputs to the customer's manufacturing process.

Conclusions

The most obvious conclusion based on this research is the need for managers to realize the interconnectedness of the design elements and management practices of a SAMP. The whole notion of configurational fit implies interdependence. As an outcome, the effective alignment of a SAMP means the simultaneous and cross-functional development of management practices. The research suggests that creating excellence in one particular design element will not improve effectiveness; what is required is the incremental and parallel development of many elements. With this systemic development view, firms can gradually secure the alignment of firm strategy and SAMP practices.

An interesting managerial question is whether elements are reinforcing and whether there are critical elements that set the foundation for configuring effective programmes. These elements could be called framing elements as they set the scene and determine the prerequisites for other elements. It is, for instance, obvious that several of the elements reinforce each other horizontally across the model. The support capabilities will have an impact on the account business planning and the planning will build support capabilities. The account-specific value proposition will form the basis for the follow-up of account performance and the metrics selected to measure account performance will influence the definition of value propositions. There is also a reinforcing effect between the account team profile and the defined account management process.

There are reinforcing effects vertically and diagonally between elements. The account business plan will obviously influence the account management process, and vice versa. The organizational integration will influence the account team's ability to create interesting value propositions and deliver them.

Based on the research process, some elements can be said to be critical or framing elements. The first element, which has already been defined and depicted as framing, is the SAMP role and goals. The issue that will frame a firm's ability to improve account performance the most is the level of coreness, i.e. how core or peripheral is the SAMP for the firm, in relation to its strategy and corporate goals. If the SAMP is peripheral, it means that the account team will not get access to the resources that need to be invested in the account in order to improve performance. The simplest way to approach this is to ask why a firm would start a SAMP. Boles et al. (1999) identified many different reasons: increase market share, change in business strategy, allow increased product/service customization, ensure better customer relationships, marketplace pressures, becoming more attractive to large clients, and a general category including issues such as gaining a competitive advantage and providing increased customer satisfaction. Many of the reasons are likely to frame the SAMP in a favourable way.

Second, the definition of the account portfolio will determine the mode of the programme. Success in selecting customers with a strategic fit, in terms of willingness to build collaborative relationships, will frame much of the other elements: the planning, definition of value proposition, the account management process, account team profile and organizational integration. Selecting accounts is certainly one of the key drivers of demand heterogeneity and will, hence, influence firm performance heterogeneity. Viewing customers as assets also implies that also strategic customers should be divided into portfolios. In the light of the customer portfolios presented by Storbacka (2004, 2006), it seems evident that a firm wishing to maximize shareholder value creation should not manage strategic accounts as one homogeneous group.

The third framing element is the value proposition. A value proposition defines both the work division and the earnings logic of the account and will, hence, drive the ability to improve the performance. At its best the value proposition can be used to decrease demand heterogeneity. In high-velocity environments, demand heterogeneity is usually greater, as there is no 'dominant design'. By collaborating in research and development with strategically important customers, a firm can create preference overlap or preference symmetry that evolves into a dominant design, decreasing demand heterogeneity, thus helping the firm to position itself in the market (Adner 2002).

Global customer team design: dimensions, determinants and performance outcomes

BY YANA ATANASOVA AND CHRISTOPH SENN

Abstract

Designing and implementing global customer teams (GCTs) represents a key task for suppliers that are expanding the scope of their customer relationships. However, research has not provided an explanation of how these teams function and what determines their performance. Using an interdisciplinary combination of concepts from customer management and organizational behaviour research streams, we develop an integrative framework of GCT design and performance. The framework is conceptualized with qualitative interview data and validated with survey data from 273 members of 113 GCTs in six multi-national companies. Our results indicate that team performance is influenced directly by three team processes: communication and collaboration, conflict management and proactiveness. Team design in terms of goal and role definition, customer coverage, empowerment, heterogeneity, skills adequacy and leadership indirectly influences performance, mediated by team processes. In addition, three factors of the organizational environment – top-management support, rewards and incentives, and training – have similar indirect effects.

Introduction

Driven by the search for both new business opportunities and competitive advantages, companies in business-to-business markets increasingly have moved away from transactional forms of exchange (Dyer 1997) to look for closer, more collaborative relationships with their customers (Cannon and Perreault 1999; Heide and John 1990; Narayandas and Rangan 2004). A common approach to exploiting the potential of long-term supplier–customer relationships (Anderson and Weitz 1992) has been to adopt various customer management techniques, such as relationship management (Subramani and Venkatraman 2003), relationship marketing (Grönroos 1994; Morgan and Hunt 1994; Webster 1992), or national and key account management (McDonald, Millman and Rogers 1997; Shapiro and Moriarty 1984; Weilbaker and Weeks 1997).

However, these approaches often become more challenging as customers become more global and powerful. With global expansion, customers establish a direct presence in more and more countries and simultaneously expect the supplier to provide consistent, coordinated service worldwide, which entails moving away from traditional relationships with local subsidiaries and towards uniform prices, terms and service in markets in which the supplier may lack operations (Montgomery and Yip 2000). Furthermore, these customers recognize the strategic value-adding potential of global procurement (Cohen and Huchzermeier 1999; Ellram and Carr 1994) and therefore adopt integrated centralized purchasing practices (Olsen and Ellram 1997; Sheth and Sharma 1997) to reduce their supplier base (Capon 2001). The resulting shift of power to the customer increases through industry consolidation (Birkinshaw et al. 2001) and advances in information and communication technologies, which enable customers to track suppliers' quality and prices globally (Narayandas et al. 2000). These factors have heightened the challenges facing suppliers and made international approaches, such as global customer management (GCM) (Birkinshaw et al. 2001; Harvey et al. 2003b; Shi et al. 2004, 2005), the new frontier in customer management (Yip and Madsen 1996).

Defined as 'an organizational form and process in multinational companies by which the worldwide activities serving one or more multinational customers are coordinated centrally by one person or team within the supplier company' (Montgomery and Yip 2000, p. 24), GCM represents a key organizational design issue for suppliers (Homburg et al. 2002). Meeting global customer demands requires a coordinated cross-functional effort, including establishing a customer dimension that crosses existing product, country or functional units and mobilizes organization-wide resources to deliver on customer expectations (Galbraith 2001). In its simplest form, this dimension might be a specialized global customer manager who plays a pivotal boundary-spanning role to manage external and internal relationships and coordinate dispersed value-adding activities (Millman 1996). As the relationship with the customer develops, the number of contacts between companies and the need for dedicated resources and relationship-specific adaptations increases (Dwyer, Schurr and Oh 1987), as does the number of people involved in the relationship. A dedicated team, possibly composed of sales representatives from various product lines and countries or with a cross-functional composition including manufacturing, distribution, finance, R&D and other functional units, works to present an integrated presence to the customer (Galbraith 2001). Ultimately, in an overall GCM organization, all customer managers and teams are integrated to reconcile external alignment requirements by the customer with the organization's existing configuration of activities.

Consequently, three main levels of analysis emerge in the context of GCM organizational solutions: the individual global customer manager, the global customer team (GCT) and the overall GCM programme. Whereas prior work addresses the role of global customer managers (Harvey et al. 2003b; Millman 1996; Wilson and Millman 2003) and structural aspects on the programme level (Birkinshaw et al. 2001; Homburg et al. 2002; Kempeners and van der Hart 1999; Shapiro and Moriarty 1984), no GCM research considers the design and functioning of the team in detail. As a result, we suffer a lack of understanding about when teams should be formed, how they should be structured and managed, and, most importantly, what determines their performance. Following the call of Workman et al. (2003) for more research that examines how team type influences effectiveness, we develop and test a framework of GCT design and performance that draws on relevant literature from the fields of GCM, team selling (Moon and Armstrong 1994; Moon and Gupta 1997; Smith and Barclay 1993) and small groups within the organization (e.g. Ancona and Caldwell 1992a; Cohen and Bailey 1997; Gladstein 1984).

Specifically, this paper aims to fill the research gap identified above by clearly delineating key GCT performance determinants. It identifies domains of GCM team functioning with their specific dimensions and tests their impact on team performance with a relatively large and truly global data sample. It contributes to the international marketing literature by narrowing the traditional focus on the overall GCM approach to concentrate on one of its less researched building blocks – the team. Moreover, it complements prior suggestions regarding the key decisions involved in designing a customer team (Kempeners and van der Hart 1999) by proposing additional design dimensions and linking them to outcomes. Finally, the novel interdisciplinary approach of combining concepts from customer management and organizational behaviour research allowed us to identify and employ team-related variables that, although used in the context of smaller teams, have never been empirically tested in the more complex, dynamic and boundary-transcending context of GCM.

Literature review

Teams in the organization

The extensive body of small group research provides valuable insights into how teams work. The broad use of teams in organizations has provoked classical team effectiveness models rooted in social psychology (McGrath 1964; Steiner 1972), socio-technical theory (Cummings 1978; Pasmore et al. 1982) and organizational psychology (Gladstein 1984; Hackman 1987), as well as myriad empirical studies in diverse organizational settings. Reviews of team research in general (Cohen and Bailey 1997; Gist et al. 1987) and team diversity in particular (Milliken and Martins 1996; Williams and O'Reilly 1998) demonstrate the bewildering range of identified constructs and relationships and provide some organizing frameworks. Although these findings can help explain some aspects of GCT interaction and performance, the special characteristics of GCTs prevent a direct transfer of the frameworks and results from small group contexts.

For example, the responsibilities of GCTs include complex interactions with groups external to both the team and the organization, whereas most small group research uses bounded or isolated groups as the unit of analysis. One exception is the stream of research that focuses on cross-functional teams, particularly in new product development contexts (Ancona and Caldwell 1992a, 1992b; Denison et al. 1996; Pelled et al. 1999), which recognizes the importance of external activities. However, its concentration remains on task-focused, limited-duration groups, which run counter to the long-term commitment expected from GCTs. Furthermore, general models of team effectiveness assume that teams exist to perform a well-defined task and have clear goals, whereas in a dynamic GCM context, tasks are likely to be unstructured, customer specific and evolving, which means they pose different challenges. This blurring of tasks and responsibilities becomes exacerbated further in GCTs by the involvement of people from different units and the complicated work matrix that may require GCM members to report to different managers (Birkinshaw et al. 2001). Therefore, small group literature cannot provide a complete answer to the question about what determines the performance of teams in more dynamic and high-velocity environments, such as GCM.

Team selling

Another body of literature tries to enhance understanding of teamwork in a more specific selling context. In response to the industrial buying centre approach (Johnston and Bonoma 1981), it follows the shift of focus away from the individual salesperson toward the collective selling effort (Weitz and Bradford 1999). Recognizing the increasing role of functions other than sales in servicing customers (Spekman and Johnston 1986), suppliers began to form selling centres to facilitate cross-functional interactions in the communication, coordination and exchange of resources and assistance (Ruekert and Walker 1987). These centres usually consist of a permanent core selling team and members of other functional groups that participate on an ad hoc basis (Moon and Gupta 1997).

Several studies examine the roles of selling centre members (Hutt et al. 1985; Moon and Armstrong 1994) and develop frameworks to incorporate the linkages among team composition, processes and effectiveness (Moon and Gupta 1997; Perry et al. 1999; Smith and Barclay 1993). These frameworks enhance understanding of how the sales division cooperates with other functions, as well as how various group and environmental factors influence team interactions and effectiveness. However, these studies contain two major limitations. First, existing models remain at a conceptual level, with no empirical support for their hypothesized relations. Second, they focus on a broader customer base that does not explicitly reflect the increased organizational complexity, cultural diversity and complexity of the solutions associated with global customers (Millman 1999). Therefore, team selling stops short of providing an explanation of the performance determinants in a GCT context.

The global customer team

Although teams facilitate the complex task of coordinating efforts by individuals across functional, product and geographic units to serve customer needs (Shapiro and Moriarty 1984) and form an integral part of many GCM programmes (Homburg et al. 2002), existing literature does not offer a precise definition of what constitutes a GCT. We might deduce that such a team comprises all persons involved in developing and maintaining relationships with one or several related key customers on a global basis and that its responsibilities include developing a customer strategy and account plan, creating innovative solutions and coordinating various networks (Galbraith 2001). Therefore, a GCT must operate in multi-actor structures with different tasks and levels of authority, and its success depends on its ability to secure continuous support and manage the various technical, legal, economic and political dimensions of the relationship (Harvey et al. 2003b). In these circumstances, the composition of the team becomes a critical managerial issue, because it determines the operating format and effectiveness of the GCM effort (Harvey et al. 2003a).

Despite the importance of this topic, research in the area remains sparse. Some studies touch on team design issues but stop short of identifying the determinants and performance effects of various team dimensions (Harvey et al. 2003a; Harvey et al. 2003b; Kempeners and van der Hart 1999). Shapiro and Moriarty (1984) note the importance of integrating two groups of support functions – sales support and other functional specialists – into the team and suggest several organizational solutions that range from using independent sales and functional forces to shared teams to fully dedicated teams. These ideas have been extended to formulate specific design decision topics (Kempeners and van der Hart 1999) and analyse the skills and knowledge diversity needed in GCT composition, depending on the challenges the team faces (Harvey et al. 2003b). Thus, several distinguishing characteristics of such groups have emerged, including geographic dispersion and multi-national composition (Harvey et al. 2003a; Montgomery and Yip 2000), cross-functional involvement (Galbraith 2001), the involvement of several hierarchical levels (Harvey et al. 2003a), full- and part-time membership (Kempeners and van der Hart 1999), parallels with competing organizational arrangements (Arnold et al. 2001) and continuous long-term tasks. However, the lack of an overarching theory or framework that consolidates these dimensions and explains how they lead to different outcomes remains a serious concern.

Furthermore, as a distinct type of group, GCTs prevent any direct extensions of frameworks and concepts from other research streams. Instead, they require a more profound investigation in the specific GCM context that includes both the integration and adaptation of existing team concepts and the identification of context-specific factors. Therefore, we develop a framework that conceptualizes some key design dimensions and performance outcomes.

Conceptual framework of GCT design and performance

Our framework proposes that the design of GCTs should incorporate six key dimensions, each of which influences team performance in terms of relational and financial outcomes through the mediating effect of three key processes: communication and collaboration, conflict management and proactiveness. In addition, three aspects of the organizational context of the GCTs – top-management support, rewards and incentives, and training – have similar effects on performance (see Figure 1).

GCT design

The GCT design construct builds on the Hackman (1987) group design concept and is similar to organizational behaviour constructs such as team structure (Gladstein 1984; Smith and Barclay 1993), team composition (Cohen and Bailey 1997; Stewart 2006) and team characteristics (e.g. Perry et al. 1999). However, it reflects the specificities of the GCT setting and the dimensions with highest relevance in this context. We define GCT design as the structural and competency characteristics of the team in terms of the distribution of skills, roles, tasks and power among the team members. Because of its practical complexity, this con-

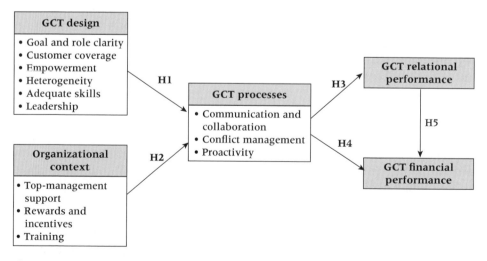

Figure 1   Conceptual framework of GCT design and performance

struct inevitably incorporates several related, but distinct, aspects. Methodologically, we tackle this issue in line with other relevant studies (Denison et al. 1996; Zou and Cavusgil 2002) modelling GCT design as a second-order variable that reflects six underlying first-order constructs: goal and role definition, customer coverage, empowerment, heterogeneity, adequate skills and leadership.

Goal and role definition

A key problem in forming groups is that team members might have conflicting group and individual goals that create mixed motives in terms of cooperating and sharing information (Bettenhausen 1991). Because GCT members often have multiple, organizationally defined roles and identities, conflicts arise, and operating managers' support for the GCT may be minimal if its role and responsibilities are not clearly delineated (Arnold et al. 2001). Aligning GCT goals with individual and overall corporate goals, as well as with customer goals, can therefore enhance collaboration, lower conflict levels and improve performance (Weldon and Weingart 1993). We therefore define this variable as the extent to which team members' goals and roles are clearly defined and aligned with team and corporate objectives.

Customer coverage

The GCT plays a boundary-spanning role, in which its ability to deal with the complexity marking the interface between the supplier and the customer depends on the extent to which it provides appropriate customer coverage across various dimensions, such as countries, divisions and functions. Structural fit between the supplier and the customer along these dimensions can improve supplier performance, because it enables the supplier to increase its information-processing capability and bargaining power in relation to its global customer (Birkinshaw et al. 2001). In addition, such fit can enhance the joint supplier–customer outcomes in terms of dyadic competitive advantages and joint profit performance (Shi et al. 2004). Therefore, customer coverage refers to the extent to which the team structure adequately corresponds to the customer's organization and its requirements.

Empowerment

Empowerment in a GCM context consists of two distinct aspects: decision-making authority and resource availability. Providing the team with sufficient authority tells the customer that customer managers have the power and resources to 'get things done' in a timely and effective manner (Homburg et al. 2002; McDonald et al. 1997). In a more general aspect, empowering teams by providing them with sufficient authority to make decisions for which they are responsible, can improve team processes (Mathieu et al. 2006), lead to greater proactiveness (Kirkman and Rosen 1999) and enhance positive customer-related outcomes such as customer service, customer satisfaction and process improvement (Kirkman et al. 2004). This empowerment requires the support derived from providing the team with sufficient resources to enable it to develop distinctive value propositions for its customers (Denison et al. 1996; Mohrman et al. 1995).

Heterogeneity

Heterogeneity refers to the diversity in skills and knowledge represented on the team. Following the resource-based view (Barney 1991; Teece et al. 1997), Harvey et al. (2003a) argue that individual and collective organizational knowledge as a resource enables the customer team to develop unique competencies valuable to global customers. Empirical evidence about the performance benefits of this type of diversity remains equivocal (Milliken and Martins 1996; Webber and Donahue 2001), but skill diversity clearly has positive performance effects on non-routine diverse tasks that require a wide range of competencies (Hambrick et al. 1996; Murray 1989) – a good description of GCT responsibilities. Therefore, incorporating a variety of backgrounds and areas of expertise within the GCT probably improves the team's performance.

Adequate skills

As opposed to skill heterogeneity, this construct focuses on individual characteristics that combine, such that more is always better for a team. The role of the global customer manager might be compared instructively to that of a political entrepreneur (Wilson and Millman 2003) who must overcome cultural barriers and navigate the sensitive political aspects of multiple interfaces while generating continuous business opportunities. These demands require a very broad range of skills that goes beyond that of a traditional salesperson, and teams whose members possess such a skill set are probably characterized by more collaborative and efficient team processes and thus superior performance.

Leadership

Because GCT leaders often have no formal authority, rely heavily on other members and are themselves contributing members to team activities, they must have strong influence both within and outside the team. Teams with leaders who can create effective working environments and motivate team members also feature more collaborative processes, reduced conflicts and higher effectiveness. Similarly, teams with leaders who exert a strong influence within the organization are more effective and collaborative because they communicate better with top management and other areas of the organization, more easily convince others that the team's activities are important, and secure more resources.

Hypothesis 1. GCT design has a positive influence on GCT processes.

Organizational context

Teams can be understood best in relation to their external surroundings and internal processes; therefore, most models of team effectiveness incorporate aspects from the organizational context of those teams (e.g. Campion et al. 1993; Denison et al. 1996; Shea and Guzzo 1987). Although there may be a large number of factors from outside the organization that play a role, it is usually the immediate surroundings within the organization that has the strongest impact (Stewart 2006). We identified three such factors that are of highest relevance in a GCT context: top-management support, rewards and incentives, and training. In line with Denison et al. (1996), we model organizational context as a second-order variable and these three factors as underlying first-order variables.

Top-management support

Top-management support often is identified as crucial for all aspects of GCM activities (Arnold et al. 2001; Homburg et al. 2002; Millman and Wilson 1999b), and some support emerges for the positive relationship between top-management support and GCM effectiveness (Workman et al. 2003), as well as marketing performance (Townsend et al. 2004) and market orientation (Jaworski and Kohli 1993). In particular, support in the form of resource allocations and public recognition of the GCT's efforts conveys the importance that top management attributes to the GCM initiative and is pivotal for overcoming potential resistance or power struggles within the firm, and legitimizing the efforts of the team as a strategic undertaking (Harvey et al. 2003b). This support enhances internal and external collaboration, reduces conflict and enforces a more proactive approach to global customers.

Rewards and incentives

A reward system that recognizes and reinforces contributions to the GCT can significantly amplify the motivational incentives provided by top-management commitment or well-designed goals and responsibilities. Because GCTs often work alongside pre-existing national sales organizations, and both units have vital roles in managing customers, it is important that the incentive structure helps reconcile any potential tensions between the units and further enhance collaboration (Arnold et al. 2001). A compensation system that enhances team processes and stimulates proactive contributions to the team usually requires two aspects: a measurement system that tracks the sales of global customers and the implied results of the GCT efforts worldwide, and an incentive system that rewards all team members appropriately.

Training

Due to the high demands on the skill sets of everyone involved with global customers, GCT members require professional development and training throughout their careers (Weeks and Stevens 1997). Even if these skills are available, team members, who come from different backgrounds and parts of the organization, need training to help them understand their tasks, processes, objectives and roles (Parker 1994). Team members who have successfully undergone rigorous training are more likely to contribute cooperatively and effectively to the team. Furthermore, external parties such as customers and other units in the supplier company probably perceive them as more competent and respectable and therefore become more willing to collaborate with them.

Hypothesis 2. The organizational context has a positive influence on GCT processes.

GCT processes

Although the team's structure and composition may have direct impacts on team outcomes, in most cases, this relationship also is mediated by the processes that characterize the interactions of team members (Lawrence 1997). We follow the definitions of Cohen and Bailey (1997, p. 244) who describe the team process as 'interactions such as communication and conflict that occur among group members and external others' and of Marks et al. (2001, p. 357) who expand the definition to 'members' interdependent acts that convert inputs to outcomes through cognitive, verbal, and behavioural activities directed toward organizing taskwork to achieve collective goals'. Consequently, our framework suggests three key mediating processes that have an impact in a GCT context: communication and collaboration, conflict management and proactiveness.

Communication and collaboration

Communication and collaboration refer to interactions both within the team and with external parties. The link between effective internal collaboration and team performance receives broad support from organizational behaviour studies (Bunderson and Sutcliffe 2002; Pinto et al. 1993), supplier–buyer relationship literature (Buvik and John 2000; Heide and John 1990; Mohr and Spekman 1994) and GCM studies (Birkinshaw et al. 2001; Shi et al. 2005). Similarly, the active management of external linkages and engagement of outsiders is crucial from a resource-dependence perspective (Pfeffer 1986) and is a key determinant of team performance (Ancona and Caldwell 1992a,b) and overall GCM performance (Homburg et al. 2002).

Conflict management

In GCTs, conflicts can arise as a result of diverse aspects of the home organizations (functions, units and regions) represented on the team, which lead to contrasting views and divergent task interpretations. Furthermore, conflicts may occur because of resource disparities or disagreements about resource allocations (Denison et al. 1996; Donnellon 1993). Therefore, we argue that the extent and frequency of conflicts, as well as the existence of working mechanisms that help resolve disputes in a timely and effective manner, influence GCT performance.

Proactiveness

Although many GCM activities result from customer demands, the potential for a cooperative and synergistic relationship is greatest when the supplier adopts more proactive behaviours (Harvey et al. 2003a; Homburg et al. 2002). Consequently, proactive team behaviours that actively seek areas for continuous improvement, identify opportunities and innovative solutions to problems and address issues before they become major problems represent a critical success factor (Bateman and Crant 1993; Hyatt and Ruddy 1997).

Hypothesis 3. GCT processes have a positive influence on GCT relational performance.

Hypothesis 4. GCT processes have a positive influence on GCT financial performance.

GCT performance

Global customer team performance often gets represented as two distinct components: financial, or quantitative, and relational, or qualitative (Birkinshaw et al. 2001).

Financial performance relates to key quantitative performance measures, such as sales growth and profitability (Birkinshaw et al. 2001; Shi et al. 2005), as well as measures such as reduced cost of sales to customers, more efficient use of salespeople's time in serving customers, cross-selling to divisions in which the supplier traditionally has been weak (Arnold et al. 2001), securing desired market share, attracting new customers (Homburg et al. 2002), or growing the share of the customer's wallet (i.e. share of the customer's total purchasing volume devoted to the supplier). Measuring GCT performance using purely quantitative criteria, however, runs the risk of missing vital aspects of customer partnerships, as well as the broader goals and objectives of developing relationships with key customers. Therefore, some qualitative performance indicators should be taken into account as well.

Relational performance refers to achieving goals such as long-term customer relationships, learning and innovation through various joint initiatives, and access to the customer's new product ideas (Birkinshaw et al. 2001). Other qualitative measures may include customer assessments of the relationship and customer satisfaction, which can increase customer value and mutual trust (Gladstein 1984; Homburg et al. 2002). In addition, the team's ability to meet its goals and objectives (Moon and Gupta 1997), gain broader market access and achieve a better competitive position in the market can indicate its performance (Smith and Barclay 1993). We expect that improvements in these indicators ultimately also enhance the team's financial performance.

Hypothesis 5. GCT relational performance has a positive influence on GCT financial performance.

Research methodology

We conduct this study in two separate stages, using both qualitative and quantitative methods. In the first stage, we conduct 15 interviews with managers in various industries, all of whom have direct responsibility for managing GCM programmes or teams. Each interview focused on the critical success factors for the customer teams in which the respondent had been involved, with the goal of better understanding the performance drivers of GCM teamwork. Through a content analysis of these interviews, we develop the questionnaire for the study. To ensure the reliability and validity of the measurements, our questionnaire development consists of several stages, following established guidelines (Churchill

1979; DeVellis 1991; Venkatraman and Grant 1986). In the first step, we review all relevant literature, with a specific focus on scales used in previous empirical research. Our analysis of the expert interviews and the thorough literature review helped us identify existing scales, adapt them where appropriate and develop new measures if no available scales existed. We pre-tested the questionnaire with several academic experts and many senior GCM executives, including managers from each of the six research companies and some of the interviewees. In accordance with their comments, we added, deleted or reworded several questions without causing a significant loss of validity in the constructs. The final versions of the scales in each of the four domains appear in Tables 2,3,4, and respectively. The coefficients alpha for all measurements is satisfactory and demonstrate their reliability.

In the second stage, we administered the questionnaire to 113 teams in six multinational companies. We followed a rigorous selection process, whereby we focused on the top companies from the *Forbes* Global 2000 list and profiled them on the basis of our understanding of their GCM practices. Following several rounds of thorough assessment and contacts with potential participant companies, we narrowed the list to the six focal companies for two main reasons. First, we aimed for an in-depth study, with the team (rather than the company) as the main unit of analysis, which required the involvement of a large number of teams within relatively similar environments. Selecting six companies helped us achieve this objective and reduced the variance in the external factors. Second, these six companies are highly representative of the population of international companies with established GCTs; all have conducted structured GCM programmes for at least six years and use GCTs extensively to manage their global customer relationships. They earn average revenues of US$18.7 billion (in 2008), employ 105,000 people on average and represent different industries, including construction equipment, engineering, hospitality services, electronics and office equipment.

Within these six companies, we targeted 425 team members in total and received 273 complete questionnaires, for an effective response rate of 64.2%, which compares favourably with similar studies (e.g. Denison et al. 1996). All respondents are qualified to complete the survey: they directly support or are involved in the GCT, in positions ranging from key or global account managers to regional or country general managers to members of the top-management team. More detailed sample characteristics appear in Table 1. The respondents' average tenure with the company is 12.5 years (SD $= 8.6$) and only 19% had been with their company for three years or less.

To test for potential non-response bias, we use an extrapolation procedure (Armstrong and Overton 1977) in which we divide the data set into thirds according to the date we received the completed questionnaire, then test for differences between the first and last third. The t-tests of the mean responses of early and late respondents indicate no significant differences ($p < .05$), suggesting non-response bias is not a concern.

Table 1:   Sample description

Positions of respondents	Total (n = 273)
Managing director, general manager, head of region/ business unit	24%
Sales director, sales manager, head of sales	17%
Global account manager, international key account manager, head of GCM	24%
Key account manager, national account manager, account manager	20%
Other	15%

Represented countries	Total (n = 273)
UK	28%
USA	23%
Germany	8%
France	7%
Rest of Europe	29%
Latin America	2%
Asia	3%

Results

We analyse the data using a three-step process. In the first step, we assess the validity of the variables suggested by the literature review and our qualitative analysis in each of the four dimensions (design, organizational context, processes and performance) on the basis of an exploratory factor analysis. In the second step, we perform separate confirmatory factor analyses (CFA) for each dimension to validate the relationships between the dimensions and the individual constructs. In the third step, we test the full structural model.

In Table 2, we provide the results of the exploratory factor analysis of the item pool for the GCT design dimension. To extract the factors, we use a principal component method, based on correlation matrices and Varimax rotation. The Kaiser criterion (i.e. factor loadings greater than or equal to .50) dictates which items we take into consideration; we highlight factor loadings above this cut-off point in bold. The six factors with eigenvalues greater than 1.0, according to our analysis, correspond directly to the proposed design constructs, namely, goal and role definition, customer coverage, empowerment, heterogeneity, adequate skills and leadership. Table 2 reports also the Cronbach (1951) coefficient alpha for the six variables. All of them are above the recommended level of .7 (Nunnally and Bernstein 1994), indicating that the measurement scales have a sufficient degree of reliability.

We present the results of the exploratory factor analysis for the organizational context dimension in Table 3. They reveal three factors, as posited by our literature review and qualitative research: top-management support, rewards and

Table 2: Results of exploratory factor analysis of team design domain

Constructs and items	1	2	3	4	5	6
Goals and roles ($\alpha = .777$)						
1. Our global customer team has well-defined goals and objectives related to our global customers.	**.763**	.031	.130	.047	.193	.070
2. Our team's goals and objectives are well aligned with our overall corporate strategies.	**.698**	.118	.202	.058	.000	.030
3. Team members' individual objectives and targets are linked to GCM team objectives.	**.716**	.061	.168	.140	.034	.121
4. The roles and responsibilities of team members are clearly defined.	**.701**	.092	−.032	.059	.176	.122
5. The team has a workable structure and clear reporting lines.	**.628**	.269	.044	−.106	.126	.159
Customer coverage ($\alpha = .714$)						
1. The team structure provides appropriate cross-geographical coverage for our customers.	.401	**.707**	.043	−.054	.124	.176
2. The team structure provides appropriate cross-functional coverage for our customers.	.172	**.822**	.214	.118	.151	.027
3. The team structure provides appropriate cross-divisional coverage for our customers.	.073	.818	.259	.061	.203	.031
Empowerment ($\alpha = .776$)						
1. Our team has sufficient authority to make important decisions about our customer business.	.209	.175	**.733**	−.045	.121	.261
2. Our team has sufficient authority to change organizational routines to achieve better results for our customers.	.083	.135	**.856**	.022	.182	.139
3. Our team has the resources required to innovate and develop our global customer relationships continuously.	.222	.214	**.646**	.144	.131	.119

Constructs and items	1	2	3	4	5	6
Heterogeneity (α = .748)						
1. Team members vary widely in their areas of expertise.	.067	.001	-.025	**.867**	-.004	.150
2. Team members have a variety of backgrounds and experiences.	-.010	.039	.001	**.859**	.154	.049
3. Team members have complementary skills and abilities.	.191	.106	.234	**.579**	.322	.023
Adequate skills (α = .893)						
The account/sales managers on our team						
1. . . . are capable of building strong and trusting relationships.	.144	-.047	.077	.012	**.733**	.329
2. . . . have a good understanding of our customer's business and organization.	.130	.055	-.061	-.062	**.765**	.152
3. . . . have a good understanding of our business and the internal capabilities of our company.	.066	.185	-.137	-.108	**.612**	.297
4. . . . are able to think and work in an interdisciplinary way.	.011	.195	.155	.028	**.749**	.011
5. . . . are able to coordinate complex networks and activities.	.072	.069	.166	.124	**.769**	.064
6. . . . are able to think creatively to deliver value to the customer.	.067	.053	.006	.143	**.802**	.032
7. . . . are able to work in a diverse and multi-cultural environment.	.053	.176	.063	.192	**.684**	.022
8. . . . employ strategic, long-term thinking.	.126	.058	.258	.078	**.726**	.049
9. . . . possess powers of persuasion.	.168	.019	.251	.167	**.651**	.123
Leadership (α = .820)						
1. Our team leader has substantial influence in the organization (even when he/she has no formal authority).	.167	.069	.216	.123	.208	**.799**
2. Our team leader has a strong relationship with top management.	.096	.093	.112	.074	.107	**.852**
3. Our team leader is able to motivate team members and create synergies within the team.	.206	.025	.172	.077	.233	**.693**
Eigenvalues	2.809	1.565	1.673	1.156	7.897	1.860
Variance explained by factor after Varimax rotation	11.5%	8.4%	8.6%	7.9%	19.9%	8.9%
Total variance explained	65.2%					

incentives, and training. All of them can be considered reliable as indicated by the high values of the coefficient alpha.

Next, in Table 4, we present the results of our exploratory factor analysis of the team processes dimension. These results support the three suggested factors – communication and collaboration, conflict management and proactiveness – and show a good level of reliability (with the exception of conflict management whose coefficient alpha is slightly below .7 but still satisfactory).

Table 3: Results of exploratory factor analysis of organizational context domain

Constructs and items	1	2	3
Top management support ($\alpha = .811$)			
1. Our top management is actively involved in the team's efforts to develop profitable, long-term relationships with global customers.	**.817**	.235	.145
2. Our top management is committed to deploying the necessary resources to make our global customer operations succeed.	**.830**	.236	.163
3. Our top management publicly promotes our team's GCM activities to others in the organization.	**.800**	.307	.113
Rewards and incentives ($\alpha = .810$)			
1. Team members' contributions to developing global customers are measured in a systematic and transparent manner.	.377	**.676**	.133
2. Our compensation system promotes global collaboration by appropriately rewarding contributions to the GCT.	.260	**.825**	.153
3. Many professional rewards (e.g. pay, promotions) are determined in large part by team members' performance on the GCT.	.240	**.804**	.145
Training ($\alpha = .790$)			
1. The company provides adequate global selling and negotiation training for our team.	.090	.434	**.690**
2. The company provides adequate team skills training for our team (e.g. communication, organization, interpersonal).	.138	.230	**.844**
3. The company provides adequate technical training for our team.	.164	−.056	**.837**
Eigenvalues	4.255	1.404	.904
Variance explained by factor after Varimax rotation	25.8%	24.8%	22.4%
Total variance explained	72.9%		

Table 4: Results of exploratory factor analysis of team processes domain

Constructs and items	1	2	3
Communication and collaboration ($\alpha = .823$)			
1. Our team regularly exchanges best practices and market knowledge with other GCTs.	**.592**	−.055	.259
2. Team members communicate proactively on issues related to our GCM activities across boundaries and hierarchical levels in the entire organization.	**.707**	.098	.291
3. Communication in the team is effective, despite the geographical distance of team members.	**.742**	.154	.043
4. Team members keep one another updated about their activities and key issues affecting the business.	**.810**	.115	.041
5. Team members are good at coordinating their efforts to serve the customer efficiently.	**.631**	.236	.287
6. Team members collaborate to achieve our global goals.	**.642**	.208	.287
Conflict management ($\alpha = .602$)			
1. Disputes between the different units represented on our team make it difficult to do our work. (reverse coded)	.050	**.802**	−.025
2. Our team is able to identify and resolve conflicts in a timely and effective manner.	.250	**.631**	.268
3. The negative politics within the team are minimal.	.125	**.701**	.274
Proactiveness ($\alpha = .721$)			
1. Team members proactively cultivate new business opportunities.	.245	.098	**.737**
2. Our team is not afraid to challenge the status quo to improve our customer relationships.	.090	.245	**.795**
3. The team is a powerful force for constructive change in the organization.	.344	.127	**.656**
Eigenvalues	4.600	1.008	1.368
Variance explained by factor after Varimax rotation	26.1%	14.7%	17.3%
Total variance explained	58.1%		

Finally, Table 5 displays the results of our exploratory factor analysis of the team performance dimension, which supports our proposed distinction between relational and financial performance.

Table 5: Results of exploratory factor analysis of team performance domain

Constructs and items	1	2
Relational performance (α = .859)		
1. Our team is characterized by strong and harmonious long-term relationships with global customers.	**.745**	.305
2. Our customers are satisfied with the overall performance of our team.	**.767**	.291
3. Our team provides real value to our customers.	**.800**	.277
4. Our team has successfully learned some critical skills or capabilities from our customer relationships.	**.728**	.211
5. Our company's competitive position has been enhanced due to our team's GCM achievements.	**.736**	.214
Financial performance (α = .826) How has your team, over the past three years, performed with respect to		
1. . . . growth in sales?	.251	**.881**
2. . . . profitability?	.296	**.779**
3. . . . growth in the share of your global customers' wallets?	.282	**.789**
Eigenvalues	40.416	1.020
Variance explained by factor after Varimax rotation	38.6%	29.4%
Total variance explained	67.9%	

In Table 6, we include the correlation matrix of the indexes from the exploratory analysis, as well as their means and standard deviations.

Following the initial exploratory factor analysis (EFA) support for the validity of the proposed constructs, we perform CFA to specify the relations of the underlying constructs to their second-order factors. This approach is in line with the recommendations for a two-step approach in which the measurement model is estimated separately prior to the simultaneous estimation of the measurement and structural submodels (Anderson and Gerbing 1988; Fornell and Yi 1992) and is consistent with other studies in the marketing area (e.g. Townsend et al. 2004; Zou and Cavusgil 2002)

Table 7 reports the results for the second-order measurement model. The chi-square/degrees of freedom ratio (χ^2/df), root mean square error of approximation

Table 6: Means, standard deviations, and correlations among constructs

	Mean	SD	1	2	3	4	5	6	7	8	9	10	11	12	13
GCT design															
1) Goals and roles	3.60	.68													
2) Customer coverage	3.50	.78	.46												
3) Empowerment	3.09	.87	.39	.47											
4) Heterogeneity	3.86	.61	.22	.19	.22										
5) Adequate skills	3.86	.53	.32	.37	.37	.30									
6) Leadership	3.81	.70	.36	.23	.35	.24	.40								
Organizational context															
7) Top-management support	3.57	.76	.43	.38	.49	.26	.31	.41							
8) Rewards and incentives	2.64	.81	.40	.27	.47	.24	.38	.39	**.58**						
9) Training	3.37	.77	.28	.21	.21	.18	.27	.27	.31	.37					
GCT processes															
10) Communication and collaboration	3.50	.59	.46	.38	.32	.21	.44	.39	.48	.42	.30				
11) Conflict management	3.66	.60	.22	.32	.35	.12	.36	.32	.27	.16	.16	.34			
12) Proactiveness	3.66	.66	.40	.41	.42	.29	**.56**	.43	.40	.41	.20	.50	.37		
GCT performance															
13) Relational performance	3.86	.61	.39	.41	.44	.21	.49	.49	.48	.44	**.27**	.49	.41	.64	
14) Financial performance	3.69	.72	.33	.21	.23	.08	.33	.41	.35	.34	.16	.36	.29	.46	**.58**

Correlations of .16 are significant at the .05 level (two-tailed). Large correlations (>.50) are indicated in bold.

Table 7: Results of the second-order CFA

Variables	Standardized loading	t-value	Fit statistics	
GCT design				
Goals and roles	.660	5.731	χ^2/df	1.587
Customer coverage	.690	6.393	RMSEA	.046
Empowerment	.710	–	RMR	.037
Heterogeneity	.273	2.534	CFI	.952
Adequate skills	.621	6.007	NFI	.883
Leadership	.515	5.855		
Organizational context			χ^2/df	1.745
Top-management support	.746	5.207	RMSEA	.052
Rewards and incentives	.938	4.641	RMR	.038
Training	.486	–	CFI	.980
			NFI	.955
GCT processes			χ^2/df	1.356
Communication and collaboration	.836	5.818	RMSEA	.036
Conflict management	.750	5.433	RMR	.029
Proactiveness	.813	–	CFI	.980
			NFI	.929
GCT performance				
Relational performance				
5.1 Long-term relationships	.737	–	χ^2/df	1.158
5.2 Customer satisfaction	.763	11.735	RMSEA	.024
5.3 Customer value	.778	11.953	RMR	.016
5.4 Learning	.673	10.390	CFI	.997
5.5 Competitive position	.672	10.371	NFI	.976
Financial performance				
5.7 Sales growth	.849	–		
5.8 Profitability	.726	11.744		
5.9 Share of wallet growth	.739	11.930		

Notes: All factor loadings are significant at the .01 confidence level. – indicates a fixed parameter.

(RMSEA), root mean square residual (RMR), comparative fit index (CFI) and goodness-of-fit index (GFI) values are satisfactory for all four dimensions and thus suggest the CFA models fit the data adequately (Hu and Bentler 1999).

Next, we assess the internal structure of the models and the convergent validity of the constructs. The loadings of all items on their respective factors are positive,

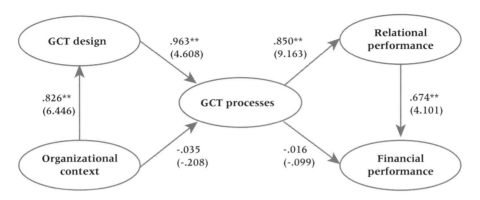

** Significant at $p < .01$.
Notes: Model fit statistics: χ^2/df= 1.469, RMSEA = .042, RMR = .041, CFI = .909, NFI = .765.

Figure 2   Structural path model

high in magnitude and statistically significant, which indicates satisfactory convergent validity (Anderson, 1987). To assess the discriminant validity of the
factors, we use the procedure recommended by Bagozzi et al. (1991) and therefore constrain the correlations between each pair of first-order factors to equal 1
and then release this restriction in a series of consecutive CFAs. In all cases, the
chi-square statistics of the nested model are significantly higher than those of the
unconstrained models, which indicates all constructs are distinct and that the
model achieves discriminant validity.

Following the purification of the measurement model through CFA, we test the
complete structural path model using the maximum likelihood procedure. The
full model includes the structural model as well as the multiple indicators of all
first- and second-order constructs obtained in the previous stages. We provide
the results in Figure 2, including the structural relationships, standardized estimates of the path coefficients and fit indexes. The *t*-values for all estimates appear
in brackets.

Furthermore, we thoroughly examine the solution by inspecting the parameter
estimates, standard errors and modification indexes, as well as any possible
irregularities. We detect no problems. The χ^2 for this model is 1,621.29, which
with 1,104 degrees of freedom results in a χ^2/df ratio of 1.469, indicating a good
fit. The other fit indexes are as follows: RMSEA = .042, RMR = .041, CFI = .909
and NFI = .765. Given the relatively complex nature of the model, with its many
indicators and three second-order factors, these indexes suggest a satisfactory fit
(Bollen 1989).

The estimates of the path coefficients in model 1 provide support for H1, H3 and
H5. Although we do not find support for H2, we identify an alternative path of
influence through which organizational context may affect the performance of
GCTs. Organizational context has a positive and significant effect on team design

and, from there, indirectly influences team processes, which supports the importance of the context construct. In addition, H4 is not supported, so team processes may influence financial performance only indirectly through their impact on relational performance.

Discussion

Global customer teams represent an important part of many GCM programmes, but existing research provides few directions for clarifying their formation, structure, composition, interaction processes or performance. Furthermore, GCTs differ from other forms of groups because of their complexity in terms of their cross-regional, cross-functional and cross-divisional span, blurred responsibilities and lines of authority, heightened external activity requirements and long-term tasks. This character of GCTs further complicates the managerial tasks of building and managing high-performance customer teams. Consequently, we examine what determines GCT performance by developing and empirically testing an integrative model of team composition, interaction and performance. On the basis of a comprehensive literature review, exploratory interview research and an analysis of survey data from six multi-national companies, we identify 12 determinants of team performance in three broad domains. We evaluate these determinants against both qualitative and quantitative performance criteria.

GCT design

The empirical results indicate that GCT design is a complex, multi-faceted construct that encompasses six key dimensions: role and goal clarity, customer coverage, empowerment, heterogeneity, adequate skills and leadership. These structural and compositional dimensions influence team performance through the mediating role of three key processes: communication and collaboration, conflict management and proactiveness. The resulting implication is that building high-performance GCTs starts with a clear specification of objectives in relation to the customer and the overall corporate goals, as well as a delineation of the roles and responsibilities that team members should fulfil. Furthermore, the team composition should receive sufficient attention to identify people with adequate skills who can develop relationships and navigate the interface between global organizations. Team performance could be enhanced further if these arrangements were accompanied by a leader with a strong presence and influence in the organization, as well as by the provision of sufficient resources and authority to the team. These factors would enable the team to make fast and efficient decisions and take courses of action that are in the best interests of the customer, even if they are unpopular or face opposition within the supplier organization. As a result, the team will experience less conflict and higher levels of collaboration and proactive behaviour. These results extend previous research in GCM by identifying a novel dimension, namely, customer coverage, as well as testing the skills-performance relationship empirically.

Organizational context

Three key elements of the organizational context of GCTs – top-management support, rewards and incentives, and training – emerge from our analysis, with the implication that developing high-performance GCTs probably will not succeed without genuine support from senior managers and proper incentives that encourage team contributions and stimulate global thinking throughout the organization. Furthermore, building strong teams requires that team members receive well-rounded training opportunities to develop their relevant selling, interpersonal and technical skills. Although a direct link to team processes is not supported (H2), we find an indirect link through team design. These constructs may contain several aspects that remain implicit in the study. For example, we predicted top-management support would influence team processes by helping the team in its work with the customer and creating a more cooperative and customer-oriented organizational environment. However, other aspects of top management support, such as involvement in the goal- and role-setting process, appointment of a team leader and members, or team empowerment, may explain these results. Therefore, this finding should prompt further investigation into the specific elements of the context dimension.

Team processes and performance

The results indicate that all design, process and context dimensions have either direct or indirect positive influences on performance. The finding that the link between design and performance is mediated by team processes falls in line with studies that call for a means to open the 'black box' of team interactions (Lawrence 1997) and implies that decisions about a team's structure and composition should be based on a careful assessment of their potential consequences for the way team members interact within the team and with their broader environment.

In addition, we find that GCT performance has two associated components, relational and financial performance, and that relational performance is only an intermediate outcome that ultimately leads to improved financial results in terms of sales growth, profitability and greater share of wallet. The lack of support for H4 suggests some interesting implications. We formulate it on the basis of prior studies that indicate a direct influence of GCM processes, such as communication and coordination, on financial measures of profitability and sales growth (Birkinshaw et al. 2001; Shi et al. 2005). Therefore, our findings suggest that prior research might have overlooked an important mediator of relational performance; we contribute to the literature by providing this missing link.

This finding also has implications for organizational behaviour research. Most studies in this research stream distinguish between performance outcomes, such as goal achievement, productivity or other relevant criteria, and attitudinal outcomes in terms of team satisfaction, commitment and trust. However, these two performance groups usually represent ultimate outcomes of effective teamwork, with no explicit interrelations. Our findings imply that the relationship between the two may require closer consideration.

Conclusions and implications

The major contribution offered by this paper is the development and empirical validation of an integrative model that sheds light on the performance determinants of a relatively new and under-researched phenomenon, namely, GCT. Its novel approach lies in the interdisciplinary combination of concepts from customer management and organizational behaviour research.

Our focus on the team level has not been investigated sufficiently in previous customer management literature. Therefore, our detailed delineation of the domains of team functions, along with their specific elements, provides a more complete set of performance determinants and extends prior research on GCT, which addresses only fundamental organizational decisions (Kempeners and van der Hart 1999). The introduction of concepts from research on organizational groups and cross-functional teams also broadens understanding of GCM teamwork by moving a step beyond purely structural issues. Moreover, we suggest and inspect variables that have never been empirically tested in a GCM context, including empowerment, leadership, conflict management and training.

Our contribution to the organizational behaviour field involves identifying factors that gain greater importance in teams with more complex and dynamic structures, tasks and environments. For example, constructs such as proactiveness, top-management support, skills and rewards have not been broadly emphasized or have produced inconclusive results in previous studies of teams with more structured and stable settings. However, they receive strong confirmation in this study, which implies a distinctive set of individual, team and organizational capabilities that may generalize to teams with similarly dynamic natures.

From a managerial viewpoint, this study highlights the importance of adopting a holistic approach to the composition and management of GCTs. As the results show, all team characteristics and the context in which the team works have important performance implications. Consequently, neglecting some or all of these issues will represent a key barrier to team effectiveness and the overall GCM operations of the supplier. Moreover, we develop a comprehensive model that can guide companies attempting to implement customer teams and help them improve their existing global customer relationships. Many of the identified elements fall directly or indirectly under the control of senior managers. Therefore, the complete set of 12 team characteristics and their corresponding questionnaire items, along with the 9 performance indicators, may serve as a practical tool for designing new GCTs or enhancing the effectiveness of existing ones, because they enable the firm to assess its current performance, map out areas for improvement, develop courses of action and track progress along each dimension.

Finally, the tested linkages among the variables illustrate the mechanisms through which different aspects of GCM teamwork are interrelated. This can help managers better understand and foresee potential consequences of their actions in each domain.

Limitations and suggestions for further research

Due to the exploratory nature of our study, we acknowledge that further research is needed to validate our proposed framework and could envisage several avenues for future investigation. First, based on our research design, most of the findings are a posteriori. Further research, however, may aim to establish additional research questions and hypotheses based on previous research and the current findings. Second, future contributions might include an analysis of the individual performance impact of each factor. The result could be a ranking or weighting of the factors depending on the magnitude of their effects, which would have important managerial implications. Third, researchers might build upon our findings to deepen the understanding of team processes which play such an important role in our framework. The conceptualization and empirical examination of complex concepts such as communication and collaboration could benefit greatly from further endeavours in this area.

In addition, some of the methodological limitations of our study could be addressed in the future. First, we use subjective performance ratings. Further research might test the effect of the identified independent variables on objective measures, such as actual sales growth, profitability, share of wallet or customer satisfaction ratings obtained in customer surveys. For measures that are rather subjective in nature (e.g. relationship building, customer value, learning, competitive position), a more objective rating might be obtained through managerial or customer assessments of these indicators. Second, our study is based entirely on data from supplier companies and lacks a customer perspective. Although some dimensions may be less visible or more difficult to evaluate from the customer side, a worthwhile extension of the findings would be to test the model with a sample of members from the customers' buying teams which work with the GCTs.

Also, due to the exploratory nature of our study, we consider the sample of six companies sufficient for the sake of depth and clarity. However, additional studies should seek to test the framework in other settings or with a larger sample of companies and thereby study each team characteristic more deeply by identifying their individual antecedents and consequences or by building on the model to identify other dimensions and measure their performance outcomes. One such research direction could be a study comparing global companies across countries to understand to what extent team design is determined by the practices in different countries. Finally, another interesting avenue for further research involves conducting a multi-level analysis to clarify the individual-, group- and organizational-level variables that may influence team performance.

Key accountization at Bosch Automotive Aftermarket Italy: managing and implementing a strategic change

BY PAOLO GUENZI

Abstract

This paper explores the implementation of a key account management programme at Bosch automotive aftermarket (BAA) Italy. Recognizing that the key accountization of a firm demands considerable organizational change, the McKinsey 7S framework was applied. It served both as a roadmap for the key account programme manager, to guide the actions he took in addressing the issues raised by a radical change in strategic direction, and as an analytical tool by the presenter of the case.

Introduction

In 1886, Robert Bosch founded the 'Workshop for Precision Mechanics and Electrical Engineering' in Stuttgart. Today, the Bosch Group is a leading global supplier of technology and services. The Bosch Group comprises Robert Bosch GmbH and its more than 300 subsidiaries and regional companies in over 60 countries. If its sales and service partners are included, then Bosch is represented in roughly 150 countries. Each year, Bosch spends more than €3.5 billion (8% of its sales revenue) for research and development and applies for over 3,000 patents worldwide. In the areas of automotive and industrial technology, consumer goods and building technology, some 280,000 associates generated sales of €45.1 billion in 2008.

Robert Bosch's market position

The automotive market is Robert Bosch's core business and consists of three interrelated markets. The first is original equipment, where Bosch is a worldwide leader in gasoline systems, diesel fuel injection systems, chassis systems brakes and chassis systems control, energy and body systems, radio navigation systems and car radios, and automotive electronics. The second is the spare parts market provided to car manufacturers and sold with their brand. The third is the independent automotive aftermarket, where all products are sold under the Bosch brand to end-users (i.e. car drivers) through car repair shops, spare parts retailers, etc.

The automotive aftermarket division supplies spare parts and information for Bosch products and systems, sells workshop and car accessories and provides after-sales service. Within the automotive technology business unit, the automotive aftermarket division is responsible for the supply, sales and logistics of automotive parts for after-sales service, as well as diagnostics plus workshop equipment (e.g. testers), technical information, training and consulting for car repair shops. Moreover, the division is responsible for the Bosch Car Service concept and the global technical after-sales service for automotive products and systems from Bosch. The global team comprises 3,700 people working worldwide in the division, in the regional subsidiaries and in the agencies located in 132 countries.

The Italian Bosch Automotive Aftermarket (BAA) division operates only in this third market and sells a broad range of spare parts (windshield wipers, fuel, oil and air filters, batteries, spark and glow plugs, ignition coils and cables, drive belts, etc.) and diagnostics equipment for repair shops (such as engine system testing, emissions analysis, brake testing, chassis geometry testing, power measurement, etc.). The division also offers a number of services, including ESI (electronic service information), that is a broad range of CD Roms with a huge amount of information and technical data on the automotive industry and products. ESI help the owners of repair shops to access all information required to do their job. These CDs provide information on Bosch products, working times, suggestions and tips for planning activities and optimizing the use of diagnostics software. In addition, Italian BAA is involved in many special projects, one example of which is Bosch Car Service, which is a sort of franchising network of specialized repair shops certified by the Bosch brand.

The independent automotive aftermarket is characterized by a complex distribution system, whose main players are:

- Wholesalers (first-tier customers).
- Spare parts retailers (5,000 outlets in Italy), which are considered second-tier customers.
- Car repair shops (about 40,000 in Italy), considered third-tier customers.

This channel structure led to difficulties in coordinating an increasingly multi-product, multi-client market. The company wanted to increase coordination and cross-functional integration, in order to boost flexibility, reduce response time and improve customer service, so in 2001 it radically changed its distribution strategy, deciding to focus exclusively on 150 big and well-structured first-level wholesalers (i.e. 'key accounts'). These customers, chosen as those with the highest levels of competency and resources, were divided into different categories:

Bosch dealer: medium-size companies with their own inventories and a well-structured organization, usually with multiple branches across Italy. They have their own sales force and technical assistance personnel for servicing their downstream customers. They sell almost exclusively Bosch branded products.

Bosch partner: smaller firms with a narrower assortment of Bosch products, as well as with lower-level technical, commercial and financial resources.

Bosch distributor: multi-brand wholesalers, who carry products manufactured by different, competing suppliers.

Special channels: larger corporate or public authority end-users (e.g. oil producers, local public transportation companies, etc.).

While BAA focused on this relatively small number of wholesaler key accounts, the management of relationships with second- and third-tier customers was left to these wholesalers. For BAA salespeople this implied a radical switch from a sell-in to a sell-out approach. This radical change was defined as a 'key accountization' of BAA Italy.

The Italian BAA division was organized into four departments:

1. *Sales*: the chief sales manager was the head of 15 employee salespeople (area managers) and about 100 independent sales reps. Their main responsibilities were supporting the growth of customers, supporting the launch of new products in the market, broadening and deepening the range of BAA products in the assortment of customers at all levels in the distribution channel, applying discounts and differentiating commercial conditions (such as payment terms, financial support, etc.) among different customers.

2. *Marketing*: one marketing manager headed about 15 people. They were mainly product managers, trade marketing managers and communication managers. Their main responsibilities were product management (positioning, pricing, advertising, etc.), driving specific marketing plans for different product lines, market research, sales forecasts, customer satisfaction analysis, supporting the sales force through the provision of technical information on all products, reports on market and financial performance of different products, joint calls to customers, etc., designing and producing all promotional supports (e.g. catalogues, leaflets, point-of-sale materials, etc.) and launching new products in the market.

3. *Sales administration*: one manager and ten people were in charge of managing all aspects regarding payments, invoices, order processing and customer service on all administrative issues. Among other things, they had to check the orders (e.g. adequacy of financial conditions, promotional prices, etc.), provide all first-level customers with information on price lists, discounts, stock availability, order processing, manage returns and delivery errors, manage claims (which in most cases have to do with logistics and delivery time) call on first-level customers to directly install software and systems for data processing and order fulfilment, as well as provide information on procedures for data processing, order processing, stock-keeping and logistics.

4. *Technical support*: this department was very important for BAA. In BAA division, all technicians in the technical support department focused on the provision of technical services to first-level customers. More specifically, their main responsibilities were managing technical training to all customers, providing continuous telephone support to all technicians of customers, contributing to creating, organizing and training all the people in the 500 repair shops involved in the Bosch Car Service Project and managing all aspects of guarantees.

The radical change in BAA distribution strategy implied switching from the traditional selling approach to a partnership approach based on the identification and implementation of win–win strategies with key accounts. As a consequence, area managers had to become relationship managers, adopting a consultative approach with first-level key accounts, developing specific business plans and creating added value for them. Traditionally, the marketing function mainly targeted end-users (car drivers) and focused on brand management and communication strategies, while the sales department focused on distributors. Moreover, the marketing function tried to strictly implement the standardized guidelines provided by the German headquarters, while the sales department called for local adaptation to the characteristics and needs of the Italian market. As a consequence, conflicts and problems of poor coordination were quite frequent.

A framework to interpret BAA Italy's KAM-focused change management

McKinsey's 7S framework, which is popular for managing change in organizations (Peters and Waterman 1982), is a way of thinking about the development

Table 1: McKinsey 7S framework

'Hard' organizational elements	*'Soft' organizational elements*
Strategy	Shared values
Structures	Style
Systems	Staff
	Skills

or remodelling of companies. The model proposes seven interdependent organizational elements that must be aligned (see Table 1). Three of these elements are perceived as *hard*: strategy, structures and systems; four are perceived as *soft*: shared values, style, staff and skills. Shared values are core to shaping all the other critical elements and are reflected in the culture of the organization.

When a company sets out to change its organization, the seven Ss are often addressed in a given sequence. The recognition that change is necessary results in new strategies emerging, a plan and series of actions designed to achieve some form of competitive advantage. The framework can then be used to analyse ways in which the other organizational elements support or block the new strategy.

Strategy tells a company how it must adapt itself to its environment and use its organizational potential, whereas the analysis of skills answers the question of how the strategy ought to be implemented. These skills define the changes that need to be made in the other five Ss: structure, systems, staff, style and shared values:

- *Structure*: the way business units are grouped in relation to each other and defines reporting lines. This is perhaps the most visible factor in the organization, and that is why it is often tempting to begin by changing the structure.
- *Systems*: defined as the procedures or processes that exist in a company and that involve many people for the purpose of identifying important issues, getting things done or making decisions. Systems provide management with a powerful tool for making changes in the organization.
- *Staff*: concerned with the question of what kind of people the company needs. It refers to the total know-how possessed by the people in the organization.
- *Style*: leaders' personal symbolic actions. Leadership and management style is not necessarily a matter of personal style but of what the executives in the organization do, how they use their personal signalling system.
- *Shared values*: one or more guiding themes of the organization's culture, things that everybody is aware of as being especially important and crucial to the survival and success of the organization.

Change management in the case example

In the following the case is used as an illustrative example of how McKinsey's 7S framework can be applied to the management of KAM-focused change in organizations.

Strategy

Radical changes entail substantial modifications of corporate strategies and goals. New strategies should be clear and easy to communicate, and new goals should be easy to justify, quantify and measure. These key success factors are apparent in the words of Mr Colabucci, sales manager at Bosch Automotive Aftermarket Italy:

> "From a strategic standpoint, change was driven by two main goals. The first one was to cut costs by reducing managerial complexity. For example, from the administrative standpoint, Bosch had to manage thousands of invoices every month and had a huge list of insolvent customers. The second goal was to increase revenues by targeting big dealers which could sell and provide service support for the whole set of Bosch products, especially technical goods, which could not be either purchased or distributed by small–medium sized distributors, due to the lack of qualified technical staff or the pretty big warehouse and financial requirements.
>
> In the process of change it was crucial to share our vision and to clearly communicate our goals to customers and employees alike. You might discuss methods, timing and tactics, but the vision must be definitely shared. In addition to this, it was of fundamental importance to root our vision of the future and our goals into hard data and objective facts. We had to support our view concretely by showing research, figures and trend analysis to justify why we thought we had to go that way."

The change management programme supporting the key accountization of the company, consistent with Kotter (1995), focused on creating a vision clarifying the direction in which the organization needed to move and developing a strategy for achieving the vision. The vision has to be simple, easy to understand and communicate, and capable of capturing the imagination of people in the organization. Without this vision, priorities are not clear and all plans, directives and projects may be confusing and perceived as incompatible: the vision should be the unifying focus of all programmes.

Skills needed to successfully redesign and manage key processes

Generally speaking, in change management initiatives companies should analyse and redesign critical processes when needed, especially to identify the critical skills needed to successfully implement the change. Such processes may refer to both back-office activities and customer interaction management of the front line. For example, Bosch mapped and redesigned some critical processes, especially to clarify roles and responsibilities, the goal being to reduce ambiguity and conflicts. Therefore, after identifying key processes, the company developed for each of them the RASIC matrix, which clearly indicated, for each phase of the process under investigation, the people involved in terms of Responsibility, Approval, Support, Information and Control.

This is in line with the recommendation made by Sirkin et al. (2005), who emphasized that radical organizational changes, such as BAA Italy's key accountization, should be characterized by a clear definition of roles and responsibilities for all the people involved.

The Bosch case highlights the critical role played by communication processes, both with internal (subordinates, colleagues from other departments, etc.) and external counterparts (e.g. customers). As Colabucci pointed out:

> "We let everybody – including customers – know about our real sales and product targets. We also wanted to inform everybody about the results of the change process. So, for instance, we immediately bought a maxi-LCD screen (which cost €10,000 at the time . . . it took me three months to have such investment approved!) and placed it right there at the entrance of our building, so that every day everybody could see at once what the target for each channel and line of products was, together with sales progress made daily. So everyone could know exactly what was happening.

> We also developed an intranet connecting all members of the sales force so that anyone could see their colleagues' results. Of course, they all remained anonymous. This was not meant to create jealousy or the like, but to let anyone have benchmarks and a clear picture of the situation. The same was true for customers who could see how they were growing compared to others: again, this was done anonymously. This gave rise to a virtuous cycle simply by letting information until then reserved circulate. Everyone knew exactly what they had to do and by when and also what the others were expected to do and the progress the others were making. This was an important achievement in a context where traditionally such type of transparency was not accepted. That was a really hard struggle . . . but it really turned out to be a key factor."

In some cases, changes in processes were only short term, tactically oriented. For example, pricing and discount policies were made very flexible at the beginning of the change initiative. The objective was to support the change process by orchestrating some early wins when needed. In fact, the company wanted to keep performance high in the short term to reinforce employees' and customers' commitment.

All this is consistent with Kotter (1995) as well as Sirkin et al. (2005), who noted that every possible communication channel should be used to make employees perceive that the change is useful and possible, and to facilitate two-way information flows to provide feedback from the both employees and customers. Kotter (1995) also pointed out that managing communication processes in radical change management initiatives like the key accountization of the firm also implies orchestrating and creating short-term wins. Meeting and celebrating short-term goals helps boost the credibility of the renewal process, keeping the urgency level high and forcing detailed analytical thinking that can clarify or revise the vision. Since big transformations take time, without some short-term success many people are at risk of giving up and losing faith in the change process. Therefore, change leaders should deliberately plan for visible and measurable performance improvements, create these improvements, and recognize and reward employees involved in such improvements. This does not mean declaring victory too soon. Rather, successful change leaders typically use the credibility gained through short-term wins to further raise the bar and start renewal projects that are even bigger in scope than the initial ones.

Improving internal communication processes also implies the modification of measurement systems (Colletti and Chonko 1997): companies should change what to measure and how it is measured. First, accurate measurement procedures can help justify why the change is needed by providing measurable goals to be accomplished. Second, if the impact of change on results can be measured, empirical testing can reveal what works well or not in the change, thus facilitating learning and continuous improvement. Third, having measurable measures of success provides opportunities for energizing the improvement process: in fact, people feel motivated by reaching quantifiable measures of performance, and demonstrated capacity to succeed reinforces employees' perceptions of their ability to succeed in the future.

Shared values and culture

Neal and Tromley (1995) suggest that when radical changes are expected, as in the case of BAA Italy's key accountization, a culture change is needed. Culture consists of the set of values, beliefs and assumptions underlying the behaviours of individuals.

When the change management process started, Bosch was changing its priorities in terms of key corporate values. Moral integrity had always been the primary value, together with a guarantee of employment to its employees. The new number one value was entrepreneurship and the spirit of initiative: the company wanted a personal contribution from its employees. This called for, among other things, an empowering leadership style, a reduction of bureaucracy in many business processes and higher job mobility, coupled with more meritocratic career advancement opportunities. The strategic change at BAA Italy also called for a stronger market-oriented culture.

To change the corporate culture, one should start from the top: it is of fundamental importance that top managers accept, witness and spread across the whole company the key values of the new culture. To do this, members of the board needed to demonstrate and embody such values by showing consistent actions, i.e. by modifying their everyday decisions and behaviours. This is not easy to accomplish. This was how Colabucci persuaded the CEO to shift from a product-oriented culture to a customer-oriented culture, which was a necessary precondition to successfully implement the change:

> "I repeatedly said that we were a product-oriented company rather than a customer-oriented one. This made the CEO criticize me. He said, 'How do you dare make such an accusation?' to which I replied, 'I have just a question for you: how many customers do we have, and how many product codes do we deal with?' Well, he knew about product codes but had no idea about customers. So I told him: 'That's the way it is, I know how many customers we have, while you don't. Yet you know how

many product codes we deal with. This means that focus is on logistics and products while you don't care about customers so much. Well . . . I guess you should!'

Since he was a smart person he realized I was right: we were not truly customer-oriented. So he started being sort of obsessed with it. He started go around asking everybody, 'How many customers do we have?' He had changed his mindset completely, and this is how some changes in mentality were introduced. In turn, this gave rise to radical changes in many key processes. For example, we completely redesigned information systems to calculate each customer's profitability. Before the change, we had no information about it, since sales statistics were organized only by product."

This statement clearly suggests that major modifications in company culture must be accompanied by substantial modifications in support systems (e.g. information systems), otherwise it is extremely difficult to implement change in practice. This is also consistent with the above mentioned need to modify measurement systems (Colletti and Chonko 1997). A typical example is the effort to calculate customer profitability to see whether the company is focusing on the right accounts, as well as to estimate the return on time invested, to make sure that salespeople are spending their time on the correct activities.

The example cited above also underlines the importance of the commitment of senior executives in implementing KAM-related change management programmes (see, for example, Sirkin et al. 2005). Furthermore, an important way to modify the corporate culture is to change some rituals. For example, to stimulate employees' entrepreneurship, Colabucci decided to change the way meetings were managed. This is how he describes this change:

"Traditionally, the company used to have meetings where some people said nothing at all. So I told them, 'Just don't come next time if you have nothing to say. Even if it was rubbish you have to say it anyway.' I used to say, 'Let's do some brainstorming because from someone's rubbish there may stem someone else's good idea.'

Yet it was not so easy to encourage brainstorming in a company with a strong hierarchical culture, where everybody tended to be reluctant. So I decided to even play games like, 'If you say nothing, you have to leave the room.' Thus, using a little bit of 'violence' we could arouse creativity and people who had always kept silent until then, when forced to speak, would often contribute the best ideas."

Another example of change in rituals refers to the challenge of stimulating a culture of interdepartmental interaction and cooperation. In Colabucci's words:

"Once there were separated dinners out for salespeople and members of the marketing department. We started to have inter-functional meetings and dinners where they all had a chance to get to know each other.

We did the same with the colleagues from information systems, who could decree success or failure of our projects, because they could dramatically facilitate the circulation of information and the possibility to have concrete data to refer to. Therefore, for example, I often invited them to our dinner meetings where we celebrated our department's accomplishments. I wanted to let them feel part of the team."

In addition, the company started to take some people from the sales department and move them to marketing and vice versa.

Corporate culture can also be changed by modifying some artifacts, such as the company language (Homburg and Pflesser 2000). An example of this is provided by Colabucci:

> "I have abolished the word 'manage' from my own vocabulary, because when you are busy managing something you have already lost ground in comparison with those who are developing their business. Therefore, one should only 'develop'. We had people in charge of 'coordinating' something. Well, a person who coordinates rarely has responsibilities, so we have renamed many of them 'business development managers' or 'channel leaders', which sound more dynamic."

Even changing the dress code was a way to try to modify culture, attitudes and behaviours. As Colabucci states:

> "We began not to wear ties because we wanted to have people feel they were part of a team where they were expected to work hard and face a change instead of feeling like managers supposed to manage business as usual. We impoverished the formal aspect in a sense while enriching the substantial one."

Consistent with Chonko et al. (2002), perceptions of organizational readiness for change and individual learning orientation were stimulated by creating a culture whose main values were market orientation and entrepreneurship. Market orientation is characterized by a continuous effort to create customer value, to collect and disseminate customer and competitor information, and by organization-wide responsiveness to customer needs. Entrepreneurship is characterized by risk tolerance, support to proactivity, receptivity to innovation and resistance to bureaucracy.

Style and leadership
Laabs (1996) reported that 20% of people in an organization are change friendly, 50% are 'fence sitters' and 30% resist or even deliberately try to make the initiative fail. Change leaders play a key role in proactively managing the meaning that people attach to change. Such meaning can be interpreted in terms of shared mental models, i.e. common perceptions, beliefs and priorities that facilitate successful change implementation. Since change implies uncertainty and ambiguity, the input of management to the construction of reality is especially important when companies undergo radical changes. Leaders should manage meanings in order to:

- Create shared perceptions and interpretations so that members' actions are guided by a common definition of the situation.
- Justify their actions and the changes they introduce to the organization.
- Recruit followers and motivate members of the organization to support their actions.

The management of meaning by strategic leaders primarily involves shaping organization members' perceptions and interpretations about (1) the environment, (2) the state of the organization and its performance, (3) the organization's vision and goals, (4) the appropriateness of various means, decisions and actions employed by the organization to achieve its goals, and (5) the ability of the organization to make progress towards meaningful goals.

Change leaders must be credible, and their leadership style should incorporate personal values and personality traits that are consistent with the values of the corporate culture. For example, as stated above, a major modification of Bosch's corporate culture was the emphasis now placed on the employees' entrepreneurial attitudes and capabilities. This calls for a leader who stimulates and supports empowerment and risk-taking. This was clearly a characteristic of Colabucci, as demonstrated by the following statement:

> "I used to say, 'Maybe at the beginning you do ten things, eight are wrong and two are right. Yet later it may go the other way round: you do eight right things and two wrong ones. If you stand still you might make no mistakes, but you don't contribute to any achievement either.' This is why I kept saying, 'Just do it, just try, we'll surely learn from our mistakes.'"

Similarly, a participative leadership style was needed to foster followers' entrepreneurial spirit. Again, this was part of Colabucci's style:

> "I remember that at first everybody said, 'Yes, sir', and at the end many would say, 'No, I disagree', which helped me grow as well."

Radical changes usually require a radical discontinuity in the management team. Hence, hiring leaders from outside can be a wise choice, as Colabucci witnessed:

> "For many customers it was important to interact with a new sales manager. I told them, 'I have nothing to do with what has been done so far. I only know that I am here to do something else.' I was credible because, while being very competent about the products and the market, I had not contributed to building up the situation like it was. Many customers understood that Bosch really wanted to change things by introducing some new managers coming from outside. They saw me as a living proof of Bosch's willingness to change."

On the other side, hiring a new leader from another company may create problems internally, because the newcomer may lack credibility. To gain credibility, the leader should be perceived as competent, honest and powerful. The company and the leaders can and should do whatever they can to improve such perceptions. Such characteristics in Colabucci's words:

> "At the beginning some people thought: this guy is too young and doesn't know the Bosch world . . . soon he won't be around any more. In Bosch, people who started a change process were rarely granted credibility as employees were generally not in

favour of it and bound to tradition. In fact, one of the main values for Bosch is: 'We have always done so successfully since 1890.' So it's truly difficult to say, 'Starting tomorrow we'll do it another way.' I had to give the impression of being appointed to a strategic mission instead of being seen as a person who, as a latecomer coming from outside, wanted to put into discussion all that had been done before introducing change processes which perhaps were not welcome and not even shared from a strategic viewpoint. I was successful especially because I was given special power on many decisions, which was highly unusual and demonstrated that I was backed by a strong commitment from the top management.

People trust you if they see that you have concrete ideas and possess the necessary competence. Fortunately enough I had technical and market competence. This helped me a lot.

Another key success factor was that I was very clear to people. If they are not aware of what is both positive and negative about the change process, they feel confused, overpowered by ambiguity and they stand still, they just don't move. You've got to be very outspoken."

The leader's communication style is especially important in change management initiatives, since it has a strong impact on the cognitive, affective and behavioural responses of individuals affected by change. A communication style characterized by clarity and openness is usually a relevant trait of successful change leaders.

Structure

In terms of organization structure, two major modifications were made at BAA. The first involved the reduction in the sales force size. In fact, since Bosch would no longer manage 4,000 customers but 150, the company needed to downsize its sales force. Therefore, Bosch decided to relocate many members of its sales force to the dealerships, thus reducing the number from 100 to 30; only 10 salespeople did not accept this proposal. To be successful, one key variable was to prove that everyone would earn more in the process. For Bosch, the main advantages were that salespeople helped convey the culture of Bosch to dealers, and that salespeople (and their customers) did not move to competitors. Salespeople did not lose their jobs and continued working with their customer base. Often they also had new career advancement opportunities in the dealers' organizations. Finally, they put their portfolio of downstream customers at the disposal of dealers, who broadened their customer base and hired experienced salespeople.

The second relevant change was that the company created formal teams (as recommended, for example, by Neal and Tromley (1995) and Beer et al. (1990)), thus giving rise to a matrix organization structure. In fact, area managers became leaders of selling teams, each one incorporating a couple of agents and one member from each of the other three departments: marketing, sales administration and technical assistance.

Staff

Bosch realized that most of its employees did not possess the set of skills and competencies needed in the new scenario. At the same time, the company understood that investing in training was a necessary step to motivate people to change. In fact, many employees felt a lack of self-confidence. Empowerment also required an increase in employees' capabilities. Therefore, most members of the organization from all four key departments were involved in inter-functional coaching, training on team building and training to develop management skills and competencies.

In short, the training process at BAA Italy consisted of the following steps:

1. Definition of the 'ideal profile' of area managers in terms of skills and competencies required by the new approach.
2. Self-evaluation of area managers on such skills and competencies.
3. Comparison of ideal and actual profile, which led to the identification of individual gaps and areas for improvement.
4. Aggregation of individual gaps and improvement priorities to identify group-level priorities (e.g. managerial competencies versus relational soft skills).
5. Application of the same process to all other members of sales teams.

All the investments of time and money made by BAA Italy with regards to the development of employees' skills, knowledge and capabilities were consistent with Beer et al. (1990), Claret et al. (2006) and Sirkin et al. (2005), who emphasized that to successfully implement profound change projects such as BAA Italy's key accountization, companies should develop new skills and competencies in those affected by change, in such a way that they feel they are ready and well prepared to deal with the challenges of the new context.

Systems
In addition to the interventions on information systems cited above, two other modifications were important to support and successfully implement change at BAA Italy. The first one involved planning: all salespeople were provided with an information-based customer planning tool aimed at setting goals, developing projects, tracking progress, monitoring problems and creating benchmarks for every single customer.

Second, consistent with the recommendation made by Beer et al. (1990), the company completely revised its incentive system. This is a critical issue in a KAM-focused change like the one made by BAA Italy. In fact, since salespeople's remuneration is typically largely related to market performance, change directly threatens the level or variability of sales force income. As a consequence, compared with other personnel, salespeople may be more reluctant to change, because unlike other employees in the organization they have to take upon themselves the risk of losing money (Hurley 1998). The challenge here was to change employees' priorities from monetary rewards to career development opportunities and professional growth. To do this, for example, the company strongly invested in cross-functional training and interdepartmental coaching, stimulated cross-functional mobility and redesigned job advancement paths.

Investing in control systems (e.g. measurement systems, reporting systems, etc.) is also a key success factor in KAM-related change management programmes – as pointed out by Sirkin et al. (2005), companies should schedule milestones and assess their impact. Carefully monitoring the change project's progress implies providing reports, determining whether achieving the milestones has had the desired impact on the company, discussing the problems, determining improvements, etc.

Conclusions

The key accountization of a company usually implies radical changes in the organization. Managing such a change in the sales force is 'special' for a number of reasons that are well exemplified by the BAA Italy case. The case is an example of the application of McKinsey's 7S model to successfully implement the change management initiatives implied by a KAM-focused strategy. The key message of this model is that a structured, integrated and consistent set of interrelated changes is needed at different levels of the organization.

The case is an empirical demonstration of the relevance of some general rules for managing KAM-focused change in sales organizations (Hurley 1998):

- The vision of the future relationship with customers should be clear and grounded in good market analysis.
- Expectations about earnings during the change process should be carefully managed.
- Complex and abstracts ideas in the vision should be translated as much as possible into concrete behaviours and actionable programmes.
- The vision and the rationale for change should be over-communicated across levels and locations.
- Salespeople's resistance to change should be reduced by involving them in the process.
- Change progress should be measured and monitored continuously.
- Specific change management structures should be created (e.g. task forces).
- Change leaders should be empowered at all levels/locations.
- Multiple parts/processes of the systems should be changed in an integrated and consistent manner.

SECTION 4

OPERATIONALIZING KSAM

Recent developments in relationship portfolios: a review of current knowledge

BY JUDY ZOLKIEWSKI

Abstract

Recent developments in relationship portfolio research are reviewed including contextuality, their significance in technology-intensive industries and innovation, portfolio dynamics and developments in customer lifetime value and other finance-based models. The interfaces between CRM, segmentation and portfolio analysis are also considered. The managerial implications are presented; these highlight the ongoing usefulness of portfolio analysis as a strategic decision-making tool.

Introduction

For business, relationship management is as central today as it was 30 years ago. Academic focus has moved from the marketing mix (e.g. Borden 1964) through relationship marketing (e.g. Grönroos 1994; Payne et al. 2005) to the current discourses on customer experience and engagement (e.g. Brodie et al. 2011), value (e.g. Ettenson et al. 2013; Ngo and O'Cass 2009; Woodruff 1997) and service-dominant logic (e.g. Grönroos 2011; Vargo and Lusch 2011). Nonetheless, it is the firms that successfully manage and meet the needs of their customers profitably that remain at the forefront of business. While customer relationship portfolios do not attract extensive attention, they remain an underlying theme in much of the research that is undertaken into strategic account management and strategy itself, and reflect the increasingly strategic role of business-to-business marketing (Wiersema 2012) and sales (Geiger and Guenzi 2009). Yorke and Wallace (1986) noted key problems in business marketing that customer selection helps to solve: achieving a true marketing orientation and strategic flexibility. Recent research by Schiele (2012) adds another perspective to this consideration with respect to the idea that customers are competing to become 'preferred customers' in an open innovation context where they are seeking the most innovative suppliers to collaborate with. Additionally, as Gök (2009) notes, portfolios form the basis of key account management (KAM), yet often KAM lacks the insight into customer needs that portfolio analysis can provide.

The importance of relationship portfolios (i.e. customer and supplier portfolios) in resource allocation decisions is recognized extensively by Industrial Marketing and Purchasing Group (IMP) researchers (e.g. Håkansson 1982; Terho and Halinen 2007; Turnbull et al. 1996) and purchasing scholars (e.g. Kraljic 1983; Krapfel et al. 1991). Pels (1992) highlights the importance of tools of this nature when dealing with concentrated demand, particularly when a firm is serving a limited number of clients either by choice or as a result of an oligopsonic market structure. However, there is also considerable evidence of the success of portfolio analysis in more competitive markets (e.g. Johnson and Selnes 2004; Turnbull and Zolkiewski 1997; Wuyts et al. 2004). From a marketing and sales management perspective, relationship portfolio analysis is important when clients are particularly active and relationships are important, and companies need to be able to identify the optimum resource allocation across their customer base. This is of central importance in KAM in that it allows account managers to actively focus on their most important accounts. Terho and Halinen (2007) suggest that viewing customer portfolio analysis simply in terms of the application of matrix-based models is inconsistent with what firms actually do. They propose a broader definition of portfolio analysis, as 'an activity by which a company analyses the current and future value of its customers for developing a balanced customer structure through effective resource allocation to different customers or customer groups' (p. 721).

The following sections present a review of the extant research into relationship portfolios and highlight the key themes that are emerging as points of discussion and practice. The managerial implications of these issues are then considered.

Review of extant research

Reviews of the work on relationship portfolios can be found in Zolkiewski and Turnbull (2002) and Terho (2009). It is not our purpose to restate this work; however, Table 1 provides an updated list of relevant research into relationship portfolios drawing on both buyer and supplier perspectives. In supplier

Table 1: Summary of customer and supplier portfolio analysis models

Author	Year	No of axes	No of steps	Suggested dimensions
Customer relationship analysis				
Cunningham and Homse	1982	2	1	Technical interaction. Sales volume.
Fiocca	1982	2	2	*Step 1: (general)* Difficulty in managing the account. Strategic importance of the account. *Step 2: (key account)* Customer's business attractiveness. Relative buyer/seller relationship.
Campbell and Cunningham	1983	2	3	*Step 1: Life cycle classification of customer relationships (tomorrow's customers, today's special customers, today's regular customer, yesterday's customers)* The classification criteria used include: sales volume, use of strategic resources, age of relationship, supplier's share of customer's purchases, profitability of customer to supplier. *Step 2: Customer/competitor analysis by market segment* Growth rate of customer's demand for product or service. Customer's share of its market. *Step 3: Portfolio analysis of key customers* Growth rate of customer's market. Competitive position (relative share of customer's purchases).
Dickson	1983	2	2	*Step 1: Distributor portfolio analysis* Distributor's rate of sales growth (adjusted for inflation). Company's share of distributor's product line sales. *Step 2: Channel dependence matrix* Manufacturer's market share. Distributor's/retailer's market share.

(Continued)

Table 1: (Continued)

Author	Year	No of axes	No of steps	Suggested dimensions
Dubinsky and Ingram	1984	2	1	Present profit contribution (contribution margin = (net sales to a particular customer − cost of goods sold)/(gross margin − direct selling expenses of salesperson)). Potential profit contribution.
Shapiro et al.	1987	2	1	Net price. Cost to serve (pre-sale costs, production costs, distribution costs and post-sale service costs).
Pels	1992	1	1	Potential to increase sales volume. Capacity to develop the seller's image. The know-how that can be created or transferred. Network effect.
Rangan et al.	1992	2	1	Price. Cost to serve.
Salle and Rost	1993	2	1	Customer attractiveness. Vulnerability of the relationship.
Yorke and Droussiotis	1994	2	2	*Step 1:* Difficulty in managing the account. Strategic importance of the account. *Step 2:* Customer profitability. Perceived strength of the relationship.
Turnbull and Zolkiewski	1997	3	1	Cost to serve. Net price. Relationship value.
Freytag and Mols	2001	2	3	*Step 1:* Divide customers to groups with regards of their importance now and in the future. *Step 2:* Net price. Cost to serve. Relationship value (note conceptualized differently to Turnbull and Zolkiewski 1997) as earnings, access to knowledge, access to certain markets, high turnover.
Ang and Taylor	2005	2	1	Gross margin. Length of tenure. Note this is operationalized in a B2C context but is derived from B2B models.

Table 1:   (Continued)

Author	Year	No of axes	No of steps	Suggested dimensions
Homburg et al.	2009	–	3	*Step 1:* Identify customer segments of different present value using customer characteristics and transaction characteristics (involves data mining using regression trees). *Step 2:* Develop empirically switching probabilities. *Step 3:* Use the material from steps 1 and 2 to calculate future contribution/predicted movements between segments.
Gök	2009	2	2	*Step 1: (current portfolio)* Relationship strength. Customer satisfaction. *Step 2: (future potential)* Business potential. Customer satisfaction.
Terho and Halinen	2012	7		*Relationship characteristics in a customer portfolio:* Relationship strength in customer portfolio. Relationship dynamism in customer portfolio. Interconnectedness of relationships in customer portfolio. *Structural characteristics of a customer portfolio:* Broadness of customer portfolio. Concentration of customer portfolio. Heterogeneity of customer portfolio. Customer turnover in customer portfolio.
Zolkiewski and Feng	2012	1	3	Sales volume. Strategic importance. Trust.
Supplier relationship analysis				
Kraljic	1983	2	1	Importance of purchasing. Complexity of the supply market.
Krapfel et al.	1991	2	1	Interest commonality. (The similarity of the economic goals of a business and its trading partner.) Relationship value (calculated using: the criticality of the goods purchased by the buyer, the quantity of the seller's output consumed by the buyer, the replaceability of this buyer and the cost savings resulting from the buyer's practices and procedures).

(Continued)

Table 1:   (Continued)

Author	Year	No of axes	No of steps	Suggested dimensions
Olsen and Ellram	1997	2	3	*Step 1: Analysis of the company's purchases* Difficulty of managing the purchase situation (includes product, supply market and environmental characteristics). Strategic importance of the purchase (includes competence, economic and image factors). *Step 2: Analyse the supplier relationships* Relative supplier attractiveness (includes financial and economic, performance, technological, organizational, cultural and strategic and other factors). Strength of relationship (includes economic factors, character of the exchange relationship, cooperation between buyer and seller and distance between buyer and seller). *Step 3: Compare the two matrices* Develop action plans (as a result of the ideal strategy suggested by step 1 and the findings from step 2).
Schiele	2012	2	2	*Step 1: Assess suppliers to determine if you have preferred customer status, criteria to be used* Technical importance. Commercial importance. Cultural fit. Past preferential treatment. Your key account status *Step 2: Develop a comparative portfolio* Buyer's status with the supplier (standard customer–preferred customer). Competitiveness of the supplier (low–high).
Relationship analysis				
Wuyts et al.	2004	2	1	Technological diversity. Level of repeated partnering.

Developed from Zolkiewski and Turnbull (2002) pp. 580–581, and Terho (2009), p. 402.

relationship management, supplier portfolios are widely adopted; for example, Gelderman and van Weele (2003) and Caniëls and Gelderman (2007) note the widespread use of Kraljic's model. However, there appears to be a wider variation in the way that customer portfolio analysis is undertaken (Terho and Halinen 2007), perhaps because many sales strategies are opportunistic in nature (Yorke and Wallace 1986). This suggests that customer portfolio analysis is not a simple implementation and adoption exercise, but rather that it needs careful planning and to be an integral part of KAM.

Talwar et al. (2008) suggest that there is limited evidence of explicit adoption of matrix-based relationship portfolio analysis in a marketing context. For example, Talwar et al.'s (2008) empirical evidence suggests that customer portfolio management is based on a division (segmentation) of customers into groups defined by their value-seeking activity. A management process is then used to allocate them into the most appropriate contact pattern, e.g. call centre versus fully fledged KAM. The selling process is also used to try to migrate customers along this continuum. This is consistent with the dichotomy proposed by Salle et al. (2000) between strategic and operational use of portfolios. Terho (2009) suggests that relationship portfolio analysis needs to be viewed as strategic, have the support of senior management and involve good cross-functional cooperation.

One practical application of customer portfolio modelling is reported by Ang and Taylor (2005). They developed a customer portfolio model for a business-to-consumer context, an Internet service provider, and utilized data on over 130,000 customers. They took a relatively simple approach by considering only gross margin (not including acquisition costs) and length of time the customer had been with the provider. They then used the results of the analysis to employ different relationship management strategies according to the quadrant in which a customer resided. For example, highly profitable short-term customers were offered an incentive to encourage them to take a longer-term contract, while stars were encouraged to become advocates by signing up a friend (Ang and Taylor 2005). Their data show some migration into the highly profitable long-term quadrant, but whether this would have happened even if no intervention had been made is not apparent. However, Ang and Taylor (2005) demonstrate that customer portfolio management can have recognized and successful outcomes.

Salle et al. (2000) observe that the different portfolio models are grounded in different perspectives on how resources should be allocated. They argue that Dubinsky and Ingram (1984), for example, use the modelling for allocation of sales resources according to assessment of profit contribution, both existing and potential. Meanwhile, the models rooted in an IMP tradition involve multi-dimensional customer–supplier relationships, which include issues such as technological interaction and the importance of the overall relationship, and could therefore be argued to be more of a strategic than tactical nature. In this respect, it can be suggested that the models rooted in a relational tradition are much more useful to key account managers, as these models allow for the identification of the critical customers for the company concerned; see, for example, how key accounts were positioned on the Shapiro et al. (1987) customer classification matrix by Turnbull and Zolkiewski (1997) in Figure 1. It can be seen how this portfolio approach highlights the accounts that deserve most attention, i.e. 'passive' and 'carriage trade'.

Understanding of broader relational constructs, such as trust, power and dependence, is also important in relationship portfolio analysis and consequently in KAM. These constructs should not be ignored when undertaking portfolio

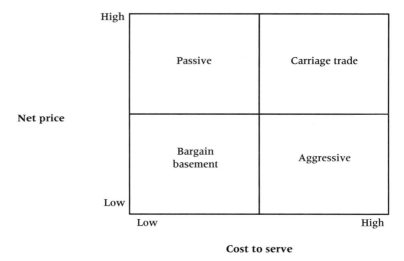

Figure 1 Key account positioning on the Shapiro et al. matrix
Source: reproduced from Turnbull and Zolkiewski (1997), p. 316

analysis. Johnson and Selnes (2004) and Zolkiewski and Feng (2012) note the importance of trust in portfolio analysis while Dickson (1983) and Caniëls and Gelderman (2007) identify the influence of power and dependency in the assessment of a portfolio. Ivens and Pardo (2007) concur; they empirically demonstrate that careful attention to managing the relationship with key customers results in increased commitment from those customers. This illustrates the complexity of portfolio dimension definition and calculation and emphasizes the need for subjective (management insight) as well as objective assessment, particularly when the portfolio analysis is being used to aid the identification of key relationships which need to be developed. Zolkiewski and Turnbull (2002) also concur with Salle et al. (2000) that portfolio analysis needs to be extended to consider the implications of the wider network within which a company, its suppliers and customers are embedded, again indicating a more strategic than operational approach to customer management.

Contextuality of portfolio analysis

Another important avenue of research has been developed by Terho and Halinen (Terho 2008, 2009; Terho and Halinen 2007, 2012), whose work explores the contextuality of portfolio analysis. Their findings suggest that in low- and medium-complexity environments more formal practices ensue, while when relationships are more intensive (highly complex contexts) management at the portfolio level is not evident (Terho and Halinen 2007). They see different customer portfolios arising to reflect different exchange conditions, and integrate perspectives from the marketing environment view and the interaction and networks perspective to analyse these (Terho and Halinen 2012). From this perspective they analyse the portfolio using seven dimensions: 'broadness, concentration, heterogeneity of the customer base, customer turnover, the strength of relationships, the dynamism of the relationships and the interconnectedness of relationships in the portfolio' (pp. 340–341) and see this as providing an empirical classification of portfolios.

Terho (2009) also develops a formative construct for customer portfolio management, comprising four dimensions: analysis efforts, analysis design, responsiveness efforts and responsiveness design. This construct highlights the multi-level and inter-functional nature of customer portfolio management. He emphasizes the need to consider both strength and style of management practices.

Portfolios in technology-intensive industries

Customer portfolios have also been specifically identified as important factors in areas such as new product development for young technology-based firms (Yli-Renko and Janakiraman 2008) and capability development for SMEs (Furlan et al. 2009), which illustrates how the identification of the key customers is critical in all sizes and types of company. Wuyts et al. (2004) observe the importance of using a portfolio approach to maximize the impact of effective knowledge transfer with respect to R&D relationships. Their findings are derived from the pharmaceutical industry where they see technological diversity as having a positive impact on both radical and incremental innovation, while the level of repeated partnering only affects radical innovations. This is argued to be because ongoing relationships facilitate complex knowledge transfer.

Wuyts et al. (2004) also find that diverse portfolios facilitate inter-organizational learning. Meanwhile, Yli-Renko and Janakiraman (2008) have observed an inverse U-shaped relationship between the number of new products developed and customer portfolio size. Additionally, they note that relational embeddedness is also a significant factor if the portfolio size is too small or large, suggesting again that factors such as relationship quality and more subjective elements relating to relationship management have to be given equal attention in portfolio management decisions.

Dynamics and portfolio analysis

Portfolio analysis is criticized for being often used as a static analysis. However, portfolios can be used effectively to monitor relationship dynamics. Indeed, it is often the key account manager's role to monitor these dynamics. For example, Furlan et al. (2009) show that as Italian SMEs develop marketing and design capabilities the composition of their customer portfolio changes, resulting in an increase in collaborative relationships. Homburg et al. (2009) argue that it is essential that the dynamic nature of customer portfolios is considered in any analysis. They suggest that there has been limited focus on capturing dynamics as part of portfolio analysis. However, some earlier work has focused on changes to the customer portfolio over time (Ang and Taylor 2005; Shapiro et al. 1987; Turnbull and Zolkiewski 1997) but this work has been retrospective rather than prospective.

Key to these dynamics is an understanding of how key account management strategies are influencing these changes. Clarke and Freytag (2013) note the importance of orchestrating the portfolio, not least by ensuring alignment with respect to key customers' strategic aims. Through introducing a customer lifetime value model that takes into account switching behaviour, Homburg et al. (2009) make the issue of dynamics into a central aspect of strategic decision-making around customer portfolios. They also force the consideration of future risk related to both individual customers and different segments. It is argued more widely that customer or segment risk analysis should be seen as one of the under-lying principles behind portfolio management (e.g. Ryals 2002). Bolton and Tarasi (2006) also highlight the balancing or optimization of risk and return as being a central managerial challenge related to portfolio management.

Homburg et al. (2009) propose two strategies for dealing with customer/segment risk: an offensive approach which seeks new customers and also focuses on developing existing customers, while a defensive approach aims not to lose cus-tomers or let their value contribution deteriorate. As part of this they see a need for observing customer behaviour to determine what the drivers are for switching and including this in the portfolio analysis, resulting in a complex three-step contextually-based analysis tool (their data show considerable differences between sectors). Such observations are essential in order to understand the value contri-bution made by key customers, especially because Homburg et al. (2009) suggest that value contribution deterioration may be more detrimental to an organization than actually losing a customer. They also discuss the importance of considering deteriorating relationships and the strategy to ensure that the decline in value of the contribution that customers, including key customers, is not overlooked. They argue that this approach highlights that marketers are in danger of focusing on inappropriate key accounts/customers/segments if they only rely on static analysis.

Switching behaviours are only one form of relationship dynamic; there are others such as changes in patterns of spending that also need to be considered. This issue of dynamics or changes that occur over the life cycle of a relationship is also beginning to be explicitly investigated in KAM, with authors such as Hsieh and Chou (2011) noting the changes in alignment between key account customers and the supplier; observing that they varied over the relationship life cycle and involved passive, opportunistic, mutualistic and compensatory forms of align-ment. These forms of alignment should also be considered as relevant to portfolio assessment.

An alternative issue relating to the dynamic nature of relationships and specifically focusing on temporality comes from Mota and De Castro (2005) who point out that due to the learning processes that take place in relationships, the dimensions used to assess customer portfolios need to be changed to reflect such learning processes. Taken to the extreme, this implies that a dynamic set of axes need to be employed to cater for learning and capability development within relationships and especially those with key customers.

Customer lifetime value and other financially derived models

The manner in which customer portfolios are used to guide the day-to-day management of relationships has also evolved into a discussion of customer lifetime value, and customer portfolio lifetime value, e.g. Johnson and Selnes (2004). Johnson and Selnes (2004) highlight the dynamic nature of such relationship management processes. They focus on value creation and the different ways in which it is created as their portfolio analysis criteria and note three different strategies for customer value creation: 'parity value, differential value and customized value' (p. 2). However, the calculation of lifetime customer value is fraught with difficulties; it relies on predictions and the categorization of customers into a typology of strangers, acquaintances, friends and partners (Johnson and Selnes 2004) and implies a progression to increased value. This progression towards increased value or profit was also included in Shapiro et al.'s (1987) work. However, Turnbull and Zolkiewski's (1997) empirical work does not reflect an upwards steady progression of profit; rather, their results show that 'partner' relationships (key accounts) may not provide the increase in value or profitability that is anticipated. It may be that this type of projection is not reflective of the dynamics and uncertainty in the environment. Additionally, it supports Håkansson and Snehota's (1995) views that close relationships can be restrictive and preclude a company from more profitable interactions. Perhaps it is more important that this type of analysis should encourage a company to consider how it can balance its stronger and weaker relationships (Johnson and Selnes 2004) and reflect critically upon which customers it identifies as key accounts.

Nonetheless, the use of financial models and theory to calculate portfolio value as a tool to optimize customer portfolio performance and management has been receiving increasing attention (Ryals 2002, 2003; Tarasi et al. 2011). Ryals (2002) considers the implications of using financial metrics to calculate the value of a customer or segment by looking at the ratio determined by comparing future cash flows with the weighted average cost of capital. She notes the difficulties of assessing customer risk and suggests that the traditional risk scorecard may not capture all the risks associated with a customer, e.g. risk related to changes in purchasing patterns. Ryals (2002) then promotes the view that incorporating an awareness of customer risk can help managers develop targeted relationship strategies to both reduce risk and increase the value of the customer/key account.

Tarasi et al. (2011) illustrate that financial portfolio theory can be used to develop an efficient customer portfolio that appears to outperform the firm in question's existing portfolio. Notwithstanding the actual limitations of the analysis undertaken, financial portfolio theory can be argued to be problematic. Selnes (2011) observes that marketers have always taken a simple diversification approach to their customer portfolios, but financial portfolios are more complex, aiming for low correlation of returns. Tarasi et al.'s (2011) approach equates customers to financial assets which, according to Selnes (2011), does not take into account issues such as how the customer portfolio relates to a company's production function or innovation. Nor does this allow for recognition of the strategic need to identify key customers. At the same time this approach adds to the complexity versus simplicity argument that relates to the dimensions used in the analysis, where too much complexity may obscure the simplicity of the portfolio approach and too little may mean that important variables are overlooked (Gök 2009; Olsen and Ellram 1997).

Using financial models to help optimize portfolios makes a number of underlying assumptions about the data that are available to a marketing or account manager. For example, it assumes that activity-based costing is being implemented by the firm and is accessible to the marketer; yet, as Yorke (1984) notes, the costs of acquiring, retaining and motivating customers to buy are lost in an amorphous and often large item called 'sales and marketing expenses' (p. 21). Billett (2011) also notes that the access and transaction costs for customer segments are not homogenous and therefore may differ from firm to firm. This is even more so for key customers. Another issue relates to the accuracy of the data in the customer relationship management (CRM) system used to support this type of analysis (Ryals 2002) and ensuring that the system is regularly updated, otherwise the data cannot give an accurate picture of the customer portfolio. The cost of data mining is another consideration; there is lack of consensus about how this can be determined but it is recognized to be significant (Marbán et al. 2008). And, of course, ability to predict the future is an art not a science; Tarasi et al. (2011) quote Bernstein (1999) who notes that even the most brilliant mathematician cannot predict the future. An additional concern is the implication that you can choose which customers you have and control the costs to serve them (cf. Shapiro et al. 1987).

Customer relationship management and relationship portfolios

IT is changing practice extensively (Geiger and Guenzi 2009) and it could be argued that technology is undermining the need for managers to understand portfolios, with more focus falling onto a discussion of CRM systems and their implicit algorithms as well as the use of other sales technology (Hunter and Perreault 2007). However, Hunter and Perreault (2007) also point out that the technology cannot manage relationships and that personnel need to be involved in it. Bolton and Tarasi (2006) also emphasize the need to consider both systems and processes as well as recognizing that, if used correctly, CRM systems can provide supporting metrics for customer portfolio management.

Bohling et al. (2006), however, note the patchy success of CRM implementation and put this down to lack of top-level management support and strategic integration. Johnson et al. (2012) also note the reluctance of firms to fully embrace CRM principles, suggesting that product and sales-led philosophies militate against true customer-centric operations.

Given the discussion that there has been about CRM, its adoption and its success, it is somewhat surprising that there is limited empirical business-to-business research into the adoption of CRM systems (Ata and Toker 2012). Hence, Ata and Toker (2012) explore the adoption of CRM in a Turkish context and demonstrate a positive impact of CRM on both customer satisfaction and organizational performance. They define CRM as 'a strategic macroprocess aiming to build and sustain a profit-maximizing portfolio of customer relationships' (p. 497) and illustrate its relationship with portfolio management. Ata and Toker (2012) also note that CRM adoption is often not a strategic decision but more tactical and see that this concurs with the findings of Bohling et al. (2006). Such views give strength to the argument that customer portfolio analysis is important as it can be argued to be more focused than CRM solutions. It is the senior managers who need to make the strategic decisions and, together with the sales force, they have to consider customer acquisition, retention and divestment, and this is where the notion of the customer portfolio has its primacy.

Segmentation and/or portfolio analysis

A perpetual question that remains when discussing customer portfolio analysis is how it is related to market segmentation. Homburg et al. (2009) and Tarasi et al. (2011) use customer segments as their unit of analysis rather than individual relationships, which suggests that customer portfolio management could be used either as a tool to focus on individual relationships or more broadly to focus on customer segments according to the size of the customer base and the characteristics of the customers. However, this moves away from the principle of using segmentation bases to analyse the majority of customers and portfolio analysis to analyse key accounts (Zolkiewski and Turnbull 2002).

Bolton and Tarasi (2006) comment on the applicability of segmentation and emphasize that the point of segmentation is to identify a group of customers who have the same needs and requirements. However, segmentation, in business-to-business markets, can be argued to be a useful but anonymous tool (Zolkiewski and Turnbull 2002) that does not focus on the inter-relationships of the customers in the target market nor allow for the identification of key customers. In many contexts it could be argued to be too simplistic an approach in an

IT-enabled global and networked world, where interconnections and competition through and between networks is shaping the competitive landscape (Gulati et al. 2000).

Tarasi et al. (2011) note that customer portfolio analysis is particularly relevant for business-to-business markets because in this arena firms tend to focus greater proportions of their resources on individual customers and key accounts, cf. consumer markets. Portfolio analysis is also considered to be preferable when distinct customers' requirements need to be considered rather than when clear segments of homogenous groups of customers can be discerned (Terho and Halinen 2007). In this case, customer portfolios could be argued simply to be identifying segmentation bases that are relationally driven. Indeed this has been suggested by Elliott and Glynn (1998) as a mechanism for segmenting retail banking relationships. Bolton and Tarasi (2006) emphasize that the central tenet of customer portfolios is to allow managers to progress beyond the traditional segmentation approach in order to consider the dynamic management of the key relationships in their portfolio.

The issue of managing relationships in a dynamic context is a central challenge in business-to-business marketing (Ford et al. 1986) and has been argued to be the main reason why portfolios are an inappropriate management tool, in that they can move the focus away from the relationship itself (Dubois and Pedersen 2002). Nonetheless, managers still need mechanisms to determine which relationships they should resource and to help in the identification of key accounts; relationship portfolio analysis is specifically designed to analyse relationships and to help with these decisions. So as long as this analysis takes dynamics into consideration it is a good mechanism to support such decision-making.

Managerial implications

The review above shows that there are multiple relationship portfolio models, covering customers, suppliers and relationships generally, which are based upon different levels of analysis, individual customers and market segments, and which can be used tactically and strategically. Hence, it is necessary to consider what this means for business-to-business marketing and key account managers.

It is important for managers to consider the insight that relationship portfolio analysis can bring to understanding their key customers' needs and also how to allocate relevant resources across their portfolio of customers/suppliers. This is particularly important when customers perceive themselves to be in a relationship with the supplier or vice versa. However, if portfolio analysis is applied retrospectively only, it brings with it the danger that the focus will be on past issues rather than understanding and meeting customers' changing needs. Additionally, there is a danger of simply focusing on existing customers and forgetting to search for new customers and/or relationships and, in turn, considering their impact on the existing portfolio. As well as encouraging managers to seek new relationships, when adopted strategically, relationship portfolio management should encourage managers to consider fading relationships as well as those that need to end because they no longer fit with the strategic direction of the company or because they are simply demanding too much resource. This should be seen as central to key account management.

Managers need to be aware that portfolios can be used on a number of different levels, for example, for allocating sales resources across key accounts, or more broadly in thinking about the overall nature of a company's complete set of resources. The importance of understanding portfolios when looking for innovative partners and in R&D contexts illustrates this point. Smackey (1977) emphasizes the importance of allocating sales resources to the customers that have the most potential to contribute to a firm's profitability. Yorke and Wallace (1986) are also early contributors to this debate, reminding us that efficient allocation of marketing resources to target customers is critical to a firm's success. However, as the discussion above about understanding the importance of customer portfolios in new product development and innovation illustrates, an understanding of customer portfolios can assist in allocation of a wide range of resources. For portfolio analysis to be effective at this level, it needs strategic-level integration, top-level management support and also consideration of the wider network implications of decisions that are made.

The discussion about the range of models and dimensions provided above demonstrates that relationship portfolio analysis requires considerable strategic and critical thinking from managers. It will never fall into the genre of simply-applied strategic tools and fixes unless it is being considered in a very simplistic fashion. The contextuality surrounding the application of relationship portfolio analysis requires managers to use their knowledge and industry insight to ensure effective application of the tool, both operationally and in strategic-level thinking.

Relationship portfolio management should not be viewed as a once-a-year planning tool. It needs to be undertaken on an ongoing basis and must be used to assist in the identification and management of key accounts, to monitor relationship dynamics and to give insight into how to react to the changes observed as well as simply assessing where the company is now. It should also not be seen as a job to be done by marketing analysts or planners; it needs to be part of all managers' remits.

The more complex customer lifetime value-based analysis tools are complicated and time consuming to develop; thus they are more expensive to implement. Managers need to be certain that they have the detailed level of data needed to calculate such factors and appropriate algorithms to make the calculations relevant as well as resources to devote to the process. They should also consider if the costs of such systems do provide the returns to justify their implementation. We would suggest that such models are best used to assist in decision-making rather than becoming prescriptive mandates. They are designed to help to manage risk and as such managers utilizing these tools need to ensure that they completely understand what the risk factors are in their contexts, so a careful analysis of the risk driving factors in the area needs to be undertaken.

Relationship portfolio analysis and CRM should not be considered to be the same. They both can be central to good customer management schemas, but cannot be simply substituted for one another. Portfolio analysis should be used to guide the assignment of key account status to specific relationships. CRM should be viewed as a complementary mechanism for dealing with customers who do not warrant such careful attention. This is not to say that any customers' needs should be treated lightly, but that CRM may be more effective for dealing with customers who are being serviced through less personalized channels.

Relationship portfolio analysis necessitates the collection of detailed information about customers and their needs; which the advent of management/marketing information systems has facilitated. However, as early as 1976 Hartley noted the importance of collecting and analysing customer data to ensure improved market penetration and customer orientation, so this is not a new idea. The approach is supported by the view that marketing is primarily an information-handling problem (Holland and Naudé 2004) and perhaps suggests that an efficient and effective information collection system is the primary tool needed to ensure the success of relationship portfolio analysis. It does not negate, however, the importance of key account managers relating to, deeply understanding and personally knowing their customers.

Relationship portfolio analysis should be seen as informing strategic direction with respect to identification of the key accounts and customers that a firm has or desires. However, while Clarke and Freytag (2013) remind us to consider how we are aligned with these key customers, we need to be aware that such alignment does not imply symmetry of the relationship. It is important to recognize that key relationships are rarely symmetrical (see, for example, Ryals and Davies (2013)), and that customers' strategic intents are not necessarily the same as those of their suppliers. Awareness of this disparity will aid managerial decision-making with respect to selection of key customers and militate understanding that, while strategic intent of customers is important, it is understanding how these strategies relate to key relationships that is important in their management and selection.

In an international context, particularly in emerging economies, the use of relationship analysis is still nascent. Contextuality can be seen to be important in this arena but the limited evidence from the research discussed above (both Zolkiewski and Feng (2012) and Talwar et al. (2008) have empirical data from BRIC countries) suggests that relationship portfolio analysis is not as apparent in such economies, probably because the markets are not yet mature and it is a seller's market. However, the situation offers an opportunity to managers in that if they can use portfolio analysis effectively here they can be in a position to 'cherry pick' the most 'profitable' accounts in these emerging markets. Tsybina and Rebiazina

(2013), meanwhile, observe that in a Russian context the interconnectedness of companies is very influential on the portfolio, resulting in smaller companies often being treated as key customers because of their relationships with large buyers, again emphasizing the need to consider the context in which the analysis is being performed.

Relationship portfolio analysis needs to be inextricably linked to an understanding that its prime purpose actually relates to profitability for the company that is utilizing it. Profitability may be in financial terms or more broadly defined as providing access to knowledge, innovation, other markets, etc. The important factor here is that managers recognize and understand the costs of looking after different customers and also the benefits that it brings to their organization. Managers should be aware when customers become too resource demanding, and they need to be in a position to apply different management strategies to reverse these situations. The findings discussed above do not point to a 'one-size-fits-all' strategy that can be applied; they show the variety of factors that needs to be considered. Managers should rely on their vision and insight to apply the most creative strategy to the context, in order that they retain the company's competitive advantage and meet their customers' needs.

Of course, the use of relationship portfolio analysis is not without critics. It can be argued that relationship portfolio analysis tools suffer from the same problems as corporate portfolio analysis tools. For example, Untiedt et al. (2012) identify problems relating to over-simplification of complex and interdependent decisions, problems with the underlying assumptions that have been made and also misapplication issues. However, Untiedt et al. (2012) also support the use of portfolio analysis and suggest that what is actually needed is research to advance it and to enable managers to understand how to differentiate between when to use the analysis diagnostically and when it should be used prescriptively. Zolkiewski and Turnbull (2002) also list additional criticisms such as problems of mixing subjective and actual data, complexity of calculating customer profitability, data distortion over time and imprecise scales. However, despite these limitations it can be argued that the benefits of formally considering and analysing your relationship portfolio far outweigh simply taking an 'anonymous' approach to customer and/ or supplier management and acquisition.

Another criticism of portfolio models is that they are unable to cope with issues such as how relationships can be used to improve efficiency and/or productivity (Mota and de Castro 2005). Similarly, Dubois and Pedersen (2002) contend that portfolio analysis actually removes focus from managing relationships in their network context and can move managers' attention away from focusing on ongoing interactions. However, Zolkiewski and Turnbull (2002) do make recommendations about how network factors can be taken into account in portfolio analysis; see Figure 2. Indeed, it could be argued that the ambition of portfolio analysis to ensure that managers consider the inter-related nature of resource decisions does force a consideration of network factors.

Step 3
Identify all portfolios and interactions
between the portfolios

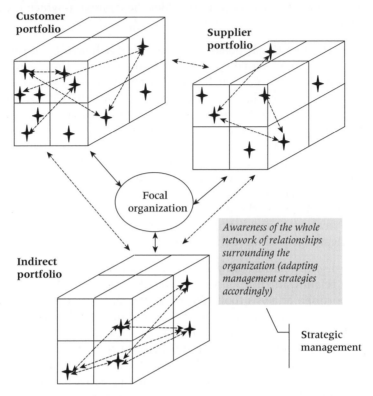

Figure 2   A network approach to portfolio analysis
Source: reproduced from Zolkiewski and Turnbull (2002), p. 587

Conclusion

The discussion above about relationship portfolios illustrates the heterogeneity in understanding of the term relationship portfolio; on the one hand these portfolios are simply analytic tools responding to faceless customers, while on the other they can be used to help determine future strategy of a firm and are central to key account management. This is a contextually-embedded phenomenon and it is in the hands of managers to exploit it correctly. Mota and de Castro (2005) support Gelderman and Van Weele's (2003) view that there is no single blueprint for portfolio management and that its use necessitates critical thinking. Using portfolio analysis requires a careful balance between selecting appropriate criteria and not over complicating the analysis so that it obscures the strategic decision-making it is designed to support.

We contend that, when used well, portfolio analysis can assist in identifying key accounts and ensuring all relationships that a firm is engaged with can be profitable, either financially or through providing access to scarce resources that the company needs for its ongoing success. Relationship portfolio analysis also forces managers to consider if the relationships they are engaged in are necessary for their firms' success, if they are really 'key' and also when they need to find additional relationships to ensure their future survival. Managers need to recognize when they are engaging in different relationships and what these relationships contribute to the firm's ongoing success.

Account portfolio management: optimizing the customer portfolio of the firm

BY OSMAN GÖK

Abstract

The account portfolio management (APM) process deals with grouping customers and developing meaningful strategies for each group incorporated into resource allocation decisions to meet marketing objectives. Portfolio techniques offer a convenient and comprehensible framework for strategic decision-making. This paper presents a comprehensive guide to developing customer portfolios using variables identified in previous studies. The paper also illustrates implications for marketing strategies and future resource allocation for the strategic account portfolio. A portfolio approach may reveal necessary actions for important relationships and may streamline the decision-making process for suppliers' account portfolios. Each customer relationship requires different types and degrees of investment and produces different outcomes (Cannon and Perreault 1999). Hence the paper emphasizes customer heterogeneity in the business-to-business (B2B) marketing context and arrives at sound evaluations of individual customers.

Introduction

The APM approach divides customers into subgroups, evaluates each group and suggests a strategic group of customers as a major output of its analysis. Such strategic groups have been variously termed 'major accounts', 'national accounts', 'key accounts', 'strategic accounts' and 'global accounts'. Pardo et al. (2006) argue that key account management originates in suppliers' recognition of the fact that not all customers are equal, as some typically represent an extremely high percentage of sales or profits (Håkansson and Snehota 1995).

Issues of strategic accounts in industrial markets have been studied for a number of years, originally in the sales management context (e.g. Churchill et al. 1993; Comer 1991; Dalrymple and Cron 1992; Kirkby 1988; Rackham 1988; Shapiro and Moriarty 1982). Both in the literature and in practice, the terms 'national accounts', 'major accounts' and 'major sales' have been used interchangeably to refer to the special clients of B2B suppliers. Early studies on the topic emphasized geographical spread and size of customers. Millman (1996) defined key accounts as those customers in industrial and B2B markets that selling companies identify as of strategic importance. This strategic importance is generally determined by volume-related considerations (Millman and Wilson 1996) and profit (McDonald et al. 1997). However, other customer characteristics can also identify an account as 'strategic'. These include accounts that provide access to new markets, technologies and/or quality systems and can give their suppliers the competitive advantage of being the first in their market, with a specific new know-how or application (Pels 1992). In some cases, a customer's referral value can be critical to the selling company's motivation to win their business, because, as a reference account, the customer can deliver a great deal more business to the company indirectly.

Account portfolio management

Increasing competition, technological change and many well-known environmental factors have encouraged companies to move away from fragile relationships between salespeople and buyers and to pursue customer retention and long-term customer relations. For the last three decades, customer relationships have been evaluated as a strategic asset for companies, particularly those competing in the B2B context, and many companies hope to gain a competitive advantage by forming stronger relationships with fewer customers and suppliers.

In recent years, the nature of buyer–seller relationships has become one of the most discussed topics in the marketing literature (e.g. Campbell 1997; Dwyer et al. 1987; Ganesan 1994; Holmlund 2004; Meehan and Wright 2012; Palmer and Bejou 1994). Unlike producers of consumer goods and services, most industrial sellers rely on a small number of key customers, and losing one may radically affect the survival of the company. Hence there is a strong link between customer portfolio management strategies and overall business strategies of B2B suppliers. Account portfolio analysis (APA) is a concept of B2B marketing used for analysing supplier–customer relationships, in order to help managers allocate scarce organizational resources (Ford 1997). Account portfolio approaches assess customer composition and develop relevant strategies for different groups of accounts. Hence, portfolio techniques offer a convenient and comprehensible framework for strategic decision-making. Johnson and Selnes (2004) argue that the relationship marketing literature recognizes the need to build portfolios of relationships or relational resources to increase a firm's return on relationships.

The portfolio approach was first studied by Markowitz (1952) to evaluate the risks of investment decisions. Following Markowitz's portfolio theory, portfolio models have been applied to strategic planning for decades (Ansoff and Leontiades 1976; Wind and Douglas 1981). Other portfolio models have been studied in business domains related to customer relationships (Campbell and Cunningham 1983; Fiocca 1982; Johnson and Selnes 2004; Krapfel et al. 1991; Yorke 1984), supplier relations (Cunningham and Homse 1982; Kraljic 1983; Wagner and Johnson 2004), technology (Capon and Glazer 1987) and new product development (Cooper et al. 1999).

Broadly defined, customer portfolio analysis refers to a company's analysis of the current and future value of its customers in order to develop a balanced customer structure through effective resource allocation to different customers or customer groups. Balancing a customer portfolio can be regarded as the central goal of customer portfolio analysis (Terho and Halinen 2007). Customer portfolio analysis has the potential to provide valuable insights for evaluating account relationships and making more efficient resource allocation decisions.

The use of a portfolio model often suggests several possible action plans from which the company must choose due to limited resources (Olsen and Ellram 1997). Hence, the value of portfolio approaches to customer relationships is strongly linked to the company's business strategies and resource allocation decisions. Portfolio analysis can therefore enhance and promote marketing planning and communication (Dubinsky and Ingram 1984). Kotler et al. (1996) point out that portfolio analysis is useful in evaluating customer relations for development and control purposes, and also in ensuring the long-term profitability of customer relationships. The portfolio concept encourages the analysis of a supplier's needs and requirements from the proposed relationship before committing resources towards these objectives (Eng 2004).

Prior portfolio studies have addressed companies' account portfolios and grouped their customers to make the relationship portfolio efficient and balanced. Fiocca (1982) suggested a two-step customer portfolio analysis: first, all customers were classified according to their strategic importance and the difficulty of managing the account; second, strategic accounts were analysed using a second portfolio, including the dimensions of customer attractiveness and strength of the buyer–supplier relationship. Fiocca (1982) then suggested marketing strategies according to the positions of customers in the two matrices. Campbell and Cunningham (1983) classified customer relations into four life cycle segments: 'yesterday's customers', 'today's regular customers', 'today's special customers' and 'tomorrow's customers'. Dubinsky and Ingram (1984) offered a profitability perspective and developed a portfolio that considered the present and potential profit contribution of customers. In addition, Krapfel et al. (1991) suggested a path to operationalize the constructs of relationship value and interest commonality, and then offer classifications for relationship types and management modes in a theoretically grounded structure.

In their case study, Yorke and Droussiotis (1994) based their portfolio dimensions on Fiocca's analysis but also included the factor of customer profitability, and offered a convenient portfolio approach. Zolkiewski and Turnbull (2002) evaluated relationship portfolios in the context of network theory and proposed that such portfolios might be a key factor in successful relationship management. Eng (2008) also presented a network approach to APA, suggesting that a firm can better enhance its competitive position with the knowledge of network effects and the interdependence of strategic actions in a business network context. Johnson and Selnes (2004) introduced a value-based approach to APA and proposed a model that links individual customer value with a firm's overall value creation and classified customers as acquaintances, friends or partners.

Some authors (Dhar and Glazer 2003; Ryals 2002, 2003; Tarasi et al. 2011) have attempted to apply financial portfolio theory to customer portfolio analysis and to formulate the risk and return characteristics of customer relationships. It is possible to conceptualize customers as financial assets, which assumes the option of applying the value concept in financial theory to marketing and customer portfolio value. Although this is a legitimate argument, marketing managers tend to take a broader view of customer portfolio value than just financial assets (Selnes 2011). Hence, identifying customer relationships as financial assets can be problematic in some ways. Marketing functions and managers have multifaceted objectives and priorities when evaluating their customer relationships, rather than the mechanistic outcomes of financial portfolio techniques. A fruitful debate on the applicability of the financial portfolio approach to customer portfolio analysis seems likely to continue in further research in the near future (see Selnes et al. (2011) for further discussion).

Another recent stream of research in account portfolio analysis deals with software-induced analytic approaches (Ang and Taylor 2005; Gopalan 2007; Homburg et al. 2009; Jouini et al. 2004; Zhiyuan et al. 2010). This research stream, which combines mathematical modelling, data-mining techniques and customer data generated by customer relationship management (CRM) software, suggests a dynamic portfolio analysis approach. Indeed, increasing the use of software technologies allows companies to store extensive customer data, and this trend is setting the stage for the implementation of analytic approaches and modelling techniques for account portfolio analysis.

Account portfolio analysis and development of customer strategies

Ford et al. (1998) suggested that relationship management is the most critical marketing challenge, particularly in a B2B situation, where firms often rely on a small number of customers and suppliers; where markets are relatively static; and where maintaining relationships is often essential to ongoing business success. In such situations, where the addition or loss of a key customer can have dramatic effects on the company's turnover, profitability and viability, portfolio analysis can act as a very useful tool by identifying key strategic relationships (Zolkiewski and Turnbull 2002). Portfolio management tools, in addition to aiding strategic planning, can potentially help businesses fine-tune their customer offerings and develop competitive advantages (Dibb and Wensley 2002).

APA involves grouping customers on a portfolio grid and developing meaningful strategies for each group incorporated into resource allocation decisions. The concept of customer portfolio analysis is similar to the concept of segmentation, but there are significant differences between the two. Portfolio analysis focuses on the value of existing customers from the focal company's point of view, whereas segmentation generally focuses on dividing the market into distinct subsets of homogeneous customers, either on the basis of specific customer needs or buying behaviours, or more generally on customers' expected response to marketing mix stimuli (Terho and Halinen 2007).

Portfolio analysis and management can be applied from multiple perspectives, at various levels of aggregation, and with different strategic variables or portfolio components, depending upon the company's objectives and specific situations (Turnbull 1990). The portfolio concept's flexibility for use at different levels of management and with different levels of sophistication makes it a powerful management tool (Turnbull 1990). Account portfolio analyses apply sound portfolio dimensions and significant indicators in order to provide a convenient and strategic framework for a company's customer relationships. The strategic variable or customer portfolio dimension may correspond to an independent variable or form part of a composite dimension (Pardo and Salle 1995). Olsen and Ellram (1997) point out the importance of complexity in the dimensions used to categorize the elements in the portfolio. On one hand, if the dimensions are overly complex, a company may focus on developing measures that do not utilize the full potential of the portfolio approach in terms of improved resource allocation and communication; on the other hand, if the dimensions are too simple, important variables may be overlooked.

Two company cases presented here demonstrate a framework for customer portfolio analysis and propose tailored relationship strategies through a convenient managerial approach. Company case studies on portfolio analysis, which have been conducted in prior research (Campbell and Cunningham 1983; Wagner and Johnson 2004; Yorke and Droussiotis 1994), have the potential to produce valuable outcomes.

Company case I: Logistics services[1]

The company used in this case study is a medium-sized logistics services provider serving 62 customers from various industries. In order to avoid disclosing customers' names, they were randomly labelled with numbers from 1 to 62 at the beginning of the portfolio analysis. The models developed by Campbell and Cunningham (1983), Fiocca (1982) and Yorke and Droussiotis (1994) are used here as a point of departure in the development of portfolio models.

Our approach employs a two-step APA. First, 62 customers of the logistics company were rated according to their strategic importance and the difficulty of managing the relationship. The resulting matrix reveals the company's strategic account portfolio and also the least strategic ones. Next, the company's strategic accounts were analysed using a second matrix, including the dimensions of customer attractiveness and strength of the buyer–supplier relationship. Simultaneous consideration of both dimensions may reveal the current situation of relationships, suggest directions for allocating resources, and generate sound strategies for strategic account relationships. Such a concurrent evaluation exposes not only the strengths and weaknesses of the company's customer relationships, but also guides accurate directions for and investments in relationships.

Variables used for portfolio analysis

Generally, industrial suppliers have a group of customers that convey much more strategic importance than others. These customers require individual attention and customized solutions throughout business relations. A customer's strategic importance might result from the dollar value of that customer's purchases, the potential of business with that customer, new market opportunities that are or may be gained by serving that customer or the prestige of the account. In addition to the account's strategic importance, the selling company should consider the difficulty of managing each customer relationship. This dimension reveals relative levels of effort and resources required for each customer relationship. Such levels of difficulty may be indicated by the complexity of a customer's product/service requirements, the intensity of competition in the account, payment problems, the customer's claiming attitudes and complaint severity/frequency, or frequent order cancellations or modifications. These variables have been used in earlier portfolio studies (Campbell and Cunningham 1983; Fiocca 1982; Yorke and Droussiotis 1994).

The account portfolio studies considered used the strength of the relationship as another portfolio dimension and proposed several indicators for measuring this dimension, such as customer share, length of the relationship, power, geographic

---

[1] This company case is partly a modified version of a proceedings paper: Gök, O. (2007) Using customer portfolio analysis for strategic business decisions: case study of a logistics company. *3rd International Strategic Management Conference*, Antalya, Turkey, 757–765.

distance, magnitude of purchases, frequency of contact, trust and cooperation. Additionally, in the light of future-related strategic considerations, companies should consider customers' business attractiveness for effective resource allocation decisions. Business attractiveness is indicative of the status/position of the customer's business in the light of future orientations. Variables used to measure a customer's business attractiveness are the dollar value of the customer's purchases, competitors' share of the customer's purchases, the growth rate of the customer's purchases, future capacity expansions, contribution margins, account prestige and the customer's sensitivity to price.

Some of the data related to the variables of the dimensions were collected from the logistics company's marketing department's reports (i.e. dollar value of purchases, age of relationships and growth rate of purchases), and the customers were categorized along a five-point scale. The remaining variables were independently rated on a five-point scale by two top managers in the company, i.e. the general manager and assistant general manager, who are the key decision-makers for managing customer relationships and who also define weighting scores for each portfolio variable. The averages of these two managers' ratings were used for analysis. All variables in the analysis were rated using a five-point scale. At the first stage of the analysis, strategic importance and the difficulty of managing each customer relationship were examined on a grid. At the second stage, only strategic accounts were positioned on another portfolio matrix with respect to the strength of the relationship and their business attractiveness. A summary of the variables used for the measurement of all four portfolio dimensions is shown in Table 1.

Analysing the general account portfolio of the firm

At this first stage, the supplier company rates the strategic importance and the difficulty of managing each customer relationship. This analysis provides a meaningful framework for the supplier in which customer relationships require individual concentration and in-depth analysis, which will result in revealing the company's strategic account portfolio. In addition to sales and volume considerations regarding the customers, the customer's business potential, prestige value and access to new markets and technologies are also substantial variables in identifying an account as 'strategic'.

Following calculations, each customer was positioned in one of Fiocca's (1982) four quadrants as shown in the difficulty–importance grid in Figure 1. The lines dividing the quadrants represent the mean scores of all customers for each dimension. After examining the position of the customers on the matrix, the supplier can decide which accounts deserve a more in-depth analysis. Normally, the customers in Cells 2 and 4 are considered 'strategic accounts' worthy of further analysis.

Cell 4 of the matrix in Figure 1 shows 14 strategic and easily managed customers who can be considered major contributors to the company's profits. The company

Table 1: Summary of the variables used for measurement

Variables	Weighting	Summary of the variable
Strategic importance of the account		
Dollar value of purchases	0.40	Average of monthly sales turnovers in the previous year.
Potential of the account	0.25	Future potential of the customer's purchases.
Open new markets	0.25	New market opportunities that are or will be gained by serving the customer.
Prestige of the account	0.10	Reputation of the customer.
Difficulty in managing the account		
Complexity of customer's service requirements	0.40	Complication of the customer's logistics services requirements.
Customer's tendency to create competition	0.30	Customer's attitude towards competition and tendency to create competition between logistics suppliers.
Payment problems	0.10	Customer's bad debts and delayed payment attitudes.
Claims put forward	0.10	Customer's claiming attitudes and complaint severity and frequency.
Frequent order cancellations or modifications	0.10	Frequency of order cancellations and modifications.
Relationship strength		
Dollar value of purchases	0.30	Average of monthly sales turnovers in the previous year.
Length of relationship	0.20	Age of the customer relationship.
Customer share	0.20	Company's share of the customer's total logistics services purchases.
Frequency of contact	0.10	Communication and contact frequency with the customer.
Degree of cooperation	0.10	Frequency and depth of cooperational business practices between parties.
Trust	0.10	Mutual trust between parties.
Customer's business attractiveness		
Competitors' share of customer's purchases	0.20	Competitors' share of the customer's total logistics services purchases.
Dollar value of purchases	0.20	Average of monthly sales turnovers in the previous year.
Growth rate of purchases	0.15	Average of percentages of increases/decreases in sales turnovers for the previous year's monthly figures.
Future capacity expansions	0.15	Capacity expansion plans of the customer and planned investments for expansion in buildings and machinery.
Contribution margins	0.15	Contribution margins of services sold to customer.
Prestige of the account	0.10	The reputation of the customer.
Sensitivity to price	0.05	Hard-bargaining attitudes of the customer and price-related tensions in the relationship.

General account portfolio analysis

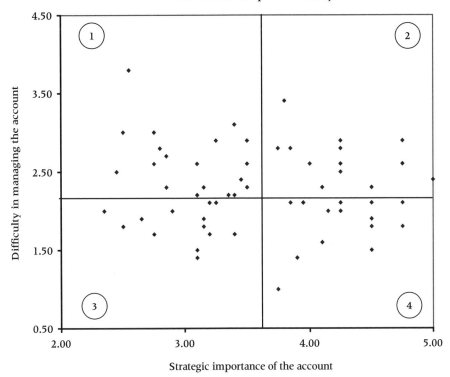

Figure 1 Difficulty–importance grid

gains larger revenues from these customers with relatively lower administration costs. Cell 2 includes 13 key customers that are relatively difficult to manage, sometimes problematic and complicated. Like those in Cell 4, these customers can have significant strategic importance for the company, but the company expends more effort to gain and retain these customers' orders. Such customers may be open to competitors' offerings, though they may not be involved in a persistent search for alternative suppliers for each logistics service requirement.

Cell 1 includes difficult/non-key customers of the company. Although some of them are profitable to some extent, company managers might conduct in-depth analyses on the contribution margins of Cell 1 customers and consider terminating some of the relationships with these customers in order to allocate scarce resources more effectively. Customers in Cell 3 are easy/non-key accounts, whose business the company may prefer to continue to enjoy without any additional marketing or managerial expenses.

Analysing the key account portfolio
The second part of the analysis focuses on evaluating strategically important account relationships with customers from Cells 2 and 4 of the first matrix. For

this purpose, the strength of the supplier–customer relationship and the customer's business attractiveness are plotted for each strategic account, which appears with its code number in the second matrix (Figure 2).

In Cell 1, there are seven key customers of the company with relatively high attractiveness and low relationship strength. Since the relationships are weak, customers in Cell 1 lack information about the selling company and perceive a high risk for the relationship. These fairly immature but promising relationships require more attention and tailor-made solutions for their logistics service requirements. Considering the future business potential of such key accounts, the logistics company should focus on the specific needs of these customers in order to advance the relationship regarding the social variables. Hence, the company's strategy for these accounts could be to allocate resources to relational dimensions and trust-creating activities, such as information sharing, timely feedback, frequency of contact, fast response to complaints and friendship.

In Cell 2, the supplier company has nine strategic accounts with relatively high business attractiveness and relationship strength. These customer relationships

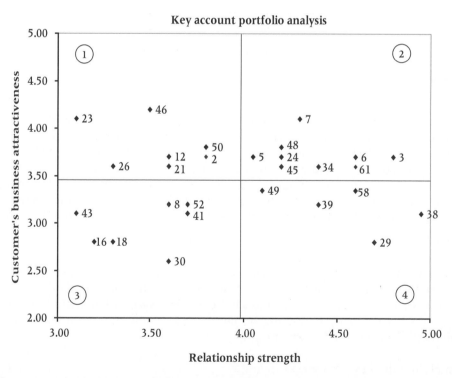

Figure 2 Relationship strength–business attractiveness grid

can be considered reasonably mature and stable in addition to their attractiveness. The easily managed accounts of this quadrant are the company's most valuable customers. The relevant strategy for this group of customers could be to defend and monitor current levels of relationship strength. The company is already strong relative to the competition for this group of customers, and the managers should focus on protecting the relationships without additional resource allocations. Maintaining strong personal relationships and levels of trust is a central course of action for the supplier. The company should pay attention to external developments related to these customers, such as competitors' actions and insistent proposals, new services and the customer's new logistics requirements.

In Cell 3, the company has seven customer relationships with low attractiveness and low strength. The recommended strategy here is to avoid allocating additional resources for these relationships. If some of them have the difficult-to-manage characteristics identified in the first analysis, resource allocation for these customers could safely be reduced, and the accounts even might be changed from strategic account status to a regular customer.

In Cell 4, the company has five customer relationships that are well established but have low attractiveness. The logistics company would be well advised to maintain the current levels of resource allocation for these accounts and refrain from marketing expenses or other additional investment in these relationships. The easily managed customers of this quadrant are cash generators for the company.

If company managers integrate the difficulty dimension into strategic account portfolio analysis on an individual customer basis, they can reach more comprehensive evaluations for strategic accounts. For instance, Customer 46, which shows low strength, high attractiveness and difficult-to-manage characteristics, requires more time, effort and resource investment to strengthen the relationship than does Customer 23, an easily managed, low-strength, high-attractiveness customer. Additionally, Customer 30, which shows low strength, low potential and highly difficult characteristics, could be another noteworthy example for further evaluations. Closer examination of this account's scores reveals that the customer has relatively low growth potential, prestige and profitability scores as well as high price sensitivity. Hence, the most suitable strategy for this customer should be withdrawal of its key account status and retreat on the resource allocation. Customers 6, 7, 24, 34 and 45, meanwhile, represent high strength, high attractiveness and easily managed characteristics, indicating robust, promising and profitable strategic account relationships for the company.

The analysis approach employed here suggests the use of portfolio analysis as a strategic management tool for decision-making, and illustrates how the customer portfolio technique can be developed by a B2B service supplier. The approach attempts to reach valuable insights for the overall customer portfolio of the logistics company and facilitates evaluation of strategic account relationships. Considering the vital importance of customer relationships for B2B suppliers, account portfolio analysis can create significant guiding principles for supplier companies' strategic business decisions. Simultaneous evaluation of the four dimensions for each customer will provide plenty of information about the customer's status, but it is important to remember that such an effort requires analysing a large amount of data. The company managers should combine their knowledge of their customers with extensive portfolio data in order to arrive at an advanced level of benefit from a portfolio approach.

The method presented here provides insights into the general framework of account relationships and forces managers to adopt a future-oriented perspective on customer relations, by evaluating customers' business attractiveness as well as the strength of the relationship, leading them to prioritize resource allocation. While the first grid shown above provides information regarding strategic and non-strategic considerations for the overall customer portfolio, the second grid points out the appropriate actions for potentially promising customer relations. Simultaneous consideration of both matrices has the potential to reveal valuable strategic insights for the company's customer portfolio. Outcomes of the method may reveal necessary actions for specific relationships and may streamline the decision-making process for suppliers' account portfolio management.

If the selling company does not have a great number of key accounts, managers ideally should evaluate their strategic customers on an individual basis in order to reach significant outcomes of portfolio analysis. If the selling company has many customers in the portfolio, the company can limit the number of accounts for the first level of analysis. It is important to note that the second step of account portfolio analysis, which involves analysing strategic accounts on an individual basis, can be costly and time consuming, particularly for big industrial sellers.

Company case II: automotive industry

Using an automotive-industry battery supplier's original equipment manufacturers (OEM) customer portfolio, this case study[2] focuses on the company's strategic accounts and explores the use of customer satisfaction (CS) metrics for managing customer relationships in the context of the portfolio approach. The case company has 12 OEM customers, who typically have a great amount of purchase volume and significant referral value for an automotive supplier.

The models developed by Fiocca (1982) and Yorke and Droussiotis (1994) were used in this case as a point of departure in the development of portfolio models. Fiocca employs the dimension of 'customer's business attractiveness' in analysing a company's key account portfolio. Since this dimension is heavily associated with the supplier's future business expectations from a customer, we have termed it 'business potential'.

---

[2] This company case is partly a modified version of a published journal article: Gök, O. (2009) Linking account portfolio management to customer information: using customer satisfaction metrics for portfolio analysis. *Industrial Marketing Management*, 38(4), 433–439.

Many companies today periodically measure the CS levels of their customer base. The CS score is a composite variable involving key aspects of the relationship and is a relevant dimension for portfolio analysis. The overall CS score calculated for each customer is a fundamental indicator of the firm's performance, owing to its links to behavioural and economic consequences for the firm (Anderson et al. 1994). The CS questionnaire used by the case company consists of 35 items and five dimensions: products and prices, quality and technical processes, sales personnel, order handling and services, and customer relationships. The satisfaction scores of the key accounts are based on weighted averages calculated from importance versus performance ratings measured on a seven-point Likert scale.

Because CS metrics convey cumulative evaluations of customers up to the time of the survey and also involve future oriented clues of customers' relationships with the supplier, it could be more significant to combine the metrics with the two relevant dimensions of the previous portfolio study. Hence, customers are positioned on grids with respect to their business potential and the strength of their relationships with the supplier along with the CS scores. These two matrices may uncover the current stability of the relationships and also provide meaningful signals in terms of strategic reallocation of resources to enhance specific relationships in order to achieve future growth.

Relationship strength–CS matrix

Prior account portfolio studies have proposed several indicators for measuring the relationship strength dimension, including customer share, magnitude of purchases, length of the relationship, frequency of contact, trust, cooperation and friendship (Campbell and Cunningham 1983; Fiocca 1982; Yorke and Droussiotis 1994). Information sharing has been cited as an indicator of relationship strength and quality in industrial supply relationships (Brennan 1997; Eckerd and Hill 2012; O'Toole and Donaldson 2002; Purdy and Safayeni 2000) and is used as a measure of strength in this study. Hence, the variables used to measure relationship strength in the present study (see Table 2) are consistent and in balance with the variables proposed by previous portfolio studies.

The data related to the first three variables of relationship strength were collected from the company's internal reports, and the customers were categorized along a five-point scale. The remaining five variables were independently rated on a scale from one to five by four managers who are key decision-makers for managing customer relationships in the company: i.e. the general manager, assistant general manager, sales manager, and key account manager. The averages of these managers' ratings were used for the analysis. The variables listed in Table 2 were weighted collectively by the four managers. It should be emphasized that this part of the implementation process, which has also been used by previous portfolio researchers (e.g. Olsen and Ellram 1997; Yorke and Droussiotis 1994), is very subjective. Although weighting the scores of indicators is also subjective and context-dependent, it is a plausible method of determining the constructs and it provides realistic evaluations.

Table 2: Variables used to measure relationship strength

Variable	Weighting
Customer share	0.20
Length of the relationship	0.15
Dollar value of purchases (sales volume of previous year)	0.15
Management distance (frequency of contact)	0.10
Degree of cooperation	0.10
Friendship	0.10
Trust	0.10
Information sharing	0.10

In Figure 3, Cell 1 includes Customers B, C and F, who all have high relationship strength and low satisfaction levels. Although these customers have established relationships with the supplier, they are relatively dissatisfied with the relationship and thus might well be open to competitors' offerings. The selling company is a preferred supplier for these customers, but they still feel the need for alternative suppliers. While they might not be actively in search of such alternatives, it would still be overly optimistic to expect a significant increase in customer share for these customers in the near future.

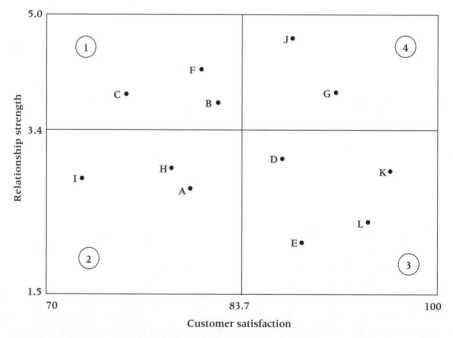

Figure 3 Relationship strength–customer satisfaction grid

Customers A, H and I, located in Cell 2 of the grid, have low relationship strength and low CS. Hence, these customers might be seen as less committed to the relationship and therefore as 'competitors' customers'. The supplier has gained some of these customers' business, although it is not the major supplier and relationships are fragile. It could be posited that their positions in the grid reflect an arm's-length relationship between parties and signify possible disloyalty in forthcoming years.

Cell 3 of the grid includes Customers D, E, L and K, all of whom have high CS levels but low relationship strength. Hence, these relatively new relationships of the company can be expected to become loyal customers in the near future as a result of their high satisfaction levels. In such relationships, volume has begun to increase and the buyer has been evaluating the supplier's performance, so the selling company needs to avoid problems and conflicts and solve them rapidly. A deeper knowledge of the customer's buying centre and an understanding of the problems that relate to the value-adding process are vital in these relationships. The supplier should offer customized solutions to the buyer's problems by concentrating on product, service and intangibles.

Since Customers G and J in the fourth quadrant of the grid have both high CS and high strength scores, they can be considered loyal customers, representing established and evolved relationships. These relationships are relatively mature, and the supplier is seen by the customer as a preferred supplier. Almost all of these customers' supply requirements are fulfilled by the selling company, and both the supplier and the customers have achieved a level of satisfaction from the relationship.

Customer's business potential–customer satisfaction matrix
Understanding both the short-term industry factors and the long-term positioning value of the customer mix is important for the management of customer portfolios (Eng 2004). As Campbell and Cunningham (1985) state, such an analysis is designed to give prominence to customers to whom the company allocates strategic funds in the hope of developing future business, as well as to emphasize those customers on which the company is dependent. Business potential refers to the status/position of the customer's business in the light of future orientations. The competitors' share of the customer's purchases represents a portion of the available business for the supplier that could be captured in the future. Obviously, if a customer has high capacity utilization, weak export links, no expansion plans, and/or low growth rate, the business potential of the customer is likely to be relatively low. If a low-potential customer has a high CS score, the selling company may decide not to spend additional resources on the customer. However, if a high-potential customer has a low satisfaction score, the selling company should pay immediate attention to the reasons for the customer's dissatisfaction and take action to correct the problem. Hence, the business potential–CS matrix might help companies to prioritize investment and resource allocation decisions in order to improve CS elements of account relationships.

Table 3: Variables used to measure customers' business potential

Variable	Weighting
Competitors' share of customer's purchases	0.15
Dollar value of customer's purchases	0.15
Growth rate of customer's purchases (per year using dollars)	0.15
Customer's capacity utilization (i.e. unemployed capacity)	0.10
Future capacity expansions (in volume terms)	0.10
Links with export markets (% exports of total turnover)	0.10
Contribution margins (of products sold to customer)	0.10
Account prestige (reputation)	0.10
Sensitivity to price	0.05

Variables used to measure customers' business potential are listed in Table 3. The figures related to competitors' customer share and customer purchase amounts were obtained using the previous year's sales data and industry statistics. The growth rate of customers' purchases was calculated as an average of the figures of the most recent three years. Information on capacity utilization, export sales, and investment and expansion plans of customers were externally gathered from the statistics issued by authoritative sectoral bodies, governmental institutions and customers' annual reports for the previous year. Using these numerical inputs, customers were grouped into intervals representing a five-point scale for each variable. Account prestige and price sensitivity were used as subjective measures, and the customers were independently rated on a scale from one to five by the four company managers.

Figure 4 shows the dispersion of the customers according to their business potential and CS scores. Customers B, C and I, located in Cell 1 of the business potential–CS grid, have relatively high levels of business potential and low levels of CS. All details regarding their satisfaction need to be examined, and corrective actions (i.e. resource allocations) should be taken for key problematic areas of the relationship. In Cell 2, Customers A, F and H have relatively low potential; thus management should not allocate additional resources for CS aspects of these accounts.

Cell 3 of the grid includes only Customer K, which has the highest CS score and the lowest potential in the account portfolio. Management should not invest extra resources in this relationship and might even consider withdrawing some resources from this account. Finally, customers D, E, G, J and L, located in Cell 4 of the grid, have both high potential and high CS scores. The relevant strategy for this group of customers could be to defend and monitor current levels of satisfaction and take moderate corrective actions if necessary to deal with significant gaps in key aspects of CS.

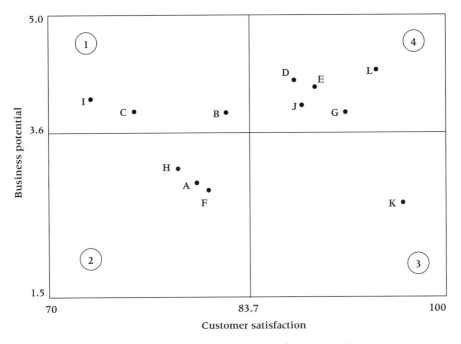

Figure 4 Account's business potential–customer satisfaction matrix

Analysis of portfolio matrices and development of marketing strategies
The two matrices proposed above offer significant insights into the customer relationships of the selling company and provide a basis for more customer-centric key account analysis. The first grid provides noteworthy indications regarding the current composition of customer relations, while the second grid forces managers to adopt a future-oriented perspective on relationships by evaluating the business potential of customers as well as their CS information, leading to prioritization with respect to resource allocation. Simultaneous consideration of both matrices has the potential to reveal valuable strategic insights for individual customer relationships and to provide pertinent managerial applications. This approach also guides accurate directions to, and investments in, relationships while improving the effectiveness of marketing decisions. It is important to note that, as pointed out by Spencer (1999), strategic account management (SAM) does not translate to 'building good, strong relationships at all costs'. Rather, it encourages companies to give each relationship the attention it merits, which might well mean reducing investment in some cases.

As shown in the results above, customers B and C are positioned in Cell 1 of both matrices, where the customer has high relative business potential and relationship strength but a low CS score. Since these customers may be open to competitors' offerings and have higher business potential, the relevant strategy for these relationships could be to allocate resources among the most unsatisfactory aspects of CS dimensions in order to increase satisfaction. A detailed examination of these customers' CS information indicates that Customer B is dissatisfied primarily with product-related technical issues, whereas Customer C is dissatisfied with complaint handling, return policies, processing of urgent orders and information sharing. Since the efforts intended to enhance the CS of these customers are likely to pay off, company managers should take corrective actions and monitor the results, especially on the dimensions of CS that are most unsatisfactory to each specific customer. For instance, the selling company's managers should enlarge the product-related interaction with Customer B, perhaps in the form of increasing technical personnel visits to the customer, providing more comprehensive product information and/or extending technical services. The relevant strategy for Customer C could be to enhance the scope of some customer service elements specific to this customer, such as expanding product return conditions, fast response, timely feedback to its complaints, and/or keeping some extra inventory for the customer.

Customers A and H are positioned in Cell 2 of both matrices. These customers are low-commitment accounts that have stronger relationships with the major competitor of the company. Since these customers also have relatively low business potential, the company should maintain their current levels of satisfaction and refrain from corrective actions or additional investment in trying to satisfy these customers. Although closer examination of these accounts' CS scores reveals that the customers are particularly dissatisfied with price levels, frequency of customer visits and sharing sensitive information, under the current circumstances the company may maintain current price ranges, communication and visit frequency with these customers.

Customer F has a longstanding relationship with the supplier but a relatively low business potential and CS score. However, examination reveals that the dissatisfaction is primarily with commercial issues and prices, so the payoff from this relationship will likely remain constant. Considering the low business potential of this price-sensitive account, the managers may decide not to take any corrective actions for CS dimensions of this relationship.

On the other hand, in the case of Customer I, relationship strength is low, CS score is low, but business potential is relatively high. The situation of Customer I should be considered exclusively in terms of key satisfaction issues, and resources should be allocated for corrective actions in order to gain future business from this potentially lucrative customer. The CS measures for this customer show greater gaps in the issues of products, quality, sales personnel and complaint handling. Managers' comments verify that in recent years there have been several conflicts on these issues between the two parties, as reflected by the satisfaction score. An advisable course for the selling company is to increase technical interaction with the customer and apply some exclusive procedures for the relationship (e.g. handling the complaints and orders at top-management levels for a reasonable period).

Customers D, E and L have relatively low relationship strength scores but high business potential and CS levels. They have no major complaints about the technical or commercial aspects of the relationships. Since these relationships are not established, the customers lack information about the selling company and perceive a high risk for the relationship. These fairly immature but promising relationships require more attention and tailor-made solutions for their product and service requirements. The strategy for these accounts could be to allocate resources to relational dimensions and trust-creating activities, such as information sharing, timely feedback, frequency of contact and friendship. The company should pursue all means of communication with these customers through regular reports, customer visits, exclusive sales promotions and meetings involving top management.

In contrast, Customer K is located in Cell 3 of both matrices. This customer has the highest CS level, but both business potential and relationship strength are low. The recommended strategy for this customer is to avoid allocating additional resources for this relationship and divest the customer's key account status. Having the highest CS level may indicate an over-allocation of resources to this relationship. Thus this allocation can safely be reduced, and the account can be removed from the key account manager's responsibility as a regular customer.

Today's loyal customers, G and J, are located in Cell 4 of both grids. Relationship strength and CS scores suggest that these relationships are mutually perceived as strong and established, making it easy for the supplier to maintain these customers' current levels of satisfaction. Because these customers already prefer the company over the competition, managers should focus on protecting these relationships without considerable resource allocations. If there are noticeable gaps in some satisfaction dimensions, the company should rectify only those issues. For example, since Customer J has somewhat lower scores in frequency of customer visits and ease of doing business, the managers could rearrange the customer visit schedule to allow for more frequent communication. Similarly, although Customer G is satisfied with almost all factors in the relationship, there is moderate dissatisfaction about delivery lead times. To rectify this, the selling company could organize new delivery schedules or retain some extra stock for the customer. In addition, the company should be mindful of external developments related to current loyal customers, such as competitors' actions and proposals and new products and service requirements.

Conclusions

This paper has attempted to present the APM approach through a comprehensive analysis of the account portfolios of two case companies, and it has also suggested strategic inferences for better CRM. The portfolio approach to account management, which emphasizes similarities and interdependencies among different customer relationships, serves as a guide for resource allocation problems pertaining to these relationships. When appropriate variables are used, portfolio analysis can reveal a company's competitive position and allow management to reconsider which customers and relationship dimensions require the most attention. The outcomes of the analysis can be used as one of the marketing metrics to support customer analysis in the strategic account management process and to design customized relationship strategies. Depending upon the company's objectives and specific situation, portfolio analysis and management strategies can be applied from multiple perspectives, at various levels of aggregation and with different strategic variables or portfolio components (Turnbull 1990). Previous portfolio models reveal that investments in a customer portfolio should be a function of underlying firm, customer and industry characteristics (Johnson and Selnes 2004), and it is likely that any specific evaluation will be context dependent.

The APM approach presented here tries to emphasize customer heterogeneity in business markets and offers managerial guidelines embracing customer-specific marketing actions instead of a one-size-fits-all approach. Since account analysis and development of customized relationship strategies are the intrinsic elements of SAM, the proposed approach can be used in SAM applications as a decision support tool. In this sense, a summarized set of the analysis outputs can be combined with marketing dashboards which present a synopsis of key performance and operational metrics of the company. In order to facilitate the analysis and accelerate reporting, data and analytical tools might be integrated with CRM software.

The normative use of CS measurement methodologies advises corrective actions for all customers and for virtually every dissatisfaction aspect of the customer in light of control theory. Similarly, account portfolio studies propose resource allocation for high-potential and high-attractiveness customers; however, such suggestions are rather naive in terms of addressing the actual direction of allocation and investment decisions. Since CS information is indicative of the customer's perspective on problematic areas in the relationship, evaluating this information in the context of the portfolio approach can provide valuable strategic inferences regarding the action necessary in specific relationships. This may lead to more efficient resource allocation decisions for suppliers.

The method proposed here involves some of the same limitations that have been acknowledged in prior portfolio studies. Inevitably, managers' ratings on some variables are subjective; however, they are based on experienced evaluations. In addition, one can offer several other criteria for measuring strategic importance, relationship strength and other dimensions in the portfolio grids.

However, account portfolio analyses are context dependent, and the variables used may differ. As Olsen and Ellram (1997) point out, using more complex measurement approaches in portfolio studies shifts the focus from decision-making to mechanistic measurement. Account portfolio analysis can provide more objective and accurate results depending on the comprehensiveness of the company's marketing intelligence data and technologies.

Strategic account management processes at corporate, relationship and annual level

BY JUKKA OJASALO

Abstract

This paper, based on literature analysis, aims to map and develop a framework of the processes central to strategic account management (SAM). So far, the literature on various SAM processes is fragmented and the big picture is lacking, so there is a clear need to structure this area further. This paper responds to this need by identifying three levels of SAM processes – corporate-, relationship- and annual-level SAM – by structuring the processes central to SAM at these levels into a framework and by discussing the nature of these processes. The theoretical implications are first, it identifies three relevant management levels of SAM as well as the main processes of these levels. Second its three-level framework contributes by showing how the different SAM processes are hierarchically subordinated to each other. Third, the framework shows the time spans of process cycles for different processes: some of them are longer and one-time processes, others are shorter and frequently repeated.

The practical implications emerging from the study are first, the proposed framework shows the hierarchical order in which these processes have to be tackled if the company is interested in introducing a systematic SAM approach in its organization. Second, as the framework maps the relevant SAM processes at different management levels and shows their hierarchical organization, it also shows how critical the commitment and effort of the whole organization are to the success of SAM.

Introduction

Systematic account management has its origins in the 1970s (Pegram 1972). The literature on management of important business-to-business customer relationships uses several terms, which have the same or very similar meaning: key account management, national account management, strategic account management, major account management, global account management, large account management, etc. This paper uses the term strategic account management but is based on any relevant literature dealing with account management.

A business process is a collection of activities that takes one or more kinds of inputs and creates an output that is of value to the customer (Hammer 1990). It is defined as structured, measured sets of activities designed to produce a specified output for a particular customer or market (Davenport 1993), and refers to a set of related tasks performed to achieve a defined business outcome (Davenport and Short 1990). It is a network of activities and buffers through which the flow units have to pass in order to be transformed from inputs to outputs (Laguna and Marklund 2005). Account management processes are those activities, mechanisms and procedures which facilitate the effective management of accounts (Millman and Wilson 1999).

As the definitions of 'business process' and 'account management process' have a rather broad scope, a great many activities are covered by them. Thus there is need to structure the large and somewhat scattered area of account management and its various processes and activities. As a result, this paper identifies three main levels of SAM and explains the main process at these levels. The levels are corporate-, relationship- and annual-level SAM. Corporate-level SAM processes set the general framework for SAM in the company, and they have the longest time horizon. Relationship-level SAM includes more detailed and concrete processes, and their time horizon is long or short, depending on the relationship length. The time horizon of annual-level SAM processes is limited to one year. This classification is intended to structure the large variety of SAM processes and illustrate their hierarchy and the big picture. The paper is based on literature analysis.

The rest of this article is organized in three sections: first, it reviews the earlier literature on account management processes and then it proposes a framework of three levels of SAM processes, maps the central processes at these levels and briefly explains their nature. Lastly, it discusses research implications and draws conclusions.

Review of earlier literature on SAM processes

The existing research literature dealing with SAM process or SAM is discussed next and summarized in Table 1. The literature includes a vast amount of material dealing with customer relationship management in general; however, the present review addresses the literature with a focus on 'account management'.

Table 1: Account management processes, findings from literature

Millman and Wilson 1995	Millman and Wilson 1996	Newbourne 1997	McDonald and Woodburn 2011/2000
• Pre-KAM • Early KAM • Mid-KAM • Partnership KAM • Synergistic KAM • Uncoupling KAM	• Evaluation of the accounts' strategic importance • Formulation/implementation of strategies for each key account • Allocation of resources	• Account targeting • Corporate account management analysis • Partnership evaluation • Account planning: objectives • Measurement of results: benefits • Validation of value exchange • Expand the field of play	• Positioning of key account planning in strategic marketing planning • Key account objectives and strategies • Marketing plan for key accounts • Measuring key account profitability
Wong 1998	Millman and Wilson 1999	Ojasalo 2001	Wilson and Weilbaker 2004
• Account positioning • Account interaction • Account outcome • Routing development	• Active participation of senior management • Definition and selection of key accounts • Forging wide and deep networks of relationships within the customer organization • Support of strong technical or product capacity • Problem identification and resolution • Development of both generic and bespoke interaction processes • Selective systems and process alignment • Performance of non-core management tasks by the supplier for the customer	• Identifying key accounts • Analysing key accounts • Selecting suitable strategies for key accounts • Developing operational-level capabilities to build, grow and maintain profitable and long-lasting relationships with key accounts (including implementation and control)	• Drivers of the GAM process • Supplier analysis • Buyer analysis • Global account definition • Global account selection • GAM strategy development • GAM operations • Organizational issues • Global account manager roles • Challenges to effective GAM • Outcomes

(*Continued*)

Table 1: (Continued)

De Backer and Van der Linden 2005	Senn 2006	Zupancic 2008	Storbacka 2012

• Commitment from top management
• Identifying key accounts
• New resources for KAM
  - new pools of knowledge
  - developing skills of sales force for selling to big buying groups
  - new compensation strategy
  - evaluation of channel and communication strategy
	• Contact planning
	• Sponsor nomination
	• Executive engagement
	• Measurement and review
		Both at single account and corporate levels:
		• strategy
		• solutions
		• people
		• management
		• screening
			• Account portfolio definition
			• Account business planning
			• Account-specific value proposition
			• Account management process
			• Account team profile and skills
			• Support capabilities
			• Account performance management
			• Organizational integration

Millman and Wilson (1995) introduced a six-stage model of key account relational development. In this model, different key account selling and management strategies and practices are applied as the relationship evolves through a number of phases:

Pre-KAM: the purpose is to identify those accounts which have the potential for moving towards key account status and to avoid wasteful investment in those accounts which do not hold that potential.

Early KAM: this phase is about exploring opportunities for closer collaboration by identifying the motives, culture and concerns of the account. It involves targeting competitor strengths and weaknesses and persuading customers of the potential benefits they might enjoy as 'preferred' customers.

Mid-KAM: trust, range of issues the relationship addresses and cross-boundary contacts increase.

Partnership KAM: the supplier is often viewed as an external resource of the customer. Sensitive information is shared and joint problem solving is common.

Synergistic KAM: relationship parties see one another not as two separate organizations but as parts of a larger entity, creating joint value (synergy) in the marketplace.

Uncoupling KAM: this phase represents relationship termination, when a planned uncoupling process and contingency planning may be needed.

Millman and Wilson (1996) argue that key account management must be driven strategically and collectively by the top team in the selling company. This means developing competencies in the three areas:

- Evaluation of the strategic importance of a portfolio of current and potential key accounts.
- Formulation/implementation of strategies for each key account which are consistent with those of the many other customers that are not designated key accounts and are also consistent with achieving overall business objectives.
- Allocation of resources to the relational mix appropriate to the stage in the relational development model outlined earlier.

Newbourne (1997) examined a global transportation company's corporate account management process and how, in this context, the company applied Lambert et al.'s (1996) partnership model, consisting of drivers, facilitators, components and outcomes. Drivers are compelling reasons to partner, while facilitators are supportive corporate environmental factors that enhance partnership growth and development. Components are joint activities and processes that build and sustain the partnership, and outcomes reflect the performance of the partnership and the extent to which performance meets expectations. Newbourne's (1997) model of corporate account management process consists of seven phases:

1. *Account targeting.* The account management process starts here, since effective targeting greatly increases the likelihood of success. The following questions are integral. Which industry segments are growing and financially stable? Which industry segments have a need for some combination of our core services? What type of products/services does the industry segment require? Who are the customers leading the industry segment in terms of product or service innovation, share of growth and financial stability? Perhaps the most important question is: which of the leading industry segment customers are driving changes in historic segment paradigms?
2. *Corporate account management analysis.* Information and insights into the target account companies that were identified in the first step are developed to help better understand the account, their business and needs. It also helps to develop an informed opinion on the account's willingness to form a partnership or strategic alliance. If the account seems to be likely to do so, then the process moves to the next step.
3. *Partnership evaluation.* This phase consists of an initial meeting to exchange business philosophy, an agreement to pursue a partnership evaluation, and

a then joint partnership evaluation session. The second partnership evaluation session should include the following actions: reviewing the current situation and a 'reality' check; evaluating the drivers and facilitators of partnership; establishing the preliminary partnership type; and reviewing the management components of the partnership. Further actions include performing partnership-type gap analysis, finalizing the initial partnership type and establishing an action plan and time lines.

4. *Account management plan.* Based on the results of the second and third phases, an account management plan can be developed to ensure execution of the strategy, action plans and partnership development. It is intended to clearly communicate important information regarding the plans for the account's business and relationship, as well as being a reference source about the account.

5. *Measuring results and benefits.* Two sets of metrics are involved: one for the account and one for our own company. The account metrics generally include savings in dollars, increased sales and non-price productivity improvements, such as changes in processes that result in cost savings. The selling company's metrics typically include their volume, revenue, margin growth and productivity improvements. Naturally, the selling company's metrics are partly driven by the account metrics.

6. *Validation of the value exchange.* The validation is made by the account, primarily using jointly developed account metrics. It is done several times a year, and written summaries are shared with the senior managers of both companies.

7. *Expanding the field of play.* This refers to the selling company's ever increasing involvement with the account. To ensure an ever expanding role with the account, it is necessary to return to the second phase of the process, the corporate account management analysis, so the result is an ongoing modified use of the process.

Wong (1998) examined the formulation and implementation of key account management strategies in China and other Asian countries. He proposed the *guanxi* (relationships) model for key account management. This model includes four major elements – positioning, interaction, outcome and routing – which are influenced by the corporate key account strategy, marketing objectives for long-term partnership, *guanxi* construct and performance indicators. The account positioning phase is based on a framework used to categorize accounts into four categories, based on two dimensions: first, the level of adaptation and commitment to the relationship, and second, whether the relationship is an 'insider' or 'outsider' type of relationship. Outsider relationships imply the interaction of parties outside any mutually defined group or network, and information is inhibited in outsider relationships. In contrast, 'insider' relationships imply the understanding of both parties involved that they share a common network, group or party of some kind, often resulting in open information exchange.

An account is positioned as *fencer, fiancé, new friend* or *old friend*. In the *fencer* category, both parties are testing the intentions or reactions of the other, regarding the other as an outsider. In the *fiancé* category, during the affirmative stage of the adaptation process, both parties bargain with their power, which depends on how each party evaluates their dependence on the other party. The continuation of the relationship depends on the exercise of power, dependence and trust on the other party. If the two parties mutually accept each other as insider friends, they are in a *new friend* situation. Furthermore, if a strong *guanxi* relationship has been established after parties enter the *new friend* quadrant, they may go to a higher stage and enter an *old friend* phase with substantial relationship-specific investment.

Account outcome positioning has the following options. The outcome of the *fencer* category is characterized by being aware of each other and 'dating', while the *fiancé* category brings benefits. *New friends* are in a de facto relationship, which is informal and does not involve total trust, and parties are still concerned about the potential impact of relationship termination costs. The relationship is characterized by belongingness, while *old friends* are characterized by 'marriage'. *Routing development* refers to the evolution of the relationship in terms of the four relationship categories. For example, parties may evolve from *fencer* to *new friend*, from *new friend* to *fiancé*, and from *fiancé* to *old friend*. The relationship may evolve through other routes as well (Wong 1998).

Millman and Wilson (1999) found that preconditions which are required to be in place in order to facilitate the implementation of KAM processes include commitment from senior management, focus on customer problem resolution, strong product and process capabilities, collaborative culture and flexibility. They (*ibid.*) brought forward eight KAM process elements:

- Active participation of senior management.
- Definition and selection of key accounts.
- Forging wide and deep networks of relationships within the customer organization.
- Support of strong technical or product capacity.
- Problem identification and resolution.
- Development of both generic and bespoke interaction processes.
- Selective systems and process alignment.
- Performance of non-core management tasks by the supplier for the customer.

McDonald and Woodburn (2011) explain planning for key accounts and measuring profitability in their book *Key Account Management: The Definitive Guide*. Their account management process is in line with the ten steps of the general strategic marketing planning process: mission, corporate objectives, marketing audit, SWOT analyses, assumptions, marketing objectives and strategies, estimation of expected results, identification of alternative plans and mixes, budget, and first-year detailed implementation programme. According to them, KAM involves positioning of key account planning in a corporate's strategic planning, setting key account objectives and strategies, developing a strategic marketing plan for each key account, and measuring key account retention and profitability.

Positioning of key account planning in a corporate's strategic planning within the hierarchy of the development of internal plans in the selling company. The corporate plan is developed first, then the marketing plan, next segment plans, and after that account plans for individual key customers.

Setting key account objectives and strategies is based on prioritizing and selecting segments in terms of the strategic attractiveness of accounts as well as the supplier's relative competitiveness.

Developing a strategic marketing plan for a key account includes an account-specific mission and purpose statement, financial summary, key account overview, client's critical success factor analysis, applications portfolio summary, assumptions, objectives and strategies, and budget.

Measuring key account retention and profitability is based on customer profit contribution over time which shows the account-specific accumulation of various costs and revenues over the time of the relationship.

Ojasalo (2001, 2002) developed a four-phase process model for elements of KAM (see Figure 1):

1. Identifying key accounts.
2. Analysing key accounts.
3. Selecting suitable strategies for key accounts.
4. Developing operational-level capabilities to build, grow and maintain profitable and long-lasting relationships with key accounts (including implementation and control).

Identifying key accounts. This phase requires answers to the following questions: Which existing or potential accounts are of strategic importance to us now and in the future? To answer this question one first needs to answer the question: What are the criteria that determine which customers are strategically important? Such account-specific criteria typically include sales volume, profitability, reference value, potential for growth in the future, share of wallet, age of the relationship, R&D cooperation, customer's buying process, customer's location, match of strategies, match of operations, replaceability, supplier's own learning and increase in competence.

Analysing key accounts. The relevant economic and activity aspects of the accounts' internal and external environment are assessed, covering the account's internal value chain, inputs, markets, suppliers, products and economic situation. This phase also includes analysing the relevant economic and activity aspects of the relationship history, addressing sales volume, profitability, key account's objectives, buying behaviour, information exchange, special needs, buying frequency and complaints. Estimating relationship value plays a particularly important role here, since the revenues from each key account should exceed the costs of estab-

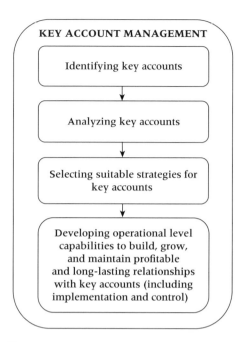

Figure 1 Elements of key account management
Source: adapted from Ojasalo (2001, p. 202)

lishing and maintaining the relationship within a certain time span. Furthermore, the level and development of commitment to the relationship, goal congruence of the parties, and switching costs (Sengupta et al. 1997) should be analysed.

Selecting suitable strategies for key accounts. Strategies depend, for example, on the supplier's competitiveness and attractiveness of the customer, power positions of the parties, and the degree of goal congruence. The strategy with the particular account may be, for example, heavy investment for deep collaboration, selective or careful investment, maintenance, avoidance, short-term dealings with cash payments, domination, submission, or dissolution of the relationship. In open and competitive markets, win–win strategies are recommended to build up long-term and mutually beneficial relationships.

Developing operational-level capabilities to build, grow and maintain profitable and long-lasting relationships with key accounts. This phase involves customization and development of capabilities related to products and services, organizational structure, information exchange and individuals. Joint R&D projects are typical between a selling company and a key account in industrial and high-tech markets. In addition, information technology applied in just-in-time production and distribution channels increases the possibilities of customizing the offering. Improving capabilities for providing services to key accounts is extremely important, because even when the core product is a tangible object, it is often the related services that differentiate the selling company from its competitors and provide competitive advantage.

The selling company's organizational ability to meet the key account's needs can be developed, for example, by adjusting the organizational structure to correspond to the key account's global and local needs, and by increasing the number of interfaces between the selling company and the account and thus also the number of interacting people. Organizational capabilities can also be developed by organizing key account teams, consisting of people with the necessary competencies and authority, to take care of key accounts. Information exchange between the selling company and a key account is a particularly important, relationship-specific task: both partners need to search, filter, judge and store information about the organizations, strategies, goals, potentials and problems of the partners. Ojasalo (2004) expanded these ideas of KAM from the dyadic relationship context into the business networks context.

Wilson and Weilbaker (2004) introduced a process model for global account management (GAM) which includes 11 elements:

- Drivers of the GAM process include economic factors, market structure, customer power and technology.
- Supplier analysis covers global capability, culture, logistics, linking systems, structure, networks and product offering.
- Buyer analysis relates to global capability, culture, logistics, linking systems, structure, networks, and received product offering.
- Global account definition is affected by global players, global transitions, global aspirants, issues of competency and culture.
- Global account selection is based in qualitative and quantitative measures, strategic fit, culture and long-term profitability.
- GAM strategy development includes strategic intent, strategic focus (economic, innovative or entrepreneurial), strategic means (problem resolution) and strategic-level decisions (partners, relationships, learning).
- GAM operations cover implementation issues, the GAM decision-making process and operational competencies.
- Organizational issues relate to structure, complexity, teamwork, culture, turf issues, information systems, connecting systems, compensation and executive support.
- Global account manager roles include political entrepreneur, communicator, team leadership, relationship, management, strategic planning, vision, problem solving and internal selling.
- Challenges to effective GAM entail blockers and systems: blockers may be political, organizational and cultural.
- Outcomes cover metrics and success factors, which involve knowledge, value, profits and customer satisfaction.

According to Backer and Linden (2005), building strategic KAM includes three steps: (1) the implementation of KAM strategy requires a clear commitment from top and their active and strong support; (2) strategic segmentation refers to the identification of key accounts, using both a priori (who the customers are) and ad hoc segmentation (how customers behave); (3) new resources for KAM include pools of knowledge, development of the skills of the sales force for selling to big buying groups, new compensation strategy, and evaluation of the channel and communication strategy.

Senn (2006) described Siemens' four-step Top Executive Relationship Process, in which account managers are required to plan executive engagements linked to their account plans, normally with the account manager in attendance and prepared with formatted documentation for both pre- and post-meeting reporting.

Contact phase. The objective is to orchestrate contact between the customer and the selling company's executives. Once a year customer objectives are formulated, sponsors and their roles are proposed, contacts in both buying and selling companies are identified and a specific contact plan is developed. This results in an overall plan for engaging top executives in the relationship and a specific contact plan.

Sponsor nomination. The purpose is to obtain executive support for the relationship process and contact plan, repeated once a year. Sponsors and key executives are evaluated, nominated and agreed. An account review is conducted, including the situation, customer, executives and sponsors' roles, and the plan for engaging top executives is updated.

Executive engagement phase. Here the purpose is to establish a consistent process for executive meetings (maybe 8–10 meetings per year) and actions, covering the scheduling of executive visits, pre-briefing, calling, post-briefing and follow-up. This phase results in complete briefing sheets and customer-specific action plans.

Measurement and review phase. The objective is to manage the information gained from executive engagement. This annual review includes looking at overall activities and results with relationship sponsors, reviewing impact with account managers and defining target achievements.

Zupancic (2008) discussed KAM at two levels: operational and corporate. Operational KAM refers to the activities of the key account manager and their team serving a specific account. In contrast, corporate KAM covers the entire KAM programme for all strategic accounts of the selling company. At both levels, the KAM process is realized through the dimensions of strategy, solutions, people, management and screening.

Operational KAM. The *strategy* dimension refers to how the company should serve the key account, while *solutions* means customizing products and services that will be offered to the account to add value and realize the chosen account strategy. It also refers to the degree to which innovations are developed in close cooperation with the key account. The *people* dimension represents the nomination of members and forming the KAM team, and *management* refers to processes that are necessary to service the account as well as coordination of interfaces and resources within the supplier company. Lastly, the *screening* dimension means measuring KAM success by various criteria, and also includes safeguarding knowledge management and corporate learning based on KAM experiences.

Corporate KAM. Here the *strategy* dimension refers to top-management support for KAM; the *solutions* dimension means willingness of the entire company to fulfil special needs of key accounts; *people* implies recognition of the importance of excellent staff in the success of KAM. The *management* dimension means support of KAM by the corporate culture as well as a formal KAM organization, while *screening* refers to corporate reporting and controlling systems for determining KAM success.

Storbacka (2012) developed a framework for strategic account management programmes, consisting of four inter-organizational and four intra-organizational elements (*ibid*).

Inter-organizational elements

Account portfolio definition relates to selecting the right customers for the strategic account portfolio.

Account business planning includes a mechanism for enhancing organizational or network learning through information acquisition, information dissemination and shared interpretation activities. It also constitutes a tool to get commitment from the firm's management to assign the resources needed to develop the account in such a way that the potential identified can be realized, and it promotes inter- and intra-organizational alignment.

Account-specific value proposition is based on the idea that developing a value proposition for the selected strategic customers is 'special', in other words, specific to the account and different from what other customers are being offered, based on solutions achievable through the integration and adaptation of firm processes to create a better fit with the customer's processes.

Account management process has four elements: (1) generating knowledge and disseminating a shared interpretation of this knowledge as a foundation for value creation; (2) the sales process, whereby value propositions are turned into orders; (3) securing the delivery of the agreed value proposition; (4) enhancement of the relationship strength and longevity, by attaining goal congruence and systematically constructing bonds consisting of mutual resource dependencies, with relationship-specific resource allocations or investments.

Intra-organizational elements

Account team profile and skills implies selection of the key account manager and members of the account team. The team can be formal or informal, and sometimes involve representatives from the customer organization as well.

Support capabilities are support systems needed in account management programmes to facilitate the account manager's work. They include information systems, administration, field and technical service, logistics, manufacturing/ operations management, application engineering, development and product engineering, finance, legal, control and marketing. Two of the necessary capabilities usually reside outside the account team, i.e. value quantification and account performance monitoring from business controllers, and contract management from legal departments.

Account performance management relates to the total value formed during the interaction between the company and its customer over time. According to Storbacka and Nenonen (2009), an important aspect is definition of how the value is shared between the firm (value capture) and its customers (value creation). They say that value capture can be measured by the discounted present value of all future economic profit that the customer relationship generates, and this can be used as a proxy for shareholder value creation. The key components of economic profit on a dyad level consist of revenue from the relationship, total cost incurred by the relationship, and the capital invested in the relationship.

Organizational integration helps account managers to build value by understanding and responding to concerns and opportunities that customers encounter. The account manager has the main responsibility for interpreting the customer's situation, making value propositions and ensuring that the promised value is delivered. The account management function should not be confined to the sales function but rather it should cross the boundaries between several functions, product areas, geographical areas and hierarchical levels.

Table 1 summarizes the principal findings from the literature on SAM processes.

SAM processes at the corporate, relationship and annual level

Based on the above literature review, a framework of SAM processes at three different levels is suggested (Figure 2). Processes at corporate-level SAM relate to making the corporate-wide grounding for SAM in the company. The time span of the management horizon at this level is the lifetime of the SAM programme in the corporation. Processes at relationship-level SAM relate to relationship management with a certain strategic account. The time horizon of the management at this level is the lifetime of the particular customer relationship, and the key processes at this level are about adjusting SAM in different phases of customer relationship. Processes at annual-level SAM involve operational and everyday serving of the account, with a maximum time span of the management horizon at this level of one year. The central processes of each of these levels are shown in Table 2.

Corporate-level SAM

Corporate-level SAM includes three eras: adopting SAM philosophy, maintaining and improving general principles of SAM, and possible abandonment of the SAM

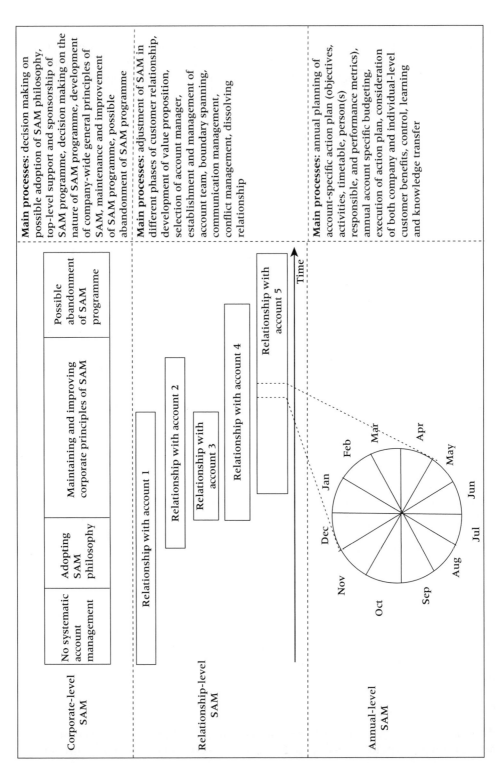

Figure 2 SAM processes at the corporate, relationship and annual level

Table 2: Central processes of SAM

Corporate-level SAM processes	Relationship-level SAM processes	Annual-level SAM processes
Decision-making on possible adoption of a SAM philosophy	Development of value proposition	Annual planning of account-specific action plan including objectives, activities, timetable, person(s) responsible and performance metrics
Top-level support and sponsorship of the SAM programme	Selection of account manager	
	Establishment and management of account team	Annual account-specific budgeting
Decision-making on the nature of the SAM programme		
Development of company-wide general principles of SAM maintenance and improvement of the SAM programme	Boundary spanning	Execution of action plan
	Communication management	Consideration of both company- and individual-level customer benefits
Possible abandonment of the SAM programme	Conflict management	Control
	Dissolving relationship	Learning and knowledge transfer

programme. It refers to account management principles in general within the whole selling company. In other words, it covers the entire KAM programme for all the strategic accounts of the selling company. The time span of the management horizon at this level is the lifetime of the SAM programme in the corporation, which is typically decades.

Adopting SAM philosophy

Should we adopt SAM philosophy in our corporation? Even though the company has strategic accounts, it may not have any systematic approach for managing them (Kempeners and Van der Hart 1999; Shapiro and Moriarty 1984). Thus, the very first SAM management decision at corporate level is to answer the question: 'Account management system or no account management system?' Some companies are reluctant to adopt account management systems, since they think that there is no strong reason for it. Some companies may even consider an account management system to be disadvantageous, because customers may exploit their power position to get discounts and extra services (Peck 1997; Rottenberger-Murtha 1992; Shapiro and Moriarty 1984). Caution against adopting systematic account management systems may also include concentration of resources on few customers, insufficient benefits to the supplier firm or accounts, limited opportunities with customers other than those who are presently strategic accounts, additional cost and bureaucracy, and significant effort in organizational change required by the account management programme due to sales force resistance and unclear responsibilities and authorities (Capon 2001).

Some main reasons for adopting a systematic account management approach in the corporation can be identified – for example, when the accounts are no longer willing to do business with several salespeople, and they demand from their suppliers one person who has the final responsibility for the relationship. Also, accounts may want to have larger national or global contracts to harmonize the purchase and delivery process, as well as other conditions. The selling company may want such contracts as well. For this reason, it becomes necessary to coordinate between several involved units and offer 'one face' to the customer (Kempeners and Van der Hart 1999; Verra 1994). When several levels, departments and decision-makers in both buying and selling companies, often located in dispersed locations, are involved, this all calls for single-point contact in relationship management (Rottenberger-Murtha 1992).

According to McDonald et al. (1994, in McDonald and Woodburn 2011), the need for account management systems stems from the need to respond to rapid change: companies must refine their processes to compete in mature and global markets with increasing customer power. They have to deal with more complex customer relationships. For example, buyers become smarter by defining the total value of the relationship, by looking for tactics to optimize this relationship, and by evaluating their suppliers to improve their own buying behaviour (De Backer and Van der Linden 2005). Large customers often rationalize their supply base to cooperate more closely with a limited number of preferred suppliers and they demand special value-adding activities, such as product development, financing services or consulting (Homburg et al. 2002). According to Wengler et al. (2006), the two most important reasons for implementing KAM are the increase in customer orientation of the supplier and increasing internationalization of customers. In addition, reasons for adopting KAM programmes entail a hope to improve internal coordination, customer segmentation, increased customer requirements, customer-induced relationship intensity, desire to improve efficiency of internal decision-making; internationalization of markets, differentiation and minimizing market risk.

What kind of corporate SAM programme should we adopt? If the company decides to adopt SAM philosophy, it needs to decide the nature of its SAM system. Four alternatives are available (Shapiro and Moriarty 1984, in Kempeners and Van der Hart 1999):

> *Part-time programme.* This is an account management system in which people with other responsibilities also accept the responsibility of looking after major accounts. This system is chosen, for example, when the selling company is small or has few accounts. Sometimes it is used in companies that are going from none to a full-time account management system (De Roos et al. 1990; Shapiro and Moriarty 1984).
>
> *Full-time programme at operating unit level – division or group.* A full-time account management system in which the account management system is decentralized at business unit or division level (related business units).

Corporate-level programme. A centralized account management system.

Account division. A separate and fully integrated operating unit serves accounts and their needs.

In the case of the latter three alternatives, the question is whether the system will be integrated in the organization or will be separated as an account division. A separate account division is chosen more frequently when the accounts are very large, or differ from other customers and buy different products, or coordination between production and sales is very important, or production scale is not important (Shapiro and Moriarty 1984). Storbacka's (2012) research finds that SAM is, to a large extent, an organizational challenge. Most organizations have product or geographical organization, and adding the account viewpoint raises questions relating to efficiency, complexity and flexibility. However, successful SAM requires designing organizational structures and management processes to be responsive to strategic customers. Strategic account management cannot be confined to the sales functions, but rather it crosses the boundaries between several functions, product areas, geographical areas and hierarchical levels (Storbacka et al. 2009). Companies use several ways to position the account managers and their teams in the organization, usually at the highest level of the organization, in business units, product divisions or regional units (Kempeners and Van der Hart 1999).

A company's scope and commitment to the account management programme may vary and evolve over the years. To be successful in account management, the company should be clear about the desired scope of the programme. When both the scope and commitment to the account management approach are limited, account management has a pilot nature with certain selected accounts. Such an ice-breaker phase may function as a starting point for further expansion of the programme scope in the corporation. If the scope of the programme is broad but the commitment is limited, this results in a dead end due to insufficient resources. When the scope of the account management programme is limited but commitment is deep, this functions like a springboard and enables efficient development of appropriate systems, processes and human resources for strategic account management in the corporation. If the firm has successfully developed and tested its account management programme, it can expand its scope substantially, even to be corporate-wide. In cases where the scope of the account management programme is broad and commitment is deep, the programme has an embedded nature and is here to stay (cf. Capon and Senn 2010).

How to adopt a corporate SAM approach. Adopting a SAM approach in the corporation requires defining certain corporate-level general principles of SAM, which are applied at a concrete level. According to Homburg et al. (2002), the key questions the corporate needs to answer while adopting a SAM approach are: What is done? (activities), Who does it? (actors), With whom is it done? (resources) and How formal is it? (formalization). This includes various alignment and integration activities, which relate to company strategy, solutions offered to customers, people in the organization, management methods and screening (Zupancic 2008).

When it concerns the company strategy, top management's commitment is very important (De Backer and Van der Linden 2005). Top management's support for adopting a SAM philosophy is needed by word and action. The importance of the SAM initiative has to be clearly prioritized alongside the other initiatives the organization is working on (Woodburn 2004): it has to be integrated in the corporate strategy, and the criteria for strategic accounts as well as the systematic method of identifying them should be defined. Related to solutions offered to customers, the willingness of the entire company to fulfil special needs of strategic accounts should be enhanced. The strategic accounts' influence on the company's product and service portfolio should be increased, including development of new products and services initiated by them. Also, corporate-level practices should be developed that help in including products and services developed specifically for certain strategic accounts into the company's general product line. Indeed, special pricing, customization of products and services, joint coordination of the work-flow, information sharing and taking over business processes that the customer outsources take place with strategic accounts. Thus, the selling company needs to define its principles in terms of the intensity of special attention given to strategic accounts. In other words, how should the servicing of strategic accounts differ from that of average customers (Homburg et al. 2002; Shapiro and Moriarty 1980)?

In terms of people, systematic methods for analysing staff's competencies and match with SAM requirements should be developed with corporate-level guidelines for recruitment of account managers and account team members, as well as their professional development and principles of remuneration. When it concerns management issues, SAM should be included as one aspect of the corporate culture programme. Principles concerning the formal organization for SAM are also needed, and acceptance of SAM processes by the whole organization should be ensured. Screening includes developing corporate and controlling systems that easily show the results of SAM and integrate SAM-specific controlling measures in the corporate's IT systems (Zupancic 2008).

Maintaining and improving corporate principles of SAM
Once the company has adopted a SAM approach, there is a natural need to maintain and improve it over time. This can happen in terms of a structured method of examining the validity of the national account organization within a specific company environment. For this purpose, Boles et al. (1994) introduced a specific audit method for critically evaluating the company's current account management programme and identifying which areas should be improved. Their audit process consists of five phases:

Environmental assessment: internal and external viability of the account management concept. This first phase addresses both the external industry conditions and senior management and inter-departmental support for the concept of account management. It focuses on the profile of the market, which includes, for example, characteristics of client companies and competitive activities.

Moreover, this examines whether the company's own culture is appropriate for successful operation of an account management programme.

Compatibility of the account management concept with the corporate mission. This phase tests not only the validity of the original purpose of the account management programme but also whether there is sufficient integration of the programme into current corporate strategy. The programme mission is reviewed as well as testing the depth of management understanding of that mission. Both quantitative and qualitative macro-objectives of the programme are addressed.

Operational and organizational assessment. Managing and motivating the national account organization is considered, alongside questioning the efficiency of the corporation's current account management programme. Organization and procedures are usually established at the inception of the account management programme, but over time, as the market and organization change, they become outdated. The assessment focuses on the structure of the marketing coverage for strategic accounts in the programme, and also addresses the positioning of the account management unit within the current company hierarchy. The characteristics of the individual account managers, their training, compensation, motivation and methods of support are exposed and analysed in light of current conditions. All these analyses result in identification of areas requiring improvement.

Analysis of individual strategic accounts. Effective account management is based on the assumption that the selling company has enough knowledge of the account. Such an assumption may be false, possibly due to the fact that account organizations change rapidly and customer knowledge loses its validity. In this fourth phase a solid and refreshed understanding of the strategic accounts is established in order to determine whether the company is able to fulfil their needs.

Evaluation of the account management programme in quantified monetary terms. In other words, the effectiveness of the current account management programme is assessed in dollars and percentages. Often the contribution of the account management programme is blurred and obscured in the consolidated financial analyses. Thus additional effort is required to isolate the contribution of the existing account management programme in quantitative measures. A periodic analysis should reveal inconsistencies or confirm adherence not only to corporate financial goals but also to the original goals which established the corporate account management programme.

Results of the account management audit should lead to improvements in the existing corporate-level account management programme. In some cases, the company may discover that strategic account management is not a feasible approach for it at this time given its level of resources, key personnel and established base of customers (Boles et al. 1994).

Abratt and Kelly (2002) give the following recommendations for improving existing account management programmes. There should be ongoing training programmes for the key account managers and for the internal personnel of both the supplier and the key account customer companies to ensure an alignment of goals, objectives and strategies. The key account manager should have a limited number of accounts to ensure focus within particular accounts. Also, strategic accounts should be correctly identified, and this is determined not only by the size or volume of the customer but also by their strategic importance. Moreover, it is important to understand strategic accounts and their main concerns, problems and strategic issues, and focus on what they see as important and what creates value for them. In addition, it is important to develop a culture of commitment to the strategic accounts, which requires all employees to understand what strategic accounts expect from their suppliers.

Possible abandonment of the SAM programme

In some cases the company may choose to abandon its SAM programme. Even though the account management concept itself receives little criticism, its implementation in the company may produce unsatisfactory results (Boles et al. 1994; Business Marketing 1988). Stevenson (1981) gives the following reasons for dropping out of the account management programme. The corporate-level organization does not allow for account organization or the existing sales force organization precludes effective implementation of the programme. It may turn out that the customer profile does not lend itself to account management or, in the search for higher levels of productivity, some companies find that the revenue and margin levels from national accounts do not warrant the added expense levels of the programme (Rottenberger-Murtha 1992). Also, firms unwilling or unable to devote sufficient resources to their national accounts are not successful in implementing the programme (Boles et al. 1994).

Piercy and Lane (2006) argue that existing SAM programmes, in practice, tend to lead to situations where a company's resources are heavily invested in that part of the business in which the customers have the lowest margins and the highest business risk. Customers who are attractive to our company are usually attractive to our competitors as well. Thus, the most attractive customers for SAM strategy are also likely to be those where competitive intensity is highest and consequently where the ability of the customer to substitute one supplier for another is highest. Moreover, customers are identified as strategic accounts often just because they are large customers. In other words, strategic accounts are not distinguished from large accounts. This should not happen with proper selection of strategic accounts with several relevant criteria, but the apparent reality tends to be that companies choose as strategic accounts those customers to which they sell most, or they respond to the demands of large customers for special treatment. In other words, their argument is that the weakness of existing SAM programmes is that the strategic account selection functions in theory but not in practice.

To deal with this problem, new business models should be developed with the help of the following advice. Alternative routes to market should be developed to reduce critical dependencies and risk, and alternative product offerings should be developed to rebuild brand strength as a counter to the power of the largest customers. Suppliers should emphasize the need for high returns to justify taking on high-risk business, not the other way around. Strategic vulnerabilities created by excessive levels of dependence on a small number of customers or distributors should be reduced. The difference between large accounts and strategic accounts should be clarified and appropriate ways of managing these different types of customers profitably should be developed. The company should also actively reject business from some sources because the customer is unattractive in terms of profitability and risk, even if the business on offer is large (Piercy and Lane 2006).

Relationship-level SAM

The implementation of the corporate-level SAM programme takes place in each strategic account relationship. The time span of the management horizon at this level is the lifetime of the particular customer relationship, which is typically several years or decades. Several integral processes of relationship-level SAM are discussed below.

Adjusting SAM in different evolutionary phases of relationship

Relationship-level SAM requires understanding the evolution of the customer relationship. The relationship marketing literature has suggested several ways in which a customer relationship may evolve over time. Ojasalo (2000) classified relationship evolution models into three different categories: episodic, phase and state approaches.

Episodic approach holds single episodes as central elements through which the relationship evolves. An episode can also be called a purchase, transaction, assignment or encounter, depending on the context: it is effectively the basic element of the relationship in which the value adding and interaction primarily take place. Episodic models do not distinguish phases or states of a relationship. Episodic orientation approaches relationships on two levels: on the episode level and on the relationship level. In other words, these models include both episode- and relationship-level elements, with episode-level elements describing what happens within a single episode, while relationship-level elements have a cumulative function which means that they 'remember' and 'sum' what has happened in previous episodes during the history of the relationship. Relationship-level elements, in some sense, represent the balance sheet of the incidents and perceptions in the relationship.

Phase approach suggests that a customer relationship develops through certain successive phases, so that one phase leads to another. The models in this approach understand the relationship as a life cycle. They typically explain what kinds of activities and incidents take place in different phases, and possibly systematically describe how certain relationship-related dimensions change in different phases. Such dimensions are sometimes called longitudinal dimensions.

State approach to relationship evolution focuses on distinguishing and characterizing different possible states which a relationship may experience. Yet state models do not suggest which of the states a relationship actually does experience and in what order, except the state of beginning. This also means that the relationship may experience the same state several times during its history. An integral part of this approach is to understand what forces drive the relationship from one state to another or what makes the relationship remain in one of them.

Different management methods are required at different evolutionary phases or states of the relationship. McDonald and Woodburn (1999) developed KAM relationship stages adapted from Millman and Wilson's (1995) model, which in Ojasalo's categorization (2000) above is an example of a phase approach. McDonald et al. (2000) describe the characteristics of the different stages or phases as follows:

Exploratory KAM
- Pre-trading.
- Customer must potentially qualify as a key account.
- Both sides are exploring.
- Signalling is important.
- Reputation is critical.
- The seller must be patient and prepared to invest.

Basic KAM
- Transactional and operational view.
- Emphasis on efficiency.
- Often low common interest.
- Buyer is multi-sourcing.
- Exit from relationship is easy.
- Driven by price.
- Little information sharing.
- Based on single-point contact.
- Reactive rather than proactive.
- Uses the standard organization of selling company.

Cooperative KAM
- Assumption of experience of performance.
- Supplier possibly has preferred status.
- Relationship is mainly with the buyer.
- Contacts are multi-functional.
- Organization is standard.
- Selling company adds value to the relationship.
- Exit from the relationship is not difficult.
- Seller is not wholly trusted by the customer.
- Visits to the customer are limited.
- Information sharing is limited.
- Based on forecasting rather than joint strategic planning.

Interdependent KAM
- Both acknowledge importance to each other.
- The selling company is the principal or sole supplier.
- Exit is more difficult.

- High level of information exchange.
- Range of joint and innovation activities is wider.
- Larger range of multi-functional contacts.
- Processes are streamlined.
- Parties are prepared to invest in the relationship.
- High volume of dialogue.
- Better understanding of the customer.
- Social relationship and trust are developed.
- Cost savings are achieved.
- Cooperation is proactive rather than reactive.
- Parties do joint strategic planning and focus on the future.
- Opportunity to grow the business.

Integrated KAM

- Real partnership, complementary and mutual dependence.
- Dedicated and cross-boundary functional or project teams established.
- Exit barriers are high and possible exit is traumatic.
- Open information sharing takes place on sensitive subjects.
- The selling company is often the sole supplier.
- Costing systems are transparent.
- Assumption of mutual trustworthiness exists at all levels.
- Opportunism does not exist, and thus protection against that is lowered.
- Joint long-term strategic planning takes place.
- Profits for both sides increase.

Finally, the relationship may disintegrate at any of the previous phases, for reasons described below. The person who was responsible for building up the relationship is not the right person to terminate it.

Disintegrating KAM

- Rarely caused by price problems.
- Often caused by changes in key personnel.
- Account manager's approach or lack of skills.
- Failure to establish multi-level links.
- Breach of trust.
- Prolonged poor performance against agreed programme.
- Changing market positions, culture, organization or ownership.
- Complacency (McDonald et al. 2000).

Developing value proposition

Each strategic account needs its own specific value proposition which is different from what other customers are being offered (Storbacka 2012). Value proposition refers to the firm's suggestion to the customer on how its resources and capabilities, expressed as artefacts (goods, services, information and experiences), can enable the customer to create value (Flint and Mentzer 2006). Frow and Payne (2011) proposed a planning framework for value propositions that consists of five steps:

1. Identify stakeholders.
2. Determine core values.
3. Facilitate dialogue and knowledge sharing.
4. Identify value co-creation opportunities.
5. Co-create stakeholders value propositions.

According to Anderson et al. (2006), a supplier's offering may have many technical, economic, service or social benefits that deliver value to customers, but so do competitors' offerings. The essential question is how the value elements compare with those of the next best alternative. To answer this question it is useful to sort value elements into three categories: points of parity, points of difference and points of contention:

- *Points of parity* are those elements with essentially the same performance or functionality as those of the next best alternative.
- *Points of difference* are elements which make the supplier's offering either superior or inferior to the next best alternative.
- *Points of contention* are elements about which the supplier and its customers disagree regarding how their performance or functionality compare with those of the next best alternative.

Either the supplier regards a value element as a point of difference in its favour, while the customer regards that element as a point of parity with the next best alternative, or the supplier regards a value element as a point of parity, while the customer regards it as a point of difference in favour of the next best alternative. In developing the value offering, the company should identify all benefits customers receive from the offering, identify the favourable points of difference, and pinpoint the one or two points of difference whose improvement will deliver the greatest value to the customer.

Storbacka's (2012) research shows that in the development of an account-specific value proposition, often the firm has to do trade-offs on its strategy. A typical example of such a trade-off relates to standardization and customization, since an increased product variation increases the average unit cost if operating policies remain unchanged. Modularization of value elements is one option to combine the efficiency of standardization and effectiveness of tailoring.

Considering the above discussion on the evolution of a relationship, a big challenge is that customer-desired value changes over time. Thus, to retain strategic accounts, suppliers are forced to either anticipate what customers will value next or be ready to react faster than competitors to these changes (Flint et al. 2002). Different people in the buying company may also value different things. The focus of a value proposition should therefore meet the initiating person's criteria, but the focus is likely to shift as the needs and demands of the other people involved in the buying process are taken into account, and the final decision criteria evolve. The initial focus may also change during the sales process as a result of the communicative interactions and dialogue between buying and selling company.

Where offerings are more extensive, it is important to maintain several customer interfaces at different organizational levels (Kowalkowski 2011).

Selecting account managers

An important relationship-level SAM measure is the appointment of an account manager to take care of the particular relationship. This involves several decisions. Is there just one or are there several accounts per account manager? Are account managers located at a new level or in the existing sales department? Is there one or are there several levels of account managers? If there are several levels of account managers, how are their hierarchies organized? For example, are the highest-level account managers selected based on the industry and the lowest-level account managers geographically (Kempeners and Van der Hart 1999)?

What are the responsibilities, skills and roles? Account managers have several roles and responsibilities and they may vary between different accounts as well as between different phases of the relationship evolution. According to Shetcliffe (2003), the key account manager's role is to be the primary link from the account into the selling organization for all matters influencing the customer relationship, the account's decision-makers and influencers. The account manager also develops proactively a continual flow of business from the account by thoroughly understanding their business, market requirements and competitive environment. Moreover, they help the account's decision-makers to exploit market opportunities through selling products and servicing them. According to Shuman (2009), an account manager:

- Builds relationships and influence with key customers.
- Lives near the customer in an ideal case.
- Provides an analysis of the account concerning market size, addressable market, mission trends, competitors and others.
- Establishes strategic intent for the account.
- Identifies growth-initiative opportunities within the account.
- Leads activities in support of achieving account quota.
- Leads the opportunity identification and qualification phases of the business-acquisition process.
- Supports the bid/no bid and proposal development phases of the business-acquisition process.
- Provides support to operations by serving as the feedback channel for performance.

Hutt and Walker (2006) emphasize the ability to build networks, and argue that by building a strong network of relationships both within their own company and within the customer organization, high-performing account managers, compared with their peers, are better able to diagnose customer requirements, mobilize internal experts and choreograph the activities that are required to out-manoeuvre rivals and create the desired customer solution.

Conflict management is a central activity of an account manager. Conflicts may be related to competition over resources, power differentials, work or role ambiguity, negative interdependence between groups, tendencies to differentiate from the group, and personal values and sensitivities (Deutsch 1973). Conflicts arise from mixed motives and goals of individuals within the account team, in other parts of the supplier organization, and in the account organization (Jones et al. 2005; Piercy 2010; Piercy and Lane 2006). Defining team members' goals and roles clearly, aligning team and corporate objectives (Atanasova and Senn 2011) and using cross-functional teams (Ryals and Bruce 2006) often help in conflict management. Account managers should also be able to adapt and use a combination of different management behaviours which can be modified throughout and across conflict episodes (Speakman and Ryals 2012).

In addition, managing communication internally and externally is one of the main responsibilities of an account manager, and customer knowledge transfer and facilitation of internal learning is one of the main aspects of internal communication management (Natti et al. 2006). External communication management involves establishing communication channels between all levels of management and across geographic boundaries with the account (Yip and Madsen 1996).

McDonald et al. (2000) bring forward five essential skills of an account manager: people skills, thinking skills, administration and project management skills, relevant knowledge and personal qualities. People skills cover communication skills, including listening and persuasion, leadership and credibility 'from boardroom to postroom'. Thinking skills include analytical skills, creativity and flexibility, strategic thinking and boundary spanning, while administration and project management skills refer to managing and organizing the key account activity. Relevant knowledge entails technical knowledge of products and applications in the customer's business, as well as subject knowledge of the industry and market, financial issues, relevant information systems, culture and language, and legal issues. Personal qualities include integrity, selling and negotiation skills, resilience and persistence, as well as likeability.

Wilson and Millman (2003) explain the behaviour of global account managers. They refer to the 'political entrepreneur' and say that a global account manager, most importantly, has a boundary-spanning role. Boundary spanning means bringing the right people together, sharing information and functioning as the organization's 'antenna' in the external business environment. Boundary spanning takes place at both internal and external interfaces of the organization. An account manager combines both the political and entrepreneurial roles and, based on their behaviour, an account manager may be classified as a *self-server, renegade, partisan* or *arbiter* (Wilson and Millman 2003).

The political behaviour of a *self-server* is manifested in manipulation of both the buyer and seller for personal advantage and protection, while a *self-server's* entrepreneurial behaviour involves seeking business opportunities to achieve personal career aspirations and objectives. A *renegade's* political behaviour is characterized by manipulation of the supplier for the customer's advantage, while the entrepreneurial behaviour includes identification of commercial advantages for the customer with little consideration of the strategic or operational impact upon the seller. The *partisan's* political behaviour is manifested in the attempt to increase personal standing with the seller. A *partisan's* entrepreneurial behaviour becomes visible in the attempt to identify commercial advantage for the seller with little consideration of the strategic or operational impact upon the customer. Finally, the *arbiter's* political behaviour means that they facilitate achievement of relational and financial goals that benefit buyer, seller and themselves, and also build multi-cultural relationships and promote meritocracy. Their entrepreneurial role becomes visible in seeking business opportunities and synergistic potentials of value to buyer, seller and self. *Renegades* and *partisans* are more suitable at the earlier evolutionary stages of the customer relationship, while *arbiters* are better suited to the later stages when cooperation is closer and more integrated.

Establishing and managing account teams

Establishing and managing an account team is often necessary for effective relationship-level SAM. This team is often cross-functional, since successful servicing of the account requires several functions and activities other than sales (Spekman and Johnston 1986). Also, the team is needed because the individual salesperson does not cover all facets of firm resources and competences, and does not possess enough intra-firm influence to propose and implement value propositions that create competitive advantage (Weitz and Bradford 1999). The work of the team includes sales, marketing, operations, finance and control, and logistics. The members of the team have relationships with members of the same team, members of different teams within the firm: i.e. the selling team and the buying centre, the selling team and other groups in the selling firm, and the selling team and the firm's strategy (Jones et al. 2005). If cooperation in the relationship has developed to be deep enough, there may be several cross-boundary teams consisting of people from both the company and its account; for example, an operation focus team, a finance focus team, an R&D focus team, a market research focus team and an environment focus team (McDonald et al. 1997). Account teams often consist of a permanent core selling team and members of other functional groups that participate on an ad hoc basis (Moon and Gupta 1997).

Account managers may operate three different forms of account team (Kempeners and Van der Hart 1999; Shapiro and Moriarty 1984): own account team, shared account team and shared account team with own manager. In the case of own account team, the account manager has their own dedicated account team with dedicated people, and the members in the team report directly and only to the account manager. Members in the shared account team option are participating in several account teams, and account managers share the services of members on a predetermined basis, while the members report to the account managers for whom they work. In the case of a shared account team with own manager, members are a pooled force under the direction of their own manager who reports to the manager of the account managers. Then the team members work only for accounts but do not report directly to the account managers.

According to Atanasova and Senn (2011), the account team management includes three main elements: team design, organizational context and processes.

Team design

> *Goal and role clarity*: aligning the team goals with individual and overall corporate goals, as well as with customer goals, enhances collaboration, lowers conflict levels and improves performance.
>
> *Customer coverage*: this refers to the extent to which the team structure adequately corresponds to the customer's organization and its requirements. The team's ability to deal with the complexity marking the interface between the supplier and the customer depends on the extent to which it provides appropriate customer coverage across various dimensions, such as countries, divisions and functions. Structural fit between the team and the customer should be ensured.
>
> *Empowerment*: empowerment of the team consists of two aspects, decision-making authority and resource availability. Providing the team with sufficient authority tells the customer that customer managers have the power and resources to get things done in a timely and effective manner.
>
> *Heterogeneity*: sufficient diversity in skills and knowledge should be represented in the team.
>
> *Adequate skills*: as opposed to skill heterogeneity, this refers to individual characteristics that combine, such that more is always better for a team.
>
> *Leadership*: leaders who can create effective working environments and motivate team members also feature more collaborative processes, reduced conflicts and higher effectiveness.

Organizational context

> *Top-management support*: this support enhances internal and external collaboration, reduces conflict and enforces a more proactive approach to customers.
>
> *Rewards and incentives*: requires a system for measuring account-specific results as well as an incentive system that rewards all team members appropriately.
>
> *Training*: team members, who come from different backgrounds and parts of the organization, need training to help them understand their tasks, processes, objectives and roles.

Processes

> *Communication and collaboration*: refers to interactions both within the team and with external parties.

Conflict management: the existence of working mechanisms that help to resolve disputes in a timely and effective manner is important.

Proactiveness: a proactive account team will be successful if it actively seeks areas for continuous improvement, identifies opportunities and innovative solutions to problems, and addresses issues before they become major problems (Atanasova and Senn 2011).

Dissolving relationships

Effective relationship management includes management of declining and dissolving relationships. The dissolution of certain relationships may even be desirable, for example if the particular relationship is not profitable enough. By uncoupling the relationship the company is able to free its resources and reallocate them to other existing or new relationships with higher profit potential (Campbell and Cunningham 1983; Fiocca 1982; Olsen and Ellram 1997; Turnbull and Zolkiewski 1997). A relationship is dissolved when all activity links are broken and no resource ties and actor bonds exist between the companies, and no mutual expectation of relationship continuity remains (Tähtinen and Halinen-Kaila 1997). A relationship may also change into a 'sleeping relationship', which is defined as preserving partners' relationships through the history of the commitment. In this case, prior commitment can be the basis for trust in the content of the relationship even in the absence of resource exchange (Cova and Salle 2000; Hadjikhani 1996; Skaates et al. 2002). It may take place at any phase of the relationship, and it may be sudden or a long process (McDonald and Woodburn 2011).

The dissolution of the relationship may be the buyer's, the seller's or a mutual decision (Hocutt 1998). Both parties may voluntarily want to end the relationship through a joint decision, but it is also possible that one may be a voluntary party to the decision while the other is involuntary, or both parties may be involuntary (Pressey and Mathews 2003).

When is careful management of relationship dissolution needed? Alajoutsijärvi et al. (2000) introduced the concept of the 'beautiful exit' to understand what type of strategy can be applied in relationship dissolution, so that any negative consequences affecting both partners and the network can be avoided. The concept also helps in recognizing early signals of potential relationship dissolution and taking actions that might still save it. The quality of relationship dissolution management is emphasized under the following conditions.

First, when the selling company has few alternative existing or potential accounts in the market, it is important for the company to ensure that reactivation of the ex-relationship is possible, if the circumstances change. Second, when the account has an influential role in the marketplace and connected network, the ex-partner may create and circulate a negative and probably one-sided aftermath story which can damage the company's image. Third, when the relationship has been public, the negative publicity may damage both partners' network image. Fourth, when the relationship has developed strong personal bonds, since business relationships are performed by individuals, avoiding hurting them is as important as avoiding hurting the partner company. Fifth, when the connected network is tightly structured, the dissolution of one relationship in a connected network is likely to have effects on other relationships in the network. Sixth, when the companies in the marketplace appreciate committed, trustworthy and other-orientated behaviour, breaking the relational norms will damage the selling company's image.

What approaches are available for relationship dissolution management? Alajoutsijärvi et al. (2000) suggested a framework for the management of relationship dissolution, based on two dimensions: directness/indirectness of communication and other/self-orientation. Indirect strategies are used when the company does not state the desire to terminate the relationship explicitly but tries to achieve the same result by different actions. Indirect communication offers the initiator a chance to respect the partner's 'face'. Indirect relationship dissolution approaches include two options: *disguised* and *silent exit*. In *disguised* exit, the desire to dissolve the relationship is communicated in words, acts or other hints, but without conveying the real message. If this is done in an other-oriented way, then the company communicates to its account that it wishes to change the relationship, but not that it wishes to exit, possibly by communicating about a reduction in investments in the relationship in the future. In the self-oriented way of relationship dissolution, the other party's relational costs are increased up to the point that the partner itself starts to dissolve the relationship, for example by increasing the price of products and services.

In the case of *silent* exit, there is no intention or need for communicating exit wishes, meaning that there is an implicit understanding that the relationship has ended. Then both parties see that the relationship has ended, but they do not bring up the subject in order to save the partner's face or to avoid hurting the partner. In the other-oriented way, relationship dissolution happens implicitly by letting the relationship just fade away. In a self-oriented way, the dissolution intention is expressed through changed behaviour, for example in the openness and frequency of communication or vanishing relationship investments.

Direct communication strategies do not leave any doubt about the desire to dissolve the relationship. Three direct communication strategies are available: *communicated exit, revocable exit* and *voice*. In the case of *communicated* exit, if the relationship is terminated in the self-oriented way, then the other party is explicitly told that the relationship is over, without giving them any chance to change their behaviour to recover the relationship. If the strategy is used in the other-oriented way, then discussion about the relationship takes place. The discussions are not hostile and both parties come to the understanding that dissolving the relationship is the right thing to do. In the case of *revocable* exit, the desire to dissolve the relationship is told explicitly, but there is still the chance to recover the relationship. The disengager may look at the problematic situation just from their own perspective (self-orientation) or take into account the other party's perspective as well (other-orientation). In the *voice* alternative, dissatisfaction with the relationship is expressed directly to the other party. The purpose may be to change the relationship (other orientation) or change the other party (self-orientation) (Alajoutsijärvi et al. 2000).

Annual-level SAM

Effective management of each relationship requires an account-specific annual plan of the various operational-level activities for the coming year. The annual-level SAM plan is subordinated to the long-term relationship-level plan, which is subordinated to the general corporate-level principles of SAM and overall corporate strategy. The time span of the management horizon at this level is from a few days to one year.

The literature of account management includes some illustrative examples of activities included in annual account plans and proposes general annual account management templates (McDonald and Woodburn 2011). An important part of strategic account management is the development of an account-specific annual plan by the account manager and their team that responds to the circumstances of the coming year. Since the accounts as well as the operating environments differ significantly, annual plans should also be very different.

An annual account management plan includes the same basic elements as any short-term action plan, such as objectives, activities, timetable, person/people responsible, costs and performance metrics. Account-specific operational objectives typically relate to sales volume, margin, new products and services sold to the customer, share of customer's total purchases in certain product or service categories, new product and services developed for the customer, learning, becoming a preferred supplier and enhancement of the supplier's image for reference purposes (Ojasalo 2001). Moreover, the annual plan may include a systematic plan to engage executives of the selling company to meet personally representatives from the account organization. A programme that involves top executives in the account management process may have a significant impact on sales growth (Senn 2006). The annual account plan also includes the account-specific budget, but it is a larger concept than just the budget. Account planning is especially concerned with identifying what and to whom sales need to be made (McDonald and Woodburn 2011).

Operational-level actions of SAM can be classified into two categories: those resulting in company-level benefits to the account organization and those resulting in individual-level benefits to the key individual in the account organization (Ojasalo 2001). Company-level benefits refer to those benefits which contribute to the customer company's organizational goals and wellbeing in a holistic sense. Individual-level benefits refer to the benefits which the individual perceives will contribute to their own wellbeing. In the case of individual-level benefits, the focus is on the individual(s) in the customer company who is/are the key decision-makers in the relationship. The following aspects are relevant when planning operational-level SAM activities providing company-level benefits:

- How could products/services be customized for the account?
- How could information exchange with the account be improved?
- How could relationship routines be improved?
- How could the organizational structure be improved to better meet the account's requirements?
- What factors make the selling company trustworthy in the eyes of the account and how could these factors be enhanced?
- What are the effective mechanisms and measures for controlling and securing the achievement of relationship goals?

The following aspects are relevant for individual-level benefits:

- How could the ease of the job and interaction with key individual(s) in the account organization be facilitated?
- What kind of social interaction styles are appreciated by the key individual(s)?
- What kind of informal social contacts and events would help in building and enhancing a friendship?
- Is there something that the key individual(s) would appreciate and that could easily be offered in terms of normal and accepted business ethics?

Organizational fragmentation and insufficient communication channels within the company, its departments, experts and subgroups cause problems in relation to internal knowledge transfer (Natti et al. 2006). The annual-level plan should include review of the operational activity during the year, as well as measures for how to learn from it. Internal knowledge transfer is vital to transform account-specific learnings into improvement at corporate, relationship and annual-level SAM.

Conclusions and research implications

The theoretical implications of this paper relate to the identification of three relevant management levels of SAM as well as the main processes at these levels. So far, the research literature has discussed the various SAM processes, but the big picture has been very unorganized and fragmented. The three-level framework contributes by showing how the different SAM processes are hierarchically subordinated to each other and the time spans of process cycles of different processes: some of them are longer and one-time processes, others are shorter and frequently repeated. The practical implication of this paper is the proposed framework of SAM processes at three levels, which not only gives a list of SAM processes but also demonstrates the hierarchical order in which these processes have to be tackled if the company is interested in introducing a systematic SAM approach in its organization. Moreover, as it maps the relevant SAM processes at different management levels and illustrates their hierarchy, it also shows that successful SAM is the effort of the whole organization and all its levels. Instead of just saying 'top management's support is required' or 'cross-functional cooperation is important', it shows that the success of front-line operational processes at the customer interface is strongly dependent on the success of corporation-wide and general processes.

This paper proposed a framework of SAM processes at the corporate, relationship and annual level. Processes at corporate-level SAM relate to establishing the corporate-wide grounding for SAM in the company. The time span of the management horizon at this level is the lifetime of the SAM programme in the corporation, which is typically decades. The central processes of this level are: decision-making on possible adoption of a SAM philosophy, top-level support and sponsorship of the SAM programme, decision-making on the nature of the SAM programme, development of company-wide general principles of SAM, maintenance and improvement of the SAM programme, and possible abandonment of the SAM programme. Processes at relationship-level SAM relate to relationship management with a certain strategic account. The time span of the management horizon of this level is the lifetime of the particular customer relationship, which is typically several years or decades. The key processes of this level are: adjustment of SAM in different phases of the customer relationship, development of value propositions, selection of the account manager, establishment and management of the account team, boundary spanning, communication management, conflict management and dissolving the relationship. Processes at annual-level SAM involve operational and everyday serving of the account and the time span of the management horizon is from a few days to one year. The main processes of this level are: annual planning of account-specific action plans, including objectives, activities, timetable, person/people responsible, and performance metrics, annual account-specific budgeting, execution of the action plan, consideration of both company- and individual-level customer benefits, control, and learning and knowledge transfer.

The following suggestions for further research stem from this paper. First, the traditional BPM/BPE (business process management/business process engineering or re-engineering) approach is not enough for understanding and developing SAM processes. Examining SAM just in terms of the process engineering philosophy gives an over-mechanistic and technical view to SAM. This is because SAM requires lots of aspects related to people and strategic management, such as leadership, entrepreneurial, political and communications skills. However, combining SAM and BPM/BPE theories has the potential to function as a fruitful starting point in examining more efficient and effective SAM processes.

Second, a business process crossing departmental lines in the organization represents a greater challenge for process management. A process crossing hierarchical layers of the organization is also challenging to manage, particularly if the process owner, in other words the person in charge of the process, is at a lower hierarchical level. Indeed, more research is needed to explore how to improve the management of SAM processes crossing departmental and hierarchical levels.

Third, the use of social media is increasingly important in managing consumer and brand relationships, and this has been widely understood. Still, so far, hardly any knowledge exists of the role and application of social media in SAM, so more research is needed in this field. Fourth, the literature includes knowledge of both evolution of relationships and value propositions in business markets. So it would be an interesting starting point for further research to examine strategies and practices for dynamic shaping of value propositions during relationship evolution. Fifth, understanding customer needs is the basis for long-term and mutually beneficial account relationships, and this includes understanding existing and future needs as well as explicit and latent needs. Simple annual customer satisfaction surveys and project feedback meetings are not enough if the selling company wants to deliver world-class quality. Better methods are required for needs analysis of strategic accounts. The use and application of new co-creation approaches in the context of SAM also clearly requires more research.

Developing strategic key account relationships in business-to-business markets

BY KEVIN WILSON

Abstract

In a series of articles and conference papers that stretch back to 1993, the author, individually and with colleagues, has explored the nature of buyer–seller interaction in organizational markets. A number of models evolving from this work have provided the foundation for the work of others in the field, most notably researchers at Cranfield University.

The result has been the development of some powerful models that have been instructive in describing the nature of buyer–seller interaction and the form that relationships take at various stages of their development.

What had been lacking was empirical evidence to link those models in a comprehensive framework that provided clues as to how buyer–seller relationships could be managed. This paper reviews the literature concerning relational development in key strategic account management (KSAM) and reports on a research project that explored how the development of buyer–seller relationships is influenced by the nature of the problems that buyers and sellers focus upon resolving during the process of interaction. This paper thus integrates the Millman–Wilson model of relational development with the problem-centred product, process and facilitation (PPF) model of buyer–seller interaction in business-to-business markets, and provides valuable insights into why and how relationships develop over time. In its revised form the paper also takes account of work that has built on the early models and other work that has contributed to our understanding of relational development.

Revision of 'A problem centred (PPF) model of buyer–seller interaction in business to business markets. *Journal of Selling and Major Account Management* (1999) 1(4).'

Introduction

This paper explores the literature concerning the nature and development of key account customer relationships in business-to-business markets. Building upon the work of a number of writers, many from the Industrial Marketing and Purchasing (IMP) Group tradition, it offers a framework for key account management (KAM) that links two previously developed models, the Millman–Wilson relational development model (1994, 1995) and the Product, Process and Facilitation model first posited by Wilson (1993), further explored by Wilson and Croom-Morgan (1993) and Millman and Wilson (1995), and operationalized by Wilson (1997).

Defining key/strategic accounts

Millman and Wilson (1994) defined a key account as a customer in business-to-business markets identified by a selling company as being of strategic importance. Although broad, the value of this definition was that it avoided linking key account status exclusively to considerations of size, geographical spread and volume of business represented by the customer, which dominated earlier definitions (Colletti and Tubridy 1987; Grickscheit et al. 1993). While important, these factors do not encompass the full range of criteria that may be used to establish the strategic importance of a customer.

Early research from Millman and Wilson (1997) suggested a far broader range of selection criteria that was later confirmed in the work of McDonald et al. (1997). The first in the following list was the most frequently cited criterion in the Millman–Wilson (1997) study, typically combined with others, depending on the characteristics of the participant's company and their industry background:

- The Pareto 80/20 rule.
- Size of purchase budget.
- Sales growth potential.
- Customer prestige.
- Account profitability (current and potential).
- The geographical spread of the customer and the potential to gain access to otherwise inaccessible markets.
- Receptivity to developing close long-term relationships.
- Access to new/complementary technology.
- Cultural 'fit'.
- Strategic 'fit'.
- Cross-selling opportunities.
- Limited customer base.

The importance of including these factors is their emphasis upon the relational issues, such as the customer receptiveness to developing close long-term relationships and cultural 'fit', as well as the transactional issues such as sales and profit potential. Some of these criteria of key account attractiveness were partly confirmed and consolidated into the following categories by McDonald et al. (1997), which, interestingly, did not include consideration of cultural 'fit' or customer receptiveness to developing closer relationships with suppliers:

- Volume-related factors.
- Profit potential.
- Status-related factors.

The more relational measures of attractiveness were explored by McDonald et al. in defining supplier attractiveness to the customer in terms of the ease of doing business, product and service quality, and people factors. The importance of these and related relational factors in determining customer attractiveness to sellers reaffirmed earlier research reported later in this paper.

The work of both Millman and Wilson (1994, 1995, 1997) and McDonald et al. (1997) serves to suggest that key accounts may be small or large compared with the seller; operate locally, nationally, regionally or globally; they may exhibit a desire for close long-term relationships or wish to remain at arm's length; or be transactional and adversarial in their dealings with suppliers. What remains critical is that they are perceived as being of fundamental importance to the selling firm in achieving its major strategic objectives.

There is a tendency in the literature to equate the terms national, key and strategic accounts, differentiating only on the basis of geographical spread through the additional descriptor 'global'. This, in my view, is an error. There is a need to differentiate between accounts that have *transactional* importance, in that they represent high levels of sales opportunity, and those that have *strategic* importance in their potential for value creation beyond product or core product offering.

Woodburn and Wilson, in the editorial to this book, imply this distinction by defining strategic key account management as 'a supplier-led process of inter-organizational collaboration that creates value for both supplier and strategically important customers by offering individually tailored propositions designed to secure long-term profitable business through the *coordinated* deployment of multifunctional capabilities'.

Gosselin and Heene (2003) distinguish between key account selling and strategic account management. They suggest that strategic accounts are those where there is mutual recognition of the strategic importance of the relationship by both buyer and seller and further suggest that while both key account selling and key account management may be involved in the creation and delivery of value, strategic account management is also concerned with building the competencies upon which that value is based.

This is an important distinction that would save much confusion in the minds of practitioners who still often mistake key account selling for key account management.

First, the transition from customer to key account and then to strategic account would be more easily facilitated, as would a downgrading of the relationship; and second, the clearer definition of client status would encourage the greater involvement of marketing in the analysis of customer relationship potential on a number of different parameters, and also provide a clearer view for senior managers of customer portfolio potential.

It is not entirely in the gift of the supplier to grant strategic account status, although there may be greater leeway in the case of key accounts. There is one other, perhaps overriding qualification: the strategic account, in order to be a strategic account, must perceive the supplier as being a real or potential source of strategic advantage – without that the relationship cannot develop beyond the *pre-* or *early KAM* relational states.

Since the late 1970s the literature on key account management appears to have emerged in parallel to, but in many ways quite separately from, the interaction, network and relationship literature, as a result of strong practitioner involvement. It is only relatively recently that academics have turned their attention to the topic and integrated the study of KAM with other bodies of theory, and have thrown valuable light on the operationalization of the principles of interaction, network theory and relationship marketing through KAM processes. The value of this literature, however, is in the descriptions that it provides of KSAM processes and related issues, rather than in the provision of an integrated model that may instruct key account management processes. It is proposed here that the integration of the PPF model with the Millman–Wilson relational development model provides just such a management tool.

Later research outlined elsewhere in this book has dealt with broader issues, but little more recent research has been reported that deals specifically with relational strategies applied at different relational stages in order to increase or diminish relational intensity, although attention has been given to relational development (Woodburn and McDonald 2011) and the appropriate economic organization that may be adopted to facilitate KSAM (Wengler 2007).

A model of relational development

The Millman–Wilson (1994) model was based on exploratory research and concepts drawn from sales strategy (Wotruba 1991), supply chain management (Lamming 1993) and interaction literature (Dwyer et al. 1987; Ford 1980). The model was adopted for further exploration by McDonald and Rogers (1996, 1998) (see Table 1). These early papers from Cranfield used the same descriptors as had been developed by Millman and Wilson, although in later iterations these were changed (e.g. Woodburn and McDonald 2011). The original descriptors are

Table 1: KSAM relationship stages in the literature

Dwyer et al. (1987) Ford (1980)	Lamming (1993)	Wotruba (1991)	Millman and Wilson (1994)	McDonald and Woodburn (2011)
Pre-relationship awareness	Traditional	Provider	Pre-KAM	Exploratory
Early stage exploration	Stress	Persuader	Early KAM	Early
Development stage expansion	Resolved	Prospector	Mid-KAM	Cooperative
Long-term commitment	Partnership	Problem solver	Partnership KAM	Interdependent
Final stage institutionalization	Beyond partnership	Procreator	Synergistic KAM	Integrated
			Uncoupling KAM	

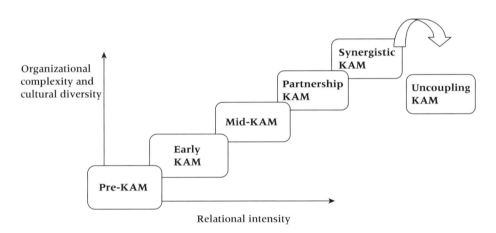

Figure 1 KSAM relational development states

retained here because of the marked similarity between the characteristics identified by the Cranfield research and the original KAM model.

The original KAM relational development model suggested that buyer–seller relationships could evolve through a number of relational states or stages (see Figure 1). Each of these states was characterized by varying degrees of dyadic complexity and relational intensity and each stage represented implications for sales strategists. The aim was to model a number of different relational states that had been observed and to suggest that it was possible to develop relationships from 'market-based', adversarial relationships towards closer 'value-laden' synergistic relationships, but not to suggest that it was necessary to adopt relational development as the sole KSAM strategy.

Attempting to develop close, trusting value-creating/sharing relationships is one strategic option for KSAM programmes, but in line with Kraljic's (1983) thoughts on supplier portfolios, account management is essentially about portfolio management. Some strategically important relationships may be close, trusting and mutually supportive, but others will be adversarial, market focused and self-interested, remaining at *pre, early* or *mid-KAM* states, but may nevertheless be of strategic importance. The model can be described as a hierarchy of relationships, one building progressively upon the other. While this appears to be intuitively attractive there is strong evidence to suggest that relationships may change their 'state' quite rapidly, skipping stages or reverting to earlier forms, despite being embedded in strong social relationships, a point endorsed by Woodburn and McDonald (2011).

Characteristics of KAM relational states adapted from Millman and Wilson (1994) are outlined below.

Pre-KAM
Not all customers are potential key accounts. The task facing the sales and marketing function in the *pre-KAM* stage is to identify those with the potential for moving towards key account status and to avoid wasteful investment in those accounts that do not hold that potential. *Pre-KAM* selling strategies are concerned with making basic product or service offerings available while attempting to gather information about the customer in order to determine whether or not they have key account potential.

Early KAM
Early KAM is concerned with exploring opportunities for closer collaboration by identifying the motives, culture and concerns of the account, with targeting competitor strengths and weaknesses, and with persuading customers of the potential benefits they might enjoy as 'preferred' customers. A detailed understanding is required of the decision-making process and the structure and nature of the decision-making unit, as well as the buyers' business and the problems that relate to the value-adding process.

At this stage, tentative adaptations will be made to the seller's offer in order to more closely match buyer requirements. The focus of the sales effort will be on building trust through consistent performance and open communications.

Key account managers will need to demonstrate a willingness to adapt their offering to provide a bespoke solution to the buyer's problems. High levels of uncertainty about the long-term potential of the relationship may mean that they will need to promote the idea for non-standard product offerings into their own company. Where these attempts are unsuccessful, then 'benefit selling' and the level of personal service provided by the salesperson may serve to differentiate the seller's offer.

Mid-KAM
As the relationship develops, so do levels of trust and the range of problems that the relationship addresses. The number of cross-boundary contacts also increases, with the salesperson perhaps taking a less central role. The account review process will tend to shift upwards to senior management level in view of the importance of the customer and the level of resource allocation, although the relationship may fall short of exclusivity and the activities of competitors within the account will require constant review.

Partnership KAM
Partnership KAM represents a mature stage of key account development. The supplier is often viewed as an external resource of the customer and the sharing of sensitive commercial information becomes commonplace as the focus for activity is increasingly upon joint problem resolution.

Synergistic KAM
At this advanced stage of maturity, key account management goes 'beyond partnership' when there is a fundamental shift in attitude on the part of both buyer and seller and they come to see each other not as two separate organizations but as parts of a larger entity creating joint value (synergy) in the marketplace.

Uncoupling KAM
Dissolution of a KAM relationship tends to be viewed in a pejorative way, as though a 'successful' relationship is by definition one of long duration. While in most cases buyers and sellers may perceive benefits in developing long-term relationships, we have uncovered some short-term relationships deemed to be successful by the participants and many others which, with the benefit of hindsight, were ill conceived.

As Low and Fullerton (1994) remind us: 'Deciding when to get out of an existing relationship and into a new one would minimize the substantial economic, political and emotional cost associated with building a relationship that was never destined to last'. In essence, many relationships are propped up beyond their relevance, or some event precipitates their termination, suggesting the need for an uncoupling process and contingency planning.

Dissolution, or *uncoupling KAM*, was ignored in the later development of the model by McDonald and Woodburn (2011) but its importance is emphasized by the observation that companies developing supplier relationships perceive three relational states (Moeller et al. 2006): those without suppliers, which are essentially geared to assessing their potential to be in suppliers (this broadly equates to *pre/early KAM*); those relationships within suppliers are focused upon collaborative co-creation of value (a number of stages are identified: set-up, development, contract and disturbance management which broadly equate to the processes involved in *mid/partnership/synergistic KAM*); and in supplier dissolution. This state recognizes that customers see that some relationships have run their course and are no longer delivering satisfaction. If customers perceive this as an important question, then perhaps account management programmes should recognize its importance.

An issue not addressed by Millman and Wilson or McDonald et al. was: 'When does the transition of responsibility take place between salesperson and account manager and how is that process managed?' Elsewhere in this book the point is made that key account managers are primarily managers, not salespeople. This is an important issue. When is an account recognized as being key or strategic, and by whom? Millman and Wilson suggested that much of the early-stage work of investigation and assessment of key account attractiveness was carried out by salespeople, but can salespeople be expected to analyse the long-term potential of their accounts, and if they do identify such potential, will they be keen to share that knowledge when the result may be that the account passes (together with its commission) into the hands of others?

Valuable though this work was in developing our understanding of the various stages of relational development, the findings were largely descriptive, and although management implications could be drawn from these findings, little insight was provided to instruct practitioners in managing the *process* of key account development.

The Millman–Wilson article (1995) had posited a link between the PPF model and the relational development model that promised to provide insights into the management of key account relationships through the development stages. Later, McDonald et al. (1997) also explored the impact upon the KSAM process of two of the underlying concepts of the model, those of product and process, although they do make mention of 'the ease of doing business' which is similar to the term 'making it easy to do business', one of the descriptors used by Wilson (1993) when explaining the meaning of facilitation within the PPF model (Table 3).

The PPF model, as presented by Wilson (1993), posited that the nature of dyadic organizational relationships was directly related to the nature of problems that the parties focused upon resolving. It was proposed that there were three orders of problem, related to product (e.g. product performance, conformance to specification, price, etc.), process (how the product offering related to the manufacturing and value-creation processes of the customer) and facilitation (the way in which business was carried out by the two parties and the strategic impact of the relationship). These problem-related issues were seen as hierarchical in that the lowest level of problems related to product was associated with more distant relationships, while the more complex higher-order problems related to process and facilitation were associated with increasing organizational closeness. They were also perceived as cumulative in that it was impossible to address higher-order problems unless lower-order problems had been resolved.

Millman and Wilson (1995) present the findings of a series of research studies that give evidence to support the validity of the PPF model and its integration

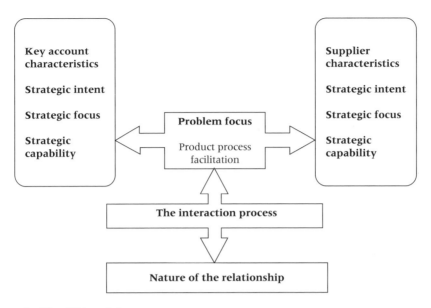

Figure 2   The PPF model

with the Millman–Wilson model in providing a framework for effective KAM. In doing so it also discusses some preliminary findings from a study into global KAM (Wilson et al. 2000).

The development of the PPF model and its integration with the relational development model

The PPF model (Figure 2) draws primarily upon the IMP model of buyer–seller interaction (Campbell 1985; Ford 1990; Håkansson 1982), the fundamental difference being that the PPF model proposes that problem resolution lies at the centre of the interaction process. The figure suggests that five major variables impact upon the nature of the interaction process within the wider industry–cultural context in which the dyadic partners operate: the prevailing atmosphere of the relationship, the characteristics of both buyer and seller, the interaction strategies that they adopt, the order of problems they choose to focus upon and the specific nature of the problem that the buyer and seller are confronted with.

The attributes that relate to the first two sets of variables draw on the Campbell (1985) model of buyer–seller interaction, the Ford (1990) representation of the IMP model and Lamming's (1993) perceptions of industry–cultural change over time. The third set of variables is based upon the strategic options defined by Håkansson (1986), refined by the addition of a number of cultural characteristics which, it is proposed, predispose either buyer or seller towards closer or more market-based relationships. The variables that relate to the nature of the problem draw on the work of Brown and Brucker (1990) in extending the RFW framework (Robinson et al. 1967) to highlight the problem-centred nature of industrial purchasing. In addition, these problem-related variables draw on Håkansson's (1982) concepts of limitation and handling problems and upon the issues of need, market and transaction uncertainty identified by Håkansson et al. (1977).

> *The environment*: the impact of the wider industry and socio-cultural environment is implicit in this model. Other factors are also acknowledged as emanating from the market environment, such as dynamism, structure, levels of internationalization and the prevailing culture within the industry. These factors effectively define the potential for relational development that exists within a given industry.
>
> *The relational atmosphere*: the atmosphere is the product of the relationship and is characterized by the level of conflict or cooperation, the overall closeness or distance of the relationship, and the companies' mutual expectations. In turn, the atmosphere will moderate both the influence of the groups of variables and the nature of the individual episodes of exchange (Håkansson 1982).
>
> *Buyer–seller characteristics*: the nature of the individual relationship is influenced by the internal characteristics of both buyer and seller. Their technological and process capabilities will prescribe the nature of problems that they can address, and their attitudes, culture and behaviours will influence the nature of the problems they may choose to address. Buyer–seller characteristics include the industries in which they operate, their relative power and dependency, the intensity of competition, the rate of technological change they are experiencing, their preferred interaction style, and the position and personal characteristics of the people involved in the exchange process (the decision-making unit and the selling team).
>
> *Buyer–seller interaction strategy*: the strategic focus adopted by buyers or sellers is a function of the interaction between the elements of the model discussed. The general strategic orientation adopted towards interaction will vary between firms on a continuum which ranges from adopting a purely transactional, arm's-length approach to relationships, through to partnership and beyond in terms of the Millman–Wilson (1994) model.
>
> *Buyer–seller focus*: this focus is represented by the way in which each dyadic partner perceives the nature of the problems they address during the interaction process. The order of problems that they address will depend upon the buyer's perception of need and the seller's ability to focus the buyer's attention upon different categories of problem. The order of problem that receives attention will be influenced by the characteristics of both buyer and seller and the relational strategies they each adopt.
>
> *Problem characteristics*: problem resolution is recognized as a major component of buyer–seller interaction by a number of writers: Håkansson (1982, 1986), Håkansson et al. (1977), Brown and Brucker (1990).

Håkansson et al. (1977) suggest that inter-organizational relationships are characterized by attempts to reduce levels of uncertainty. Where high levels of uncertainty exist about buyer need (*need uncertainty*), there is a tendency for organizational interaction to increase in order to solve buyer need-related problems. *Market uncertainty* represents the dilemma faced by buyers when choosing one supplier over another: the very act of choosing will preclude their receiving the benefits represented by alternative sources of supply. Håkansson et al. (1977) suggested that levels of uncertainty were reduced through the application of the need-serving abilities and handling capabilities of the supplier.

Håkansson (1982) identified two groups of problems of concern to dyadic partners: *limitation* and *handling* problems that are closely related to the need-solving and transfer capabilities discussed by Håkansson et al. (1977). *Limitation* problems are identified as being concerned with resolving issues relating to technology, organizational structure and knowledge, and both determine which types of customers will be served, for example price or value seekers, and whether to differentiate between customers in terms of the level of service offered. It is suggested that the level of internal competence displayed by the seller in meeting customer need, or the demands made by the seller upon suppliers, effectively limit the range of suitable relationships. While not confined to being transaction specific, these elements are concerned with the relatively short-term issues of delivering product and service offerings, and with determining whether transformation and process capabilities may be applied to specific relationships.

Handling problems, however, are identified as being concerned with the long-term development of the relationship. They centre upon relative power and dependency and upon issues of conflict and cooperation. As such they may be viewed as occurring within the cultural and social context of the relationship reflecting the atmosphere in which business is done; the strategic orientation of each party, and the nature of the social interaction, experiences and personal relationships represented within the relationship. The importance of these observations to the development of the PPF model is two-fold:

1. Although these two sets of problems cannot be divided (they are affected by and affect each other), they do represent two approaches to the study of inter-organizational relationships: the transaction costs economic perspective of the new institutionalist and the social systems perspective. *Limitation* problems may be viewed as impacting directly upon transaction costs and essentially prescribe the range of potential relationships open to the seller, while *handling* problems are related to how the relationship is managed within a socio-economic context. This paper represents an attempt to better understand the nature of *handling* problems as they might be applied to the management and development of key accounts while at the same time recognizing the *limitations* imposed by buyer capabilities, seller demands, strategic orientation and industry atmosphere.

2. Håkansson's focus upon the nature and importance of problem resolution to the development of inter-organizational relationships provides a major contribution to the development of a problem-centred model of buyer–seller interaction.

The concept that problem resolution is at the heart of buyer–seller interaction is addressed by other writers. Using the analogy of a river, Brown and Brucker (1990) perceived the industrial buying process as a problem-solving stream of behaviour, with industrial buyers being differentiated by their function and location in relation to what they call the 'channels' and 'bars' that mark the flow of the decision-making process.

The value of this model is that it focuses the process of buyer–seller interaction upon problem resolution and recognizes that both buyer and seller are active within that process. It also suggests that there is a hierarchy of problems, with some requiring greater allocation of resources than others. It further suggests that the seller is able to influence the buyer's perception of the nature of the problem by focusing upon the differing needs of functional specialists throughout the problem-solving process, and thus provides a framework within which the seller may identify potentials for competitive advantage.

In bringing together the concepts of uncertainty (*need, market and transaction*), *handling* and *limitation* problems and the problem-solving stream of buyer behaviour, three central themes may be identified. Levels of uncertainty will influence the nature of relationships that develop between buyers and sellers. For example:

*   High *need uncertainty* will tend to create closer relationships.
*   High levels of *market uncertainty* will tend to create more switching between suppliers and less close dyadic relationships.
*   *Transaction uncertainty* will be reduced by greater levels of cultural, linguistic and organizational congruence which in turn lead to greater closeness between trading partners.

Firms are faced with the problems of who to do business with and on what basis (*limitation* problems), and how to manage relationships as they evolve (*handling* problems). Problems which buyers and sellers focus jointly upon resolving are hierarchical in nature.

The PPF model identifies three orders of problem associated with managing ongoing relationships and classifies these as *product, process* and *facilitation* (see Table 2). These problem areas are hierarchical, in that problems related to *product* and base technology issues are of a relatively low order and are associated with shallow inter-organizational relationships. *Process*-related issues reflect an interest in systems and process capabilities which require closer relationships for their realization, while *facilitation* problems are concerned with strategic

Table 2: Nature of problem by category

Problem category	Nature of problem
Product	Availability
	Performance
	Features
	Quality
	Design
	Technical support
	Order size
	Price
	Terms
Process	Speed of response
	Manufacturing process issues
	Application of process knowledge
	Changes to product
	Project management issues
	Decision-making process knowledge
	Special attention in relation to deliveries, design, quotes
	Cost reduction
Facilitation	Co-value creation
	Compatibility and integration of systems
	Alignment of objectives
	Integration of personnel
	Managing processes peripheral to customer core activity
	• Addressing customer's strategic issues
	• Making it easy to do business

issues whose resolution requires high levels of integration and commonality of purpose.

Product need-related problems: these are related to issues of conformance to specification, quality, consistency, continuity of supply and suitability for use. Product needs are met by the attributes of the product. They are the elements of exchange most often given attention by marketers and may be equated to Hill's (1985) order-qualifying criteria. The elements of *need uncertainty* are also perceived to be covered by this problem category.

Process need-related problems: the incorporation of supplier goods and services in the buyer's own market offering involves a transformation process. Problems in this area relate to ensuring that inbound logistics are compatible with the processes adopted by the buyer, or that they enhance the manufacturing process in terms of delivering higher quality, lower costs, or greater efficiency or effectiveness. The application of process capabilities to buyer problems tends to move the relationship to a deeper level and switches the focus of negotiations from price to overall system cost. The exchange relationship also suffers less from the threat of competitive offerings which occurs where they focus exclusively upon product-related problem resolution.

Facilitation need-related problems: problems arise for both buyer and seller in terms of how to manage the development of relationships, the process of transformation and the creation of value. Varying levels of adaptation are required to facilitate the process and this may be described as the way business is done. Facilitation is essentially concerned with resolving issues related to trust, the reduction of uncertainty, developing a common culture and language, and developing congruence of systems, structure and strategic orientation. Sellers wishing to forge exceptionally close and competitively exclusive relationships with customers need to address problems that have direct impact upon their customers' ability to achieve their strategic organizational objectives, while at the same time making it easy to do business. Facilitation need-related problems are the highest order of problem that can be addressed by dyadic partners.

These constructs have received considerable support from empirical observation and the resolution of different orders of problem closely related to the different stages of relational development posited by the Millman–Wilson model of relational development. There are also obvious links with the concept of the role of the political entrepreneur mentioned elsewhere in this book.

Selected findings from the work of Millman and Wilson support the overall validity of the PPF model and link orders of problem resolution to the various stages of relational development.

- Buyers and sellers in industrial and organizational markets interact within the context of problem resolution, and product or service acquisition is incidental, not central to that process.
- Industry culture acts as a constraint upon the types of relationships that develop between buyers and sellers in a given industry.
- Company characteristics influence the nature of inter-organizational relationships and, in particular, are related to management style and attitudes towards salespeople and customers.
- Three orders of problem were identified from the data, which refined the concepts of *product, process* and *facilitation*-related need.
- There was strong support for the contention that these three types of problem are hierarchical, that they are associated with different levels of relational closeness and with different negotiation concerns.
- While hierarchical, these problem foci are also cumulative in that it is not possible to focus only upon *facilitation* issues without resolving issues related to *product* and *process*.

Discussion

Relationships between buyers and sellers grow progressively closer as the problem focus moves from *product* through *process* to encompass *facilitation* issues. Their effect is cumulative in that higher levels of relational interaction are not associated with an exclusive focus upon process or facilitation but upon facilitation, process and product issues. The association between problem focus and relational development is represented in Figure 3.

Millman and Wilson suggest that where sellers concentrate upon meeting only the *product*-related needs of their customers, the relationships they have tend to conform to *pre-* and *early KAM* relational forms. Relationships will be essentially arm's-length, transaction focused and display low levels of customer involvement. Only where suppliers have exclusive (monopoly) ownership of product technology can they hope to achieve sustainable competitive advantage solely through product-related problem resolution. Increasing product homogeneity in many markets suggests that this is not often the case and, in the absence of clear product differentiation, the tendency is to compete on the basis of price. Where price becomes the main focus for negotiation, relationships are likely to be increasingly transactional and arm's-length.

The development of *process* capabilities appears to be associated with the ability to manage the firm's supply chain, to forge alliances with other players in the

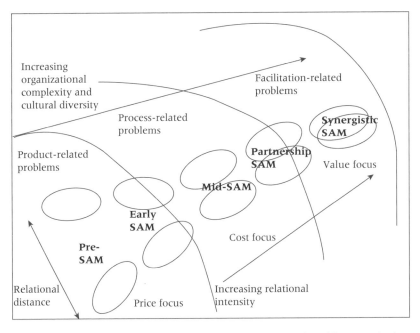

Figure 3 The relational impact of focus on different forms of problem resolution

marketplace and to enhance internal process capabilities. Suppliers that recognize the importance to customers of reducing cost within their value-creation process, and can convince their customers of the value of addressing those process-related issues, tend to develop closer relationships with their customers and are less often the victim of competitor activity. Problem-solving activity at this level is associated with buyer–seller relationships that have reached the *mid-KAM* stage and may be developing towards *partnership KAM*. Increasing organizational closeness is both a cause and an effect of focusing upon process-related issues. As the seller demonstrates their ability to solve problems of this order, so trust develops and inter-organizational contact networks grow, but access to personnel and information within the client organization is also a prerequisite for understanding process-related need. Neither does performance in this area reduce the importance of meeting the buyer's product need. High levels of product performance are a given at this stage.

It also became clear that the focus of negotiation is no longer price but the total system cost that the buyer will bear. The resolution of process-related problems that deliver substantial cost savings to the buyers allows sellers to charge premium prices for their base product offering, or to charge management fees for facilitating the process of employing commodity products in customer processes.

Facilitation issues are addressed at the *mid, partnership* and *synergistic* phases of the KSAM development process. Facilitation problems were found to be associated with the way business was done: it involves adaptation on both sides of the dyad, a drawing together, both in physical terms through modifications to internal systems processes and organizational structures, and in cultural and strategic terms. At this stage the seller is addressing the fundamental strategic needs of the buyer through a focus upon joint value creation (partnership), the creation of inter-organizational teams (virtual organizations), the performance of non-core management functions, and the joint development and exploitation of technologies and markets. Through addressing facilitation issues relationships become extremely close, the subject of negotiation moves from cost to value, and the danger from competition is slight because of the difficulty of replicating the benefits that are embedded in the relationship. Table 3 summarizes the link between KAM relational states and PPF strategies appropriate to them.

More recent research

Evidently, some important elements of KSAM relational development were not addressed by the original model and much useful work has subsequently been done to flesh out the bones. One such body of work is that emanating from Cranfield and summarized in Woodburn and McDonald (2011). They identify 11 relationship features that vary with specific KAM relational states (see Table 4).

Table 3: KAM relational states and PPF strategies

Development stage	Objectives	PPF strategies
Pre-KAM	Identify/disqualify as potential key account Establish account potential Secure initial order	Identify key contacts Establish nature of product need Identify decision-making process Display willingness to make product adaptations Advocate key account status 'in house'
Early KAM	Account penetration Increase volume of business/share of wallet Become preferred supplier	If attractive, invest in building social relationships If unattractive, serve through low-cost channels, e.g. telephone or intermediaries Identify process-related problems and show willingness to provide cost-effective solutions Extend social network Build trust through performance and open communication
Mid-KAM	Build towards partnership Become first-tier or single-source supplier Establish key account status If limited potential for development then evolve a standard offering	Focus upon process-related problems Manage the implementation of process improvements Build teams between the two organizations Establish joint systems Perform management tasks for the customer
Partnership KAM	Develop spirit of partnership Lock in customer by providing external resource base	Integrate processes Extend joint problem-solving teams Focus upon cost reduction and value creation Address facilitation issues relating to culture, language, etc.
Synergistic KAM	Continuous improvement Shared rewards Quasi-integration	Focus upon joint value creation for the end user (customer's customer) Establish semi-autonomous project teams Establish cultural congruence

Table 4: Relationship features that vary with specific KAM relational states

Relationship feature	Ranging from:	To:
Relationship emphasis	Research and reputation at *pre-KAM*	Open and strategically focused at *synergistic KAM*
Supplier status	One of several/many	Sole, possibly primary
Ease of exit	Easy, not started trading	High exit barriers, separation traumatic
Information sharing	Careful, as necessary	Open, even on sensitive subjects
Contact	Channelled through individual key account manager	Intimate: focus groups and teams
Access to customer	Customer request only	Constant both sides
Adaptation of organization and process	Standard	Joint processes, new organization
Relationship costs	May be small or large, speculative investment	Major running costs, larger sums but easier to identify
Level of trust	Exploring reputation and 'signals'	Trustworthiness assumed at all levels
Planning	Variable	Joint strategic long-term planning
Relationship potential	Important to qualify as key account	Very good/excellent in revenue and profits

These conclusions strongly support the earlier findings of Millman and Wilson as presented below.

While providing more detail characterizing the various ways in which key dyadic relationships develop, it is still in relatively broad brushstrokes and it would be interesting to map each of the 11 elements in Table 4 to problem focus.

The work of Ryals and Humphries (2007) is also of interest and, in exploring the links between the perception of relationship development from both a supply chain and key account management perspective, opens a rich area of potential research that may provide further insights into how and why relationships between key suppliers and their customers develop over time. Again, it may well be fruitful to explore the issues of value creation and exchange, trust and reliability, flexibility and responsiveness, stability and communication from the perspective of problem resolution and from both the key account and supply chain management side.

Conclusions

The PPF model, when linked to the Millman–Wilson relational development model, becomes a powerful tool for key account managers. It provides a diagnostic tool for analysing the present stage that a particular relationship has reached, for analysing the potential for relational development that exists both in particular industries and within the context of specific dyads, and for managing that relationship over time.

Many companies have been observed using problem resolution to develop relationships with their customers, but few were observed to do this in a deliberate or structured way. The PPF model offers a conceptual framework within which this may take place. The development of capabilities in the areas of *product, process* and *facilitation* expands the range of relationships that a company can form, and a focus upon resolving different orders of problem allows those relationships to be developed.

Product-related capabilities are relationship-qualifying criteria. If a company cannot offer a product or service that meets consistently high-quality, performance and cost criteria, then it will not remain in the market for long.

Process capabilities offer the seller a first step towards achieving competitive advantage and customer loyalty. Process capabilities are normally perceived as those internal abilities that allow the firm to improve its market offering. The PPF model, in contrast, extends the concept of process capability to include the ability to help customers enhance their process capabilities.

In many industries this may require firms to adopt a fundamentally different approach to the market from their competitors. It requires that they facilitate the ease with which their customers can do business with them. It requires that suppliers provide their customers with a bespoke offering aimed at joint value creation, the alignment of objectives and often the sharing of managerial responsibility. Sellers must perceive themselves not as separate from their customers but as part of their total organization, intimately involved in providing value for their customers' customer. This is not to argue that all relationships should be treated alike, rather that each relationship should be judged on the basis of its potential for (co-)value creation through problem resolution and strategies adopted accordingly (see Table 3).

The PPF/relational states model further offers a conceptual framework within which new approaches to the development of competitive strategies may be forged, one that focuses upon managing relationships rather than products.

Within industries that are short termist and which retain a strong focus upon transactions rather than relationships, this may well be difficult. However, as is the case with new products, so it may be with new ways of doing business, that the first to market gain enormous advantage over their competitors. The potential certainly exists within niche markets and among smaller, flexible companies to experiment with this form of account management, identifying and solving bespoke problems for their customers in order to help them compete better in their own markets.

The role of the key/strategic account manager

BY KEVIN WILSON AND SUE HOLT

Abstract

The role of the manager of relationships with strategic accounts has received little attention in the literature encompassing the topic of national/key/global and strategic account management. Indeed, where it has been discussed, much of this literature has generally seen the role as an extension of the role of the salesperson. This paper explores and reviews the extant literature and research about the role, and the authors conclude that this is a new and emerging position that is fundamentally different from more traditional sales and account management roles.

We therefore wanted to differentiate this emerging role and have adopted the term *key strategic account manager (ksam)*. When referring to the work of the authors cited here we will, in the main, retain the terms they used, but when describing our perception of the role we will use the term *ksam*.

We end this paper by discussing the important managerial implications of the *ksam* role and propose a conceptual framework that attempts to explain this new and complex role.

Introduction

The role of the key strategic account manager[1] (*ksam*), whether operating at local, national or global levels, must be viewed as evolving. Its roots are embedded in the sales function, but there is increasing evidence to suggest that in its evolving form, the role of account manager is much more than the creator of sales, reflecting an increasingly strategic importance of the key account management (KAM) function within the firm.[2] This paper aims to explore and draw together the extant literature about the role of the *ksam* and presents a conceptual framework that attempts to explain this complex and strategic role. Implications for researchers and managers are discussed and areas requiring further research are identified.

Long-term relationships characterized by high levels of interaction, interdependence and collaboration have long been the norm in business-to-business (B2B) markets (Ford 1990), but a number of factors have increased their level of intensity and strategic importance in recent years, giving rise to the growing importance of the role played by key strategic account managers. Interest in the implementation of KAM processes was driven by changing economic and market conditions in the USA and Europe, starting in the 1950s and impacting to the present day (Wengler 2005), i.e. market saturation and uncertainty, increased demand for cost reduction and avoidance (Shapiro and Wyman 1981), increased pressure for quality and service improvement (Bragg 1982), reduced customer supplier base (Bragg 1982; Shapiro and Wyman 1981), increasing sophistication of buyers (Mayer 1984) and, more recently, increasing levels of globalization. These environmental changes led directly to the adoption of account management processes by many major US companies (Weilbaker and Weeks 1997), a practice that has spread, certainly in the last 20 years, beyond the confines of the USA. Over this time there has been a move towards relational rather than transactional exchange that has resulted in changes in the role span of account managers, reflected in the tasks they perform.

Thus, the role of the key strategic account manager encompasses much more than a strategic selling approach and may be seen as the operationalization, on the supply side, of the interaction, networks and relationships approach to marketing and purchasing that emerged from the work of the Industrial Marketing

---

[1] This paper draws on previously published work by Wilson and Millman (2000, 2003), Wilson (2001) and Holt (2001, 2003).

[2] We use the term key strategic account manager in our discussion to differentiate between those who manage the relationship with strategically important customers and those whose role is merely to increase sales. The term stands in place of the terms national, key, strategic and global account manager except where these terms reflect the usage of the various authors discussed. The use of upper or lower case differentiates between process and role, thus KAM represents key account management while *kam* denotes key account manager. In our later discussion we also use the term key strategic account manager (*ksam*).

and Purchasing (IMP) Group over the past 30 years (drawing upon transaction cost economics and inter-organizational theoretical perspectives for its foundations) (Ford 1990), and the relationship marketing approach (Grönroos 1994; Gummesson 1987; Sheth and Parvatiyar 1995).

While relationship marketing encompasses approaches to consumer, services and B2B markets, the IMP model is focused on exploring industrial marketing and purchasing, the domain of the key strategic account manager (Davies et al. 2010; Holt 2003). Both stress the importance of long-term relationships built on individual exchanges, but where the IMP approach brings greater insights is in the additional emphasis placed upon interaction – both buyers and sellers are active – and upon networks (Ford 1990). Dyadic exchange takes place within the context of industry-wide networks of relationships that constrain or facilitate the actions of buyers and sellers (Ford 1990). The role of boundary spanners in linking and facilitating exchange is evident in the IMP approach, which also underpinned the seminal early research in KAM by Millman and Wilson (1995, 1996a).

The evolution of key account management

The importance of interpersonal communication in B2B relationships, though not in the role of the account manager, was recognized early in the IMP literature. Interpersonal relationships were associated with the roles of adaptation, crisis management, insurance, ego-enhancement and sociability (Cunningham and Turnbull 1982). However, it would be some time before attention turned to the role played by account managers in inter-organizational relationships.

Although KAM may be traced back to the 1960s, the first recognition of the singularity of the role performed by account managers may be seen in the formation of the National Account Marketing Association[3] in 1964 in the USA, and although it did not represent a departure from a focus upon increased sales towards broader value creation, it did herald a change in emphasis in its recognition that customers, as well as products and markets, were important (Homburg et al. 2000, 2002). It also recognized that not all customers are equal in B2B markets, that some require more attention than others. It was some years later that the academic community recognized the phenomenon (Anderluh 1968; Barrett 1986; Shapiro 1979; Shapiro and Moriarty 1982; Stevenson and Page 1979) and a management book on the topic of key account selling appeared (Hanan 1985).

The literature has reflected the growing interest in KAM but has largely ignored the role performed by individual account managers as organizational boundary

---

[3] The National Account Marketing Association, later changed in 1979 to the National Account Management Association and then to the Strategic Account Management Association (SAMA)

spanners (Holt 2003) and the skills, above and beyond those of the salesperson, that they must possess in order to perform their developing role.

Weilbaker and Weeks (1997) identified three stages in the development of interest in KAM, reflected in the literature. They identify an introductory stage between the 1960s and 1984 where the focus was on description of existing account management programmes, disseminating information about account management and providing a macro view of the concept. A growth stage was seen between 1985 and 1994 when empirical studies emerged with a growing recognition of the importance of performance and a focus on micro issues such as customer selection and process improvement. Wotruba and Castleberry's (1993) paper from this period reflects interest in our topic. They discussed the selection of national account managers, recognizing that specialist skills were required beyond those related to selling. A late growth phase in interest in KAM was identified running from 1995, where the literature focused upon some of the theoretical foundations of KAM and the assessment of the performance of different types of account management. Here the issues addressed concentrate on coordination and alignment, value-chain management and performance measures of account managers. Little reference is found to the roles performed by account managers or other players in the account management process.

Nevertheless, Weilbaker and Weeks (1997) conclude their paper with a call to academics to address a number of key issues related to key account management, among which are the topics 'role of the key account person or team in strategic alliances' and 'cross-functional roles and responsibilities and their impact on key account recruitment, training and assessment', a clear recognition that research in these areas was scant but needed.

The evolving role of the account manager from key account sales to key strategic account manager

The term 'key account management' first gained currency in Europe in the 1990s (Kempeners 1997; McDonald and Rogers 1998; McDonald et al. 1997; Millman and Wilson 1995, 1996a; Pardo et al. 1993) but most of the literature focused upon KAM processes rather than upon the role of the account manager, with the tacit assumption, made by many, that the role was an extension of the sales role. McDonald et al. (1997) observed that most companies adopted a key account selling approach and, despite a growing literature on the process of strategic account management (SAM), many companies still assume the role to be primarily associated with sales and the increase in business volume won from major customers (Wilson and Woodburn 2014), using key account salespeople who operate in much the same way as traditional territory-based sales. They may have a number of accounts, with limited points of contact in any of them, and are focused on product sales. These are not the focus of this paper.

Our aim is to discuss the role of those account managers that operate in more complex inter-organizational environments and are concerned with problem resolution and value creation 'beyond sales', because the need for value-adding key account management approaches is increasingly evident (Wengler 2005). In order to differentiate them from key account salespeople we use the term key strategic account managers (*ksam*).

Millman and Wilson (1995, 1996a) were the first to highlight the importance of recognizing KAM as a management, not a sales, process and warned that many account managers were ill prepared for the wider and more demanding roles that take them into areas of business development, industry/market analysis, bench-marking, relationship management and so on.

> "We have argued that (the role of) *kam* should be regarded as an activity carrying responsibilities and requiring competencies closer to the general management func-tion or senior marketing function, in preference to its current location in sales."
> *(Millman and Wilson 1996)*

Acknowledging the difficulty of separating organizational from managerial com-petencies, Millman and Wilson (1999) identified a top ten of global account management competencies. These contrasted interestingly with those skills seen to be highly valued at national account management level (see Table 1). These differences are not surprising in the light of the then newly emerging strategic importance of global account management (GAM), and the long history of national account management (NAM). The emphasis for national account man-agers (NAMS) was placed upon skills associated with traditional sales roles, the emphasis for global account managers (GAMS) widened to encompass skills more associated with general management.

Table 1: *gam* vs. *nam* competencies

	Top ten gam competencies	Most highly rated nam competencies
1	Communication skills	Selling/negotiation skills
2	Global team leadership and management skills	Industry/customer knowledge
3	Business and financial acumen	Product/service knowledge
4	Relationship management skills	
5	Strategic vision and planning capabilities	
6	Problem-solving capabilities	
7	Cultural empathy	
8	Selling skills (internal and external)	
9	Industry and market knowledge	
10	Product service knowledge	

Source: Millman and Wilson (1999)

While some practitioners may still view the *ksam* role as being primarily concerned with sales, this view is increasingly challenged as inadequate in light of increasing levels of competition and the demands placed upon suppliers by customers (Wengler 2007). Wengler also argues that research into the account management role must evolve beyond the confines of 'the traditions of personal selling research' and encompass the context of relationship management. The early distinctions between national, key and global account management are also challenged on the basis that they are different only in the degree of complexity imposed by internationality (Napolitano 1997), a view supported by Wilson et al. (2001) and one that we endorse now. However, there are differences in the role demanded of account managers that are reflected in the different relational 'states' that may exist between buyer and seller, and these are discussed later.

In his comprehensive review of the literature relating to key account management, Wengler (2005) devotes only one small section to the tasks of account management. He refers to the four tasks that must be performed by the account manager or account management teams identified by Diller (1989): informing, planning, coordinating and controlling, each with an internal and external aspect. This reflects a 'Janus' role performed by account managers or account teams (Kleintenkamp and Ricker 1997).

> "The Janus head with his two faces, one for the internal processes, and one for the external processes, perfectly symbolizes the future of key account management processes." *(Wengler 2005)*

This highlights a fundamental difference between the role performed by salespeople and that performed by the key strategic account manager. We contest the idea that salespeople are boundary 'spanners'; they are better likened to boundary 'connectors' in that they tend to have limited contact networks within the customer organization and rarely penetrate deeply. Direct contact within their own organization may also be shallow, limited to colleagues in similar roles and line management relationships. Contrast this with the true boundary-spanning role of the key strategic account manager who is expected to have multiple contacts within the client organization, spanning function (broad) and hierarchy (deep). *Ksams* must also reach back into their own organizations, not just to manage multi-functional 'virtual' teams but also to access resources and influence decisions impacting on client relationships. We contend that it is this boundary 'spanning' role, as opposed to the boundary 'connecting' role performed by traditional salespeople, that differentiates the role of key strategic account managers.

Factors that influence the nature of the role of the key strategic account manager

We propose that a number of interwoven factors influence the competency needs of *ksams*. The relational context, the degree of relational intensity, organizational complexity and cultural diversity, and the demands customers place on their strategic suppliers, all shape the nature of the multiple roles played by account managers and determine the competency requirements of both organizations and individual account managers.

Millman and Wilson (1996a), referring to their six-stage relational development model (Millman and Wilson 1995[4]), identified that both organizational and management competency requirements may depend upon the nature of the relationship that exists, or is intended to exist, between buyer and seller. In the early 'states' of key account development they suggested that companies can migrate some way along the relational development continuum by making only minor adaptations to their organizational infrastructure, but eventually a point is reached when major changes are required that transform rather than merely extend traditional organizational structures and processes.

Similarly, the competencies required of account managers may relate strongly to the traditional sales role in the early relational states but, as the role becomes increasingly embedded in complex networks of interaction, so the need to understand the organizational context as well as the characteristics of each participant becomes increasingly important, which has implications for the selection and development of key strategic account managers.

Later, Millman and Wilson (1996b) specifically address the changing role of *kams* together with an analysis of the inherent conflicts/ambiguities associated with their boundary-spanning role. They suggest that the growth in buyer–supplier partnerships has led to a need for industry and customer knowledge that they perceive as being much deeper than in the traditional sales role. They observe, referring to their 1995 article, that there was a general belief that KAM had its natural home in 'sales', but warned that if that belief were perpetuated there was a danger that *kams* would be perceived as merely 'sales managers dealing with large customers'.

They also refer to the danger of promoting the best salespeople to KSAM roles and expecting them to 'grow into the role' of 'farmer' rather than 'hunter' salespeople. They challenged this practice, saying, 'in our view, these changes are necessary for the sales role, but insufficient for the broader and more demanding role of key account manager'.

In discussing the changing role of the *kam* they noted that the *kam* operates within a network of other managerial activities, and that these existing structures make it difficult to initiate development of the *kam* role where it threatens the status quo and traditional power bases. Organizational complexity can also cause difficulty as there may be vast differences, for example, in the state of readiness

---

[4] The model, based on exploratory research, identified six relational stages of development: *Pre-KAM; Early KAM; Mid-KAM; Partnership KAM; Synergistic KAM;* and *Uncoupling KAM*. This model was adopted and subsequently the stages were reduced and re-named in work by McDonald and Woodburn(1999).

to accept KSAM where organizations have many different divisions, countries and cultures. Even where the KSAM relationship seems to have reached a stable state which is developing mutual advantage, this can be adversely affected by such dynamics as acquisitions, mergers, strategic alliances, changing top-down edicts, imposition of systems, changes in personal/corporate alignments and changes in key personnel.

Clearly this early work recognized that the role of the *kam* was not the extension of a sales role but a role requiring much higher levels of authority, status and reward. This view is supported by Millman and Wilson's (1996b) identification of the growing importance of managing the support for strategic customer and supplier relationships, often involving large numbers of people: even if they are not directly managed by the *kam/gam*, they are certainly orchestrated by them.

Gosselin and Heene (2003) also distinguish between key account selling and strategic account management. They suggest that strategic accounts are those where there is mutual recognition of the strategic importance of the relationship by both buyer and seller and further suggest that while both key account selling and key account management may be involved in the creation and delivery of value, strategic account management is also concerned with building the competencies upon which that value is based.

> "It is clear that the competencies and skills needed to perform the task of account manager are far beyond those of a sales person." *(Gosselin and Heene 2003)*

The political entrepreneur

The term 'political entrepreneur' first appeared in an IMP paper presented by Wilson and Millman (2000). It emerged from discussion following the Strategic Account Management Association/Sales Research Trust Global Account Management Research Study published later in the same year (Wilson et al. 2000) and owed much to the discussion of the role of global account manager presented by Croom et al. (1999). The account managers observed were entrepreneurial in the sense that they had the ability to recognize and realize the potential for innovation and value creation through the combination of existing inputs in the sense suggested by Schumpeter (2012). They realized value by combining the operational and core competencies of both buyer and seller (see Figure 1). Their political capabilities were observed in their understanding of how organizations worked and their ability to manage people and resources, and influence decisions through networking in both buyer and seller organizations.

Croom et al. (1999) identified three managerial roles performed by global account managers, which we consider to be equally applicable to all key strategic account managers, i.e. those of *analyst, politician* and *entrepreneur*. This theme was later elaborated upon in the Wilson and Millman papers (2000, 2003), where they explore the nature of boundary-spanning roles and identify the *gam* as performing a boundary-spanning role across two important interfaces – the *internal*

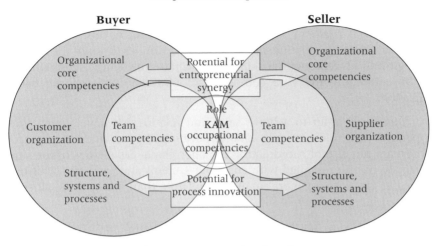

The political entrepreneur

Complex inter-organizational environment

Figure 1   The role of the political entrepreneur
Source: adapted from Wilson and Millman (2003)

interface between global and national account management, which is often embedded in the headquarters/subsidiary relationship, and the *external* interface between the selling company and the dispersed activities of the global account – thus recognizing what Kleintenkamp and Ricker (1997) subsequently identified as the 'Janus' nature of the key account manager role.

> "In recognition of the need to navigate sensitive commercial/political aspects of these interface relationships, we have dubbed the global account manager as performing the role of *Political Entrepreneur*." *(Wilson and Millman 2000)*

To the three roles identified by Croom et al. (1999), a further role, that of coordinator, was added. These roles, while distinct, are not mutually exclusive, and the political entrepreneur (PE) can be expected to perform all these roles as the situation demands. This is a reflection of the overall ambiguity under which they operate.

In their role as *analysts*, PEs tend to be team-orientated trouble-shooters possessing outstanding knowledge of products/services, technologies and customer industries. Analysts perceive themselves primarily as international sales managers focusing on global sales targets, sales from regional/national territories and share of customer spend, rather than on opportunities for enhancing levels of value creation and customer profitability.

As *politicians* they combine diplomatic and linguistic skills with cultural empathy and knowledge of global business trends/opportunities. They engage their senior managers in the GAM process and are adept at achieving objectives via influence/persuasion, both in their own and in the customer organization.

As *entrepreneurial strategists* they are seen as looking beyond the immediate transactional exchange relationship to seek opportunities through the application of strategic and entrepreneurial skills that facilitate the synergistic realization of value by combining the core competencies of their own and the customer organization.

As *coordinators*, in order to achieve sales and relationship development targets, they perform the role not only of orchestrating the activities of the account support team but also of coordinating the operational capabilities of the supplier organization in order to align with customer systems and processes. This may be perceived as closer to a general management role than a sales role, albeit often with limited line authority.

The role of the PE is clearly a boundary-spanning role, performed at both the internal interface between corporate and local account management (embedded in the headquarters/subsidiary relationship) and at the external interface between the selling company and the dispersed activities of its strategic account. Political and entrepreneurial skills are applied at both these interfaces by this new breed of manager. The internal interface is where much of the *gam*'s or *ksam*'s ability to manage potential conflict/ambiguity depends on positive or negative perceptions of their mediating role, and thus where political skills may be of primary importance. Those political skills include the ability to walk the corridors of power, to know the people to speak to, the buttons to press and the strings to pull, in both their own organization and that of the customer. The external interface provides the forum within which both political and entrepreneurial skills may be applied (Croom et al. 1999; Wilson and Millman 2000, 2003).

The role of the PE is represented in Figure 1. It represents the main elements of the role and its contextual complexity. The importance of this model is that it presented the role of the *ksam/gam* as being concerned primarily with value creation rather than with the creation of sales.

First, as analyst, the *ksam/gam* identifies, through their intimate knowledge of customer, industry and process, not only opportunities for increased share of wallet but also the potential for creating process-related innovation in manufacturing, logistics and organizational interaction. As coordinator they manage the integration and realization of synergistic value arising from the operational capabilities of both buyer and seller.

As entrepreneurial strategist, the *ksam/gam* role is focused upon realizing entrepreneurial opportunity offered by accessing and using the combined core competencies of both organizations. The entrepreneur sees things that other people do not and acts upon those insights in order to create new value. Within the context of KSAM/GAM, the knowledge and resources from which entrepreneurial opportunity is created are the core competencies embedded in the relationship. At an operational level, the PE recognizes the potentials inherent in

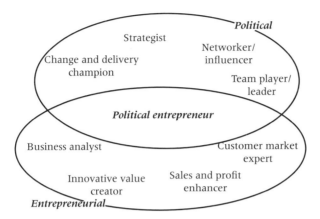

Figure 2   Political entrepreneur (PE) behaviours and competencies

marrying the core competencies of both the buyer and seller teams to create process innovations that enhance the product/service offering by creating greater efficiencies within the supply chain. At a strategic level, the political entrepreneur sees opportunities to create entrepreneurial synergy from the core competencies of both organizations.

In both value-creation roles the *ksam/gam* must manage people over whom they may have no direct authority, certainly within the client organization and, more often than not, within their own. They must also gain access to resources which, unlike the general manager, they do not 'own', and be adept at influencing the decision-making process at senior managerial level in order to realize opportunity.

These 'mega' skills were refined into eight operational competencies (Wilson 2006, borrowing from Bradford and Minshul 2001): strategist, networker/influencer, change and delivery champion, team player/leader (reflecting the political elements of the role); business analyst, customer market expert, sales and profit enhancer, and innovative value creator (reflecting the entrepreneurial elements) (see Figure 2).

Political roles

Strategist: we argue that strategy is essentially a political process and that the role of the key strategic account manager is strategic rather than operational. They are involved in developing strategies for both relational management (aimed at developing, sustaining or diminishing relational inter-dependence) and, perhaps more fundamentally, profitable value co-creation.

Networker/influencer: one operational role of the *ksam* is to influence the decision-making process within their own organization and within the client company, in order to gain access to resources and implement relational and value-creation strategies. This can be achieved only where there is detailed understanding of how organizations work, how the decision process operates and where networks of contacts exist that can be recruited in the support of strategic objectives.

Change and delivery champion: within their own organization the *ksam* often faces resistance to the implementation of customer-centric initiatives, either because they run contra to existing product-, production- or technology-led cultures or because they threaten existing power bases. Managing change and delivering results are thus essential elements of the role.

Team player/leader: this element reflects the fact that often the *ksam* must manage those over whom they have little or no line authority, creating virtual teams from geographically and functionally dispersed players from their own organization, as well as working with and adopting a leadership role with people from the customer organization.

Evidently these political competencies are interlinked and provide support for the entrepreneurial activities embedded in the remaining four attributes.

Entrepreneurial roles

Business analyst: this role reflects the PE as identifying process innovation and improvement opportunities (Figure 1). A major source of value creation is the identification of ways in which interconnecting processes can be streamlined to effect cost and efficiency savings.

Innovative value creator: the entrepreneurial process is essentially concerned with value creation, not just at process level but also through combining organizational core competencies—the link with business analysis skills is evident.

Customer market expert: the *ksam*'s intimate knowledge of the customer's business and the industry in which they operate is one of the foundations of their ability to create entrepreneurial value, applying entrepreneurial skills to the reallocation of core competencies to realize business opportunities.

Sales and profit enhancer: while the primary focus of the PE is not increased sales, nevertheless are one result, along with enhanced levels of profitability, that derive from their performance of these operational roles and form part of the overall strategic approach that they adopt.

These combined roles, both political and entrepreneurial, have significant implications for managers in recruiting, developing and deploying key strategic account managers, issues that will be addressed later in our discussion.

The impact of contextual factors on the role of the political entrepreneur

Wilson and Millman (2000, 2003) and Wilson (2001) further explored the boundary-spanning role of the political entrepreneur and the impact of contextual factors upon the application of political and entrepreneurial skills, and how the application of those skills may be related to stages of relational development.

The demand for political capabilities and the opportunity to apply entrepreneurial skill, they suggest, is dependent upon the context within which the global buyer–seller relationship exists. The relational context is defined by the degree of organizational complexity and cultural diversity that surrounds the global relationship and by the degree of organizational interdependence and integration.

Where the customer operates in many different countries, where those operations include multiple functions and where the global account manager is required to have many multi-functional relationships at different levels within the client organization, then the organizational context may be perceived as highly complex. Conversely, where there are few touch points and penetration is low, the organizational context is low in complexity.

Where the organizational context is complex, there tend to be higher levels of political activity with divergent views, competing factional interests and different cultural perspectives influencing the global buyer–seller relationship. In order to operate effectively within this context, the global account manager must be capable of applying high levels of diplomacy, cultural sensitivity, networking and political skill.

Entrepreneurship is about using existing knowledge and resources to develop new and innovative opportunities for value creation. This is clearly dependent upon the closeness of the relationship and the degree of integration achieved by the account manager into both organizations.

The degree to which entrepreneurial skills can be exercised is dependent upon the global account manager's level of access to specialized knowledge about the resources of both their own organization and that of the client. If the global account manager is to be able to identify entrepreneurial opportunity they must have detailed knowledge of organizational, team and individual competencies, the resources of both organizations and a clear understanding of the strategic imperatives facing the client. Such knowledge (which allows the identification of the potential for problem resolution, process innovation and the creation of entrepreneurial value) grows as relationships evolve in terms of entanglement and interdependence. This in turn depends upon the level of organizational interdependence and integration. In other words, the closer the relationship, the more access there is to specialized knowledge and the more opportunity to exercise entrepreneurial skill (see Figure 3).

Figure 3 illustrates that where there are high levels of organizational complexity and cultural diversity, there is a strong need to exercise political skills (P). Where the organizational context is simple, then there is little need for political activity (p). Figure 3 also shows that the opportunity for exercising entrepreneurial skills varies depending upon the closeness of the buyer–seller relationship. Where the

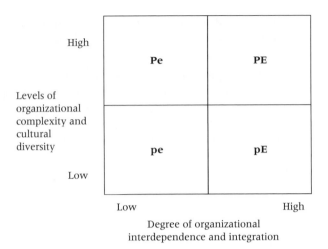

Figure 3   The impact of context on the role of the political entrepreneur

relationship is well developed, the entrepreneurial opportunities are high (E), where the relationship is new or under-developed, then those opportunities are low (e).

What this suggests is that different levels of political and entrepreneurial skill can be applied at different stages in the development of global relationships and other key strategic relationships. Figure 4 links varying levels of political and entrepreneurial behaviour to stages in the Millman–Wilson (1995) relational development model.

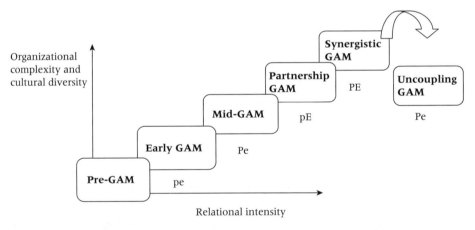

Figure 4   Linking PE behaviours and the relational development model
Source: Millman and Wilson (1995)

At *pre-GAM* to *early GAM* stages, there is a need to develop networks of contacts, to gain knowledge about the customer's operations and to begin to assess the potential for relational development. It is unlikely that concepts of value creation can go much beyond assessing the global client's need for the basic product–service offering of the supplier. At this stage, the organizational–cultural context is relatively simple and the relationship is poorly developed. The demand for political skills and the opportunity to apply entrepreneurial skills is low (pe).

From *early* to *mid-GAM* there is an increasing need for political skills to be applied as the potential of the account is identified, and the global account manager is called upon to ensure that the supplier's resources are configured to best serve the needs of the customer. Detailed knowledge of the global customer and their core competencies, the depth of the relationship and the potential for creating relationship-specific entrepreneurial value are all limited at this stage and the requirement is greater for political than entrepreneurial skill (Pe).

Mid- to *partnership GAM* may be characterized by the global account manager having developed a strong vertical and horizontal network of relationships within the client organization. As the relationship has developed in closeness, so the need to promote the client's interests within the selling company also recedes and political activity becomes less necessary for gaining access to resources and support.

As the relationship has developed, so has the knowledge about the account and, in order to consolidate or grow the relationship, further opportunities for joint value creation must be identified that go beyond the effective delivery of the global product/service offering. It is at this stage that entrepreneurial skill comes into play (pE), in terms of being able to recognize the potential for creating opportunities for value creation that address both the core competencies and the strategic interests of both buyer and seller. This stage is also pivotal in terms of the need to build a strong internal understanding of GAM and the need to develop processes and boundary-spanning activities that cut across the traditional silos present in many organizations.

Partnership and *synergistic GAM* increases the demand for political skill and the opportunity to apply entrepreneurial skills also increases. The closer the relationship, the greater is the opportunity to acquire knowledge of the customer and the greater the potential for creating entrepreneurial value. At the same time, the realization of entrepreneurial opportunity will involve fundamental changes in the way each organization operates and the need for political skills to drive those changes increases (PE).

At any stage in the relationship it may be necessary to disengage and *uncoupling GAM/KSAM* occurs. It is suggested that when this stage is reached the *GAM/KSAM* may need to apply high levels of political expertise (Pe) in order to extricate their company from the relationship at minimum cost.

One final point made by Millman and Wilson (1995) was that the relational development model was not intended to suggest that all relationships should, or can, develop through all stages. Some will never develop beyond the *pre-GAM* stage, others will rest in the early stages of *mid-* or *partnership GAM* and by their nature, very few will develop to *synergistic GAM*. This suggests that different relationships may allow for the deployment of *GAMs/KSAMs* with different levels of political and entrepreneurial skill.

The importance of the boundary-spanning role

Research by Holt (2001, 2003) took a dyadic approach to exploring the role of the *GAM* based on a boundary role theory perspective. A boundary position is defined by Kahn et al. (1964) as one which requires extensive interaction with people who occupy positions in another system, either another unit within the same organization or another organization altogether (Organ and Greene 1972). Boundary role theory (e.g. Kahn et al. 1964; Singh and Rhoads 1991; Spekman 1979) finds that those in boundary roles have to manage a number of different expectations, which in the GAM/KSAM context includes those of managers, co-workers and customers.

Organ (1971) also argues that these types of roles are strategically important for several reasons:

- It is through their behaviour that the organization adapts (or fails to adapt) to changes in the environment.
- It is through reports of the boundary spanners that other organization members acquire their knowledge, perceptions and evaluations of the organization's environments.
- It is through vigilance of these roles that the organization is able to monitor and screen important happenings in the environment.
- They function as 'sensory organs' for the organization.

Spekman (1979) extended Organ's largely one-sided view to include the 'role sender' aspect of the boundary spanner; an influence agent attempting to influence the decisions and behaviours of those individuals with whom they interact, both inter-organizationally and within their organization. This very much supports the political entrepreneur *gam/ksam* profile.

The empirical study by Holt (2003) involved interviewing *gams*, their customers, managers and their virtual team members, across a number of case study organizations from different industries, and found that the role of the *gam* was indeed that of a strategic boundary spanner. The final set of roles that emerged from this study is shown in Figure 5.

There are strong similarities with the Wilson and Millman (2003) political entrepreneur model. A key contribution of the study by Holt (2003) was to firmly establish that a major part of the *gam* role is managing the internal interfaces. While this had been suggested in the literature and anecdotally, the inclusion of customer respondents, who articulated a number of key activities that they

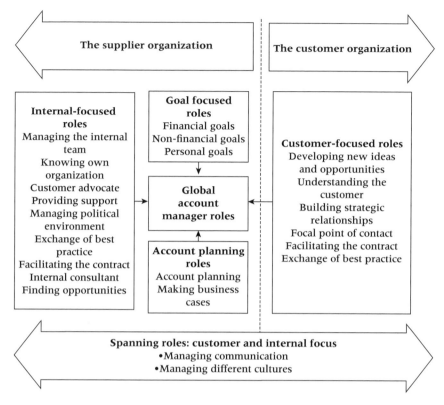

Figure 5 A boundary role theory perspective of the role of the global account manager
Source: Holt (2003)

expected the *gam* to go back and facilitate in their own organization, finally established the legitimacy of the internal role of the *gam*.

Customer impact on the role

Holt's (2003) study also found that the *gam* role may be subject to change, depending on the degree of sophistication of the customer in global account relationships, and the degree of sophistication of the *gam* in the role, as shown in Figure 6.

Where the level of sophistication of the customer is high, and so is the level of the global account manager, then the *gam* is likely to be able to adopt the role of the *global strategist*. The *gam* would be operating at a very strategic level internally and externally, having a fully effective account team, be seeking business opportunities for both organizations, and be involved at senior management level with the customer and internally.

Where the sophistication of the *gam* is high but the level of sophistication of the customer organization is low, then the role of the *gam* is more likely to be that

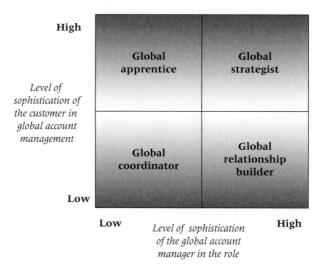

Figure 6   A typology of global account manager roles

of the *global relationship builder*. The role here would be to build the relationship with the customer to a more strategic level. Activities might include developing some new opportunities to move the customer forward, building up some key relationships, helping to set up their teams, doing some consultancy, and facilitating meetings between the organizations at senior level.

Where the sophistication of the customer in GAM is high but the level of the *GAM* is low, then the role is more likely to be that of the *global apprentice*. As many customers are driving GAM, this type of situation is likely to exist, although the customer is not likely to be satisfied with it for long.

Finally, where the level of sophistication is low for both the customer organization and the global account manager, the *GAM* role is likely to be more of a *global coordinator*. In this role the *GAM* would be focused on coordinating the customer relationship, ensuring the operations and service delivery, building the internal teams and facilitating the contracts.

The study also suggested that the *GAM* role was becoming more like a managing director for the customer role rather than anything to do with transactional selling. It suggests that the *GAM* may yet evolve into a role that heads up a strategic business unit (SBU) with sole responsibility for a customer, rather than for a line of business or a product, as suggested conceptually in the literature (Homburg et al. 2000). One of the cases in the study was already taking this approach.

More recently, a small study by Li (2012) suggested that when looking at the competencies for *kams, ksams* and *gams* it made sense to divide the competencies and skills into those needed for the strategic selling part of the roles and those needed for the management part of the role. The more strategic the relationship, the more important the management part of the role becomes, with far less focus on the strategic selling part of the role. This study, therefore, also supports our conjectures in this paper.

The Strategic Account Management Association (SAMA), based in Chicago, USA, has also recently published some work in this area. The strategic account management core competencies identified by SAMA (2011) are not based upon a single research project but represent a synthesis of the accumulated body of research supported by SAMA over a number of years reflecting its members' collective and evolving views, which indicate considerable growth in the complexity of the role in recent times. Previously named the National Account Management Association (NAMA), the change of the name to SAMA also reflected the growing recognition of the strategic and complex nature of strategic account management. Indeed, SAMA has supplied much of the access to practitioners that has facilitated the work of researchers such as Millman and Wilson, and it has had a fundamental role in disseminating widely the output from such research.

> 'While job requirements for Strategic Account Managers (aka *ksam, kam, gam* et al.) can vary among different businesses and industries, a number of core competencies, knowledge areas and skills are essential for strategic customer management in a majority of companies.' *(SAMA 2013)*[5]

SAMA identifies five essential skill sets:

1. Understanding organizational priorities: customer orientation, company knowledge, industry knowledge and customer knowledge.
2. Strategic account and opportunity planning: strategic thinking, financial business acumen, value analysis and opportunity insight.
3. Joint solution development, co-creation and reaching agreement: communication and influencing skills, value co-creation, negotiation skills.
4. Multi-functional account team leadership: interpersonal relationship skills, team leadership, cultural knowledge and sensitivity.
5. Overall relationship and outcome management: responsible for corporate customer relationship, process discipline, accountability for business outcomes.

While not supported by direct reference to formal research, the views of SAMA conform broadly to the views we have presented here, placing much greater emphasis upon managerial skills than upon those related to personal selling. The position of SAMA as a major thought leader in the field, coupled with its support for research in the general field of account management, adds weight to its views.

In the next section we discuss the ramifications and implications from the above literature review.

---

[5] This quotation and the five skills are taken from publicity material on the SAMA website https//strategicaccounts.org/samau/(critical skills for *sams*).

Discussion

Our work has figured prominently in this paper and we make no apology for that, as there is little other research extant in the literature. What we would say is that although the work of Millman and Wilson and Holt has focused upon the role of the global account manager, the increasing strategic importance of all forms of account management leads us to the belief that their observations now hold true for many, though perhaps not all, occupying the role of account managers, be they key, strategic or global.

A major difference between key strategic account management and most other traditional managerial roles is that normally managers are charged with managing people and resources that are allocated to them. There are clear reporting structures and delineated responsibilities, which does not seem to be the case, certainly with *gams* and, we believe, increasingly with other *ksams*. They must manage people and resources over which they have no direct authority in conditions often redolent with ambiguity, and are charged with the realization of entrepreneurial value not often demanded of others. This, we believe, suggests the emergence of a new managerial role embodied in the concept of the boundary-spanning political entrepreneur and in our renaming the role as that of the key strategic account manager (*ksam*).

We suggest that these observations, together with the material we have presented in the main body of the text, hold significant implications for managers and offer considerable opportunity for future research.

Implications for managers

A number of issues arise from this discussion for senior managers: the realization of the strategic nature of both KSAM programmes and the role performed by *ksams*, the recruitment of people to fulfil the role, provision for the development of the necessary skill sets, and how best to deploy them to meet the strategic needs of the firm.

Strategic positioning: the positioning of the account manager within the hierarchy of the firm and the consistency of senior management in their support of KSAM initiatives have a direct impact upon the *ksam's* ability to perform their role effectively. Senior managers need to realize that in spite of the discomfort that realignment around customers may bring the organization, it is increasingly imperative that organizations are structured in this way to maximize the potential from a KSAM programme. If this does not happen, KSAM programmes will remain cyclical in nature and will fail to realize their full potential. Senior managers also need to recognize that this is a fundamentally different role from that of a traditional senior salesperson, and that this has implications for the levels of authority and scope that are given to *ksams*.

Boundary and scope: by its nature the role of the *ksam* stretches far beyond the sales function where it has traditionally been seen as residing. As we have explained, the *ksam* generally needs to lead and manage supply chain teams internally, the members of which do not report to them and may be geographically dispersed. This has implications for internal relationships and organization that cut across traditional boundaries and effectively change the whole way of working across the company.

Recruitment: the role of the *ksam* is not that of a salesperson, nor is it that of a general manager. Recruitment should be for the skills that we have discussed here, and the role should be perceived as a career path to senior managerial status, just as country or divisional management has been perceived traditionally. Human resource (HR) departments too have their role to play in developing job specifications and recruitment programmes that reflect the complexity and importance of the role.

Development: clearly the skills required to perform this role are complex. The higher levels of KSAM require *ksams* to develop meta-skills and competencies, as illustrated by Millman and Wilson and Holt, which HR departments need to recognize. Development programmes should acknowledge that a new managerial role is emerging that will have significant impact within the firm and within the marketplace. The task is to develop managers who can manage the complexity and ambiguity of the future, not just of today. For both recruitment and development, *ksams* need to be tested not only for their competency as managers but also for their political and entrepreneurial capabilities.

Deployment: the ideal may be one account manager for one strategic customer. The reality reflects pragmatic necessity, so account managers are often responsible for managing the relationships their company enjoys with multiple customers. This emphasizes the need to choose people who can reconcile the demands of customers at different relational stages and manage for profit, whatever the nature of the relationship. Senior managers and HR need to appoint *ksams* to different types of customer relationship depending on their competencies.

Compensation and rewards: managers need to radically review the compensation and reward mechanisms for *ksams*. Anecdotal research suggests that many *ksams* are still rewarded through totally inappropriate mechanisms that work against much of what we have said needs to happen, if KSAM programmes are to be successful and maximize both the contribution of the *ksam* and the KSAM programme.

Implications for researchers and a research agenda

The role of the key strategic account manager is still under-researched and even less understood by both academics and practitioners alike. The potential for research and the importance of understanding the multiple roles performed by key strategic account managers (and how they interface with other functions such as supply chain managers) is enormous. It is our view that this role is a model that will be used for the future management of inter-organizational

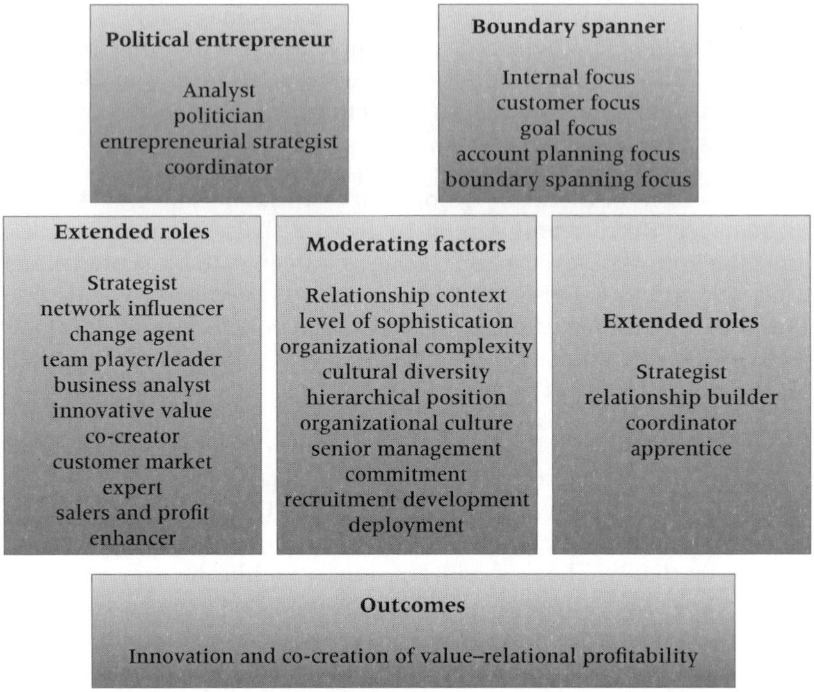

Political entrepreneur	Boundary spanner
Analyst politician entrepreneurial strategist coordinator	Internal focus customer focus goal focus account planning focus boundary spanning focus

Extended roles	Moderating factors	Extended roles
Strategist network influencer change agent team player/leader business analyst innovative value co-creator customer market expert salers and profit enhancer	Relationship context level of sophistication organizational complexity cultural diversity hierarchical position organizational culture senior management commitment recruitment development deployment	Strategist relationship builder coordinator apprentice

Outcomes

Innovation and co-creation of value–relational profitability

Figure 7 A conceptual framework summarizing the role of the key strategic account manager

relationships, not only of buyer–seller relationships but for a wide range of collaborative inter-organizational projects.

The work of Millman and Wilson, of Holt and others presented here suggests a framework (see Figure 7) that may provide the impetus for future academic endeavour, inform practitioners and help in facilitating the process of value co-creation beyond the concept of simple product or relational exchange.

It is becoming increasingly clear that, with the emergence of networks of customer–supplier relationships and more complex supply chains, the role of the *ksam* will continue to evolve in its complexity and breadth of focus. For example, the role of *ksams* in the orchestration of supply chains requires further research.

The conceptual framework presented in Figure 7 summarizes the role of the key strategic account manager as both political entrepreneur and boundary spanner, as discussed in the literature, and suggests a number of contextual variables dealt with in the text that impact upon those roles. We propose that this conceptual framework should act as a starting point for a future research agenda. For example, research to test the validity of the roles, to understand the impact of intervening contextual factors and to explore the impact upon outcomes needs to be carried out using more positivist quantitative approaches than research studies have hitherto deployed. It is particularly important to research and understand the effects of the moderating factors shown in Figure 7, as these would appear to be the factors upon which the success or failure of KSAM programmes is dependent. Also the degree and level of importance of these factors needs to be determined. Research needs to be carried out on the relationships between the moderating factors and the outcomes.

Other key areas for the future research agenda include topics such as:

- The compensation and reward systems for *ksams* and their teams.
- Team structures and team leadership of KSAM teams.
- Competences of KSAM team members in complex customer relationships.
- The personal qualities that *ksams* need to do their role competently.

Conclusion

This paper has raised the importance of further researching the role and competences of the *ksam, gam* and *kam*. To date, there has been little research in this area and much of what has been done, while empirically sound, has been largely qualitative. A conceptual framework is presented from the extant literature that may act as the starting point for further, more rigorous academic research.

We believe that these roles will continue to evolve as companies move away from traditional buyer–supplier relationships to those involving multiple supply-chain relationships and networks, where all parties are seeking value and are more focused on co-creation of value and more collaborative ways of working. It is proposed that a new role has emerged in response to the changing nature of buyer–seller relationships, a role that is fundamentally different from that of a traditional salesperson, and that organizations need to recognize this if they are to be successful in managing their supply chains and networks in the future.

The influence of personality on the job performance of strategic account managers

BY TOMMI MAHLAMÄKI, OLAVI UUSITALO AND
TONI MIKKOLA

Abstract

Strategic account management (SAM) is a current and relevant topic in the business-to-business marketing context. SAM is a management process that consists of identifying and serving strategically important customers of a company, which aims for a company to have a cooperative relationship with its customer with a unique value proposition. One key determinant of the SAM process's success is the strategic account manager. This paper focuses on the job performance of the strategic account manager, more precisely on the influence of such a manager's personality on job performance. The paper reports the results of a survey study whose purpose was to examine the relationship between personality traits and strategic account managers' job performance. The analysed data consists of the responses of 143 account managers. The results show that three personality traits – extraversion, conscientiousness and agreeableness – have a significant relationship with job performance.

Introduction

The financial performance of a large number of companies is dependent on their customers who are strategically most important – in other words, their strategic accounts. Strategic accounts are assigned a manager, often called a strategic account manager or key account manager, who works as a contact point between the customer and the selling organization. It can be argued that the performance of these strategic account managers is paramount to the success of companies with strategic account programmes.

Even though the role of strategic account manager is seen as important, little research has focused on the identification of factors affecting their job performance. McDonald and Rogers (1998) list the qualities, knowledge and skills that key account managers need in order to fulfil the expectations of selling and buying organizations. Still, empirical research into those qualities and skills has been largely neglected. Some exceptions exist: Sengupta et al. (2000) developed and tested a model of key account salesperson effectiveness, although their model focused on individual abilities only, namely the manager's strategic and intrapreneurial ability. Hutt and Walker (2006) researched the performance of key account managers from a network perspective, such as how the social network of a manager affects their work performance. Sharma (2006) studied the success factors in key accounts, but the study concentrated on the accounts themselves rather than on the manager's handling of the accounts.

Unlike the strategic account manager job performance/personality relationship, the salesperson job performance/personality relationship has been studied extensively (Barrick and Mount 1991; Hurtz and Donovan 2000). The results show a relationship between extraversion and sales job performance and between conscientiousness and sales job performance. It is clear that the job description of a strategic account manager is different from that of a salesperson; therefore, it is interesting to know whether a strategic account manager benefits from having different personality traits. In conclusion, the main goal of this paper is to study the effect of personality on the strategic account manager's job performance.

Theoretical background

In this paper, the theoretical background of this research is covered. First, the field of strategic account management is explored briefly. Second, the strategic account manager roles and skills are explained. Strategic account manager job performance-related issues are then explained. Finally, the Five Factor Model (FFM) of personality is introduced.

Strategic account management

In essence, strategic account management consists of identifying and serving a company's strategically important customers. SAM aims for a cooperative relationship with the customer, a relationship that has a unique value proposition. While SAM is an important topic, academia has no clear definition or universally agreed name for the management process. One of the first concepts depicting the theory was national account management (NAM), which has been the subject of academic research since the 1970s (see Napolitano 1997; Pegram 1972). International account management and global account management are also widely used terms (see Millman 1996; Montgomery and Yip 2000; Shi et al. 2004). Maybe the term most widely used by academics and practitioners is key account management (KAM). These different account-management concepts differ with regard to their geographical scope (national, global, etc.) and in their research focus. Reisel et al. (2005) state that NAM literature focuses largely on individuals in dyadic relationships with customers. KAM literature, meanwhile, focuses on the selling team and its support role across the organization being studied. Because KAM and key account managers are the predominant terms used in the literature, they are used in the theory parts of this paper.

Because a KAM programme requires an exceptional commitment of different resources in order to serve a customer, selecting the most essential organizations as key accounts is extremely important (Capon 2001). The criteria for selecting key accounts should help a firm identify a customer's attractiveness in terms of its specific potential for the selling company (McDonald and Woodburn 2007). Different types of selection criteria exist when choosing key accounts for the company. Cheverton (2008) identified five factor groups: (1) attractiveness of the customer, (2) likelihood of success, (3) compatible business objectives, (4) specific customer opportunities, and (5) own resources and capabilities. These groups of specific attractiveness factors can be used to evaluate potential key accounts. In addition to the previous five groups of factors, McDonald and Woodburn (2007) cited an additional group for identifying whether a customer has great potential to be good for the company. These factors include a customer being a reference value for the whole company or being able to act as an important partner in research and development projects.

KAM relationships typically progress through certain stages. Millman and Wilson (1995) arrange the relationship levels along a transactional–collaborative continuum: *pre-KAM, early KAM, mid-KAM, partnership KAM* and *synergistic KAM*. McDonald and Rogers (1998), McDonald and Woodburn (2007) and Cheverton (2008) have further developed the model.

Recent research on KAM has concentrated on issues such as the creation of a comprehensive KAM framework (Homburg et al. 2002; Shi et al. 2004; Zupancic 2008), the problems and challenges of KAM strategies (Piercy and Lane 2006), implementation issues of KAM programmes (Davies and Ryals 2009; Wengler et al. 2006; Woodburn 2006), and empirical testing of the common assumptions that academia has made during the past years (Ivens and Pardo 2008).

Roles and skills of the strategic account manager

The role of the key account manager changes according to the stage of the relationship between buyer and seller organizations (McDonald and Rogers 1998). This means that the skills needed to perform well as a key account manager also change. Identifying the roles of the key account manager is difficult. First, the roles of key account manager can take a number of different forms (McDonald and Woodburn 2007). To further complicate the task, the roles and responsibilities of key account managers change from relationship to relationship (Capon 2001). However, even with the challenges of changing situations, some general roles can be identified.

McDonald and Woodburn (2007) divided the job of key account managers into implementation and facilitation roles. The implementation role includes tasks that are related to the selection of the relationship tactics and the fulfilment of those tactics. First, the implementation role can be further divided into three sub-categories:

1. *An expert in the customer*: this means understanding the customer's business.
2. *A value developer*: this means helping the company create value for the customer and itself. The value developer also anticipates future customer needs and works continuously to add value to the customer.
3. *A point of accountability*: this means ensuring that the customer gets things delivered to it that have been promised. The role requires defining, briefing and coordinating commitments on the company's side.

Second, the facilitation role is about developing the customer relationship on a cross-functional level. The facilitation role can also be divided into three sub-categories:

1. *A boundary spanner*: this means expanding the relationship within the key customer account. The boundary spanner can seek out cross-selling opportunities in the customer organization.
2. *A conduit*: this means representing the customer in the manager's own organization and working as an ambassador. The conduit also works in the other direction, building up the company brand in the customer organization.
3. *A focal point of contact*: this means acting as a single contact point for the customer and for one's own organization. The focal-point-of-contact role works as a reference point.

Wilson and Millman (2003) stress that the performance of global account managers is closely related to their ability to manage the boundary-spanner role. The authors also identify four boundary-spanning behaviours: (1) *self-server*, (2) *renegade*, (3) *partisan*, and (4) *arbiter*. They continue to raise political and entrepreneurial skills as major contributors in global account manager job performance.

Another way to categorize the key account manager roles from the supplier viewpoint is to divide them into internal and customer-facing roles. For the internal role, McDonald and Woodburn (2007) included doing resource-manager, risk-manager and team-leader tasks. Customer-facing roles include being a salesperson, competition monitor and lever for a full range of capabilities and tasks.

Cheverton (2008) described the general skill set required for KAM tasks. This skill set includes strategic thinking, strategic influencing, business management, project management, team leadership, teamwork, innovation and creativity, coordination, managing change, managing diversity, coaching and political entrepreneurship. Cheverton continues that KAM tasks are sometimes mistakenly considered just an extension of traditional sales tasks, while Davies et al. (2010) portray the clearly different roles of traditional salesperson and relationship manager. Nonetheless, the selling skills should not be forgotten.

McDonald and Rogers (1998) profile the ideal key account manager. They identify four skills or qualities that enable the manager to fulfil the expectations of both the selling and the buying company at higher relationship levels (i.e. *mid-KAM*, *partnership KAM* or *synergistic KAM*). The four attributes are personal qualities, subject knowledge, thinking skills and managerial skills.

Abratt and Kelly (2002) studied the perceptions of both customers and suppliers in the KAM context. The most important aspect, in both the suppliers' and customers' opinion, was the ability to identify problems and provide solutions. Understanding the customer was also an important aspect, alongside having strong interpersonal skills and the right kind of personality. Schultz and Evans (2002) presented evidence on key account manager communication activities and performance.

Not only do different relationship stages demand different sets of skills but so do different selling environments. Millman (1996) studied the key account manager's role in systems selling (selling comprehensive packages of products and services). Millman found seven requirements for the key account manager: coordination, key account planning, external relationship management, internal relationship management, sales and profit responsibility, negotiation and multi-cultural teamwork.

Strategic account manager job performance

A limited number of studies exist with regard to the job performance of the strategic account manager or to closely related topics. Sengupta et al. (2000) created a model concerning the performance of key account salespeople. Their model consisted of strategic ability, communication quality, intrapreneurial ability and customer trust as factors that affect the perceived effectiveness of key account salespeople. In the model, communication quality and customer trust had direct influences on perceived effectiveness.

In a different study, Wotruba and Castleberry (1993) used a performance scale for NAM managers and salespeople. The scale consisted of nine questions that asked NAM people to evaluate their performance compared with other national-account salespeople. The questions concerned sales performance, the quality and execution of account plans, the development of customer relationships, competitive-account conversations and overall performance.

Based on the previously identified roles and requirements of strategic account managers, strategic account manager job performance can be defined as consisting of two broad but distinct dimensions: sales performance and relationship performance. Sales performance is quite easy to define. It includes such aspects as closing deals, closing profitable deals and meeting sales goals. Relationship performance is more complex than sales performance and includes aspects such as the successful management of customer relationships and building relationships that have good potential. Sharma (2006) discovered that a social and personal bond between the selling and buying companies increases the success of KAM. Relationship performance as a concept includes the creation of these social and personal bonds. Hutt and Walker (2006) also hypothesized that relationship building within the organization and towards customers is influential in key account manager performance. The two dimensions of strategic account manager job performance – sales performance and relationship performance – are considered equal in weight with regard to the total strategic account manager job performance.

Five-Factor Model of personality

As individuals, we have personality traits that distinguish us from each other. These same traits also make us more or less suited for working with customers. It is important, therefore, to understand how significantly these different factors contribute to a person's performance when managing customer relationships. This knowledge is valuable in terms of employee selection and training, for example. The Big Five, or Five-Factor Model (FFM), is one of the most highly regarded trait theories of personality. In this model, variations of personality are explained by five orthogonal factors: extraversion, agreeableness, conscientiousness, emotional stability (or neuroticism) and openness to experience (Saucier and Goldberg 2002).

Categorizing personality into five independent personality factors is not a new concept. The first time five common personality factors were described was when Thurstone conducted factor analytical studies in the 1930s (Scroggins et al. 2009). Another manifestation of the five factors of personality came from a United States Air Force technical report from 1961, in which Tupes and Christal (1961) used factor analysis to identify five personality factors: surgency, agreeableness, dependability, emotional stability and culture.

A major development for the FFM occurred when five individual personality factors emerged from Goldberg's lexical research in the early 1980s (Goldberg 1981), and the final step in the development of the FFM arrived when Costa and McCrae revised their three-factor model. They had previously developed a three-factor model of personality using the questionnaire approach, while the redeveloped model included the two additional factors of agreeableness and conscientiousness, which were based on Goldberg's research (Costa et al. 2002). Later, McCrae, Costa and Martin developed yet another version of the inventory: NEO-PI-3. In that model, 37 of the NEO-PI-R items were replaced in order to improve the psychometrics and reliability of the inventory (McCrae and Costa 2007).

Goldberg continued his work on the FFM and developed the International Personality Item Pool (IPIP) inventory, which was introduced in 1996 (Goldberg 1999; Goldberg et al. 2006). Currently, the IPIP is one of the most utilized personality inventories in the world; it has been translated into over 25 languages and been completed more than 500,000 times over the Internet, where it has been open to the public for over ten years (Goldberg et al. 2006). A major reason for its success on such a scale is its public-domain nature. Individuals can complete and get results from the test for free. Researchers can also use the IPIP scales freely.

Since the early 1990s, many factor analytic studies of personality have been conducted (Pervin 2003). These studies have concentrated on personality ratings and self-report questionnaire responses. Such factor analyses and other statistical analyses have strengthened the credibility and influence of trait-based personality models such as the Five Factor Model (see Fruyt et al. 2004; Heuchert et al. 2000; Hong et al. 2008; Lim and Ployhart 2006; McCrae and Costa 2004; Tokar et al. 1999). In addition, during the last three decades, the validity of the FFM framework has been widely studied. The FFM framework has shown validity across sex, age, and culture (Heuchert et al. 2000; John and Srivastava 1999; McCrae and Costa 1998; McCrae and Costa 2004; Nye et al. 2008).

Before the 1990s, the evidence for personality characteristics or traits that predict job performance was not strong (Reilly and Chao 1982; Schmitt et al. 1984). The situation changed after Barrick and Mount (1991) and Tett et al. (1991) published the first comprehensive meta-analyses concentrating on FFM traits as predictors of job performance. The results of both analyses were that statistically significant relationships emerged between some personality traits and job performance. One of the strongest and generalized relationships was between conscientiousness and job performance. After the analyses of Barrick and Mount (1991) and Tett et al. (1991) were published, more research on the topic was conducted. Salgado (1997) examined FFM traits and job performance with a European sample, while Hurtz and Donovan (2000) conducted their meta-analysis, concentrating on criterion-related validity. Salgado's (1997) and Hurtz and Donovan's (2000) results were closely in line with the previous analyses by Barrick and Mount (1991) and Tett et al. (1991).

Research hypotheses

The objective of the research was to identify the relationships between strategic account manager performance and personality. After defining strategic account manager performance, we can now formulate the research hypotheses. The hypotheses are divided according to the five personality factors introduced earlier.

Extraversion has been found to correlate with manager and salesperson job performance (Barrick and Mount 1991). Wanberg et al. (2000) found that people with higher levels of extraversion were more comfortable networking and that they displayed more networking behaviour. This suggests that extraversion would also correlate with relationship performance. Thus, the following hypothesis can be formulated:

> *Hypothesis 1:* Extraversion is positively related to (a) relationship performance, (b) sales performance and (c) overall job performance.

People with high agreeableness are sympathetic to others and eager to help them (Costa and McCrae 2006). It is likely that this helps strategic account managers form better relationships with co-workers and customers. Still, Barrick and Mount (1991) and Salgado (1997) concluded that agreeableness is not a strong predictor of job performance. Rather, Organ and Lingl (1995) found that agreeableness was linked to job satisfaction in the work relationship context.

> *Hypothesis 2*: Agreeableness is positively related to (a) relationship performance and (b) overall job performance.

People with high conscientiousness are purposeful, strong willed and determined (Costa and McCrae 2006). Therefore, it can be theorized that conscientiousness has a strong relationship with job performance. In addition, in empirical work, conscientiousness has been consistently found to correlate with job performance in different fields (Barrick and Mount 1991; Hurtz and Donovan 2000; Salgado 1997, 2003). From this, the following hypothesis can be formulated:

> *Hypothesis 3*: Conscientiousness is positively related to (a) relationship performance, (b) sales performance and (c) overall job performance.

Emotional stability manifests itself as a tendency to cope in stressful situations. This quality might be helpful in professions such as surgeon or truck driver, but its usefulness is somewhat limited in the strategic account manager context. The research findings on this subject are mixed. According to Barrick and Mount (1991), emotional stability cannot be considered to be a valid predictor of job performance for managers or for salespeople. Meanwhile, based on a European sample, Salgado (1997) concluded that emotional stability would be a valid predictor of job performance across occupational groups. Still, the following hypothesis is presented:

> *Hypothesis 4*: Emotional stability is not related to job performance.

Studies have shown that openness to experience is not a good predictor of job performance (Barrick and Mount 1991; Hurtz and Donovan 2000; Salgado 2003). That provides the basis for proposing the following hypothesis:

> *Hypothesis 5*: Openness to experience is not related to job performance.

Sample and research design

The population under research was Finnish key account managers working for companies operating in business-to-business markets. Because it was very difficult to identify all the key account managers in Finland, thus making the size of the population unclear, a non-probability sample was used. The national contact information provider, Fonecta, was chosen to be the source of key account manager name and address information. The selection was based on the fact that the provider had one of the largest databases of company contact information in Finland. Names of more than 700 people with a job title of 'key account manager' or the equivalent Finnish titles 'Avainasiakaspäällikkö' or 'Avainasiakasjohtaja' were obtained. These people were approached by printed mail questionnaires. A reminder letter was sent three weeks after the first letter (and one week after the requested submission deadline). The reminder letter also had an address to a web page, through which respondents could fill in the same questionnaire online if they thought it would be more convenient (or if they had misplaced the original questionnaire).

Within two weeks of posting the questionnaire, 132 responses were received. After the reminder letter, an additional 56 responses were received, 22 of which came from the online questionnaire. Therefore, the total number of responses was 188, which amounts to a response rate of 27%. Of the responses received, eight were discarded as incomplete and four on suspicion of socially desirable responding. Altogether, 176 usable responses were received.

Closer analysis of the key account managers revealed that some of their work descriptions did not match the description based on the SAM and KAM literature. The biggest concern was with the number of key accounts for which an individual key account manager was responsible. It was decided that managers who had more than 20 key customers were excluded from the data set. This led to 33 excluded responses. The resulting 143 responses represent managers that conform more to the theoretic model of strategic account managers.

The key account managers' average age was 43 years. Of the respondents, 30% were female and 70% were male. The average experience in SAM (or account management in general) was 14 years, and within the current organization it was 9 years. The average number of key accounts per manager was seven.

Measures

As mentioned earlier, the FFM is one of the most utilized trait theories concerning personality. According to the theory, personality can be explained by five factors: extraversion, agreeableness, conscientiousness, emotional stability (or neuroticism) and openness to experience (Saucier and Goldberg 2002). The FFM model is used in this research as the main tool for assessing personalities.

Relationship performance was measured by using a scale validated by Sengupta et al. (2000). Even though the authors named the construct 'key account salesperson perceived effectiveness', it concentrates on the performance of relationship management. The scale items were originally measured using a five-point Likert scale ranging from 1 = Strongly disagree to 5 = Strongly agree. The same scale was used in the current research. Sales performance was measured using a modified performance scale originally developed by Sujan et al. (1994). The original scale went from −5 = Much worse to 5 = Much better. The scale used in this research was a five-point Likert scale ranging from 1 = Strongly disagree to 5 = Strongly agree. Furthermore, the original scale consisted of seven items, but in order to have a scale applicable to all types of industries, companies of all sizes and all types of markets, four of the items were omitted. For example, the item 'assisting your sales supervisor to meet his or her goals' could have been difficult to answer for the employee of a very small company where no sales supervisors exist. Wording was slightly modified to better suit the different answer choices, the Finnish environment and the SAM context.

Socially desirable responding

In the present research, strategic account manager job performance is measured and personalities are assessed with the help of self-report instruments. Self-reporting as a business research method has its advantages, but it also brings certain challenges. One of these is socially desirable responding, which can be defined as an inclination to respond in a way that will present the respondent in a favourable manner (Donaldson and Grant-Vallone 2002; Thompson and Phua 2005). This research uses a short version of the Marlowe–Crowne social-desirability measure in order to screen the responses for elevated scores on the social-desirability measure. The short-form Marlowe–Crowne scale that was used was developed by Rudmin (1999). The measure ranges from −20 to 20 (positive 20 indicating the respondent with the most socially desirable responses).

In the screening process, it was decided that the cut-off level should be placed at 16, meaning that if a respondent received a social-desirability score of 16, 17, 18, 19 or 20, the whole response would be removed from the data set. When the data were analysed, four responses were found that met the cut-off criteria. In all the deleted responses, the respondents rated themselves above average in terms of job performance. This provides evidence that the screening process improved the data quality.

Results

This section describes the results of the analysis of the questionnaire data. The objective of the research was to examine the relationship between personality traits and strategic account manager job performance. Before the examination of the correlation between personality traits and job performance, the correlations between job performance and background variables – such as age, gender and work experience – are presented.

Table 1: Correlation of background variables and job performance

Background variable	Statistic	Relationship performance	Sales performance	Overall performance
Age (N = 142)	Pearson corr.	−.04	−.06	−.06
	Significance	.6509	.4796	.5065
Gender (N = 143)	Spearman corr.	−.03	−.04	−.04
	Significance	.7399	.6617	.6591
Education (N = 143)	Spearman corr.	−.11	−.1100	−.13
	Significance	.1771	.2004	.1322
Work experience with company (N = 143)	Pearson corr.	.15	.07	.12
	Significance	.0819	.4176	.1456
Customer work experience (N = 143)	Pearson corr.	−.06	−.05	−.06
	Significance	.4630	.5595	.4511

Table 1 shows the correlations between the background variables and strategic account manager job performance. Correlations were calculated with overall job performance and two of its dimensions: relationship performance and sales performance. Spearman correlations were calculated between job performance and gender and education level. This was because gender and education level were not continuous variables. For the other variables, the more common Pearson correlation calculation was used.

The correlations between job performance and age, gender, education level and customer work experience were not statistically significant. One of the closest correlations to a significant level was between education level and job performance. Somewhat surprisingly, the correlation was −.13, suggesting that having a relatively higher education level is not a factor in strategic account manager performance. Also surprising was the lack of correlation between customer work experience and job performance. The results suggest that life experience or experience working with customers does not necessarily lead to a better-performing strategic account manager.

Extraversion

When the survey data were analysed, strong correlations were found between extraversion and relationship performance, sales performance and overall performance. From Table 2, it can be seen that all correlations are statistically significant at the $p<.001$ level. The correlation between extraversion and relationship performance is .28. Based on this, *Hypothesis 1a: Extraversion is positively related with relationship performance* can be accepted. A stronger correlation of .36 exists between extraversion and sales performance. Correspondingly, *Hypothesis 1b: Extraversion is positively related with sales performance* is accepted. Lastly, the

Table 2: Correlation of five factors and job performance

		Relationship performance	Sales performance	Overall performance
	Correlation (N = 143)			
Extraversion	Pearson correlation	**.28**	**.36**	**.37**
	Significance	.0006	.0001	<.0001
Agreeableness	Pearson correlation	.18	.18	.21
	Significance	.0321	.0271	.0125
Conscientiousness	Pearson correlation	**.18**	**.22**	**.24**
	Significance	.0274	.0070	.0047
Emotional stability	Pearson correlation	.09	.12	.12
	Significance	.2829	.1714	.1618
Openness to experience	Pearson correlation	.13	.08	.12
	Significance	.1314	.3582	.1673

correlation between extraversion and overall job performance is .37. Therefore, *Hypothesis 1c: Extraversion is positively related with overall job performance* is also accepted.

Based on the results, it can be concluded that extraversion is a contributing factor for strategic account manager job performance. Of the five personality traits, extraversion showed the strongest relationships with job performance.

Agreeableness

Hypothesis 2a: Agreeableness is positively related with relationship performance is supported with the results of the correlation analysis. The correlation coefficient between agreeableness and relationship performance is .18 at the $p<.05$ significance level. A stronger relationship was found between agreeableness and overall job performance. The coefficient is .21 at the $p<.05$ significance level. Therefore, *Hypothesis 2b: Agreeableness is positively related with overall job performance* is accepted. In addition, an unhypothesized correlation with agreeableness and sales performance was found. The correlation between the two variables is .18 with a significance level of $p<.05$. Agreeableness showed the third-strongest correlation with job performance, after extraversion and conscientiousness.

Conscientiousness

When the relationship between conscientiousness and job performance was analysed, statistically strong correlations were found. The correlation between conscientiousness and relationship performance is .18 at the $p<.05$ level. Therefore, *Hypothesis 3a: Conscientiousness is positively related with relationship performance* is accepted. The correlation between sales performance and conscientiousness was stronger, being .22 at the $p<.01$ level. Based on the results, *Hypothesis 3b: Conscientiousness is positively related with sales performance* is accepted. The correlation between conscientiousness and overall job performance is .24. This leads to the acceptance of *Hypothesis 3c: Conscientiousness is positively related with overall job performance*.

Emotional stability

The analysis did not reveal statistically significant relationships between emotional stability and job performance. The correlation coefficients range from .09 to .12. Based on this, *Hypothesis 4: Emotional stability is not related to job performance* is accepted.

Openness to experience

It was hypothesized that *openness to experience is not related to job performance* (Hypothesis 5). The analysis revealed a non-significant correlation of .13 between openness to experience and relationship performance with a *p* value of .1341. Similarly, sales performance and overall job performance did not show statistically significant relationships with openness to experience.

Conclusions

Previous research has constantly shown a relationship between conscientiousness and job performance. The results confirm this relationship. Strategic account manager job performance and its sub-components, relationship performance and sales performance, all have statistically significant correlations with conscientiousness at significance levels ranging from $<.05$ to $<.001$.

Another result that was expected because of earlier research was the non-existent relationship with strategic account manager job performance and emotional stability. It is possible that people with low emotional stability will never apply or qualify for a strategic account manager position. This might bias the results, especially in the case of non-linear relationships between emotional stability and strategic account manager job performance. An example of this would be a relationship in which a certain threshold score of emotional stability is needed for a strategic account manager to perform well.

The extraversion trait was found to have the strongest relationship with strategic account manager job performance. Prior studies have shown the relationship between performance in sales work and extraversion. The current research further confirms this and identifies a link between performance in relationship management and extraversion.

Agreeableness was also found to have a statistically significant relationship with strategic account manager job performance and its two sub-components. The relationship is not as strong as the relationships between strategic account manager job performance and extraversion or conscientiousness. Previous research has failed to find the relationship between job performance and agreeableness. The reason might be the unique job profile of the strategic account manager, in which getting along with very different stakeholders is essential. These stakeholders include, for example, the individual's own organization and members in the customer organization.

Openness to experience does not exhibit a statistically significant correlation with strategic account manager job performance. Indeed, only a few research results have identified statistically significant relationships between openness and job performance (Bing and Lounsbury 2000). Thus, it is not a surprise that the relationship between strategic account manager job performance and openness to experience is not present in the current results.

Managerial implications

This research has shown that in order to build a successful KAM programme, a company needs to concentrate on finding the right people (in terms of their personality). Out of all the analysed factors, key account manager job performance had strong relationships with certain personality traits. Moreover, the result showed that age, gender, education level or customer work experience do not have a significant effect on job performance. Overall, it is evident that companies should pay a great deal of attention to personality during the employee-selection processes. The most important personality traits that companies should look for in potential employees are extraversion, conscientiousness and agreeableness.

In addition to improving the employee-selection process, employees should be encouraged to behave according to certain personality traits that improve job performance. Employees could, for example, be trained to pay more attention to details, to be more socially open, polite or concerned with other people's feelings or interests. Some behaviours could be described in work manuals and could be introduced to new employees in their orientation phase. Companies could create measures based on some of the desired behaviours and perhaps, to some extent, base employee compensation on these measures.

Limitations and future research

One major limitation of the research is that the sample consists of individuals from only one country. It is possible that some tasks or requirements are more important in a Finnish context than, for example, in the United States. It could be that in some cultures, extraversion or emotional stability is more important in order to achieve good job performance. In other cultures, agreeableness could be the key trait. These possible cultural differences could also limit being able to generalize the results.

Regarding future research, it would be interesting to see comparative studies in which the success factors for strategic account manager job performance are compared across different cultures or countries. It is clear that cultural differences exist, but it is unclear whether they affect the personality traits, behaviours or skills that are required of strategic account managers.

The definition of strategic account manager job performance used in this research is not comprehensive. Compromises had to be made in order to achieve a widely applicable definition of strategic account manager job performance. For assessing individuals, a more comprehensive model should be created. Emphasis should also be put on valid and reliable measures that could be used in the research.

Because of self-reporting respondents, the research results may have biases. Even when the results are supported by previous research and logical reasoning, replicating the research with actual performance data would provide a greater amount of evidence concerning this research issue. A good way to repeat the research would be by obtaining objective measures of sales performance, which might be possible by cooperating with larger companies employing a large number of strategic account managers. In this case, relationship performance would be more difficult to measure. Measuring the length of a strategic-account relationship or strategic-account satisfaction could be done to obtain useful data.

References

Bold type: cited by 10 or more of the 24 papers in the Handbook
Italic type: cited by 5–9 of the 24 papers in the Handbook
Normal type: cited by 1–4 of the 24 papers in the Handbook

Aaronson, S.A. (2005) 'Minding our business': What the United States government has done and can do to ensure that U.S. multinational act responsibly in foreign markets. *Journal of Business Ethics.* 59(1/2), 175–198.

Abrahamsson, M. & Brege, S. (2005) Dynamic effectiveness improved industrial distribution from interaction between marketing and logistics strategies. *Journal of Marketing Channels.* 12(2), 83–112.

Abratt, R. & Kelly, P.M. (2002) Customer–supplier partnerships: Perceptions of a successful key account management program. Industrial Marketing Management. 31(5), 467–476.

Achrol, R.S. (1991) Evolution of the marketing organization: New forms for turbulent environments. *Journal of Marketing.* 55(4), 77–93.

Achrol, R.S. (1997) Changes in the theory of interorganizational relations in marketing: Toward a network paradigm. *Journal of the Academy of Marketing Science.* 25(1), 56–71.

Achrol, R.S. & Kotler, P. (1999) Marketing in the network economy. *Journal of Marketing.* 63(Fundamental Issues and Directions for Marketing), 146–163.

Achrol, R.S. & Stern, L.W. (1988) Environmental determinants of decision-making uncertainty in marketing channels. *Journal of Marketing Research.* 25(2), 36–50.

Adner, R. (2002) When are technologies disruptive? A demand-based view of the emergence of competition. *Strategic Management Journal.* 23(8), 667–688.

Alajoutsijärvi, K., Möller, K. & Rosenbröijer, C.J. (1999) Relevance of focal nets in understanding the dynamics of business relationships. *Journal of Business-to-business Marketing.* 6(3), 3–35.

Alajoutsijärvi, K., Möller, K. & Tähtinen, J. (2000) Beautiful exit: How to leave your business partner. *European Journal of Marketing.* 34(11/12), 1270–1289.

Alejandro, T.B. et al. (2011) The outcome of company and account manager relationship quality on loyalty, relationship value and performance. *Industrial Marketing Management.* 40(1), 36–43.

Al-Hasan, F.B. & Brennan, R. (2009) Strategic account management in an emerging economy. *Journal of Business & Industrial Marketing.* 24(8), 611–620.

Aliouat, B. (1996) *Les stratégies de coopération Industrielle.* Paris: Economica.

Ancona, D.G. & Caldwell, D.F. (1992) Bridging the boundary: External activity and performance in organizational teams. *Administrative Science Quarterly.* 37(4), 634–665.

Ancona, D.G. & Caldwell, D.F. (1992a) Bridging the boundary: External activity and performance in organizational teams. *Administrative Science Quarterly*. 37(4), 634–665.

Ancona, D.G. & Caldwell, D.F. (1992b) Demography and design: Predictors of new product team performance. *Organization Science*. 3(3), 321–341.

Anderluh, J.R. (1968) National account marketing: Top management expectations. *The 24th Annual National Account Marketing Association Conference*. San Diego, California.

Anderson, E. (1996) Marketing and transaction cost economics. In: Groenewegen, J. (ed.), *Transaction Cost Economics and Beyond*. Boston: Springer.

Anderson, E. (1998) Customer satisfaction and word of mouth. *Journal of Service Research*. 1(1), 5–17.

Anderson, E. & Jap, S.D. (2005) The dark side of close relationships. *MIT Sloan Management Review*. 46(3), 75–82.

Anderson, E. & Oliver, R.L. (1987) Perspectives on behaviour-based versus outcome-based sales force control systems. *Journal of Marketing*. 51(4), 76–88.

Anderson, E. & Sullivan, M. (1993) The antecedents and consequences of customer satisfaction for firms. *Marketing Science*. 12(2), p.125–143.

Anderson, E. & Weitz, B. (1989) Determinants of continuity in conventional industrial channel dyads. *Marketing Science*. 8(4), 310–323.

Anderson, E. & Weitz, B. (1992) The use of pledges to build and sustain commitment in distribution channels. *Journal of Marketing Research*. 29(1), 18–34.

Anderson, E.W. & Mittal, V. (2000) Strengthening the satisfaction–profit chain. *Journal of Service Research*. 3(2), 107–120.

Anderson, E.W., Fornell, C. & Lehmann, D.R. (1994) Customer satisfaction, market share, and profitability. *Journal of Marketing*. 56(3), 53–66.

Anderson, J.C. (1987) An approach for confirmatory measurement and structural equation modelling of organizational properties. *Management Science*. 33(4), 525–524.

Anderson, J.C. (1995) Relationships in business markets: Exchange episodes, value creation, and their empirical assessment. *Journal of the Academy of Marketing Science*. 23(4), 346–350.

Anderson, J.C. & Gerbing, D.W. (1988) Structural equations modelling in practice: A review and recommended two-step approach. *Psychological Bulletin*. 103(3), 411–423.

Anderson, J.C. & Narus, J.A. (1991) Partnering as a focused market strategy. *California Management Review*. 33(3), 95–113.

Anderson, J.C. & Narus, J.A. (1998) Business marketing: Understand what customers value. *Harvard Business Review*. 76(6), 53–65.

Anderson, J.C. & Narus, J.A. (1999) *Business Market Management: Understanding, Creating, and Delivering Value*. (1st edition) Upper Saddle River: Prentice-Hall.

Anderson, J.C. & Narus J.A. (2004) *Business Marketing Management: Understanding, Creating and Delivering Value* (2nd edition). Upper Saddle River: Pearson Education.

Anderson, J.C., Håkansson, H. & Johanson, J. (1994) Dyadic business relationships within a network context. *Journal of Marketing*. 58(4), 1–15.

Anderson, J.C., Narus, J.A. & van Rossum, W. (2006) Customer value propositions in business markets. *Harvard Business Review*. 84(3), 91–99.

Andersson, D., Pruth, M. & Rehme J. (2007) Coordinate to enhance third party logistics relationships. *International Journal of Integrated Supply Management*. 3(1), 69–85.

Ang, L. & Taylor, B. (2005) Managing customer profitability using portfolio matrices. *The Journal of Database Marketing & Customer Strategy Management*. 12(4), 298–304.

Ansoff, H.I. & Leontiades, J. (1976) Strategic portfolio management. *Journal of General Management*. Autumn, 13–29.

Ariely, D. (2008) *Predictably Irrational: The Hidden Forces that Shape Our Decisions*. New York: HarperCollins Publishers LLC.

Armstrong, J.S. & Overton, T.S. (1977) Estimating nonresponse bias in mail surveys. *Journal of Marketing Research*. 14(3), 396–402.

Arnett, D.B. & Badrinarayanan, V. (2005) Enhancing customer needs-driven CRM strategies: Core selling teams, knowledge management competence, and relationship marketing competence. *Journal of Personal Selling and Sales Management* .25(4), 329–341.

Arnett, D.B., Macy, B.A. & Wilcox, J.B. (2005) The role of core selling teams in supplier–buyer relationships. *Journal of Personal Selling & Sales Management*. 25(1), 27–42.

Arnold, D., Birkinshaw, J. & Toulan, O. (1999) Implementing global account management in multinational corporations. *Thexis*. 16(4), 14–17.

Arnold, D., Birkinshaw, J. & Toulan, O. (2001) Can selling be globalized? The pitfalls of global account management. California Management Review. 44(1), 8–20.

Aroujo, L. & Muzas, S. (1995) Category management in marketing and purchasing: Formal structure as representation and adaption. *Proceedings of the 11th IMP Conference*. Manchester, United Kingdom. 67–94.

Arrow, K.J. (1969) The organization of economic activity: Issues pertinent to the choice of market versus nonmarket allocation. In: U.S. Joint Economic Committee (ed.), *The Analysis and Evaluation of Public Expenditure: The PPB System*. Washington: Congress of the United States.

Asanuma, B. (1989) Manufacturer–supplier relationships in Japan and the concept of relation specific skill. *Journal of the Japanese and International Economies*. 3, 1–30.

Ata, Z. & Toker, A. (2012). The effect of customer relationship management adoption in business-to-business markets. *Journal of Business and Industrial Marketing (SSCI)*. 27(6), 497–507.

Atanasova, Y. & Senn, C. (2011) Global customer team design: Dimensions, determinants, and performance outcomes. *Industrial Marketing Management*. 40(2), 278–289.

Auguste, B.G., Harmon, E.P. & Pandit, V. (2006) The right service strategies for product companies. *McKinsey Quarterly*. 1, 41–51.

Axelrod, R. (1980) Effective choice in the prisoner's dilemma. *The Journal of Conflict Resolution*. 24(1), 3–25.

Axelrod, R. & Hamilton, W.D. (1981) The evolution of cooperation. *Science*. 211(4489), 1390–1396.

Babakus, E. et al. (1996) Investigating the relationships among sales management control, sales territory design, salesperson performance, and sales organization effectiveness. *International Journal of Research in Marketing*. 13(4), 345–363.

Baccarini, D. (1996) The concept of project complexity – a review. *International Journal of Project Management*. 14(4), 201–205.

Backer, Y. & Linden, C.V. (2005) Key account management: Creating added value in European hospitals. *Journal of Medical Marketing*. 3(3), 219–229.

Bagozzi, R. (1978) Sales force performance and satisfaction as a function of individual difference, interpersonal, and situational factors. *Journal of Marketing Research*.15(4), 517–53l.

Bagozzi, R.P. & Youjae, Y. (1988) On the evaluation of structural equation models. *Journal of the Academy of Marketing Science*. 16(1), 74–94.

Bagozzi, R.P., Yi, Y. & Phillips, L.W. (1991) Assessing construct validity in organizational research. *Administrative Science Quarterly*. 36(3), 421–458.

Balakrishnan, S. & Wernerfelt, B. (1986) Technical change, competition, and vertical integration. *Strategic Management Journal*. 7(4), 347–359.

Baldwin, C.Y. & Clark, K.B. (2000) *Design Rules. Volume 1: The Power of Modularity*. Cambridge: The MIT Press.

Ballantyne, D. & Varey, R.J. (2006) Creating value-in-use through marketing interaction: The exchange logic of relating, communicating and knowing. *Marketing Theory*, 6(3), 335–348.

Ballantyne, D. et al. (2011) Value propositions as communication practice: Taking a wider view. *Industrial Marketing Management*. 40(2), 202–210.

Barney, J.B. (1986) Organizational culture: Can it be a source of sustained competitive advantage. *Academy of Management Review*. 11(3), 656–665.

Barney, J.B. (1991), Firm resources and sustained competitive advantage. *Journal of Management*. 17(1), 99–120.

Barney, J.B. (2001) Is the resource-based 'view' a useful perspective for strategic management research? Yes. *The Academy of Management Review*. 26(1), p.41–56.

Barrett, J. (1986) Why major account selling works. Industrial Marketing Management. 15(1), 63–73.

Barrick, M.R. & Mount, M.K. (1991) The big five personality dimensions and job performance: A meta-analysis. *Personnel Psychology*. 44(1), 1–26.

Bateman, T.S. & Crant, J.M. (1993) The proactive component of organizational behaviour: A measure and correlates. *Journal of Organizational Behaviour*. 14(2), 103–118.

Bauer, G.J. et al. (1998) *Emerging Trends in Sales Thought and Practice*. Westport: Praeger.

Beer, M., Eisenstat, R.A. & Spector, B. (1990) Why change programs don't produce change. *Harvard Business Review*. 68(6), 158–166.

Bellizzi, J.A. & Bristol, T. (2005) Supervising the unethical selling behaviour of top sales performers: Assessing the impact of social desirability bias. *Journal of Business Ethics*. 57(4), 377–388.

Bellizzi, J.A. & Hasty, R.W. (2003) Supervising unethical sales force behaviour: How strong is the tendency to treat top performers leniently? *Journal of Business Ethics*. 43(4), 337–351.

Bengtsson, M. & Kock, S. (1999) Cooperation and competition in relationships between competitors in business networks. *Journal of Business & Industrial Marketing*. 14(3), 178–193.

Bengtsson, M. & Kock, S. (2000) 'Coopetition' in business networks – To cooperate and compete simultaneously. *Industrial Marketing Management*. 29(5), 411–426.

Bensaou, M. (1999) Portfolios of buyer–supplier relationships. *Sloan Management Review*. 40(4), 35–44.

Benson, P. et al. (1987), Manage customers for profits (not just sales). *Harvard Business Review*. September, 101–108.

Bentler, P.M. (1995) *EQS Structural Equations Program Manual*, Encino, CA: Multivariate Software, Inc.

Berger, P.D. & Nasr, N. (1998) Customer lifetime value: Marketing models and applications. *Journal of Interactive Marketing*. 12(1), 17–30.

Berger, P.D., Eechambadi, N., George, M., Lehmann, D.R., Rizley, R. & Venkatesan, R. (2006) From customer lifetime value to shareholder value. *Journal of Service Research*. 9(2), 156–167.

Berghman, L., Matthyssens, P. & Vandenbempt, K. (2006) Building competences for new customer value creation: An exploratory study. *Industrial Marketing Management*. 35(8), 961–973.

Bernstein, P.L. (1999) Wimps and consequences. *The Journal of Portfolio Management*. 26(1), 1.

Berry, L.L. (1983) Relationship marketing. In: Berry, L.L., Shostack, G.L. & Upah, G.D. (eds.), *Emerging Perspectives of Services Marketing*. Chicago: American Marketing Association. 25–28.

Beth, S. et al. (2003) *Building Relationships*. [Online] July 2013. Available from: http://hbr.org/2003/07/building–relationships/ar/1.

Bettenhausen, K.L. (1991) Five years of groups research: What we have learned and what needs to be addressed. *Journal of Management*. 17(2), 345–381.

Biggart, N.W. & Delbridge, R. (2004) Systems of exchange. *Academy of Management Review*. 29(1), 28–49.

Billett, M.T. (2011) Balancing risk and return in a customer portfolio: A comment. *Journal of Marketing*. 75(3), 21–23.

Bing, M.N. & Lounsbury, J.W. (2000) Openness and job performance in U.S.-based Japanese manufacturing companies. *Journal of Business and Psychology*. 14(3), 515–522.

Biong, H. & Selnes. F. (1996) *The Strategic Role of the Salesperson in Established Buyer–Seller Relationships*. Report No. 96–118 (December), Cambridge: Marketing Science Institute.

Birkinshaw, J., Toulan, O. & Arnold, D. (2001) Global account management in multinational corporations: Theory and evidence. Journal of International Business Studies. 32(2), 231–248.

Bititci, U.S. Martinez, V., Albores, P. & Parung, J. (2004) Creating and managing value in collaborative networks. *International Journal of Physical Distribution and Logistics Management*. 34(3/4), 251–268.

Blattberg, R.C., Getz, G. & Thomas, J. (2001) *Customer Equity*. Boston, MA: Harvard Business School Press.

Blattberg, R.C. & Deighton, J. (1996) Manage marketing by the customer equity test. *Harvard Business Review*. July, 136–144.

Blois, K. (1996) Relationship marketing in organisational markets: When is it appropriate? *Journal of Marketing Management*. 12(1–3), 161–173.

Blois, K. (1997) Are business to business relationships inherently unstable? *Journal of Marketing Management*. 13(5), 367–382.

Blois, K. (1999a) Relationships in business-to-business marketing – How is their value assessed? *Marketing Intelligence and Planning*. 17(2), 91–99.

Blois, K. (1999b) Trust in business-to-business relationships: An evaluation of its status. *The Journal of Management Studies*. 36(2), 197–215.

Blois, K. & Ramirez, R. (2006) Capabilities as marketable assets: A proposal for a functional categorization. *Industrial Marketing Management*. 35(8), 1027–1031.

Bohling, T. et al. (2006) CRM implementation: Effectiveness issues and insights. *Journal of Service Research*. 9(2), 184–194.

Boles, J.S., Barksdale, H.C. & Johnson, J.T. (1996) What national account decision makers would tell salespeople about building relationships. *Journal of Business & Industrial Marketing*. 11(2), 6–19.

Boles, J.S., Johnston, W. & Gardner, A. (1999) The selection and organization of national accounts: A North-American perspective. *Journal of Business & Industrial Marketing*. 14(4), 264–275.

Boles, J.S., Pilling, B.K. & Goodwyn, G.W. (1994), Revitalizing your national account marketing program: The NAM audit. *Journal of Business & Industrial Marketing*. 9(1), 24–33.

Bollen, K.A. (1989) *Structural Equations with Latent Variables*. New York: John Wiley & Sons.

Bolton, R.N. (1998) A dynamic model of the duration of the customer's relationship with a continuous service provider: the role of satisfaction. *Marketing Science*. 17(1), 45–65.

Bolton, R.N. (2006) Foreword. In: Lusch, R.F. & Vargo, S.L. (eds.), The *Service Dominant Logic of Marketing: Dialog, Debate and Directions*. New York: M.E. Sharpe.

Bolton, R.N., Tarasi, C.O. (2006) Managing customer relationships. *Review of Marketing Research*. 3, 3–38.

Borden, N.H. (1964) The concept of the marketing mix. *Journal of Advertising Research*. June, 2–7.

Böttcher, M. & Klingner, S. (2011) Providing a method for composing modular B2B services. *Journal of Business & Industrial Marketing*. 26(5), 320–331.

Bournay, E. (2007) *In Dead Water – Climate Change, Pollution, Over-Harvest, and Invasive Species in The World's Fishing Grounds*. [Online] Available from: http://www.grida.no/publications/rr/in–dead–water/.

Bowersox, D., Closs, D. & Drayer, R. (2005) The digital transformation: Technology and beyond. *Supply Chain Management Review*. 9(1), 22–29.

Bowman, D. & Narayandas, D. (2004) Linking customer management effort to customer profitability in business markets. *Journal of Marketing Research*. 41(4), 433–447.

Boyer, K.K. & McDermott, C. (1999) Strategic consensus in operations strategy. *Journal of Operations Management*. 17(3), 289–305.

Braddach, J.L. & Eccles, R.G. (1989) Price, authority, and trust: From ideal types to plural forms. *Annual Review of Sociology*. 15, 97–118.

Bradford, E. & Minshul, J. (2001) Beyond the competent key account manager – Building a competency based SAM programme. *Focus Europe*. 2(4), 8–12.

Bradford, E. et al. (2001) Realising relationship potential at Henkel: Using account profitability to upgrade customer relationships. *Focus Europe*.1(3), 1–4.

Bradford, E., Erickson, S. & McDonald, M. (2012) *Marketing Navigation*. Oxford: Goodfellow Publishers.

Bradford, K., Brown, S., Ganesan, S., Hunter, G., Onyemah, V., Palmatier, R., Rpouziēs, D., Spiro, R., Sujan, H. & Weitz, B. (2010) The embedded sales force: Connecting buying and selling organizations. *Marketing Letters*. 21(3), 239–253.

Brady, N. (2004) In search of market orientation – An experiment in key account management. *Marketing Intelligence & Planning*. 22(2), 144–159.

Brady, T., Davies, A. & Gann, D. (2004) Creating value by delivering integrated solutions. *International Journal of Project Management*. 23(5), 360–365.

Bragg, A.J. (1982) National account management to the rescue. *Sales and Marketing Management*. 16, 30–34.

Brandenburger, A.M. & Nalebuff, B.J. (1995) The right game: Use game theory to shape strategy. *Harvard Business Review*. [Online]. Available from: http://hbr.org/1995/07/the –right–game–use–game–theory–to–shape–strategy/ar/1.

Brehmer, P.-O. & Rehme, J. (2009) Proactive and reactive: drivers for key account management programmes. *European Journal of Marketing*. 43(7/8), 961–984.

Brennan, R. (1997) Buyer/supplier partnering in British industry: The automotive and telecommunications sectors. *Journal of Marketing Management*. 13(8), 759–775.

Brewer, G. (1997) Brain power. *Sales and Marketing Management*. 149(May), 38–45.

Brodie, R.J., Hollebeek, L.D., Juric', B. & Ilic', A. (2011) Customer engagement: Conceptual domain, fundamental propositions, and implications for research. *Journal of Service Research*.14(3), 252–271.

Brown, H.E. & Brucker, R.W. (1990) Charting the industrial buying stream. *Industrial Marketing Management*. 19(1), 55–61.

Brown, S.L. & Eisenhardt, K.M. (1995) Product development: Past research, present findings, and future directions. *Academy of Management Review*. 20(2), 343–378.

REFERENCES

Brown, S.P. & Peterson, R.A. (1993) Antecedents and consequences of salesperson job satisfaction: Meta-analysis and assessment of causal effects. *Journal of Marketing Research.* 30(1), 63–77.

Brown, S.P., Cron, W.L. & Slocum, J.W. (1998) Effects of trait competitiveness and perceived intraorganizational competition on salesperson goal setting and performance. *Journal of Marketing.* 62(4), 88–98.

Buchanan, L. (1992) Vertical trade relationships: The role of dependence and symmetry in attaining organizational goals. *Journal of Marketing Research.* 29(1), 65–75.

Buck, T. (2005) Boost for big companies in EU antitrust reforms. *Financial Times.* October, 8.

Bucklin, L. & Sengupta, S. (1993) Organizing successful co-marketing alliances. *Journal of Marketing.* 57(2), 32–46.

Bunderson, J.S. & Sutcliffe, K.M. (2002) Comparing alternative conceptualizations of functional diversity in management teams: Process and performance effects. *Academy of Management Journal.* 45(5), 875–893.

Bunn, M.D. (1993) Taxonomy of buying decision approaches. *Journal of Marketing.* 57(1), 38–56.

Burnett, K. (1992) *Strategic Customer Alliances: How to Win, Manage and Develop Key Account Business in the 1990's.* London: Financial Times Prentice-Hall.

Burt, D.N., Dobler, D.W. & Starling, S.L. (2003) *World Class Supply Management: The Key to Supply Chain Management.* New York: McGraw–Hill/Irwin.

Busch, P. (1980) The sales manager bases of social power and influence. *Journal of Marketing.* 44(3), 91–101.

Bush, A.J. & Grant, E.S. (1994) Analysing the content of marketing journals to assess trends in sales force research. *Journal of Personal Selling & Sales Management.* 14(Summer), 57–68.

Business Marketing (1988) National account marketers want more support. *Business Marketing.* 72(Aug), 26.

Buvik, A. & John, G. (2000) When does vertical coordination improve industrial purchasing relationships? *Journal of Marketing.* 64(3), 52–64.

Buzzell, R.D. (1985) *Citibank: Marketing to Multinational Customers.* Harvard Business School Case No. 9-584-016. Boston: Harvard Case Services.

Campbell, A.J. (1997) Buyer–supplier partnerships: flip sides of the same coin? *Journal of Business & Industrial Marketing.* 12(6), 417–434.

Campbell, A.J. (2003) Creating customer knowledge competence: Managing customer relationship management programs strategically. *Industrial Marketing Management.* 32(5), 375–383.

Campbell, N.C.G. (1985) An interaction approach to organizational buying behavior. *Journal of Business Research.* 13(1), 35–48.

Campbell, N.C.G. & Cunningham, M.T. (1983) Customer analysis for strategy development in industrial markets. *Strategic Management Journal.* 4(4), 369–380.

Campbell, N.C.G. & Cunningham, M.T. (1985) Managing customer relationships: The challenge of deploying scarce managerial resources. *International Journal of Research in Marketing.* 2(4), 255–262.

Campion, M.A., Medsker, G.J., & Higgs, A.C. (1993) Relations between work group characteristics and effectiveness: Implications for designing effective work groups. *Personnel Psychology.* 46(4), 823–847.

Caniëls, M. & Gelderman, C. (2007) Power and interdependence in buyer–supplier relationships: A purchasing portfolio approach. *Industrial Marketing Management.* 36(2), 219–229.

Cannon, J. & Homburg, C. (2001) Buyer–supplier relationships and customer firm costs. *Journal of Marketing*. 65(1), 29–43.

Cannon, J. & Narayandas, N. (2000) Relationship marketing and key account management. In: Sheth, J.N. & Parvatiyar, A. (eds.), *Handbook of Relationship Marketing*. Thousand Oaks, CA: Sage Publications.

Cannon, J. & Perreault, W.D. (1999) Buyer–seller relationships in business markets. *Journal of Marketing Research*. 36(4), 439–460.

Capon, N. (2001) Key Account Management and Planning: The Comprehensive Handbook for Managing Your Company's Most Important Strategic Asset. New York: Free Press.

Capon, N. (2012) *Managing Marketing in the 21st Century*. New York: Wessex Press.

Capon, N. & Glazer, R. (1987) Marketing and technology: A strategic coalignment. *Journal of Marketing*. 51(3), 1–14.

Capon, N. & Senn, C. (2010) Global customers management programs: How to make them really work. *California Management Review*. 52(2), 32–55.

Capon, N. & Tubridy, G.S. (2010) *Sales Eats First*. New York: Wessex Press.

Capron, L. & Hulland, J. (1999) Redeployment of brands, sales forces, and general marketing management expertise following horizontal acquisitions: A resource-based view. *Journal of Marketing*. 63(2), 41–54.

Cardozo, R.N., Shipp, S.H. & Roering, K.J. (1987) Implementing new business-to-business selling methods. *Journal of Personal Selling & Sales Management*. 7(2), 17–26.

Cardozo, R.N., Shipp, S.H. & Roering, K.J. (1992) Proactive strategic partnerships: A new business markets strategy. *Journal of Business and Industrial Marketing*. 7(1), 51–64.

Carroll, A.B. (1991) The pyramid of corporate social responsibility: Toward the moral management of organizational stakeholders. *Business Horizons*. 34(4), 39–49.

Carroll, A.B. (1993) *Business and society: Ethics and stakeholder management*. Cincinnati, OH: South-Western Publishing.

Cater, T. & Cater, B. (2010) Product and relationship quality influence on customer commitment and loyalty in B2B manufacturing relationships. *Industrial Marketing Management*. 39(8), 1321–1333.

Cespedes, F.V. (1992), Sales coordination: An exploratory study. *Journal of Personal Selling & Sales Management*. 12(3), 13–29.

Cespedes, F.V. (1993) Coordinating sales and marketing in consumer goods firms. *Journal of Consumer Marketing*. 10(2), 37–55.

Cespedes, F.V. (1995), *Concurrent Marketing: Integrating Product, Sales, and Service*. Boston, MA: Harvard Business School Press.

Cespedes, F.V., Doyle, S.X. & Freedman, R.J. (1989) Teamwork for today's selling. *Harvard Business Review*. 67(2), 44–56.

Chandler, A.D. (1962) *Strategy and Structure*. Cambridge: MIT Press.

Chandler, A.D. (1998) Corporate strategy and structure: Some current considerations. *Society*. 35(2), 347–350.

Chapman, S. (2004) Socially responsible supply chains: Marks & Spencer in historic perspective. *International Centre for Corporate Social Responsibility Research Paper Series*, No 26, Nottingham University Business School.

Chesbrough, H. (2010) Business model innovation: Opportunities and barriers. *Long Range Planning*. 43(2/3), 354–363.

Cheverton, P. (2008) *Key Account Management, Tools and Techniques for Achieving Profitable Key Supplier Status*. London: Kogan.

Chonko, L.B., Jones, E., Roberts, J.A. & Dubinsky, A.J. (2002) The role of environmental turbulence, readiness for change, and salesperson learning in the success of sales force change. *Journal of Personal Selling and Sales Management*. 22(4), 227–245.

Churchill, G.A. (1979) A paradigm for developing better measures of marketing constructs. *Journal of Marketing Research*. 16(1), 64–73.

Churchill, G.A., Ford, N.M. & Walker, O.C. (1993) *Sales Force Management*. New York: Irwin Professional Publishing.

Churchill, G.A., Ford, N.M., Hartley, S.W. & Walker, O.C. (1985) The determinants of salesperson performance: A meta-analysis. *Journal of Marketing Research*. 22(2), 103–118.

Claret, J., Mauger, P. & Roegner, E.V. (2006), Managing a marketing and sales transformation. *The McKinsey Quarterly*. 111–121.

Clarke, A.H. & Freytag, P.V. (2013) Orchestration of customer portfolios – Challenges of internal and external alignment. *29th IMP Conference*. Atlanta, Sweden.

Claycomb, C. & Frankwick, G.L. (2004) A contingency perspective of communication, conflict resolution and buyer search effort in buyer–seller relationships. *Journal of Supply Chain Management*. 40(1), 18–34.

Cohen, A.R. & Bradford, D.L. (2005) *Influence without Authority*, (2nd edition). Hoboken, NJ: John Wiley & Sons.

Cohen, M.A. & Huchzermeier, A. (1999) Global supply chain management: A survey of research and applications. In: Tayur, S.R., Ganeshan, R. & Magazine, M. (eds.), *Quantitative Models for Supply Chain Management*. Boston, MA: Kluwer Academic Publishers.

Cohen, S.G. & Bailey, D.E. (1997) What makes teams work: Group effectiveness research from the shop floor to the executive suite. *Journal of Management*. 23(3), 239–290.

Colletti, J.A. & Chonko, L.B. (1997) Change management initiatives: Moving sales organizations from obsolescence to high performance. *Journal of Personal Selling & Sales Management*. 17(2), 1–30.

Colletti, J.A. & Tubridy, G.S. (1987) Effective major account sales management. *Journal of Personal Selling and Sales Management*. 7(2), 1–10.

Collis, D. & Rukstad, M.G. (2008) Can you say what your strategy is? *Harvard Business Review*. 82–91.

Comer, J.M. (1991) *Sales Management*. Needham Heights, MA: Allyn and Bacon.

Comer, L.B. & Drollinger, T. (1999) Active empathetic listening and selling success: A conceptual framework. *Journal of Personal Selling and Sales Management*. 29(1), 15–29.

Commission of the European Communities (2001) *Green Paper: Promoting a European framework for corporate social responsibility*. [Online] Available from: http://eur–lex.europa.eu/LexUriServ/site/en/com/2001/com2001_0366en01.pdf.

Cooper, R.G. & Kaplan, R.S. (1991) Profit priorities from activity-based costing. *Harvard Business Review*. 69(May–June), 130–135.

Cooper, R.G., Edgett, S.J. & Kleinschmidt, E.J. (1999) New product portfolio management: Practices and performance. *Journal of Product Innovation Management*. 16(4), 333–351.

Corbin, A. & Corben, C. (1973) *Implementing the Marketing Concept*. London: British Institute of Management.

Corominas-Bosch, M. (2004) Bargaining in a network of buyers and sellers. *Journal of Economic Theory*. 115(1), 35–77.

Corsaro, D. & Snehota, I. (2010) Searching for relationship value in business markets: Are we missing something? *Industrial Marketing Management*. 39(6), 925–935.

Costa, P. & McCrae, R. (2006) *Revised NEO personality inventory (NEO PI–R) Manual (UK Edition)*. Oxford: Hogrefe.

Costa, P., McCrae, R. & Jonsson, F. (2002) Validity and utility of the revised NEO personality inventory: Examples from Europe. In: Raad, B. & Perugini, M. (eds.), *Big Five Assessment*. Washington: Hogrefe & Huber Publishers.

Cousins, P.D. & Spekman, R. (2003) Strategic supply and the management of inter- and intra-organizational relationships. *Journal of Purchasing and Supply Management*. 9(1), 19–29.

Cousins, P.D. & Stanwix, E. (2001) It's only a matter of confidence: A comparison of relationship management between Japanese- and UK non-Japanese-owned vehicle manufacturers. *International Journal of Operations & Production Management*. 21(9), 1160–1180.

Cousins, P.D., Lawson, B. & Squire, B. (2008) Performance measurement in strategic buyer–supplier relationships. *International Journal of Operations and Production Management*. 28(3), 238–258.

Cova, B. & Salle, R. (2000) Rituals in managing extra-business relationships in international project marketing: A conceptual framework. *International Business Review*. 9(6), 669–685.

Cova, B. & Salle, R. (2008) Marketing solutions in accordance with the S-D logic: Co-creating value with customer network actors. *Industrial Marketing Management*. 37(3), 207–77.

Covey, S.M.R. & Merrill, R.R. (2008) *The Speed of Trust: The One Thing that Changes Everything*. New York: The Free Press.

Coviello, N.E. & Joseph, R.M. (2012) Creating major innovations with customers: Insights from small and young technology firms. *Journal of Marketing*. 76(6), 87–104.

Cravens, D.W. (1995) The changing role of the sales force. *Marketing Management*. 4(2), 48–57.

Cravens, D.W. & Piercy, N. (2013) *Strategic Marketing*. Englewood Cliffs, NJ: McGraw-Hill/ Irwin.

Cravens, D.W., Ingram, T.N., Laforge, R.W. & Young, C.E. (1993) Behavior-based and outcome-based salesforce control systems. *Journal of Marketing*. 57(4), 47–59.

Cronbach, L.J. (1951) Coefficient alpha and the internal structure of tests. *Psychometrika*. 16(3), 297–334.

Croom, S.R. (2001) The dyadic capabilities concept: Examining the processes of key supplier involvement in collaborative product development. *European Journal of Purchasing and Supply Management*. 7(1), 29–37.

Croom, S.R., Svetina, M. & Betts, A. (2014) The process of strategic prioritization. How operations align priorities to customer or competitor performance. [Online] Available from: http://www.futurepurchasing.com/content/private/ProcTrans/Exploiting _Strategic_Power_Report.pdf.

Croom, S.R., Wilson, K., Millman, T., Senn, C. & Weilbaker, D. (1999) How to meet the challenge of managing global customers. *Velocity*: SAMA. 33–46.

Cummings, T.G. (1978) Self-regulating work groups: A socio-technical synthesis. *Academy of Management Review*. 11(3), 625–634.

Cunningham, M.T. & Homse, E. (1982) An interaction approach to marketing strategy. In: Håkansson, H. (ed.), *International Marketing and Purchasing of Industrial Goods*. New York: John Wiley & Sons.

Cunningham, M.T. & Turnbull, M.W. (1982) Inter-organizational contact patterns. In: Håkanssen, H. (ed.), *International Marketing and Purchasing of Industrial Goods*. New York: John Wiley & Sons.

Daboub, A.J. (2002) Strategic alliances, network organizations, and ethical responsibility. *SAM Advanced Management Journal*. 67(4), 40–48.

Daboub, A.J. & Calton, J.M. (2002) Stakeholder learning dialogues: How to preserve ethical responsibility in networks. *Journal of Business Ethics*. 41(1/2), 85–98.

Dalrymple, D.J. & Cron, W.L. (1992) *Sales Management: Concepts and Cases*. New York: John Wiley & Sons.

Danneels, E. (2003) Tight–loose coupling with customers: The Enactment of Customer Orientation. *Strategic Management Journal*. 24(6), 559–576.

Das, T.K. & Teng, B.S. (2001) Relational risk and its personal correlates in strategic alliances. *Journal of Business and Psychology*. 15(3), 449–465.

Dastmalchian, A. & Boag, D.A. (1990) Environmental dependence and departmental structure: Case of the marketing function. *Human Relations*. 43(12), 1257–1276.

Davenport, T.H. (1993) *Process Innovation: Reengineering Work through Information Technology*. Boston, MA: Harvard Business School Press.

Davenport, T.H. & Short, J.E. (1990) The new industrial engineering: Information technology and business process redesign. *Sloan Management Review*. 31(4), 11–27.

Davies, A., Brady, T. & Hobday, M. (2006) Charting a path toward integrated solutions. *MIT Sloan Management Review*. 47(3), 39–48.

Davies, I. & Ryals, L. (2009) A stage model for transitioning to KAM. *Journal of Marketing Management*. 25(9–10), 1027–1048.

Davies, I., Holt, S. & Ryals, L. (2007) *GAMs, KAMs & Relationship Managers*. Cranfield University Press.

Davies, I., Ryals, L. & Holt, S. (2010) Relationship management: A sales role, or a state of mind? An investigation of functions and attitudes across a business-to-business sales force. *Industrial Marketing Management*. 39(7), 1049–1062.

Davis, H.T. (1941) *The Analysis of Economic Time Series*. Bloomington, IN: Principia Press.

Day, G.S. (1994) The capabilities of market driven organizations. *Journal of Marketing*. 58(4), 37–52.

Day, G.S. (1997) Aligning the organization to the market. In: Lehmann, D.R. & Jocz, K.E. (eds.), *Reflections on the Futures of Marketing*. Cambridge: Marketing Science Institute. 67–93.

Day, G.S. (2000) Managing market relationships. *Journal of the Academy of Marketing Science*. 28(1), 24–30.

Day, G.S. (2003) Creating a superior customer-relating capability. *MIT Sloan Management Review*. 44(3), 77–82.

Day, G.S. (2006) *Aligning the Organization with the Market. Working Paper*. Cambridge: Marketing Science Institute.

Day, G.S. (2011) Closing the marketing capabilities gap. *Journal of Marketing*. 75(4), 183–195.

Day, G.S. & Klein, S. (1987) Cooperative behavior in vertical markets: The influence of transaction costs and competitive strategy. In: Houston, M. (ed.), *Review of Marketing*. Chicago: American Marketing Association. 39–66.

Day, G.S. & Montgomery, D.B. (1999) Charting new directions for marketing. *Journal of Marketing*. 63(Special Issue), 3–13.

de Boer, L., Labro, E. & Morlacci, O. (2001) A review of methods supporting supplier selection. *European Journal of Purchasing & Supply Management*. 7(2), 75–89.

de Roos, H.J., Sweerman, S.D. & de Koning, R.A. (1990) *Het Managen Van Industriâle Accounts: Veeleisend, Maar VeelbelovendReport*. Diemen: Bakkenist Management Consultants.

de Ruyter, K., Moorman, L. & Lemminck, J. (2001) Antecedents of commitment and trust in customer–supplier relationships in high technology markets. *Industrial Marketing Management*. 30(3), 271–286.

Dell, M. (2007) *Everyone Has A Choice*. Financial Times Digital Business – Special Report, April.

Demsetz, H. (1992) *The Emerging Theory of The Firm*. Uppsala: Acta Universitatas Uppsaliensis.

Denison, D.R., Hart, S.L. & Kahn, J.A. (1996) From chimneys to cross-functional teams: Developing and validating a diagnostic model. *Academy of Management Journal*. 39(4), 1005–1023.

Deshpande, R. (1982) The organizational context of market research use. *Journal of Marketing*. 46(4), 91–101.

Dess, G.G. & Beard, D.W. (1984) Dimensions of organizational task environments. *Administrative Science Quarterly*. 29(1), 52–73.

Deutsch, M. (1973) *The Resolution of Conflict*. New Haven, CT: Yale University Press.

Devellis, R.F. (1991) *Scale Development: Theory and Applications*. Thousand Oaks, CA: Sage Publications.

Dhanaraj, C. & Parkhe, A. (2006) Orchestrating innovation networks. *Academy of Management Review*. 31(3), 659–669.

Dhar, R. & Glazer, R. (2003) Hedging customers. *Harvard Business Review*. May. 86–92.

Dibb, S. & Wensley, R. (2002) Segmentation analysis for industrial markets: Problems of integrating customer requirements into operations strategy. *European Journal of Marketing*. 36(1), 231–251.

Dickson, P.R. (1983) Distributor portfolio analysis and the channel dependence matrix: New techniques for understanding and managing the channel. *Journal of Marketing*. 47(3), 35–44.

Diller, H. (1989) Key account management als verticalis Marketingkonzept. *Marketing – Zeitschift Fur Forschung und Praxis (ZFP)*. 11(4), 213–223.

Dishman, P. & Nitse, P.S. (1998) National accounts revisited: New lessons from recent investigations. *Industrial Marketing and Management*. 27(1), 1–9.

Dolan, R.J. (1995) Black & Decker Corp. (B): Operation Sudden Impact, Case No. 595060, Cambridge, MA: Harvard Business School Publishing.

Donaldson, S. & Grant-Vallone, E. (2002) Understanding self-report bias in organizational behavior research. *Journal of Business and Psychology*. 17(2), 245–260.

Donaldson, T. & Dunfee, T. (1999) *Ties That Bind: A Social Contracts Approach To Business Ethics*. Boston, MA: Harvard Business School Press.

Doney, P.M. & Cannon, J.M. (1997) An examination of the nature of trust in buyer–seller relationships. *Journal of Marketing*. 61(2), 35–51.

Donnellon, A. (1993) Cross functional teams in product development: Accommodating the structure to the process. *Journal of Product Innovation Management*. 10(5), 377–392.

Dorsch, M.J., Swanson, C.R. & Kelley, S.W. (1998) The role of relationship quality in the stratification of vendors as perceived by customers. *Journal of the Academy of Marketing Science*. 26(2), 128–142.

Dowling, G.R. & Uncles, M. (1997) Do customer loyalty programs really work? *Sloan Management Review*. 38(4), 71–82.

Doyle, P. (2002) *Marketing Management and Strategy* (3rd edition). London: Prentice-Hall.

Dubinsky, A.J. (1999) Salesperson failure: Sales management is the key. *Industrial Marketing Management*. 28(1), 7–17.

Dubinsky, A.J. & Ingram, T.N. (1984) A portfolio approach to account profitability. *Industrial Marketing Management*. 13(1), 33–41.

Dubinsky, A.J., Howell, R.D., Ingram, T.N. & Bellenger, D.N. (1986) Sales force socialization. *Journal of Marketing*. 50(4), 192–207.

Dubois, A. & Gadde, L.E. (2002) Systematic combining: An abductive approach to case research. *Journal of Business Research*. 55(7), 553–560.

Dubois, A. & Pedersen, A.C. (2002) Why relationships do not fit into purchasing portfolio models – A comparison between the portfolio and industrial network approaches. *European Journal of Purchasing and Supply Management*. 8(1), 35–42.

Dunn, D. & Thomas, C. (1994) Partnering with customers. *Journal of Business and Industrial Marketing*. 9(1), 34–40.

Durman, P. & Box, D. (2005) *Cut Off*. London: The Sunday Times.

Dwyer, F.R. (1989) Customer lifetime valuation to support marketing decision making. *Journal of Direct Marketing*. 3(4), 8–15.

Dwyer, F.R., Schurr, P. & Oh, S. (1987) Developing buyer–seller relationships. Journal of Marketing. 51(2), 11–27.

Dyer, J.H. (1997) Effective interfirm collaboration: How firms minimize transaction costs and maximize transaction value. *Strategic Management Journal*. 18(7), 535–556.

Dyer, J.H. (2000) *Collaborative Advantage: Winning Through Extended Enterprise Supplier Networks*. Oxford University Press.

Dyer, J.H. & Hatch, N.W. (2006) Relation-specific capabilities and barriers to knowledge transfers: Creating advantage through network relationships. *Strategic Management Journal*. 27(8), 701–719.

Dyer, J.H. & Nobeoka, K. (2000) Creating and managing a high-performance knowledge sharing network: The Toyota case. *Strategic Management Journal*. 21(3), 345–367.

Dyer, J.H. & Singh, H. (1998) The relational view: Cooperative strategy and sources of interorganizational competitive advantage. *Academy of Management Review*. 23(4), 660–679.

Dyer, J.H., Cho, D.S. & Chu, W. (1998) Strategic supplier segmentation: The next 'best practice' in supply chain management. *California Management Review*. 40(2), 57–77.

Eckerd, S. & Hill, J.A. (2012) The buyer–supplier social contract: Information sharing as a deterrent to unethical behaviors. *International Journal of Operations & Production Management*. 32(1–2), 238–255.

Edvardsson, B., Tronvoll, B. & Gruber, T. (2011) Expanding understanding of service exchange and value co-creation: a social construction approach. *Journal of the Academy of Marketing Science*. 39(2), 327–339.

Eggert, A., Ulaga, W. & Schultz, F. (2006) Value creation in the relationship cycle: A quasi-longitudinal analysis. *Industrial Marketing Management*. 35(1), 20–27.

Ehret, M. (2004) Managing the trade-off between relationships and value networks. Towards a value-based approach of customer relationship management in business-to-business markets. *Industrial Marketing Management*. 33(6), 465–473.

Eisenhardt, K.M. (1985), Control: Organizational and economic approaches. *Management Science*. 31(February), 134–149.

Eisenhardt, K.M. (1989) Building theories from case study research. *The Academy of Management Review*. 14(4), 532–551.

Eisenhardt, K.M. (2002) Has strategy changed? *Sloan Management Review*. 43(2), 88–91.

Eisenhardt, K.M. & Martin, J.A. (2000) Dynamic capabilities: What are they? *Strategic Management Journal*. 21(10–11), 1105–1121.

Elliott, G. & Glynn, W. (1998) Segmenting financial service markets for customer relationships: A portfolio-based approach. *The Service Industries Journal*. 18(3), 38–54.

Ellram, L.M. (1991) Key success factors and barriers in international purchasing partnerships. *Management Decision*. 29(7), 38–44.

Ellram, L.M. & Carr, A. (1994) Strategic purchasing: A history and review of the literature. *International Journal of Purchasing and Materials Management*. 30(2), 10–18.

Emberson, C. & Storey, J. (2006) Buyer–supplier collaborative relationships: Beyond the normative accounts. *Journal of Purchasing and Supply Management*. 12(5), 236–245.

Emshwiller, J.R. (1991) Suppliers struggle to improve quality as big firms slash their vendor roles. *Wall Street Journal*. B1. August 16.

Eng, T.Y. (2004) Does customer portfolio analysis relate to customer performance? An empirical analysis of alternative strategic perspective. *Journal of Business & Industrial Marketing.* 19(1), 49–67.

Eng, T.Y. (2008) Customer portfolio planning in a business network context. *Journal of Marketing Management.* 24(5–6), 567–587.

Ettenson, R., Conrado, E. & Knowles, J. (2013) Rethinking the 4 P's. *Harvard Business Review.* January–February, 26.

Fiocca, R. (1982) Account portfolio analysis for strategy development. *Industrial Marketing Management.* 11(1), 53–62.

Fisher, R.J., Maltz, E. & Jaworski, B.J. (1997) Enhancing communication between marketing and engineering: The moderating role of relative functional identification. *Journal of Marketing.* 61(3), 54–70.

Fitzsimmons, J.A. (1985), Consumer participation and productivity in service operations. *Interfaces.* 15(3), 60–67.

Flint, D.J. & Mentzer, J.T. (2006) Striving for integrated value chain management given a service–dominant logic for marketing. In: Lusch, R.F. & Vargo, S.L. (eds.), *The Service Dominant Logic of Marketing: Dialog, Debate and Direction.* New York: ME Sharpe. 139–149.

Flint, D.J., Woodruff, R.B. & Gardial, S.F. (2002) Exploring the phenomenon of customers' desired value change in a business-to-business context. *Journal of Marketing.* 66(4), 102–117.

Fontenot, R.J. & Hyman, M.R. (2004) The anti-trust implications of relationship marketing. *Journal of Business Research.* 57(11), 1211–1221.

Ford, D. (1980) The development of buyer seller relationships in industrial markets. *European Journal of Marketing.* 14(5/6), 339–354.

Ford, D. (1990) *Understanding Business Markets.* Waltham: Academic Press.

Ford, D. (1997) *Understanding Business Markets: Interaction, Relationships and Networks.* London: Academic Press.

Ford, D., (2001) The development of buyer–seller relationships in industrial markets, *European Journal of Marketing.* 14(5/6).

Ford, D. & Håkansson, H. (2006) The idea of interaction. *The IMP Journal.* 1(1), 4–27.

Ford, D., Gadde, L-E., Håkansson, H., Snehota, I., Turnbull, P. & Wilson, D. (1998) *Managing Business Relationships.* Chichester: John Wiley & Sons.

Ford, D., Gadde, L-E., Håkansson, H. & Snehota, I. (2003) *Managing Business Relationships.* Chichester: John Wiley & Sons.

Ford, D., Gadde. L.-E., Håkansson, H. & Snehota, I. (2011) *Managing Business Relationships.* Chichester: Wiley.

Ford, D., Håkansson, H. & Johanson, J. (1986) How do companies interact? *Industrial Marketing and Purchasing.* 1(1), 26–41.

Fornell, C. & Wernerfelt, B. (1988) A model for customer complaint management. *Marketing Science.* 7(3), 287–298.

Fornell, C. & Yi, Y. (1992) Assumptions of the two-step approach to latent variable modeling. *Sociological Methods and Research.* 20(3), 291–320.

Foxall, G. (1986) A conceptual extension of the customer active paradigm. *Technovation.* 4(1), 17–27.

Foxall, G. & Johnston, B. (1987) Strategies of user initiated product innovation. *Technovation.* 6(2), 77–102.

Francis, K. (2004) Should senior managers be actively involved in sales account management? *Journal of Personal Selling and Sales Management.* 24(3), 235–246.

Frankwick, G.L., Ward, J.C., Hutt, M.D. & Reingen, P.H. (1994) Evolving patterns of organizational beliefs in the formation of strategy. *Journal of Marketing.* 58(2), 96–110.

Frazier, G. (1983) On the measurement of interfirm power in channels of distribution. *Journal of Marketing Research*. 20(2), 158–166.

Frazier, G., Gill, J.D. & Kale, S.H. (1989) Dealer dependence levels and reciprocal actions in a channel of distribution in a developing country. *Journal of Marketing*. 53(1), 50–69.

Frazier, G., Spekman, R.E. & O'Neal, C.R. (1988) Just-in-time relationships in industrial markets. *Journal of Marketing*. 51(4), 52–67.

Freytag, P. & Mols, N. (2001) Customer portfolios and segmentation. In: Freytag, P. (ed.), *Portfolio Planning in a Relationship Perspective*. Copenhagen: Forlaget Thomson. 93–123.

Friedman, T.L. (2005) *The World is Flat: A Brief History of the Twenty-First Century*. New York: Farrar, Straus and Giroux.

Friedman, T.L. (2007) *The World is Flat 3.0: A Brief History of the Twenty-First Century*. New York: Picador.

Frow, P. & Payne, A. (2011) A stakeholder perspective of the value proposition concept. *European Journal of Marketing*. 45(1), 223–240.

Fruyt, F., McCrae, R., Szirmak, Z. & Nagy, J. (2004) The five-factor personality inventory as a measure of the five-factor model: Belgian, American, and Hungarian comparisons with the NEO-PI-R. *Assessment*. 11(3), 207–215.

Fry, M.L. & Polonsky, M.J. (2004) Examining the unintended consequences of marketing. *Journal of Business Research*. 57(11), 1303–1306.

Furlan, A., Grandinetti, R. & Camuffo, A. (2009) Business relationship portfolios and subcontractors' capabilities. *Industrial Marketing Management*. 38(8), 937–945.

Futrell, C.M. & Parasuraman, A. (1984) The relationship of satisfaction and performance to sales force turnover. *Journal of Marketing*. 48(4), 33–40.

Gadde, L.E. & Snehota, I. (2000) Making the most of supplier relationships. *Industrial Marketing Management*. 29(4), 305–316.

Galbraith, J.R. (1995) *Designing Organizations: An Executive Briefing on Strategy, Structure, and Process*. San Francisco: Jossey-Bass.

Galbraith, J.R. (2001) Building organizations around the global customer. *Ivey Business Journal*. 66(1), 17–24.

Gallagher, T.A. (2000) *Financial Management* (2nd edition). New Jersey: Prentice-Hall.

Ganesan, S. (1994) Determinants of long-term orientation in buyer–seller relationship. *Journal of Marketing*. 58(2), 1–19.

Gao, T. & Shi, L.H. (2011) How do multinational suppliers formulate mechanisms of global account coordination? An integrative framework and empirical study. *Journal of International Marketing*. 19(4), 61–87.

Gardner, A., Bistritz, S.J. & Klopmaker, J.E. (1998) Selling to senior executives: Part 2. *Marketing Management*. 7(3), 18–27.

Garrette, B. & Dussauge, P. (1995) *Les stratégies d'alliance*. Paris: Editions d'organisation. 283.

Gaski, J.F. (1984) The theory of power and conflict in channels of distribution. *Journal of Marketing*. 48(3), 9–29.

Gebert, H., Geib, M., Kolbe, L. & Brenner, W. (2003) Knowledge-enabled customer relationship management: Integrating customer relationship management and knowledge management concepts. *Journal of Knowledge Management*. 7(5), 107–123.

Geiger, S. & Guenzi, P. (2009) The sales function in the twenty-first century: Where we are and where we do go from here? *European Journal of Marketing*. 43(7/8), 873–889.

Gelderman, C.J. & van Weele, A.J. (2003) Handling measurement issues and strategic directions in Kraljic's purchasing portfolio model. *Journal of Purchasing & Supply Management*. 9(4/5), 207–216.

Georges, L. (2006) Delivering integration, value, and satisfaction through key account managers' communication. *Journal of Selling & Major Account Management.* 6(1), 6–21.

Georges, L. & Eggert, A. (2003) Key account managers' role within the value creation process of collaborative relationships. *Journal of Business-to-business Marketing.* 10(4), 1–22.

Germain, R. & Dröge, C. (1997) Effect of just-in-time purchasing relationships on organizational design, purchasing department configuration, and firm performance. *Industrial Marketing and Management.* 26(2), 115–125.

Germain, R., Dröge, C. & Daugherty, P.J. (1994) The effect of just-in-time selling on organizational structure: An empirical investigation. *Journal of Marketing Research.* 31(4), 471–483.

Geyskens, I., Steenkamp, J.E.M. & Kumar, N. (1998) Generalizations about trust in marketing channel relationships using meta-analysis. *International Journal of Research in Marketing.* 15(3), 223–248.

Geyskens, I., Steenkamp, J.E.M. & Kumar, N. (1999) A meta-analysis of satisfaction in marketing channel relationships. *Journal of Marketing Research.* 36(2), 223–238.

Geyskens, I., Steenkamp, J.E.M., Scheer, L.K. & Kumar, N. (1996) The effects of trust and interdependence on relationship commitment: A trans-Atlantic study. *International Journal of Research in Marketing.* 13(4), 303–317.

Ghemawat, P. (1993) Commitment to a process innovation: Nucor, USX, and Thin-Slab casting. *Journal of Economics & Management Strategy.* 2(1), 135–161.

Gibson, C.B. & Birkinshaw, J. (2004) The antecedents, consequences, and mediating role of organizational ambidexterity. *Academy of Management Journal.* 47(2), 209–226.

Gist, M.E., Locke, E.A. & Taylor, M.S. (1987) Organizational behavior: Group structure, process, and effectiveness. *Journal of Management.* 13(2), 237–257.

Giunipero, L. & Pearcy, D. (2000) World class purchasing skills: An empirical investigation. *Journal of Supply Chain Management.* 36(4), 4–13.

Gladstein, D.L. (1984) Groups in context: A model of task group effectiveness. *Administrative Science Quarterly.* 29(4), 499–517.

Godfrey, P.C. (2006) Strategic account development workshop. Unpublished. Halcrow.

Godfrey, P.C. & Hatch, N.W. (2007) Researching corporate responsibility: An agenda for the 21st Century. *Journal of Business Ethics.* 70(1), 87–98.

Gök, O. (2007) Using customer portfolio analysis for strategic business decisions: Case study of a logistics company. *3rd International Strategic Management Conference.* Antalya, Turkey. 757–765.

Gök, O. (2009) Linking account portfolio management to customer information: Using customer satisfaction metrics for portfolio analysis. *Industrial Marketing Management.* 38(4), 433–439.

Goldberg, L. (1981) Language and individual differences: the search for universals in personality lexicons. *Review of Personality and Social Psychology.* 2, 141–165.

Goldberg, L. (1999) A broad-bandwidth, public-domain, personality inventory measuring the lower-level facets of several five-factor models. In: Mervielde, I. & Goldberg, L. (1981) Language and individual differences: The search for universals in personality lexicons. In: Wheeler, L. (ed.), *Review of Personality and Social Psychology.* Beverly Hills, CA: SAGE Publishing. 295.

Goldberg, L., Johnson, J.A., Eber, H.W., Hogan, R., Ashton, M.C., Cloninger, C.R. & Gough, H.G. (2006) The international personality item pool and the future of public-domain personality measures. *Journal of Research in Personality.* 40(1), 84–96.

Goldberg, L.R. & Deary, I. (eds.), *Personality Psychology in Europe.* Tilburg University Press. 399.

Golfetto, F. & Gibbert, M. (2006) Marketing competencies and the sources of customer value in business markets. *Industrial Marketing Management.* 35(8), 904–912.

Gopalan, R. (2007), Customer portfolio management using Z-ranking of customer segments and the LTV perturbation method. *Database Marketing & Customer Strategy Management.* 14(3), 225–235.

Gosman, M.L. & Kelly, T. (2000) Increased buyer concentration and its effects on profitability in the manufacturing sector. *Review of Industrial Organization.* 17(1), 41–59.

Gosselin, D. & Bauwen, G.A. (2006) Strategic account management: Customer value creation through customer alignment. *Journal of Business & Industrial Marketing.* 21(6), 376–385.

Gosselin, D. & Heene, A. (2003) A competence-based analysis of account management: Implications for a customer-focused organization. *Journal of Selling and Major Account Management.* 5(1), 11–31.

Gounaris, S. & Tzempelikos, N. (2012) Conceptualization and measurement of key account management orientation. *Journal of Business Market Management.* 5(3), 173–194.

Grant, J. (2005) Mr Daley's mission: To reach 6bn shoppers and make money. *Financial Times.* July 15. 32.

Greenwald, J. (1996) Frito-Lay Under Snack Attack. *Time.* (June 10), 62–63.

Greer, C.R. & Lei, D. (2011) Collaborative innovation with customers: A review of the literature and suggestions for future research. *International Journal of Management Reviews.* 14(1), 63–84.

Grickscheit, G.M., Cash, H.C., & Young, C.E. (1993) *Handbook Of Selling: Psychological, Managerial and Marketing Dynamics.* New York: John Wiley & Sons.

Grönroos, C. (1994a) Quo vadis marketing? Towards a relationship marketing paradigm. *Journal of Marketing Management.* 10(5), 347–360.

Grönroos, C. (1994b) From marketing mix to relationship marketing – Towards a paradigm shift in marketing. *Asia–Australia Marketing Journal.* 2(1), 322–340.

Grönroos, C. (1997) Value-driven relational marketing: From products to resources and competencies. *Journal of Marketing Management.* 13(5), 407–419.

Grönroos, C. (1999) Relationship marketing: Challenges for the organization. *Journal of Business Research.* 46(3), 327–335.

Grönroos, C. (2008) Service logic revisited: Who creates value and who co-creates? *European Business Review.* 20(4), 298–314.

Grönroos, C. (2011) A service perspective on business relationships: The value creation, interaction and marketing interface. *Industrial Marketing Management.* 40(2), 240–247.

Grönroos, C. & Ravald, A. (2011) Service as business logic: Implications for value creation and marketing. *Journal of Services Management.* 22(1), 5–22.

Guenzi, P., Georges, L. & Pardo, C. (2009) The impact of strategic account managers' behaviors on relational outcomes: An empirical study. *Industrial Marketing Management.* 38(3), 300–311.

Guesalaga, R. & Johnston, W. (2010) What's next in key account management research? Building the bridge between the academic literature and the practitioners' priorities. *Industrial Marketing Management.* 39(7), 1063–1068.

Guinipero, L. & Pearcy, D. (2000) World class purchasing skills: An empirical investigation. *Journal of Supply Chain Management.* 36(4), 4–13.

Gulati, R., Nohria, N. & Zaheer, A. (2000) Strategic Networks. *Strategic Management Journal.* 21, 203–215.

Gummesson, E. (1987) The new marketing: Developing long-term interactive relationships. *Long Term Planning.* 20(4), 10–20.

Gummesson, E. (1991) Marketing-orientation revisited: The crucial role of the part-time marketer. *European Journal of Marketing*. 25(2), 60–75.

Gummesson, E. (1997) In search of marketing equilibrium: Relationship marketing versus hypercompetition. *Journal of Marketing Management*. 13(5), 421–430.

Gummesson, E. (2000) *Qualitative Methods in Management Research*. Thousand Oaks, CA: Sage Publications.

Gummesson, E. (2005) Qualitative research in marketing – Road-map for a wilderness of complexity and unpredictability. *European Journal of Marketing*. 39(3/4), 309–327.

Gundlach, G.T. & Cadotte, E.R. (1994) Exchange interdependence and interfirm interaction: Research in a simulated channel setting. *Journal of Marketing Research*. 31(4), 516–532.

Gundlach, G.T. & Murphy, P.E. (1993) Ethical and legal foundations of relational marketing exchanges. *Journal of Marketing*. 57(4), 35–46.

Gundlach, G.T., Achrol, R.S. & Mentzer, J.T. (1995) The structure of commitment in exchange. *Journal of Marketing*. 59(1), 78–92.

Gupta, A.K., Raj, S. & Wilemon, D.L. (1986) A model for studying the R&D–marketing interface in the product innovation process. *Journal of Marketing*. 50(2), 7–17.

Gupta, S. & Lehmann, D.R. (2003) Customers as assets. *Journal of Interactive Marketing*. 17(1), 9–24.

Gupta, S. & Lehmann, D.R. (2005) *Managing Customers as Investments: The Strategic Value of Customers in the Long Run*. Upper Saddle River, NJ: Wharton School Publishing.

Gupta, S. & Lehmann, D.R. (2007) *Managing Customers as Investments*. Upper Saddle River, NJ: Pearson Education, Inc.

Gupta, S. & Zeithaml, V. (2006) Customer metrics and their impact on financial performance. *Marketing Science*. 25(6), 718–739.

Gupta, S., Hanssens, D., Hardie, B., Kahn, W., Kumar, V., Lin, N., Ravishanker, N. & Sriram, S. (2006) Modeling customer lifetime value. *Journal of Service Research*. 9(2), 139–155.

Gupta, S., Lehmann, D.R. & Stuart, J.A. (2004) Valuing customers. *Journal of Marketing Research*. 41(February), 7–18.

Haas, A., Snehota, I. & Corsaro, D. (2012) Creating value in business relationships: The role of sales. *Industrial Marketing Management*. 41(1), 94–105.

Hackman, J.R. (1987) The design of work teams. In: Lorsch, J.W. (ed.), *Handbook of Organizational Behaviour*. Englewood Cliffs, NJ: Prentice-Hall. 315–342.

Hadjikhani, A. (1996) Project marketing and the management of discontinuity. *International Business Review*. 5(3), 319–336.

Håkansson, H. (1982) An interaction approach. In: Håkansson, H. (ed.), *International Marketing and Purchasing of Industrial Goods*. Chichester: John Wiley & Sons, 10–27.

Håkansson, H. (1982) *International Marketing and Purchasing of Industrial Goods*. Chichester: John Wiley & Sons.

Håkansson, H. (1986) The Swedish approach to Europe. In: Turnbull, P., Valla, J. & Croom, H. (eds.), *Strategies for Industrial Marketing*. London: Croom Helm.

Håkansson, H. & Olsen, P.I. (2012) Innovation management in networked economies. *Journal of Business Marketing Management*. 5(2), 79–105.

Håkansson, H. & Pedersen, A.C. (1999) Learning in networks. *Industrial Marketing Management*. 28, 443–452.

Håkansson, H. & Snehota, I. (1995) *Developing Relationship in Business Networks*. London: Routledge.

Håkansson H. & Snehota, I. (1998) The burden of relationships or who's next? In: Naude, P. & Turnbull, P.W. (eds.), *Network Dynamics in International Marketing*. Oxford: Elsevier Science.

Håkansson, H. & Snehota, I. (2006) No business is an island: The network concept of business strategy. *Scandinavian Journal of Management.* 22(3), 256–270.

Håkansson, H., Ford, D., Gadde, L-E. & Snehota, I. (2009) *Business in Networks.* Chichester: John Wiley & Sons.

Håkansson, H., Havila, V. & Pedersen, A.-C. (1999) Learning in Networks. *Industrial Marketing Management.* 28, 443–452.

Håkansson, H., Johansson, J. & Wootz, B. (1977) Influence tactics in buyer–seller processes. *Industrial Marketing Management.* 5(6), 319–332.

Hallen, L., Johanson, J. & Sayed-Mohamed, N. (1991) Interfirm adaptation in business relationships. *Journal of Marketing.* 55(2), 29–37.

Hambrick, D.C. & Mason, P.A. (1984) Upper echelons: The organization as a reflection of its top managers. *Academy of Management Review.* 9(2), 193–206.

Hambrick, D.C., Cho, T. & Chen, M. (1996) The influence of top management team heterogeneity on firms' competitive moves. *Administrative Science Quarterly.* 41(4), 659–684.

Hamel, G. & Välikangas, L. (2003) The quest for resilience. *Harvard Business Review.* 81(9), 52–63.

Hammer, M. (1990) Reengineering work: Don't automate, obliterate. *Harvard Business Review.* 68(4), 104–112.

Hammersley, M., & Atkinson, P. (1991) *Ethnographic Principles in Practice.* London: Routledge.

Hanan, M. (1985) *Key Account Selling.* New York: American Management Association.

Hannan, M.T., Burton, M.D. & Baron, J.N. (1996) Inertia and change in the early years: Employment relations in young, high-technology firms. *Industrial and Corporate Change.* 5(2), 503–536.

Harrigan, K.R. (2001) Strategic flexibility in the old and new economies. In: Hitt, M.A., Freeman, R.E. & Harrison, J.S. (eds.), *The Blackwell Handbook of Strategic Management.* Hoboken, NJ: John Wiley & Sons.

Harris, I.C. & Ruefli, T.W. (2000) The strategy/structure debate: An examination of the performance implications. *Journal of Management Studies.* 37(4), 587–603.

Harrison, D. & Finch, J. (2009) New product development when you have to: Frames and temporary collaboration in industrial nets. *IMP Journal.* 3(3), 35–52.

Harrison, D. & Waluszewski, A. (2008) The development of a user network as a way to re-launch an unwanted product. *Research Policy.* 37(1), 115–130.

Hartley, R.F. (1976) Use of customer analysis for better market penetration. *Industrial Marketing Management.* 5, 57–62.

Harvey, M. & Speier, C. (2000) Developing an inter-organization relational management perspective. *Journal of Marketing Channels.* 7(4), 23–44.

Harvey, M., Myers, M.B. & Novicevic, M.M. (2003a) The managerial issues associated with global account management: A relational contract perspective. *Journal of Management Development.* 22(2), 103–129.

Harvey, M., Novicevic, M.M., Hench, T. & Myers, M.B. (2003b) Global account management: A supply-side managerial view. *Industrial Marketing Management.* 32(7), 563–571.

Hawkes, S. (2008) 'M&S supplier scraps dividend as costs rise', *Times Business Section,* March 25.

Heide, J. B. & Wathne, K.H. (2006) Friends, businesspeople, and relationship roles: A conceptual framework and a research agenda. *Journal of Marketing.* 70(3), 90–103.

Heide, J.B. (1994) Interorganizational governance in marketing channels. *Journal of Marketing.* 58(1), 71–85.

Heide, J.B. & John, G. (1988) The role of dependence balancing in safeguarding transaction-specific assets in conventional channels. *Journal of Marketing.* 52(1), 20–35.

Heide, J.B. & John, G. (1990) Alliances in industrial purchasing: The determinants of joint action in buyer–supplier relationships. *Journal of Marketing Research*. 27(1), 24–36.

Heide, J.B. & Stump, R.L. (1995) Performance implications of buyer–seller relationships in industrial markets. *Journal of Business Research*. 32(1), 57–66.

Heikkilä, J. & Holmström, J. (2006) The impact of RFID and agent technology innovation on cost efficiency and agility. *International Journal of Agile Manufacturing*. 9(1), 3–9.

Helgesen, Ø. (2006) Are loyal customers profitable? Customer satisfaction, customer loyalty and customer profitability at the individual level. *Journal of Marketing Management*. 22(3–4), 245–266.

Helper, S. (1993) An exit-voice analysis of supplier relations: The case of the automobile industry. In Grabner, G. (ed.), *The Embedded Firm: On the Socioeconomics of Industrial Networks*, London: Routledge.

Helper, S. & Sako, M. (1995) Supplier relations in Japan and the United States: Are they converging? *Sloan Management Review*. 97(8), 77–84.

Helsing, J., Geraghty, B. & Napolitano, L. (2003) *Impact Without Authority*. Chicago: SAMA.

Hempel, J. (2011) IBM's super second act. *Fortune*. March 21, 55–61.

Henneberg, S.C., Pardo, C., Mouzas, S. and Naudé, P. (2005) Value dimensions and strategies in dyadic 'key relationships programmes', Paper presented at the 21st IMP Conference, Rotterdam.

Henneberg, S.C., Pardo, C., Mouzas, S. & Naudé, P. (2009) Value dimensions and relationship postures in dyadic 'key relationship programmes'. *Journal of Marketing Management*. 25(5–6), 535–550.

Hennessey, H.D. & Jeannet, J. (2003) *Global Account Management: Creating Value*. New York: John Wiley & Sons.

Heuchert, J., Parker, W., Stumpf, H. & Myburgh, C. (2000) The five-factor model of personality in South African college students. *American Behavioral Scientist*. 44(1), 112–125.

Hill, T. (1985) *Manufacturing Strategy. The Strategic Management of the Manufacturing Function*, Open University Book.

Hilton, R.W. (2008) *Managerial Accounting*. New York: McGraw-Hill/Irwin.

Hinterhuber, A. & Liozu, S. (2012) *Is It Time to Rethink Your Pricing Strategy?MIT Sloan Management Review*. [Online]. Available from: http://sloanreview.mit.edu/the –magazine/2012–summer/53413/is–it–time–to–rethink–your–pricing–strategy/

Hocutt, M.A. (1998) Relationship dissolution model: Antecedents of relationship commitment and the likelihood of dissolving a relationship. *International Journal of Service Industry Management*. 9(2), 189–200.

Hoekstra, J.C. & Huizingh, E.K. (1999) The lifetime value concept in customer-based marketing. *Journal of Market-Focused Management*. 3(3–4), 257–274.

Hoholm, T. & Olsen, P.I. (2012) The contrary forces of innovation: A conceptual model for studying networked innovation processes. *Industrial Marketing Management*. 41(2), 344–356.

Holbrook, M.B. (1994) The nature of customer value: Axiology services in the consumption experience. In: Rust, R.T. & Oliver, R.L. (eds.), *Service Quality: New Directions in Theory and Practice*. Thousand Oaks, CA: Sage.

Holland, C. & Naudé, P. (2004) The metamorphosis of marketing into an information-handling problem. *Journal of Business & Industrial Marketing*. 19(3), 167–177.

Holmlund, M. (2004) Analyzing business relationships and distinguishing different interaction levels. *Industrial Marketing Management*. 33(4), 279–287.

Holt, S. (2003) The role of the global account manager: A boundary role theory perspective. Unpublished PhD Thesis. Cranfield University.

Holt, S. & McDonald, M. (2001) A boundary role theory perspective of the global account manager. *Journal of Selling and Major Account Management*. 3(4), 9–31.

Homburg, C. & Baumgartner, H. (1998) Beurteilung von Kausalmodellen. Bestandsaufnahme und Anwendungsempfehlungen. In: Hildebrandt, L. & Homburg, C. (eds.), *Die Kausalanalyse*. Stuttgart: Instrument derempirischenbetriebswirtschaftlichenForschung. 343–370.

Homburg, C. & Pflesser, C. (2000), A multiple-layer model of market-oriented organizational culture: Measurement issues and performance outcomes. *Journal of Marketing Research*. 37(4), 449–462.

Homburg, C., Hoyer, W. & Koschate, N. (2005) Customers' reactions to price increases: do customer satisfaction and perceived motive fairness matter? *Journal of Academy of Marketing Science*. 33(1), 36–49.

Homburg, C., Steiner, V.V. & Totzek, D. (2009) Managing dynamics in a customer portfolio. *Journal of Marketing*. 73(5), 70–89.

Homburg, C., Workman, J. & Jensen, O. (2000) Fundamental changes in marketing organization: The movement towards customer focused organizational structures. *Journal of the Academy of Marketing Science*. 28(4), 459–478.

Homburg, C., Workman, J. & Jensen, O. (2002) A configuration perspective on key account management. *Journal of Marketing*. 66(2), 38–60.

Homburg, C., Workman, J. & Krohmer, H. (1999) Marketing's influence within the firm. *Journal of Marketing*. 63(2), 1–17.

Hong, R., Paunonen, S. & Slade, H. (2008) Big five personality factors and the prediction of behavior: A multitrait–multimethod approach. *Personality and Individual Differences*. 45(2), 160–166.

Hooley, G., Piercy, N.F. & Nicoulaud, B. (2012) *Marketing Strategy and Competitive Positioning*. Harlow: FT/Prentice-Hall.

Howard, M., Miemczyk, J. & Graves, A. (2006) Automotive supplier parks: An Imperative for Build-to-Order. *Journal of Purchasing and Supply Management*. 12(2), 91–104.

Hsieh, M.H. & Chou, W.C. (2011) Managing key account portfolios across the process of relationship development: A value proposition-desired value alignment perspective. *Journal of Business-to-business Marketing*. 18(1), 83–119.

Hu, L. & Bentler, P.M. (1999) Cutoff criteria for fit indexes in covariance structure analysis: Conventional criteria versus new alternatives. *Structural Equation Modeling*. 6(1), 1–55.

Hui Shi, L., Zou, S. & Cavusgil, S.T. (2004) A conceptual framework of global account management capabilities and firm performance. *International Business Review*. 13(5), 539–553.

Hult, G.T., Hurley, R.F. & Knight, G.A. (2004) Innovativeness: Its antecedents and impact on business performance. *Industrial Marketing Management*. 33(5), 429–438.

Hunt, S.D. (1991) *Modern Marketing Theory: Critical Issues in the Philosophy of Marketing Science*. New York: South-Western.

Hunt, S.D. (1999) The strategic imperative and sustainable competitive advantage: Public policy implications of resource-advantage theory. *Journal of the Academy of Marketing Science*. 27(2), 144–159.

Hunt, S.D. (2000) A *General Theory of Competition: Resources, Competences, Productivity, Economic Growth*. Thousand Oaks, CA: Sage Publications.

Hunter, G.K. & Perreault, W.D. (2007) Making sales technology effective. *Journal of Marketing*. 71(1), 16–34.

Hunter, M.W. (1987) Getting started in national account marketing. *Business Marketing*. 61–64.

Hurley, R.F. (1998) Managing change: an ethnographic approach to developing research propositions and understanding change in sales organizations. *Journal of Personal Selling and Sales Management.* 18(3), 57–71.

Hurtz, G. & Donovan, J. (2000) Personality and job performance: The big five revisited. *Journal of Applied Psychology.* 85(6), 869–879.

Hutt, M.D. & Walker, B.A. (2006) A network perspective of account manager performance. *Journal of Business & Industrial Marketing.* 21(7), 466–473.

Hutt, M.D., Johnston, W.S. & Ronchetto, J.R. (1985) Selling centres and buying centres: Formulating strategic exchange patterns. *Journal of Personal Selling & Sales Management.* 5(1), 33–40.

Hutt, M.D., Reingen, P.H. & Ronchetto, J.R. (1988) Tracing emergent processes in marketing strategy formation, *Journal of Marketing.* 52(1), 4–19.

Hyatt, D.E. & Ruddy, T.M. (1997) An examination of the relationship between work group characteristics and performance: Once more into the breach. *Personnel Psychology.* 50(3), 553–585.

Ingemansson, M. & Waluszewski, A. (2009) The relative benefits of an innovation: Its appearance in the academic, venture capital and user setting. *The IMP Journal.* 3(2), 20–56.

Ivens, B.S. & Pardo, C. (2003) Are key account relationships different? Empirical results on supplier strategies and customer reactions. *Proceedings of the 19th Annual IMP Conference, Lugano, September 4–6, 2003.*

Ivens, B.S. & Pardo, C. (2005) When a relationship is 'transactionalized': The introduction of reverse auctions in a key account relationship. *The 21st Annual IMP Conference.* Rotterdam, Netherland.

Ivens, B.S. & Pardo, C. (2007, 2003) Are key account relationships different? Empirical results on supplier strategies and customer reactions. *Industrial Marketing Management.* 36(4), 470–482.

Ivens, B.S. & Pardo, C. (2008) Key account management in business markets: An empirical test of common assumptions. *Journal of Business & Industrial Marketing.* 23(5), 301–310.

Jackson, B.B. (1985) *Winning and Keeping Industrial Customers: The Dynamics of Customer Relationships. Lexington,* MA: D.C. Heath and Company.

Jacobs, F.A., Johnston, W. & Kotchetova, N. (2001) Customer profitability: Prospective vs. retrospective approaches in a business-to-business setting. *Industrial Marketing Management.* 30(4), 353–363.

Jagdish, S. & Sharma, A. (1997), Relationship marketing: An agenda for inquiry. *Industrial Marketing Management.* 26(2), 87–89.

Jain, D. & Singh, S.S. (2002), Customer lifetime value research in marketing: A review and future directions. *Journal of Interactive Marketing.* 16(2), 34–46.

Janda, S. & Seshadri, S. (2001) The influence of purchasing strategies on performance. *Journal of Business & Industrial Marketing.* 16(4), 294–308.

Jap, S.D. (1999) Pie-expansion efforts: Collaboration processes in buyer–supplier relationships. *Journal of Marketing Research.* 36(4), 461–475.

Jap, S.D. (2001) 'Pie sharing' in complex collaboration contexts. *Journal of Marketing Research.* 38(1), 86–99.

Jap, S.D. (2003) An exploratory study of the introduction of online reverse auctions. *Journal of Marketing.* 67(3), 96–107.

Jap, S.D. & Ganesan, S. (2000) Control mechanisms and the relationship life cycle: Implications for safeguarding specific investments and developing commitment. *Journal of Marketing Research.* 37(2), 227–245.

Jaworski, B.J. & Kohli, A.K. (1993) Market orientation: Antecedents and consequences. *Journal of Marketing.* 57(July), 53–70.

Johanson, J., Hallen, L., & Seyed-Mohamed, N. (1991) Interfirm Adaptation in Business Relationship. *Journal of Marketing.* 55(2), 29–37.

John, G. & Reve, T. (1982) The reliability and validity of key informant data from dyadic relationships in marketing channels. *Journal of Marketing Research.* 19(4), 517–524.

John, O. & Srivastava, S. (1999) The big five trait taxonomy: History, measurement, and theoretical perspectives. In: Pervin, L. & John, O. (eds.), *Handbook of Personality: Theory and Research.* New York: Guilford Press.

Johnson, D.S., Clark, B.H. & Barczak, G. (2012) Customer relationship management processes: How faithful are business-to-business firms to customer profitability? *Industrial Marketing Management.* 41(8), 1094–1105.

Johnson, J. & Duyn, A.V. (2007) Pressure on clothes retailers after gap child labour allegation. *Financial Times.* October 29, 6.

Johnson, M.D. & Selnes, F. (2004) Customer portfolio management: Toward a dynamic theory of exchange relationships. *Journal of Marketing.* 68(2), p.1–17.

Johnson, T. & Ford, D. (2007) Customer approaches to product development with suppliers. *Industrial Marketing Management.* 36(3), 300–308.

Johnston, D.A., Mccutcheon, D.M., Stuart, F.I. & Kerwood, H. (2004) Effects of supplier trust on performance of cooperative supplier relationships. *Journal of Operations Management.* 22(1), 23–38.

Johnston, W.J. & Bonoma, T.V. (1981) The buying center: Structure and interaction patterns. *Journal of Marketing.* 45(3), 143–156.

Jolson, M.A. (1997) Broadening the scope of relationship selling. *Journal of Personal Selling & Sales Management.* 17(4), p.75–88.

Jones, E., Brown, S.P., Zoltners, A.A. & Weitz, B.A. (2005) The changing environment of selling and sales management. *Journal of Personal Selling & Sales Management.* 25(2), 105–111.

Jones, E., Dixon, A.L., Chonko, L.B & Cannon, J. (2005) Key accounts and team selling: A review, framework, and research agenda. *Journal of Personal Selling & Sales Management.* 25(2), 181–198.

Jones, E., Roberts, J.A. & Chonko, L.B. (2000) Motivating sales entrepreneurs to change: A conceptual framework of factors leading to successful change management initiatives in sales organizations. *Journal of Marketing Theory & Practice.* 8(2), 37–50.

Jones, T.M. (1991) Ethical decision making by individuals in organizations: An issue-contingent model. *Academy of Management Review.* 16(2), 366–395.

Joshi, A.W. & Stump, R.L. (1999a) The contingent effect of specific asset investments on joint action in manufacturer–supplier relationships: An empirical test of the moderating role of reciprocal asset investments, uncertainty, and trust. *Journal of the Academy of Marketing Science.* 27(3), 291–305.

Joshi, A.W. & Stump, R.L. (1999b) Transaction cost analysis: Integration of recent refinements and an empirical test. *Journal of Business-to-business Marketing.* 5(4), 37–72.

Jouini, O., Dallery, Y. & Nait, A.R. (2004) Stochastic models of customer portfolio management in call centers. *Annual International Conference of the German Operation Research Society.* Tilburg, Netherlands.

Jüttner, U., Godsell, J. & Christopher, M.G. (2006) Demand chain alignment competence delivering value through product life cycle management. *Industrial Marketing Management.* 35(8), 989–1001.

Kaario, K., Pennanen, R. & Storbacka, K. (2004) *Selling Value – Maximize Growth by Helping Customers Succeed.* Helsinki: WSOY.

REFERENCES

Kahn, K.B. & Mentzer, J.T. (1998) Marketing's integration with other departments. *Journal of Business Research*. 42(1), 53–62.

Kahn, R.L., Wolfe, D.M., Quinn, R.P. and Snoek, J.D. (1964) *Organisational Stress: Studies in Role Conflict and Ambiguity*. New York: John Wiley & Sons.

Kalafatis, S. & Denton, A. (2000) A method for estimating the profit impact of a discount scheme. *Journal of Business-to-business Marketing*. 7(1), 19–43.

Kalwani, M.U. & Narayandas, N. (1995) Long-term manufacturer–supplier relationships: Do they pay off for supplier firms? Journal of Marketing. 59(1), 1–16.

Kaplan, R.S. (2005a) *A Balanced Scorecard Approach to Measure Customer Profitability*. Harvard Business School.

Kaplan, R.S. (2005b) How the balanced scorecard complements the McKinsey 7–S Model. *Strategy & Leadership*. 33(3), 41–46.

Kaplan, R.S. & Norton, D. (2006) *Alignment–Using the Balanced Scorecard to Create Corporate Synergies*. Harvard Business School Press.

Kaufman, A., Wood, C. H. & Theyel, G. (2000) Collaboration and technology linkages: A strategic supplier typology. *Strategic Management Journal*. 21(6), 649–663.

Kempeners, M.A. (1997) Key account management: Between failure and success. *13th IMP conference*. Lyon, France.

Kempeners, M.A. & van der Hart, H.W. (1999) Designing account management organizations. Journal of Business & Industrial Marketing. 14(4), 310–335.

Kerin, R.A., Varadarajan, P.R. & Peterson, R.A. (1992) First-mover advantage: A synthesis, conceptual framework, and research propositions. *Journal of Marketing*. 56(4), 33–52.

Kim, K.K., Park, S-H., Ryoo, S.Y. & Park, S.K. (2010) Inter-organizational cooperation in buyer–supplier relationships: Both perspectives. *Journal of Business Research*. 63(8), 863–869.

Kirkby, (1988) Creating major sales. In: Forsyth, (ed.), *Sales Management Handbook*. Hoboken, NJ: John Wiley & Sons Ltd.

Kirkman, B.L. & Rosen, B. (1999) Beyond self-management: Antecedents and consequences of team empowerment. *Academy of Management Journal*. 42(1), 58–74.

Kirkman, B.L., Rosen, B., Tesluk, T. & Gibson, C. (2004) The impact of team empowerment on virtual team performance: The moderating role of face-to-face interaction. *Academy of Management Journal*. 47(2), 175–192.

Kirkpatrick, D. (2005) IBM shares its secrets. *Fortune*. September 5, 60–67.

Kirwan, J. (1992) The precision selling payoff. *Sales & Marketing Management*. 144(January), 58–61.

Klein, B. (1996) Why hold-ups occur: The self-enforcing range of contractual relationships. *Economic Inquiry*. 34(3), 444–463.

Kleinaltenkamp, M. & Ehret, M. (2006) The value added by specific investments – A framework for managing relationships in the context of value networks. *Journal of Business and Industrial Marketing*. 21(2), 65–71.

Kleintenkamp, M. & Ricker, S.A. (1997). Kundenovientierte Organisation. In: Kleintenkamp, M. & Plinke, W. (eds.) *Strategisches Business to Business Marketing*. Berlin: Springer.

Kohli, A.K. (1985) Some unexplored supervisory behaviors and their influence on salespeople's role clarity, specific self-esteem, job satisfaction, and motivation. *Journal of Marketing Research*. 22(4), 424–433.

Kohli, A.K. & Jaworski, B.J. (1990) Market orientation: The construct, research propositions, and managerial implications. *Journal of Marketing*. 54(2), 1–18.

Koopmans, T. (1957) *Three Essays on The State of Economic Science*. New York: Martino Fine Books.

REFERENCES

Kotler, P. (1997) *Marketing Management: Analysis, Planning, Implementation, and Control* (9th edition). Upper Saddle River, NJ: Prentice-Hall, Inc.

Kotler, P., Armstrong, G., Saunders, J. & Wong, V. (1996) *Principles of Marketing*. London: Prentice-Hall.

Kotter, J. (1995) Leading change. Why transformational efforts fail. *Harvard Business Review*. March–April, 59–67.

Kowalkowski, C. (2011) Dynamics of value propositions: Insights from service-dominant logic. *European Journal of Marketing*. 45(1/2), 277–294.

Kowalkowski, C., Kindström, D. & Brehmer, P.O. (2011) Managing industrial service offerings in global business markets. *Journal of Business & Industrial Marketing*. 26(3), 181–192.

Kraljic, (1983) Purchasing Must Become Supply Management. [Online] Available from http://hbr .org/1983/09/purchasing–must–become–supply–management/ar/1.

Kranton, R.E. & Minehart, D.F. (2001) A theory of buyer–seller networks. *The American Economic Review*. 91(3), 485–508.

Krapfel, R.E., Salmond, D. & Spekman, R. (1991) A strategic approach to managing buyer–seller relationships. *European Journal of Marketing*. 25(9), 22–37.

Kumar, N., Scheer, L.K. & Steenkamp, J.E.M. (1995) The effects of perceived interdependence on dealer attitudes. *Journal of Marketing Research*. 32(3), 348–356.

Kumar, V. & Shah, D. (2009) Expanding the role of marketing: From customer equity to market capitalization. *Journal of Marketing*. 73(6), 119–136.

Kumar, V., Bohling, T.R. & Ladda, R.N. (2003) Antecedents and consequences of relationship intention: Implications for transaction and relationship marketing. *Industrial Marketing Management*. 32(8), 667–676.

Kumar, V., Venkatesan, R. & Reinartz, W. (2008) Performance implications of adopting a customer-focused sales campaign. *Journal of Marketing*. 72(5), 50–68.

Kumar, V., Venkatesan, R., Bohling, T. & Beckmann, D. (2008) The power of CLV: Managing customer lifetime value at IBM. *Marketing Science*. 27(4), 585–599.

Kuratko, D.F., Montagno, R.V. & Hornsby, J.S. (1990) Developing an intrapreneurial assessment instrument for an effective corporate entrepreneurial environment. *Strategic Management Journal*. 11, 49–58.

Kurzrock, W. (1983) Key account sales: A high payoff training challenge. *Training and Development Journal*. 37(11), 41–46.

La Rocca, A. & Snehota, I. (2012) Sales outside-in and inside-out. 28th IMP Conference. Rome, Italy.

La Rocca, A. & Snehota, I. (2014) Value creation and organisational practices at firm boundaries. *Management Decision*.

La Rocca, A., Caruana, A. & Snehota, I. (2012) Measuring customer attractiveness. *Industrial Marketing Management*. 41(8), 1241–1248.

Laabs, J.J. (1996) Expert advice on how to move forward with change. *Personnel Journal*. 75(7), 54–62.

Laguna, M. & Marklund, J. (2005) *Business Process Modelling, Simulation, and Design*. Upper Saddle River, NJ: Pearson Education, Inc.

Lambe, C.J. & Spekman, R.E. (1997a) National account management: Large account selling or buyer supplier alliance? Journal of Personal Selling & Sales Management. 17(4), 61–74.

Lambe, C.J. & Spekman, R.E. (1997b) Alliances, external technology acquisition, and discontinuous technological change. *Journal of Product Innovation Management*. 14(2), 102–116.

Lambe, C.J., Spekman, R.E. & Hunt, S.D. (2000) Interimistic relational exchange: Conceptualization and propositional development. *Journal of the Academy of Marketing Science*. 28(2), 212–225.

Lambert, D.M., Emmelhainz, M.A. & Gardner, J.T. (1996) Developing and implementing supply chain partnerships. *International Journal of Logistics*. 7(2), 1–17.

Lamming, R. (1993) *Beyond Partnership: Strategies for Innovation and Lean Supply*. London: Prentice-Hall.

Lamont, W.D. (1955) *The Value Judgment*. Westport, CT: Greenwood Press.

Landry, J.T. (2000) Trusted partners: How companies build mutual trust and win together. *Harvard Business Review*. 78(2), 179.

Lang, R. (1973) National account selling. *American Management Association Seminar*. Chicago.

Lawrence, A. & Taylor, B. (2005) Managing customer profitability using portfolio matrices. *Database Marketing & Customer Strategy Management*. 12(4), 298–304.

Lawrence, B.S. (1997) The black box of organizational demography. *Organization Science*. 8(1), 1–22.

Lawrence, P.R. & Lynch, R.P. (2011), *Leadership and The Structure of Trust*. [Online] Available from: http://www.europeanbusinessreview.com/?p=3900.

Leake, J. (2005) Picky stores force farmers to dump veg. *The Sunday Times*. July 17, 1–6.

Leigh, T.W. & Marshall, G.W. (2001) Research priorities in sales strategy and performance. *Journal of Personal Selling & Sales Management*. 21(2), 83–93.

Lerner, A.(1934) The concept of monopoly and the measurement of monopoly power. *The Review of Economic Studies*. 1(3), 157–175.

Levitt, T. (1960) Marketing myopia. *Harvard Business Review*. July–August, 45–56.

Lewin, K. (1946) Action research and minority problems. *Journal of Social Issues*. 2(4), 34–46.

Lewis, J.D. (1990) *Partnerships for Profit: Structuring a Managing Strategic Alliances*. New York: Free Press.

Li, F. & Nicholls, J.A.F. (2000) Transactional or relationship marketing: Determinants of strategic choices. *Journal of Marketing Management*. 16(5), 449–464.

Li, Y. (2012) *The Competence Profile of The Key Account Manager*. Unpublished MSc Thesis. Cranfield University.

Lieberman, M.B. & Montgomery, D.B. (1988) First-mover advantages. *Strategic Management Journal*. 9(special issue), 41–58.

Liedtka, J.M. (1996) Collaborating across lines of business for competitive advantage. *Academy of Management Executive*. 10(2), 20–37.

Lim, B.C. & Ployhart, R. (2006) Assessing the convergent and discriminant validity of Goldberg's international personality item pool: A multitrait–multimethod examination. *Organizational Research Methods*. 9(1), 29–54.

Lin, C.Y. (2002) Empowerment in the service industry: An empirical study in Taiwan. *Journal of Psychology*. 136(5), 533–555.

Lincoln, Y.S. & Guba, E.G. (1985) *Naturalistic Inquiry*. Newbury Park, CA: Sage Publications.

Lindgreen A. & Wynstra, F. (2005) Value in Business Markets: What do we Know? Where are we Going? *Industrial Marketing Management*. 34(7), 732–748.

Lindgreen, A., Palmer, R., Vanhamme, J. & Wouters, J. (2006) A relationship-management assessment tool: Questioning, identifying, and prioritizing critical aspects of customer relationships. *Industrial Marketing Management*. 35(1), 57–71.

Lovelock, C.H. & Young, R.F. (1979) Look to consumers to increase productivity. [Online]. Accessible from: *Hardvard Business Review*, http://hbr.org/1979/05/look–to –consumers–to–increase–productivity/ar/1.

Low, G.S. & Fullerton, R.A. (1994) Brands, brand management, and the brand manager system: A critical-historical evaluation. *Journal of Marketing Research*. 31(2), 173–190.

Lusch, R.F. & Vargo, S. (2006) Service-dominant logic: Reactions, reflections and refinements. *Marketing Theory*. 6(3), 281–288.

REFERENCES

Lynette, J.R. & Humphrey, A.S. (2007) Managing key business-to-business relationships: What marketing can learn from supply chain management. *Journal of Service Research.* 9(4), 312–326.

Macauley, S. (1963) Non-contractual relations in business: A preliminary study. *American Sociological Review.* 28(1), 55–67.

Macinnis, D.J. (2011) A framework for conceptual contributions in marketing. *Journal of Marketing.* 75(4), 136–154.

Mackintosh, J. & Simon, B. (2005) Ford to focus on business from key suppliers. *Financial Times.* September 30, 32.

Macneil, I. (1978) Contracts: Adjustment of long term economic relations under classical, neoclassical and relational contract law. *Northwestern University Law Review.* 72(6), 854–906.

Macneil, I. (1980) Power, contract, and the economic model. *Journal of Economic Issues.* 14(4), 909–923.

Mahajan, J. & Churchill, G.A. (1990) Alternative approaches for investigating contingency-based organizational predictions in personal selling. *International Journal of Research in Marketing.* 7(2–3), 149–169.

Maignan, I., Ferrell, O.C. & Ferrell, L. (2005) A stakeholder model for implementing social responsibility in marketing. *European Journal of Marketing.* 39(9/10), 956–977.

Maister, D.H. (1999) Key account management. *CPA Journal.* 69(3), 62–64.

Maltz, E. & Kohli, A. (1996) Market intelligence dissemination across functional boundaries. *Journal of Marketing Research.* 33(1), 47–61.

Marbán, O., Menasalvas, E. & Fernández-Baizán, C. (2008) A cost model to estimate the effort of data mining projects (DMCoMo). *Information Systems.* 33(1), 133–150.

Marchetti, M. (1999) A hiring decision you can't afford to screw up. *Sales and Marketing Management.* 151(6), 13.

Markowitz, H. (1952) Portfolio selection. *The Journal of Finance.* 7(1), 77–91.

Marks, M.A., Mathieu, J.E. & Zaccaro, S.J. (2001) A temporally based framework and taxonomy of team processes. *Academy of Management Review.* 26(3), 356–376.

Marshall, G.W., Moncrief, W.C. & Lassk, F.G. (1999) The current state of sales force activities. *Industrial Marketing and Management.* 28(1), 87–98.

Mathieu, J.E., Gilson, L. L. & Ruddy, T.M. (2006) Empowerment and team effectiveness: An empirical test of an integrated model. *The Journal of Applied Psychology.* 91(1), 97–108.

McCrae, R. & Costa, P. (2004) A contemplated revision of the NEO five-factor inventory. *Personality and Individual Differences.* 36(3), 587–596.

McCrae, R. & Costa, P. (2007) Brief versions of the NEO-PI-3. *Journal of Individual Differences.* 28(3), 116–128.

McCrae, R., Costa, P., Pillar, G., Rolland, J. & Parker, W. (1998) Cross-cultural assessment of the Five-Factor Model: The revised NEO Personality Inventory. *Journal of Cross-Cultural Psychology.* 29(1), 171–188.

McDonald, M. (1986) *The Theory and Practice of Marketing Planning in Industrial Markets.* Cranfield University.

McDonald, M. (2000) Key account management: A domain review. *Marketing Review.* 1(1), 15–35.

McDonald, M. (2012) *Marketing Plans: How To Prepare Them; How To Profit From Them.* Oxford: Wiley.

McDonald, M. & Rogers, B. (1996) Key account management: Learning from supplier and customer perspectives. *Cranfield School of Management Research Report.* Cranfield University.

McDonald, M. & Rogers, B. (1998) Key Account Management – Learning From Supplier and Customer Perspectives. Oxford: Butterworth Heinemann.

McDonald, M. & Woodburn, D. (1999) Key account management: Building on supplier and customer perspectives, *Financial Times*, Prentice Hall.

McDonald, M. & Woodburn, D. (2007) *Key Account Management. The Definitive Guide* (2nd edition). Oxford: Elsevier.

McDonald, M. & Woodburn, D. (2011) *Key Account Management: The Definitive Guide* (3rd edition). Oxford: Wiley.

McDonald, M., Millman, T. & Rogers, B. (1997) Key account management: Theory, practice and challenges. Journal of Marketing Management. 13(8), 737–757.

McDonald, M., Rogers, B. & Woodburn, D. (2000) *Key Customers: How to Manage Them Profitably* (CIM Professional Development), Oxford: Butterworth-Heinemann.

McDonald, M., Ryals, L., Dennison, T., Yallop, R. & Rogers, B. (1994) *Marketing the Challenge of Change*. Cranfield University.

McGrath, J.E. (1964) *Social Psychology: A Brief Introduction*. Holt: Rinehart and Winston.

McKelvey, B. (1975) Guidelines for the empirical classification of organizations. *Administrative Science Quarterly*. 20(4), 509–525.

McKinney, G. & McKinney, M. (1989) Forget the corporate umbrella–entrepreneurs shine in the rain. *Sloan Management Review*. 30(4), p.77–82.

Meehan, J. & Wright, G.H. (2012) The origins of power in buyer–seller relationships. *Industrial Marketing Management*. 41(4), 669–679.

Menard, C. (2004) The economics of hybrid organizations. *Journal of Institutional and Theoretical Economics*. 160(3), 1–32.

Menguc, B. & Barker, T. (2005) Re-examining field sales unit performance: Insights from the resource-based view and dynamic capabilities perspective. *European Journal of Marketing*. 39(7/8), 885–909.

Menon, A., Jaworski, B.J. & Kohli, A. (1997) Product quality: Impact of interdepartmental interactions. *Journal of the Academy of Marketing Science*. 25(3), 187–200.

Meyer, A.D., Tsui, A.S. & Hinings, C.R. (1993) Configurational approaches to organizational analysis. *Academy of Management Journal*. 39(6), 1175–1195.

Miles, M. & Huberman, M. (1994) *Qualitative Data Analysis: An Expanded Sourcebook*. Thousand Oaks, CA: Sage Publications.

Miles, M.B. & Huberman, M. A. (2003) *Analyse des données qualitatives* (2nd edition). Brussels: De Boeck.

Miles, R.E. & Snow, C.C. (1978) *Organizational Strategy, Structure, and Process*. New York: McGraw-Hill.

Miller, D. (1996) Configurations revisited. *Strategic Management Journal*. 17(7), 505–512.

Miller, D. & Friesen, P.H. (1984) A longitudinal study of the corporate life cycle. *Management Science*. 30(10), 1161–1183.

Miller, D., Hope, Q., Eisenstat, R., Foote, N. & Galbraith, J. (2002) The problem of solutions: Balancing clients and capabilities. *Business Horizons*. 45(2), 3–12.

Miller, R.B. & Heiman, S.E. (1985) *Strategic Selling*. New York: William Morrow & Co. Inc.

Miller, R.B. & Heiman, S.E. (1987) *Conceptual Selling*. New York: Harry Halt & Co Inc.

Miller, R.B. & Heiman, S.E. (1991) *Successful Large Account Management*. New York: Henry Holt and Company, Inc.

Milliken, F. & Martins, L. (1996) Searching for common threads: Understanding the multiple effects of diversity in organizational groups. *Academy of Management Review*. 21(2), 402–433.

Millman, T. (1996) Global key account management and systems selling. International Business Review. 5(6), 631–645.

Millman, T. (1999) From national account management to global account management in business-to-business markets. *Thexis*. 16(4), 2–9.

Millman, T. & Wilson, K. (1994) From key account selling to key account management. *Proceedings of the 10th IMP Conference*. Bath.

Millman, T. & Wilson, K. (1995a) From key account selling to key account management. Journal of Marketing Practice: Applied Marketing Science. 1(1), 9–21.

Millman, T. & Wilson, K. (1995b) Developing key account managers. In: Turnbull, P., Yorke, D. & Naude, P. (eds.), *The 11th IMP International Conference*. Manchester.

Millman, T. & Wilson, K. (1996a) Developing key account management competencies. Journal of Marketing Practice Applied Marketing Science. 2(2), 7–22.

Millman, T. & Wilson. K. (1996b) *Contentious Issues in Key Account Management*. [Online] Available from: https://www.escholar.manchester.ac.uk/api/datastream?publicationPid =uk–ac–man–scw:2n1053&datastreamId=FULL–TEXT.PDF.

Millman, T. & Wilson, K. (1997) Defining key account management attractiveness in business to business markets. *Proceedings of the 33rd NAMA Conference*. Fort Lauderdale, Florida.

Millman, T. & Wilson, K. (1999a) *Developing Global Account Management Competencies*. Available from: https://www.escholar.manchester.ac.uk/api/datastream?publicationPid =uk–ac–man–scw:2n923&datastreamId=FULL–TEXT.PDF.

Millman, T. & Wilson, K. (1999b) Processual issues in key account management: Underpinning the customer-facing organisation. Journal of Business & Industrial Marketing. 14(4), 328–337.

Mills, P. & Morris, J. (1986) Clients as 'partial' employees of service organizations: Role development in client participation. *Academy of Management Review*. 11(4), 726–735.

Miner, A.S., Basoff, P. & Moorman, C. (2001) Organizational improvisation and learning: A field study. *Administrative Science Quarterly*. 46(2), 304–337.

Missirilian, O. & Calvi, R. (2004) Key supplier manager (KSM): An emerging function in purchasing. *The 20th IMP Conference*. Copenhagen.

Moeller, S., Fassnacht, M. & Klos, S. (2006) A framework for supplier relationship management (SRM), *Journal of Business to Business Marketing*. 13(4), 69–94.

Mohr, J. & Spekman, R. (1994) Characteristics of partnership success: Partnership attributes, communication behavior, and conflict resolution techniques. *Strategic Management Journal*. 15(2), 135–152.

Mohr, J.J. & Nevin, J.R. (1990) Communication strategies in marketing channels: A theoretical perspective. *Journal of Marketing*. 54(4), 36–51.

Mohr, J.J., Fisher, R.J. & Nevin, J.R. (1996) Collaborative communication in interfirm relationships: Moderating effects of integration and control. *Journal of Marketing*. 60(3), 103–115.

Mohrman, S.A., Cohen, S.G. & Mohrman, A.M. (1995) *Designing Team-Based Organizations: New Forms For Knowledge Work*. San Francisco: Jossey-Bass.

Möller, K.E. (2006) Role of competence in creating customer value: A value-creation logic approach. *Industrial Marketing Management*. 35(8), 913–924.

Möller, K.E. & Törrönen, P. (2003) Business suppliers. Value creation potential: A capability-based analysis. *Industrial Marketing Management*. 32(2), 109–118.

Möller, K.E., Rajala, A. & Svahn, S. (2005) Strategic business nets – their type and management. *Journal of Business Research*. 58(3/4), 1274–1284.

Möllering, G. (2003) A typology of supplier relations: From determinism to pluralism in inter-firm empirical research. *Journal of Purchasing and Supply Management*. 9(1), 31–41.

Momani, F. & Richter, T. (1999) Standardization versus differentiation in European key account management: The case of Adidas–Salomon AG. *Thexis*. 4, 44–47.

Moncrief, W.C. (1986) Selling activity and sales position taxonomies for industrial salesforces. *Journal of Marketing Research*. 23(3), 261–270.

Moncrief, W.C. & Marshall, G.W. (2005) The evolution of the seven steps of selling. *Industrial Marketing Management*. 34(1), 13–22.

Monczka, R. & Morgan, J. (2000) Competitive supply strategies for the 21st century. *Purchasing*. 128(1), 48–59.

Monroe, K.B. (1990), *Pricing: Making Profitable Decisions*. (3rd edition). New York: McGraw-Hill.

Montgomery, D.B. & Yip, G.S. (2000) The challenge of global customer management. Marketing Management. 9(4), 22–29.

Montgomery, D.B., Yip, G.S. & Villalonga, B. (1998) *The Use And Performance Effect Of Global Account Management: An Empirical Analysis Using Structural Equation Modelling*. Unpublished working paper. Stanford University Graduate School of Business.

Moon, M.A. & Armstrong, G.M. (1994) Selling teams: A conceptual framework and research agenda. *Journal of Personal Selling and Sales Management*. 14(1), 17–30.

Moon, M.A. & Gupta, S.F. (1997) Examining the formation of selling centers: A conceptual framework. *Journal of Personal Selling and Sales Management*. 17(2), 31–41.

Moorman, C. & Rust, R.T. (1999) The role of marketing. *Journal of Marketing*. 63(Special Issue), 180–197.

Moorman, C., Deshpandé, R. & Zaltman, G. (1993) Factors affecting trust in market research relationships. *Journal of Marketing*. 57(1), 81–101.

Morgan, R. & Hunt, S. (1994) The commitment trust theory of relationship marketing. Journal of Marketing. 58(3), 20–38.

Morgan, R. & Hunt, S. (1999) Relationship-based competitive advantage: The role of relationship marketing in marketing strategy. *Journal of Business Research*. 46(3), 281–290.

Morrison, S. & Waters, R. (2005) Time comes to think different. *Financial Times*. June 7, 25.

Moss Kanter, R. (2009) *Supercorp: How Vanguard Companies Create Innovation, Profits, Growth and Social Good*, London: Profile Books.

Mota, J. & de Castro, L.M. (2005) Relationship portfolios and capability development: Cases from the moulds industry. *Journal of Purchasing & Supply Management*. 11(1), 42–54.

Mouzas, S. & Araujo, L. (2000) Implementing programmatic initiatives in manufacturer–retailer networks. *Industrial Marketing Management*. 29(4), 293–303.

Mouzas, S. & Ford, D.(2006) Managing relationships in showery weather: The role of umbrella agreements. *Journal of Business Research*. 59(12), 1248–1256.

Mouzas, S., Henneberg, S. & Naudé, P. (2007) Developing network insight. *Industrial Marketing Management*. 37(2), 167–180.

Mulhern, F. (1999) Customer profitability analysis: Measurement, concentration, and research. *Journal of Interactive Marketing*. 13(1), 25–40.

Mundt, J. (1993) Externalities: Uncalculated outcomes of exchange. *Journal of Macromarketing*. 13(2), 46–53.

Murray, A.I. (1989) Top management group heterogeneity and firm performance. *Strategic Management Journal*. 10, 125–141.

Murray, S. (2006) Alliances heed anti–trust traps. *Financial Times*. January 5, 10.

Myhr, N. & Spekman, R.E. (2005) Collaborative supply-chain partnerships built upon trust and electronically mediated exchange. *Journal of Business and Industrial Marketing*. 20(4/5), 179–186.

Nachnani, A. (1998) Restoring the balance of power: Profiting from strategic customer relationships. *USA: Sales Executive Council Report*.

Nahapiet, J. (1994) Servicing the global client: Towards global account management? In *14th Annual Conference of the Strategic Management Society*. Jouy en Josas, France.

Naidu, A.P., Sheth, J.N. & Westgate, L. (1999) Does relationship marketing pay? An empirical investigation of relationship marketing practices in hospitals. *Journal of Business Research*. 46(3), 207–218.

REFERENCES

Nambisan, S. (2002) Designing virtual customer environment for new product development: Toward a theory. *Academy of Management Review*. 27(3), 392–413.

Napolitano, L. (1997) Customer supplier partnering: A strategy whose time has come. Journal of Personal Selling and Sales Management. 17(4), 1–8.

Narayandas, D. & Rangan, V. K. (2004) Building and sustaining buyer–seller relationships in mature industrial markets. *Journal of Marketing*. 68(3), 63–77.

Narayandas, D., Quelch, J. & Swartz, G. (2000) Prepare your company for global pricing. *Sloan Management Review*. 42(1), 61–70.

Narus, J.A. & Anderson, J.C. (1995) Using teams to manage collaborative relationships in business markets. *Journal of Business to Business Marketing*. 2(3), 17–46.

Narver, J.C. & Slater, S.F. (1990) The effect of a market orientation on business profitability. *Journal of Marketing*. 54(October), 20–35.

Natti, S. & Ojasalo, J. (2008) What prevents effective utilisation of customer knowledge in professional B-to-B services? An empirical study. *Services Industry Journal*. 28(9), 1199–1213.

Natti, S. & Palo, T. (2006) Key account management in business-to-business expert organizations: an exploratory study on the implementation process. *Service Industries Journal*. 32(11), 1837–1852.

Natti, S., Halinen, A. & Hanttu, N. (2006) Customer knowledge transfer and key account management in professional service organizations. *International Journal of Service Industry Management*. 17(4), 304–319.

Neal, J.A. & Tromley, C.L. (1995) From incremental change to retrofit: Creating high-performance work systems. *Academy of Management Executive*. 9(1), 42–53.

Netemeyer, R.G., Boles, J.S., Mckee, D. & Mcmurrian, R. (1997) An investigation into the antecedents of organizational citizenship behaviors in a personal selling context. *Journal of Marketing*. 61(3), 85–98.

Nevin, J.R. (1995) Relationship marketing and distribution channels: Exploring fundamental issues. *Journal of the Academy of Marketing Science*. 23(4), 327–334.

Newbourne, P.T. (1997) The role of partnerships in strategic account management. The *International Journal of Logistics Management*. 8(1), 67–74.

Newman, R.G. (1989) Single sourcing: Short-term savings versus long-term problems. *Journal of Purchasing and Materials Management*. 25(2), 20–25.

Ngo, L.V. & O'Cass, A. (2009) Creating value offerings via operant resource-based capabilities. *Industrial Marketing Management*. 38(1), 45–59.

Ngobo, P. (2005) Drivers of upwards and downward migration in the theatre context. *International Journal of Research in Marketing*. 22 April, 183–210.

Nicolajsen, H. W. & Scupola, A. (2011) Investigating issues and challenges for customer involvement in business services innovation. *Journal of Business & Industrial Marketing*. 26(5), 368–376.

Nidumolo, R., Prahalad, C.K. & Rangaswami, M.R. (2009) Why sustainability is now the key driver of innovation. *Harvard Business Review*. September, 56–64.

Niraj, R., Gupta, M. & Narasimhan, C. (2001) Customer profitability in a supply chain. *Journal of Marketing*. 65(3), 1–16.

Noordewier, T.G., John, G. & Nevin, J.R. (1990) Performance outcomes of purchasing arrangements in industrial buyer–vendor relationships. *Journal of Marketing*. 54(4), 80–93.

Normann, R. (2001) *Reframing Business: When the Map Changes the Landscape*. Chichester: John Wiley & Sons Ltd.

Nunnally, J.C. (1978) *Psychometric Theory* (2nd edition). New York: McGraw-Hill.

Nunnally, J.C. & Bernstein, I.H. (1994) *Psychometric Theory* (3rd edition). New York: McGraw-Hill.

Nye, C., Roberts, B., Saucier, G. & Zhou, X. (2008) Testing the measurement equivalence of personality adjective items across cultures. *Journal of Research in Personality*. 42(6), 1524–1536.

O'Callaghan, R., Kaufman, P.J. & Konsynski, B.R. (1992) Adoption Correlates and Share Effects of Electronic Data Interchange Systems in Marketing Channels. *Journal of Marketing*. 56(April), 45–56.

O'Connor, G.C. & Rice, M.(2001) Opportunity recognition and breakthrough innovation in large established firms. *California Management Review*. 43(2), 95–116.

O'Toole, T. & Donaldson, B. (2002) Relationship performance dimensions of buyer–supplier exchanges. *European Journal of Purchasing & Supply Management*. 8(4), 197–207.

Odell, M. (2005) Convergence is the key to Ericsson's Marconi move. *Financial Times*. October 26, 23.

Ojasalo, J. (2000) The episodic, phase, and state approaches to customer relationships. In: Cooley, F.V.G. (ed.) *Marketing in a Global Economy*. Chicago: AMA American Marketing Association, 363–370.

Ojasalo, J. (2001) Key account management at company and individual levels in business-to-business relationships. *Journal of Business & Industrial Marketing*. 16(3), 199–218.

Ojasalo, J. (2002) Key account management in information–intensive services. *Journal of Retailing and Consumer Services*. 9(5), 269–276.

Ojasalo, J. (2004) Key network management. *Industrial Marketing Management*. 33(3), 195–205.

Oliva, R. & Kallenberg, R. (2003) Managing the transition from products to services. *International Journal of Service Industry Management*. 14(2), 160–172.

Oliver, R. & Winer, R.S. (1987) A framework for the formation and structure of consumer expectations: Review and propositions. *Journal of Economic Psychology*. 8(4), 469–499.

Oliver, R.L. (1997) *Satisfaction: A Behavioral Perspective on the Consumer*. New York: Irwin/McGraw-Hill.

Olsen, R.F. & Ellram, L.M. (1997) A portfolio approach to supplier relationships. Industrial Marketing Management. 26(2), 101–113.

Olson, E.M., Walker, O.C. & Rueckert, R.W. (1995) Organizing for effective new product development. The moderating role of product innovativeness. *Journal of Marketing*, 59(1), 48–62.

Organ, D.W. (1971) Linking pins between organizations and environment. *Business Horizons*. 14(December), 73–80.

Organ, D.W. & Lingl, A. (1995) Personality, satisfaction, and organizational citizenship behavior. *Journal of Social Psychology*. 135(3), 339–350.

Organ, D.W. & Greene, C.N. (1972) The boundary relevance of the project manager's job: findings and implications for R & D management. *R & D Management*. 3(1), 7–11.

Orwell, G. (1945) *Animal Farm*. London: Secker & Warburg.

Oswald, A. (1997) Happiness and economic performance. *Economic Journal*. [Online] Available from: http://www2.warwick.ac.uk/fac/soc/economics/staff/academic/oswald/happecperf.pdf.

Owen, L., Goldwasser, C., Choate, K. & Blitz, A. (2008) Collaborative innovation throughout the extended enterprise. *Strategy & Leadership*. 36(1), 39–45.

Palmatier, R. (2008) Interfirm relational drivers of customer value. *Journal of Marketing*. 72(4), 76–89.

Palmer, A. & Bejou, D. (1994) Buyer–seller relationships: A conceptual model and imperical investigation. Journal of Marketing Management. 10(6), 495–512.

Palmer, R. (2007) The transaction-relational continuum: Conceptually elegant but empirically denied, *Journal of Business & Industrial Marketing*, 22(7), 439–451.

Pardo, C. (1997) Key account management in the business to business field: The key account's point of view. *Journal of Personal Selling & Sales Management.* 17(Fall), 17–26.

Pardo, C. (1999) Key account management in the business-to-business field: A French overview. *Journal of Business & Industrial Marketing.* 14(4), 276–290.

Pardo, C. (2006) Key account management in the industrial field. In: Sarathy, V. & Balakhrishna, A.V. (eds.), *Key Accounts Management: Concepts and Applications.* Hyderabad: The ICFAI University Press. 111–131.

Pardo, C. & Salle, R. (1995) Defining customer boundaries: The first step in customer portfolio management. In: Turnbull, P.W., Yorke, D. & Naude, P. (eds.), *Interaction, Relationships and Networks: Past–Present–Future.* 11th IMP International Conference. Manchester. 962–978.

Pardo, C., Henneberg, S.C., Mouzas, S. & Naude, P. (2006) Unpicking the meaning of value in key account management. European Journal of Marketing. 40(11/12), 1360–1374.

Pardo, C., Salle, R. & Spencer, R. (1993). The key accountisation of the firm, a case study. 9th IMP Conference, Bath, UK, September 23–25.

Pardo, C., Salle, R. & Spencer, R. (1995) The key accountization of the firm in industrial markets. *Journal of Marketing Management.* 22(2), 123–134.

Parker, G.M. (1994) *Cross-Functional Teams: Working With Allies, Enemies, and Other Strangers.* San Francisco: Jossey-Bass.

Parolini, C. (1999) *The Value Net.* Chichester: Wiley.

Pasmore, W., Francis, C. & Haldeman, J. (1982) Sociotechnical systems: A North American reflection on empirical studies of the seventies. *Human Relations.* 35(12), 1179–1204.

Patton, M.Q. (2002), *Qualitative Research & Evaluation Methods.* Thousand Oaks, CA: Sage Publications.

Payne, A. & Holt, S. (1999) A review of the 'value' literature and implications for relationship marketing. *Australian Marketing Journal.* 7(1), 41–51.

Payne, A., Ballantyne, D. & Christopher, M. (2005) A stakeholder approach to relationship marketing strategy. *European Journal of Marketing.* 39(7/8), 855–871.

Payne, A., Christopher, M., Clark, M. & Peck, H. (1995) *Relationship Marketing for Competitive Advantage.* Oxford: Elsevier Butterworth-Heinemann.

Payne, A., Storbacka, K. & Frow, P. (2008) Managing the co-creation of value. *Journal of the Academy of Marketing Science.* 36(1), 83–96.

Peck, M.A. (1997) *Integrated Account Management: How Business-to-business Marketers Maximize Customer Loyalty and Profitability.* New York: Amacom.

Pegram, R.M. (1972) *Selling and Servicing the National Account.* Report No. 557. New York: The Conference Board, Inc.

Pelham, A.M. (1999) Influence of environment, strategy, and market orientation on performance in small manufacturing firms. *Journal of Business Research.* 45(1), 33–46.

Pelled, L.H., Eisenhardt, K.M. & Xin, K.R. (1999) Exploring the black box: An analysis of work group diversity, conflict, and performance. *Administrative Science Quarterly.* 44(1), 1–28.

Pels, J. (1992) Identification and management of key clients. *European Journal of Marketing.* 26(5), 5–21.

Perks, H. & Moxey, S. (2011) Market-facing innovation networks: How lead firms partition tasks, share resources and develop capabilities. *Industrial Marketing Management.* 40(8), 1224–1237.

Perret, V. & Josserand E. (2003) *Le paradoxe: Penser et gérer autrement les organisations.* Paris: Elllipses.

Perry, M.L., Pearce. C.L. & Sims, H.P. Jr (1999) Empowered selling teams: How shared leadership can contribute to selling team outcomes. *Journal of Personal Selling & Sales Management.* 19(3), 35–51.

Pervin, L. (2003) *The Science of Personality* (2nd edition). New York: Oxford University Press. 528.

Peterat, M.A. & Helfatl, C.E. (2003) The dynamic resource-based view: Capability lifecycles. *Strategic Management Journal.* 24(10), 997–1010.

Peters, L.D., Johnston, W.J., Pressey, A.D. & Kendrick, T. (2010) Collaboration and collective learning: networks as learning organizations. *Journal of Business & Industrial Marketing.* 25(6), 478–484.

Peters, T.J. & Waterman, R.H. (1982) How the best-run companies turn so-so performers into big winners. *Management Review.* 71(11), 8–17.

Peters, T.J. & Waterman, R.H. (1982) *In Search of Excellence – Lessons from America's Best Run Companies.* London: HarperCollins.

Pfeffer, J. (1986) A resource dependence perspective on intercorporate relations. In: Mizruchi, M.S. & Schwartz, M. (eds.), *Structural Analysis of Business.* New York: Academic Press. 117–132.

Pfeffer, J. & Salancik, G.R. (1978) *The External Control of Organizations – A Resource Dependence Perspective.* New York: Harper & Row.

Piercy, N.F. (2006), The strategic sales organization. *The Marketing Review.* 6(1), 3–28.

Piercy, N.F. (2009a) *Market-Led Strategic Change: Transforming the Process of Going to Market* (4th edition). Oxford: Elsevier.

Piercy, N.F. (2009b) Strategic relationships between boundary-spanning functions: Aligning customer relationship management with supplier relationship management. *Industrial Marketing Management.* 38(8), 857–864.

Piercy, N.F. (2010) Evolution of strategic sales organizations in business-to-business marketing. *Journal of Business & Industrial Marketing.* 25(5), 349–359.

Piercy, N.F. & Lane, N. (2003) Transformation of the traditional sales force: Imperatives for intelligence, interface and integration. *Journal of Marketing Management.* 19(5/6), 563–582.

Piercy, N.F. & Lane, N. (2006a) The hidden risks in strategic account management strategy. *Journal of Business Strategy.* 27(1), 18–26.

Piercy, N.F. & Lane, N. (2006b) The underlying vulnerabilities in key account management strategies. *European Management Journal.* 24(2–3), 151–162.

Piercy, N.F. & Lane, N. (2006c) Ethical and moral dilemmas associated with strategic relationships between business-to-business buyers and sellers. *Journal of Business Ethics.* 72(1), 87–102.

Piercy, N.F. & Lane, N. (2007) Ethical and moral dilemmas associated with strategic relationships between business-to-business buyers and sellers. *Journal of Business Ethics.* 72, 87–102.

Piercy, N.F. & Lane, N. (2009a) Corporate social responsibility: Impacts on strategic marketing and customer value. *The Marketing Review.* 9(4), 335–360.

Piercy, N.F. & Lane, N. (2009b) *Strategic Customer Management: Strategizing the Sales Organization.* Oxford University Press.

Piercy, N.F. & Lane, N. (2011a) Corporate social responsibility initiatives and strategic marketing imperatives. *Social Business.* 1(4), 325–345.

Piercy, N.F. & Lane, N. (2011b) The evolution of the strategic sales organization. In: Cravens, D.W., Le Meunier-Fitzhugh, K. & Piercy, N.F. (eds.), *The Oxford Handbook of Strategic Sales and Sales Management.* Oxford University Press.

REFERENCES

Piercy, N.F. & Lane, N. (2014) Social and ethical concerns in strategic account management: Emerging opportunities and new threats. In: Woodburn, D. &Wilson, K. (eds.), *Handbook of Key Account Management*. Oxford: John Wiley.

Pillai, K.G. & Sharma, A. (2003) Mature relationships: Why does relational orientation turn into transaction orientation? *Industrial Marketing Management*. 32(8), 643–651.

Pinchott, G. (1985) *Intrapreneuring*. New York: Harper & Row.

Pinto, M.B., Pinto, J.K. & Prescott, J.E. (1993) Antecedents and consequences of project team cross–functional cooperation. *Management Science*. 39(10), 1281–1297.

Platzer, L.C. (1984) *Managing National Accounts*. Report No. 850. New York: The Conference Board.

Plender, J. & Persaud, A. (2005) Good ethics means more than ticking boxes. *Financial Times*. August 23, 10.

Plender, J. & Persaud, A. (2006) *The Missing Moral Compass: A Reality Check On Business and Finance Ethics*. London: Longtail Publishing.

Plouffe, C.R. & Barclay, D.W. (2007) Salesperson navigation: The intraorganizational dimension of the sales role. *Industrial Marketing Management*. 36(4), 528–539.

Pollitt, M. (2002) The economics of trust, norms and networks. *Business Ethics*. 11(2), 119–128.

Porter, M. (1979) How competitive forces shape strategy. *Harvard Business Review*. March/April.

Porter, M. (1980) *Competitive Strategy – Techniques for Analyzing Industries and Competitors*. New York: Free Press.

Porter, M. (1996) What is strategy? *Harvard Business Review*.

Porter, M. (2008) The five competitive forces that shape strategy. *Harvard Business Review*. January.

Porter, M. & Kramer, M.R. (2002) The competitive advantage of corporate philanthropy. *Harvard Business Review*. December, 57–68.

Porter, M. & Kramer, M.R. (2011) Creating shared value. *Harvard Business Review*. January–February, 62–77.

Prahalad, C.K. & Ramaswamy, V. (2000) Co-opting customer competence. *Harvard Business Review*. August, 2000.

Prahalad, C.K. & Ramaswamy, V. (2005) Co-creation experiences: The next practice in value creation. *Journal of Interactive Marketing*. 8(3), 5–14.

Prahalad, C.K. & Krishnan, M.S. (2008) *The New Age of Innovation: Driving Co-Created Value Through Global Networks*. New York: McGraw-Hill.

Pressey, A.D. & Mathews, B. (2003) Jumped, pushed or forgotten? Approaches to dissolution. *Journal of Marketing Management*. 19(1/2), 131–55.

Prévot, R. & Spencer, R. (2006)Supplier competence alignment: Cases from the buyer perspective in the Brazilian market. *Industrial Marketing Management*. 35(8), 944–960.

Punj, G. & Stewart, D.W. (1983) Cluster analysis in marketing research: Review and suggestions for application. *Journal of Marketing Research*. 20(2), 134–148.

Purdy, L. & Safayeni, F. (2000) Strategies for supplier evaluation: A framework for potential advantages and limitations. *IEEE Transactions on Engineering Management*. 47(4),. 435–443.

Rackham, N. (1988) *Account Strategy for Major Sales*. Aldershot: Gower.

Rackham, N., Friedman, L. & Ruff, R (1996) *Getting Partnering Right*. New York: McGraw-Hill.

Raddats, C. (2011) Aligning industrial services with strategies and sources of market differentiation. *Journal of Business & Industrial Marketing*. 26(5), 332–343.

Ramani, G. & Kumar, V. (2008) Interaction orientation and firm performance. *Journal of Marketing*. 72(1), 27–45.

Rangan, K.V., Moriarty, R.T. & Swartz, G.S. (1992) Segmenting customers in mature industrial markets. *Journal of Marketing*, 56(4), 72–82.

Rappaport, A. (1986) *Creating Shareholder Value*. New York: Free Press.

Read, S., Dew, N., Sarasvathy, S.D., Song, M. & Wiltbank, R. (2009) Marketing under uncertainty: The logic of an effectual approach. *Journal of Marketing*. 73(3), 1–18.

Rehme, J. (2001) *Sales coordination in multinational corporations: Development and management of key account programmes*. A Thesis Submitted in Linköping Institute of Technology for the Degree of Doctor of Philosophy. Linköping University.

Reichheld, F. (1996) *The Loyalty Effect: The Hidden Force Behind Growth, Profits, and Lasting Value*. Boston, MA: Harvard Business School Press.

Reichheld, F. & Sasser, W. (1990) Zero defections: Quality comes to services. *Harvard Business Review*. 68(5), 105–111.

Reid, D.A. & Plank, R.E. (2000) Business marketing comes of age: A comprehensive review of the literature. *Journal of Business-to-business Marketing*. 7(2/3), 9–185.

Reilly, R. & Chao, G. (1982) Validity and fairness of some alternative employee selection procedures. *Personnel Psychology*. 35(1), 1–62.

Reinartz, W. & Kumar, V. (2000) On the profitability of long-life customers in a noncontractual setting: An empirical investigation and implications for marketing. *Journal of Marketing*. 64(4), 17–35.

Reinartz, W. & Kumar, V. (2002) The mismanagement of customer loyalty. *Harvard Business Review*. 80(7), 86–94.

Reinartz, W. & Kumar, V. (2003) The impact of customer relationship characteristics on profitable lifetime duration. *Journal of Marketing*. 67(1), 77–99.

Reinartz, W., Thomas, J. & Kumar, V. (2005) Balancing acquisition and retention resources to maximize customer profitability. *Journal of Marketing*. 69(1), 63–79.

Reisel, W., Chia, S.L. & Maloles, C. (2005) Job insecurity spillover to key account management: Negative effects on performance, effectiveness, adaptiveness, and esprit de corps. *Journal of Business and Psychology*. 19(4), 483–503.

Rich, P. (1992)The organizational taxonomy: Definition and design. *Academy of Management Review*. 17(4), 758–781.

Rindfleisch, A. (2000) Organizational trust and interfirm cooperation: An examination of horizontal versus vertical alliances. *Marketing Letters*. 11(1), 81–95.

Rindfleisch, A. & Heide, J.B. (1997) Transaction cost analysis: Past, present, future applications. *Journal of Marketing*. 61(4), 30–54.

Ritter, T. (1999) The networking company. Antecedents for coping with relationships and networks effectively. *Industrial Marketing Management*. 28(5), 467–479.

Ritter, T. & Gemünden, H.G. (2003a) Inter-organizational relationships and networks. *Journal of Business Research*. 56(9), 691–697.

Ritter, T. & Gemünden, H.G. (2003b) Network competence: Its impact on innovation success and its antecedents. *Journal of Business Research*. 56(9), 745–755.

Ritter, T., Wilkinson, I.F. & Johnston, W.J. (2004) Managing in complex business networks. *Industrial Marketing Management*. 33(3), 175–183.

Robin, D. & Reidenbach, R.E. (1987) Social responsibility, ethics, and marketing strategy: Closing the gap between concepts and applications. *Journal of Marketing*. 51(1), 44–58.

Robinson, P.J., Faris, C.W. & Wind, Y. (1967) Industrial buying and creative marketing. Boston. Allyn and Bacon. Cited in Anderson, E., Chu, W. & Weitz, B. Industrial purchasing: an empirical exploration of the buyclass framework. *Journal of Marketing*. 51, 71–86.

Rokkan, A., Heide, J.B., & Wathne, K.H. (2003) Specific investments in marketing relationships: Expropriation and bonding effects. *Journal of Marketing Research*. 40(2), 210–224.

REFERENCES

Roman, S. & Ruiz, S. (2005) Relationship outcome of perceived ethical sales behavior: The customer's perspective. *Journal of Business Research.* 58(4), 439–445.

Romelaer, P. (2005) L'entretien de recherche. In: Roussel, P. & Wacheux, F. (eds.), *Management des Ressources Humaines: Méthodes de Recherche en Sciences Humaines et Sociales.* Paris: De Boeck. 101–137.

Rosenberg, L.J. & Czepiel, J.A. (1984) A marketing approach to customer retention. *Journal of Consumer Marketing.* 1(2), 45–51.

Rottenberger-Murtha, K.J. (1992), A 'NAM' by any other name. *Sales & Marketing Management.* 144(December), 40–44.

Rudmin, F. (1999) Norwegian short-form of the Marlowe–Crowne social desirability scale. *Scandinavian Journal of Psychology.* 40(3), 229–233.

Rueckert, R.W. & Walker, O.C. (1987) Marketing's interaction with other functional units: A conceptual framework and empirical evidence. *Journal of Marketing.* 51(1), 1–19.

Rueckert, R.W., Walker, O.C. & Roering, K.J. (1985)The organization of marketing activities: A contingency theory of structure and performance. *Journal of Marketing.* 49 (Winter), 13–25.

Russel, A. & Kelly, P.M. (2002) Customer–supplier partnerships perceptions of a successful key account management program. *Industrial Marketing Management.* 31(5), 467–476.

Rust, R.T., Lemon, K.N. & Zeithaml, V.A. (2001) Where should the next marketing dollar go? *Marketing Management.* 10(3), 24–28.

Rust, R.T., Lemon, K.N. & Zeithaml, V.A. (2004) Return on marketing: Using customer equity to focus marketing strategy. *Journal of Marketing.* 68(1), 109–127.

Ryals, L. (2002) Measuring risk and returns in the customer portfolio. *Journal of Database Marketing.* 9(3), 219–227.

Ryals, L. (2003) Making customers pay: Measuring and managing customer risk and returns. *Journal of Strategic Marketing.* 11(3), 165–175.

Ryals, L. (2005) Making customer relationship management work: The measurement and profitable management of customer relationships. *Journal of Marketing.* 69(4), 252–261.

Ryals, L. (2008) *Managing Customers Profitability.* Chichester: John Wiley & Sons.

Ryals, L. & Bruce, L. (2006) Key account management: Overcoming internal conflict. *Journal of Direct, Data and Digital Marketing Practice.* 7(4), 344–351.

Ryals, L. & Davies, I.A. (2013) Where's the strategic intent in key account relationships? *Journal of Business & Industrial Marketing.* 28(2), 111–124.

Ryals, L. & Holt, S. (2007) Creating and capturing value in KAM relationships. *Journal of Strategic Marketing.* 15(5), 403–420.

Ryals, L. & Rodgers, B. (2006) Sales compensation plans – One size does not fit all. *Journal of Targeting, Measurement and Analysis for Marketing.* 13(4), 354–362.

Ryals, L.J. & Humphries, A.S. (2007) Managing key business-to-business relationships: What marketing can learn from supply chain management. *Journal of Service Research.* 9, 312.

Sahay, B.S. (2003) Understanding trust in supply chain relationships. *Industrial Management & Data Systems.* 103(8), 553–563.

Sako, M. & Helper, S. (1998) Determinants of trust in supplier relations: Evidence from the automotive industry in Japan and the United States. *Journal of Economic Behavior & Organization.* 34(3), 387–417.

Salgado, J. (1997) The five factor model of personality and job performance in the European Community. *Journal of Applied Psychology.* 82(1), 30–43.

Salgado, J. (2003) Predicting job performance using FFM and non–FFM personality measures. *Journal of Occupational and Organizational Psychology.* 76(3), 323–346.

Salle, R. & Rost, C. (1993) Une méthode de gestion des portefeuilles de clients en milieu industriel. A method to manage portfolios of clients in the industry]. *Gestion.* 2, 69–87.

Salle, R., Cova, B. & Pardo, C. (2000) Portfolios of supplier–customer relationships. In: Woodside, A. (ed.), *Advances in Business Marketing and Purchasing.* 9. Amsterdam: Elsevier.

SAMA (Strategic Account Management Association) (2013) http://www.strategicaccounts .org/certification/samas-certified-strategic-account-manager-(csam)-certification -overview.aspx

Sanchez, R. (1993) Strategic flexibility, firm organization, and managerial work in dynamic markets: A strategic options perspective. *Advances in strategic management.* 9, 251–291.

Sanchez, J.A.L., Vijande, M.L.S. & Guttierez, J.A.T. (2010) Organizational learning and value creation in business markets. *European Journal of Marketing.* 44(11/12), 1612–1641.

Saucier, G. & Goldberg, L. (2002) Assessing the big five: Applications of 10 psychometric criteria to the development of marker scales. In: Raad, B. & Perugini, M. (eds.), *Big Five Assessment.* Washington: Hogrefe & Huber Publishers.

Sawhney, M. (2004) *Going Beyond the Product: Defining, Designing and Delivering Customer Solutions.* New York: SD Logic.

Schiele, H. (2012) Accessing supplier innovation by being their preferred customer. *ResearchTechnology Management.* 55(1), 40–50.

Schmitt, N., Gooding, R., Noe, R. & Kirsch, M. (1984) Metaanalyses of validity studies published between 1964 and 1982 and the investigation of study characteristics. *Journal of Applied Psychology.* 37(3), 407–422.

Schön, D. (1983) The Reflective Practitioner: How Professionals Think in Action. In: Schreyögg, G. (2003) (ed.) *Organisation* (4th edition). New York: Wiesbaden.

Schreyögg, G. (2003) *Organisation.* 4th edition, Wiesbaden 2003.

Schultz, R.J. & Evans, K. (2002) Strategic collaborative communication by key account representatives. *Journal of Personal Selling & Sales Management.* 22(1), 23–31.

Schumpeter, J.A. (2012) *Capitalism, Socialism and Democracy.* London: Routledge.

Scroggins, W., Thomas, S. & Morris, J. (2009) Psychological testing in personnel selection: The resurgence of personality testing. *Public Personnel Management.* 38(1), 67–77.

Selnes, F. (2011) A comment on 'balancing risk and return in a customer portfolio'. *Journal of Marketing.* 75(May), 18–21.

Selnes, F. & Sallis, J. (1999) *Relationship Learning with Key Customers.* Report No. 99–103. Cambridge: Marketing Science Institute.

Selnes, F., Billett, M.T., Tarasi, C.O., Bolton, R.N., Hutt, M.D. & Walker, B.A. (2011) Commentaries and rejoinder to 'balancing risk and return in a customer portfolio'. *Journal of Marketing.* 75(3), 18–26.

Senge, P.M. (1990)*The Fifth Discipline.* New York: Doubleday Currency.

Senge, P.M., Smith, B., Kruschwitz, N., Laur, J. & Schley, S. (2008) *The Necessary Revolution: How Individuals and Organizations are Working Together to Create a Sustainable World.* London: Nicholas Brealey Publishing

Sengupta, S., Krapfel, R.E. & Pusateri, M.A. (1997a) The strategic sales force. *Marketing Management.* 6(2), 29–34.

Sengupta, S., Krapfel, R.E. & Pusateri, M.A. (1997b) Switching costs in key account relationships. *Journal of Personal Selling & Sales Management.* 17(4), 9–16.

Sengupta, S., Krapfel, R.E. & Pusateri, M.A. (2000) An empirical investigation of key account salesperson effectiveness. *Journal of Personal Selling & Sales Management.* 20(4), 253–261.

Senn, C. (1999) Implementing global account management: A process oriented approach, *Journal of Selling and Major Account Management.* 1(3), 10–19.

Senn, C. (2006) The executive growth factor: How Siemens invigorated its customer relationships. *Journal of Business Strategy*. 27(1), 27–34.

Senn, C. & Atanasova, Y. (2011) Global customer team design: Dimensions, determinants, and performance outcomes. *Industrial Marketing Management*. 40(2), 278–289

Shapiro, B. (1977) Can marketing and manufacturing coexist? *Harvard Business Review*. 55(4), 104–114.

Shapiro, B. (1979) Account management and sales organization, new developments in practice. In: Bagozzi, R. (ed.), *Sales Management–New Developments from Behavioral and Decision Model Research*. Cambridge: Management Science Institute.

Shapiro, B. (2001), Sprint sell to close sales quickly. *Harvard Business Review*. [Online]. Available from: http://hbr.org/product/sprint–sell–to–close–sales–quickly/an/999004 –PDF–ENG.

Shapiro, B. & Moriarty, R.T. (1980) National Account Management. *Marketing Science Institute Working Paper No. 80–104*. Cambridge: Marketing Science Institute.

Shapiro, B. & Moriarty, R.T. (1982) National Account Management: Emerging Insights. Cambridge: Marketing Science Institute.

Shapiro, B. & Moriarty, R.T. (1984a) Organizing the National Account Force. Working Paper, No. 84–101. Cambridge: Marketing Science Institute.

Shapiro, B. & Moriarty, R.T. (1984b) *Support Systems for National Account Management Programs: Promises Made – Promises Kept*. Working Paper, No. 84–102. Cambridge: Marketing Science Institute.

Shapiro, B. & Wyman, J. (1981) New ways to reach your customers. *Harvard Business Review*. 59(4), 103–110.

Shapiro, B., Rangan, V.K., Moriarty, R.T. & Ross, E.B. (1987) Manage customers for profits (not just sales), *Harvard Business Review*. September, 101–108.

Shapiro, B., Slywotzky, A. & Doyle, S. (1997) *Strategic Sales Management*. Virginia: Booz Allen and Hamilton.

Sharma, A. (1997) Who prefers key account management programs? An investigation of business buying behavior and buying firm characteristics. *Journal of Personal Selling & Sales Management*. 17(4), 27–39.

Sharma, A. (2003) Are you selecting the right key accounts? Examining the relationship between account sales and profitability. *Journal of Selling and Major Account Management*. October, 29–39.

Sharma, A. (2006a) Success factors in key accounts. *Journal of Business and Industrial Marketing*. 21(3), 141–150.

Sharma, A. (2006b) Strategies for maximizing customer equity of low lifetime value customers. *Journal of Relationship Marketing*. 5(1), 59–83.

Shea, G. & Guzzo, R.A. (1987) Group effectiveness: What really matters? *Sloan Management Review*. 3, 25–31.

Sherman, S., Sperry, J. & Reese, S. (2003), *The Seven Keys to Managing Strategic Accounts*. New York: McGraw-Hill.

Shetcliffe, J. (2003) Key account management. *Insurance Brokers' Monthly*. 53(10), 22–23.

Sheth, J.N & Sharma, A. (2008) The impact of the product to service shift in industrial markets & the evolution of the sales organization. *Industrial Marketing Management*. 37(3), 260–269.

Sheth, J.N. (2000) *Clients For Life: How Great Professionals Develop Breakthrough Relationships*. New York: Simon & Schuster.

Sheth, J.N. & Parvatiyar, A. (1995) The evolution of relationship marketing. *International Business Review*. 4(4), 397–418.

Sheth, J.N. & Parvatiyar, A. (2002) Evolving relationship marketing into a discipline. *Journal of Relationship Marketing.* 1(1), 3–36.

Sheth, J.N. & Sharma, A. (1997) Supplier relationships: Emerging issues and challenges. *Industrial Marketing and Management. 26(2), 91–100.*

Sheth, J.N. & Sisodia, R. (2002) *The Rule of Three – Surviving and Thriving in Competitive Markets.* New York: Free Press.

Sheth, J.N., Sisodia, R.S. & Sharma, A. (2000) The Antecedents and Consequences of Customer-Centric Marketing. *Journal of the Academy of Marketing Science.* 28, 55.

Shi, L.H., White, J.C., Zou, S. & Cavusgil, S.T. (2010) Global account management strategies: Drivers and outcomes. *Journal of International Business Studies.* 41(4), 620–638.

Shi, L.H., Zou, S. & Cavusgil, S.T. (2004) A conceptual framework of global account management capabilities and firm performance. *International Business Review.* 13(5), 539–553.

Shi, L.H., Zou, S., White, J.C., Mcnally, R.C. & Cavusgil, S.T. (2005) Global account management capability: Insights from leading suppliers. *Journal of International Marketing.* 13(2), 93–113.

Shultz, R. & Evans, K. (2002) Strategic collaborative communication by key account representatives. *Journal of Personal Selling & Sales Management.* 22(1), 23–31.

Shuman, J. (2009) The account manager role: Key to a successful customer interface. *People & Strategy.* 32(2), 36–53.

Siggelkow, N. (2002) Evolution toward fit. *Administrative Science Quarterly.* 47(1), 125–159.

Simon, B. (2005) Suppliers reorder priorities for survival. *Financial Times.* June 10, 28.

Simon, B. (2010) Carmakers explore fresh terrain with suppliers. *Financial Times.* May 5, 23.

Simon, B. & Mackintosh, J. (2009) Chrysler turns the screw on beleaguered parts makers. *Financial Times.* February 2, 20.

Simon, H.A. (1959) Theories of decision-making in economics and behavioural science. *American Economic Review.* 49(3), 253–283.

Simon, H.O. (1978) Rationality as Process and as Product of Thought. The American Economic Review Vol 68 No 2 Papers and Proceedings of Nineteenth Annual Meeting of the American Economic Association (May) 1–16.

Singh, J. (1993) Boundary role ambiguity: Facets, determinants, and impacts. *Journal of Marketing.* 57(2), 11–31.

Singh, J. & Rhoads, G.K. (1991) Boundary role ambiguity in marketing-oriented positions: A multidimensional, multifaceted operationalization. *Journal of Marketing Research.* 28(3), 328–338.

Singh, J., Verbeke, W. & Rhoads, G.K. (1996) Do organizational practices matter in role stress processes? A study of direct and moderating effects for marketing-oriented boundary spanners, *Journal of Marketing.* 60(3), 69–86.

Singhapakdi, A. (1999) Perceived importance of ethics and ethical decisions in marketing. *Journal of Business Research.* 45(1), 89–99.

Singhapakdi, A. & Vitell, S.J. (1990) Marketing ethics: Factors influencing perceptions of ethical problems and alternatives. *Journal of Macromarketing.* Spring, 10(1), 4–18.

Sirkin, H.L., Keenan, & Jackson, A. (2005) The hard side of change management. *Harvard Business Review.* 83(10), 109–118.

Skaates, M.A., Tikkanen, H. & Alajoutsiärvi, K. (2002) Social and cultural capital in project marketing service firms: Danish architectural firms on the German market. *Scandinavian Journal of Management.* 18(4), 589–609.

Skapinker, M. (2008) Why companies and campaigners collaborate. *Financial Times.* July 8, 15.

Slack, N.D.C. & Lewis, M. (2002) *Operation Strategy* (1st edition). London: Prentice-Hall.

REFERENCES

Slack, N.D.C. & Lewis, M. (2008) *Operation Strategy* (2nd edition). London: Prentice-Hall.

Slack, N.D.C. & Lewis, M. (2011) *Operation Strategy* (3rd edition). London: Prentice-Hall.

Slack, N.D.C., Chambers, S. & Johnston, R. (2001) *Operations Management* (3rd edition). London: Prentice-Hall.

Slater, S.F. & Narver, J.C. (1995) Market orientation and the learning organization. *Journal of Marketing.* 59(3), 63–74.

Sluyts, K., Matthyssens, P.R. & Streukens, S. (2011) Building capabilities to manage strategic alliances. *Industrial Marketing Management.* 40(6), 875–886.

Smackey, B.M. (1977) A profit emphasis for improving sales force productivity. *Industrial Marketing Management.* 6(2), 135–140.

Smart, A. & Harrison, A. (2003) Online reverse auctions and their role in buyer–supplier relationships. *Journal of Purchasing and Supply Management.* 9(5–6), 257–268.

Smith, J. B. & Barclay, D.W. (1990) Theoretical perspectives on selling center research. In: Lichtenthal, D. et al. (eds.), *1990 AMA Winter Educators' Conference Marketing Theory and Applications.* Chicago.

Smith, J.B. (1997) Selling alliances. *Industrial Marketing Management.* 26(March), 149–161.

Smith, J.B. (2003) The effectiveness of strategy making in medical markets. Cranfield University.

Smith, J.B. & Barclay, D.W. (1993) Team selling effectiveness: A small group perspective. *Journal of Business-to-business Marketing.* 1(2), 3–33.

Smith, J.B. & Barclay, D.W. (1993) Team selling effectiveness: A small group perspective. *Journal of Business-to-Business Marketing.* 1(2), 3–32.

Smith, J.B. & Barclay, D.W. (1997) The effects of organizational differences and trust on the effectiveness of selling partner relationships. *Journal of Marketing.* 61(1), 3–21.

Sneath, P.H. & Sokal, R.R. (1973) *Numerical Taxonomy: The Principles and Practice of Numerical Classification.* San Francisco: W.H. Freeman & Co Ltd.

Soderlund, M. & Vilgon, M. (1995) Buyer–seller relationships in 'cyberspace', customer satisfaction loyalty, and profitability. *COTIM.* November, 93–101.

Speakman, J.I.F. & Ryals, L. (2012) Key account management: The inside selling job. *Journal of Business & Industrial Marketing.* 27(5), 360–369.

Spekman, R.E. (1979) Influence and information: An exploratory investigation of the boundary role person's basis of control, *Academy of Management Journal.* 22, (1), 104–117.

Spekman, R.E. & Carraway, R. (2006) Making the transition to collaborative buyer–seller relationships: An emerging framework. *Industrial Marketing Management.* 35(1), 10–19.

Spekman, R.E. & Johnston, W.J. (1986) Relationship management: Managing the selling and the buying interface. *Journal of Business Research.* 14(6), 519–531.

Spekman, R.E. & Strauss, D. (1986) An exploratory investigation of a buyer's concern for factors affecting more cooperative buyer–seller relationships. *Industrial Marketing & Purchasing,* 1(3), 26–43.

Spencer, R. (1999) Key accounts: Effectively managing strategic complexity. *Journal of Business & Industrial Marketing.* 14(4), 291–309.

Spiggle, S. (1994) Analysis and interpretation of qualitative data in consumer research. *Journal of Consumer Research.* 21(3), 491–503.

Spiro, L.N. (1996) Panic in the Year Zero Zero. *Business Week.* (August 12), 72–73.

Srivastava, R. & Shocker, A. (1997) Strategic challenges in the financial services industry. In: Pettigrew, A. (ed.), *The Management of Strategic Change.* Oxford: Basil Blackwell.

Srivastava, R., Faehy, L. & Christensen, H.K. (2001) The resource-based view of marketing: The role of market-based assets in gaining competitive advantage. *Journal of Management.* 27(6), 777–802.

Srivastava, R., Fahey, L. & Shervani, T. (2001) Building and leveraging market-based assets to drive marketplace performance and value. [Online]. Available from: http://mthink.com/article/building-and-leveraging-market-based-assets-drive-marketplace-performance-and-value/

Srivastava, R., Shervani, T.A. & Fahey, L. (1998) Market-based assets and shareholder value: A framework for analysis. *Journal of Marketing.* 62(1), 2–18.

Stahl, H.K., Matzler, K. & Hinterhuber, H.H. (2003) Linking customer lifetime value with shareholder value. *Industrial Marketing Management.* 32(4), 267–279.

Steiner, I.D. (1972) *Group Process and Productivity.* New York: Academic Press.

Stevens, M. (2009) Sprouting a strategic account management program: how to build one from the ground up. *Velocity,* Q3&4, 25.

Stevenson, T.H. (1980) Classifying a customer as a national account. Industrial Marketing Management. 9(2), 133–136.

Stevenson, T.H. (1981) Payoffs from national account management. *Industrial Marketing and Management.* 10(2), 119–124.

Stevenson, T.H. & Page, A.L. (1979) The adoption of national account management by industrial firms. Industrial Marketing Management. 8(1), 94–100.

Stewart, G.L. (2006) A meta-analytic review of relationships between team design features and team performance. *Journal of Management.* 32(1), 29–54.

Storbacka, K. (2004) Create your future by investing in customers. *Velocity.* 6(1), 19–25.

Storbacka, K. (2006) *Driving Growth with Customer Asset Management.* Helsinki: WSOY Pro.

Storbacka, K. (2012) Strategic account management programs: Alignment of design elements and management practices. *Journal of Business & Industrial Marketing.* 27(4), 259–274.

Storbacka, K. & Nenonen, S. (2009) Customer relationships and the heterogeneity of firm performance. *Journal of Business and Industrial Marketing.* 24(5/6), 360–372.

Storbacka, K. & Nenonen, S. (2010) Scripting markets: From value propositions to market propositions. *Industrial Marketing Management.* 40(2), 255–266.

Storbacka, K., Ryals, L., Davies, I.A. & Nenonen, S. (2009) The changing role of sales: Viewing sales as a strategic, cross-functional process. *European Journal of Marketing.* 43(7/8), 890–906.

Storbacka, K., Sivula, P. & Kaario, K. (2000) A strategic perspective on the most valuable customers. *Velocity,* Q2.

Strauss, A. & Corbin, J. (1990) *Basics of Qualitative Research, Grounded Theory Procedure and Techniques.* Newbury Park, CA: Sage Publications.

Strutton, D., Pelton, L.E. & Lumpkin, J.R.(1995) Personality characteristics and salespeople's choice of coping strategies. *Journal of the Academy of Marketing Science.* 23(2), 132–140.

Stump, R.L. (1995) Antecedents of purchasing concentration: A transaction cost explanation. *Journal of Business Research.* 34(2), 145–157.

Subramani, M.R. & Venkatraman, N. (2003) Safeguarding investments in asymmetric interorganizational relationships: Theory and evidence. *Academy of Management Journal.* 46(1), 46–62.

Sujan, H., Weitz, B.A. & Kumar, N. (1994) Learning orientation, working smart, and effective selling. *Journal of Marketing.* 58(3), 39–52.

Sullivan, U., Peterson, R.M. & Krishnan, V. (2012) Value creation and firm sales performance: The mediating roles of strategic account management and relationship perception. *Industrial Marketing Management.* 41(1), 166–173.

REFERENCES

Swoboda, B., Schluter, A., Olejnik, E. & Morschett, D. (2012) Does centralising global account management activities in response to international retailers pay off? *Management International Review*. 52(5), 727–756.

Sydow, J. (1992) On the management of strategic networks. In Ernste, H. and Meier, V. (eds.), *Regional Development and Contemporary Industry Response*. London. Pinter 113–129.

Sydow, J. (1992) *Strategische Netzwerke*. Wiesbaden 1992.

Sydow, J. (2001) Understanding the constitution of interorganizational trust. In Lane, C. & Bachmann, R. (eds.), *Trust Within and Between Organizations: Conceptual Issues and Empirical Applications*. Oxford University Press.

Szymanski, D.M. (1988) Determinants of selling effectiveness: the importance of declarative knowledge to the personal selling concept. *Journal of Marketing*, 52(1), January, 64–77.

Tähtinen, J. & Halinen-Kaila, A. (1997) The death of business triads: The dissolution process of a net of companies. In Mazet, F., Salle, R. & Valla, J. (Eds.), *Interaction, Relationships and Networks*. The 13th IMP International Conference, Lyon, 553–590.

Talluri, S. & Narasimhan, R. (2004) A methodology for strategic sales alignment. *European Journal of Operational Research*. 154(1), 236–250.

Talwar, V., Burton, J. & Murphy, J.A. (2008) A non-matrix approach to customer relationship portfolio management: A case study from the UK industrial market context. *Journal of Customer Behaviour*. 7(3), 231–255.

Tarasi, C.O., Bolton, R.N., Hutt, M.D. & Walker, B.A. (2011) Balancing risk and return in a customer portfolio. *Journal of Marketing*. 75(3), 1–17.

Taylor, A. (2007) Microsoft drops supplier over diversity policy. *Financial Times*. March 24, 5.

Teece, D., Pisano, G. & Shuen, A. (1997) Dynamic capabilities and strategic management. *Strategic Management Journal*. 18(7), 509–533.

Terho, H. (2008) *Customer Portfolio Management – The Construct and Performance*. Turku School of Economics.

Terho, H. (2009) A measure for companies' customer portfolio management. *Journal of Business-to-business Marketing*. 16(4), 374–411.

Terho, H. & Halinen, A. (2007) Customer portfolio analysis practices in different exchange contexts. *Journal of Business Research*. 60(7), 720–730.

Terho, H. & Halinen, A. (2012) The nature of customer portfolios: Towards new understanding of firms' exchange contexts. *Journal of Business-to-business Marketing*. 19(4), 335–366.

Tett, R., Jackson, D. & Rothstein, M. (1991) Personality measures as predictors of job performance: A meta-analytic review. *Personnel Psychology*. 44(1), 703–742.

Thomas, J., Reinartz, W. & Kumar, V. (2004) Getting the most out of all your customers. *Harvard Business Review*. 82(7–8), 116–23.

Thompson, E. & Phua, F. (2005) Reliability among senior managers of the Marlowe–Crowne short-form social desirability scale. *Journal of Business and Psychology*. 19(4), 541–554.

Tice, T.E. (1997) Managing compensation caps in key accounts. *Journal of Personal Selling & Sales Management*. 17(4), 41–47.

Tokar, D., Fischer, A., Snell, A. & Harik-Williams, N. (1999) Efficient assessment of the five-factor model of personality: Structural validity analyses of the NEO five-factor inventory (Form S). *Measurement and Evaluation in Counseling and Development*. 32(1), 14–30.

Tooher, P. (2005) Supply firms hit out as DIY giant turns the screw. *Financial Mail*. July 10, 2.

Tosdal, H. (1950) *Introduction To Sales Management*. New York: McGraw-Hill.

Toulan, O., Birkinshaw, J. & Arnold, D. (2002) *The role of inter-organizational fit in global account management*. Unpublished Working Paper. London: London Business School.

Townsend, J., Yeniyurt, S., Deligonul, S. & Cavusgil, S.T. (2004) Exploring the marketing program antecedents of performance in a global company. *Journal of International Marketing.* 12(4), 1–24.

Trompenaars, F. & Hampden-Turner, C. (1998) *Riding the Waves of Culture* (2nd edition). London: Nicholas Brealey Publishing.

Tsoukas, H. (1996) The firm as a distributed knowledge system: A constructionist approach. *Strategic Management Journal.* 17(Special Issue), 11–25.

Tsybina, E. & Rebiazina, V. (2013) Managing portfolios of interconnected customers: Evidence from Russian B2B market. *Journal of Business & Industrial Marketing.* 28(3), 229–239.

Tubridy, G. (1986) How to pay national account managers. *Sales and Marketing Management.* (January 13), 51–53.

Tuli, K.R., Kohli, A.K. & Bharadwaj, S.G. (2007) Rethinking customer solutions: From product bundles to relational processes. *Journal of Marketing.* 71(3), 1–17.

Tupes, E. & Christal, R. (1961) *Recurrent personality factors based on trait ratings.* Technical Report, ASD-TR-61-97. Texas: Aeronautical Systems Division, Personnel Laboratory, Lackland Air Force Base.

Turnbull, P.W. (1979) Roles of personal contacts in industrial export marking. In: Ford, D. (ed), *Understanding Business Markets: Interaction, Relationships and Networks.* Waltham: Academic Press.

Turnbull, P.W. (1990) A review of portfolio planning models for industrial marketing and purchasing management. *European Journal of Marketing.* 24(3), 7–22.

Turnbull, P.W. & Zolkiewski, J.M. (1997) Profitability in customer portfolio planning. In: Ford, D. (ed.), *Understanding Business Markets* (2nd edition). London: Dydren Press.

Turnbull, P.W., Ford, D. & Cunningham, M. (1996) Interaction, relationships and networks in business markets: An evolving perspective. *Journal of Business & Industrial Marketing.* 11(3), 44–62.

Tutton, M. (1987) Segmenting a national account, *Business Horizons,* 30, 61–68.

Tuusjärvi, E. & Möller, K. (2009) Multiplicity of norms in inter-company cooperation. *Journal of Business & Industrial Marketing.* 27(7), 519–528.

Ulaga, W. (2003) Capturing value creation in business relationships: A customer perspective. *Industrial Marketing Management.* 32(8), 677–693.

Ulaga, W. & Chacour, S. (2001) Measuring customer perceived value in business markets. *Industrial Marketing Management.* 30(6), 525–540.

Ulaga, W. & Eggert, A. (2005) Relationship value in business markets: The construct and its dimensions. *Journal of Business-to-Business Marketing.* 12(1), 73–99.

Ulaga, W. & Eggert, A. (2006) Value-based differentiation in business relationships: Gaining and sustaining key supplier status. *Journal of Marketing.* 70(1), 119–136.

Ulrich, D. & Barney, J.B. (1984) Perspectives in organizations: Resource dependence, efficiency and population. *Academy of Management Review.* 9(3), 471–481.

Untiedt, R., Nippa, M. & Pidan, U. (2012) Corporate portfolio analysis tools revisited: Assessing causes that may explain their scholarly disdain. *International Journal of Management Reviews.* 14(3), 263–279.

Valenzuele, J.L.D. & Villacorta, F.S. (1999) The relationships between the companies and their suppliers. *Journal of Business Ethics.* 22(3), 273–280.

van de Ven, A.H. & Ferry, D.L. (1980) *Measuring and Assessing Organizations.* New York: John Wiley & Sons.

van der Sande, D., Bradford, E. and Davidson, R. (2001) Realising relationship potential at Henkel: using account profitability to upgrade customer relationships. *Focus Europe (Velocity),* 1(3), 1–4, Strategic Account Management Association, USA.

van Raaij, E.M., Vernooij, M.J.A. & van Triest, S. (2003) The implementation of customer profitability analysis: A case study. *Industrial Marketing Management*. 32(7), 573–583.

Vandermerwe, S. (1999) *Customer Capitalism*. London: Nicholas Brealey Publishing Ltd.

Varadarajan, R. & Jayachandran, S. (1999) Marketing strategy: An assessment of the state of the field and outlook. *Journal of the Academy of Marketing Science*. 27(2), 120–143.

Vargo, S.L. & Lusch, R.F. (2004) Evolving to a new dominant logic of marketing. *Journal of Marketing*. 68(1), 1–17.

Vargo, S.L. & Lusch, R.F. (2008) Service-dominant logic: Continuing the evolution. *Journal of the Academy of Marketing Science*. 36(1), 1–10.

Vargo, S.L. & Lusch, R.F. (2011) It's all B2B . . . And beyond: Toward a systems perspective of the market. *Industrial Marketing Management*. 40(2), 181–187.

Velasquez, M. (1996) Why ethics matter: A defence of ethical business organizations. *Business Ethics Quarterly*. 6(2), 201–214.

Venkatesan, R. & Kumar, V. (2004) A customer lifetime value framework for customer selection and resource allocation strategy. *Journal of Marketing*. 68(4), 106–125.

Venkatraman, N. & Grant, J.H. (1986) Construct measurement in organizational strategy research: A critique and proposal. *Academy of Management Review*. 11(1), 71–87.

Verhoef, P.C., Franses, P.H. & Donkers, B. (2001) Changing perceptions and changing behaviour in customer relationships. *Marketing Letters*. 13(2), 121–134.

Verra, G.J. (2003) *Global Account Management*. London: Routledge.

Verra, G.J.(1994) *Account Management: Filosofie, Instrumenten en Implementatie*. Kluwer Bedrijfswetenschappen, Deventer (in Dutch).

Villanueva, J., Yoo, S. & Hanssens, D.M. (2008) The impact of marketing-induced versus word-of-mouth customer acquisition on customer equity. *Journal of Marketing Research*. 45(1), 48–59.

von Hippel, E. (1978) A customer active paradigm for industrial product idea generation. *Research Policy*. 7(3), 240–266.

von Hippel, E. (1985) Learning from lead users. In: *Marketing In an Electronic Age*. In: Buzzell, R.D. (ed.), Boston, MA: Harvard Business School Press.

von Hippel, E. (1986) Lead users: A source of novel product concepts. *Management Science*. 32(7), 791–805.

von Hippel, E. (1988) *The Sources of Innovation*. New York: Oxford University Press.

Waddock, J. (2002) *Leading Corporate Citizens: Vision, Values, Value-Added*. Boston, MA: McGraw-Hill/Irwin.

Wagner, S.M. & Hoegl, M. (2006) Involving suppliers in product development: insights from R&D directors and project managers. *Industrial Marketing Management*. 35(8), 936–943.

Wagner, S.M. & Johnson, J.L. (2004) Configuring and managing strategic supplier portfolios. *Industrial Marketing Management*. 33(8), 717–730.

Wagner, S.M., Eggert, A. & Lindemann, E. (2010) Creating and appropriating value in collaborative relationships. *Journal of Business Research*. 63(8), 840–848.

Walker, O.C. Jr, Churchill, G.A. & Ford, N.M. (1977) Motivation and performance in industrial selling: present knowledge and needed research. *Journal of Marketing Research*. 14(2), 156–168.

Wallendorf, M. & Belk, R.W. (1989) Assessing trustworthiness in naturalistic consumer research. In Hirschman, E. (ed.), *Interpretive Consumer Research*. New Jersey: Association for Consumer Research.

Walter, A. & Ritter, T. (2003) The influence of adaptations, trust and commitment on value-creating functions of customer relationships. *Journal of Business & Industrial Marketing*. 17(4/5), 353–365.

Walter, A., Müller, T.A., Helfert, G. & Ritter, T. (2003) Functions of industrial supplier relationships and their impact on relationship quality. *Industrial Marketing Management.* 32(2), 159–169.

Walter, A., Ritter, T. & Gemünden, H.G. (2001) Value creation in buyer–supplier relationships: Theoretical considerations and empirical results from a supplier's perspective. *Industrial Marketing Management.* 30(4), 365–377.

Walters, D. & Halliday, M. (1997) *Marketing and Finance: Working the Interface.* London: Allen and Unwin.

Wanberg, C., Kanfer, R. & Banas, J. (2000) Predictors and outcomes of networking intensity among unemployed job seekers. *Journal of Applied Psychology.* 85(4), 491–503.

Wang, G. & Netemeyer, R.G. (2004) Salesperson creative performance: conceptualization, measurement, and nomological validity. *Journal of Business Research.* 57(8), 805–813.

Wathne, K.H. & Heide, J.B. (2000) Opportunism in interfirm relationships: Forms, outcomes and solutions. *Journal of Marketing.* 64(4), 36–51.

Webber, S.S. & Donahue, L.M. (2001) Impact of highly or less job-related diversity on work group cohesion and performance: A meta-analysis. *Journal of Management.* 27(2), 141–162.

Webster, F.E. (1984) *Industrial Marketing Strategy.* New York: John Wiley & Sons.

Webster, F.E. (1992) The changing role of marketing in the corporation. *Journal of Marketing.* 56(4), 1–17.

Webster, F.E. (2000) Understanding the relationships among brands, consumers, and resellers. *Journal of the Academy of Marketing Science.* January, 28(1), 17–23.

Weeks, W.A. & Stevens, C.G. (1997) National account management sales training and directions for improvement: A focus on skills/abilities. *Industrial Marketing Management.* 26(5), 423–431.

Weick, K.E. (1995) *Sensemaking in organization.* Thousand Oaks, CA: Sage Publishing.

Weick, K.E., Sutcliffe, K.M. & Obstfeld, D. (2005) Organizing and the process of sensemaking. *Organization Science.* 16(4), 409–421.

Weilbaker, D. & Weeks, W.A. (1997) The evolution of national account management: A literature perspective. Journal of Personal Selling and Sales Management. 17(4), 49–59.

Weiss, A.M. & Anderson, E. (1992) Converting From Independent to Employee Salesforces: The Role of Perceived Switching Costs. *Journal of Marketing Research.* 29(1), 101–115.

Weitz, B.A. (1981) Effectiveness in sales interactions: A contingency framework. *Journal of Marketing.* 45(1), 85–103.

Weitz B.A. & Bradford. K.D. (1999) Personal selling and sales management: A relationship marketing perspective. Journal of Personal Selling & Sales Management. 27(Spring), 241–254.

Weitz, B.A. & Jap, S.D. (1995) Relationship marketing and distribution channels. *Journal of the Academy of Marketing Science.* 23(4), 305–320.

Weitz, B.A., Sujan, H. & Sujan, M. (1986) Knowledge, motivation, and adaptive behavior: A framework for improving selling effectiveness. *Journal of Marketing.* 50(4), 174–191.

Weldon, E. & Weingart, L.R. (1993) Group goals and group performance. *The British Journal of Social Psychology.* 32(4), 307–334.

Wengler, S. (2005) *Key Account Management in Business-to-business Markets: An Assessment of Its Economic Value.* [Online] Available from: http://books.google.fr/books/about/Key _Account_Management_in_Business_to_Bu.html?id=SE_34ZF8WSEC&redir _esc=y.

Wengler, S. (2007) The appropriateness of key account management organization. *Journal of Business Marketing.* 1(4), 253–272.

Wengler, S., Ehret, M. & Saab, S. (2006) Implementation of key account management: Who, why, and how? An exploratory study on the current implementations of key account management programs. Industrial Marketing Management. 35(1), 103–112.

Werner, H. (1997) Relationalesbeschaffungsverhalten.Ausprägungen und Determinanten ('Relational Purchasing Behavior: Forms and Determinants'), GablerVerlag: Wiesbaden.

Wiersema, F. (2012) The B2B Agenda: The Current State of B2B Marketing and a Look Ahead. SMEAL College of Business: ISBM.

Wieseke, J., Ahearne, M., Lam, S.K. & Dick, R. (2009) The role of leaders in internal marketing. Journal of Marketing. 73(2), 123–145.

Wiessmeier, G.F.L, Thoma, A. & Senn, C. (2012) Leveraging synergies between R&D and key account management to drive value creation. Research Technology Management. 55(3), 15–22.

Wiggins, J. & Rigby, E. (2006) New neighbour Disney knocks at Tesco's door. Financial Times. December 9/10, 3.

Wilkinson, I.F. & Young, L.C. (2002) On cooperating: Firms, relationships and networks. Journal of Business Research. 55(2), 123–133.

Williams, K.Y. & O'Reilly, C.A. (1998) Demography and diversity in organizations: A review of 40 years of research. In: Staw, B.M. & Cummings, L.L. (eds.), Research in Organizational Behavior. Greenwich, CT: JAI Press. 77–140.

Williams, T.M. (1999) The need for new paradigms for complex projects. International Journal of Project Management. 17(5), 269–273.

Williamson, O.E. (1975) Markets and hierarchies – analysis and antitrust implications, London 1975.

Williamson, O.E. (1979) Markets and Hierarchies: Analysis and Anti-Trust Implications. New York: The Free Press.

Williamson, O.E. (1985) The Economic Institutions of Capitalism: Firms, Markets, Relational Contracting. New York: The Free Press.

Williamson, O.E. (1996) The Mechanisms of Governance. New York: Oxford University Press.

Wilson, C. (1996) Profitable Customers. London: Kogan Page.

Wilson, D.T. (1978) Dyadic interactions: Some conceptualisations. In: Bonoma, T.V. & Zaltman, G. (eds.), Organizational Buying Behavior. Chicago: American Marketing Association. 31–48.

Wilson, D.T. (2000) Deep relationships: The case of the vanishing salesperson. Journal of Personal Selling and Sales Management. 20(1), 53–61.

Wilson, D.T. & Mummalaneni, V.V. (1986) Bonding and commitment in buyer–seller relationships: A preliminary conceptualisation. Industrial Marketing and Purchasing. 1(3), 44–58.

Wilson, K. (1993) A problem centred approach to key account management. Proceedings of the National Sales Management Conference. Atlanta.

Wilson, K. (1997) An interaction approach to key account management. Unpublished Ph.D Thesis. University of Nottingham.

Wilson, K. (1999) Developing global account management programmes: Observations from a GAM panel presentation. Thexis. 4, 30–35.

Wilson, K. (2001) The Political Entrepreneur: Are we seeing a new management role? Focus Europe: Strategic Account Management Association.

Wilson, K. (2006) Using the concept of the political entrepreneur to enhance your gam recruitment and development program. Velocity: Strategic Account Management Association.

Wilson, K. & Croom-Morgan, S. (1993) A problem centred approach to buyer seller interaction. Proceedings of the 9th IMP Conference. Bath.

Wilson, K. & Millman, T. (2000) Career development of global account managers: The dilemma of the political-entrepreneur. *Proceedings of the 16th IMP Conference.* Phuket, Thailand.

Wilson, K. & Millman, T. (2003) The global account manager as political entrepreneur. ***Journal of Industrial Marketing Management.*** **32(2), 151–158.**

Wilson, K. & Weilbaker, D. (2004) Global account management: A literature based conceptual model. *Mid-American Journal of Business.* 19(1), 13–21.

Wilson, K. & Woodburn, D. (2014) The impact of organisational context in the failure of key and strategic account management programs. *Journal of Business and Industrial Marketing,* 29(5).

Wilson, K., Croom, S., Millman, T., Senn, C. & Weilbaker, D. (2000) *Global Account Management Study Report: Executive Summary of the Preliminary Findings of the SAMA/SRT GAM Project.* The Sales Research Trust.

Wilson, K., Millman, T., Weilbaker, D. & Croom, S. (2001) *Harnessing Global Potential: Insights into Managing Customers Worldwide.* Chicago: Strategic Account Management Association.

Wilson, K., Speare, N. & Reese, J.S. (2002) *Successful Global Account Management: Key Strategies and Tools for Managing Global Customers.* London: Miller Heiman.

Wind, Y. & Douglas, S. (1981) International portfolio analysis and strategy: The challenge of the '80s. *Journal of International Business Studies.* 12(2), 69–82.

Windsperger, J. (1996) Transaktionskostenansatz der Entstehung der Untemehmensorganisation, Heidelberg.

Windsperger, J. (1998) Ungeloste Problems der Transaktionskostentheorie. *Journal fur Betriebswirtshaft,* 4(5–6), 266–276.

Wise, R. & Baumgartner, P. (1999) Go downstream: The new profit imperative in manufacturing. *Harvard Business Review.* 77(5), 133–141.

Wong, Y.H. (1998) Key account management: Relationship (guanxi) model. *International Marketing Review.* 15(3), 215–231.

Wood, D.J. & Logsdon, J.M. (2002) Business citizenship: From individuals to organizations. [Online]. Available from: http://papers.ssrn.com/sol3/papers.cfm?abstract_id =1512277

Woodburn, D. (2004) Key account management in financial services: Poised between desire and fulfilment. *Interactive Marketing.* 6(1), 9–20.

Woodburn, D. (2006a) *Competencies for Key Account Managers.* Warwick Strategic Sales and Customer Management Network report. Warwick Business School.

Woodburn, D. (2006b) *Transitioning to Key Account Management.* Cranfield School of Management Research Report. Cranfield University.

Woodburn, D. (2008a) *Marketing Accountability – How to Work with Finance to Get Your Marketing Plans Approved: A guide for practitioners.* Cranfield Centre for Business Performance Research Report. Cranfield University.

Woodburn, D. (2008b) *Rewarding Key Account Management.* Cranfield School of Management Research Report. Cranfield University.

Woodburn, D. (2009) *Organising for Key Account Managers.* Warwick Strategic Sales and Customer Management Network Report. Warwick Business School.

Woodburn, D. & McDonald, M. (2001) *Key Customers. World-leading Key Account Management: Identification and Development of Strategic Relationships.* Cranfield School of Management Research Report. Cranfield University.

Woodburn, D. & McDonald, M. (2011) *Key Account Management: The Definitive Guide* (3rd edition). Chichester: John Wiley & Sons.

Woodburn, D., Holt, S. & McDonald, M. (2004) *Key Customer Profitability – Making Money in Strategic Customer Partnership*. Cranfield School of Management Research Report. Cranfield University.

Woodruff, R.B. (1997) Customer value: The next source for competitive advantage. *Journal of the Academy of Marketing Science*. 25(2), 139–153.

Workman, J. (1993) Marketing's limited role in new product development in one computer systems firm. *Journal of Marketing Research*. 30(4), 405–421.

Workman, J.P., Homburg, C. & Gruner, K. (1998) Marketing organization: An integrative framework of dimensions and determinants. *Journal of Marketing*. 62(3), 21–41.

Workman, J.P., Homburg, C. & Jensen, O. (2003) Intraorganizational determinants of key account management effectiveness. *Journal of the Academy of Marketing Science*. 31(1), 3–21.

Wotruba, T.R. (1990) A comprehensive framework for the analysis of ethical behavior, with a focus on the sales organization. *Journal of Personal Selling & Sales Management*. 10(2), 29–42.

Wotruba, T.R. (1991) The evolution of personal selling. *The Journal of Personal Selling and Sales Management*. 11(3), 1–12.

Wotruba, T.R. & Castleberry, S.B. (1993) Job analysis and hiring practice in national marketing positions. Journal of Personal Selling and Sales Management. 13(3), 49–65.

Wright, R. (2006) Competition spotlight could fall on partners. *Financial Times*. April 22/23.

Wuyts, S., Shantanu, D. & Stremersch, S. (2004) Portfolios of inter firm agreements in technology-intensive markets: Consequences for innovation and profitability. *Journal of Marketing*. 68(2), 88–100.

Yadav, M.S. (2010) The decline of conceptual articles and implications for knowledge development. *Journal of Marketing*. 74(1), 1–19.

Yao, Z., Holmbom, A.H. & Eklund, T. (2010) Combining unsupervised and supervised data mining techniques for conducting customer portfolio analysis. *Proceedings of 10th Industrial Conference on Data Mining*. Berlin, Germany. 292–307.

Yin, R.K. (2003) *Case Study Research – Design and Methods* (3rd edition). London: Sage Publications.

Yip, G.S. & Bink, A. (2007) Managing global accounts. *Harvard Business Review*. 85(9), September, 102–111.

Yip, G.S. & Madsen, T.L. (1996) Global account management: The new frontier in relationship marketing. International Marketing Review. 13(3), 24–42.

Yip, G.S., Hult, T. & Bink, A. (2007) Static triangular simulation as a methodology for strategic management research. In: Ketchen, D.J. & Bergh, D.D. (eds.), *Research Methodology in Strategy and Management*. Oxford: Elsevier. 121–160.

Yli-Renko, H. & Janakiraman, R. (2008) How customer portfolio affect a new product development in technology-based entrepreneurial firms. *Journal of Marketing*. 72(September), 131–148.

Yorke, D. (1984) An interaction approach to the management of a portfolio of customer opportunities. In: Turnbull, P.W. & Paliwoda, S.J. (eds.), *Proceedings of Research Developments in International Marketing*. Manchester: UMIST.

Yorke, D. (1986) The application of customer portfolio theory to business markets – A review. *Proceedings of IMP Group Conference*. Lyon, France.

Yorke, D. & Droussiotis, G. (1994) The use of customer portfolio theory: An empirical survey. *Journal of Business & Industrial Marketing*. 9(3), 6–18.

Yorke, D. & Wallace, K. (1986) A customer selection strategy for business markets. *Journal of Marketing Management*. 2(2), 181–191.

Young, L. & Freeman, L. (2008) A case for contrast as a catalyst for change. *International Journal of Learning*. 15(3), 295–304.

Zaheer, A., Mcevily, B. & Perrone, V. (1998) Does Trust Matter? Exploring the effects of interorganizational and interpersonal trust on performance. *Organizational Science*. 9(2), 141–159.

Zeithaml, V. (1988) Consumer perceptions of price, quality, and value: A means-end model and synthesis of evidence. *Journal of Marketing*. 52(3), 2–22.

Zerbini, F. & Castaldo, S. (2007) Stay in or get out the Janus? The maintenance of multiplex relationships between buyers and sellers. *Industrial Marketing Management*. 36(7), 941–954.

Zeynep, A. & Toker, A. (2012) The effect of customer relationship management adoption in business-to-business markets. *Journal of Business & Industrial Marketing*. 27(6), 497–507.

Zhang, J.Q., Dixit, A. & Friedmann, R. (2010) Customer loyalty and lifetime value: An empirical investigation of consumer pacakaged goods. *Journal of Marketing Theory and Practice*. 18(2), 127–139.

Zhiyuan, Y., Holmbom, A.H., Eklund, T. (2010). Combining unsupervised and supervised data mining techniques for conducting customer portfolio analysis. *10th Industrial Conference on Data Mining Proceedings*. Berlin, Germany, 292–307.

Zhizhong, J., Henneberg, S. & Naudé, P. (2011) The importance of trust vis-à-vis reliance in business relationships: Some international findings. *International Marketing Review*. 28(4), 318–339.

Zolkiewski, J.M. (1999) *Purchaser/Provider Relationships in the UK National Health Service: A Marketing Perspective*. PhD Thesis. Manchester: UMIST.

Zolkiewski, J.M. & Feng, J. (2012) Relationship portfolios and Guanxi in Chinese business strategy. *Journal of Business & Industrial Marketing*. 27(1), 16–28.

Zolkiewski, J.M. & Turnbull, P. (2002) Do relationship portfolios and networks provide the key to successful relationship management? *Journal of Business & Industrial Marketing*. 17(7), 575–597.

Zou, S. & Cavusgil, S.T. (2002) The GMS: A broad conceptualization of global marketing strategy and its effect on firm performance. *Journal of Marketing*. 66(4), 40–56.

Zupancic, D. (2008) Towards an integrated framework of key account management. *Journal of Business & Industrial Marketing*. 23(5), 323–331.

Zupancic, D. & Mullner, M. (2008) International key account management in manufacturing companies: An exploratory approach of situative differentiation. *Journal of Business-to-Business Marketing*. 15(4), 455–475.

Author profiles

ATANASOVA, Yana PhD
Director and Head of EMEA In-house Mergers & Acquisitions at Credit Suisse, Switzerland.

Previously, Yana Atanasova held positions at Account Management Center, Lehman Brothers and the University of St Gallen where she completed her PhD in the area of global account management.

BINK, Audrey MSc
Marketing and Communications Manager at Delft University of Technology in the Netherlands.

a.j.m.bink@tudelft.nl

Audrey Bink is the author of *Managing Global Customers* and a *Harvard Business Review* article on the same subject. She has also been active in global account management in earlier positions at ingredients company DMV-International.

BREHMER, Per-Olof PhD
Professor in Industrial Marketing and head of the Department of Management and Engineering at Linköping University, Sweden.

per−olof.brehmer@liu.se

His research interests are value-creation strategies, industrial services and KAM, and innovation, marketing and sales strategies in knowledge-intensive industries.

CAPON, Noel
R.C. Kopf Professor of International Marketing, Columbia Business School, New York, USA.

www.axcesscapon.com and nc7@columbia.edu

Noel Capon teaches and writes extensively in the field of key, strategic and global account management. His books include *Key Account Management and Planning,*

Managing Global Accounts, Strategic Account Strategy and *Case Studies in Managing Key, Strategic, and Global Customers*. Capon also offers world-class textbooks, in particular, *Managing Marketing in the 21st Century, Capon's Marketing Framework* and *The Virgin Marketer*.

CROOM, Simon BA, MSc, PhD, FRSA, FCIPS, CPSM

Professor of Supply Chain Management in the Supply Chain Management Institute, University of San Diego, USA, and Quondom Executive Director of the Supply Chain Management Institute.

scroom@sandiego.edu

Simon Croom started out as a student apprentice in purchasing and supply chain at Jaguar Cars before setting up and growing his own retail businesses for ten years. He joined Warwick Business School as faculty where he established and directed the Supply Strategy Research Unit, moving to the University of San Diego in 2005, where he is now USD Distinguished University Professor.

GÖK, Osman PhD

Associate Professor of Marketing, Yasar University, İzmir, Turkey.

osman.gok@yasar.edu.tr

Osman Gök has worked as sales manager, product manager and marketing research specialist and also as a consultant and educator to companies in marketing management, key account management and CRM. He studied key account management as a graduate researcher at De Montfort University, Leicester, and his research and publications focus on customer portfolio management and managing the marketing function in organizations.

GUENZI, Paulo

Associate Professor in the Department of Marketing, Università Bocconi, Milano, Italy.

Paolo Guenzi's primary research interest is salesforce and key account management. He recently co-authored books on *Sales Management: A Multinational Perspective* and *Leading Teams*. He is on the editorial board of *Journal of Personal Selling & Sales Management*, is track chair of Personal Selling & Sales Management of European Marketing Academy Conference, and has been Visiting Professor and Research Associate in Canada, New Zealand and Belgium.

HENNEBERG, Stephan PhD

Chair Professor of Marketing and Strategy at Queen Mary University of London.

Stephan has degrees in management studies, economics, philosophy and political sciences. Before coming back to academia, Stephan was a management consultant with A.T. Kearney and McKinsey & Co. His research focuses on business marketing, supply chain management and strategy, particularly business relationships, business networks, innovation capabilities and business model development. He has published more than 200 articles in international journals and conference proceedings.

HOLT, Sue BA MBA PhD

Visiting Fellow, Cranfield School of Management, UK and Visiting Professor, IESEG School of Management, Lille, France.

s.holt@cranfield.ac.uk

Following a successful career in industry, Sue has been involved for the last 15 years in lecturing, research, writing and consultancy in key and global account management. As well as her visiting positions at Cranfield and IESEG, Sue has worked with many organizations in many different industries, helping them to implement key account management.

HOMBURG, Christian PhD

Professor of Marketing, Chair of the Marketing Department, and Director of the Institute for Market-Oriented Management, University of Mannheim, Germany.

homburg@bwl.uni−mannheim.de

Christian Homburg, currently one of the most productive marketing researchers worldwide, has published more than 20 books and 50 articles in *Journal of Marketing, Journal of Marketing Research, Strategic Management Journal* and *Journal of the Academy of Marketing Science*. Key clusters of his work include market orientation of the firm, organization of marketing and sales, management of pricing, and the management of the customer interface.

IVENS, Björn PhD

Professor of Marketing and Head of the Marketing Department at Otto-Friedrich-University Bamberg, Germany, and visiting professor at EM Lyon Business School, France and Wirtschaftsuniversität Wien, Austria.

Björn Ivens' work focuses on customer management, price management and marketing organization, with specific interest in key account management and business relationships. He has published in *Journal of Business Research* and *Industrial Marketing Management*, among others, and is a founding member of European Foundation for Key Account Management, a think tank on KAM comprised of practitioners, consultants and academics.

JENSEN, Ove PhD

Professor of Marketing, Chair of Sales Management and Business-to-Business Marketing at WHU – Otto Beisheim School of Management, Vallendar, Germany.

ove.jensen@whu.edu

Ove Jensen's PhD (University of Mannheim) was based on research reported here. He is dedicated to sales management: the organization of marketing and sales activities, price management, and sales force management. He has published in *Journal of Marketing* and *Journal of the Academy of Marketing Science*, and hosts companies at the Campus for Sales community and edits *Springer's Sales Management Review* magazine in Germany.

KRAPFEL, Robert PhD

Former Chair of the Marketing Department and former Associate Dean for MBA/MS degree programmes at the Smith School of Business, University of Maryland.

bkrapfel@umd.edu

Robert Krapfel's work focuses on organizational buyer behaviour and relationship marketing issues in business-to-business settings. Author or co-author of more than 20 refereed publications, he has published in the *Journal of Marketing, Journal of Retailing* and *Journal of Transportation*, and serves on the editorial review board of the *Journal of Business-to-Business Marketing*.

LA ROCCA, Antonella PhD

Research Fellow, University of Lugano – USI, Switzerland.

antonella.la.rocca@usi.ch

Antonella La Rocca's current research interests are in innovation and entrepreneurship in B2B businesses and in particular in the interplay between intra- and inter-organizational processes. She is marketing consultant for the university start-up promotion center. She was visiting research fellow at Graz University and at BI Norwegian Business School. She has published in *IMP Journal, Industrial Marketing Management* and *Management Decision*.

LACOSTE, Sylvie PhD

Associate Professor, NEOMA Business School, Rouen, Reims and Paris, France.

sylvie.lacoste@profecogest.com

Sylvie Lacoste held senior positions in key account management in multinational companies before moving to academia. She has published a book entitled *Key Account Management*, and her paper on supplier and key account interactions in *Industrial Marketing Management* was nominated for best academic article award in France, 2012.

LANE, Nikala BSc, PhD

Reader in Marketing and Strategy in the School of Management, Swansea University, previously Associate Professor at Warwick Business School.

N.Lane@swansea.ac.uk

Research interests are strategic sales and account management, including ethical and gender issues therein, publishing in journals such as *Journal of the Academy of Marketing Science, Journal of Personal Selling and Sales Management, Journal of Business Ethics*, and the *Journal of Management Studies*. Nikala Lane recently co-authored *Strategic Customer Management: Strategizing the Sales Organization* with Nigel Piercy and edited *Strategic Sales and Sales Management*.

LEMMENS, Régis PhD

Partner, Sales Cubes, Belgium, and Visiting Fellow at Cranfield University and TiasNimbas Business School in the Netherlands.

regis.lemmens@salescubes.com

Régis Lemmens is a consultant, author and teacher on sales and sales management, focusing his research on managing key account managers. His sales management consulting firm specializes in sales and key account management.

MAHLAMÄKI, Tommi MBA, MSc, Dr Tech

Lecturer at Tampere University of Technology, Industrial Management, Finland.

tommi.mahlamaki@tut.fi

Tommi Mahlamäki's research focuses on key account management, customer relationship management, sales management and supply chain management. As a consultant, he helps companies with their marketing and account management programmes. Mahlamäki earned his MBA at Eberly College of Business and finished his doctoral dissertation on key account management at Tampere University of Technology.

McDONALD, Malcolm MA (Oxon) MSc PhD DLitt DSc

Emeritus Professor of Marketing, Cranfield School of Management, Cranfield University.

m.mcdonald@cranfield.ac.uk

Formerly Marketing Director of Canada Dry, followed by 27 years at Cranfield University School of Management, where he was Professor of Marketing and Deputy Director. He has written numerous books and articles, particularly on marketing planning, marketing value and key account management. He is also a Visiting Professor at Henley, Warwick, Aston and Bradford Business Schools.

MIHOC, Florin PhD

Researcher/lecturer in marketing and sales, and senior corporate account manager for a *Fortune* 500 company in Romania.

Florin Mihoc's PhD focused on relationship marketing and strategic account management in Romania, with potential to be the foundation for a transforming concept in both academia and business practices. His areas of expertise are strategic account management, international business and sales/marketing, from both academic and managerial perspectives. He has lectured at Emanuel University and numerous other universities and business schools in the USA and Europe.

MIKKOLA, Toni

Researcher and doctoral candidate at Tampere University of Technology, Finland.

toni.mikkola@tut.fi

Toni Mikkola's research interests are related especially to value-based sales and marketing communications in industrial B2B settings. His research topics also cover areas of B2B relationships and networks, customer and relationship value, and industrial services.

MOUZAS, Stefanos BSc LLM PhD
Professor of Marketing, Lancaster University, UK, Visiting Fellow Harvard University Law School.

Stefanos Mouzas has wide-ranging research interests in business-to-business markets, currently exploring corporate responses to contemporary challenges. Before joining the academic world he gained corporate experience with a number of leading global companies, including Kellogg and Procter & Gamble. He has held five visiting professorships in Europe and the Far East and is on the editorial boards of several academic journals.

NAUDÉ, Peter PhD
Professor of Marketing and Deputy Director of Academic Programmes at Manchester Business School.

Peter Naudé gained degrees in Marketing and in Operations Research. He lectured at the University of Cape Town's Graduate School of Business (1983–1988) before joining the Doctoral Programme at Manchester Business School. He joined the staff there, later moving to the University of Bath, and returning to MBS in 2005. He has been involved in organizing three Industrial Marketing and Purchasing (IMP) Group conferences.

OJASALO, Jukka PhD
Professor, Laurea University of Applied Sciences, Espoo, Finland, and Adjunct Professor of Professional Services Management, Aalto University, Helsinki.

jukka.ojasalo@laurea.fi

Jukka Ojasalo has published several articles dealing with key account management, for example in *Journal of Business & Industrial Marketing, Journal of Retailing and Consumer Services*, and *Industrial Marketing Management*. He has also worked for several years in the IT/software industry doing product development and relationship management with large B2B customers.

PARDO, Catherine PhD
Professor of Business-to-Business Marketing, CGI/EMLYON Research Chair in BtoB Intermediation, at EMLYON Business School, Lyon, France.

pardo@em−lyon.com

Catherine Pardo teaches B2B marketing. Her main research interests are B2B marketing in general and, specifically, supplier−customers relationships, key account management, marketing organization and B2B intermediation (wholesaling). Her work has been published in international reviews such as *Industrial Marketing Management, Journal of Business and Industrial Marketing, Journal of Personal Selling and Sales Management, European Journal of Marketing*, and she frequently presents her research at conferences in France and Europe.

PIERCY, Nigel BA, MA, PhD, DLitt

Dean and Professor of Marketing and Strategy in the School of Management, Swansea University. Previously Professor of Marketing and Strategy at Warwick Business School.

Nigel.Piercy@Swansea.ac.uk

Current research interests are strategic sales and account management, publishing in journals such as *Journal of the Academy of Marketing Science, Journal of Personal Selling and Sales Management*, and *Journal of World Business*. Recent relevant books include *Strategic Customer Management: Strategizing the Sales Organization* with Nikala Lane, and with co-editors Cravens and Fitzhugh, *The Oxford Handbook of Strategic Sales and Sales Management*.

PUSATERI, Michael

Formerly Vice-President of Interactive Account Sales and Marketing at Marriott Hotels, USA.

Michael Pusateri was a pioneer in the travel and distribution industry. He joined Marriott following extensive experience within the travel industry. He was COO of the US Travel Association, and President/CEO of hospitality and tourism consulting group Vantage Strategy. He worked with Cornell, Maryland and George Washington Universities, and participated in many research projects, particularly during his time at Marriott. Michael died prematurely in 2012.

REHME, Jakob

Associate Professor in Industrial Marketing at Linköping University, Sweden.

jakob.rehme@liu.se

Jakob Rehme's research interests include B2B sales and purchasing management, with a focus on complex business dealings such as KAM. He has published in journals such as *Journal of Business & Industrial Marketing, European Journal of Marketing, Supply Chain Management: An International Journal* and *Journal of Service Management*. Before joining academia he worked in various sales and marketing positions in the high-tech industry.

SENGUPTA, Sanjit PhD

Professor in the Marketing Department at San Francisco State University.

Sanjit Sengupta has taught strategic marketing, B2B marketing and marketing of high-technology products and services in Finland, India, New Zealand, the USA and South Korea. His research interests include new product development and technological innovation, strategic alliances, sales management and international marketing. His award-winning research has been published in many journals, including *Academy of Management Journal, Journal of Marketing* and *Journal of Product Innovation Management*.

SENN, Christoph PhD

Director of the Competence Center for Global Account Management (CGAM) at the Research Institute for International Management, University of St Gallen, Switzerland.

Christoph Senn joined academia after having worked as project manager and later global sales and marketing director of a leading European high-tech company. He has taught strategic and global customer management at Columbia Business School, New York, and Rotterdam School of Management and Technical University of Hamburg. He is also Chairman of the Account Management Center (AMC), a spin-off consultancy firm from St Gallen University.

SNEHOTA, Ivan

Professor of Marketing at the University of Lugano – USI, Switzerland.

ivan.snehota@usi.ch

Ivan Snehota has previously taught at Uppsala University and Stockholm School of Economics. His research interests focus on market strategy development in B2B. He is a founding member of IMP group and co-author of several books on business networks and papers in *Scandinavian Journal of Management, Industrial Marketing Management* and *Journal of Business Research*.

STORBACKA, Kaj PhD

Professor of Marketing at University of Auckland Business School, New Zealand.

k.storbacka@auckland.ac.nz

Kaj Storbacka has previously held professor chairs at Hanken School of Economics in Finland and Nyenrode Business Universiteit in the Netherlands. In 1994 he founded Vectia Ltd (now Talent Vectia Ltd), a management consultancy focusing on customer-oriented strategy, solution business development and strategic account management. He is on the board of the Strategic Account Management Association (SAMA).

UUSITALO, Olavi MSc (power electronics), MBA, PhD

Professor of Marketing, Tampere University of Technology, Industrial Management, Finland.

olavi.uusitalo@tut.fi

Olavi Uusitalo holds a PhD in Marketing from Helsinki School of Economics. His field of research lies in innovation, industrial marketing, networks and international business. Before an academic career he worked for 12 years in Finnish international companies. He has 20 years' experience in running international business simulation courses in several universities in Finland, Germany, Switzerland and Estonia.

VANDERBIESEN, Tom MSc (Business Administration)

Associate, Sales Cubes, Belgium and researcher and doctoral candidate at UBI Brussels, Belgium.

Tom.Vanderbiesen@salescubes.com

Tom Vanderbiesen is a consultant and researcher on the topic of performance management. He has worked on customer profitability management projects in major European banks and he is currently doing a DBA on the topic of customer value management at UBI Brussels (University of Wales).

WENGLER, Stefan PhD

Professor of Marketing at Hof University, Germany, head of the MBA programme 'German Indian Management Studies' and a regular Visiting Professor at PSG Institute of Management, Coimbatore, India.

stefan.wengler@hof−university.de

Stefan Wengler's main research interest is on B2B marketing, especially the implementation of key account management programmes as well as its management in globalizing companies like globalized pricing and organization. Further research interests are international marketing (i.e. marketing strategies in India) and sports marketing. His research has been published in journals such as *Industrial Marketing Management* and *Journal of Business Market Management*.

WILSON, Kevin MBA PhD

Chair of Selling and Client Relationships at KEDGE Business School, Bordeaux, France.

kevin.wilson@kedgebs.com

Kevin Wilson is a researcher, writer and presenter of more than 20 years' standing in the field of strategic account management, a past board member of the Strategic Account Management Association USA and founder of the Sales Research Trust. He has published over 70 academic and practitioner articles and two books on the subject, *Harnessing Global Potential* for SAMA (2000) and *Successful Global Account Management* (2002).

WOODBURN, Diana BSc MSc MBA PhD

Principal, Marketing Best Practice and Visiting Fellow at Cranfield School of Management, Cranfield University.

woodburn@marketingbp.com

Diana Woodburn researches, writes, teaches and consults in key/strategic account management. She started exploring the subject in 1997, and in 1998 she set up Cranfield's KAM Best Practice Club. She has taught thousands of key account managers and directors about KSAM and developed much of the teaching material used in the subject. Her prior career in marketing covered a wide range of sectors and continents.

WORKMAN, John BS, MBA, PhD

Professor of Marketing at Creighton University, Omaha, USA.

workman@creighton.edu

John Workman received his PhD from MIT and his research has been published in journals such as the *Journal of Marketing, Journal of Marketing Research* and *Strategic Management Journal*. His research interests include new product development, the organization and role of marketing, key account management, qualitative methods, academic integrity, and public policy and marketing.

YIP, George PhD

Professor and Co-Director, Centre on China Innovation, at China Europe International Business School in Shanghai, China, and Visiting Professor at Imperial College Business School in London.

gyip@ceibs.edu

George Yip is the author of a recent book, *Managing Global Customers*, and a recent *Harvard Business Review* article on global account management, and has advised numerous major companies on this subject. Former positions include Vice-President Research and Innovation at Capgemini Consulting.

ZOLKIEWSKI, Judy PhD

Professor, Manchester Business School, University of Manchester.

judy.zolkiewski@manchester.ac.uk

Before becoming an academic in 1999, Judy had 15 years' technical, sales and marketing experience in real-time computing. She is an internationally recognized scholar, with research interests focusing on understanding the operation of B2B marketing, selling and purchasing, in manufacturing and in the B2B services sector.

Index